HANDBOOK OF I … N

Handbook of Inclusive Innovation

The Role of Organizations, Markets and Communities in Social Innovation

Edited by

Gerard George

Dean and Lee Kong Chian Chair Professor of Innovation and Entrepreneurship, Lee Kong Chian School of Business, Singapore Management University, Singapore

Ted Baker

George F. Farris Professor of Entrepreneurship, Rutgers Business School – Newark and New Brunswick, USA and Honorary Professor at the University of Cape Town, South Africa

Paul Tracey

Professor of Innovation and Organization, Cambridge Judge Business School, University of Cambridge, UK and Professor of Entrepreneurship, Department of Management and Marketing, University of Melbourne, Australia

Havovi Joshi

Director, Centre for Management Practice, Singapore Management University, Singapore

EE Edward Elgar PUBLISHING

Cheltenham, UK • Northampton, MA, USA

Published by
Edward Elgar Publishing Limited
The Lypiatts
15 Lansdown Road
Cheltenham
Glos GL50 2JA
UK

Edward Elgar Publishing, Inc.
William Pratt House
9 Dewey Court
Northampton
Massachusetts 01060
USA

Paperback edition 2020

A catalogue record for this book
is available from the British Library

Library of Congress Control Number: 2019930683

This book is available electronically in the **Elgar**online
Business subject collection
DOI 10.4337/9781786436016

MIX
Paper from responsible sources
FSC® C013604

ISBN 978 1 78643 600 9 (cased)
ISBN 978 1 78643 601 6 (eBook)
ISBN 978 1 80088 132 7 (paperback)

Typeset by Servis Filmsetting Ltd, Stockport, Cheshire

Printed and bound by CPI Group (UK) Ltd, Croydon, CR0 4YY

Contents

PART IV SYSTEMS, INSTITUTIONS AND INFRASTRUCTURE

PART V INDIVIDUALS, ORGANIZATIONS AND ORGANIZING

PART VI NETWORKS AND SOCIAL CHANGE

About the editors

Gerard (Gerry) George is Dean and Lee Kong Chian Chair Professor of Innovation and Entrepreneurship at Lee Kong Chian School of Business at Singapore Management University. Previously, he was Deputy Dean of Imperial College Business School and Director of the Gandhi Centre. Before Imperial, he held tenured positions at the London Business School and at University of Wisconsin-Madison. From 2013 to 2016, he served as Editor of the *Academy of Management Journal*, the flagship empirical journal in the field of management. An award-winning researcher and teacher, Professor George has published over 100 articles in leading journals. His areas of interest are in innovation, entrepreneurship, sustainability and tackling grand challenges in society. He was awarded a prestigious Professorial Fellowship from the UK's Economic and Social Research Council to work on socially inclusive innovation in areas such as natural resources, healthcare and energy. George serves on the Board of AACSB International. Established in 1916, AACSB provides quality assurance, business education intelligence and professional development services to over 800 accredited business schools worldwide. He helped create BML Munjal University, near New Delhi, and serves on its Board of Governors. He serves on the Management Committee of Global Compact Network Singapore, which facilitates companies committed to aligning with the United Nations Global Compact principles in the areas of human rights, labor, environment and anti-corruption at the country level. He was a member of the Corporate Governance Council of Monetary Authority of Singapore tasked to redraft the Corporate Governance Code in 2017–18. Professor George was awarded Fellowship of the City & Guilds of London Institute. He is Fellow of the Royal Society of Arts, Manufactures and Commerce. He was conferred an honorary doctorate in Economics from the University of St. Gallen for intellectual contributions to the fields of strategic management, innovation and entrepreneurship. He is a Visiting Professor at Imperial College London and Erasmus University.

Ted Baker, the George F. Farris Professor of Entrepreneurship, leads entrepreneurship efforts at Rutgers Business School – Newark & New Brunswick. He is also Honorary Professor at the University of Cape Town. He spent much of the first half of his adult life building a variety of technology-rich entrepreneurial ventures. His research explores entrepreneurship under resource constraints and adversity (for example, in the informal settlements around Cape Town, South Africa and in the US textile industry), focusing in particular on sources and patterns of resourceful behavior and organizational resilience. His recent work builds on the social psychology of identity to explain founders' responses to adversity, continuation of organizing efforts and choices of organizational structure. His research has been published in leading academic journals such as the *Academy of Management Journal*, *Administrative Science Quarterly*, *Small Business Economics*, *Journal of Business Venturing* and *Strategic Entrepreneurship Journal*.

Paul Tracey is Professor of Innovation and Organization at the Cambridge Judge Business School (CJBS). He is also Professor of Entrepreneurship in the Department of Management and Marketing, University of Melbourne. His work focuses on how entrepreneurs and established organizations create value of different kinds. In 2014, he co-founded the Centre for Social Innovation and is currently Co-Director. The Centre creates new knowledge about social innovation and social change, offers a Masters in Social Innovation and supports social entrepreneurs through its social enterprise incubator (Cambridge Social Ventures). Prior to joining CJBS, Tracey was Assistant Professor of Entrepreneurship at Warwick Business School. He has published widely on many aspects of innovation, including papers in the *Academy of Management Journal*, *Academy of Management Review*, *Organization Science* and *Journal of Marketing*.

Havovi Joshi is the Director of the Centre for Management Practice at Singapore Management University (SMU). She is the Editor-in-Chief of *Asian Management Insights*, and has served as a chief collaborator and editor on several book projects. Joshi is a widely published award-winning case author and has led numerous professional development workshops on case writing and teaching. Her knowledge and understanding of business practice is backed by several years of experience in international banking, internal auditing and consulting services in India, Australia, Hong Kong and Mauritius. In 2012, she helped establish the Centre for Management Practice at SMU to promote two-way learning between academia and business through research, case studies and management articles. Her areas of interest include social and inclusive innovation and global competitiveness in emerging markets.

Contributors

Luis Ballesteros is Assistant Professor of Global Strategy at the George Washington University School of Business. His research centers on the individual and institutional drivers of organizational decision making and the economic consequences of firm strategy. He has focused on organizational choices during episodes of exogenous uncertainty and risk shocks and the consequences of such choices for firm performance and economic welfare. Prior to joining academia, he worked with financial derivatives for two private banks and with policy instruments to finance catastrophic risk for two multilateral agencies.

Harry Barkema is Professor of Management at the London School of Economics (LSE). His current research and teaching focus on (social) entrepreneurship trajectories in incubators in South Asia (India, Bangladesh), West (Nigeria), East (Kenya) and Southern (South) Africa. He is the founder and Director of the LSE's Innovation Co-Creation Lab (which creates and shares evidence-based knowledge, globally, on how to design, improve/learn and scale up social enterprises/social businesses/non-governmental organizations (NGOs)). He is also the founder and Director of the LSE's Masters program on Social Innovation and Entrepreneurship. He has given numerous design/field workshops for new social enterprises/social businesses/NGOs in South Asia, Africa and South America. He also recently edited (with Xiao-Ping Chen, Gerry George, Yadong Luo, Anne Tsui) the *Academy of Management Journal*'s first special issue on theories from Asia. Previously, he has published extensively on organizational learning and international acquisitions of multinational corporations, and served in various roles in the Academy of Management: (first European) Associate Editor (twice), Board of Governors, and other.

Julie Battilana is the Joseph C. Wilson Professor of Business Administration in the Organizational Behavior unit at Harvard Business School and the Alan L. Gleitsman Professor of Social Innovation at Harvard Kennedy School, where she is also the founder and faculty chair of the Social Innovation and Change Initiative. Her research examines the processes by which organizations and individuals initiate and implement social changes that diverge from the taken-for-granted norms in society. She received a joint PhD in Organizational Behavior from INSEAD and in Management and Economics from Ecole Normale Supérieure de Cachan.

Marya Besharov is Associate Professor of Organizational Behavior at the ILR School at Cornell University. She earned her PhD in Organizational Behavior from Harvard University. An organizational theorist with a background in organizational sociology, she studies how organizations and their leaders sustain competing goals. Much of her research focuses on hybrid organizations such as social enterprises and mission-driven businesses that seek to address deeply rooted societal challenges while also making a financial profit. Besharov's work has been published in journals such as the *Academy of Management Journal*, *Academy of Management Review*, *Administrative Science Quarterly*, *Business Ethics Quarterly*, *Academy of Management Learning and Education*, *Research in Organizational*

Behavior and *Research in the Sociology of Organizations*. She is currently an Associate Editor for the *Academy of Management Annals*, and serves on the editorial boards of the *Academy of Management Journal*, *Administrative Science Quarterly* and *Organization Science*.

Yasser Bhatti conducts research in the fields of innovation, entrepreneurship and strategy with a focus on innovation under constraints, the localization and globalization of innovation, and the role of emerging market economies and situated actors (such as social entrepreneurs) in emerging trends in innovation, particularly frugal and reverse innovation. He originally trained as a mechanical engineer at the University of Oklahoma and received postgraduate Computer Science and Management degrees from the Georgia Institute of Technology. Subsequently, he trained as a social scientist in Management Studies at the University of Oxford, jointly at Said Business School and Green Templeton College. He holds academic affiliations with Queen Mary University of London, University of Oxford, Imperial College London and Warwick University. Prior to his academic career, he worked in the USA at IBM, Met-Pro Corporation and the United Nations (UNDP and UNICEF). Bhatti served as an advisor on Frugal Innovation for the European Commission (along with Jaideep Prabhu) and has recently co-authored the book *Frugal Innovation: Models, Means, Methods* (2018).

Christian Busch is Clinical Assistant Professor at New York University (NYU), where he leads the Center for Global Affairs' Global Economy concentration. He teaches on alternative growth strategies, purpose-driven leadership, impact entrepreneurship, social innovation, and emerging markets at NYU and at the London School of Economics (LSE). Christian is a co-founder of Leaders on Purpose and the Sandbox Network, and served as Deputy Director at the LSE's Innovation and Co-Creation Lab. His research has been published in outlets such as the Academy of Management Best Paper Proceedings and the *International Journal of Entrepreneurial Venturing*, and has been featured by platforms such as TEDx and the World Economic Forum. He is a member of the World Economic Forum's Expert Forum, and his upcoming book on 'cultivating serendipity' (Penguin, June 2020) has been a finalist for the Financial Times/McKinsey Bracken Bower Prize. Busch received his PhD from the LSE. Twitter: @ChrisLSE.

Brittany Butler is Adjunct Lecturer in Public Policy at Harvard Kennedy School, where she also provides programming and strategic direction as the Executive Director of the Social Innovation and Change Initiative. She received an MPP from Harvard Kennedy School.

M. Tina Dacin is Professor of Strategy and Organizational Behavior at Queen's University where she is the Stephen J.R. Smith Chair and the Director of the Centre for Social Impact. Her research interests include traditions, place, social entrepreneurship and strategic collaboration. Her work has been published in management journals such as the *Academy of Management Journal*, *Academy of Management Review*, *Academy of Management Perspectives*, *Organization Science*, *Journal of International Business Studies*, *Journal of Business Ethics* and the *Strategic Management Journal*. She received her doctorate from the University of Toronto and prior to joining Queen's University, she spent nine years at Texas A&M University.

Peter A. Dacin is Professor of Marketing at Queen's University. His research interests focus on issues of corporate reputation, traditions, social enterprise and consumer behavior. His work has appeared in several marketing and management journals including the *Journal of Marketing*, *Journal of Marketing Research*, *Journal of Consumer Research*, *Journal of the Academy of Marketing Science*, *Organization Science*, *Journal of Business Ethics*, *Journal of Business Research* and the *Academy of Management Perspectives*. He received his doctorate from the University of Toronto and prior to joining Queen's University, he taught at Texas A&M University and University of Wisconsin–Madison.

Tiffany Darabi is a PhD student in Organizational Behavior at Cornell University in the ILR School. She previously worked as a research assistant at the McDonough School of Business at Georgetown University and the Ross School of Business at the University of Michigan. Her research focuses on how individuals engage in meaningful work, how social impact organizations apply their values in a coherent fashion, and how conceptualizations of social value are shaped by the practice of social impact investing. Prior to her academic career, she spent nearly a decade and a half working for and consulting with mission-driven organizations in the international development sector on developing management systems and effective organizational practices. She holds a BA in International Relations from Johns Hopkins University.

Gerald F. (Jerry) Davis received his PhD from the Graduate School of Business at Stanford University and taught at Northwestern and Columbia before moving to the University of Michigan, where he is Associate Dean for Business+Impact, the Gilbert and Ruth Whitaker Professor of Business Administration and Professor of Sociology. He has published widely in management, sociology and finance, and was Editor-in-Chief of *Administrative Science Quarterly*. Books include *Social Movements and Organization Theory* (2005); *Organizations and Organizing* (2007); *Managed by the Markets: How Finance Reshaped America* (2009); *Changing Your Company from the Inside Out: A Guide for Social Intrapreneurs* (2015); and *The Vanishing American Corporation* (2016). Davis's research is broadly concerned with the effects of finance on society, changes in the corporate economy and new forms of organization.

Silvia Dorado is Associate Professor of Management at the University of Rhode Island. She is also Associate Editor of *Business & Society* and a board member of DePaul Industries (a social enterprise). In her research, Dorado has explored topics around processes of social innovation within markets as well as the founding, management and challenges of social enterprises. She has published on these topics in several top journals including the *Academy of Management Journal*, *Business & Society*, *Journal of Business Venturing* and *Organization Studies*.

Elizabeth Embry is a PhD student at the University of Colorado, Boulder, studying entrepreneurship and management. Her research interests include topics related to social entrepreneurship, leadership and identity, specifically in healthcare and international development. Prior to beginning at CU, Embry was the Director of Global Health at Saint Louis University's College for Public Health and Social Justice. She has also worked in program development and disaster management with the World Health Organization and Catholic Health Association. She holds a Masters of Business Administration in International Business from the John Cook School of Business at Saint Louis University and a Masters of Public Health in International Health and Complex Humanitarian Aid from Boston University.

Michelle Fava is Head of Knowledge Transfer at the Cambridge Centre for Social Innovation. She is also co-founder of the Thinking through Drawing project, a symposium series and professional development provider that seeks to apply cognitive principles to the practical application of drawing and visualization. Fava's research explores the use of visual methods for organizational research and educational development. Previously, Fava was Junior Research Fellow in Drawing at the Cambridge School of Art, Anglia Ruskin University.

Pablo D. Fernández is Assistant Professor of Business, Society & Economics at IAE Business School, Universidad Austral, Argentina. His research centers on processes of social inclusion in which marginalized actors seek to organize and work together to regain their dignity. At a broader level, he is interested in understanding issues of power and resistance in and around organizations. Part of his research has appeared in *Organization Studies* and *Business & Society*.

Ann Florini is Visiting Professor at the University of Maryland School of Public Policy, where she is also Academic Director of the Intersector Initiative. She was previously Professor of Public Policy, Singapore Management University, where she created and ran the Masters of TriSector Collaboration, a Senior Fellow at the Brookings Institution and Professor of Public Policy at the National University of Singapore. She is an authority on new approaches to global governance. Her research and teaching focus on collaborations involving government, civil society and the private sector. Her books include *China Experiments: From Local Innovation to National Reform* (with Hairong Lai and Yeling Tan, 2012); *The Right to Know: Transparency for an Open World* (2007); *The Coming Democracy: New Rules for Running a New World* (Brookings, 2005); and *The Third Force: The Rise of Transnational Civil Society* (2000). Florini received her PhD in Political Science from UCLA and a Masters in Public Affairs from Princeton University.

Nuno Gil is Professor of New Infrastructure Development at the Alliance Manchester Business School. He is a design scholar with a research focus on the design of structures and processes to tackle today's big issues facing humanity, including population growth, climate change, world poverty and antimicrobial resistance. With his PhD students and collaborators, he has developed theory, conceptual framing and methods for communicating with key societal actors on new forms of organizing to develop effectively capital-intensive technologies. Gil was born in Lisbon, Portugal, where he trained as a civil engineer. He joined the University of Manchester, after earning a PhD from the University of California at Berkeley in 2002. Gil is the Research Director of the AMBS Infrastructure Development Research Group, and the leading editor of the book *Duality by Design: The Global Race to Build Africa's Infrastructure* (forthcoming, 2019).

Helen M. Haugh is Senior Lecturer and Research Director for the Centre for Social Innovation at the Cambridge Judge Business School, University of Cambridge. She received her PhD from the University of Aberdeen. Haugh's research interests focus on community enterprise, development and sustainability. Her research has been published in several leading journals, including the *Academy of Management Journal*, *Organization Studies*, *Journal of Business Venturing* and *Journal of Business Ethics*.

Todd Inouye joined the Niagara University faculty in September 2016 after receiving his PhD in Business Administration. He holds an Executive MBA in Business Administration, a BA in Psychology and certificates in International Management and Ethnic Studies, all from the University of Hawai'i at Mānoa. His primary research interests lie at the intersection of competitive context and firm-level strategy for small and medium-sized enterprises. He also engages in the scholarship of teaching and learning within the management discipline as a secondary research stream. Inouye's research has appeared in *Small Business Economics: An Entrepreneurship Journal* and peer-reviewed proceedings of the Hawai'i International Conference on System Sciences and the Association of Japanese Business Studies.

Jessica Jones is a PhD candidate at the University of Colorado, Boulder, studying Entrepreneurship and Management. Her research interests include topics related to entrepreneurial financing, entrepreneurial identity and impact entrepreneurship with a focus on understanding how entrepreneurs in marginalized contexts access important sources of capital (mentors, investment and so on). Prior to beginning at CU, Jones was Assistant Director for the Page Center for Entrepreneurship at Miami University. She has also worked in a variety of global and local entrepreneurial contexts concerned with entrepreneurial solutions to poverty.

Amol M. Joshi (PhD, UNC Chapel Hill) is Assistant Professor of Strategy and Entrepreneurship in the Oregon State University College of Business. Joshi researches how inventors create and commercialize new technologies. He developed his expertise in innovation management over a 13-year career as an engineer, entrepreneur and executive in venture capital-funded startups and high-growth public companies in Silicon Valley. He is the co-inventor of two patents for voice products. Joshi co-founded BeVocal, a speech recognition software startup (acquired by Nuance Communications) and served as Vice President of Sales & Marketing (1999–2003). He is a 2016 Kauffman Foundation Junior Faculty Fellow and a 2010 Kauffman Dissertation Fellow in Entrepreneurship Research. Since joining OSU's faculty in 2014, Joshi was honored with the Betty and Forrest Simmons Award for Excellence in Graduate Teaching (2017), the Byron L. Newton Award for Excellence in Undergraduate Teaching (2016) and a Newcomb Associates Award for Outstanding Research (2015).

Yong H. Kim received his PhD from Stephen M. Ross School of Business, University of Michigan where he was also a Dow Sustainability Doctoral Fellow from 2015 to 2016. He is currently Assistant Professor at Hong Kong University of Science and Technology's Department of Management. Kim's dissertation investigated the interplay between supply chain visibility and supply chain dynamics in the context of the global mobile handset industry. His broader research interests include social networks (interpersonal and interorganizational), organizational accountability, sustainability and 'big data' applications to organizational research.

Marissa Kimsey is a research associate at Harvard Business School. She studies the growing blurring of the boundaries between the social and business sectors around the globe. She received an MPhil in Development Studies from the University of Cambridge.

Arno Kourula is Associate Professor (tenured) of Strategy at the University of Amsterdam Business School and a Docent at Aalto University. Previously, he has been a Postdoctoral

Fellow at Stanford University and a Visiting Fellow at Copenhagen Business School. Kourula's primary research interest is corporate sustainability through cross-sector interactions. He has published widely in academic journals in the fields of management, international business, business ethics, political science and environmental studies. He is the special issues Co-editor for *Journal of Business Ethics* and an Associate Editor for *Business & Society*. He has won multiple awards for his research, teaching and reviewing, including the 2017 International Association for Business & Society Best Published Paper Award.

Johanna Mair is Professor of Organization, Strategy and Leadership at the Hertie School of Governance in Berlin and co-directs the Global Innovation for Impact Lab at the Stanford Center on Philanthropy and Civil Society. She studies how organizations address societal challenges and contribute to economic and social progress. Mair received a PhD in Management from INSEAD.

Ana Cristina Campos Marques has worked in private, non-profit and government sectors for nearly 20 years in Brazil. Currently living in the Netherlands, she is the founder of Lumina Perspectives (Curitiba, Brazil and Amsterdam), an online startup on sustainability education. Marques believes in new sustainability narratives where individuals, organizations, society and the planet can thrive together. To that end, she designs development programs, delivers keynote speeches, mentors practitioners and academics, and supports new ways of thinking. She blends perspectives from several fields of knowledge with a driving quest for deeper ways to sustainability. She has a Bachelor's degree in Chemical Engineering from the Federal University of Parana, an MBA from Fundação Getúlio Vargas, a Masters in Design for the Environment from the Technological Federal University of Parana (Brazil) and is completing a PhD from Erasmus University Rotterdam.

Christopher Marquis is the Samuel C. Johnson Professor in Sustainable Global Enterprise at Cornell University. He studies how the interaction between civil society, governments and corporations leads to socially and environmentally beneficial outcomes, with a particular emphasis on how these processes unfold in China. He received a PhD in Sociology and Business Administration from the University of Michigan.

Anita M. McGahan is Professor and George E. Connell Chair in Organizations and Society at the Rotman School of Management at the University of Toronto. She is cross appointed to Toronto's Medical School, School of Public Health, and Munk School of Global Affairs. In 2014, she joined the MacArthur Foundation's Research Network on Opening Governance. McGahan is a Fellow and past President of the Academy of Management, and is a Fellow of the Strategic Management Society.

Murdith McLean is associated with the Department of Philosophy at the University of Victoria, with a particular interest in business ethics and the role of business in society. He holds a DPhil from the University of Oxford, and was for 17 years head of St John's College at the University of Manitoba. He has held visiting appointments at New College, University of New South Wales in Sydney and at the Research School for Social Sciences, the Australian National University in Canberra. More recently, McLean was Associate Director, and then Acting Director, for the Centre for Studies in Religion and Society at the University of Victoria. He has taught courses and supervised graduate students in Philosophy of Religion, Critical Thinking and Applied Ethics; and published in a number of scholarly journals including *Business & Society*, *Journal of Vocational Behavior*, *Canadian Journal of Philosophy*, *Religious Studies*, *Philosophical Quarterly* and *Journal of World Business*.

Greg Molecke is Lecturer in Social Entrepreneurship and Philanthropy at the University of Exeter Business School. He holds a PhD from the Grenoble Ecole de Management and an MBA and dual Bachelor's degree in Literature and Philosophy from the University of New Mexico. Molecke's research interests focus on organizational decision making in relation to social impact performance, social innovation, paradox theory and scaling-up processes in organizations. Prior to embarking on an academic career, He has held positions in people, project and program management at a Fortune 50 media and entertainment company, an energy company, a hospital and a research university.

Warren Nilsson is Associate Professor of Social Innovation at the University of Cape Town Graduate School of Business, where he also serves as the Academic Director of the MPhil in Inclusive Innovation program. He holds a PhD in Management from McGill University. Nilsson's research focuses on the organizational dynamics of social change. He is particularly interested in the relationship between positive organizing and social innovation. Why are some organizations so good at disrupting previously intractable patterns of behavior, belief and relationship? How can social purpose organizations develop a sustained capacity for ongoing institutional reimagination? His research developing the concept of 'positive institutional work' has appeared in the *Academy of Management Review* and the *Stanford Social Innovation Review*, and he is a faculty affiliate of the Center for Positive Organizations at the University of Michigan.

Daniel Nyberg is Professor of Management at the University of Newcastle Business School, an honorary professor at the University of Sydney, and guest professor at Malmö University. His research explores responses to climate change in projects on the transition to a low carbon economy, the politics of adaptation and how corporate political activities influence public policy. He has published widely on these topics in journals including the *Academy of Management Journal*, *British Journal of Sociology*, *Organization* and *Organization Studies*.

Maggie O'Carroll is CEO and founder of The Women's Organisation, an award-winning charity and social enterprise, working in the UK and internationally for the economic and social advancement of women. O'Carroll is actively involved in female economic development service design, delivery and policy influencing and is a regular contributor to conferences in the UK and in other countries on issues relating to women's education, employment, entrepreneurship and social enterprise. She is a business graduate and holds a Masters in Community Enterprise from the Cambridge Judge Business School, University of Cambridge, a visiting scholar at the Haydn Green Institute for Innovation and Entrepreneurship, Nottingham University, and an Entrepreneurial Scholar in residence at Simmons College, Boston, Massachusetts. She also holds several non-executive roles including social economy lead for a £2 billion European Structural Investment Fund Programme and transformational Health Provider Alliance.

Anne-Claire Pache is Chaired Professor in Social Innovation and Philanthropy at ESSEC Business School in Paris. She holds a Masters in Management from ESSEC (1994), a Masters in Public Administration from Harvard Kennedy School (2001) and a PhD in Organizational Behavior from INSEAD (2010). Her research interests lie at the intersection of organizational theory and social innovation, with a particular emphasis on pluralistic environments, hybrid organizations and scaling-up processes in organizations. She has authored several books and articles, including in the *Academy of Management Review*, *Academy of Management Journal*, *Journal of Business Ethics*, *California Management Review* and *Leadership Quarterly*. Before embarking on an academic career, Pache was part of the co-founding team of Unis-Cité, a French non-profit organization that pioneered youth civil service in France.

Ana María Peredo is Professor in the School of Environmental Studies at the University of Victoria. She is former Director (2008–14) of the Centre for Co-operative and Community-Based Economy, and Professor (2000–16) in the Peter B. Gustavson School of Business, also at the University of Victoria. Drawing on her background in social and cultural anthropology, and experience as a journalist in her native Peru, Peredo's research focuses on the role of collective, co-operative enterprise in fostering sustainable communities, especially among impoverished peoples. She has a strong interest in community alternatives and participatory action research among Indigenous people. She has published widely in high-ranking scholarly journals and presented at numerous national and international academic conferences. She has won a number of research and dissemination awards; most recently, the 2013 recipient of both the University of Victoria's Craigdarroch Award for Excellence in Knowledge Mobilization and a University of Victoria Community Leadership Award.

Yves Plourde is Assistant Professor of Strategy and International Business at HEC Montréal. He received his PhD in General Management from the Ivey Business School, Western University. His research interests lie at the intersection between international business, strategic management and organization studies. He is particularly interested in how organizations leverage their scope to achieve a global impact. Plourde's current research explores how Greenpeace became more effective at organizing for global change, focusing on how the organization identified the problems to focus on, the impact of its internal resource allocation processes on its performance, and the different structures and practices it implemented over the years to increase collaboration across its worldwide network of national organizations.

Jaideep Prabhu is Professor of Marketing, Jawaharlal Nehru Professor of Indian Business and Enterprise, and Director of the Centre for India & Global Business at Cambridge Judge Business School, University of Cambridge. His research interests are in marketing, innovation, strategy and international business. He has published in and is on the editorial board of leading international journals such as the *Journal of Marketing*. He has appeared on BBC News24, BBC Radio 4 and Bloomberg BusinessWeek, and his work has been profiled in *BusinessWeek*, BBC World Service, *The Economist*, *Financial Times*, *Le Monde*, *New York Times* and *The Times*. Prabhu has consulted with, taught executives from or given talks at ABN Amro, Bertelsmann AG, Barclays, BP, BRAC, BT, GE, IBM, ING Bank, Marks and Spencer, the NHS,

Pearson, Roche, Shell, Siemens, Unilever and Vodafone, among others. He is the co-author of *Jugaad Innovation: Think Frugal, Be Flexible, Generate Breakthrough Growth* (2012), described by *The Economist* as 'the most comprehensive book yet' on the subject of frugal innovation. His most recent book *Frugal Innovation: How to Do More With Less* was published in February 2015 and won the CMI's Management Book of the Year Award 2016.

Jeffrey A. Robinson (PhD) is an award-winning business school professor, international speaker and entrepreneur. Since 2008, he has been a leading faculty member at Rutgers Business School where he is Associate Professor of Management and Entrepreneurship and the Academic Director of the Center for Urban Entrepreneurship & Economic Development. Robinson is a passionate advocate for social entrepreneurship, inclusive innovation and economic development. He is the author of books and articles on such topics as social entrepreneurship, African American women in entrepreneurship and inclusive innovation. Emerging from his pioneering research, the New Jersey Social Innovation Institute and the CUEED Pipeline to Inclusive Innovation are national and international models for economic development and social problem solving using entrepreneurial approaches. He is an editorial board member for *Academy of Management Perspectives* and the *Social Entrepreneurship Journal*.

Christian Seelos is a Distinguished Fellow at the Stanford University Center on Philanthropy and Civil Society (PACS) and co-directs the Global Innovation for Impact Lab at PACS. He studies organizational processes of social innovation and system change and explores their causal powers for generating positive impact. He received a PhD in Molecular Biology from Baylor University.

Jason D. Shaw is Professor and Shaw Foundation Chair in Business in the Nanyang Business School at the Nanyang Technological University. He is currently Editor-in-Chief of the *Academy of Management Journal*. His research interests include employment relationships, pay structures, financial incentives and social networks.

Natalie Slawinski is Associate Professor of Strategic Management at the Memorial University of Newfoundland. She earned her PhD from the Richard Ivey School of Business at the University of Western Ontario. Slawinski's research focuses on understanding sustainability, temporality and paradoxes in organizations. Her most recent research examines these themes in the context of social enterprise. She serves as Academic Advisor to Memorial's Centre for Social Enterprise and is a Research Fellow at the Cambridge Judge Business School's Centre for Social Innovation, University of Cambridge. Her research appears in such journals as *Organization Science*, *Strategic Management Journal* and *Organization Studies*.

Wendy Smith earned her PhD in Organizational Behavior at Harvard Business School, and is Professor of Management at the Lerner School of Business, University of Delaware. Her research on the nature and management of strategic paradoxes has been published in journals such as the *Academy of Management Journal*, *Academy of Management Review*, *Harvard Business Review*, *Organization Science*, *Management Science* and *Academy of Management Learning and Education*. Smith is currently an Editor at the *Academy of Management Journal*, co-founder of the Lerner Women's Leadership Initiative and co-founder of the blog www.leveragingtensions.com, which shares ideas between practitioners and scholars about managing paradox.

David Souder is the Interim Dean of the University of Connecticut School of Business where he has taught courses in Strategy, Entrepreneurship and Statistics. He has published a dozen research articles focusing mainly on organizations' long-term decision processes and outcomes, and regularly engages with industry leaders on this topic. Souder earned his PhD in Strategic Management and Organization from the Carlson School at the University of Minnesota and his BS in Economics from the Wharton School of the University of Pennsylvania. Earlier in his career, he worked as a strategy consultant and helped launch one of the first charter schools in New York.

Neil Stott is Faculty (Reader level) in Management Practice and Co-director of the Centre for Social Innovation at the Cambridge Judge Business School, University of Cambridge. He is also Director of the Masters in Social Innovation. Prior to joining JBS, Stott worked in charities, local government and led a development trust. His research examines social innovation, community social organizing and the role of organizations in poor places. He is a Visiting Social Innovator at the Memorial University of Newfoundland and Visiting Fellow at Anglia Ruskin University.

Hwee-Pink Tan is Associate Professor at Singapore Management University (SMU), where he leads a team of technology and social science researchers to bring together Internet of Things technologies, and social-behavioral research to enable and sustain ageing-in-place, leading to intelligent and inclusive societies, in partnership with public and private entities, as well as voluntary welfare organizations. At SMU, he teaches a new Information Systems Depth Elective on Internet of Things: Technology and Applications, targeted at senior undergraduate students, as well as students pursuing the Professional Masters of IT and Business. He has been a member of the Adjunct Faculty of the Geriatric Education and Research Institute since May 2017. He obtained his PhD from Technion, Israel Institute of Technology in 2004. He is a Senior Member of the IEEE, and has performed executive roles for various conferences on wireless sensor networks, and is currently an Editor of the *Journal of Wireless Communications and Mobile Computing*.

Hwee-Xian Tan is Assistant Professor of Information Systems (Practice) at Singapore Management University (SMU). She co-leads the SmartBFA (Smart Accessibility & Mobility for Barrier-free Access) team, which aims to find barrier-free access routes for Singaporeans through crowdsourced sensor data. She was also part of the SHINESeniors (Smart Homes and Intelligent Neighbors to Enable Seniors) project team, which aims to improve the effectiveness of healthcare and caregiver support for the elderly, through the use of sensor-enabled homes and other forms of technology. She obtained her PhD from the School of Computing, National University of Singapore in 2011. Her current research interests are in tech-enabled inclusive societies, Internet of Things (IoT), smart city applications, wireless networking, as well as embedded systems.

Madeline Toubiana is Assistant Professor of Strategic Management and Organization at the University of Alberta, School of Business, and is the current Southam Faculty Fellow. Her research focuses on the role that emotions, complexity and stigmatization play in processes of social change and innovation. To understand the dynamics of social change and innovation, Toubiana examines the intersection and interaction between social actors and institutional systems. Some of her previous and current work examines this topic in the context of social entrepreneurship, academia, social media, the Canadian prison system and the sex trade. Her research has been published in the *Academy of Management Journal*, *Academy Management Review*, *Organization Studies*, *Journal of Management History* and *Management Learning*, among others.

Crystal Tremblay is Assistant Professor in Geography and Special Advisor on Community Engaged Scholarship at the University of Victoria. She is a community-based scholar with over a decade of international experience in the areas of environmental sustainability, participatory governance and livelihood enhancement. She specializes in using participatory video and arts-based methods for community engagement, capacity building and program evaluation working across the public, private and non-profit sectors. Strongly rooted in the investigation of innovation in community-based development, Tremblay is passionate about cultivating new spaces for creative citizen engagement and the co-creation of knowledge leading to environmental and social equity. She is the co-founder and academic lead of the emerging UNESCO Chair in CBR Salish Sea Community-based Research Hub, a partnership between the University of Victoria and civil society organizations in the Greater Vancouver Island region.

Lutisha Vickerie-Dearman is Assistant Professor in the Management & Entrepreneurship Department at Hofstra University's Zarb School of Business. Her research interests include examining the institutional logics supporting policy initiatives and the influence on entrepreneur responses. Prior to joining Hofstra, she taught various Entrepreneurship, Ethics and Negotiation courses as a part-time lecturer at Rutgers and as an assistant Adjunct Professor at Baruch College Zicklin School of Business. Vickerie also worked as an attorney, representing a multinational firm and its subsidiaries on international business regulation and policy matters. She served as co-founder and Vice President of Fair To Women, Inc., where she advocated on behalf of women across the world facing socio-economic marginalization. She received her PhD in Management from Rutgers School of Business and her JD from Rutgers School of Law.

Christopher Wright is Professor of Organisational Studies at the University of Sydney Business School and a key researcher at the Sydney Environment Institute. His research explores organizational responses to climate change, with a particular focus on corporate environmentalism, risk, identity and future imaginings. His research has appeared in a broad range of leading journals including *Academy of Management Journal*, *Organization Studies*, *Journal of Management Studies*, *Research Policy*, *Environment & Planning A* and *Human Relations*. Wright is the author of several monographs including *The Management of Labour: A History of Australian Employers* (1995), *Management as Consultancy: Neo-bureaucracy and the Consultant Manager* (2015) and most recently, with Daniel Nyberg, *Climate Change, Capitalism and Corporations: Processes of Creative Self-destruction* (2015).

Jeffrey G. York is Associate Professor of Strategy and Entrepreneurship, Research Director for the Deming Center for Entrepreneurship, and Shane Faculty Scholar at the Leeds School of Business at the University of Colorado, Boulder. He received his PhD from the Darden School of Business at the University of Virginia. His teaching and research are focused on how and why entrepreneurs create new products, services and industries that reduce environmental degradation. York teaches classes in Business Planning, Entrepreneurial Thinking and Environmental Ventures at the undergraduate, MBA and PhD levels. He has published research in journals such as the *Academy of Management Journal*, *Academy of Management Review*, *Journal of Business Venturing*, *Organization Science* and *Strategic Management Journal*. He serves as a Field Editor for the *Journal of Business Venturing* and is on the editorial boards of the *Academy of Management Journal*, *Entrepreneurship Theory & Practice* and *Strategic Entrepreneurship Journal*.

Xiang Zhou is a PhD student at the Nanyang Business School at the Nanyang Technological University. She is interested in compensation studies and has a background in human resource management and organizational behavior.

Charlene Zietsma is Associate Professor, Management and Organization at the Smeal College of Business, Pennsylvania State University. She earned her doctorate from the University of British Columbia. Zietsma studies emotions and institutions, social innovation, institutional change processes, field theory and entrepreneurship. She has lectured extensively on these topics around the world and her work has been published in *Administrative Science Quarterly*, *Academy of Management Journal*, *Academy of Management Review*, *Organization Science*, *Organization Studies*, *Journal of Business Venturing*, amongst others. In 2016, she was awarded the ASQ Scholarly Contribution Award for the paper published in 2010 that has had the most significant impact on the field of Organization Studies. She is a Senior Editor for *Organization Studies*, has been guest Editor for *Business & Society*, *Research in the Sociology of Organizations*, *Strategic Organization* and *Organization Studies*, and serves on the editorial board for several other journals.

Acknowledgements

Gerard George gratefully acknowledges the generous support of The Lee Foundation, Singapore.

Ted Baker thanks the Rutgers Advanced Institute for the Study of Entrepreneurship and Development (RAISED) for its support.

Paul Tracey thanks Sir Harvey McGrath for his generous support of the Cambridge Centre for Social Innovation at the Cambridge Judge Business School.

Havovi Joshi thanks the Centre for Management Practice at Singapore Management University for its support.

PART I

INTRODUCTION

1. Inclusion and innovation: a call to action

Gerard George, Ted Baker, Paul Tracey and Havovi Joshi

Social inclusion is at the heart of sustainable development. Inclusion implies that a concerted effort is required to bring in the "excluded," marginalized or disenfranchised. Inclusion implies that there are structural and systemic barriers that reinforce this exclusion, making it challenging to be inclusive. The United Nations (UN) 2015 Sustainable Development Goals keeps social inclusion at the core of its 17 goals, that sustainability, prosperity and growth should be shared across all inhabitants of this world. Social indicators reveal that while we are living longer and, in many countries, healthier lives, the distribution of wealth has become less equal, and social and economic opportunities for growth and wellbeing are becoming unequally accessible to large proportions of our global population. It would suffice to say that inclusion has become one of the most pressing political and economic problems of society today.

GRAND CHALLENGES AND SOCIAL INCLUSION IN MANAGEMENT RESEARCH

A core focus of business schools is the preparation of students for careers within organizations that value a certain set of functional competences and soft skills that help business create economic value. Traditionally, much management research has also been oriented toward the instrumental needs of these employer organizations to innovate in the marketplace and in how they manage their organizations to create and capture economic value (Tracey and Stott, 2017, p. 51). Increasingly, however, a subgroup of management researchers has engaged with broader questions of value creation, moving beyond the goals of Pareto efficiency and optimization bequeathed to management research by the field of economics (George et al., 2012), to consider broader questions of social value creation (Di Domenico et al., 2010). Much of this work has considered one or more of a very wide variety of "social purpose organizations" (Tracey and Stott, 2017, p. 52), but it also extends to traditional organizations that are tightly focused on economic value appropriation, but which at the same time engage in some social purpose activities either as part of profit-seeking or in addition to it (Aguinis and Glavas, 2012). For those of us interested in having our work be of some use in addressing both societal grand challenges (Eisenhardt et al., 2016; George et al., 2016) and their more local instantiations, a simple question underlies all of this work: What can we, as management scholars, do to both *help* and *encourage* those who are creating and leading organizations engage in forms of innovation that bring benefit to people and communities that have been excluded or marginalized from socio-economic resources and opportunities?

Grand challenges – such as poverty, extreme inequality, climate change and hunger – require insights and actions at every level from changing individual behavior to changing international relations (George et al., 2012). In terms of the sorts of organizations that management scholars are accustomed to studying, such challenges call for solutions that involve social entrepreneurship, social intrapreneurship and also "social extrapreneurship," which refers to forms of inter-organizational action that facilitate "alternative combinations of ideas, people, places and resources to address social challenges" (Tracey and Stott, 2017, p. 53).

Because of the breadth of issues and the stacked height of the levels of analysis invoked in studying grand challenges, this work opens up a vast array of opportunities for management scholars to pursue novel questions in novel contexts within the bounds of their disciplinary frameworks. One could readily build a successful career by examining grand challenges through the single disciplinary lens of sociology, economics, psychology, organization theory, strategy, organizational behavior or entrepreneurship. Indeed, given the structure of academic careers, including those in business schools, there are strong incentives for people to stay largely within their disciplines. Unfortunately, the sorts of wicked problems (Dorado and Ventresca, 2013) we face are very unlikely to yield much ground to insights bounded within any single discipline. Such self-imposed limitations therefore squander much of the opportunity we face to help entrepreneurs and leaders engage in beneficial social action.

The argument is commonly made that much of management research is too "theoretical" and distant from practice to allow us to be of much help even with regard to our traditional clients: large, profit-oriented corporations (Baker and Pollock, 2007; George, 2014). Our approach to privileging theory, which Hambrick (2007, p. 1346) described as "religious fervor," often seems to provide a poor fit with Lewin's (1943) maxim that "there is nothing as practical as a good theory." Instead, it often seems to be theory for the sake of theory. Yet, it is not clear that either recurring criticisms or the dedication of Academy of Management conferences to themes about practical relevance have made much of a dent in this issue. The same concern extends to our work on social innovation. Despite encouraging moves toward broadening the domain of what "counts" as good management research by some elite journals (George, 2014), journal gatekeepers and tenure committees are slow to change and continue to focus on traditional notions of theoretical contribution. This, in turn, is likely to slow the movement of young researchers toward pursuing the sorts of questions and engaging in the sorts of fraught cross-disciplinary approaches that might contribute directly toward addressing societal grand challenges. Not to put too fine a point on it, if we are unable as a professional community to change the largely self-imposed institutional constraints of our own career and reward systems, how can we reasonably hope to help bring the sorts of institutional changes that grand challenges seem to demand (Ferraro et al., 2015; Fligstein and McAdam, 2012)?

THE CHALLENGES OF BOUNDEDNESS AND THEORIZING

Relatively speaking, inclusive innovation represents a somewhat more tractable subset of work on social challenges and innovation. Defined as "the development and implementation of new ideas which aspire to create opportunities that enhance social and economic well-being for disenfranchised members of society" (George et al., 2012, p. 663), inclusive innovation refers to "grassroots" efforts at innovation in which those driving the innovation may include the "disenfranchised" people for whom the innovation seeks to provide opportunities. It also refers to more market-driven approaches in which companies, frequently multinational corporations (MNCs), provide goods and services that help to improve the circumstances of the disenfranchised, sometimes also inviting their participation in the provision of such products and services (Pansera and Owen, 2018).

There seems to be some sort of underlying belief or hope – if not faith – that grand challenges require and will therefore somehow call forth grand responses. But what if the more probable response in most cases is a patchwork of many, many more bounded efforts? While the search for "scalability" in social innovation remains the touchstone for dealing with grand challenges, "replicability" of solutions may be the more realistic, albeit prosaic path. From this perspective, inclusive innovation may be an important pathway toward dealing with some of the thorniest social problems the world faces.

Much of the research on inclusive innovation is quite local and bounded. It is about whether and how relatively contained and focused efforts can bring progress against social challenges. For example, Petersen et al. (2018) compared the efforts of two sub-Saharan universities to improve small-scale farmer livelihoods by building their innovation capacity and found that small differences in their approaches to learning seemed to make substantial differences in outcomes. Such studies can suggest relatively replicable approaches to social innovation when they identify common elements that lead to success or obstacles that can be overcome. Similarly, Powell et al. (2018) conducted a longitudinal study of eight cross-sector partnerships in South Africa in which the interests of disenfranchised people were juxtaposed against the interests of an assortment of government, business and civil society participants. They uncovered a pattern in which greater progress was achieved in dealing with zero-sum tradeoffs involving inequality, poverty and environmental degradation when the participants dealt explicitly with their conflicting material interests rather than treating them as differences of perspective. Such conflicting material interests and zero-sum tradeoffs are likely to be common across many kinds of social innovation.

We might think of the myriad local efforts at inclusive innovation as sets of experiments in social inclusion. From this perspective, the proliferation of studies of more bounded examples of inclusive innovation may be a path to discoveries about what can work and gain traction more broadly, through replication. In this *Handbook*, Stott, Fava and Salwinski (2019), develop the important point that community enterprises are often resilient to "the feast and famine of public policy attention" and that they "proffer solutions." Peredo, McClean and Tremblay (2019) take this approach to broadening local social innovation one step further by asking "what we can learn from distinctively indigenous social innovation that could inform our attack on social problems faced not only by the indigenous but by other disadvantaged peoples and communities?"

ABCD

Lest we become too optimistic and start thinking that because it may be the most feasible path to scale, replication is somehow "easy," other studies such as Dacin and Dacin's examination of collective social innovation on Fogo Island (2019) highlight the importance of deep contextualization to the success of localized efforts. While their finding that "place embeddedness, community identity and community character" matter may provide general lessons, it also suggests the challenging and detailed work that would be required for replication elsewhere. This resonates as well with McGahan's argument (2019) that inclusive innovation in healthcare requires that we "evaluate, community by community, whether and how health can be supported using currently available tools and technologies . . ." Even less Panglossian, Hall et al.'s (2012) study of the Brazilian tourist industry shows how policies encouraging inclusive innovation can lead to destructive outcomes in the face of "weak institutions." They outlined how well-meaning attempts to attract travelers to the beaches of Recife and create jobs for local residents inadvertently turned the city into a magnet for "sex tourism," increasing street crime and leading to thousands of children being forced into the sex trade. Of course, the manifold replication of local solutions is hardly a panacea when we are talking about challenges of global proportions.

PATHWAYS FROM SOCIAL INCLUSION TO LARGE-SCALE, SOCIAL CHANGE

We therefore inevitably return to questions about the role of inclusive innovation in large-scale, innovative social change. There appear to be at least three important pathways to explore. The first is the provisioning of new infrastructure that can potentially level the playing field for opportunities between haves and have not. Development projects that provide access to clean water and electricity can sometimes emancipate residents (and perhaps especially female residents) from endless hours of backbreaking labor, freeing up time and energy to pursue other activities. In some cases, such large-scale projects underwritten by governments or public–private partnerships can be implemented in ways that are sensitive to local contexts and invite participation (Powell et al., 2018). One form of public infrastructure provision that has received substantial attention is access to internet connectivity. Concerns over the "digital divide" between poorer and wealthier individuals and communities also led to the idea that the internet could be a source of information, education and market access that would allow poor people and communities to improve their socio-economic status, in part through promoting entrepreneurship. Provision of telecommunication utilities can also support the provision of telemedicine into rural areas, allowing greater inclusivity in medical care (McGahan, 2019). Research on each of these topics has pointed to both successes and failures (Cumming and Johan, 2010; Warschauer, 2003), leaving open the window for research that improves our understanding of how best to deploy ICT infrastructure to support inclusivity.

A second pathway connecting inclusive innovation to large-scale, innovative social change is through corporate action (either "intrapraneurship" or "extrapreneurship" as described by Tracey and Stott, 2017). Research along these lines includes work stemming from the bestselling *Fortune at the Bottom of the Pyramid* (Prahalad, 2004) that views social engagement around inclusivity as a corporate strategic activity, as well as later work on topics such as "intrapreneurial bricolage" (Halme et al., 2012) that put the locus of activity supporting inclusivity at middle management levels. Here, too, the evidence paints a mixed picture of the success of corporate bottom of the pyramid (BoP) programs, which have also generated criticisms that they may sometimes do more harm than good for the people "at the bottom of the pyramid" (Kolk et al., 2014). An individual we know who has led dozens of BoP training programs involving immersion in poor communities put one criticism to us pretty bluntly: "It becomes like a corporate retreat for executives, like one of those ropes training trust-building weeks. They love it. Then nothing comes of it."

Finally, several bodies of research examine pathways to institutional and political change. A substantial body of work by institutional theorists has examined the institutional conditions of exclusion and inclusion and the possibilities of change (Khan et al., 2007; Lawrence and Suddaby, 2006; Mair and Marti, 2009; Tracey et al., 2011). For example, Maguire et al. (2004) studied institutional entrepreneurship in the emergence of inclusive approaches to treatment advocacy in Canada. Battilana and Dorado (2010) examined the early processes through which commercial microfinance, an intentionally inclusive and large-scale innovation, emerged and moved toward institutionalization in Bolivia.

In parallel with work on institutional innovation and entrepreneurship, a promising and somewhat critical body of work is emerging based on so-called "field theory," which focuses on the importance of social movements to broadening the impact of social innovation (Fligstein and McAdam, 2012). From this perspective, many different forms of social benefit organizations (Tracey and Stott, 2017) could be viewed as distributed instantiations of social movements. This work could lead us to treat the creation of social movement organizations as an important form of entrepreneurship (Baker and Powell, 2019). It is probably fair to say that none of the larger-scale social innovations connected to inclusive innovation has yet made any substantial dent in the list of grand challenges the world faces. It is also not yet fair to judge the contributions of management scholarship on this basis. But eventually, it will be fair to make such judgments.

Much work on inclusive innovation is in fact nicely problem-focused, rooted in concern for social issues and empathy for those who suffer most directly from Grand Challenges (e.g., Souder, 2019, Tan and Tan, 2019; Zhou and Shaw, 2019). To be only slightly irreverent, an increasing number of management and entrepreneurship scholars find themselves moved by the promise of inclusive innovation more than they find themselves moved by the promise of increasing the bottom line of multinational corporations. If, however, we want to do research that actually makes a real and positive difference, this probably has to become a main focus of our work, and achieving this focus probably requires institutional entrepreneurship closer to home.

Obviously, we cannot let go of theorizing, because we have no other vehicle for cumulating and challenging the results of research, but the theories we privilege should probably be tethered to more practical metrics than those we celebrate now. In addition, the imaginary division of labor we now sometimes describe between management researchers and those who "translate" this research to practitioners may need to be supplanted to some extent by rules for tenure, promotion and other rewards that value not only fundamental research but also getting our hands dirty doing "engaged" research and even participating in and studying "implementation."

While Grand Challenges provide a rich tableau of opportunities *for us* to build our careers by focusing on contributions to elite disciplinary journals, it may be time that we start thinking more about the opportunities our work can provide to those outside of the academy. If our underlying goal is to both *help* and *encourage* an array of players to entrain themselves to efforts to deal with grand challenges, we need to show that such efforts are opportunities – that is, that they are both desirable and feasible (Stevenson and Jarillo, 1990) – not just for us, but *for everyone else*.

EMERGENT RESEARCH THEMES IN INCLUSIVE INNOVATION

In this *Handbook*, we curate 26 contributions organized around five core themes and, in doing so, highlight the approaches by which scholars are taking up this challenge.

Social Innovation in Practice

The constituent chapters of Part II offer a range of insights pertaining to this theme: two of the chapters encourage us to question the very basis of social innovation as a "tool" for inclusion, and focus on the issue of sustainability to illustrate their arguments. Another provides a framework for rethinking social innovation pedagogy, while the remaining two chapters, respectively, focus on the distinctive challenges of social innovation in the context of healthcare and the complex web of issues surrounding social impact measurement.

In her chapter "A Silent Evolution: Innovative and Inclusive Narratives on Sustainability," Ana Cristina Campos Marques draws on complexity and chaos theories to argue that we are currently witnessing the emergence of a "new narrative" on sustainability. Based on interviews from leading figures in the sustainability field, she identifies a set of "microstories" on sustainability, contrasting them with the "grand narratives" that currently frame social understanding of the relationship between people and the natural environment. She builds a framework – the "social attractor framework" – which seeks to explain how microstories can challenge, and ultimately radically alter, dominant conceptions of sustainability. Her framework is designed to explain how deep-rooted change can unfold from micro-level action.

Christopher Wright and Daniel Nyberg's chapter on "Climate Change and Social Innovation" also focuses on sustainability, but they adopt a very different approach than the previous chapter, one based on political economy. For these authors, current approaches to sustainability – rooted in the notion of social innovation – are premised on neo-liberal myths about the role of markets, corporate self-regulation and the potential of social enterprise to offer ready-made "solutions." There is an urgent need, these authors argue, to reflect more critically on social innovation, and to view it as part of "a hegemonic political project." Their core argument is that we need an alternative conception of social innovation, one in which "social movements and communities reclaim a central role in shaping our climate future, and social innovation re-emphasizes themes of justice, equality and human rights."

Julie Battilana, Brittany Butler, Marissa Kimsey, Johanna Mair, Christopher Marquis and Christian Seelos are concerned with how to best support practitioners in their quest to address intractable social problems, and to do so at the "relevant scale." As the title of the chapter suggests – "Problem, Person, and Pathway: A Framework for Social Innovators" – the authors present a framework based around "3Ps," each of which offers a different lens that social innovators can draw upon to augment their effectiveness. They involve (1) unpacking the nature of the focal problem and the risks associated with it; (2) reflecting on the motivations and power position of the person leading the innovation; and (3) conceptualizing a pathway for change – the social innovator's position in the broader ecosystem. This distinct pedagogical approach offers rich insights for educators seeking to support social innovators.

Anita McGahan focuses her chapter on the critically important topic of "Inclusion and Innovation in Healthcare." She argues powerfully that there is a moral imperative to promote inclusion with regard to healthcare: that so many people in the world's poorest countries can live their lives without direct experience of professional healthcare is a fundamental injustice. Moreover, a core message of the chapter is that innovation is required not only in the Global South, but also the Global North: healthcare systems in many of the world's richest countries have become unaffordable. While global inequality in healthcare may be shocking, there is an opportunity for governments and organizations of different kinds to "cultivate stability and prosperity." The author offers "an agenda for research on the role of organizations, markets, and communities in social innovation in healthcare" which can help push forward knowledge in this area and which have crucial implications for practice.

Few topics are as debated in the world of social innovation as social impact measurement – an issue that tends to raise the temperature in a room of practitioners whenever it is discussed. In their chapter "How Do We Know When Social Innovation Works? A Review and Contingency Model of Social lmpact Assessment," Greg Molecke and Anne-Claire Pache tackle the core issues head on. They acknowledge that social impact is "tricky" and "ambiguous." Their chapter is important because it represents one of the few attempts to "map the current knowledge on social impact to allow researchers and innovators alike to make sense of the multiplicity of approaches currently available and to overcome the challenges associated with their implementations." The end result is a contribution which brings much needed clarity to a contested set of ideas, and which has significant implications for the study and practice of impact measurement.

Community and Place

The second core theme is community and place. As this set of chapters makes clear, communities can take many different forms, and the challenges of social inclusion and social innovation may vary dramatically across time and place. That said, there are also some commonalities, and a core insight from the contributions in the *Handbook* is that harnessing shared experience of hardship and a common identity are at the heart of effective efforts to promote social and economic inclusion in marginalized communities of all kinds.

In their chapter "Indigenous Social Innovation: What is Distinctive? And a Research Agenda," Ana María Peredo, Murdith McLean and Crystal Tremblay focus on a topic that has been sorely neglected by management and innovation researchers. As the authors make clear, social innovation in the context of indigenous communities is distinct. While these communities are many and varied, and therefore defy straightforward classification, they tend to face a particular configuration of challenges that are rooted in colonialism and racism. The authors are interested in the question of "what specifically indigenous social innovation (ISI) might look like, and whether something like that is already taking place." The specific example of T'Sou-ke – "a small, Canadian First Nation of approximately 250 members located on the southern tip of Vancouver Island" – is used to help answer this question and to show how the study of ISI has the potential to shed light on the challenges faced by other disadvantaged communities.

Jeffrey Robinson, Amol Joshi, Lutisha Vickerie-Dearman and Todd Inouye are interested in innovation in a very different context – that of urban neighborhoods. In their chapter, "Urban Innovation: At the Nexus of Urban Policy and Entrepreneurship," the authors focus on the challenges and opportunities of social inclusion through urban innovation. The overarching aim is to "synthesize the current attempts to encourage social innovation from a policy perspective and to describe the various business models that are used to enact innovative solutions to urban challenges." The particular models discussed in the chapter include social enterprise, venture accelerators, triple bottom line ventures, benefits corporations and technology parks.

Neil Stott, Michelle Fava and Natalie Slawinski's chapter – "Community Social Innovation: Taking a Long View on Community Enterprise" – explores community social innovation in its historical context with a particular focus on geographical communities. As the authors point out, while the language of community enterprise, entrepreneurship and innovation may be new, the core ideas are not. Indeed, these ideas have existed in various guises for many generations. However, academic interest appears to have waned in recent years – with attention focused instead on the apparently heroic actions of individual social entrepreneurs. The aim of the chapter is to "reinvigorate scholarly interest in community social innovation and community enterprise." To do so, the authors review the work on community economic development stretching back to the 1970s, offer a framework to support theory building around community social innovation that is rooted in practice, and offer an agenda for future research.

The contribution by Tina Dacin and Peter Dacin – "Collective Social Innovation: Leveraging Custodianship, Tradition and Place on Fogo Island" – also focuses on social innovation at the community level, but with a specific focus on how tradition and place interact to provide resources for communities. A core part of the argument is that community members can act as "vested custodians" through the reinvention and renewal of traditions, offering the possibility of "inclusive prosperity." This leads to a framework for collective social innovation with three key elements – place embeddedness, community identity and community character – each of which are "inextricably intertwined through their rootedness in place." To illustrate these arguments, the authors draw on the community of Fogo Island, a small and remote island situated off the coast of Newfoundland, which offers an interesting example of collective social innovation dynamics.

Systems, Institutions and Infrastructure

The third theme is systems, institutions and infrastructure. These chapters highlight the challenges of making the systemic social change required to tackle the most intractable social problems, whether that be supporting older people, creating public infrastructure in resource-poor environments or reconfiguring global supply chains. At the same time, however, each of the chapters in this part points to the opportunities – rooted in part in changing technology – open to social innovators, and the potential to make radical change at varying levels of scale.

David Souder's chapter on "Coordinating Infrastructure Changes to Meet Retiring Baby Boomers' Needs" is focused on a specific, but often neglected, social innovation challenge: how to cater for people's changing circumstances as they transition from employment to retirement. In the United States, as in much of the Western world, the proportion of retirement age people is set to rise dramatically. Many live in suburban areas which were designed for families rather than for older people, but the baby boomers entering retirement do not want to move, which presents a complex set of planning and infrastructure challenges. The author argues, however, that these challenges also represent an opportunity: "Done well, catering to the needs of baby boomers can jump-start demand and ultimately promote inclusion across age and income demographics, generating spillover benefits . . . and revitalizing city centers for generations to come."

Hwee-Pink Tan and Hwee-Xian Tan are also focused on issues connected to ageing, and the desire of older people to remain living independently in their homes throughout their later years. The authors' chapter, "Sustainable Technology-Enabled Innovations for Ageing-in-Place: The Singapore Example," focuses on the role of technological change, and in particular the rise of artificial intelligence, to support older people. The authors review existing initiatives designed to leverage technology to support senior citizens and introduce a framework that the authors hope will facilitate the sustainability of these efforts. They also share their own experiences of initiatives that combine technology with socio-behavioral sciences and clinical validation, backed by a collaborative ecosystem of key stakeholders, for vulnerable seniors to age well and gracefully in their own homes and local community. The chapter concludes with a set of recommendations for future research in this important area of inquiry.

In his chapter on "How Firms Bring Social Innovation and Efficiency to the Global Effort to Recover from National Uncertainty Shocks," Luis Ballesteros offers an optimistic view on the role that corporations can play in times of crisis such as natural disasters, terrorist attacks, technological accidents, pandemics and sustained episodes of violent crime. As the author notes, these crises bring with them a set of economic issues with the potential to devastate communities. More often than not, the author argues, governments, non-profits and multilateral agencies simply do not have the capabilities to meet such challenges – challenges imbued with increasing complexity as commercial activity becomes more globalized. The arguments contained in the chapter have important policy implications, and raise questions about how best to incorporate business organizations into relief efforts in an efficient and effective manner.

Nuno Gil's chapter on "The Lack of Public Goods in Emergent Economies: A Call for Research and a Case Study of an Innovative Organisational Design" addresses the thorny issue of how emerging economies can effectively provide the basic infrastructure required to meet the needs of growing populations. This is particularly challenging because policy makers in these economies are operating in the context of institutional voids – inefficient markets, ill-defined property rights, poor regulation and weak judiciary and contract-enforcement mechanisms. In developing his arguments, the author connects to the organizational design literature, contrasting the inclusive, market-based approach of Western governments to infrastructure development with the centralized, state-led approach found in China. The author introduces a research agenda based around the concept of "ambidextrous systems." In doing so, he draws on the "extreme" case of the upgrading of Cairo's "garbage cities" – a project that effectively and quickly promoted the development of much needed infrastructure while at the same time challenging and changing key elements of the institutional environment.

Silvia Dorado and Pablo Fernández focus on a core question in social innovation research: How can we replicate – and therefore magnify the impact of – effective solutions to social problems? Their chapter – "An Institutional Framework to the Scaling Up of Inclusive Social Innovations: The Case of La Salada" – draws on core ideas from institutional theory in order to address this question. They focus in particular on the importance of two concepts: (1) justification – the arguments that actors use "to frame and gain support for innovations" and (2) cooptation – the power dynamics "that frame the negotiations required for a social innovation to gain permanency and diffuse." To illustrate their arguments, the authors draw on the fascinating case of La Salada, a market located in a "dodgy" municipality on the outskirts of Buenos Aires, which provides opportunities for marginalized people to "create, develop, and grow their businesses from backroom workshops to legal or paralegal establishments."

Warren Nilsson also draws on institutional theory, and particularly the notion of institutional work, to explore social innovation and radical social change. His chapter, "Social Innovation as Institutional Work," conceptualizes social innovation as a kind of social movement. The overarching goal of this movement is to promote "everyday systemic agency," and the core challenge involves connecting "macro-systemic grand challenges to micro-praxis." An institutional work lens is particularly useful, it is argued, because such a lens helps to reveal the complex power dynamics and vested interests that are inevitably implicated when actors engage in deliberate institutional change. Five "performative dimensions" of institutions are outlined – roles, social identities, resource flows, authority processes and meanings – which can be used by researchers and practitioners to investigate whether a particular social innovation is creating deep-rooted change at the level of the system.

In their chapter "Challenges for Global Supply Chains and Opportunities for Social Innovation," Yong Kim and Gerald Davis suggest that the increasingly dispersed nature of supply chains in the global economy presents an intriguing set of issues and possibilities for those seeking to make positive social change. Specifically, the fragmentation of supply chains renders monitoring and control very difficult; indeed, even ascertaining the identity of supply chain members is far from straightforward in some industries. However, it is this very disaggregation that presents opportunities for social innovators, because it allows them to enter supply chains with relatively few resources. The effects of social innovations can also be amplified in a way that was unthinkable when the traditional Chandlerian approach to supply chain organization was predominant: "the impact of small-scale innovative activities and services with social purposes may be transferred to different parts of global supply chains due to the complexity and interdependencies among the related companies."

Individuals, Organizations and Organizing

The chapters that constitute the fourth core theme are diverse in the topics they cover and the theories they draw upon, but collectively they show the multi-level nature of inclusive and social innovation. Charlene Zietsma and Madeline Toubiana begin this part with a contribution that unpacks the crucial, but often neglected, role that emotion can play in social change. Their chapter on "Emotion as the Glue, the Fuel and the Rust of Social Innovation" draws attention to a range of affective dynamics that can shape the nature of social innovation in fundamental ways. Crucially, these dynamics can both facilitate and impede efforts to create positive social outcomes. The chapter is structured around three different types of social innovation – social entrepreneurship, social intrapreneurship and social extrapreneurship. It draws on three discrete metaphors – social innovation as glue, fuel and rust – to explore the emotional underpinnings of each of these forms of social innovation. The metaphors are used to derive a research agenda which highlights a fascinating set of issues for social innovation researchers to explore.

Xiang Zhou and Jason Shaw focus on a topic that goes to the heart of inclusive and social innovation: inequality. Indeed, much of the motivation to engage in social and inclusive innovation stems from a desire to address this issue. The authors begin their chapter – "Income Inequality: Consequences and Implications for Social Innovation" – by considering definitions of income inequality and the challenges of measuring it. They then review the outcomes of inequality at two different levels: within organizations and within nations. They conclude with a powerful research agenda on income inequality and social innovation, and offer a series of "social-innovation-based actions that organizations and governments may take to address income inequality." In doing so, they point out that management research has not engaged systematically on the topic of inequality, and highlight a range of opportunities to make important contributions – both practical and theoretical.

Yasser Bhatti and Jaideep Prabhu focus on the interrelationship between three influential concepts: social innovation, frugal innovation and inclusive innovation. In their chapter, "Frugal Innovation and Social Innovation: Linked Paths to Achieving Inclusion Sustainably," the authors offer a theoretical model that connects social innovation and frugal innovation using the concept of inclusion as a "common denominator." The core argument is that, when these concepts are combined into an overarching framework, new opportunities arise to solve the Grand Challenges of our time and improve social and economic inclusion sustainably around the world. In addition, the authors highlight a range of possibilities for future research at the intersection of social, frugal and inclusive innovation, and consider their potential implications.

Elizabeth Embry, Jessica Jones and Jeff York focus on "one of the greatest managerial challenges of our time": the role of entrepreneurship of different kinds – economic, social, institutional and environmental – as a way of tackling human-induced climate change, a problem that is set to worsen as the global population grows and consumption increases. In their chapter on "Climate Change and Entrepreneurship," these authors argue that, while management research has focused mainly on corporations and policy makers, the limitations of these actors in meaningfully addressing the problem have become all too apparent. Their core argument is that there is a set of entrepreneurial opportunities embedded in the ecological, societal and human health impacts of human-induced climate change, and that we urgently need to understand more about the nature of these opportunities and how entrepreneurs can exploit them. The theory offered in the chapter represents a starting point for entrepreneurship research that may help to find solutions to climate change impacts.

Marya Besharov, Wendy Smith and Tiffany Darabi consider a specific organizational form deeply implicated in addressing social issues – social enterprise – and a specific theoretical perspective that has played a key role in illuminating social enterprise dynamics – paradox theory. Their chapter, "A Framework for Sustaining Hybridity in Social Enterprises: Combining Differentiating and Integrating," focuses on the challenge of how organizations can sustain two apparently conflicting logics over time. To do this successfully, the authors argue, social enterprises need to combine features that "*both* differentiate *and* integrate logics." Interestingly, the authors show how this can be done at the individual, group and organizational levels. They construct a framework that highlights the potential for social enterprises to combine logic differentiation and integration. This framework allows the authors to offer a research agenda on social enterprise sustainability, which contains valuable suggestions for moving research on this topic forward.

The last chapter in this part is by Yves Plourde and is concerned with "Organizing for Global Change." As the author makes clear, there is no shortage of seemingly intractable global problems – problems that are "systemic and structural," meaning that "despite their urgency there is a tendency to deny that they even exist." Addressing such problems requires global change organizations with the ability to collaborate across organizational and sectoral boundaries, but this is far from straightforward. Drawing on sensemaking theory, the chapter outlines three fundamental challenges inherent in organizing for global change (making sense of the focal problem, the construction of an action plan to deal with it, and the organization of people and resources). To illustrate these challenges, three discrete episodes in the history of a high-profile global change organization – Greenpeace – are explored and discussed.

Networks and Social Change

The final theme of the *Handbook* contains four chapters concerned with relationships and ways of organizing within and between organizations. A key theme that emerges from these chapters is that addressing the most deep-rooted social issues requires collaborations across organizations of very different kinds. At the same time, such collaborations are far from straightforward and bring with them many challenges that need to be navigated and negotiated. Ann Florini begins the part with a chapter on "Collaborative Governance," which she defines as a type of governance that "goes beyond the traditional governmental hierarchies and market-based approaches" to collaboration. The concept is connected to a range of practices that have emerged in multiple domains including public management, corporate social responsibility and multi-stakeholder collaboration, and is seen as essential to the achievement of global goals. It is, the author argues, an important social innovation in its own right because it represents a novel way of organizing designed to address deep-rooted social problems involving a range of actors including communities, foundations, corporations and governments. The chapter builds new theory about collaborative governance and suggests research opportunities designed to help scholars shed new light on it.

Arno Kourula's contribution considers a related set of issues to Ann Florini's: it focuses on alliance networks as an emerging and increasingly common type of collaboration designed to addresses the "grand challenges" of our time. His chapter, "Inclusive Innovation Through Alliance Networks," begins by outlining what he terms "the collaborative imperative" and the need to move beyond conventional approaches to collaboration if we are to address these grand challenges. It then explores research to date in the field of alliance network studies, highlighting in particular the concept of an organizational role as a key element in the functioning of alliance networks "as drivers of inclusive innovation." The author concludes the chapter by offering a research agenda to help guide scholars in their study of alliance networks from a role-based perspective.

The chapter by Christian Busch and Harry Barkema focuses on the role of social networks in social innovation. Their chapter – "Social Entrepreneurs as Network

Orchestrators: A Framework and Research Agenda on Networks and Leadership in the Context of Social Innovation" – makes the case that social networks are fundamental to any meaningful attempts to address social problems, and that these networks inevitably cut across sectoral boundaries. The authors make the important point that while there has been a burgeoning of research about the role of social networks in the creation and scaling of commercial ventures, network dynamics in the context of social innovation remain poorly understood. In response, the authors develop a framework of "transformative network orchestration" that builds on and extends existing work on networks and leadership, and applies them to social innovation. As well as offering an intriguing set of ideas for the study of social innovation, the chapter offers important opportunities for future research.

The final chapter in the *Handbook* by Helen Haugh and Maggie O'Carroll, "Empowerment, Social Innovation and Social Change," focuses on the key issue of empowerment – arguably a building block of social innovation, albeit one that is often ignored or glossed over by researchers in management and organization studies. As the authors point out, this concept is often considered in the context of women in the Global South, but applies irrespective of gender and country setting. It begins by critically analysing the concept, including with respect to its definition and measurement. A novel framework that helps to make sense of and organize empowerment research is then offered, as are some "cautionary tales for empowerment researchers."

Together, these chapters provide a comprehensive coverage of levels of analyses, contexts and applications of inclusive innovation and social change. Whereas each chapter acts as a call for research, we now discuss how a research agenda on social inclusion and innovation can also address on-the-ground problems.

A RESEARCH AGENDA ON SOCIAL INCLUSION AND INNOVATION

Social inclusion and innovation has been a topic that management scholars have taken up with significant enthusiasm, mostly over the past two decades. Yet, other social and applied sciences have championed this effort for much longer. Our focus as management scholars has been to integrate some of these views on how businesses and organizations can become actors for social change. Furthermore, innovation as a domain of study can also be applied to organizing processes. By building on management research on innovation, we can then focus on social inclusion as the core phenomenon of interest. In doing so, management scholars can systematically engage with other social and applied science disciplines to define research questions, examine empirical contexts and generate replicable, scalable, customizable solutions to the seemingly intractable problem of social inclusion. In this section, we highlight the persistent barriers to inclusion as a phenomenon of study.

Our chapters draw on a rich diversity of theoretical lenses. With previous calls for management research on inclusive innovation, the focus has been on achieving theoretical richness – by explaining problems and contexts with potential for social impact (e.g., George and Schillebeeckx, 2018; George et al., 2012; George et al., 2016). The response to these calls for research on framing theoretical problems around "Grand Challenges" has been strong. Yet, as we mention in the introduction of this chapter, scholarly attention has been on the theoretical development and richness rather than on highlighting potential ways to solve the problem itself. The maturity of the management field in understanding such grand challenges has also commensurately increased. In this *Handbook*, we now call for a shift from *theoretical focus* to *practical action*.

Tractable Problems of Inclusion and Social Change

Our chapters in this *Handbook* draw from a rich repertoire of theories, and tackle wide-ranging phenomena and contexts where inclusion and social change are the key outcomes. Our scholarly training encourages us to frame a social problem through a theoretical lens, because theoretical contribution is the currency that is carried from one context to another, and one article to a subsequent article. Another, perhaps less traditional, approach is to highlight the problem itself. If we could focus our energies on the problem itself, then perhaps we could similarly generate a compendium of solutions to the problem across contexts – allowing a cumulativeness in our energies to tackle societal maladies. We hope that as students become professors, they will devote greater energies and define their own work through the problems they seek to solve. This problem-solving orientation in management could someday soon become the primary pathway to impact and relevance of our academic scholarship.

Problems of access

When is inclusion defined to be a problem? When not everyone has access to a product or service that is generally seen as a meaningful enhancer of social or economic wellbeing. Perhaps then some scholars in the management field could champion systematic efforts at addressing problems of access as their singular focus of research. Some chapters provide frameworks and outcomes by which inequality is perpetuated and can be addressed (e.g., Zhou and Shaw, 2019). In many studies on financial inclusion, for example, the fundamental problem of growth is access to banking facilities. But more powerful in the individual's economic wellbeing is when individuals can then access credit facilities such as microfinance loans. The "digital divide" is a problem of accessing the internet or other mobile-based services, and even more so, accessing information and knowledge that could lead to more productive activities, for example, access to weather information, seeds or pesticides for improving the productivity of farming practices.

Substantial research on gender issues in the workplace is framed around fairness and opportunities for growth for women, and thereby highlights one form of the problem of access (e.g., Joshi et al., 2015). More recent access problems are seen in housing, health-care and urban infrastructure where significant potential for community and perhaps world-saving solutions exist; several are highlighted in contributions in this *Handbook* (e.g., McGahan, 2019; Robinson et al., 2019; Souder, 2019; Tan and Tan, 2019). Our theoretical approaches to access can be translated into solutions or perspectives on access. Scholars can address the challenges of access by asking questions about: (1) the physical and social barriers to access; (2) the seeking or the provisioning of access (or the lack thereof); and (3) the behavioral and socio-economic impact of access.

Problems of scale

Often, large-scale social change requires systems or macro-level changes in values, norms and institutions. A substantial literature exists on institutional theory approaches to social change and social movements. Institutional theory has been a popular lens because of its flexibility to explain multi-level change across multiple actors and multiple time frames. The problem of scale, however, is a substantive issue. A problem of scale might require solutions of scale, making scalability of field-level interventions an important selection criterion. In this *Handbook*, Dorado and Fernández (2019) and Nilsson (2019) suggest institutional approaches to social innovation and change, and provide avenues for future research.

Significant institutional infrastructure weakness, such as lack of healthcare, or sudden shocks, such as currency devaluation or civil strife, might challenge the entire system and trigger mass migration for economic or political reasons. Such substantial shifts that affect the social fabric while causing systemic upheaval call for institutional solutions to alleviate suffering and declining quality of life. In contrast, it is perhaps misconstrued that large-scale problems require commensurately complex and large-scale solutions. This might not be the case – not all problems require complex, institutional change. Energy access issues, such as rural electrification, and slum infrastructure upgradation through combinations of interventions such as solar installations, lamps and toilets are simple and yet effective ways of addressing social problems (e.g., Parikh et al., 2012; Parikh et al., 2015). Although climate change is a large-scale problem, it can be tackled in part by local entrepreneurship efforts (Embry et al., 2019). The presence of large-scale problems provides a new focus for scholars in search of solutions: (1) What attributes of large-scale problems might influence the nature of solutions for social innovation? (2) When do institutional solutions provide more sustainable outcomes and impact relative to speedier interventions? (3) Are there patterns of institutional change in social innovation exemplars? (4) What factors make for scalable solutions, and what influences their success?

Problems of localization

Social change, irrespective of scale, is implemented at the local or community levels, which raises important challenges of rejection or acceptance of solutions, as well as adaptation of solutions to local mores, values and customs. Peredo et al. (2019) ask the question of what makes for indigenous social innovation. Frugal innovation (e.g., Bhatti and Prabhu, 2019) emphasizes local solutions to local problems. Besharov and colleagues (2019) suggest that there is a need to differentiate and integrate solutions in social enterprises. Similarly, Stott and colleagues (2019) articulate the need for community-level enterprises in social innovation. Dacin and Dacin (2019) provide a rich case study of Fogo Island where solutions leverage the community's distinct identity and traditions.

Perhaps the localization problem is addressed when we adopt the Problem, Person, Pathways framework proposed by Battilana and colleagues (2019). Busch and Barkema (2019) suggest that solutions require individual leadership and mobilization of resources across local networks. The challenge of localization could imply the lack of scalability of solutions, which raises an important paradox for social innovation scholars: (1) What are the nature of tradeoffs between localization and globalization of social impact solutions? (2) How do successful projects navigate the localization problem through customization? (3) When is it necessary to localize solutions? (4) How do we leverage local solutions for global impact? (5) What modifications in organization or behaviors are needed to effectively scale local solutions to global problems?

Problems of behavioral change

Social science scholars have dedicated decades of effort in understanding behavioral change. The provision of public goods and services is not uniform across countries and contexts, and in many places the expectations of such services are non-existent (e.g., Gil, 2019). Changing individual, firm and community-level behaviors has been noted as the root cause of sustainability challenges, for example, in natural resource consumption and degradation on non-renewable natural resources (e.g., George and Schillebeeckx, 2018). One approach to changing behaviors for social change is through empowerment (e.g., Haugh and O'Carroll, 2019). Zietsma and Toubiana (2019) point to emotions as the core driver of behavioral change. Yet, as our chapters note, the challenges of empowerment and sustaining emotional commitment through these efforts remain significant.

Every day we hear news of floods, fires and natural calamities – and often these events are blamed on climate change. More detailed analyses will shed light on contributing local causes such as excessive housing construction in flood plains, or over-farming and depletion of natural barriers such as trees and forests. Climate change and sustainability are significant domains where social innovation and inclusivity become critical drivers (e.g., Marques, 2019; Wright and Nyberg, 2019). Those of us living in coastal communities would vouch for the plastic crisis in our rivers and oceans. European countries have implemented supplementary charges for use of plastic bags for grocery shopping in order to curtail rubbish disposal. Recently, Thailand and the Philippines closed several of their scenic islands that have been ravaged by tourism in order to allow replenishment of natural habitats. Innovative efforts by Ant Forest, a division of the Chinese payments giant Ant Financial, have adopted a mobile gamification approach to instil sustainability sensibilities and a savings mentality in their customers, and correspondingly create real world impact by planting trees commensurate to their customers' virtual world behaviors. These are examples where behavioral changes are needed, and are being implemented.

The solutions for behavioral change could well involve a multipronged approach, which correspondingly raises interesting problems to study and solve: (1) When do different behavioral change efforts succeed, and why? (2) What motivates individuals to change behaviors, and what are the different behavioral responses to change stimuli? (3) What factors influence thresholds or tipping points for behavioral change and attention allocation to problem solving?

Problems of collaboration and coordination

Collective action and common resource problems have been highlighted with the award of the Nobel Prize for Elinor Ostrom's work. Yet, this is just the beginning as shown by the chapters on collaborative and network models of governance for new models to organize for impact (e.g., Florini, 2019; Kourula, 2019; Plourde, 2019). Collaboration and coordination highlight fundamental challenges in organizing collective action where goals and incentives differ among parties. Studies have examined contexts such as disaster aid or the coordination of medical supplies (e.g., Ballesteros, 2019). We need more efforts in understanding how collaboration can be successful in a tri-sector context. The Sustainable Development Goals list Partnerships as a priority area – to highlight the need for collaboration between the private sector (business), the public sector (government) and civil society (non-governmental organizations, communities and individuals). This tri-sector collaboration becomes the bedrock of social innovation and change. Yet, management research provides very limited understanding of how collaboration between multiple parties can be structured, aligned and executed successfully. Though there are some works on public–private partnerships, for example, in healthcare (e.g., Caldwell et al., 2017; Roehrich et al., 2014), there is a substantive lack of attention on solutions by which private and public coordination and collaboration can be made successful. The problems of coordination and collaboration raise several attendant challenges requiring organizational solutions: (1) How do we create goal congruence among actors with divergent interests and backgrounds? (2) How do we structure relationships, contracts and mechanisms to reinforce collective action for the collective good? (3) What types of problems require tri-sector collaboration, and when is it better for public–private, public–civic, private–civic dyadic forms of organizing?

Problems of transparency and impact

Trust is at a deficit. Societal trust in business and government are at historic lows. In such an environment, asking individuals to rise above their misgivings to solve a collective problem is a challenge – and this influences whether individuals and firms engage. The lack of trust also suggests that individuals no longer find credible the promises of firms when they advertise products as sustainable. In some cases, firms are culpable when they claim more sustainable processes than they actually use, labeled "greenwashing." Kim and Davis (2019) point out that the "Nikefication" of global supply chains means that the production of goods through globally sourced and distributed processes further reduces the verifiability of sustainable practices. Even if not deterred by lack of trust, individuals might believe that the scale of the problem is so large that their individual effort is meaningless. These issues suggest that if solutions could provide easier ways to assess impact or verify corporate claims on sustainability this might support engagement in positive change behaviors.

Molecke and Pache (2019) provide frameworks that begin to unpack the problems of social impact assessment. New technologies, such as blockchain, offer new solutions to the trust and verifiability of impact assessment. For example, blockchain is now being used to verify farm-to-fork sustainability practices in farming, logistics and packaging in grocery chains. New financial models of "tokens" allow tokenizing of forests and promote sustainable forestry or natural resource consumption. Such new technologies and new models of assessment provide avenues to assess impact easily and inexpensively, which raises new questions for management scholars: (1) How can impact assessment be done more efficiently and effectively? (2) How do verifiability and trust impact behaviors and engagement? (3) What factors influence the credibility of corporate claims on sustainability or social impact? (4) When do new technologies allow for creative new models of social change at large scale?

CALL TO ACTION

Our introductory chapter and this *Handbook* provide a call to action. Each chapter in the *Handbook* provides fresh insight into a global problem and associated solutions to tackling it. Inclusive innovation is the development of new ideas which aspire to create opportunities that enhance social and economic wellbeing for disenfranchised members of society – it has action and actionability at the core of its definition. The *Handbook* is organized into distinctive themes: (1) social innovation in practice; (2) community and place; (3) systems, institutions and infrastructure; (4) individuals, organizations and organizing; and (5) networks and social change. These five themes reflect current theoretical approaches and frameworks, cut across levels of analysis, and provide a rich tapestry of problem-solution contexts that can guide future research.

Our emphasis on action suggests a fundamental shift in management scholarship by focusing sustained scholarly effort on deep-rooted and seemingly intractable global problems, with the explicit aim of social impact. To catalyse our conversations, we have provided six classes of problems: (1) access, (2) scale, (3) localization, (4) behavioral change, (5) collaboration and coordination, and (6) transparency and impact. While these six problems are not meant to be comprehensive, they provide a foundation to begin an exploration of solutions. When a former UN Secretary General launched the Sustainable Development Goals he provided a call to action by saying, "There is no Plan B, because there is no Planet B." We are hopeful that management researchers, and business scholars more broadly, will adopt an action-oriented approach to their scholarship, and define the success of their work through its social impact outcomes.

REFERENCES

Aguinis, H. and Glavas, A. 2012. What we know and don't know about corporate social responsibility: a review and research agenda. *Journal of Management*, 38(4), 932–68.

Baker, T. and Pollock, T.G. 2007. Making the marriage work: the benefits of strategy's takeover of entrepreneurship for strategic organization. *Strategic Organization*, 5, 297–312.

Baker, T. and Powell, E. 2019. Entrepreneurship as a new liberal art. *Small Business Economics*, 52(2), 405–18.

Ballesteros, L. 2019. How firms bring social innovation and efficiency to the global effort to recover from disasters. In G. George, T. Baker, P. Tracey and H. Joshi (eds), *Handbook of Inclusive Innovation: The Role of Organizations, Markets and Communities in Social Innovation*. Cheltenham, UK and Northampton, MA, USA: Edward Elgar Publishing, pp. 225–47.

Battilana, J. and Dorado, S. 2010. Building sustainable hybrid organizations: the case of commercial microfinance organizations. *Academy of Management Journal*, 53(6), 1419–40.

Battilana, J., Butler, B., Kimsey, M., Mair, J., Marquis, C. and Seelos, C. 2019. Problem, person and pathway: a framework for social innovators. In G. George, T. Baker, P. Tracey and H. Joshi (eds), *Handbook of Inclusive Innovation: The Role of Organizations, Markets and Communities in Social Innovation*. Cheltenham, UK and Northampton, MA, USA: Edward Elgar Publishing, pp. 61–74.

Besharov, M., Smith, W. and Darabi, T. 2019. A framework for sustaining hybridity in social enterprises: combining differentiating and integrating. In G. George, T. Baker, P. Tracey and H. Joshi (eds), *Handbook of Inclusive Innovation: The Role of Organizations, Markets and Communities in Social Innovation*. Cheltenham, UK and Northampton, MA, USA: Edward Elgar Publishing, pp. 394–413.

Bhatti, Y. and Prabhu, J. 2019. Frugal innovation and social innovation: linked paths to achieving inclusion sustainably. In G. George, T. Baker, P. Tracey and H. Joshi (eds), *Handbook of Inclusive Innovation: The Role of Organizations, Markets and Communities in Social Innovation*. Cheltenham, UK and Northampton, MA, USA: Edward Elgar Publishing, pp. 354–76.

Busch, C. and Barkema, H. 2019. Social entrepreneurs as network orchestrators: a framework and research agenda on networks and leadership in the context of social innovation. In G. George, T. Baker, P. Tracey

and H. Joshi (eds), *Handbook of Inclusive Innovation: The Role of Organizations, Markets and Communities in Social Innovation*. Cheltenham, UK and Northampton, MA, USA: Edward Elgar Publishing, pp. 464–85.
Caldwell, N., Roehrich, J. and George, G. 2017. Social value creation and relational coordination in public–private collaborations. *Journal of Management Studies*, 54(6), 906–28.
Cumming, D. and Johan, S. 2010. The differential impact of the internet on spurring regional entrepreneurship. *Entrepreneurship Theory & Practice*, September, 857–83.
Dacin, M.T. and Dacin, P.A. 2019. Collective social innovation: leveraging custodianship, tradition and place on Fogo Island. In G. George, T. Baker, P. Tracey and H. Joshi (eds), *Handbook of Inclusive Innovation: The Role of Organizations, Markets and Communities in Social Innovation*. Cheltenham, UK and Northampton, MA, USA: Edward Elgar, pp. 167–84.
Di Domenico, M., Haugh, H. and Tracey, P. 2010. Social bricolage: theorizing social value creation in social enterprises. *Entrepreneurship Theory and Practice*, 34(4), 681–703.
Dorado, S. and Fernández, P.D. 2019. An institutional framework to the scaling up of inclusive social innovations: the case of La Salada. In G. George, T. Baker, P. Tracey and H. Joshi (eds), *Handbook of Inclusive Innovation: The Role of Organizations, Markets and Communities in Social Innovation*. Cheltenham, UK and Northampton, MA, USA: Edward Elgar Publishing, pp. 266–83.
Dorado, S. and Ventresca, M.J. 2013. Crescive entrepreneurship in complex social problems: institutional conditions for entrepreneurial engagement. *Journal of Business Venturing*, 28, 69–82.
Eisenhardt, K.M., Graebner, M.E. and Sonenshein, S. 2016. Grand challenges and inductive methods: rigor without rigor mortis. *Academy of Management Journal*, 59(4), 1113–23.
Embry, E., Jones, J. and York, J.G. 2019. Climate change and entrepreneurship. In G. George, T. Baker, P. Tracey and H. Joshi (eds), *Handbook of Inclusive Innovation: The Role of Organizations, Markets and Communities in Social Innovation*. Cheltenham, UK and Northampton, MA, USA: Edward Elgar Publishing, pp. 377–93.
Ferraro, F., Etzion, D. and Gehman, J. 2015. Tackling grand challenges pragmatically: robust action revisited. *Organization Studies*, 36(3), 363–90.
Fligstein, N. and McAdam, D. 2012. *A Theory of Fields*. New York: Oxford University Press.
Florini, A. 2019. Collaborative governance. In G. George, T. Baker, P. Tracey and H. Joshi (eds), *Handbook of Inclusive Innovation: The Role of Organizations, Markets and Communities in Social Innovation*. Cheltenham, UK and Northampton, MA, USA: Edward Elgar Publishing, pp. 433–50.
George, G. 2014. Rethinking management scholarship. *Academy of Management Journal*, 57(1), 1–6.
George, G. and Schillebeeckx, S. 2018. *Managing Natural Resources: Organizational Strategy, Behavior and Dynamics*. Cheltenham, UK and Northampton, MA, USA: Edward Elgar Publishing.
George, G., McGahan, A.M. and Prabhu, J. 2012. Innovation for inclusive growth: towards a theoretical framework and research agenda. *Journal of Management Studies*, 49(4), 661–83.
George, G., Howard-Grenville, J., Joshi, A. and Tihanyi, L. 2016. Understanding and tackling societal grand challenges through management research. *Academy of Management Journal*, 59(6), 1880–95.
Gil, N. 2019. The lack of public goods in emergent economies: a call for research and a case study of an innovative organisational design. In G. George, T. Baker, P. Tracey and H. Joshi (eds), *Handbook of Inclusive Innovation: The Role of Organizations, Markets and Communities in Social Innovation*. Cheltenham, UK and Northampton, MA, USA: Edward Elgar Publishing, pp. 248–65.
Hall, J., Matos, S., Sheehan, L. and Silvestre, B. 2012. Entrepreneurship and innovation at the base of the pyramid: a recipe for inclusive growth or social exclusion? *Journal of Management Studies*, 49(4), 785–812.
Halme, M., Lindeman, S. and Linna, P. 2012. Innovation for inclusive business: intrapreneurial bricolage in multinational corporations. *Journal of Management Studies*, 49(4), 743–84.
Hambrick, D.C. 2007. The field of management's devotion to theory: too much of a good thing? *Academy of Management Journal*, 50(6), 1346–52.
Haugh, H.M. and O'Carroll, M. 2019. Empowerment, social innovation and social change. In G. George, T. Baker, P. Tracey and H. Joshi (eds), *Handbook of Inclusive Innovation: The Role of Organizations, Markets and Communities in Social Innovation*. Cheltenham, UK and Northampton, MA, USA: Edward Elgar Publishing, pp. 486–502.
Joshi, A., Neely, B., Emrich, C., Griffiths, D. and George, G. 2015. Gender research in AMJ: an overview of five decades of research and call to action. *Academy of Management Journal*, 58(5), 1459–75.
Khan, F.R., Munir, K.A. and Willmott, H. 2007. A dark side of institutional entrepreneurship: soccer balls, child labour and postcolonial impoverishment. *Organization Studies*, 28, 1055–77.
Kim, Y.H. and Davis, G.F. 2019. Challenges for global supply chains and opportunities for social innovation. In G. George, T. Baker, P. Tracey and H. Joshi (eds), *Handbook of Inclusive Innovation: The Role of Organizations, Markets and Communities in Social Innovation*. Cheltenham, UK and Northampton, MA, USA: Edward Elgar Publishing, pp. 305–20.
Kolk, A., Rivera-Santos, M. and Rufín, C. 2014. Reviewing a decade of research on the "Base/Bottom of the Pyramid" (BOP) concept. *Business & Society*, 53(3), 338–77.
Kourula, A. 2019. Inclusive innovation through alliance networks. In G. George, T. Baker, P. Tracey and H.

Joshi (eds), *Handbook of Inclusive Innovation: The Role of Organizations, Markets and Communities in Social Innovation*. Cheltenham, UK and Northampton, MA, USA: Edward Elgar Publishing, pp. 451–63.
Lawrence, T.B. and Suddaby, R. 2006. Institutions and institutional work. In S.R. Clegg, C. Hardy, T.B. Lawrence and W.R. Nord (eds), *Handbook of Organization Studies*, 2nd edn. London: Sage, pp.215–54.
Lewin, K. 1943. Psychology and the process of group living. *Journal of Social Psychology*, 17, 113–31.
Maguire, S., Hardy, C. and Lawrence, T.B. 2004. Institutional entrepreneurship in emerging fields: HIV/AIDS treatment advocacy in Canada. *Academy of Management Journal*, 47(5), 657–79.
Mair, J. and Marti, I. 2009. Entrepreneurship in and around institutional voids: a case study from Bangladesh. *Journal of Business Venturing*, 24, 419–35.
Marques, A.C.C. 2019. A silent evolution: innovative and inclusive narratives on sustainability. In G. George, T. Baker, P. Tracey and H. Joshi (eds), *Handbook of Inclusive Innovation: The Role of Organizations, Markets and Communities in Social Innovation*. Cheltenham, UK and Northampton, MA, USA: Edward Elgar Publishing, pp. 24–46.
McGahan, A.M. 2019. Inclusion and innovation in healthcare. In G. George, T. Baker, P. Tracey and H. Joshi (eds), *Handbook of Inclusive Innovation: The Role of Organizations, Markets and Communities in Social Innovation*. Cheltenham, UK and Northampton, MA, USA: Edward Elgar Publishing, pp. 75–82.
Molecke, G. and Pache, A.C. 2019. How do we know when social innovation works? A review and contingency model of social impact assessment. In G. George, T. Baker, P. Tracey and H. Joshi (eds), *Handbook of Inclusive Innovation: The Role of Organizations, Markets and Communities in Social Innovation*. Cheltenham, UK and Northampton, MA, USA: Edward Elgar Publishing, pp. 83–105.
Nilsson, W. 2019. Social innovation as institutional work. In G. George, T. Baker, P. Tracey and H. Joshi (eds), *Handbook of Inclusive Innovation: The Role of Organizations, Markets and Communities in Social Innovation*. Cheltenham, UK and Northampton, MA, USA: Edward Elgar Publishing, pp. 284–304.
Pansera, M. and Owen, R. 2018. Framing inclusive innovation within the discourse of development: insights from case studies in India. *Research Policy*, 47, 23–34.
Parikh, P., Chaturvedi, S. and George, G. 2012. The effects of energy provision on individual aspiration in slum communities. *Energy Policy*, 50, 477–85.
Parikh, P., Fu, K., Parikh, H., McRobie, A. and George, G. 2015. Infrastructure provision, gender and poverty in Indian slums. *World Development*, 66, 468–86.
Peredo, A.M., McLean, M. and Tremblay, C. 2019. Indigenous social innovation: what is distinctive? And a research agenda. In G. George, T. Baker, P. Tracey and H. Joshi (eds), *Handbook of Inclusive Innovation: The Role of Organizations, Markets and Communities in Social Innovation*. Cheltenham, UK and Northampton, MA, USA: Edward Elgar Publishing, pp. 107–28.
Petersen, I., Kruss, G., Gastrow, M. and Nalivata, P.C. 2018. Innovation capacity-building and inclusive development in informal settings: a comparative analysis of two interactive learning spaces in South Africa and Malawi. *Journal of International Development*, 30(5), 865–85.
Plourde, Y. 2019. Organizing for global change. In G. George, T. Baker, P. Tracey and H. Joshi (eds), *Handbook of Inclusive Innovation: The Role of Organizations, Markets and Communities in Social Innovation*. Cheltenham, UK and Northampton, MA, USA: Edward Elgar Publishing, pp. 414–31.
Powell, E.E., Hamann, R., Bitzer, V. and Baker, T. 2018. Bringing the elephant into the room? Enacting conflict in collective prosocial organizing. *Journal of Business Venturing*, 33, 623–42.
Prahalad, C.K. 2004. *The Fortune at the Bottom of the Pyramid*. Philadelphia, PA: Wharton School Publishing.
Robinson, J.A., Joshi, A.M., Vickerie-Dearman, L. and Inouye, T. 2019. Urban innovation: at the nexus of urban policy and entrepreneurship. In G. George, T. Baker, P. Tracey and H. Joshi (eds), *Handbook of Inclusive Innovation: The Role of Organizations, Markets and Communities in Social Innovation*. Cheltenham, UK and Northampton, MA, USA: Edward Elgar Publishing, pp. 129–44.
Roehrich, J., Lewis, M. and George, G. 2014. Are public–private partnerships a healthy option? A systematic review. *Social Science & Medicine*, 113, 110–19.
Souder, D. 2019. Coordinating infrastructure changes to meet retiring baby boomers' needs. In G. George, T. Baker, P. Tracey and H. Joshi (eds), *Handbook of Inclusive Innovation: The Role of Organizations, Markets and Communities in Social Innovation*. Cheltenham, UK and Northampton, MA, USA: Edward Elgar Publishing, pp. 186–205.
Stevenson, H.H. and Jarillo, J.C. 1990. A paradigm of entrepreneurship – entrepreneurial management. *Strategic Management Journal*, 11, 17–27.
Stott, N., Fava, M. and Slawinski, N. 2019. Community social innovation: taking a long view on community enterprise. In G. George, T. Baker, P. Tracey and H. Joshi (eds), *Handbook of Inclusive Innovation: The Role of Organizations, Markets and Communities in Social Innovation*. Cheltenham, UK and Northampton, MA, USA: Edward Elgar Publishing, pp. 145–66.
Tan, H-P. and Tan, H-X. 2019. Sustainable technology-enabled innovations for ageing-in-place: the Singapore example. In G. George, T. Baker, P. Tracey and H. Joshi (eds), *Handbook of Inclusive Innovation: The Role*

of Organizations, Markets and Communities in Social Innovation. Cheltenham, UK and Northampton, MA, USA: Edward Elgar Publishing, pp. 206–44.
Tracey, P. and Stott, N. 2017. Social innovation: a window on alternative ways of organizing and innovating. *Innovation*, 19(1), 51–60.
Tracey, P., Phillips, N. and Jarvis, W. 2011. Bridging institutional entrepreneurship and the creation of new organizational forms: a multilevel model. *Organization Science*, 22(1), 60–80.
Warschauer, M. 2003. *Technology and Social Inclusion: Rethinking the Digital Divide*. Cambridge, MA: MIT Press.
Wright, C. and Nyberg, D. 2019. Climate change and social innovation. In G. George, T. Baker, P. Tracey and H. Joshi (eds), *Handbook of Inclusive Innovation: The Role of Organizations, Markets and Communities in Social Innovation*. Cheltenham, UK and Northampton, MA, USA: Edward Elgar Publishing, pp. 47–60.
Zhou, X. and Shaw, J.D. 2019. Income inequality: consequences and implications for social innovation. In G. George, T. Baker, P. Tracey and H. Joshi (eds), *Handbook of Inclusive Innovation: The Role of Organizations, Markets and Communities in Social Innovation*. Cheltenham, UK and Northampton, MA, USA: Edward Elgar Publishing, pp. 342–53.
Zietsma, C. and Toubiana, M. 2019. Emotions as the glue, the fuel and the rust of social innovation. In G. George, T. Baker, P. Tracey and H. Joshi (eds), *Handbook of Inclusive Innovation: The Role of Organizations, Markets and Communities in Social Innovation*. Cheltenham, UK and Northampton, MA, USA: Edward Elgar Publishing, pp. 322–41.

PART II

SOCIAL INNOVATION IN PRACTICE

2. A silent evolution: innovative and inclusive narratives on sustainability

Ana Cristina Campos Marques

INTRODUCTION

> We hear the noise of the falling oak, but we do not hear the noise of the growing forest. Today, much is said about things that are falling apart, that make noise, but the most important is what we do not hear. We need to pay attention to the seeds of awareness that are sprouting. (Jean-Yves Leloup)

Humanity is going through a unique moment, a time of sustainability challenge so complex that it can influence all life on the planet. Scholars named this epoch the Anthropocene because of the likely influence of humankind on the planet's natural systems. This sustainability challenge is manifested in many interdependent social, environmental and economic crises. Examples are biodiversity loss, poverty, climate change, corruption, refugees, pollution, natural disasters, among many others. With all these challenges it seems that chaos has taken over the world, and that the challenges are so complex that it does not seem possible to solve them. To complicate matters further, the mainstream media invariably focus on mass dissemination of chaos on sustainability in every corner of the planet and narrate these challenges in such a way that they appear even more complex and impossible to tackle. Perhaps the mainstream media are not focusing on the different emerging narratives because, while they are still sparse and not widespread, they do not seem to have much impact on solving the complex sustainability challenge. Additionally, mainstream research in sustainability is trying to tackle the challenges, but due to their complexity, it seems that the results are not provided fast enough to be applied in society. These complex challenges call for different scientific approaches to tackle them.

Meanwhile, there is a different narrative on sustainability emerging worldwide. Small groups of people are silently innovating, and solving the various challenges of society, in an inclusive way. It seems like a silent evolution, which is not printed on the covers of newspapers and is not widely disseminated in scientific journals. The purpose of this study is to shed light on these new narratives on sustainability that are emerging from the social field in business, civil society and education/science. Additionally, in order to study the innovative and inclusive narratives on sustainability, I focus this research on the narratives that simultaneously benefit individuals, society and the planet. To understand these narratives on sustainability along with the actual chaos of the social systems, this study has a theoretical basis on complexity and chaos theories. These theories show that change emerges from micro to macro. Accordingly, this research is about change emerging from micro, that is, narratives by small groups of people that are not part of the mainstream narratives. In other words, this research is about microstoria (Boje, 2001) as it focuses on the emerging narratives on sustainability rather the mainstream ones. To understand the emerging narratives, I interviewed sustainability experts and change makers. I also collected insights from different conferences on sustainability and management.

In addition to shedding light on the innovative and inclusive narratives on sustainability, another purpose of this study is to understand the deeper patterns of these emerging narratives. Once these patterns are understood, more people can be made aware of them and might be inspired to make more positive changes in their communities. Moreover, according to complexity and chaos theories, the effects of small changes can be amplified through phenomena like the butterfly effect (Lorenz, 1963), positive feedbacks and self-organizing systems. Inspired by the language of this relatively new science of chaos, I call the main framework – the combination of patterns in the emerging narratives – the social attractor. To understand the narratives and their patterns I use hermeneutics (Gadamer, 1976 [2013]; Heidegger, 1953 [2010]; Ricoeur, 1981 [2016]). Then, combining my observations with key constructs from complexity science, I present some initial ideas about this pattern. Finally, I reflect on a research agenda, through the emerging pattern, for tackling the sustainability challenge in more innovative and inclusive ways.

THEORETICAL PERSPECTIVES

> He who wants to have right without wrong,
> Order without disorder,
> Does not understand the principles
> Of heaven and earth.
> He does not know how
> Things hang together
> (Chuang Tzu, Chinese philosopher, fourth century BC)

Narratives on Sustainability

Narratives come after living stories, they narrate them. According to Boje, narrative "adds 'plot' and 'coherence' to the story line" (2001, p. 1). Flory complements this by defining narrative as the "reflective product of looking back and making sense of stories constructed to making sense of life" (2008, p. 70). This study focuses on the narratives that are related to sustainability. Scharmer (2017) classifies these narratives as muddling through, moving backward and moving forward.

The muddling through narratives are the ones that maintain the status quo or business as usual (Scharmer, 2017). Examples of muddling through narratives on sustainability are corporate social responsibility and sustainability as small practices, that is, not integrated in the core business of the company. Another example is research on the business case for sustainability, which aims to understand if sustainability pays off while maintaining the narrative of business as usual. This narrative seems to understand the limits of the planet, but does not make the necessary changes to sustain life within these planetary limits. Elkington and Braun (2013) describe this kind of narrative of change as business as usual, stating that it "works for 30–40% of 7 billion people" (p. 47). Therefore, it is an exclusive narrative as it neither works for the majority of people nor for the planet.

The moving backward narratives are the "making X great again" (Scharmer, 2017) ones. This kind of narrative wants to bring back a narrative from the past. Examples of moving backward narratives on sustainability are climate change denial, which reduces investments in clean energy and allocates investments in dirty energy, like oil and coal. This narrative denies the limits of the planet and assumes an endless use of resources – perhaps because this kind of narrative seems to assume fast and magical technological solutions for challenges. Elkington and Braun (2013) name this narrative as breakdown and show that it worked for the "wealthy 1% of 1–2 billion of people" (p. 47) in the past. Therefore, it is an extremely exclusive narrative, as it excludes the vast majority of people and it also denies the limits of the planet.

The moving forward narratives are concerned with disruption and breakthrough (Elkington and Braun, 2013). According to Scharmer, these narratives lean "into the unknown to co-sense and co-create the future" (2017). Examples of moving forward narratives on sustainability are circular economy, collaborative consumption, new technologies contributing to positive externalities, amongst others. The moving forward narratives understand the limits of the planet and change the paradigms to sustain life within these limits. According to Elkington and Braun (2013), this type of narrative will work for a "growing majority of 9–10 billion people" (p. 47). Therefore, this is a more inclusive narrative, as it works for people and the planet. Thus, the moving forward narratives are the focus of this study. To further explore the moving forward narratives, I discuss the concept of social innovation. Social innovation may be defined as "a broad range of organizational and inter-organizational activity that is ostensibly designed to address the most deep-rooted 'problems' of society, such as poverty, inequality and environmental degradation" (Tracey and Stott, 2017, p. 51). This research studies the narratives of this kind of innovation by small groups of people. Furthermore, the focus of this research is on the innovative narratives which are inclusive, that is, the ones that benefit simultaneously individuals, society and the planet. Figure 2.1 shows these inclusive dimensions. It is noteworthy that there is a broad range of different narratives co-existing in the chaos of society nowadays.

Figure 2.1 Inclusive dimensions of the narratives in this study

The Dance of Chaos and Order

New ways to understand chaos and change emerged from the study of complex systems (Wheatley, 2006). Complexity science "seeks to understand how the complex behavior of a whole system arises from its interacting parts" (Complexity Explorer, 2017). In this study the whole system is the entire society and the interacting parts are small groups of people. Additionally, for the complexity theorists change emerges from micro to macro. In the words of Auster and Freeman (2013): "What seem to be more macro issues, whether they are external 'forces,' 'big challenges' or 'them' or positive change, are actually the aggregated result of people making choices" (p. 43). In this research, I study the changes that are occurring in society as a whole through the analysis of innovative and inclusive narratives on sustainability which are emerging from small groups of people.

Although this study focuses on the innovative and inclusive narratives on sustainability, there are different narratives which are metaphorically dancing with each other. Some examples of these different narratives are presented above as the muddling through and moving backward narratives. These diverse narratives also help the chaotic societal system to see itself and may provide the information for the entire system to evolve, or not. The dance of these contrasting narratives, then, is full of possibilities, the chaotic system is experiencing itself in different ways. Thus, each person in the social field makes choices, moment by moment. And from thousands of seemingly antagonistic choices, the human system dances and develops. This is nothing new. The difference now is what some scholars call the Anthropocene. It is a time when the human community has enough technology to unbalance the systems that sustain life on the planet, including human life. However, the incredible moment of this chaos can be used in other ways. Using the existing technology and knowledge of humanity, the experience of this chaos can be used to evolve as a society in a way that we could never have imagined before. We might have the opportunity to end hunger, misery and to live in harmony with the systems that sustain life on the planet. This is because chaotic moments can shake off old assumptions and paradigms, creating the opportunity for new possibilities to materialize in the social field.

With that said, the purpose of this study is not to deny the importance of all the different narratives of this moment of societal chaos, but to shed light on the inclusive and innovative ones, as a way to inspire people to see other possibilities. As mentioned above, other narratives are very well observed in the mainstream media and elsewhere. This study gives voice to the inclusive and innovative narratives on sustainability which are silently emerging in different parts of the world. In order to delve deeper into these innovative and inclusive narratives on sustainability, in the following I present the concepts of antenarrative and social attractor.

Antenarrative and Social Attractor

Antenarratives come before the narratives (Boje, 2001). In this study, antenarratives are the fragmentary formative ideas in the interviews, lectures and documents analysed, the building blocks of stories and narratives (Boje, 2001; Perey, 2014). Figure 2.2 presents antenarratives in reference to living stories and narratives. Next, I present the deeper level of the antenarratives, part of complexity and chaos theories, which in this study I call the social attractor.

Complexity theory is technically known as nonlinear dynamics, which is computer-based mathematics that allows scientists to handle the enormous complexity of some systems (Capra and Luisi, 2016). An important aspect of complexity theory is that it involves non-linear mathematics. When a nonlinear equation is solved, the result is not a formula but a geometric pattern (Capra, 2016). It is more qualitative than quantitative mathematics. It is a mathematics of relationships and patterns (Capra, 1996). In the case of chaotic systems, the patterns formed are called strange attractors (in this research I call this the social attractor), which can be defined as trajectories in the phase space that exhibit fractal geometry (Capra, 1996). If we observe a chaotic system over time, it demonstrates an inherent state of order; its actions remain within an invisible boundary. It is worth mentioning that in a chaotic system it is impossible to predict the values of the variables at a given moment, but it is possible to predict the qualitative characteristics of the system (Capra, 1996), which is the objective of this study. This means that this study is qualitative; it does not concentrate on the quantitative characteristics of the narratives studied (for example, statistics), but on their qualitative characteristics and their main pattern, the social attractor.

Social science researchers (for example, Boje, 2001; Perey, 2014) have studied patterns in the antenarratives of systems in a normal state. Following the discoveries of mathematics, physics and natural sciences, they called these patterns fractals. However, according to the relatively new discoveries of these sciences, in the case of chaotic systems, another kind of pattern is formed, the strange attractor, which in this study I call the social attractor. I named the main pattern the social attractor because this research is related to the new narratives emerging from the social field, which seem attracted by the actual moment of chaos in society. Still, like the fractals, I assume that the social attractor is dispersed in the antenarratives (Boje, 2001; Perey, 2014). Figure 2.2 schematizes the position of the

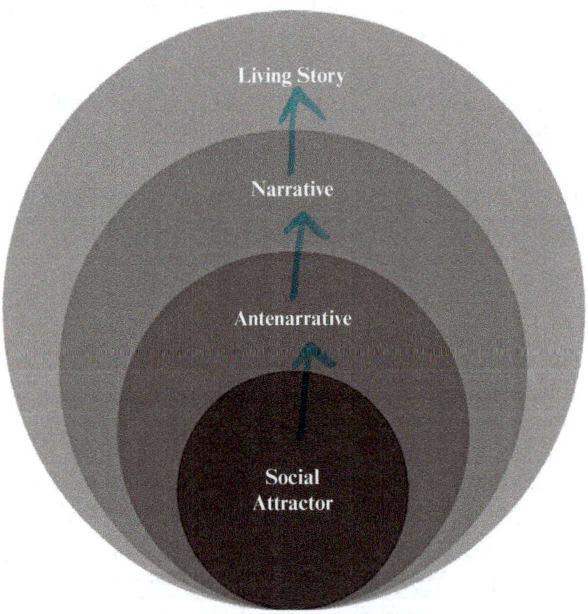

Figure 2.2 Social attractor pattern in reference to living story, narrative and antenarrative

social attractor within the concepts of living story, narrative and antenarrative. In this research, then, I aim to understand this social attractor, that is, the pattern of innovative and inclusive narratives on sustainability by small groups of people. Once the pattern is understood, people might be inspired by it to make more positive changes in their communities.

INNOVATIVE AND INCLUSIVE NARRATIVES

> But, caution is in order. If we just replace one centre with our own authoritative centre, we have fallen into our own trap. The point then is not to replace one centre with another, but to show how each centre is in a constant state of change and disintegration. (Boje, 2001, p. 19)

A Time of Transition and Change?

This study was inspired by the surprising and growing moments that I have encountered on innovative and inclusive narratives on sustainability. This type of narrative seems to have increased in recent years. Below are some examples of these narratives.

In 2016, during the organization of an online conference on sustainability and corporate responsibility (Cosustentare, 2016) for Portuguese-speaking countries, several times I heard about transition and change through innovative and inclusive narratives.

> I assume that we are facing a major transition that is complete and goes through different spheres. (Leticia, professor, October 2016)

> But have no doubt that I think this change is occurring, it leads us to give up some things, to leave the old, and this doesn't necessarily have suffering, but it has pain. It's almost a movement of death, a feeling that something must die. (Eva, entrepreneur, January 2015)

Similarly, I again heard about these narratives during recent conferences I attended, for example:

> If we know where to look, we can see the new emerging. (Frederic Laloux, consultant, Power & Care, September 2016)

Additionally, from another source, this narrative appears again:

> Everyone knows that we live in a moment of profound disruption. An old order is about to end. And something new is about to be born. (Otto Scharmer, researcher, November 2017)

As mentioned above, innovative and inclusive narratives on sustainability are the focus of this study. Of course, narratives such as muddling through and moving backward continue to be present in the mainstream media and society. These narratives dance with one another, and they are all part of the current chaos of the societal system. In the following, I present the concept of the microstoria, which is the basis of the narratives discussed in this study.

Microstoria

Innovative and inclusive narratives on sustainability are not the mainstream narratives, or in the vocabulary of Boje the "grand narratives" (2001, p. 45). This study is about the microstories of small groups of people. It is noteworthy that "microstory is often about resisting a grand narrative" (Boje, 2001, p. 60). The research is thus about broadening the perspectives of actual mainstream narratives on sustainability. Microstorians do not select the narratives "for their statistical frequency, but because they constitute the 'apparently exceptional'" (Boje, 2001, p. 45). In this study, then, I select the innovative and inclusive narratives on sustainability. My purpose is to shed light on these innovative and inclusive narratives on sustainability and their metaphorical dance with the other types of narratives, not to control or to impose any kind of narrative. In the words of Boje, the "more a narrative works to control a centre, even one with a grain of truth, the more the narrative spirals out of control" (2001, p. 19). In addition, I do hope that society will develop in a moving forward way and in the following present the basis for this hope.

Hope through Complexity and Chaos Theories?

The new understandings of complexity and chaos theories may give some hope for the evolution of the societal system. Below are some concepts of these theories that are related to this study.

The butterfly effect

Chaotic systems are characterized by extreme sensitivity to the initial conditions, so small changes in the initial state of the system can lead to large-scale consequences over time (Capra, 1996). This is known as the butterfly effect, from the famous statement of the meteorologist Edward Lorenz (1963) that the flap of a butterfly's wings in one part of the world could create a storm somewhere else (Capra, 1996). This is because chaotic systems are nonlinear and so small events can have huge consequences. Conversely, sometimes big events can have small consequences. This is the beauty and also the difficulty of a chaotic system, which is full of possibilities for better or worse. After the chaos, the societal system has two main possibilities: self-transcendence or self-dissolution (Pozzati, 2007). In self-transcendence, the system comes into equilibrium again, but in a different form, which is generally more complex and evolved than the previous one. In self-dissolution, the system disintegrates. My purpose in this study is to shed light on the inclusive and innovative narratives on sustainability. And perhaps this tiny contribution can also help the actual chaotic system of society to self-transcend, a moving forward way.

Feedback and amplification

In a nonlinear system, such as the chaotic one, very tiny variations can amplify into completely unexpected results (Wheatley, 2006), such as the butterfly effect. This is due to the repeated amplification by means of self-reinforcing feedback (Capra, 1996). The feedback effect is studied by cybernetics, which uses negative feedback to bring a system back to equilibrium. But in the case of nonlinear systems, the focus is on the positive feedback that amplifies the change and moves the system even further from equilibrium. Exemplifying this effect of positive feedback in social systems in the words of Plowman et al.: "When social systems experience stress, people or groups that were independent become highly interdependent, often as the result of a crisis or turbulence of some sort. In highly interconnected systems, positive feedback reinforces an initial signal and can amplify small changes" (2007, p. 520). These nonlinear feedback processes are the basis of the evolution of systems for new forms of organization (Capra, 1996), as described below.

Self-organizing systems

When a nonlinear system receives positive feedback, it chooses to react to it or not. However, if the positive feedback becomes a disturbance of such magnitude that the system can no longer ignore it, there is a real change. At a point with many internal disturbances and far from equilibrium, the system disintegrates, but this disintegration does not mean its end (Wheatley, 2006). If it can keep its own identity, the system can reconfigure itself in a higher level of complexity (Capra, 1996), that is, an evolved form. This characteristic of nonlinear systems is studied in different areas of science. The following examples are in chemistry, physics and neuroscience. In chemistry, Ilya Prigogine received the Nobel Prize in 1977 for his work that demonstrated how certain chemical systems reorganize themselves in a more complex order, when faced with changes. Prigogine and Stengers (1984) created the term "dissipative structures" to describe the contradictory nature of these systems. The dissipation describes a loss, a process of gradual flow of energy, while the structure describes the order embodied (Wheatley, 2006). In a dissipative structure, anything that disturbs the system (positive feedbacks) has the crucial role of helping it to self-organize into a new and evolved form. In physics, Hermann Haken studied the laser. He discovered that when a beam of light is bombarded energetically (positive feedback) to get out of equilibrium, it self-organizes into a new and evolved form, the laser light (Capra, 1996). In neuroscience, Humberto Maturana and Francisco Varela coined the term *Autopoies*es (Varela et al., 1974), which means self-creation. This means that a living system modifies itself for self-preservation (Wheatley, 2006).

The actual chaos of the societal system with different and seemly opposite narratives may help the system, through positive feedbacks, to self-organize into a new form. Maybe the following patterns in the analysis of the microstories of this study might be a preview of what is coming as the next main narratives in our society. Of course, there are no guarantees that this will happen, but the innovative and inclusive narratives assessed in this study combined with complexity and chaos theories indicate some hope.

THE SOCIAL ATTRACTOR FRAMEWORK

In this section, I describe how I found the patterns of the innovative and inclusive narratives on sustainability. Then, combining these patterns with the chaos and complexity theories, I develop a comprehensive pattern, the social attractor framework.

Data Sources

The initial insights on the innovative and inclusive narratives on sustainability were obtained through interviews with sustainability experts and change makers. Additionally, I have also collected insights from a number of international sustainability and management conferences that I have attended in the last couple of years. This study aims to understand the pattern of these narratives through the following perspectives: business, civil society and science/education. I chose these perspectives because generally they are where the sustainability narratives are originally formed, before the interpretation of the mainstream media. In what follows, I describe more about the sources of the narratives in the study.

Interviewees

I interviewed 42 sustainability experts and change makers. These respondents work as consultants, entrepreneurs, executives and professors. Some of these interviews were conducted through questions and others through lectures on a theme related to sustainability. The lectures were initially intended for an online conference on sustainability and corporate responsibility (Cosustentare, 2016) that I organized. The respondents come from a variety of national, ethnic and educational backgrounds and age groups. Although most of the interviewees are Brazilians, there were also four Americans (Central, North and South America) and seven Europeans. A total of 19 interviewees were conducted with men and 23 with women. All respondents have at least a Bachelor's degree and eight have a PhD degree. The interviews were all voice-recorded, most of them were video-recorded, and all were transcribed in full. To protect the respondents' identity, they were all assigned pseudonyms when quoted. Also, particular personal episodes were concealed and only their principal groups were mentioned (consultant, entrepreneur, executive or professor).

Conferences

I also collected insights about the patterns from the following conferences:

- 7th International Conference on Corporate Sustainability and Responsibility at Humboldt-Universität zu Berlin, 14–16 September 2016.
- Power & Care – A Mind & Life Dialogue with HH The Dalai Lama at Bozar Center for Fine Arts, Brussels, 9–11 September 2016.
- Academy of Management Conference at Anaheim, California, 4–9 August 2016.

It is worth pointing out that although I have nearly 20 years of experience in the field of sustainability and have had access to a great diversity (people, cultures and countries) of narratives in this area, this study is limited to my own experience and interpretation of these narratives.

Hermeneutics

The analysis was guided by hermeneutics, which derives from the Greek term *hermeneuein* that means "to interpret." In this research I use hermeneutics to go deeper, to understand the deep pattern of the innovative and inclusive narratives on sustainability. Therefore, to interpret the pattern of the narratives on sustainability in this study, I use the following principles of hermeneutics.

Part and whole: in a chaotic system, according to Wheatley (2006), it is important to focus on the whole to understand how these systems reveal their patterns. Moreover, since a large amount of information is analysed in this study, great care is needed to not get lost in the details of the narratives, seeing only the chaos. Therefore, I use the hermeneutics principle of part and whole, considering the parts as the single narratives and the whole as all the analysed narratives, their context and my own experience on sustainability. To find the patterns, I searched in the narratives analysed for the themes that were repeated. I agree with Wheatley (2006) that to find the patterns in chaotic systems one must assume an attitude of reflection and patience. This is because it is difficult to see a pattern when one is very close to the details of the narratives, the patterns take time to reveal themselves. But with patience and reflection, the patterns start to reveal themselves and elegantly show another way of seeing chaos. Table 2.1 shows each of the 13 patterns found, along with some exemplary quotes. It is noteworthy that these patterns were not developed by any central organization (for example, government, business, etc.), but are emerging from the social field in different parts of the world.

Pre-understanding and understanding: the process of understanding as more important than its results, or the process as its own result (Alvesson and Sköldberg, 2009). Additionally, introducing Paul Ricoeur's (1974a, 1974b, 1981 [2016]) hermeneutic arc between explanation and understanding (Alvesson and Sköldberg, 2009), in this study I combined complexity and chaos theories with the narratives on sustainability. Thus, combining scientific theories (explanation) with narratives (understanding).

Pattern of interpretation: in the words of Alvesson and Sköldberg, it is "the coherent whole of partial interpretations" (2009, p. 99). In this study, the global pattern of interpretations is the social attractor, which I looked for within the innovative and inclusive narratives on sustainability. This main pattern is discussed next.

The Main Pattern: The Social Attractor

Analysing the data (from the sources described above) through hermeneutics, I found 13 patterns emerging on the innovative and inclusive narratives for sustainability (Table 2.1). I focused on understanding how these patterns could combine into one main pattern. It was not an easy task to combine all these emerging patterns into a comprehensive one. First, inspired by the dissipative structures of the Nobel Prize laureate Ilya Prigogine (Prigogine and Stengers, 1984), I put the patterns in an initial framework resembling the dissipative structures. However, after feedback from fellow researchers, I realized that the framework did not consider the relationships among the patterns nor resemblance to a strange attractor, the main pattern in complex systems. I therefore tried different combinations of the patterns, but again without success to find a comprehensive one. Then, I focused more on the attractor, which is a set of states (patterns in this study) which a system tends towards, cycling through it for some time (Complexity Explorer, 2017; Complexity Labs, 2018). Thus, a social attractor in this research is the set of patterns which a societal system tends towards, cycling through it for some time (Complexity Labs, 2018). Then, combining the definition of social attractor with the shapes of chaotic attractors (mainly inspired by the Lorenz, 1963 attractor) and the patterns emerging in the innovative and inclusive narratives for sustainability, I came up with the main pattern in this study. Figure 2.3 shows the social attractor framework, the comprehensive pattern in this study. On the left side of Figure 2.3 are the patterns that are more related to inner dimensions in society, and on the right side are the ones more related to the outer dimensions in society. In between the inner and outer patterns is the "Openness to Review Beliefs

Table 2.1 Patterns in the inclusive and innovative narratives on sustainability

Pattern	Exemplary Narratives
Openness to Review Beliefs and to Evolve	We can't create health organizations if we can't imagine health organizations. We continue to create social systems that require us to be aggressive, because this is what we believe. (Robert Quinn, AOM, 2016)
	If an organization wants to attract talent and bring in people who are capable of promoting transformation and responding in the context of sustainability; but it is not willing to change, then it will not work. So, organizations also need to be open to transforming themselves into this process. (Leticia, professor, 2016)
	Most CEOs who are purpose driven, they did not start with this mindset, they were mainly in mindset economics. They become purpose driven through crisis, personal transformation. (Robert Quinn, AOM, 2016)
	Instead of continuing to look outside, looking at the objective aspects – which are important. There is a fundamental dimension to happen, which is how each one makes his evolutionary process, enters and honors his journey of personal transformation. (Andre, consultant, 2016)
Authenticity and Vulnerability	We see being authentic as an ongoing process of conversation that not only starts with perceived values but also involves one's history, relationships with others, and aspirations. Authenticity entails acting on these values for individuals and organizations and thus also becomes a necessary starting point for ethics. (Freeman and Auster, 2011, p. 15)
	One side effect of a purpose driven company is that CEOs open themselves and become vulnerable. (Robert Quinn, AOM, 2016)
	What is a leader's ability to be vulnerable? We leave a little of that history, that model, the leader who is a hero, who knows everything, who will solve everything, who will account, who will teach, and come to a leader who is vulnerable after all. And being vulnerable in a scenario of transition, uncertainty, complexity, it also opens space for other people to contribute and bring their best to help, since he will not handle everything alone. (Leticia, professor, 2016)
Balance, Care and Respect	If you do not have balance you do not sustain, because the support has to be in time, it has a time, it cannot sink in the moment, so, you see that there is no sustainability. You see that the basis, the fundamentals are very solid, are balanced, so will sustain. (Gabriel, professor, 2015)
	Because if you do not take care of yourself, of your universe, how can you care for the planet? (Alice, entrepreneur, 2015)
	I need to work to make my business fit into nature. (Amelia, consultant, 2015)
	I cannot say that I will call my employees to save energy, it is not because I want to get richer. It's because I want to make my company steal less energy from the collective. (Gabriel, professor, 2015)
	I work a lot from the human point of view, from respect, from opening the spaces, from respecting the local culture, the local infrastructure. And logically, bring out what is the original culture of the parent company of the country where this company comes from, but harmonize with what there is here. That is, you have to have this respect, this bridge. (Patricia, consultant, 2015)
	Responsibility to ensure a balance in the source and the resource from where it comes . . . So I think you have to figure out a formula to understand how far an enterprise, a project, an action can grow. Respecting a cycle and giving space to others, transforming what could be competition into partnerships, in cooperation. (Davi, professor, 2015)

Ethics and Values	Therefore, I advise students everywhere that if they cannot find the company that matches their way of seeing the world, their purpose and values, start a new one! (Genaro, professor, 2016) So the company has this obligation because it is occupying a space in society, it is occupying an economic space. So I think the company has an obligation to have an emblematic and symbolic role of values that help build society. (Gabriel, professor, 2015) There is a disintegration agreement, let's put it this way, between people and business. I invite you to investigate a little better where these points of attention are and to think together ways to get out of this corporate hypocrisy towards people. These are the practices that invite people to disintegrate in the name of sustaining their vacancies and the progression of their careers, based on incredible personal, family, and social sacrifice. (Sandra, consultant, 2016) Economic growth alone by growth does not makes sense. We have already seen this. So, if we could think of a growth of value, if we were more aware of our own existence on this planet, how should you cohabit with your fellows on this planet, I think there would be a big step. (Gabriel, professor, 2015)
Compassion and Wisdom	My first principle or personal vision statement, in few words, is to expand the world's collective wisdom and compassion . . . Wisdom without compassion is ruthlessness, and compassion without wisdom is folly. (Weiner and Gordhamer, 2013) I have to meditate, but I also have to learn differential and integral calculus. (Amelia, consultant, 2015) The exact sciences must leave this Cartesian view and integrate more in the one of the natural capitalism, is no longer only technology, money; but it's people and it's environment. (Cesar, professor, 2015) So, the university is very good and improving for the knowledge of the rational and intellectual world. But, let's put to people the importance of self-knowledge too, take care of the inner landscapes. If you do not have these two things balanced, neither process is sustainable. Neither do I just grow growing self-knowledge, spiritual elevation, stay in that unsustainable lightness of being. That's sustainable, these two things going together. (Sofia, professor, 2015)
Mindset of Abundance and Prosperity	What we want is to live in a happy world, to live in a world that has for all and that has abundance for all. (Beatriz, entrepreneur, 2015) They do not know, but it has for everyone. Then, collaborate, do not compete, share, do not hold knowledge, share. Why do I put this up? Because we work together and it's these paradoxical things or paradigms that are changing . . . (Arthur, entrepreneur, 2015) There is much talk today about sustainable prosperity and not just about sustainable development. What is the point of prosperity and not running after development, perhaps growth, which in the long run is unsustainable? I believe that the word prosperity reflects this much more. We have a prosperous company, which does not mean that it is a company that is growing at a rate of 20 or 30% a year. The prosperous company is the one that manages to compensate the people who are there, manages to deliver a positive thing to society, it manages to make the world better. (Airton, professor, 2016) I have a company, I am prosperous, but the country is not prosperous. I am prosperous, and the country is miserable, it's not nice, what can I do to help? (Diego, consultant, 2015)

Table 2.1 (continued)

Pattern	Exemplary Narratives
Collaboration and Multiple Value Creation	I am not a competitive being, I am a collaborative being. Also, if I am a collaborative being I live more in peace. (Helena, consultant, 2015)
	We are moving from a modus operandi of serving myself to a modus operandi of contribution. Where I can contribute individually with my talent, with my competencies and we collectively within the organization with the talents and competencies of the organization, with the essence and purpose of the organization. (Samuel, consultant, 2016)
	I have learned to do a lot with little, to listen more than to talk, to work cooperatively, to think along with people. And I have freed myself from my arrogance to think that I know everything, and I have all the answers and started to build the answers collaboratively. (Mauro, consultant, 2016)
Freedom, Reflection and Dialogue	If you take care of freedom, truth will take care of itself. (Ed Freeman, AOM, 2016)
	I am becoming more willing to promote reflection spaces, where people can work and rescue this kind of reflective and autonomous human. (Manuela, consultant, 2015)
	Reflection allows you to open up possible paths that you can choose because you begin to think of everything that you are generating. Why am I here? Or why do I make a lot of sustainable waste or not? What do I do? This question of how we do what we do in a way that manages a more sustainable world or not? . . . How do we live what we live in a way that generates suffering? (Manuela, consultant, 2015)
	There is no time when people are debating this issue, wondering what action we should take now, what impacts it has in the future. In an ideal organization you should have more time for this. (Carlos, executive, 2015)
	So I believe that sustainability is with this deep look, beyond the surface. (Eva, entrepreneur, 2015)
	The sustainability of an organization, it has to go through the review of power models, basically, is the history of dialogue, co-creation. (Camila, consultant, 2015)
Networks and Interdependence	I believe a lot in networks, and networks in different ways. I do not believe there has to be a person who decides everything, I believe the whole knows more than the unity. (Arthur, entrepreneur, 2015)
	I think the correct would be small or medium enterprises and organizations to act in network. But each respecting a sustainable limit, not only in the sense of profit. Sustainable in the sense of the bigger more imbalance it can cause, including economic. (Davi, professor, 2015)
	If I try to pull a supplier a lot, if I try to make the most out of it, he will have to take it from someone, and that's not win–win relationships . . . And it's important that both grow together, so that I can have a long-term maintenance of a company . . . If I make win–lose relationships, in which only I win, they are not sustainable relationships and I cannot grow. (Helena, consultant, 2015)

Blurring of Borders	I believe that I cannot really differentiate my professional from my personal. As I told you, we begin to realize this relationship in everything, which you will hardly be able to separate into fragments, you will have to understand the dynamics. So, every customer that comes, it generates a new dynamic and that's life! There is a movement for sustainability, because when it comes we both create a new relational dynamic. (Eva, entrepreneur, 2015)
	These identity issues are very dangerous, who am I? I am important, I am the employer, and you are the employee. I am the contractor and you are the staff. I am the owner of the company and the rest is stone, the rest is tree. So this type of relationship that puts us as distant, they cannot keep up, they cannot handle long-term maintenance. (Helena, consultant, 2015)
	So, I also see that all this is going to have to make people move, multidisciplinary, is going to have to have this look, call several people to look at different possibilities. (Eva, entrepreneur, 2015)
	Because this story of speaking in country also no longer makes much sense. Sustainability no longer depends on one country. Economically everything is so interconnected, socially everything is so connected and environmentally everything so connected, that it no longer makes sense if you talk about country policies. It makes sense to talk about global policies. (Carlos, executive, 2015)
Diversity and Culture	I think the first thing in terms of organizational management, which is essential for sustainability, is the one dealing with the difference. Because three people in a room already have diversity, imagine two thousand. And then our model (patriarchal, military, industrial revolution) is to flatten diversity and homogenize people. (Camila, consultant, 2015)
	Much emphasis was given to the external issue, to the technical question of sustainability, which is important. But an important question that is the internal question, both individual and collective, has been left aside. So now is the time to develop the inner self, the awareness of sustainability. And in a collective way, we work on the sustainability culture of organizations. (Airton, professor, 2016)
	And we humans think we can go to any system with the same posture, and sometimes it is not. You need to find your place within that new system, that it has another story, another pattern. So this I find a respect for life, you fit in, you dance with the system. (Eva, entrepreneur, 2015)

Table 2.1 (continued)

Pattern	Exemplary Narratives
Circular and Exponential	All businesses must strive to become completely circular. (Volans, 2016, p. 7) A circular economy is one that is restorative and regenerative by design and aims to keep products, components, and materials at their highest utility and value at all times, distinguishing between technical and biological cycles. (MacArthur Foundation, 2015, p. 3) Circular economy in much more than waste, it is about: Wasted resources, Wasted capacity, Wasted embedded values, Wasted lifecycles. (CSR Berlin, 2016) Use of the forest what is necessary for a given cycle . . . There is no exaggeration of accumulation and there is no feeling of lack. There is a feeling that the forest, it gives according to needs, according to the cycles, then we respect needs and cycles. (Davi, professor, 2015) A shift from incremental to exponential mindsets and ambitions; from our current focus on the negative impacts of economic activity to the deliberate generation of positive impacts; and from the business case for action to a reconsideration of business models that ensures industries are fit for tomorrow's very different market and geopolitical realities. (Volans, 2016, p. 3)
Purpose and Positive Impact	[The purpose of] organizations are for us to create the conditions for societies to develop. (Carlos, executive, 2015) What enables transformation are resilient and healthy communities. That is to say, the sense of community, of being together at the service of a cause, of a purpose, and of making that cause and purpose the agglutinating element that makes the whole greater than the sum of the parts, this is a key step in the sustainability agenda. (Andre, consultant, 2016) What good is it to sell my time to this company in exchange for a salary? Does that dignify my life? Does this accomplish my purpose? What is my purpose? How much is there a connection between my personal purposes, my personal values, the way I want to live my life and the values of the company where I am hired? (Sandra, consultant, 2016) The company is a means to find solutions to society. (Gabriel, professor, 2015)

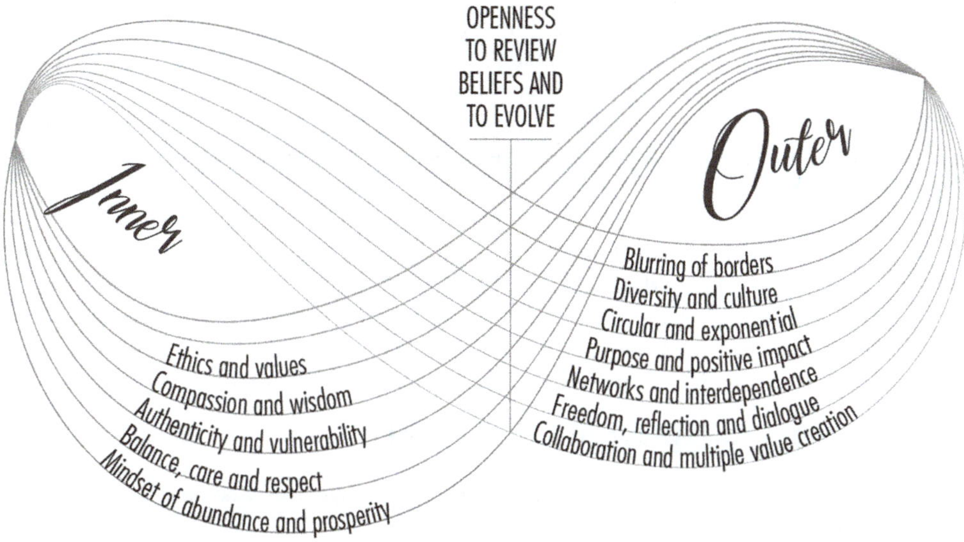

Figure 2.3 The social attractor framework

and to Evolve," which "attracts" the other patterns. Thereafter, the pattern goes to the inner dimensions (inner developments) to the outer dimensions (outer expressions), and so on, cycling though both sides of the social attractor framework. Through the openness to review beliefs and to evolve, the patterns continuously evolve until the balance of the social attractor breaks again to open in a way that reviews itself and evolves into new forms and dimensions.

REFLECTIONS ON A RESEARCH AGENDA

This time of chaos, in both social and natural systems, is an important moment to rethink the current form of tackling the sustainability challenge, doing it in a more innovative and inclusive way. In this section I propose some ideas for reflection. However, it is worth mentioning that these ideas are to inspire and broaden the possibilities and perspectives, not to act as restrictive models. I do not believe in these kinds of models, especially in the case of the complex and chaotic sustainability challenge. One of the interviewees describes it in an interesting way:

> I think it comes out of the linear, because it's an observation in the present, you do not have more models, you're going to have to drop models. You'll have to have a look at it, go in like a dance, see what's going on, and go that way or that or that one, watch the endless possibilities you have. (Eva, entrepreneur, January 2015)

Tackling the Sustainability Challenge in Innovative and Inclusive Ways

The following ideas for reflection were inspired by the 13 patterns emerging on innovative and inclusive narratives for sustainability, which formed the social attractor framework – the comprehensive pattern in this study. To better understand this section, I recommend reading it together with Table 2.1 and Figure 2.3. In the following, I present a number of reflections on research insights and inspirations.

Openness to Review Beliefs and to Evolve: according to the complexity and chaos theories, when a system is in a chaos state, it is experimenting with itself in different configurations. This chaos may also help the societal system to be open in a way that reviews itself and evolves. It is noteworthy that this openness can be both involuntary (through crisis and chaos) or voluntary (through personal choice). This is the pattern in between the inner and outer dimensions of the strange attractor framework because it is through this openness to review beliefs that society and science evolve. Thus, I suggest that it is important for the researcher to often question how open she or he is to new ways of understanding the so-called reality. In the words of different scholars:

> The theory of progress is the process of revising beliefs. (Edward Freeman, AOM, 2016)

> We continue to create social systems that require us to be aggressive, because this is what we believe. (Robert Quinn, AOM, 2016)

To create research that helps society to tackle the sustainability challenge in an innovative and inclusive way, it is also important for the researchers to be open to review their own beliefs and to evolve. Examples of instruments to assist in this process of opening up are appreciative inquiry (Cooperrider and Whitney, 2005) and theory U (Scharmer, 2018). Appreciative inquiry can help to access new possibilities for change and transformation in a positive way. Theory U can help to understand what is trying to emerge as a future possibility to tackle the sustainability challenge.

I also suggest that the researcher should be open to self-development, to improve as a human being. In this way, discovering inner truths and reviewing own beliefs. In the words of one of the interviewees:

> Our limit of mind is the limit that we think it is, so we have to have a more extensive limit, think of other possibilities, so that other possibilities are constructed. (Helena, consultant, 2015)

Authenticity and Vulnerability: authenticity can be traced back to aphorisms from centuries ago (Gardner et al., 2011). Examples are: "know thyself" from the Temple of Apollo at Delphi and "an unexamined life is not worth living" from the philosopher Socrates. Authenticity means the researcher going deeper into one's self-knowing and finding one's own voice to develop research that matters for both society and the planet. This is not an easy process and it might involve vulnerability due to different demands in life. However, researchers who embrace this challenge seem to have a more fulfilling work and life. For example, Waddock (2015), an important sustainability researcher, describes the narratives of several successful researchers who followed the path of authenticity and vulnerability in her book about scholars making a difference. In her words:

> We "simply" need to have the courage to answer the call to become who we really are, to work in service of something beyond ourselves that tries to make the world or something in it better, and follow that call in our life's work by doing work that matters, makes a difference. (Waddock, 2015, p. 7)

Authenticity and vulnerability might be interesting areas for sustainability research. For example, to understand how to help sustainability professionals (for example, experts, researchers, teachers and practitioners) become increasingly authentic and open to vulnerability. And how this authenticity and vulnerability may help people around them strengthen ties to jointly develop solutions to the sustainability challenge. In the words of one of the interviewees:

> What is a leader's ability to be vulnerable? [. . .] And being vulnerable in a scenario of transition, uncertainty, complexity, it also opens space for other people to contribute and bring their best to help, since he [the leader] will not handle everything alone. (Leticia, professor, 2016)

Additionally, I suggest research on understanding how an authentic and vulnerable organization would be; and what are the gains for people, society and planet of such organizations.

Balance, Care and Respect: sustainability is related to balance, not static balance but dynamic balance. In the words of one interviewee:

> When you have dynamic balance, everything is in a right measure, things do not overlap excessively, one part does not enslave the other part. When you see this within business management, it is the company interacting with the environment, the inner world and the outside world in a way that does not prey, what is outside, nor what is inside, not to sacrifice a part in function of another. (Camila, consultant, 2015)

This balance includes care and respect for both people and the planet. Research might be undertaken on how organizations, through care and respect, can restore balance for individuals, society and the planet and on enhancing balance, care and respect for employees, supply chains, different cultures, natural systems and so on.

Ethics and Values: to realize values it is important first to be aware of one's own values. In the words of Klamer (2016a):

> Realizing values in the sense of being aware of them, and the actions that follow as the realization of those values in the sense of valorizing them or making them real. (Klamer, 2016a, p. 19)

Then, I suggest investigating how organizations and individuals understand their own values, and how they can make these values real while making contributions to tackle the sustainability challenge. Education programs could be developed on values, ethics and so on at universities. Also of value might be research on how organizations can help to strength societal values. In the words of an interviewee:

> So the company has this obligation because it is occupying a space in society, it is occupying an economic space. So I think the company has an obligation to have an emblematic and symbolic role of values that help build society. (Gabriel, professor, 2015)

Compassion and Wisdom: in the words of the CEO of LinkedIn, Jeff Weiner:

> Wisdom without compassion is ruthlessness, and compassion without wisdom is folly. (Weiner and Gordhamer, 2013)

Wisdom here is what Aristotle calls phronesis, which "involves the weighing of values, conditions, interests and findings in order to do the right thing" (Klamer, 2016b, p. 372). I suggest that universities also include compassion and wisdom in their education program. In the words of an interviewee:

> One of the things masters, MBAs and doctoral degrees in management . . . are forgetting. They have turned a lot to the technical side and have forgotten the human part. (Arthur, entrepreneur, 2015)

Additionally, I argue that research on tackling the sustainability challenge through compassion and wisdom could perhaps access inclusive and innovative ways of achieving this.

Mindset of Abundance and Prosperity: in the words of an interviewee:

> Several people don't know, but there's enough for everyone. Then, collaborate, do not compete; share, do not hold knowledge, share. Why do I suggest this? Because we work together and it's these paradoxical things or paradigms that are changing. (Arthur, entrepreneur, 2015)

Research may be undertaken on how to help people to change their paradigms and beliefs from scarcity and competition to abundance and prosperity for all. As well as research on new ways of understanding organizations and growth. In the words of an interviewee:

> There is much talk today about sustainable prosperity and not just about sustainable development. What is the point of prosperity and not running after development, perhaps growth, which in the long run is unsustainable? I believe that the word prosperity reflects this much more. We have a prosperous company, which does not mean that it is a company that is growing at a rate of 20 or 30% a year. The prosperous company is the one that manages to compensate the people who are there, manages to deliver a positive thing to society, it manages to make the world better. (Airton, professor, 2016)

Collaboration and Multiple Value Creation: research themes might, for example, be how different organizations can collaborate to solve the sustainability challenge instead of competing between them and also understanding new social contracts between business and society, such as sustainability beyond the business case and beyond eco-efficiency, to a way of multiple value creation. According to Volans:

> There is a growing shift in focus away from the business case and towards the role of business models in delivering multiple forms of value. (Volans, 2016, p. 12)

As a practical example Jeff Weiner, the CEO of LinkedIn, explains:

> The creation of long-term value is aligned with creating value for our membership, for our customers and that ultimately create value for the entire ecosystem which we all operate. (Weiner and Gordhamer, 2013)

Freedom, Reflection and Dialogue: I would suggest as research topics here to better understand how to facilitate freedom, reflection and dialogue for tackling the sustainability challenge. In the words of Professor Edward Freeman:

> If you take care of freedom, truth will take care of itself. (Edward Freeman, AOM, 2016)

I suggest that universities should give more freedom for researchers to conduct research on issues that matter for the researcher, society and the planet. In addition, the pressure for publication in 'A' journals should be rethought because the goal should be to develop research and ideas that matter rather than collect points from publications that may be forgotten and not used. I think that if universities, and specifically business schools, continue to focus on these kinds of publications instead of research that matters, they could be in danger of becoming irrelevant to society. In the words of the founder of the VISA organization:

> Science should be judged by whether it has diminished violence, eliminated war, enhanced justice, insured freedom, improved happiness, equitably distributed power and wealth, and protected the environment. By any such standard it has been an abysmal failure. (Dee W. Hock, 2017)

Networks and Interdependence: this pattern seems to have strengthened with new technologies, like the internet. One example is the Nobel Peace Prize 2017 to the International Campaign to Abolish Nuclear Weapons (ICAN), which is a network of 468 non-governmental organizations in 101 countries (Nobel Prize, 2017). According to complexity theory, change emerges from micro to macro, so instead of concentrating sustainability studies in top-down approaches, I suggest studying more about networks and interdependence of people for sustainability. This is because the role of leadership for sustainability is overrated, and the role of networks and interdependence of people for tackling the sustainability challenge is bigger, but less studied. Further suggestions of themes to be studied include: networks of trust and interdependence, such as the supply chain beyond audit and control and multi-stakeholder approaches to tackle the sustainability challenge; understanding ways of empowering poor people, women and the vulnerable; studying decentralized and self-organizing social systems for sustainability; and instead of externalities, how to solve sustainability problems as a whole. In the words of an interviewee:

> Interdependence, which means the following: we are all interconnected and what I do here in my company, it will have an effect on my community, my neighborhood, my city, my country and maybe even the world. Thus, there is no longer the outside and the inside and there is no longer what we once called as externality. (Mauro, consultant, 2016)

Blurring of borders: it seems there is a removal of borders for people, organizations and society, for example, the blurring of borders between professional and personal life and between disciplines, and even countries. The scholar Josep Lozano refers to it as creating bridges:

> I'm strongly interested in understanding education as creating bridges between organizations, creating bridges between disciplines, creating bridges between ideologies and mindsets, or religions, and so on. (Waddock, 2015, p. 305)

There are important and unexplored possibilities for sustainability research in the interactions between disciplines. Multi-, inter- and transdisciplinary research are important to tackle the complex sustainability challenge. Gladwin et al. (1995) argue that the "idea of sustainable development pushes management research toward interdisciplinary and transdisciplinary modes of inquiry" (p. 897). Research to tackle the sustainability challenge would include different areas of knowledge, for example, understanding the same sustainability challenge through different perspectives such as philosophy, natural and social sciences. It would also include combining methods for understanding it, for example, philosophical, qualitative and quantitative as well as combining different ontologies and epistemologies in the same research.

Diversity and Culture: I suggest research that celebrates diversity and honors different cultures. Mainstream research is mainly conducted using the Western worldview and paradigms. In the words of an interviewee:

> I think the first thing in terms of organizational management, which is essential for sustainability, is the dealing with differences . . . And our organizational model – which is still patriarchal, military, industrial revolution – is to flatten diversity and homogenize people. (Camila, consultant, 2015)

It is possible that we are not seeing the solution to our most challenging sustainability problems because we are not looking from the perspectives of different cultures and traditions in the world. Additionally, research that celebrates diversity and honors different cultures does not suggest that only one way is the truth, nor does it suggest that all other perspectives are irrelevant or wrong. I would argue that research should broaden horizons and not homogenize people or limit worldviews.

Circular and Exponential: tackling the sustainability challenge in an inclusive way has to respect natural systems, such as being circular like in nature. It means including all people in the solutions, and therefore exponential. Thus, I suggest research that better understands the circular economy:

> A circular economy is one that is restorative and regenerative by design and aims to keep products, components, and materials at their highest utility and value at all times, distinguishing between technical and biological cycles. (MacArthur Foundation, 2015, p. 3)

There might be research to help organizations become circular:

> All businesses must strive to become completely circular, their operations designed to sustain products, components, and material inputs and outputs at their highest utility and value at key points in the cycle. (Volans, 2016, p. 7)

Additionally, research for exponential solutions:

> A shift from incremental to exponential mindsets and ambitions; from our current focus on the negative impacts of economic activity to the deliberate generation of positive impacts; and from the business case for action to a reconsideration of business models that ensures industries are fit for tomorrow's very different market and geopolitical realities. (Volans, 2016, p. 3)

Purpose and Positive Impact: research that matters creates positive impact for individuals, society and the planet. Research possibilities for this abound in the actual chaos of societal and natural systems. As an example, to understand better how to change the narrative of business as usual to one that is more purposeful in generating a positive impact, as shown in the following:

> We need to reframe business as a high purpose organization, that creates value for the stakeholders. And we need to figure out how to create millions of new entrepreneurs who start with a high purpose orientation. (Edward Freeman, CSR Berlin, 2016)

Additionally, research to understand business models that are more fit for human beings and have a positively impact. As an example:

> Tomorrow's business models must deliver financial and extra-financial value by generating positive social impact. (Volans, 2016, p. 7)

These are some reflections about different possibilities for developing research to tackle the sustainability challenge in inclusive and innovative ways. These reflections are based on the social attractor pattern (Figure 2.3) on innovative and inclusive narratives on sustainability that are emerging worldwide. This pattern was inspired by complexity and chaos theories, which indicate that the human society already seems to be in a silent evolution. These reflections are intended to inspire and broaden perspectives. However, there are infinite possibilities to develop research that matters for individuals, society and the planet. Here, the words of the thirteenth-century poet Rumi seem relevant:

> There is a voice that doesn't use words. Listen.

ACKNOWLEDGMENTS

I would like to thank the editors for the invitation to contribute this chapter and for helpful feedback on earlier versions of this chapter. I am grateful to Arjo Klamer, Marja Flory, Ynze Alkema, Erwin Dekker and Christian Handke for valuable comments and discussions on this study. I would also like to express my gratitude to the scholars who provided valuable feedback on a previous version of this chapter at the Economics and Culture Seminar at Erasmus University Rotterdam.

REFERENCES

Alvesson, M. and Sköldberg, K. (2009). *Reflexive Methodology: New Vistas for Qualitative Research*, 2nd edn. London: Sage.

Auster, E.R. and Freeman, R.E. (2013). Values and poetic organizations: beyond value fit toward values through conversation. *Journal of Business Ethics*, 113, 39–49.

Boje, D.M. (2001). *Narrative Methods for Organizational & Communication Research*. London: Sage.

Capra, F. (1996). *The Web of Life*. London: HarperCollins.

Capra, F. (2016). *Capra Course*, participation and accessed February to August 2016 at http://www.capracourse.net

Capra, F. and Luisi, P.L. (2016). *The Systems View of Life: A Unifying Vision*. Cambridge: Cambridge University Press. Reprint edition.

Complexity Explorer (2017). *Glossary*, accessed 23 October 2017 at https://www.complexityexplorer.org/explore/glossary

Complexity Labs (2018). *Social Attractors and Chaos Theory*, accessed 18 May 2018 at http://complexitylabs.io/social-attractors-chaos-theory/

Cooperrider, D. and Whitney, D.D. (2005). *Appreciative Inquiry: A Positive Revolution in Change*. San Francisco, CA: Berrett-Koehler Publishers.

Cosustentare (2016). *Conferência Online de Sustentabilidade e Responsabilidade Corporativa*, developed and accessed January to December 2016 at http://www.cosustentare.com

Elkington, J. and Braun, S. (2013). *Breakthrough: Business Leaders, Market Revolutions*. London: Volans.

Flory, M. (2008). The never-ending story: narrating the paradox of self-management in organizations. Unpublished doctoral dissertation, Erasmus University Rotterdam, Rotterdam, the Netherlands.

Freeman, R.E. and Auster, E.R. (2011). Values, authenticity, and responsible leadership. *Journal of Business Ethics*, 98, 15–23.
Gadamer, H.-G. (1976 [2013]). *Truth and Method*. London: Bloomsbury Academic. Second revised edition.
Gardner, W.L., Cogliser, C.C., Davis, K.M. and Dickens, M.P. (2011). Authentic leadership: a review of the literature and research agenda. *The Leadership Quarterly*, 22, 1120–45.
Gladwin, T.N., Kennelly, J.J. and Krause, T.S. (1995). Shifting paradigms for sustainable development: implications for management theory and research. *Academy of Management Review*, 20, 874–907.
Heidegger, M. (1953 [2010]). *Being and Time*. New York: State University of New York. A revised edition of the Stambaugh translation.
Hock, D.W. (2017). *Reflections*, accessed 5 October 2017 at http://www.deewhock.com/quotations/
Klamer, A. (2016a). *Doing the Right Thing: A Value-Based Economy*. London: Ubiquity Press.
Klamer, A. (2016b). The value-based approach to cultural economics. *Journal of Cultural Economics*, 40, 365–73.
Lorenz, E.N. (1963). The mechanics of vacillation. *Journal of the Atmospheric Sciences*, 20, 448–64.
MacArthur Foundation (2015). *Towards a Circular Economy: Business Rationale for an Accelerated Transition*, accessed 30 November 2017 at https://www.ellenmacarthurfoundation.org/assets/downloads/TCE_Ellen-MacArthur-Foundation_9-Dec-2015.pdf
Nobel Prize (2017). *International Campaign to Abolish Nuclear Weapons (ICAN) – Interview*, accessed 5 December 2017 at https://www.nobelprize.org/nobel_prizes/peace/laureates/2017/ican-interview.html
Perey, R. (2014). Organizing sustainability and the problem of scale: local, global, or fractal? *Organization & Environment*, 27(3), 215–22.
Plowman, D.A., Baker, L.T., Beck, T.E., Kulrarni, M., Solansky, S.T. and Travis, D.V. (2007). Radical change accidentally: the emergence and amplification of small change. *Academy of Management Journal*, 50(3), 515–43.
Pozzati, M. (2007). *Buscando a inteireza do Ser: Proposições para o desenvolvimento sustentável da consciência humana*. Porto Alegre: Gênese Editora.
Prigogine, I. and Stengers, I. (1984). *Order Out of Chaos: Man's New Dialogue With Nature*. Boulder, CO: New Science Library.
Ricoeur, P. (1974a). Metaphor and the main problem of hermeneutics. *New Literary History*, 6(1), 95–110.
Ricoeur, P. (1974b). *The Conflict of Interpretations: Essays in Hermeneutics*. Evanston, IL: Northwest University Press.
Ricoeur, P. (1981). *Hermeneutics and the Human Sciences*, reprinted in J.B. Thompson (ed. and trans.) (2016), Cambridge Philosophy Classics edition. New York: Cambridge University Press.
Scharmer, O. (2017). *Trump and Transforming Capitalism: Making Our Movement See Itself*, accessed 23 October 2017 at https://www.huffingtonpost.com/entry/5a06ef9ce4b0f1dc729a6b39
Scharmer, O. (2018). *The Essentials of Theory U: Core Principles and Applications*. Oakland, CA: Berrett-Koehler Publishers.
Tracey, P. and Stott, N. (2017). Social innovation: a window on alternative ways of organizing and innovating. *Innovation*, 19(1), 51–60.
Varela, F.G., Maturana, H.R. and Uribe, R. (1974). Autopoiesis: the organization of living systems, its characterization and a model. *BioSystem*, 5, 187–96.
Volans (2016). *Breakthrough Business Models: Exponentially More Social, Lean, Integrated and Circular*, accessed 20 November 2017 at https://volans.com/wp-content/uploads/2016/09/Volans_Breakthrough-Business-Models_Report_Sep2016.pdf
Waddock, S. (2015). *Intellectual Shamans: Management Academics Making a Difference*. Cambridge: Cambridge University Press.
Weiner, J. and Gordhamer, S. (2013). *The Art of Conscious Leadership: Jeff Weiner*, accessed 25 June 2014 at http://www.youtube.com/watch?v=2x0fOLqj2Zw
Wheatley, M.J. (2006). *Leadership and the New Science*. San Francisco, CA: Berrett-Koehler Publishers.

3. Climate change and social innovation

Christopher Wright and Daniel Nyberg

INTRODUCTION

Climate change is perhaps the greatest challenge facing humanity. Humanity's rampant use of fossil fuels and the destruction of forests and peatlands has over the last two centuries altered the chemistry of the atmosphere and oceans. As climate and Earth System scientists have highlighted, this human perturbation to the carbon cycle is now resulting in increasingly severe storms, droughts and heatwaves, the melting of glaciers and ice-shelves, a sixth mass extinction of animal and plant species and escalating sea-level rise (IPCC, 2013; Mann and Kump, 2015). Future projections based on the current path of carbon emissions suggest an average global temperature increase of as much as 4 degrees Celsius this century, which is incompatible with continued human civilization (New et al., 2011).

As a number of recent key texts have highlighted (Angus, 2016; Klein, 2014; Wright and Nyberg, 2015), responding to this threat requires a radical decarbonization of global energy, transport and industrial systems, the mass replacement of coal, oil and gas by renewable energy technologies such as solar and wind, and the reinvention of established economic and political conventions. The scale and pace of such change is daunting, particularly given the way in which such changes fundamentally threaten the business and political interests of the most powerful industry in the world, the fossil fuel sector.

In this chapter, we use a political economy approach to consider the role of social innovation in responding to the climate crisis. 'Social innovation' has become a fashionable buzzword for political and business elites in responding to emerging social and environmental problems. In its narrow, contemporary usage, social innovation implies a neoliberal policy agenda of market mechanisms, corporate self-regulation and the encouragement of social enterprise 'solutions' (Jessop et al., 2013). By contrast, we argue that responses to 'grand challenges' such as climate change need to go well beyond the current market fetish and adopt more fundamental and systemic forms of social change. This involves embracing a broader conception of social innovation in which social movements and communities reclaim a central role in shaping our climate future, and social innovation re-emphasizes themes of justice, equality and human rights. We begin by first outlining how the concept of social innovation interacts with the emerging climate crisis, by focusing on current climate policy responses and the maintenance of 'business as usual' outcomes. We then outline possibilities for a broader conception of social innovation in relation to climate change which goes beyond neoliberal conceptions and embraces earlier ideas of systemic social change, social justice and social movements. We provide examples of these broader conceptions of social climate innovation, before outlining specific recommendations for expanding future research.

SOCIAL INNOVATION AND THE CLIMATE CRISIS

Social innovation is a broad and potentially all-encompassing concept of social change. Given the ambiguity of the concept, a wide range of definitions of social innovation exist (for overviews, see Edwards-Schachter and Wallace, 2017; Moulaert et al., 2013). Four key themes of social innovation are often stressed. First, the *social* nature of innovation, that is, the development of ideas, practices and processes focused on new forms of social interaction and organization as opposed to technological innovation. Second, the *objective* of social innovation should respond to social needs and problems rather than economic or profit-maximizing goals. Third, the *source and process* of social innovation should derive from social groups in civil society rather than from government or business. And fourth, that the *goals and objectives* of social innovation explicitly adopt an ethical position of social justice, seeking to overcome inequality and promote the inclusion of excluded groups in improving overall human well-being.

Indeed, as Jessop et al. (2013) note, the broad concept of social innovation underpins the work of many of the founding theorists of political economics such as Marx (1976), Weber (1947), Schumpeter (1942) and Polanyi (1957). This extends not only to an understanding of how powerful social groups (for example, the aristocracy, capitalists, bureaucrats) have shaped political and economic outcomes in their favour, but also how the disenfranchised (such as workers, migrants and women) organized and resisted their exploitation through combination and collective action. Thus a subset of traditional social innovation research explores the role of industrial and political movements for social reform and radical change/revolution, focusing on worker democracy, student activism, feminism and civil rights (Chambon et al., 1982).

However, in recent years the term 'social innovation' has been embraced by governments, corporations and think-tanks and the concept has narrowed towards a far more conservative vision of market relations of enterprise and exchange (Fougère et al., 2017; Jessop et al., 2013). 'Social enterprises' and 'social entrepreneurs' are now presented as the key agents of this new narrow form of social innovation, which it is argued bring together the advantages of business acumen with a concern for specific social issues (Mulgan, 2006; Mulgan et al., 2007). Examples of the new social innovation include the development of microfinance, the Fairtrade movement, socially responsible investing and emissions trading mechanisms (Phills et al., 2008). Business corporations have also become increasingly focused on social innovation through their adoption of the discourse and practices of corporate social responsibility (CSR) (Crane et al., 2008), corporate citizenship (Matten and Crane, 2005) and, most recently, Creating Shared Value (CSV) (Porter and Kramer, 2011). Combined with the decline of the state provision of social welfare and the 'marketization' of the third-sector (Fougère et al., 2017), this focus upon an enterprise culture of social innovation is viewed by critics as an expression of 'caring liberalism' in which new 'social enterprises' have become the key actors for social change in an increasingly 'market society' (Jessop et al., 2013; Sandel, 2012).

Of the many 'grand challenges' facing human society (George et al., 2016), perhaps none are more profound than climate change (Klein, 2014). Despite the science of anthropogenic climate change dating back over two centuries, it has only been in the last 30 years that climate change has emerged as an increasingly urgent political and economic concern, evident in the formation of the Intergovernmental Panel on Climate Change

(IPCC) and ongoing international negotiations over climate change policy (Edwards, 2010; Weart, 2003). Often tagged a 'wicked problem' (Lazarus, 2009; Levin et al., 2012), climate change represents a classic 'tragedy of the commons' dilemma in that economic development based on fossil fuel use has greatly benefited developed nations at the cost of long-term global environmental destruction. Taking meaningful action to respond to this threat requires dramatic and rapid reductions in the global production of greenhouse gas (GHG) emissions, which in turn requires government regulation of fossil fuel use. Not surprisingly, climate change has become a highly partisan political issue as vested interests in industry and politics have vigorously fought to prevent any restrictions on fossil fuel use (Dunlap and McCright, 2011).

Climate change has thus become a key arena for social innovation in that: (1) the climate crisis is primarily a social and political issue rather than a technical problem; (2), it requires a focus on social and environmental concerns beyond economic and profit-maximizing goals; (3) much of the demand for progress comes from social movements rather than governments or business; and (4) there are clear ethical concerns and social justice imperatives in responding to climate change. In the section that follows, we set out a typology of divergent paths of climate response and examples of the forms of social innovation they propose.

DIVERGENT CLIMATE RESPONSES AS FORMS OF SOCIAL INNOVATION

While the responses of governments, businesses and civil society to climate change are complex and vary significantly in different countries and regions, three general types of political-economic response can be discerned. We have labelled these three forms of climate response as 'business as usual', 'green economy' and 'climate mobilization'. As set out in Table 3.1, each of these responses are examples of social innovation aimed at broad social and economic change and each also exhibit a form of social inclusivity in that they seek to engage business, government and civil society to differing degrees in their proposed response to climate change. In the following subsections we outline how each of these responses has evolved and how different examples of social innovation have been used in seeking to achieve their goals.

Business as Usual

The first and most common social response to climate change has been what can be characterized as 'business as usual'; that is, a continuation of the economic path set out since the end of the Second World War involving a commitment to compound economic growth and the unending expansion of fossil fuel-based energy. This dominant model of economic development has been reinforced since the late 1980s with the rapid globalization of economic activity, the rise of neoliberalism, and the emergence of developing nations such as China and India as fast-growing industrial economies (Klein, 2014). The business as usual response explicitly rejects the threat posed by climate change and the need for any form of carbon regulation. As Levy and Spicer (2013, p. 663) argue, it can be characterized as a 'fossil fuels forever' imaginary, in that proponents argue there is no need

Table 3.1 Political-economic models of social innovation in response to climate change

	Business as usual	Green economy	Climate mobilization
Ideological narrative	'Free market' capitalism and neoliberalism; conquest of nature is central to human progress	Corporations and markets benefit both shareholders and society/environment	Environmental sustainability underpins social well-being
Response to climate change	Rejection of climate science and carbon regulation	Acceptance of climate science and acknowledgement of the need to reduce carbon emissions	Climate change as an existential threat requiring radical decarbonization
Innovation focus	Expansion of fossil fuel extraction via technological innovation in new carbon frontiers	Corporate leadership via technological and entrepreneurial innovation in new products and services	Opposition to fossil fuel industry through protest, divestment and alternative models (e.g., community-owned renewable energy)
Role of business	Corporations create social and economic prosperity through expanding fossil fuel use	Corporations as leaders in developing a green economy through corporate environmentalism	Small business and social entrepreneurs can partner with communities in renewable reinvention
Role of government	Government regulation of the environment should be reduced, governments need to protect fossil fuel extraction from civil society opposition	Governments create the architecture for 'market mechanisms' (e.g., carbon pricing)	Governments should encourage and plan for a 'just transition' from fossil fuel economy
Role of civil society	Citizens as supporters of industrial expansion	Citizens as consumers, ecopreneurs and campaigners for green market innovation	Civil society leading opposition to environmental destruction and developing collective, democratic alternatives

to depart from the economic trajectory already laid out and societies should continue to exploit all possible sources of fossil fuels for the economic well-being of society (see, for example, Epstein, 2014).

Examples of the business as usual response to climate change began soon after the political recognition of the issue in the late 1980s when proposals for government regulation of carbon emissions met with organized resistance from the fossil fuel sector (Levy and Egan, 1998). Over the next decades an increasingly powerful climate change denial movement developed in anglophone economies such as the United States, Canada, Australia and Britain consisting of major fossil fuel corporations, industry groups, conservative think-tanks and politically aligned media organizations (Dunlap and McCright, 2011; Oreskes and Conway, 2010). This increasingly political movement lobbied government and political parties, and sought to sway public opinion by questioning climate science, highlighting the economic costs of cutting emissions, and promoting the views of so-called climate 'sceptics'. Following the failure of the 2009 Copenhagen climate talks, right-wing politicians and media in the United States propagated a narrative of climate change as a 'hoax' and conspiracy (Mann, 2012). This found political voice in industry-funded social movements such as the Tea Party in the United States which gained increasing control over Republican Party policy (Brulle, 2014; Dunlap and McCright, 2011). With the election of Donald Trump in 2016 as President of the United States, the business as usual response to climate change became the official policy of the most powerful country in the world. This has been evident in the withdrawal of the United States from the Paris Climate Agreement, the expansion of coal, oil and gas extraction, removal of environmental regulations and the promotion of prominent climate change deniers to key government positions (De Pryck and Gemenne, 2017).

Underpinning the business as usual response is a founding ideological narrative that dates back to the scientific revolution of the seventeenth century, that the conquest of nature is central to human progress (Foster et al., 2010). Innovations in fossil fuel use during the Industrial Revolution led to the belief that human society could free itself from the limits of natural laws and bend nature to our will (Klein, 2014). This belief in human progress over the natural environment underpinned the economic expansion of the twentieth century and was celebrated in the ideological belief in the merits of 'free market capitalism' as the finest expression of human innovation. The rise of neoliberalism from the mid-1970s onwards expanded this view through commitments to 'free trade', reducing the role of government and the public sector, cutting corporate taxation and promoting corporate self-regulation (Harvey, 2007).

This narrative promotes a particular vision of social innovation based upon corporate capitalism ensuring human progress via fossil fuel-based expansion. As Wright and Nyberg (2015, p. 25) argue, this involves a form of 'creative self-destruction' in which economic expansion *relies on* the continued exploitation and degradation of natural resources and where 'businesses are encouraged to further devour the very life-support systems of a habitable environment'. Here, the climate crisis results not so much in attempts to reduce our society's carbon emissions but rather in a doubling down of the bet that we can master nature. Technological and social innovation is directed towards finding more efficient and effective ways of sourcing and extracting new, unconventional fossil fuel resources evident in the expansion of deep-water and Arctic oil drilling, tar sands processing, gas fracking and new mega coal mines (Kitchen, 2014).

These developments highlight how business as usual encapsulates a particularly powerful form of social innovation which now dominates the global economy. For instance, when challenged by critics over the climate destruction they are unleashing, proponents of the business as usual model respond that they are not only benefiting corporate shareholders but also advancing social progress by addressing 'energy poverty' in developing economies (Goldenberg, 2015). Moreover, when climate change is acknowledged, the response quickly pivots towards advocacy for future large-scale technological innovations such as geo-engineering and carbon capture and storage as viable solutions. This imaginary of a business as usual future thus embraces continued expansion in fossil fuel use and the human consumption of the last vestiges of the natural environment with the negative side-effects managed through stratospheric sulphur injection, solar dimming, ocean fertilization and other likely disastrous 'solutions'. As critics have noted, rather than a technological utopia, this form of climate response appears more akin to chemotherapy for a dying planet (Hamilton, 2013; Wagner and Weitzman, 2012).

Green Economy

While the business as usual response rejects the issue of climate change as a pressing social concern and focuses innovation towards greater fossil fuel use, alternative responses have also emerged. Within the business and policy community a different reaction has been what can be characterized as a 'green economy' vision of social innovation (Esty and Winston, 2006; Orsato, 2009). Advocates of this view accept climate science and in many cases emphasize the urgency of the climate crisis. In response, they argue that technological and entrepreneurial innovation is needed to decouple economic growth from its material impacts, viewing climate change as 'the greatest market failure the world has ever seen' (Stern et al., 2006, p. viii). Here, however, market forces and business are seen as the best response, through the pricing of carbon emissions and the creation of a carbon market or 'cap and trade' system (World Bank Group/Ecofys, 2014). Added to this, entrepreneurial know-how and innovation are seen as the best ways to reduce carbon emissions via improved eco-efficiency, 'smart' technologies, and a shift from fossil fuels to renewable energy sources such as solar and wind. From this perspective, climate change becomes not only a business risk but also a business opportunity as companies develop new products and services and market themselves as 'green' companies (Wright and Nyberg, 2017). Indicative of this perspective, business tycoon Richard Branson has argued that 'our only option to stop climate change is for industry to make money from it' (Neubacher, 2012).

The key expression of the green economy can be found amongst businesses which profess their concern for the natural environment and promote practices which seek to benefit their shareholders *and* the climate; what is termed 'corporate environmentalism' (Jermier et al., 2006). Corporate environmentalism promotes a vision of global corporations as saviours; reinventing capitalism and providing environmental and social benefit through innovation and economic growth. This draws on a broader vision of ecological modernization which argues that increasing economic development, technological innovation and environmental reform serve to minimize pollution and environmental harm over time (Hajer, 1995; Mol, 2002).

The practice of corporate environmentalism is diverse including both internally and externally focused innovations. These include: reducing operational costs through improved eco-efficiency and waste reduction; promoting 'green' and environmentally responsible products and services; marketing and branding as 'green' companies to consumers and the public; and developing corporate cultures and engaging employees around environmental activities (Dauvergne and Lister, 2013; Wright and Nyberg, 2015; Wright et al., 2012). Corporate environmentalism also extends to political action in lobbying government over environmental regulations, and developing political coalitions that promote the vision of business as environmentally and economically progressive (Nyberg et al., 2013). As evident in companies such as GE, Walmart, Virgin, Nestlé and Unilever, corporate environmentalism thus presents an image of business leadership on the environment, and promotes the merits of corporate self-regulation, innovation and technology in solving key environmental challenges (Esty and Winston, 2006; Hart, 1997; Hoffman, 2001).

The green economy vision of social innovation is particularly evident in sectors of industry which promote a renewable energy transition. Here, entrepreneurs such as Tesla's Elon Musk present a vision of a future low-carbon, technologically innovative world built around renewable energy, electric cars and battery storage (Battisti and Giulietti, 2015). The dramatic increases in renewable energy investment and the falling costs of solar, wind and other renewable energy technologies, particularly in countries like China, highlight how such an energy transition could eventuate (Mathews, 2014).

However, critics argue that the practice of corporate environmentalism often fails to live up to its pro-environmental rhetoric (Banerjee, 2001). At one level, critics point to the potential for corporate environmental claims to amount to little more than 'greenwashing'; fictitious and misleading marketing which masks a darker reality of environmental degradation (Ramus and Montiel, 2005). More substantively, others point to the way in which corporate environmentalism involves practices which incorporate the environment more completely within business activities. For instance, Dauvergne and Lister (2013) demonstrate how major corporations have used 'green' business strategies to reduce costs and increase productivity across global supply chains. Here, efficiency improvements and cost reductions paradoxically increase aggregate environmental harm through encouraging greater consumption. Similarly, the focus on demonstrating a 'business case' for environmental initiatives and pricing natural resources as market commodities reveals how the tensions between the values of the market and nature are all but erased in favour of a dominant business logic (Nyberg and Wright, 2013). More importantly, the scale and speed of decarbonization necessary to avoid hazardous climate change is frequently ignored in optimistic interpretations of the future 'green' economy. Although the cost of solar-based and wind-based technologies continues to drop – often exceeding projections – renewables still constitute only a small proportion of our overall energy needs, and the escalation of GHG emissions continues even at a time when substantial reductions are needed in a relatively short period (Tollefson, 2018).

Climate Mobilization

While both the 'business as usual' and 'green economy' approaches to the climate crisis prioritize the interests of corporate capitalism and the market economy, 'climate mobilization' represents a third alternative form of climate response that adopts a far more critical approach to business and economics. Consisting of a diverse range of non-government organizations (NGOs), grassroots activists, local communities, religious institutions, charities and indigenous communities, the climate mobilization movement stresses the need for urgent and radical reductions in carbon emissions and employs a range of strategies including political action, protest, civil disobedience and community engagement (for an overview, see Dietz and Garrelts, 2014).

Building on an earlier tradition of environmentalism which highlighted how industrialization had degraded nature (Carson, 1962; Radkau, 2014), climate mobilization emphasizes the existential threat posed by humanity's reliance on fossil fuel-based energy and ever-expanding consumption. As environmentalist Bill McKibben (2012) has argued, the mathematics of the climate crisis are simple. Humanity has a set 'carbon budget' if global warming is not to exceed 2° Celsius; we have already burned two-thirds of this budget, and the remainder is exceeded more than fivefold by remaining reserves of fossil fuel; therefore, around 80 per cent of known fossil fuel resources must stay in the ground – a proposition that raises fundamental economic and moral arguments.

First, the political recognition that existing fossil fuel reserves are unrecoverable if a habitable climate is to be maintained raises the likelihood of a 'carbon bubble' and 'stranded assets' (Carbon Tracker Initiative, 2012). Second, recognition of the fundamental conflict between continued fossil fuel extraction and humanity's future has driven a growing political movement for fossil fuel divestment (Ansar et al., 2013). Popularized by NGO 350.org through a programme directed at US colleges and local government, fossil fuel divestment has swiftly gained international traction and earned the backing of many high-profile organizations. To date, around 180 organizations, most of them from civil society, have committed to divest from fossil fuel stocks. These include Stanford University, the cities of Seattle, San Francisco and Portland, the World Council of Churches, Glasgow University, the British Medical Association and, perhaps most symbolically, the Rockefeller Foundation. While still far from the type of market and regulatory disruption needed to trigger a wholesale move from fossil fuels to renewable energy, divestment is undoubtedly an alternative narrative to the mainstream model of 'business as usual'.

Climate mobilization as a form of social innovation has also involved direct resistance and civil disobedience (della Porta and Parks, 2014). So, for example, Greenpeace has spearheaded campaigns against oil extraction in the Arctic (Vidal, 2014); UK group Plane Stupid has occupied London's Heathrow Airport to condemn the climate impact of an ever-growing airline industry (Topham, 2016); and indigenous communities and NGOs have led protests and occupations to delay the US government's construction of new oil pipelines (Bradshaw, 2015). This opposition has also emerged spontaneously from within local communities that are rising up against the expansion of fossil fuel extraction. For instance, Klein (2014, pp. 293–336) has characterized this phenomena as 'Blockadia' evident in: Greek villagers protesting the destruction of their forests by a Canadian mining company; running battles between police and anti-fracking protesters in Romania and England; indigenous communities fighting oil extraction in the Amazon; blockades against huge new coal mines in Australia; and protests and sit-ins over proposed pipelines to transport Canadian tar sands bitumen to processing plants in the southern United States and export terminals in British Columbia. Across the most diverse locations, companies accustomed to buying consent with the promise of jobs and government royalties are facing concerted resistance that goes beyond traditional localism. As Klein (2014, p. 335) notes:

> More and more these communities are simply saying 'No'. No to the pipeline. No to Arctic drilling. No to the coal and oil trains. No to the heavy hauls. No to the export terminal. No to fracking. And not just 'not in my backyard' but, as the French anti-fracking activists say, *ni ici, ni ailleurs* – neither here nor elsewhere. In other words: no new carbon frontiers.

However, beyond divestment, protest and opposition, climate mobilization as a form of social innovation has also sought to provide alternatives to the current dominance of top-down industrial development. So, for instance, examples such as community-owned renewable energy production (Maruyama et al., 2007; van der Schoor and Scholtens,

2015), 'transition towns' (Smith, 2011), food cooperatives and concepts such as the 'circular economy' (Murray et al., 2017) are increasingly promoted by communities as more sustainable economic models to follow. More broadly, the environmental movement has also started to explore possibilities for a 'just transition' away from fossil fuel-based energy systems including alternative employment options that can be generated in the switch to community-based renewable energy systems (Evans and Phelan, 2016).

This comes at a time when many local communities are also confronting the physical impacts of a climate-changed world. For coastal populations now exposed to increasingly severe storms, flooding and sea-level rise, rural communities confronting record-breaking droughts and fires or urban centres dealing with summer heatwaves and power outages, adapting to the shifting baselines of a changed climate will require new forms of social interaction and collaboration (IPCC, 2014; Newman et al., 2017). Here, a newly emerging social movement for 'climate justice' is evident in a wide range of communities focused on local climate impacts and vulnerabilities, inequality of resources and demands for community action and control (Schlosberg and Collins, 2014). This focus on climate justice highlights the reality that the poor and economically marginalized around the world are not only the most vulnerable to climate change impacts, but also the least responsible for contributing to it. Evident in the formation of groups such as the Climate Justice Alliance (Quinn-Thibodeau and Wu, 2016), this broad-based transformation in social and economic relations is a huge undertaking requiring cooperation across traditionally separated policy concerns such as energy, housing, transport and poverty alleviation. It is, however, indicative of where social innovation needs to be centred in the coming decades in an increasingly climate-challenged world.

A FUTURE RESEARCH AGENDA

Climate change provides a critical context within which to expand our understanding of social innovation. While more recent interpretations of social innovation have emphasized market relations of enterprise and entrepreneurship in addressing social issues, this ignores earlier understandings of social innovation as part of the contested nature of social change, power and politics (Fougère et al., 2017; Jessop et al., 2013). Reducing social innovation to the 'caring liberalism' of social enterprises or, for that matter, the corporate benevolence of CSR and 'shared value' initiatives ignores the far more substantive processes of social innovation evident in current debates over social and political change. Of the many 'grand challenges' humanity now faces (George et al., 2016), climate change highlights the need to interpret social innovation in this broader, more politically informed way. In this final section of the chapter, we outline a number of areas where we see an urgent need to expand the research agenda on social innovation in the area of climate change response.

First, we would argue there is a need to approach the topic of social innovation in a far more critical and reflexive manner and locate current understandings within the broader political context of neoliberalism as a hegemonic political project (Brown, 2015; Harvey, 2007). Seen in this light, the redefinition of social innovation as solely the preserve of 'social entrepreneurs' and 'social enterprises' aims at papering over the growing inequality caused by neoliberal policies of economic austerity, labour market deregulation, globalization and the demise of state-provided social welfare. From this perspective, critical research is needed in revealing the processes through which the contemporary neoliberal discourse of 'social innovation' has evolved, the key actors involved, and the interests and purposes such a narrow conception serves (see, for example, Fougère et al., 2017).

Possible theoretical framings here include the way in which the current market focus of social innovation (and aligned concepts of CSR and corporate citizenship) act as forms of justification and response to growing social critique and resistance (Boltanski and Thévenot, 2006). For instance, recent treatises on the need to redefine business and corporate purpose around 'shared value' and collaboration with civil society have explicitly acknowledged the growing social opposition to economic austerity and inequality (Barton, 2011; Porter and Kramer, 2011). Viewed in this way, a critical reading of current conceptions of social innovation would explore how such justifications serve to incorporate critique and bring it within a more market-friendly framework.

For instance, despite growing public concern over climate change, governments and businesses avoid any serious attempts to curtail escalating carbon emissions via fossil fuel use, while at the same time promoting 'green' consumption, recycling and eco-efficiency as 'solutions' (Hamilton, 2010). We are encouraged as individuals to find ways to reduce our carbon footprints and buy ethical and environmentally friendly products from companies (and social enterprises) that express a social purpose (Wright and Nyberg, 2015). 'Green' innovation is promoted by companies and governments and the 'ecopreneur' celebrated as a viable response to environmental degradation (Phillips, 2013). As a result, social innovation in its narrow market sense acts as a justification for maintaining existing economic interests and avoiding systemic change. This feeds into both the 'business as usual' and 'green economy' climate responses we have outlined earlier where entrepreneurship, individualism, products and markets feature prominently as preferred themes of innovation.

Second, more work is needed in bringing together research on social innovation and social movements (Benford and Snow, 2000; de Bakker et al., 2013; della Porta and Diani, 2015). This harks back to the work of earlier theorists such as Marx (1976) and Polanyi (1957) who explicitly emphasized how social change was based upon resistance and contestation between classes over the future path of social progress. Social movements have also featured prominently in the work of earlier innovation researchers who explored the dynamics of innovation diffusion as a political process (see, for example, Rogers, 1995). By broadening current writing on social innovation to include social movements we can move beyond the current fetish for innovation as solely a corporate/market phenomenon and better understand the broader political dynamics of social change.

In terms of environmental politics and climate change, as we have seen there is already a growing literature exploring the dynamics, processes and efficacy of different social movements in areas such as climate activism, fossil fuel divestment and climate justice. However, more work is needed in identifying what makes for effective climate mobilization in terms of message framing, political strategy and civic engagement (della Porta and Parks, 2014). Moreover, these issues are more salient given the increasingly hostile and contested political context these emergent groups now operate within. The growing securitization of the state acting on behalf of fossil fuel interests raises particular challenges for those seeking to halt the slide towards further 'creative self-destruction'. For instance, many developed economies have already begun to categorize civil protest and environmental activism as potential threats to national security (Potter, 2011). Examples of this more authoritarian response to climate mobilization can be seen in the Russian arrest of the *Arctic 30* (Vidal, 2014), the imprisonment of fossil fuel protestors in the United States (Dietz, 2014; Whyte, 2017), and the repression and death of environmental protestors in developing economies in Asia and South America (Holmes, 2016). Just as previous generations of social activists put their bodies on the line fighting for the abolition of slavery, universal franchise and civil rights, so the current fight to challenge the power of fossil fuels will also involve increasingly conflictual strategies and choices.

Finally, considerations of a broader vision of social innovation require engagement with both the material and discursive dimensions of our increasingly climate-challenged world. In contrast to the Enlightenment assumption that humans are masters of nature, climate change reveals we are in fact highly dependent and interlinked with the natural world. The belief that humankind could free itself from nature's laws has been revealed as a fantasy and nature is now biting back! This materiality of the climate crisis is evident both in the tangible physical impacts of climate change that are now unfolding (for example, sea-level rise, melting glaciers, heatwaves, hurricanes, floods, fires and droughts) and the dramatic scale of decarbonization required to avoid existential harm. The laws of physics and chemistry do not respond to the politically convenient spin of 'business as usual' or the 'green economy'. Indeed, future research will need to contend with far more substantive social innovations around climate adaptation, reimagining and retrofitting cities and energy systems, and, ultimately, retreat (Koslov, 2016).

Moreover, rather than simply re-embracing the same technological mythology that has caused this dilemma (via geo-engineering and other proclaimed techno-fixes), we need to step back and reconsider basic assumptions about our relationship to the natural world. The all-powerful discourses of 'the market', 'shareholder value' and 'economic growth' frame our thinking in particular, narrow ways. Real social innovation requires alternative discourses which acknowledge our place within a wider web of life on this planet (Devall and Sessions, 1985; Lovelock, 2000; Naess, 1973). Importantly, this needs to acknowledge a broader set of values beyond just economic value. These include the values of nature, other species and human community. Future research in social innovation thus needs to contend with both the material realities of our climate-changed world and the way in which this materiality is also forcing people and communities to re-evaluate their identities and understandings of a very different future.

REFERENCES

Angus, I. (2016), *Facing the Anthropocene: Fossil Capitalism and the Crisis of the Earth System*. New York: Monthly Review Press.

Ansar, A., Caldecott, B. and Tilbury, J. (2013), *Stranded Assets and the Fossil Fuel Divestment Campaign: What Does Divestment Mean for the Valuation of Fossil Fuel Assets?* Oxford: Smith School of Enterprise and Environment, University of Oxford.

Banerjee, S.B. (2001), Managerial Perceptions of Corporate Environmentalism: Interpretations from Industry and Strategic Implications for Organizations, *Journal of Management Studies*, **38**(4), 489–513.

Barton, D. (2011), Capitalism for the Long Term, *Harvard Business Review*, **89**(3), 84–91.

Battisti, G. and Giulietti, M. (2015), Tesla is Betting on Solar, Not Just Batteries, *Harvard Business Review*, https://hbr.org/2015/07/tesla-is-betting-on-solar-not-just-batteries (accessed 17 November 2017).

Benford, R.D. and Snow, D.A. (2000), Framing Processes and Social Movements: An Overview and Assessment, *Annual Review of Sociology*, **26**, 611–39.

Boltanski, L. and Thévenot, L. (2006), *On Justification: Economies of Worth*. Princeton, NJ: Princeton University Press.
Bradshaw, E.A. (2015), Blockadia Rising: Rowdy Greens, Direct Action and the Keystone XL Pipeline, *Critical Criminology*, **23**(4), 433–48.
Brown, W. (2015), *Undoing the Demos: Neoliberalism's Stealth Revolution*. New York: Zone.
Brulle, R.J. (2014), Institutionalizing Delay: Foundation Funding and the Creation of US Climate Change Counter-Movement Organizations, *Climatic Change*, **122**(4), 681–94.
Carbon Tracker Initiative (2012), *Unburnable Carbon: Are the World's Financial Markets Carrying a Carbon Bubble?* London: CTI.
Carson, R. (1962), *Silent Spring*. Boston, MA: Houghton Mifflin.
Chambon, J.-L., David, A. and Devevey, J.-M. (1982), *Les Innovations Sociales*. Paris: Presses universitaires de France.
Crane, A., McWilliams, A., Matten, D., Moon, J. and Siegel, D.S. (2008), The Corporate Social Responsibility Agenda. In A. Crane, A. McWilliams, D. Matten, J. Moon and D.S. Siegel (eds), *The Oxford Handbook of Corporate Social Responsibility*. Oxford: Oxford University Press, pp. 3–17.
Dauvergne, P. and Lister, J. (2013), *Eco-Business: A Big-Brand Takeover of Sustainability*. Cambridge, MA: MIT Press.
de Bakker, F.G.A., den Hond, F., King, B. and Weber, K. (2013), Social Movements, Civil Society and Corporations: Taking Stock and Looking Ahead, *Organization Studies*, **34**(5–6), 573–93.
De Pryck, K. and Gemenne, F. (2017), The Denier-in-Chief: Climate Change, Science and the Election of Donald J. Trump, *Law and Critique*, **28**(2), 119–26.
della Porta, D. and Diani, M. (2015), *The Oxford Handbook of Social Movements*. Oxford: Oxford University Press.
della Porta, D. and Parks, L. (2014), Framing Processes in the Climate Movement: From Climate Change to Climate Justice. In M. Dietz and H. Garrelts (eds), *Routledge Handbook of the Climate Change Movement*. Abingdon: Routledge, pp. 19–30.
Devall, B. and Sessions, G. (1985), *Deep Ecology: Living as if Nature Mattered*. Salt Lake City, UT: Gibbs Smith.
Dietz, M. (2014), Activist Profile – Tim DeChristopher. In M. Dietz and H. Garrelts (eds), *Routledge Handbook of the Climate Change Movement*. Abingdon: Routledge, pp. 231–2.
Dietz, M. and Garrelts, H. (eds) (2014), *Routledge Handbook of the Climate Change Movement*. Abingdon: Routledge.
Dunlap, R.E. and McCright, A.M. (2011), Organized Climate Change Denial. In J.S. Dryzek, R.B. Norgaard and D. Schlosberg (eds), *The Oxford Handbook of Climate Change and Society*. Oxford: Oxford University Press, pp. 144–60.
Edwards, P.N. (2010), *A Vast Machine: Computer Models, Climate Data and the Politics of Global Warming*. Cambridge, MA: MIT Press.
Edwards-Schachter, M. and Wallace, M.L. (2017), 'Shaken, but Not Stirred': Sixty Years of Defining Social Innovation, *Technological Forecasting and Social Change*, **119**(Suppl C), 64–79.
Epstein, A. (2014), *The Moral Case for Fossil Fuels*. New York: Portfolio.
Esty, D.C. and Winston, A.S. (2006), *Green to Gold: How Smart Companies Use Environmental Strategy to Innovate, Create Value, and Build Competitive Advantage*. Hoboken, NJ: John Wiley & Sons.
Evans, G. and Phelan, L. (2016), Transition to a Post-Carbon Society: Linking Environmental Justice and Just Transition Discourses, *Energy Policy*, **99**(Suppl C), 329–39.
Foster, J.B., Clark, B. and York, R. (2010), *The Ecological Rift: Capitalism's War on the Earth*. New York: Monthly Review Press.
Fougère, M., Segercrantz, B. and Seeck, H. (2017), A Critical Reading of the European Union's Social Innovation Policy Discourse: (Re)Legitimizing Neoliberalism, *Organization*, **24**(6), 819–43.
George, G., Howard-Grenville, J., Joshi, A. and Tihanyi, L. (2016), Understanding and Tackling Societal Grand Challenges through Management Research, *Academy of Management Journal*, **59**(6), 1880–95.
Goldenberg, S. (2015), The Truth Behind Peabody's Campaign to Rebrand Coal as a Poverty Cure, *Guardian*, 19 May, https://www.theguardian.com/environment/2015/may/19/the-truth-behind-peabodys-campaign-to-rebrand-coal-as-a-poverty-cure (accessed 17 November 2017).
Hajer, M. (1995), *The Politics of Environmental Discourse: Ecological Modernization and the Policy Process*. Oxford: Oxford University Press.
Hamilton, C. (2010), *Requium for a Species: Why We Resist the Truth About Climate Change*. London: Earthscan.
Hamilton, C. (2013), *Earthmasters: Playing God with the Climate*. Sydney: Allen & Unwin.
Hart, S.L. (1997), Beyond Greening: Strategies for a Sustainable World, *Harvard Business Review*, **75**(1), 66–77.
Harvey, D. (2007), Neoliberalism as Creative Destruction, *The ANNALS of the American Academy of Political and Social Science*, **610**(1), 21–44.

Hoffman, A.J. (2001), *From Heresy to Dogma: An Institutional History of Corporate Environmentalism*. Stanford, CA: Stanford University Press.
Holmes, O. (2016), Environmental Activist Murders Set Record as 2015 Became Deadliest Year, *Guardian*, 21 June, https://www.theguardian.com/environment/2016/jun/20/environmental-activist-murders-global-witness-report (accessed 17 November 2017).
IPCC (2013), *Climate Change 2013: The Physical Science Basis. Working Group I Contribution to the Fifth Assessment Report of the Intergovernmental Panel on Climate Change*. Cambridge: Cambridge University Press.
IPCC (2014), *Climate Change 2014: Impacts, Adaptation, and Vulnerability. Part A: Global and Sectoral Aspects. Contribution of Working Group II to the Fifth Assessment Report of the Intergovernmental Panel on Climate Change*. Cambridge: Cambridge University Press.
Jermier, J.M., Forbes, L.C., Benn, S. and Orsato, R.J. (2006), The New Corporate Environmentalism and Green Politics. In S.R. Clegg, C. Hardy, T.B. Lawrence and W.R. Nord (eds), *The Sage Handbook of Organization Studies*. London: Sage, pp. 618–50.
Jessop, B., Moulaert, F., Hulgård, L. and Hamdouch, A. (2013), Social Innovation Research: A New Stage in Innovation Analysis? In F. Moulaert, D. MacCallum, A. Mehmood and A. Hamdouch (eds), *The International Handbook on Social Innovation: Collective Action, Social Learning and Transdisciplinary Research*. Cheltenham, UK and Northampton, MA, USA: Edward Elgar Publishing, pp. 110–26.
Kitchen, C. (2014), *To the Ends of the Earth: A Guide to Unconventional Fossil Fuels*. London: Corporate Watch.
Klein, N. (2014), *This Changes Everything: Capitalism vs. the Climate*. New York: Simon & Schuster.
Koslov, L. (2016), The Case for Retreat, *Public Culture*, **28**(2), 359–87.
Lazarus, R.J. (2009), Super Wicked Problems and Climate Change: Restraining the Present to Liberate the Future, *Cornell Law Review*, **94**, 1153–234.
Levin, K., Cashore, B., Bernstein, S. and Auld, G. (2012), Overcoming the Tragedy of Super Wicked Problems: Constraining Our Future Selves to Ameliorate Global Climate Change, *Policy Sciences*, **45**(2), 123–52.
Levy, D.L. and Egan, D. (1998), Capital Contests: National and Transnational Channels of Corporate Influence on the Climate Change Negotiations, *Politics and Society*, **26**(3), 337–61.
Levy, D.L. and Spicer, A. (2013), Contested Imaginaries and the Cultural Political Economy of Climate Change, *Organization*, **20**(5), 659–78.
Lovelock, J. (2000), *Gaia: A New Look at Life on Earth*. Oxford: Oxford University Press.
Mann, M. (2012), *The Hockey Stick and the Climate Wars: Dispatches from the Front Lines*. New York: Columbia University Press.
Mann, M.E. and Kump, L.R. (2015), *Dire Predictions: Understanding Climate Change*. New York: DK Publishing.
Maruyama, Y., Nishikido, M. and Iida, T. (2007), The Rise of Community Wind Power in Japan: Enhanced Acceptance through Social Innovation, *Energy Policy*, **35**(5), 2761–9.
Marx, K. (1976), *Capital: A Critique of Political Economy*. Harmondsworth: Penguin.
Mathews, J. (2014), *Greening of Capitalism: How Asia is Driving the Next Great Transformation*. Stanford, CA: Stanford University Press.
Matten, D. and Crane, A. (2005), Corporate Citizenship: Toward an Extended Theoretical Conceptualization, *Academy of Management Review*, **30**(1), 166–79.
McKibben, B. (2012), The Reckoning, *Rolling Stone*, **1162**, 52–8, 60.
Mol, A.P.J. (2002), Ecological Modernization and the Global Economy, *Global Environmental Politics*, **2**(2), 92–115.
Moulaert, F., MacCallum, D. and Jean, H. (2013), Social Innovation: Intuition, Precept, Concept, Theory and Practice. In F. Moulaert, D. MacCallum, A. Mehmood and A. Hamdouch (eds), *The International Handbook on Social Innovation: Collective Action, Social Learning and Transdisciplinary Research*. Cheltenham, UK and Northampton, MA, USA: Edward Elgar Publishing, pp. 13–24.
Mulgan, G. (2006), The Process of Social Innovation, *Innovations: Technology, Governance, Globalization*, **1**(2), 145–62.
Mulgan, G., Tucker, S., Ali, R. and Sanders, B. (2007), Social Innovation: What It Is, Why It Matters and How It Can Be Accelerated, Skoll Centre for Social Entrepreneurship Working Paper, http://eureka.sbs.ox.ac.uk/761/1/Social_Innovation.pdf (accessed 30 April 2018).
Murray, A., Skene, K. and Haynes, K. (2017), The Circular Economy: An Interdisciplinary Exploration of the Concept and Application in a Global Context, *Journal Of Business Ethics*, **140**(3), 369–80.
Naess, A. (1973), The Shallow and the Deep, Long-Range Ecology Movement. A Summary, *Inquiry*, **16**(1–4), 95–100.
Neubacher, A. (2012), Interview with Richard Branson: 'Climate Change is a Huge Opportunity', *Spiegel International*, 21 June, http://www.spiegel.de/international/business/richard-branson-discusses-climate-change-business-opportunities-a-839985.html (accessed 17 November 2017).
New, M., Liverman, D., Schroeder, H. and Anderson, K. (2011), Four Degrees and Beyond: The Potential for a

Global Temperature Increase of Four Degrees and Its Implications, *Philosophical Transactions of the Royal Society A: Mathematical, Physical and Engineering Sciences*, **369**(1934), 6–19.
Newman, P., Beatley, T. and Boyer, H. (2017), *Resilient Cities: Overcoming Fossil Fuel Dependence*. Washington, DC: Island Press.
Nyberg, D. and Wright, C. (2013), Corporate Corruption of the Environment: Sustainability as a Process of Compromise, *The British Journal of Sociology*, **64**(3), 405–24.
Nyberg, D., Spicer, A. and Wright, C. (2013), Incorporating Citizens: Corporate Political Engagement with Climate Change in Australia, *Organization*, **20**(3), 433–53.
Oreskes, N. and Conway, E.M. (2010), *Merchants of Doubt: How a Handful of Scientists Obscured the Truth on Issues from Tobacco Smoke to Global Warming*. New York: Bloomsbury Press.
Orsato, R.J. (2009), *Sustainability Strategies: When Does it Pay to Be Green?* London: Palgrave Macmillan.
Phillips, M. (2013), On Being Green and Being Enterprising: Narrative and the Ecopreneurial Self, *Organization*, **20**(6), 794–817.
Phills, J.A., Deiglmeier, K. and Miller, D.T. (2008), Rediscovering Social Innovation, *Stanford Social Innovation Review*, **6**(4), 34–43.
Polanyi, K. (1957), *The Great Transformation*. Boston, MA: Beacon Press.
Porter, M.E. and Kramer, M.R. (2011), Creating Shared Value, *Harvard Business Review*, **89**(1/2), 62–77.
Potter, W. (2011), *Green is the New Red: The Journey from Activist to 'Eco-Terrorist'*. San Francisco, CA: City Lights.
Quinn-Thibodeau, T. and Wu, B. (2016), NGOs and the Climate Justice Movement in the Age of Trumpism, *Development*, **59**(3), 251–6.
Radkau, J. (2014), *The Age of Ecology: A Global History*. Cambridge: Polity Press.
Ramus, C.A. and Montiel, I. (2005), When are Corporate Environmental Policies a Form of Greenwashing?, *Business & Society*, **44**(4), 377–414.
Rogers, E.M. (1995), *Diffusion of Innovations*. New York: Free Press.
Sandel, M.J. (2012), *What Money Can't Buy: The Moral Limits of Markets*. New York: Farrar, Straus and Giroux.
Schlosberg, D. and Collins, L.B. (2014), From Environmental to Climate Justice: Climate Change and the Discourse of Environmental Justice, *Wiley Interdisciplinary Reviews: Climate Change*, **5**(3), 359–74.
Schumpeter, J.A. (1942), *Capitalism, Socialism, and Democracy*. New York: Harper & Brothers.
Smith, A. (2011), The Transition Town Network: A Review of Current Evolutions and Renaissance, *Social Movement Studies*, **10**(1), 99–105.
Stern, N., Peters, S., Bakhshi, V. et al. (2006), *Stern Review: The Economics of Climate Change*. London: HM Treasury.
Tollefson, J. (2018), Can the World Kick Its Fossil-Fuel Addiction Fast Enough?, *Nature*, **556**(7702), 422–5.
Topham, G. (2016), Heathrow 13 Likely to Become UK's First Climate Change Protesters to Be Jailed, *Guardian*, 24 February, https://www.theguardian.com/environment/2016/feb/24/heathrow-13-likely-to-become-uks-first-climate-change-protesters-to-be-jailed (accessed 17 November 2017).
van der Schoor, T. and Scholtens, B. (2015), Power to the People: Local Community Initiatives and the Transition to Sustainable Energy, *Renewable and Sustainable Energy Reviews*, **43**(Suppl C), 666–75.
Vidal, J. (2014), Arctic 30: Russia Releases Greenpeace Ship, *Guardian*, 6 June, https://www.theguardian.com/environment/2014/jun/06/arctic-30-sunrise-russia-to-release-greenpeace-ship (accessed 17 November 2017).
Wagner, G. and Weitzman, M.L. (2012), Playing God, *Foreign Policy*, 24 October, http://www.foreignpolicy.com/articles/2012/10/22/playing_god (accessed 30 April 2018).
Weart, S.R. (2003), *The Discovery of Global Warming*. Cambridge, MA: Harvard University Press.
Weber, M. (1947), *The Theory of Social and Economic Organization*. New York: Free Press.
Whyte, K.P. (2017), The Dakota Access Pipeline, Environmental Injustice, and US Colonialism, *Red Ink: An International Journal of Indigenous Literature, Arts, & Humanities*, **19**(1), 154–69.
World Bank Group/Ecofys (2014), *State and Trends of Carbon Pricing 2014*. Washington, DC: World Bank Group.
Wright, C. and Nyberg, D. (2015), *Climate Change, Capitalism and Corporations: Processes of Creative Self-Destruction*. Cambridge: Cambridge University Press.
Wright, C. and Nyberg, D. (2017), An Inconvenient Truth: How Organizations Translate Climate Change into Business as Usual, *Academy of Management Journal*, **60**(5), 1633–61.
Wright, C., Nyberg, D. and Grant, D. (2012), 'Hippies on the Third Floor': Climate Change, Narrative Identity and the Micro-Politics of Corporate Environmentalism, *Organization Studies*, **33**(11), 1451–75.

4. Problem, person and pathway: a framework for social innovators

Julie Battilana, Brittany Butler, Marissa Kimsey, Johanna Mair, Christopher Marquis and Christian Seelos

INTRODUCTION

In the last decade, the appetite for learning about social innovation has intensified, and universities around the world have tried to keep up by creating an array of new courses, certificates, and degree programs (Lawrence et al., 2012). As researchers, educators, and advisers, how can we better prepare social innovators for the work of addressing the world's pressing social problems at the relevant scale? We undertook this inquiry in recent years as we researched, taught, and advised social innovators around the globe. Broadly, we view social innovation as innovation with the intent to address social problems. Rather than assuming that creating something new is good, we consider innovation in light of its potential to lead to positive social impact, that is, to improve the lives of individuals and communities (Seelos and Mair, 2017). From our experience, we identified three key lenses to help social innovators contribute to social change, which culminated in what we call the "3P" framework that considers the nature of: the *problem* at hand, the *person* pursuing change, and the *pathway* to change (see Figure 4.1). For both new and experienced social innovators, considering the alignment of these 3Ps can provide an organizing template that helps them to think and act in ways more likely to benefit individuals and communities. We find that exploring the problem, person, and pathway in turn can also shed light on the corresponding interrelationships, and where there may or may not be overlap. Rather than providing a one-size-fits-all blueprint, at its core the 3P framework offers sets of questions for social innovators to unpack and update iteratively. This approach encourages individuals and groups to find the "fit" between different elements.

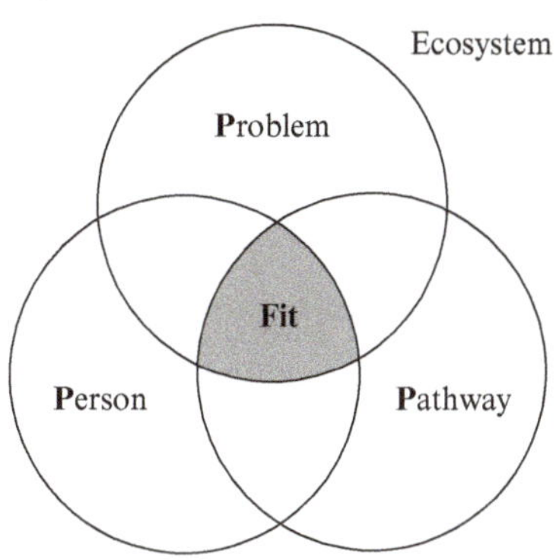

Figure 4.1 The 3P framework

The 3P framework is based on a situational approach (Hersey and Blanchard, 1977) to social innovation that accounts for ways in which different contexts may call for different responses. It also accounts for the politics of change. Addressing social problems often requires coordinating shifts in behavior across diverse individuals and institutions, and sometimes even sectors (see Alinsky, 1971; Battilana, 2015; Snow and Soule, 2010). Accordingly, accounting for the situational, interpersonal, and structural dynamics of power is key as a basis for realistic understanding and action (Pfeffer, 1992). This does not mean that the 3Ps is a tool meant for those who already have power. Social innovators often challenge power hierarchies. Even when they do not already have the power to do so, those seeking change can work to build their power bases in order to enhance their impact. From that standpoint, we view the 3Ps as an inclusive tool that also aims to help empower marginalized individuals and groups aspiring to participate in a movement for change. Furthermore, although the 3P framework is meant as a tool to help guide the thinking and action of individual social innovators, a single individual very rarely succeeds in developing and disseminating social innovations alone. As we elaborate below, such an adoption most often involves collective action. Accordingly, each social innovator is part of a broader movement toward social change (Battilana and Kimsey, 2017). In presenting the 3Ps below, we emphasize the importance of thinking beyond the individual level and accounting for the cultivation of collective capacities often critical for social change.

In the chapter, we delve into each element of the 3P framework – problem, person, and pathway – in turn. Although our discussion proceeds in a linear sequence, we intend the learning journey to be iterative, whereby social innovators regularly revisit their assumptions and the sets of questions posed over time. We illustrate how we engage new and experienced social innovators in this journey by discussing our pedagogical approach as educators in universities. In conclusion, we highlight future research directions based on our experience developing the 3P framework.

PROBLEM

Social innovators often approach issues with interventions already in mind. However, enacting a prespecified solution without thoroughly understanding the problem risks causing negative unintended consequences. The stakes are high for social innovators, whose mistakes can incur not only costs for themselves, but also costs for those they seek to serve. To unpack the problem in the 3P framework, we put forward the questions: What is the nature of the problem? What is the problem statement?

What Is the Nature of the Problem?

Social innovators may feel emboldened when they think that they know more than they do, or, on the flip side, feel paralysed by the web of interconnected moving pieces. Intractability is a common reason given to delay action and diminish aspirations. In a middle way between naivety and paralysis, we encourage social innovators to identify sets of stakeholders and come to recognize their distinct perspectives. This exploration can provide an entry point into understanding the material and social conditions of the particular locality of the problem that social innovators seek to address.

Such an exploration is critical for social innovators to understand the nature of the problem at hand. Specifically, it can help them identify the various factors that contribute to the problem's reproduction. These factors may be economic, cognitive, normative, and/or political. For many problems, such dynamics are intertwined – with, for instance, deeply rooted gender roles (normative) intertwined with insecure property rights (political), and low levels of income (economic) intertwined with people's ability to make decisions about the future (cognitive). Yet, depending on the problem, each kind of factor may be more or less important as barriers to change than others. Mapping these factors and understanding how they contribute to the problem can help social innovators to overcome them (Seelos and Mair, 2017).

Our experience suggests that in order to fully understand the nature of the problem, there is no replacement for social innovators immersing themselves in the places where the problem exists, getting to know firsthand the distinct social norms, power hierarchies, legal rules, economic systems, historical legacies, and physical landscapes. Various established techniques for such immersion have grown out of the study of ethnography, which grounds interpretations of the perspectives of those under study in firsthand experiences of the setting (see Atkinson et al., 2001). Action research, dating back to Lewin (1951), has sought "to take knowledge production beyond the gate-keeping of professional knowledge makers . . . to the people" (Bradbury-Huang, 2010, pp. 93–4). In participatory systemic inquiry, people try to find out everything possible about what, how, why, where, and with whom issues unfold in a specific ecosystem. Such an approach can help outsiders and insiders alike learn about the setting with the use of open-ended prompts that try to ascertain what is present, rather than focusing on what is missing. Being intentional about expanding the reference frame beyond "people like you" also helps reveal hidden narratives, besides dominant ones that maintain existing norms and hierarchies (Burns and Worsley, 2015).

Engaging in field-based inquiry is critical for social innovators to uncover stakeholders' habits of thought and action that contribute to perpetuating the status quo. Habits of action refer to the sequences of steps underlying flows of materials, money, and information. Habits of thought encompass people's narratives of themselves, each other, and the wider context (Forrester, 1971). When considered together, these habits can surface underlying distributions of power that reproduce asymmetries (Battilana, 2015). In the 3P framework, we encourage social innovators to create, and update, stakeholder maps that account for these habits of thought and action and demarcate the array of interrelated individuals and groups: who is harmed by the current reality (potential beneficiaries), who cares about an alternative future (potential allies), who benefits from the current reality (potential resistors), and who observes the current reality without particularly caring about it (potential fence sitters)? Crucially, these categories are neither mutually exclusive nor static. A potential beneficiary may also be an ally, and a potential fence sitter may become a resistor.

At the same time that we encourage social innovators to investigate what stakeholders take for granted, we also encourage social innovators to revisit their own assumptions. Cognitive scientists and psychologists widely accept that people create and use mental models of external reality to help them engage with the world (Craik, 1943; Johnson-Laird, 1983). Yet, people's ability to represent reality accurately is inherently limited and context-dependent (see Jones et al., 2011). Without reflection on their own mental models, social innovators risk blocking their way, and even exacerbating problems as they interact with and on behalf of others. To meet this challenge, social innovators can approach iterations of their stakeholder maps as hypotheses to test further rather than facts to validate firmly. In the process, they may compare whether potential beneficiaries, allies, resistors, and fence sitters share their own internal representations or not. Social innovators may also work to apply the notion of "unlearning." As they surface their particular ways of relating to the world, social innovators not only can come to discard unhelpful mental models, but also can cultivate new openness to not knowing (Brook et al., 2016).

What Is the Problem Statement?

A clearly formulated problem statement is an underappreciated tool (Astor et al., 2016), both as an internal compass for individual social innovators and for external communication to cement a shared purpose and mobilize collective resources inclusively. Psychologists have long found that individuals exert more effort and focus in the face of understandable goals (see Locke and Latham, 2002). A growing body of evidence suggests that mental contrasting in particular can help spur action, whereby individuals juxtapose positive aspects about a desired future with negative aspects of the status quo (Oettingen et al., 2000). A corresponding way to approach problem formulation is to demarcate the gap between the current reality and a goal state. The current reality captures how the world is, while a goal state captures a notion of how the world could be different. That gap is a source of creative tension, with tension dissipating either when reality rises to the level of a goal state or a goal state lowers to the level of reality (Senge, 1990).

Such problem formulation is a delicate dance. Imagining a goal state can easily lead to presupposing a solution, yet a problem statement loses its potency when it is actually a solution in disguise (Astor et al., 2016). For example, saying "most Ugandans still do not live near an electric grid" assumes that access to an electric grid leads to reliable power, that proximity to a grid guarantees connection, that a connection guarantees the necessary power, and that power is affordable. A broader formulation – such as "just 30 percent of Ugandans have a reliable supply of energy throughout the day" – leaves room for more open investigation of the problem, as well as pathways to change.

In our experience, social innovators very rarely formulate a problem once and leave that statement static. Instead, they iterate and adjust their formulations of the problem over time, based on both their more nuanced understandings of the current reality and fresh visions of alternative futures. One common theme of effective problem statements, though, is that they enable social innovators to distinguish the direction of progress (Astor et al., 2016). In the energy example, it is clear that the goal state involves an increase in the number of Ugandans whose access to energy is affordable, continuous, and reliable.

PERSON

In addition to understanding and communicating about the problem, social innovators often need to understand and communicate about themselves as individuals. Rather than such introspection amounting to indulgent navel-gazing, we find the opposite – that it can help social innovators contribute more effectively to collective action when they can be both inward- and outward-looking. Addressing social problems often requires breaking with existing norms, and a single individual rarely succeeds alone. Instead, social innovators contribute to collective movements toward change (Ganz and McKenna, 2019). To do so, we encourage social innovators to probe how they can harness their motivations and sources of power to benefit individuals and communities, while ensuring their efforts have the necessary legitimacy and support (Moore, 1997). To understand person in the 3P framework, we invite the questions: What are the motivations? What are the sources of power? In answering both, we encourage social innovators to look inwardly at themselves as well as outwardly to account for other stakeholders' motivations and sources of power.

What Are the Motivations?

Social innovators need to persevere when uncertainty looms, momentum slows, new obstacles arise, and critics become louder. Such perseverance requires passion and courage (see Kanter, 2005b). One side of this coin is emotional. Marshall Ganz, for example, suggests combatting inertia with urgency, apathy with anger, fear with hope, isolation with solidarity, and self-doubt with the belief that an individual can make a difference (Ganz, 2011). Another dimension is mindset. Carol Dweck has pioneered a growing body of research on the growth mindset, showing that when people perceive failure as an opportunity to learn and strengthen themselves, rather than a sign of permanent inadequacy, they are more likely to exert additional effort, take risks, and achieve long-term goals (Dweck, 2007). For new and experienced social innovators alike, such a growth mindset can help in the face of complexity and resistance.

Furthermore, the public never recognizes the many who contribute to collective action, and the level of control of a single individual in a movement for change is often limited. While some motivations may inevitably ebb and flow over time, we find that people who can tap into a lasting personal sense of purpose are more likely to persevere in the face of setbacks, or when their work does not receive the anticipated public recognition.

Moreover, because social innovators often coordinate with others to be able to improve the lives of individuals and communities, we encourage them not only to examine their own motivations, but also to consider the motivations of others from their perspectives. Such understanding of others is critical in order to mobilize and organize effectively as part of a movement for change (Benford and Snow, 2000; Bernstein, 1997; Tilly, 1999). Doing so requires tailoring communication accordingly such that it provides potential partners with resonant meanings and shared identities to help bring them into a coalition (Snow and Soule, 2010). When social innovators can connect their own motivations to values shared by the coalition, this alignment of feeling can also help the alignment of action.

What Are the Sources of Power?

In our experience, social innovators too often underestimate political considerations in pursuit of their noble goals. Many gravitate to the technical aspects of a perceived solution while discounting relational elements. Take the example of a mobile application for farmers in India that reports up-to-date levels of local agricultural prices. While the technical aspect of this social innovation may function brilliantly on mobile phones, its ability to empower farmers also inextricably depends on the relational dynamics of the relative bargaining power between farmers and middlemen who sell their products to restaurants and grocery stores. Underestimating the political aspect of empowering farmers, and what is at stake for those involved, can render social innovators ineffective, or even harmful. Ultimately, power is not a possession that some people have inherited or accumulated while others lack it. Power depends on the situation and the extent to which people therein control access to resources, tangible or intangible, that others value.

We encourage social innovators to think systematically about the sources of power available to contribute to social change, both their own as individuals and those of existing and potential partners. In the 3P framework, we distinguish between personal, positional, and relational sources of power. Each is important to consider with respect to individual social innovators as well as those who make up their coalitions. Personal sources of power are internal, deriving from personality, experience, and expertise. Positional sources come from formal roles in organizations and society. Relational sources come from connections with family, friends, and colleagues (Battilana, 2015). We encourage social innovators to map all of these sources of power, assessing themselves individually, as well as their influence on others and the strength or weakness of their social ties. Besides creating their own map, we also encourage social innovators to map the sources of power of potential beneficiaries, allies, resistors, and fence sitters.

Overall, sources of power are far from fixed. They often change over time and space, across different relationships and as the problem statement or proposed vehicle for change shifts. It is thus critical for social innovators to update their stakeholder analysis regularly in order to more accurately capture stakeholder orientations toward the proposed change and their sources of power. The effectiveness of various sources of power will accordingly also depend on the context. Different sources may be more or less critical for different tasks and across different relationships. Influencing others and convincing them to join a movement for change draws heavily on relational sources of power in the form of strong social ties (see Battilana and Casciaro, 2012, 2013). If social innovators do not have the dispositions and networks to build coalitions, they may grow them over time, and/or team up with others who do, to bring these strengths into the movement.

PATHWAY

Besides the problem and person, the remaining P of the 3Ps is the pathway to change. Because social change often results from coordinated action, we encourage social innovators to account systematically for how their efforts can most effectively complement other existing ones in the ecosystem and, in particular, respond to perspectives of potential beneficiaries who have been grappling with the problem, often over lifetimes. To help guide social innovators in assessing different pathways to change in the 3P framework, we pose the questions: What are possible vehicles for social impact? What could scaling social impact look like?

What Are Possible Vehicles to Social Impact?

The universe of potential entry points to push for social change tends to be manifold (Kanter, 2005a; Tracey and Stott, 2017). At one end of the spectrum, some occupy themselves with "arranging the deck chairs on the Titanic" (Meadows, 1999, p. 6). Indeed, taking the existing rules of the game for granted can translate into smaller social impact. At the other end of the spectrum, social innovators may utilize leverage points to try and alter the goals of the system as well as the mindsets that perpetuate it (see Meadows, 2008). Such divergent changes that break with taken-for-granted ways of thinking and behaving are especially challenging to push, because they tend to face more resistance (see Battilana and Casciaro, 2012, 2013).

In the 3P framework, we encourage social innovators to consider multiple possible vehicles to social change in light of their potential to improve the lives of individuals and communities. This exploration goes against the impulses of social innovators to latch onto to their first idea for a solution, or to bend to the wills of donors and investors who can provide financing but whose stipulations compromise social impact. In different settings, the route to social impact may be on the back of individual or collective action, starting new initiatives or working within existing ones, a single organization or collaboration across organizations, cooperation that is officially or loosely bound, or some combination.

Individually, social innovators may try to push for change as authors, speakers, performers, legislators, organizers, or investors (among many other personas). As a scientist, Rachel Carson sought to alert the American public that pesticides were toxic in the 1950s and 1960s. Through her writing, speeches, and Congressional testimony, she helped spur new policies to protect people's health and the environment. At the same time, the limits of individual action tend to be stark. Social impact needs a movement toward change to launch and develop. Carson's work had impact precisely because it gave rise to such a collective movement in the United States and beyond (Kisfalvi and Maguire, 2011).

Some social innovators jump to the conclusion that they need to create a new organization to address the problem at hand. Yet, in some contexts, the sources of power available through existing organizations or movements may outweigh the flexibility of creating a new entity. There are increasingly institutional channels for such "social intrapreneurship" across organizational structures and sectors (Davis and White, 2015). Among collective movements, social innovations such as fair trade agreements have emerged out of movements for ethical international development and solidarity. Among businesses, new strategies have tried to take sustainability seriously, like the Sustainable Living Plan at the multinational corporation Unilever. In governments and not-for-profits, innovation labs are emerging, including across the European Union and in the large not-for-profit BRAC based in Bangladesh (Tracey and Stott, 2017). Whichever the sector, social intrapreneurship may take place as part of internal operations in a single division or multiple; in a subsidiary that is partial, complete, or a joint venture; as part of a partnership that is formal or informal; or some combination of arrangements (Kistruck and Beamish, 2010).

Alternatively, social innovators may realize that they need to start new organizations to enhance their social impact – a typical not-for-profit, business, public entity, or some hybrid of these traditional organizational forms, like social enterprises. To compare across different possible vehicles for social change, we encourage social innovators to map how different options could create value and for whom (Mair and Martí, 2006). The rapid prototyping that characterizes design thinking can be helpful when it comes to experimenting with various kinds of pathways. The process of engaging beneficiaries and/or customers early and often can help reveal unexpected opportunities and challenges, including at "the edges, the places where 'extreme' people live differently, think differently, and consume differently" (Brown and Wyatt, 2010, p. 32).

Regardless of the vehicle, social innovators will need to chart a path that involves collaborating and coordinating with others, often across sectors, to address social problems. While governmental contracting and community development projects involving both the corporate and social sectors have become more mainstream, cross-sector work can still be difficult to organize and sustain. Different missions, values, accountabilities, and constituencies can make the task of aligning interests formidable (Bryson et al., 2006). Yet, examples of effective models to reconcile fundamental partner differences do exist, such as the partnership between the Norwegian corporation Telenor and the Bangladeshi social enterprise Grameen Bank (Seelos and Mair, 2007).

What Could Scaling Social Impact Look Like?

Scale is a hot topic in research and practice (see Shah and Han, 2018). Our approach focuses on expanding and/or adapting to match the magnitude of the problem at hand. One aspect of such scale may be organizational growth – increasing revenue, staff, and offices. However, growing an organization does not always translate to scaling social impact (Gugelev and Stern, 2015). In the 3P framework, we encourage social innovators to investigate the gamut of scaling options in light of their potential to match the magnitude of the problem in its entirety. Besides options in terms of what to scale – a product, program, model, organization, principles, or some combination – social innovators also face the choice of how to scale – across geographies, activities, and/or collaborations.

Geographically, social innovators may try to replicate what they already do in new communities, provinces, countries, and/or regions. Such expansion might happen in new branches, franchises, or subsidiaries. A particular risk here is not accounting for the context-specific nature of some innovations' initial successes that could prevent growth. Even BRAC, often considered one of the most effective and experienced international development organizations, struggled after it expanded its Bangladeshi operations to new countries. Despite decades of experience and a large cadre of professional staff, the organization had to stop or spin off programs that it failed to adapt to new contexts (Seelos and Mair, 2017).

Changing the parameters of activities and collaborations also requires attention to the different sources of power necessary to understand these different kinds of tasks and relationships, as well as balancing more or less control over outcomes. In terms of activities, social innovators may grow their operations by expanding the range of activities that they undertake, either upstream or downstream. In terms of collaborations, social innovators may grow their operations by working with new stakeholders – in the arenas of government, business, not-for-profits, and/or social enterprise – in new kinds of arrangements. Through open source platforms, social innovators may disseminate their innovations for free. With affiliations, social innovators may create networks with external partners to replicate or adopt their innovations for fees. A team led by medical doctors Atul Gawande and Bill Berry, for example, collaborated with the World Health Organization to leverage its global influence to disseminate the first Surgical Safety Checklist for operating rooms around the world. After rapid iterations of the design and content, the World Health Organization issued the first edition of this checklist in 2008. Today, operating rooms across the globe, in developed and developing countries alike, are utilizing the checklist, the implementation of which was associated with a 36 percent drop in postoperative complications in diverse settings (Haynes et al., 2009).

To consider different scaling trajectories side-by-side, social innovators have multiple tools at their disposal. Through research and evaluation, they can better understand which aspects of their innovations are core and which can be flexible. Through enabling adaptation, they can support modifications that meet the needs of a growing number of beneficiaries. Through reducing the resources required for implementation, they can lower some of the burden of dissemination. Through willingness to rethink their innovations, they can enhance their ability to evolve as the context evolves. Through empowering users, they can inclusively, and powerfully, harness users' knowledge as "co-evaluators," "co-designers," and "co-scalers" (see Clarke and Dede, 2009).

FINDING THE FIT

Rather than providing definite or prescriptive answers, the 3P framework draws attention to essential sets of questions for investigation. The culmination of the framework is the intersection between the problem, person, and pathway. At this intersection is the locus of action that accounts for the fit of each element in relation to each other.

How do the problem and pathway fit? Some vehicles for social change may address the symptoms of the problem but not its root causes. The way that particular resistors think and act may make some pathways especially difficult to champion. How do the problem and person fit? Individuals' levels of direct experience with the problem are likely to inflect not only their understandings and motivations internally, but also their sources of power and perceived legitimacy externally. How do the person and pathway fit? Some pathways may require sources of power that individuals do not currently have, while some motivations may lead people to other vehicles for change. Altogether, how do the problem, person, and pathway fit? This question is literally the center of the 3P framework (see Figure 4.1), whereby we encourage social innovators to understand and undertake their roles in movements for change attuned to the dynamic interplay across the problem, person, and pathway.

OUR PEDAGOGY

The responses to such questions of alignment across the 3Ps will inevitably change over time for social innovators. As educators in universities, we have accordingly tried to design our pedagogy to encourage social innovators to embrace a learning perspective, whereby they test their assumptions and update their emerging knowledge to help them find the fit across the 3Ps. As we teach new and experienced social innovators, we have sought to meet them where they are: as changemakers with their own histories, motivations, and communities, whose actions carry consequences and whose assumptions require testing in dynamic settings. Before concluding this chapter with a discussion of future research directions, we illustrate how we help our students find such fit across the 3Ps. Our approach emphasizes self-direction, connection to the real world, iteration, and ongoing evaluation.

To start, we ask our students to create and execute individualized game plans, where they choose their own goals and actions for their social change work. This simple, self-directed, experiential tool allows for relevant customization, while placing responsibility with the learners to find and work at their own expanding edges (Knowles, 1970). This teaching approach is consistent with a constructionist view of learning, whereby educators help learners cultivate understanding and skills through a problem-solving project of the learners' choosing (Harel and Papert, 1991), in this case a social innovation.

Correspondingly, in most of our sessions with students, we carve out time for them to apply taught material to their own projects. After teaching a case and outlining research on the relationship between social network composition and social change, for example, we ask students to map how their own approach to stakeholder engagement may advance or hinder their social change projects. This format creates space to surface tensions between research and practice in real time, while producing something "useful" for the learner. Research on adult learning suggests that students exert more effort and prefer learning experiences with direct and immediate relevance for their social and professional worlds (Knowles, 1970). As such, we find that requesting assignments in formats that most closely resemble "real life" deliverables yields greater attention than papers that seem like "homework." At the end of our time with students, we ask them to compose a slide deck that summarizes their work, as professional settings will call upon them to share slides with that same content. This is not simply about efficiency; it is about learning through practice in an area that feels relevant.

We present material on the problem, person, and pathway through a spiraled rather than linear sequence of sessions. For example, rather than spending many consecutive sessions focused on the problem, the fundamentals of creating a tight problem statement reappear throughout the year – when students conduct a root cause analysis of the problem, present a theory of change, and consider social performance measurement. By spacing out conversations about the problem (and similarly the person and pathway), students have time to integrate and try out what they have learned. At the same time, we encourage students to take action to test their thinking in the field. Practice with the rhythm of an iterative learning process not only advances their understandings, but also builds the muscles necessary for competence as a practitioner (Seelos and Mair, 2016). Such a learning approach depends on social innovators' willingness to revisit their assumptions, which can be more difficult to entertain as they build experience.

Our core objective as educators is to enhance the potential for our students to improve the lives of individuals and communities. To build this potential, learners can accumulate more valid and comprehensive knowledge about the 3Ps, in addition to developing broader and deeper sources of power. We assess progress by tracking the learning effort of our students and the effectiveness of the learning trajectory we steward. At the start and end of our courses we ask students to articulate what they know about each of the 3Ps, as well as gaps in their understandings and their processes for testing their assumptions over time. As their projects gain momentum, signals of project progress can shift to more tangible inputs and outputs, as well as outcomes related to their projects (Ebrahim, 2019; Ebrahim and Rangan, 2010).

FUTURE RESEARCH

As researchers, educators, and advisers, we are still learning how to support social innovators effectively, which content to select, and how to sequence pedagogy in a mix of customized and general experiences. To answer such questions, we need more knowledge about social innovation. From our experience, the following three areas for future research stand out as critical: examining the effectiveness of social innovation in context, measuring social performance, and creating and sustaining cross-sector collaboration.

Over the past decade, research on social innovation has produced rich ethnographies and in-depth case studies to better understand phenomena (Mair et al., 2012; Mair et al., 2016). Leveraging such qualitative data and analysis is important to specify the mechanisms triggering and enabling social change (Seelos and Mair, 2014), particularly when individuals do not know much yet about the phenomena at hand (Edmondson and McManus, 2007). However, as the field of research on social innovation matures, it is equally important to compare more systematically the effectiveness of different approaches across contexts. While there have been many calls for these studies (for example, Lee et al., 2014), we are only starting to design large-scale research examining the effectiveness of different social innovation approaches (Huysentruyt et al., 2016). The challenge going forward will be in collecting data systematically over time, and in a way that captures differences across social change projects and the individuals involved, as well as their cultural contexts.

Another critical, and related, area of inquiry relates to how we measure and evaluate performance when it comes to social innovation, both in the realm of practice (how should social innovators measure progress in their own efforts?) and in the realm of teaching (how should educators assess student progress?) (Ebrahim, 2019). One obstacle is that social change efforts rarely have "dependent variables" that lend themselves to quantification and comparative work across different initiatives, problem spaces, or geographies. We also lack an understanding of the "independent variables" that drive social performance. For example, how does context influence the importance of resource acquisition (for example, in contexts of low resource munificence) or particular resource configurations (for example, in contexts with competitive social sectors) to explain social performance? Currently, several donors are enacting big-bet strategies, such as Co-Impact, that concentrate resources around particular approaches intended to generate tremendous social change. Such allocations of massive amounts of resources to big-bets have generated high expectations of positive impact. These initiatives accordingly offer unique opportunities to understand the potential of various resource configurations to generate social impact and to identify intended benefits as well as possible unintended harms.

We also recognize that the most intractable social problems today require solutions that engage deeply rooted systems of power and traverse sectors. Since the 1992 Rio World Summit, the international community has called for more cross-sectoral efforts to foster sustainable development. Billions of dollars now flow to public–private partnerships, yet cross-sector work remains difficult to organize and sustain. Besides different goals, regulations, and norms, each sector tends to have different accountabilities – public organizations to political and legal systems, not-for-profits to donors, and corporations to shareholders (Bryson et al., 2006; Seelos and Mair, 2007). Future research is necessary to help identify the enabling conditions, processes, and structures underlying cross-sector work, as well as their associated outcomes.

CONCLUSION

Each year students join the ranks of our universities with aspirations to make the world a better place. Given the scale, scope, and persistence of the world's most pressing social problems, we have joined together with them in serious consideration of this premise and have committed as researchers, teachers, and advisers to support social innovators navigating the complexities of initiating and implementing social change, while in school and beyond. Over time, our hope is that insights produced through these efforts will contribute to a dynamic knowledge base that accelerates learning in the field of social innovation, grounded in a better understanding of the role that social innovators can play in creating and sustaining a more just and livable world.

REFERENCES

Alinsky, Saul (1971), *Rules for Radicals: A Pragmatic Primer for Realistic Radicals*. New York: Random House.

Astor, T., Michael Morales, Don Kieffer and Nelson Repenning (2016), "What problem are you trying to solve: an introduction to structured problem solving", MIT Sloan Working Paper 5175-16, MIT Sloan School of Management, Cambridge, MA.

Atkinson, Paul, Amanda Coffey, Sara Delamont, John Lofland and Lyn Lofland (eds) (2001), *Handbook of Ethnography*. London: Sage.

Battilana, Julie (2015), "Power and influence in society", Harvard Business School Module Note 415-055, Harvard Business School Publishing, Boston, MA.

Battilana, Julie and Tiziana Casciaro (2012), "Change agents, networks, and institutions: a contingency theory of organizational change", *Academy of Management Journal*, **55** (2), 381–98.

Battilana, Julie and Tiziana Casciaro (2013), "Overcoming resistance to organizational change: strong ties and affective cooptation", *Management Science*, **59** (4), 819–36.

Battilana, Julie and Marissa Kimsey (2017), "Should you agitate, innovate, or orchestrate?", *Stanford Social Innovation Review*, 18 September, accessed 11 May 2018 at https://ssir.org/articles/entry/should_you_agitate_innovate_or_orchestrate.

Benford, Robert D. and David A. Snow (2000), "Framing processes and social movements: an overview and assessment", *Annual Review of Sociology*, **26** (1), 611–39.

Bernstein, Mary (1997), "Celebration and suppression: the strategic uses of identity by the lesbian and gay movement", *American Journal of Sociology*, **103** (3), 531–65.

Bradbury-Huang, Hilary (2010), "What is good action research? Why the resurgent interest?", *Action Research*, **8** (1), 93–109.

Brook, Cheryl, Mike Pedler, Christine Abbott and John Burgoyne (2016), "On stopping doing those things that are not getting us to where we want to be: unlearning, wicked problems and critical action learning", *Human Relations*, **69** (2), 369–89.

Brown, Tim and Jocelyn Wyatt (2010), "Design thinking for social innovation", *Stanford Social Innovation Review*, **8** (1), 31–5.

Bryson, John M., Barbara C. Crosby and Melissa Middleton Stone (2006), "The design and implementation of cross-sector collaborations: propositions from the literature", *Public Administration Review*, **66** (s1), 44–55.

Burns, Danny and Stuart Worsley (2015), *Navigating Complexity in International Development: Facilitating Sustainable Change at Scale*. Rugby, UK: Practical Action Publishing.

Clarke, Jody and Chris Dede (2009), "Design for scalability: a case study of the River City curriculum", *Journal of Science Education and Technology*, **18** (4), 353–65.

Craik, K.J.W. (1943), *The Nature of Explanation*. Cambridge: Cambridge University Press.

Davis, Gerald F. and Christopher J. White (2015), *Changing Your Company from the Inside Out: A Guide for Social Intrapreneurs*. Boston, MA: Harvard Business Review Press.

Dweck, Carol (2007), *Mindset: The Psychology of Success*. New York: Ballantine Books.

Ebrahim, Alnoor (2019), *Measuring Social Change: Designing for Performance and Accountability in a Complex World*. Redwood City, CA: Stanford University Press.

Ebrahim, A. and V.K. Rangan (2010), "What impact? A framework for measuring the scale and scope of social performance", *California Management Review*, **56** (3), 118–41.

Edmondson, Amy C. and Stacy E. McManus (2007), "Methodological fit in management field research", *Academy of Management Review*, **32** (4), 1246–64.
Forrester, Jay W. (1971), "Counterintuitive behavior of social systems", *Theory and Decision*, **2** (2), 109–40.
Ganz, Marshall (2011), "Public narrative, collective action, and power", in Sina Odugbemi and Taeku Lee (eds), *Accountability Through Public Opinion: From Inertia to Public Action*. Washington, DC: The International Bank for Reconstruction and Development/The World Bank, pp. 273–90.
Ganz, Marshall and Elizabeth McKenna (2019), "Bringing leadership back in", in David A. Snow, Sarah A. Soule, Hanspeter Kriesi and Holly J. McCammon (eds), *The Wiley Blackwell Companion to Social Movements*, 2nd edn. Hoboken, NJ: Wiley-Blackwell, pp. 185–202.
Gugelev, Alice and Andrew Stern (2015), "What's your endgame?", *Stanford Social Innovation Review*, **13** (1), 41–7.
Harel, Idit and Seymour Papert (eds) (1991), *Constructionism*. Norwood, NJ: Ablex Publishing.
Haynes, Alex B., Thomas G. Weiser, William R. Berry et al. (2009), "A surgical safety checklist to reduce morbidity and mortality in a global population", *New England Journal of Medicine*, **360** (5), 491–9.
Hersey, P. and K.H. Blanchard (1977), *Management of Organizational Behavior*, 3rd edn. Englewood Cliffs, NJ: Prentice Hall.
Huysentruyt, M., J. Mair and U. Stephan (2016), "Market-oriented and mission-focused: social enterprises around the globe", *Stanford Social Innovation Review*, accessed 19 October 2017 at https://ssir.org/articles/entry/market_oriented_and_mission_focused_social_enterprises_around_the_globe.
Johnson-Laird, Philip N. (1983), *Mental Models*. Cambridge: Cambridge University Press.
Jones, Natalie, Helen Ross, Timothy Lynam, Pascal Perez and Anne Leitch (2011), "Mental models: an interdisciplinary synthesis of theory and methods", *Ecology and Society*, **16** (1), 46.
Kanter, Rosabeth M. (2005a), "Even bigger change: a framework for getting started at changing the world", Harvard Business School Background Note 305-099, Harvard Business School Publishing, Boston, MA.
Kanter, Rosabeth M. (2005b), "Leadership for change: enduring skills for change masters", Harvard Business School Note 304-062, Harvard Business School Publishing, Boston, MA.
Kisfalvi, Veronika and Steve Maguire (2011), "On the nature of institutional entrepreneurs: insights from the life of Rachel Carson", *Journal of Management Inquiry*, **20** (2), 152–77.
Kistruck, Geoffrey M. and Paul W. Beamish (2010), "The interplay of form, structure, and embeddedness in social intrapreneurship", *Entrepreneurship Theory and Practice*, **34** (4), 735–61.
Knowles, M.S. (1970), *The Modern Practice of Adult Education: From Pedagogy to Andragogy*. Englewood Cliffs, NJ: Prentice Hall Regents.
Lawrence, Thomas, Nelson Phillips and Paul Tracey (2012), "From the guest editors: educating social entrepreneurs and social innovators", *Academy of Management Learning & Education*, **11** (3), 319–23.
Lee, Matthew, Julie Battilana and Ting Wang (2014), "Building an infrastructure for empirical research on social enterprise: challenges and opportunities", in Jeremy Short, David J. Ketchen and Donald D. Bergh (eds), *Social Entrepreneurship and Research Methods*, Vol. 9. Bingley, UK: Emerald Group Publishing, pp. 241–64.
Lewin, Kurt (1951), *Field Theory in Social Science: Selected Theoretical Papers*. New York: Harper.
Locke, Edwin A. and Gary P. Latham (2002), "Building a practically useful theory of goal setting and task motivation: a 35-year odyssey", *American Psychologist*, **57** (9), 705–17.
Mair, Johanna and Ignasi Martí (2006), "Social entrepreneurship research: a source of explanation, prediction, and delight", *Journal of World Business*, **41** (1), 36–44.
Mair, Johanna, Ignasi Martí and Marc J. Ventresca (2012), "Building inclusive markets in rural Bangladesh: how intermediaries work institutional voids", *Academy of Management Journal*, **55** (4), 819–50.
Mair, Johanna, Miriam Wolf and Christian Seelos (2016), "Scaffolding: a process of transforming patterns of inequality in small-scale societies", *Academy of Management Journal*, **59** (6), 2021–44.
Meadows, Donella H. (1999), *Leverage Points: Places to Intervene in a System*. Hartland, VT: Sustainability Institute.
Meadows, Donella H. (2008), *Thinking in Systems: A Primer* (ed. Diana Wright). White River Junction, VT: Chelsea Green Publishing.
Moore, Mark H. (1997), *Creating Public Value: Strategic Management in Government*. Bridgewater, NJ: Replica Books.
Oettingen, Gabriele, Gaby Hönig and Peter M. Gollwitzer (2000), "Effective self-regulation of goal attainment", *International Journal of Educational Research*, **33** (7–8), 705–32.
Pfeffer, Jeffrey (1992), *Managing with Power: Politics and Influence in Organizations*. Boston, MA: Harvard Business School Press.
Seelos, C. and J. Mair (2007), "Profitable business models and market creation in the context of deep poverty: a strategic view", *Academy of Management Perspectives*, **21** (4), 49–63.
Seelos, C. and J. Mair (2014), "Organizational closure competencies and scaling: a realist approach to theorizing

social enterprise", in J.C. Short (ed.), *Social Entrepreneurship and Research Methods.* Bingley, UK: Emerald Group Publishing, pp. 147–88.
Seelos, C. and J. Mair (2016), "When innovation goes wrong", *Stanford Social Innovation Review*, Fall, 27–33.
Seelos, Christian and Johanna Mair (2017), *Innovation and Scaling for Impact: How Effective Social Enterprises Do It*. Stanford, CA: Stanford Business Books.
Senge, Peter M. (1990), "The leader's new work: building learning organizations", *Sloan Management Review*, **32** (1), 7–23.
Shah, Sonal and Jun Han (2018), "The ecosystem of scaling social impact: a new theoretical framework and its application", Working Paper.
Snow, David A. and Sarah A. Soule (2010), *A Primer on Social Movements*. New York: W.W. Norton & Company.
Tilly, Charles (1999), "From interactions to outcomes in social movements", *How Social Movements Matter*, **10**, 253–70.
Tracey, Paul and Neil Stott (2017), "Social innovation: a window on alternative ways of organizing and innovating", *Innovation*, **19** (1), 51–60.

5. Inclusion and innovation in healthcare

Anita M. McGahan

Inclusion in healthcare is a moral imperative. It's simply not fair for those of us who were born in wealthy countries to have access to knowledge, information, medicines, and technologies that are not available elsewhere. Many people – especially in rural communities in low-income countries – live their entire lives without encountering professional healthcare. This is simply not right.

Inclusion is a pragmatic imperative because the health of each one of us depends in great part on the health of all of us. This principle is acutely clear during epidemics of infectious disease, but it's also relevant in many other situations – such as when food shortages arise, or when victims of human trafficking land on foreign shores, or when a newfound awareness of others' excruciating pain moves us to want fundamental change both because the suffering is morally intolerable and because it will lead to conflict on a large scale.

Inclusion in healthcare is also an economic opportunity for the organizations that seek to deliver healthcare, and for the politicians who seek to cultivate stability and prosperity. Many private companies have internationalization as a centerpiece of their strategies. Politicians around the world have decried the high cost of healthcare as destabilizing and unsustainable.

Innovation in healthcare – in developed-market countries as well as emerging-market countries – is essential for continued prosperity. This is partly because the cost of the system in the West has become unaffordable. In the United States, for example, the healthcare bill is fast approaching $10,000 per person per year on average. This figure has made healthcare reform and cost control a central element of the national agenda. And the United States is not alone among developed countries in spending unsustainably on healthcare.

The imperative for innovation in healthcare is not only a matter of cost. Studies have shown that suffering in the healthcare system of the West – especially among the elderly – is tragically heightened by the ways that choices are structured and healthcare is delivered (Gawande, 2014). For what we spend, we could have better and more humane outcomes. We could live longer at less expense. What's required is innovation in the ways in which choices are made, the way that technologies are deployed, and especially in the ways that organizations have evolved.

This chapter describes an agenda for research on the role of organizations, markets, and communities in social innovation in healthcare. The purpose is to describe the kinds of insights required to make progress on an agenda that considers both the imperative for inclusion and the imperative for innovation. The next section is a brief survey of some of the major themes of research on these topics in the field of management. Subsequently, I discuss a series of big issues on the agenda of inclusion and innovation in healthcare. The next section is a theoretical framework that describes relationships between major constructs in this agenda. The final section deals with some of the most important and immediate opportunities for research in this domain.

A VERY BRIEF SURVEY OF THE LITERATURE

The literature on healthcare inclusion and innovation is enormous. Indeed, many universities host public health schools that are entirely focused on the organization and operation of health delivery. Schools of pharmacy, dentistry, nursing, and medicine all support research and teaching on the organization of their domains.

This topic also has a long history in the social sciences. Scholars in the fields of global affairs, public policy, and economics have long sought to investigate and document the impact of specific initiatives to improve health, such as smoking cessation programs, various vaccines, malaria controls, HIV education – to name just a few. Many other fields – medical anthropology, political science, health metrics, statistics, engineering, and the law immediately come to mind – have also focused on these issues.

Even within the field of management, the agenda on healthcare organization and outcomes is extensive. For example, a well-established group of scholars – many associated with the National Bureau of Economic Research – have theorized and conducted empirical studies on the incentives for innovation arising from the privatization of intellectual property under a patent system. Hundreds if not thousands of papers on patents have been published in the field. As another example, a large group of scholars grounded in organization theory and sociology have studied diverse topics in healthcare, including "bricolage" – that is, the cobbling together of solutions to healthcare problems using available resources; the institutional foundations of healthcare decision-making; and the relationships between organization structure and outcomes. Others have examined how the structures of various health systems – such as the system for allocating organs to patients in need of transplantation – operate under various conditions.

Indeed, the literature on healthcare innovation and inclusiveness is so extensive that I imagine it would be virtually impossible to survey comprehensively in any outlet other than a book, and even then it would be difficult. So instead, I will focus on several recent studies in management that deal specifically with the problem of integrating inclusiveness and innovation in healthcare. My goal is to demonstrate the range of insights that have evolved in different corners of the field to illustrate the questions that have been raised.

First, George et al. (2012) identify three enablers of inclusive innovation: reframing constraints, enacting new business models, and bridging access for the disenfranchised. The emphasis in the article is on a synthetic approach that first sets out a fundamental tradeoff between innovation and inclusion that must be broken. The tradeoff arises because, when proprietary new technologies are made accessible through mechanisms such as compulsory licenses, the incentive for innovation is blunted. George et al. (2012) argue that this tradeoff can be broken through organizational breakthroughs that allow for both broadened access and incentives for future research.

Second, Kyle and Williams (2017) analyse whether the US healthcare system is uniquely inefficient in the distribution of high-quality pharmaceuticals by comparing the country's systems to those in other countries. The results demonstrate that, indeed, low-quality drugs do diffuse through the US system more readily than in other countries. These results point to the central role of healthcare institutions – including not only salient governmental agencies, such as the Patent Bureau and the Food and Drug Administration, but also decision-making norms that are amplified by organizations such as medical schools, physician associations, and the governors of reimbursement guidelines.

Third, Rosabeth Moss Kanter has made a life's work of understanding the challenges of healthcare innovation and how organizations overcome them. Kanter (2011) suggests that prodding at one facet of the system carries less promise than systemic change. She writes that "Complex systems of multiple actors and interest groups rarely change by fiat; they are more likely to change because of the accumulation of many positive deviations from tradition that prove themselves and gain support."

Finally, Kellogg (2009) uses ethnographic methods to show how the uptake of innovation in healthcare rests on complex interdependencies between professionals that rely on varying routines to assure safety, efficacy, and efficiency. The implementation of innovation in healthcare settings requires a thoughtful assessment of the range of procedural and professional systems affected by the change.

These examples demonstrate that innovation in healthcare systems is as complex as health itself. Barriers to change arise from a wide range of factors, including those that have been implemented to preserve patient safety, protect physicians against claims of malpractice, and assure continuity of practice. At the same time, opportunities arise for innovation in the construction of new types of systems – ones that may rest on new principles, including of inclusion.

BIG QUESTIONS

The literature on health outcomes makes clear that three major questions must guide advances in health systems. These are:

1. How can health systems deliver better outcomes at lower cost? What is the business model for prevention?
2. What constitutes inclusiveness in healthcare?
3. How can digitization and other breakthrough technologies advance health?

How Can Health Systems Deliver Better Outcomes at Lower Cost? What is the Business Model for Prevention?

This question suggests that the field would benefit from greater clarity about what constitutes health itself. This seemingly simple question is, in fact, quite complex. The World Health Organization defines health as "complete physical, mental, and social well-being . . ." Critics have suggested that this definition encourages endless investments in health technologies that offer incremental improvements in health. The endlessness arises because the goal of complete well-being is unattainable. Alternative definitions – developed more recently than the World Health Organization's charter in 1948 – point to the importance of resilience and self-sufficiency.

Understanding outcomes is equally complex. Despite the legions of studies on this question, the field has not converged on a unified and comprehensive approach to assessment. Studies of mortality are important, but are difficult to link to specific interventions. Investigations based on disability-adjusted life years and quality-adjusted life years are also difficult to use for discerning the specific impact of particular programs.

Finally, the boundaries on health systems are not well defined. Scholars have asked whether and how to measure the effectiveness of interventions that prevent illness. Studies have shown that improvements in sanitation, infrastructure, electricity, education, and entrepreneurship all improve the health of the most disenfranchised. In places of relative wealth, many of the interventions designed to improve the health of the elderly are ineffective. When many of the most important opportunities for reducing healthcare costs involve prevention, what is the business model? How can incentives be designed to reward the absence of an adverse outcome?

What Constitutes Inclusiveness in Healthcare?

Many of the world's most vulnerable people do not have access to essential medicines for a whole range of reasons. These include gaps in the institutional environment arising from the absence or failure of clinics, hospitals, medical care, training, and pharmacies. Advocates for these patients have long argued that this situation is unfair, and sought to address these gaps. A profound weakness in this approach is that replication of the systems of the West in settings of poverty is destined to fail simply because the system is too expensive and insufficiently effective. What often happens as healthcare systems develop in emerging-market countries is a dramatic resource crisis.

Against this background, innovation is central to an agenda of inclusiveness. This is because we know that extending the existing system for accessibility cannot succeed because the system's cost is too high and the outcomes are unacceptable. We have to move the frontier on quality while lowering cost simultaneously to make healthcare accessible to the poor. The challenge of moving the frontier is at the heart of innovation. Better protocols, approaches, and delivery are essential even for making existing medicines and other essential tools available in resource-limited settings. The challenge is at the level of the system itself. Inclusion is more than a conversation or a process. To make the system inclusive, we have to make the system better.

How Can Digitization and Other Breakthrough Technologies Advance Health?

Perhaps in no other field has the promise of digitization been greater. Investments in digital health of all types – including, for example, electronic medical records, tele-medicine, the medicalized home, and improved decision support for both doctors and patients – carry promise for streamlining systems and improving outcomes. A central challenge, of course, is that these systems are costly to design, implement, and monitor. And they must operate in parallel with long-standing, inefficient, analog systems that constitute the core of the health delivery system precisely because system failure is not tolerable. The net result of this is that, in the short term, the investments required to digitize core processes are nearly as daunting. Innovation through digitization is thus a political, economic, medical, and social mountaintop that is extremely difficult to reach. Despite the challenges, however, most health professionals could easily rattle off ten major opportunities for digitizing the systems on which they regularly rely. The issue is that the potential failure of core systems during the implementation process stalls and even stops progress. How can this problem be overcome?

A THEORETICAL FRAMEWORK

The challenge of inclusive innovation has several major facets that reflect the enormity of the task of building the institutional environment to achieve better outcomes at lower costs and farther reach. The first major facet is a clearer definition of the goal of effective healthcare. We know, in the first instance, that prevention of injuries and aversion of avoidable deaths – especially from infection, nutritional conditions, and the conditions around birth – is universally desirable. Yet most healthcare costs in developed countries are related to end-of-life care. Understanding what constitutes health in this important phase of life is the starting point for the agenda. And because of the diversity of answers to this question, the unit for effective innovation is endogenous. In short, a shared understanding of what constitutes health and prosperity is fundamental to the identity of the community that the health system serves.

Strategy Map

The second major facet is to evaluate, community by community, whether and how health can be supported using currently available tools and technologies, including especially digital tools for communication, resource allocation, and intelligent decision-making. A great deal of opportunity lies in developing a comprehensive and well-considered point of view about what types of interventions would deliver optimal health if the transition to the new system were not constraining. We need to know what we are shooting for. Organizing and managing this conversation is essential to progress, and will be ongoing. Inclusion in the conversation itself is critical to the legitimacy of every investment that will come in its wake. Indeed, the processes of allocating scarce and essential resources can be conceptualized as the health system itself. In other words, the reason that we need a health system is because resources are scarce. The purpose of the system is to allocate them effectively to cultivate and support health. Thus, innovation in the system involves making better decisions about how and where to channel scarce, essential resources.

A third facet is to develop a shared, inclusive understanding of paths for change in current healthcare systems toward the effective implementation of new approaches with the potential for delivering better health. This in and of itself is a massive task that will require decades of deliberation, research, experimentation, and investment. Indeed, this facet of the challenge of innovation to resolve the three major questions described above is so extensive – so complex – that it will require extraordinary insight by dedicated and heroic leaders. Much of the opportunity for contribution by scholars of management and organization is in the interests of this task of adaptation.

Finally, the health system must be adaptive at its core to fulfill the promise of inclusive innovation. The technological innovations that advance health – as the definition is refined over time by a community – will strain the resources of every system. Identifying and prioritizing opportunities for system improvement will require a procedural roadmap that considers the implications of change for everyone affected by it. Constructing such a roadmap for inclusive governance over the management of healthcare system improvements is a priority for effective innovation.

THE RESEARCH AGENDA

For scholars of organization and management, the research agenda on inclusive innovation in healthcare is extensive. Indeed, given that the healthcare sector constitutes some 20 percent of the international economy, the opportunities for research in this domain are as broad and deep as the field of management itself. There are virtually no limits for scholars in our field interested in any theory, empirical question, or methodology. Some of these opportunities may be most appropriately pursued in collaboration with scholars in related fields: public policy, medicine, and healthcare administration, to name a few. We need to understand, for example, how the organization and management of particular types of public policies – consider smoking cessation programs, for instance – shape their impact and success. The entire gamut of questions outlined in the prior sections of this chapter engages issues that are of central concern to health practitioners, and thus to researchers concerned with the efficacy of health practices. The broad range of theoretical, empirical, and methodological lenses of our field can be fruitfully applied to the agenda in collaboration with scholars from cognate disciplines.

However, for researchers interested specifically in an agenda of inclusive innovation, the opportunities come into a somewhat sharper focus. Given the sprawling diversity of the issues of inclusive innovation in health, the field would benefit from phenomena-based studies that seek to identify relevant constructs through qualitative approaches of all types. We need an empirical understanding of efforts to advance inclusive innovation in healthcare in practice – such as in India over the past ten years.

The field of management would benefit as well from comprehensive analyses of the psychological, behavioral, and social processes associated with a community's shared understanding of what constitutes health itself. What are the various ways in which communities assemble such a shared understanding? What are the implications of different routes to an assessment of health for inclusion? How is dissension managed? When is inclusiveness in the process of discerning a shared understanding of health sufficient to justify considering the system itself as inclusive? What if some members of the community do not want to participate?

Understanding inclusive innovation in healthcare also rests on deploying the lenses of management and organization to understand – theoretically and empirically – how the institutional systems required to deliver health (however defined) can be governed and managed for inclusivity. What models have emerged for inclusion in governance? Can these models be compared across geographies and over time? What are the costs and consequences of various models of resource allocation that prioritize inclusion in the processes of decision-making? Do healthcare institutions with inclusive governance models resist change more deeply than those that are run by a small group of experts? What are the tradeoffs?

An understanding of inclusive innovation in healthcare is incomplete without considering change at the level of patient care itself. How and when should consideration of the needs of a patient's family and friends be integrated into models of care? Where are the boundaries on inclusion at this level for elders, children, and the disabled? The social, psychological, economic, and managerial consequences of inclusion are so complex at this level that they require extensive analysis by researchers in our field. Much more theoretical work is needed, for example, to understand the boundaries on inclusion when the target of a health intervention is an individual.

The agenda on inclusive innovation in healthcare also engages a large range of issues related to digitization, privacy, transparency, and the boundary between private and public health. Research is needed on the implications of disclosure and non-disclosure through electronic systems when health conditions are infectious; or when they reveal potential errors of practice; or when they point to underlying causes that may or may not be remediated through further intervention. The issues on privacy alone could constitute a life's work. How are we to balance considerations of inclusion against privacy when the dissemination of health information in the interests of inclusion would expose a patient to potential discrimination, abuse, or bias, for example?

The role of public and private institutions in advancing inclusive innovation is another major opportunity for research. What types of organizational models are most effective for promoting innovations in the interests of preventing onsets into a community of infectious and communicable conditions? Which are better suited for promoting universal access to various options for end-of-life care? Comparative governance analysis on the agenda of inclusion would seem to depend on whether a health concern is communicable. How have various communities dealt with this problem?

The inclusive innovation agenda also raises questions for scholars of innovation itself. To what extent – and under what conditions – does inclusion in the innovation process yield better, faster, or more legitimate advances? What types of innovations are most amenable to inclusion? Answers to these questions have profound implications for the organization of healthcare systems both in emerging-market countries that seek to build inclusiveness at the core and in developed-market countries that seek to improve health systems.

Inclusion in health also depends on universal insurance. Questions arise regarding the allocation of health risks across communities. Behavioral analysis is needed to evaluate how the availability of different types of insurance changes the incentives of patients to invest in health and to avail themselves of health services. Structural analysis of the competitive environment both among insurers and among service providers would also yield critical insights on inclusion.

Engagement with these issues also carries promise for deepening the theoretical, empirical, and methodological agenda of the field of management and organization. First, scholars engaging in these domains inevitably confront – and must resolve – fundamental multi- and inter-disciplinary challenges. Second, the agenda for inclusiveness drives us to consider a different objective for organizational performance than we normally consider. Finally, the consequences of the research for public policy are profoundly important.

REFERENCES

Gawande, Atul (2014). *Being Mortal: Illness, Medicine, and What Matters in the End*. New York: Metropolitan Books.

George, Gerard, Anita M. McGahan, and Jaideep Prahbu (2012). Innovation for Inclusive Growth: Towards a Theoretical Framework and a Research Agenda, *Journal of Management Studies*. doi: 10.1111/j.1467-6486.2012.01048.x.

Kanter, Rosabeth Moss (2011). Why Innovation is So Hard in Health Care – and How to Do It Anyway. https://hbr.org/2011/02/why-innovation-is-so-hard-in-h.html (accessed 25 February 2019).
Kellogg, Katherine (2009). Operating Room: Relational Spaces and Micro-Institutional Change in Surgery, *American Journal of Sociology*, 115 (3), 657–711.
Kyle, Margaret K. and Heidi Williams (2017). Is the US Healthcare System Uniquely Inefficient: Evidence from Prescription Drugs, *American Economic Review*, 107 (5), 486–90.

6. How do we know when social innovation works? A review and contingency model of social impact assessment

Greg Molecke and Anne-Claire Pache

In the face of contemporary societal challenges as widespread and taxing as poverty, illiteracy, health epidemics, and climate change (George et al., 2016), policy makers, civil society leaders, business leaders, and citizens alike place high hopes in the ability of so-called "social entrepreneurs" to craft social innovations that will contribute scalable solutions to these enduring societal problems (Mair and Marti, 2006; Venkataraman, 1997). Whether they take root in the traditional nonprofit, business and government sectors, or in emerging hybrid spaces that cut across these sectors, these social innovations bring about novel ways to address societal challenges and ultimately aim at creating social good by improving the condition of individuals, communities, and the planet (Kroeger and Weber, 2014; Venkataraman, 1997). In a context of growing inequalities, social innovation may act as a powerful driver of inclusion, contributing to promote belonging, equality, and access to resources and capabilities for underserved and marginalized groups in society (George et al., 2012).

Like those aimed at generating profits, social innovations require significant support and interventions to take off, grow, thrive, and scale. Gaining this support from various resource providers, at the most general level, is the same for social and for-profit innovations: innovators must demonstrate the "pull" of a need or demand they aim to address, their potential to implement their innovation, and an expected return for their supporters (Ebrahim, 2003; Molecke and Pinkse, 2017). Where social and profit-oriented innovations differ, however, comes most distinctly in the final objectives pursued as well as in the way in which the achievement of these objectives may be assessed. While profit motives underlie the motivations for undertaking and investing in many innovations, social innovators aim at bringing about a positive change in the world and evaluate the achievement of this goal by assessing the social impact generated by the introduction of the innovation.

Social impact, however, is a tricky concept. It is ambiguous and contested (Rawhouser et al., 2017), as illustrated by the proliferation of related yet distinct concepts, such as "social value" (Santos, 2012), "social performance" (Mair and Marti, 2006), or "social returns" (Emerson, 2003). While initial research on the topic attempted to reduce that complexity by developing a unique and universal approach to measuring social impact (Arvidson et al., 2013; Emerson, 2003; Millar and Hall, 2013; Nicholls, 2009), recent articles have, in contrast, recognized the proliferation of alternative yet complementary approaches to assessing social impact, acknowledging the absence of an agreed upon definition, unit of measurement, or of standard conventions for its valuation or evaluation (Ebrahim and Rangan, 2014; Kroeger and Weber, 2014; Stievenart and Pache, 2014).

Given the importance of social impact assessment in helping social innovators achieve positive social change in a sustainable way, an important challenge is to map the current knowledge on social impact to allow researchers and innovators alike to make sense of the multiplicity of approaches currently available and to overcome the challenges associated with their implementations, particularly when it comes to promote inclusion of the most disenfranchised. With this chapter, we hope to make a step in this direction. To do so, we start with reviewing the main approaches to assessing social impact. Next, we discuss the challenges associated with social impact assessment. Building upon this analysis, we then propose a model that relates stages and needs in the innovation cycle with relevant social impact assessment approaches. Finally, we discuss future research directions that could help social impact assessment better drive social innovation and impact.

SOCIAL IMPACT ASSESSMENT: A REVIEW OF CURRENT APPROACHES

Although we recognize that multiple terms are used to refer to the creation of positive social change, we decided, for the sake of clarity and consistency, to rely on the notion of "social impact" that we define as improvements in wellbeing, quality of life, life satisfaction, or living standards (Campbell et al., 1976; Kroeger and Weber, 2014), or, in an inverse view, reductions in social needs or hindrances that deprive one of the capability to live a good life (Kroeger and Weber, 2014; Sen, 2001).

Social impact is often conceived to be the ultimate step in a value chain, transforming "inputs" (i.e., the resources devoted to the innovation) into "outputs" (i.e., what is produced by the innovation), "outcomes" (i.e., the short-term effects produced by the innovation on its intended beneficiaries) and ultimately "social impact" (i.e., the significant or lasting changes in people's lives, directly attributable to the innovation) (Roche, 1999). For example, the value chain of a social enterprise that introduces low-cost toilet systems in areas that lack running water would regard financial and material resources as the inputs, the new toilet facilities as the output, whereas the immediate improvements to convenience, sanitation, and privacy would be outcomes. The lasting repercussions to public health, changes in behavior from greater self-esteem, and improved environment and social status would be the social impact (Millar and Hall, 2013).

Multiple frameworks have been developed in recent decades to evaluate the extent of social impact generated by social innovators. Underlying the question of how to approach social impact assessment is the question of "What is the purpose of evaluating social impact?" Two fundamental purposes are recognized in the literature: proving impact and improving impact (Lall, 2017). First, innovators may evaluate their social impact as a way of *proving* to themselves as well as to internal and external stakeholders that the innovation has created social impact (Nicholls, 2009; Rawhouser et al., 2017). When the goal is to prove impact, the primary question is whether and how much social impact an innovation has created. Second, innovators find it useful to evaluate the social impact of their innovation as a way of *improving* the level of social impact generated (Behn, 2003; Millar and Hall, 2013). When the goal is impact improvement, the primary question is not whether an innovation creates positive social impact, but how can the impact of the innovation be improved over time by optimizing its means of value creation.

While in reality these two purposes often intermingle and meld into a combined social impact regime, it is important to understand the general principles that underlie each objective as well as their implications in terms of what assessment approaches may be more suited to achieve this objective. The review below outlines the specificities of each objective as well as their associated methods, highlighting that while some methods may be available to achieve both objectives, they may then be used in different ways.

Approaches to Prove Social Impact

In a resource-constrained world where there are more potential social innovations than there are resources to support them all, social innovators may need to *prove* that their innovation is worthwhile enough to gain a portion of the resources available (Ebrahim, 2003). This need may be partly driven by requests from funders, regulators, or policy makers, but also by internal stakeholders such as the innovators themselves or their boards. When the purpose of the impact evaluation is to prove social impact, innovators need to rely on approaches that measure the effect of an innovation on its intended targets or on society. These approaches are referred to, in the literature, as "outcome-based" approaches (Rawhouser et al., 2017).

Monetary metrics use monetary amounts as their unit of measurement to evaluate the amount of social value created by an innovation. One of the most visible outcome-based approaches to accounting for social impact is the Social Return on Investment (SROI), which attempts to compute the ratio of the social impacts generated by an intervention (e.g., increase in wages of beneficiaries, reduced reliance on government assistance, and so on), expressed in monetary terms, divided by the costs required to produce the intervention (Arvidson et al., 2013; Millar and Hall, 2013). Alternatively, the Trucost Environmental Impact Metrics approach calculates the dollar costs to society of a firm's environmental emissions (Jo et al., 2015). More broadly, Avoided Cost Methods calculate what costs are alleviated by the innovation and assign them a monetary value. Gas and solar cooking stoves, for example, alleviate the need to collect firewood and tend a fire, saving many hours of labor primarily for women. Multiplying the number of hours saved by an estimated hourly wage in that region can result in an avoided cost estimate. Economists have also developed increasingly savvy statistical analysis techniques to convert social impact into financial terms (Kroeger and Weber, 2014). An example is to measure the value of a given impact by revealing people's actual willingness to pay, in financial terms, for the perceived benefits of the impact. Contingent valuation and stated preference models use survey data to translate changes in wellbeing or satisfaction into economic values: one such survey might ask individuals in malaria zones how much they would be willing to pay for anti-malaria bed nets, and considers this price as a proxy for the value of the bed net innovation, as assessed by its main beneficiaries. Once value has been converted to a monetary proxy, it is generally evaluated using cost–benefit analysis, (S)ROI, cost-effectiveness, and other financial and accounting techniques (Arvidson et al., 2013; Stievenart and Pache, 2014).

Non-monetary metrics do not reduce the social value created to a financial amount but to some other unit of measurement. For example, the United Nations (UN), World Health Organization, World Bank, and many other public health organizations measure impact in terms of gains of Disability-Adjusted-Life-Years (DALYs). The DALY measure converts the burdens experienced by health issues into a single simple unit: the number of years of life lost due to sickness, disability, or early death. Different health issues are given different "disability weights" to adjust for the severity of the burden they impose. Innovations that prevent, cure, or treat these health burdens can then calculate the numbers of DALYs they regain for their beneficiaries as their social impact (Anand and Hanson, 1997).

Other non-financial measures of social impact assess how an innovation triggers changes in units of Personal Wellbeing, Quality of Life, or Happiness (Kroeger and Weber, 2014; Ura et al., 2012), relative Level of Poverty (Schreiner, 2014), or in one's Capabilities to be and do what one values (Nussbaum and Sen, 1993). Such indexes may be computed through the use of surveys that ask a series of simple, factual questions about a beneficiary's lifestyle and wellbeing. The Grameen Foundation's Poverty Probability Index, for example, asks ten questions such as "What material is your roof made out of?" and "What toilet facility does the household have?" to create a poverty score for individual families and then uses this data to assess how this score is impacted by access to microcredit.

Social value, once converted to a non-monetary proxy unit may be evaluated by net unit changes attributed to the innovation, or Incremental Cost Effectiveness Ratios (ICERs), which can compare innovations based on their relative costs to increases in selected unit of measure by one unit. For example, a recent study in the Gambia found that three different innovations in pneumococcal conjugate vaccines had cost-effectiveness ratios of $570:1 DALY, $670:1 DALY, and $910:1 DALY, respectively. Health organizations then selected the innovation with the lowest cost per DALY (Kim et al., 2010).

Combined indicators and scorecards consist of collections of metrics that monitor the level achieved on various operational dimensions, in relationship to intended achievement levels. Although primarily used for the purpose of monitoring and improving performance, indicators and scorecards may nevertheless be used by social innovators to prove their impact by using measures of outcomes as a proxy for social impact. However, this may only be relevant when the causal link between outcome and impact is clear and direct. For example, solar lamp projects often develop scorecards to prove their impact which include the number of lamps sold, the number of hours of light provided by the lamps, the number of kerosene lamps replaced, and the amount of extra income small resellers have earned selling the lamps. While none of these truly describe the impact of the innovation, which would require assessing the combination of effects on the users, the sellers, and the environment, some of these indicators may be used as proxies given the direct causal link between the use of the lamps and environmental impact.

Experimental approaches are often seen as the gold standard for proving social impact because their protocols are the more robust to demonstrate causal relationships. Large field-based experiments using Randomized Controlled Trials (RCTs) compare different groups of individuals who are equally affected by the myriad of changes in an environment. In a basic field experiment, the groups are controlled so that the only difference between them is whether they are in the treatment group that receives the innovation or the control group that does not. When these groups are later compared, differences in results between the groups should be directly attributable to the intervention. One prominent field experiment introduced microcredit programs in 52 (out of 104) randomly selected urban slums in Hyderabad, India. Surprisingly, after following the experiment for four years, the study found no differences between areas with and without microfinance opportunities in terms of household consumption, profitability of family businesses, or "any of the development outcomes that are often believed to be affected by microfinance, including health, education, and women's empowerment" (Duflo et al., 2013, p. 22). This experiment, and others like it, led a wave of rethinking regarding whether microfinance was the miracle social innovation many believed it was (Ali et al., 2017; Duflo et al., 2013). Conversely, another randomized study of educational interventions of a randomly selected group of Indian school children did find lasting effects on their literacy (Banerjee and Duflo, 2012). Additional experimental structures can also be used to help improve performance and are discussed in the next section.

Sociological and ethnological techniques, when employed to prove impact, capture the outcomes of an intervention through narrative, holistic descriptions of the changes in the lives and capabilities of individuals and their broader communities. These approaches address the limitations of quantitative approaches which have been criticized for missing the breadth, complexity, and nuance of the social impacts (Behn, 2003; Hall, 2004), and for myopically focusing on those forms of social impact that most easily lend themselves to being represented financially or quantitatively (Ebrahim, 2005; Ebrahim and Rangan, 2014; Molecke and Pinkse, 2017). These rich qualitative methods may involve interviews, participant observation, content analysis of consumed media, observational field notes, and other forms of gaining up-close personal experience (Mulgan, 2006; Taylor et al., 2015). A skilled qualitative researcher can uncover and triangulate patterns among multiple individual accounts and observations to develop rigorous, rational findings. Social impact, in these methods, is proven not through numbers, but through "thick" accounts of impact (narratives, anecdotes, testimonials, pictures) that have a much greater ability to appeal to individuals' intuitive and emotional perceptions of impact (Dickert et al., 2011; Slovic, 2007).

Approaches to Improve Social Impact

In addition to proving their social impact, social innovators may find it useful to evaluate their achievements relative to set social goals in order to continually *improve* the efficiency and effectiveness of their operations in creating social impact (Behn, 2003; Millar and Hall, 2013). Improving a venture's social impact involves evaluating and optimizing the procedures and activities along the steps of the social value chain that transforms inputs into outputs, outcomes and ultimately, social impact. In comparing actual to desired or expected social performance at each step, social innovators may be able to identify barriers and hindrances and to devise potential remedies (Behn, 2003; Hubbard, 2009; Margolis et al., 2007; Wood, 1991). This may allow them to avoid poor performance or mission drift (Battilana et al., 2015; Christensen and Ebrahim, 2006; Ebrahim et al., 2014). Evaluation approaches that view and support performance gains as impact gains are referred to in the literature as "activity-based" approaches (Rawhouser et al., 2017).

Theories of change and logic models form the backbone of the activity-based approaches (Chen and Rossi, 1983; Rogers, 2008). They create a map or flowchart of the multiple paths that could lead the innovation to generate the desired social changes (Kaplan and Garrett, 2005; W.K. Kellogg Foundation, 2006; Wry and Haugh, 2018). Theories of change are often complex with feedback loops and interconnected parts (Rogers, 2008). Logic models, on the other hand, focus on just one specific pathway for impact within an overall theory of change (Bakewell and Garbutt, 2005; Kaplan and Garrett, 2005).

Innovations can then be measured for how successfully they accomplish each of the steps through a variety of performance indicators determined by the organization and its stakeholders. The performance indicators for individual steps draw heavily from the outcome-based methodologies previously discussed. The difference is in how and where the methodologies are applied, as discussed in the following sections.

Combined indicators and scorecards, when used for performance improvement, are collections of Key Performance Indicators that audit performance for either an individual step of the value chain or across the major elements that lead to an innovation's performance in achieving social impact (Parmenter, 2015; Rogers, 2008). Alternatively, they may be designed at the level of an organization or a social problem as a whole. Many different groups have worked to design such metrics as well as balanced scorecards (Kaplan and Norton, 1995) to assist organizations and funders in finding and implementing them, such as the UN Millennium Development Goals (MDGs), the Outcomes Star, the Impact Reporting and Investment Standards (IRIS), the Global Reporting Initiative's (GRI) Sustainability Reporting Standards, or B Analytics' Global Impact Investing Rating System (GIIRS). Quality control measures (e.g., TQM, Six Sigma, Lean) and methodologies also fall within this category (Andersson et al., 2006). These metrics can then be evaluated through standardized social accounting and audit practices (Gray, 2001).

Other metrics are created by third-party ratings and certification agencies that create their own independent ratings of organizations. These may include the MSCI/KLD 400 Social Index and the Ethical Investment Research Service (EIRIS) ratings used by financial markets to assess public firms' Environmental, Social, and Governance risks and opportunities (Rawhouser et al., 2017). Organizations such as Charity Navigator and GiveWell also rank nonprofit organizations according to their own social impact methodologies to help guide donors to the most effective interventions (Lowell et al., 2005).

Sociological and ethnological techniques, when used to improve performance, gather "thick" descriptive feedback and insights into how and why specific processes are working or not and to identify barriers to performance and opportunities for improvement. A social business providing clean water in a rural village in Bangladesh, for instance, relied on an extensive ethnographic field study two years after its founding to understand lower than expected consumption rates of available clean water by villagers (André et al., 2018). These techniques involve the mobilization of skilled individuals talking to the intended beneficiaries, either informally or through structured surveys, about their problems and the organization's innovation to address it. Alternatively, innovators' daily lived experience interacting with beneficiaries to design, market, sell, and support their innovations provides rich data as well.

Experimental methods, when designed to help improve performance, create experiments that compare different factors that can be varied in value creation processes. Improvement-based experiments generally have multiple treatment groups that each receive different variations of the innovation. A/B testing of different product design variations, different pricing options, different locations, or different types of target beneficiaries are all examples. One notable study found that cash transfers given to women generated large improvements in the development of girls but had little effect on boys. Money given to men did not improve the development of either boys or girls (Duflo, 2003). In experimentation developed to improve performance, the value of the experiments is not in the additional validity it provides to outcome evaluations of the studied interventions, but in how the experiments inform innovators' understanding of the theory of change an innovation has developed and the optimal processes and activities that support it. Table 6.1 summarizes all these methods and their potential goals.

Impact and Legitimacy

It is important to emphasize, at this point, that while social innovators may earnestly engage in assessing their impact to prove or improve it, they may also engage in assessing their impact ritually, for the main purpose of being perceived as legitimate by important institutional referents, such as regulators, funders, or peers (Lall, 2017). Social impact assessment may be undertaken, then, not as appraisals of social impact per se, but as symbolic displays or rituals aimed at producing legitimacy (Nicholls, 2009; Power, 1997; Zott and Huy, 2007).

For example, nonprofit organizations may signal that they "run their organization like a business" by implementing financialized reporting and performance monitoring practices (e.g., SROI calculations) imported from for-profit accounting and finance functions (Brest et al., 2012; DiMaggio and Powell, 1983; Nicholls, 2009, 2010). They may further rely on assessments conducted by external groups (such as rating or certification agencies) to demonstrate that they meet certain minimum standards of behavior and/or embrace socially desirable principles (Doh et al., 2010; Rawhouser et al., 2017). Impact assessments that appear systematic and rigorous may also project a sense of professionalism and analytic capabilities, characteristics increasingly necessary as the social sector has undergone a strong trend towards rationalization and professionalization (Brest et al., 2012; Ebrahim et al., 2014; Eikenberry and Kluver, 2004; Rourke, 2014).

As such, legitimacy concerns act as a moderator that can affect not only which methodologies and tools are used for proving and improving social impact, but also how they are used. Legitimacy pressures exerted by powerful stakeholders (such as funders) may lead innovators to embrace methods that are poorly suited to address their real needs at a given point in time. Legitimacy concerns can further affect how methodologies and tools are used and the manners in which they are presented. As widely recognized in the institutional literature (Meyer and Rowan, 1977), legitimacy concerns lead actors exposed to conformity pressures from important stakeholders to decouple their formal policies from their actual practices. In the context of social impact assessment, this may lead social innovators to symbolically commit to engage in a given impact assessment approach, while not actually implementing it in practice.

Impact and Inclusion

Given the focus of this book on "inclusive innovation," it is important to discuss relevant approaches to assess inclusion as a specific form of social impact. Inclusive innovation aims at generating improvements in the social and economic wellbeing of communities that have been denied access to resources, capabilities, and opportunities (George et al., 2012). Assessing the impact of inclusive innovation thus requires paying specific attention to which groups receive benefits, how different groups may benefit unevenly from an innovation, as well as how the groups impacted improve their ability to access the resources, capabilities, and opportunities that they were once denied. As such, an innovation's

Table 6.1 Social impact assessment approaches and their purposes

Methods Used	Purpose		Examples
	Prove Impact Demonstrate achievement of results	Improve Impact Monitor and optimize performance of activities theorized to lead to impact	
Monetary metrics	Prove impact using monetary units of measurement. Evaluated using cost–benefit analysis and other financial/accounting techniques.		• Social Return on Investment (SROI) (Arvidson et al., 2013) • Trucost Environmental Impact (Jo et al., 2015) • Avoided cost methods (De Groot et al., 2002) • Contingent valuation (Carson & Hanemann, 2005)
Non-monetary metrics	Prove impact using single units of measurement adapted to specific innovation. Evaluated by net unit changes or cost-effectiveness per unit of change.		• Disability-Adjusted-Life-Years (DALYs) (Anand & Hanson, 1997) • Personal wellbeing/quality of life (Kroeger & Weber, 2014) • Level of poverty (Schreiner, 2014) • Capabilities (Nussbaum & Sen, 1993) • Gross national happiness (Ura et al., 2012) • Incremental Cost Effectiveness Ratios (ICERs) (Gafni & Birch, 2006)
Combined indicators and scorecards	Prove impact using a combined set of units of measurement adapted to specific innovation.	Improve impact by clarifying and monitoring performance of individual activities/steps along the value chain.	• Key Performance Indicators (KPIs) (Parmenter, 2015) • Balanced scorecards (Kaplan & Norton, 1995)

Types of

	Used when causal link between outcome and impact is clear and direct and outcome can thus be used as a proxy for impact.		• UN Millennium Development Goals (MDGs) (Sachs, 2012) • Outcomes Star (MacKeith, 2011) • Impact Reporting and Investment Standards (IRIS) (GIIN, 2011) • MSCI/KLD 400 Social Index (Sun et al., 2011) • Third-party raters – Charity Navigator/GiveWell (Lowell et al., 2005)
Experimental approaches	Prove impact of innovation with additional validity by controlling for omitted variables and other biases. Experiments structured to control for differences between treated and non-treated groups.	Improve impact by experimenting with different factors that can be varied in value creation processes (e.g., design variations, beneficiary characteristics, implementation approaches) to validate and refine assumptions in theories of change.	• Randomized Controlled Trials (RCTs) (Banerjee & Duflo, 2012) • Statistical analysis of correlations/causations, statistically significant differences among groups (Kirk, 1982)
Sociological and ethnological approaches	Prove impact through "thick" holistic descriptions of changes in behavior and wellbeing.	Improve performance through gathering feedback and insights to identify barriers to performance and opportunities for improvement.	• Interviews • Participant observation • Content analysis of media/artifacts • Observational field notes • Action learning (Corbin & Strauss, 2014; Taylor et al., 2015)
Theories of change and logic models		Improve impact by developing theoretical models of the critical activities and steps along the value chain and establishing performance metrics.	• Theory of change • Maps/flowcharts • Logic models (Chen & Rossi, 1983; Rogers, 2008)

inclusivity can be assessed on the basis of how inclusive the innovation process is, as well as how much inclusion is created as a result of the innovation (Foster and Heeks, 2013).

Assessing the degree to which the innovation process promotes inclusion requires looking at how well marginalized groups targeted by an innovation are involved in its development (Altenburg et al., 2009; Cozzens and Sutz, 2012; Utz and Dahlman, 2007). Specific participation indicators may be designed and monitored to assess the degree to which the disenfranchised populations targeted by the innovation are invited to participate (i.e., to contribute their ideas, experience, or time) in the innovation process. Stakeholder analysis exercises can provide a useful tool to assess which groups are potentially relevant and affected by an innovation, and can indicate which groups are currently over- or underrepresented (McKinley, 2010).

Assessing the inclusivity of an innovation further requires assessing the degree to which the innovation has generated improvements in the wellbeing of marginalized groups. This includes assessing the degree to which the innovation targeted the populations with most needs as well as whether the situation of those impacted really improved as a result of the innovation. A common issue for many social innovations (like, for instance, microfinance) is that they may fail to target those at the very base of the economic pyramid, targeting instead those in slightly higher economic strata. And when they do target the groups with the most needs, assessing the degree to which they have truly improved their condition is not an easy task. Relevant metrics to assess the degree to which an innovation truly fostered inclusion of the disenfranchised include the UN Human Poverty Index, Grameen's Poverty Probability Index, the Organisation for Economic Co-operation and Development's Better Life Index, and the Oxford Global Multidimensional Poverty Index. These indexes assess potential improvements in the wellbeing of marginalized groups through economic measures such as household income, un/under/informal employment, and the percentage of a group with electricity, mobile phone, or internet (McKinley, 2010). Building upon the "capabilities approach" developed by Sen and Nussbaum (Nussbaum, 2001; Sen, 2001), alternative approaches have proposed more comprehensive measures, such as the Human Development Index, the more granular Basic Capabilities Index, the Asian Development Bank Capabilities Indicators, the Social Progress Index, and, to some extent, the UN Millennial Development Goals. All focus on measuring changes in capabilities rather than changes in wealth or specific wellbeing.

CONTEMPORARY CHALLENGES IN SOCIAL IMPACT ASSESSMENT

Despite the growing efforts deployed by social innovators, funders of social innovation, policy makers, and scholars alike to develop our understanding and mastery of social impact assessment, it is important to recognize that important conceptual and practical challenges remain.

Complexity

A first important challenge to acknowledge is the complexity of the practice. This complexity is experienced first-hand by social innovators, who reported to Molecke and

Pinkse (2017) that social impact metrics were immeasurable, irrelevant, and incomplete. The reported "immeasurability" of social impact assessment is due to its computational complexity (DiMaggio, 2002; Kroeger and Weber, 2014). Assessing the social impact of a social innovation requires considering a wide range of elements: different individuals and groups impacted, different ways in which they are impacted, and different natures of impact. These various elements are very difficult to add up and account for in a simple way.

Social impact assessment may further be perceived as irrelevant because of epistemic complexity (Choi and Majumdar, 2014; Kroeger and Weber, 2014; Molecke and Pinkse, 2017; Nicholls, 2009). Assessing social impact entails measuring effects as subtle as individual increases in self-respect, happiness, or competence. Choosing a framework to report on these impacts necessarily relies on an interpretation of human realities, inherently partial and biased, from which it is difficult to predict future success or guide decision making.

Finally, the depiction of social impact assessment as "incomplete" may be due to its systemic complexity: assessment methods may not easily establish the interrelated causal relationships between inputs, outputs, outcomes, and net impacts. Any actor engaging in social impact assessment thus needs to acknowledge these different levels of complexity, and to accept that any outcome of an assessment endeavor is likely to be imperfect, subjective, and malleable (Mulgan, 2006; Murray et al., 2010).

Causality

Causality challenges are so central to any work on social impact assessment that it is worth elaborating on that issue. A fundamental challenge for social innovators is to demonstrate that the changes measured in the social impact assessment process are indeed caused by the intervention, and not by other factors. While outcome-based evaluations look for observable changes once an innovation has been launched, these methods are rarely fully reliable because they cannot control for all of the other environmental factors that also affect the beneficiaries' lives such as changing environmental or political conditions or parallel interventions by other actors. Thus, omitted variable biases significantly complicate organizations' ability to create accurate, valid evaluations of a specific intervention's effects (Kroeger and Weber, 2014). Experimental methods are the only methods that are able to address this bias. If they are not available because they are too costly or too technical, social innovators have to acknowledge that any measure that they develop to assess impact will only be a "best estimate" for the real net impact of the innovation.

Comparability

Another important challenge for impact assessment is that despite recent methodological developments, it remains very difficult to compare the social impact of different, heterogeneous interventions even when narrowing the scope of the comparison to a single issue (Kroeger and Weber, 2014, p. 513; Nicholls, 2009; Polonsky and Grau, 2011). This challenge is particularly critical for any private or public actor intending to make informed decisions about how to best allocate resources to maximize social impact. For instance, a charitable foundation intending to positively impact elementary education will have a hard time comparing an intervention focusing on training teachers to enhance their effectiveness in the classroom, with an intervention focusing on involving parents in the school community. The challenge of comparability is compounded when attempting to compare social innovations across various contexts (Mair and Marti, 2006; Molecke and Pinkse, 2017). It would be difficult to make sense of an increase in students' achievements in a rural school in Burkina Faso with a similar increase in an urban school in France. Attempts at addressing this challenge, either through the development of sector-specific metrics or through the use of common metrics such as SROI, have so far remained insufficient.

Conflicting Demands

A final central challenge is that assessing social impact is not merely a technical endeavor but a socio-political one (Ansari and Euske, 1987; Barman, 2017; Lamont, 2012). Social innovators are subject to a wide variety of accountability pressures, as both internal and external stakeholders expect them to report on their activities and performance. Yet what matters to one stakeholder may differ substantially from what matters to another, leaving social innovators confronted with diverse and sometimes conflicting demands for accountability (Ebrahim 2003; Nicholls, 2009). Social innovators will thus face the challenge of adjudicating between these competing demands while avoiding the risk of losing important institutional support. Some of these demands may even press for metrics that serve the strategic or reputational needs of stakeholders themselves, at the expense of the needs of the innovation's beneficiaries (Frumkin, 2008). In the face of these demands, social innovators may find it difficult to make sense of the information generated through impact assessment and to use it to implement meaningful changes in their organizations (Hall, 2005; Hendricks et al., 2008; Kramer et al., 2007).

TOWARDS A CONTIGENCY MODEL OF SOCIAL IMPACT ASSESSMENT

Given the wealth of social impact assessment approaches available and the challenges associated with their use, social innovators face the difficult task of identifying which approach is best suited to their needs. As previously highlighted in the innovation literature (Greiner, 1972; Murray et al., 2010; Van de Ven and Poole, 1995), organizational priorities and resource needs vary drastically at different stages in the life of an innovation. We thus propose a contingency model that relates innovation stages with assessment objectives and their associated social assessment methods as a framework to enrich our understanding of the social impact assessment approaches innovators are likely to choose at different times.

We rely on Santos et al.'s (2013) life cycle model of social innovation to highlight the specific needs associated with each stage, and build upon this analysis to propose the impact assessment approaches most likely to be employed at each social innovation stage. Taking stock of the debate regarding the number of stages and the location of the boundaries between them, Santos et al. (2013) surveyed prior social innovation life cycle models and incorporated these insights into their model (Elkington et al., 2010; Murray et

Table 6.2 Towards a contingency model of social impact assessment

Social Innovation Stage	Focus		Available Resources	Likely Social Impact Assessment Approaches
	Improve	Prove		
Problem	**High**	Low	Very scarce	• Theory of change • Logic models • Sociological studies – improving • Establishing baselines for before/after comparisons • Improving experiments (e.g., A/B testing of designs)
Business model	**High**	Medium	Limited	• Theory of change • Logic models • Sociological studies – improving • Improving experiments (e.g., testing of markets, processes, pricing) • Combined indicators and scorecards – for proving & improving • Monetary metrics • Non-monetary metrics
Scaling up	Medium	**High**	Medium	• Theory of change • Logic models • Sociological studies – improving & proving • Combined indicators and scorecards – for proving & improving • Monetary metrics • Non-monetary metrics • Proving experiments
Mainstreaming	Low	**High**	High	• Monetary metrics • Non-monetary metrics • Proving experiments

al., 2010) with an eye towards balancing insight and parsimony. This led them to identify four stages: Problem, Business Model, Scaling, and Mainstreaming (Table 6.2).

Problem Stage

In the first stage of the social innovation cycle, innovators identify a societal problem and come up with a preliminary idea (or ideas) for a potential solution. This stage is marked by uncertainty and experimentation. Much of the innovators' time is spent iteratively designing their solution and getting feedback from various stakeholders, in particular from beneficiaries. At this stage, the innovators' goal is to better understand the problem they are addressing, as well as the strengths and weaknesses of the solution that they are designing. Their objective is also to articulate the hypothesized relationships between specific interventions and the expected social impact. This stage often includes several cycles of failure and changes in approach before the outlines of a workable solution come into focus. This stage is traditionally characterized by scarce resources, making expenses a concern.

At this stage, innovators are thus likely to prioritize the objective to improve their internal operations to ensure the relevance of their solution. In contrast, given that the solution remains largely theoretical at this point, innovators may neither be motivated nor able to prove their social impact to external constituencies. At best will they be able to formulate the level of social impact that they intend to generate. Given these priorities, in a context of very scarce resources, relevant impact assessment methods at this stage are thus likely to include methods that help innovators fully understand the needs of beneficiaries as well as the potential obstacles to their changes in behavior and explicate the value chain leading to the desired change. Theories of Change approaches and qualitative sociological studies are thus anticipated to be prominent at this stage.

Business Model Stage

Social innovations enter the business model stage once the uncertainties and questions from the problem stage are resolved to a degree that the innovation becomes workable in practice. With a minimally viable product, innovators turn their attention to simplifying, codifying, and architecting their value chain to optimize its efficiency and effectiveness. In the business model stage, innovators refine and elucidate their business model and theory of change to create a clear and compelling understanding of how the innovation works as well as how it can be sustained. These models and theories also help organizations craft indicators and scorecards to monitor and optimize their activities. During that phase, social innovators focus on "selling" their innovation to the external world, not only to raise funds, but also to mobilize the committed human resources as well as the political support that is required to implement the innovation. While the innovator may access some resources at this point, they remain limited.

During the business model stage, innovators are thus likely to focus on improving the processes and theoretical models by which the innovation will succeed, but they may also start proving to the external world that the innovation is worth supporting and endorsing (Santos et al., 2013). Yet, given the relative small scale of the initiative at this point, the need to prove the performance is likely to be only moderate. During this phase, social innovators are thus likely to continue to rely on impact assessment approaches that focus on the explication of the desired social change, such as theory of change or qualitative methods to refine their models. If the pressure to prove their social impact is strong enough, they may also resort to a simple results-based approach, such as custom-made indicators which allow, with limited time and resources, to share easy metrics as proxies of their social impact to generate the support that they need. If they have the resources available, they may attempt experiments with different possible variations of product attributes to test their designs and business model.

Scaling Stage

Innovations that have successfully mapped and optimized the activities in their business model and value chain, and that are sustainably generating small-scale impact may decide to scale and expand their impact. Scaling increases the complexity of the organization and requires the organization to develop new activities, processes, and models to support and control work with new branches, partners, and stakeholders. A common risk is that the process of scaling will "pull the organization away from its original mission, vision, and values and strain scarce financial and human resources" (Santos et al., 2013, p. 189). One key factor for deciding an innovation's readiness to scale is when it has a demonstrable track record of success over time (Clark et al., 2012). The scaling phase traditionally requires substantial financial and human resources to bring the innovation to more beneficiaries.

As they enter the scaling stage, social innovators are thus likely to start focusing on proving their performance to external audiences as a means to convince outside stakeholders to grant them the required resources to scale. The focus on improving their internal operations may not be totally abandoned though, but maintained at a medium level because the process of scaling requires ventures to re-architect their processes and models once again to adapt them and make them more robust to handle the additional complexity. During the scaling phase, social innovators are thus likely to primarily rely on methods that allow for the quantification of social impact such as monetary and non-monetary metrics, or combined indicators or scorecards. As innovations reach scale, institutional investors and partnerships with other organizations may bring the expertise and resources needed to progress to more sophisticated assessment methodologies such as experiments to prove outcomes and assumptions.

Mainstreaming Stage

Although only few social innovations reach the mainstreaming stage, those that successfully scaled up may turn their attention to enlisting others in their industry as well as broader social institutions and policy makers to adopt the innovation (Christensen and Ebrahim, 2006; Westley and Antadze, 2010). At this stage, innovators transition from being social entrepreneurs to institutional entrepreneurs (DiMaggio and Powell, 1983; Murray et al., 2010; Westley and Antadze, 2010). As they rely on processes and activities that have been tested, refined, and improved over previous phases, social innovators thus focus on holding their innovations up as successful and disruptive, and advocate for their adoption by others.

During the mainstreaming phase, social innovators' priority is thus likely to fully switch to proving their innovation's ability to generate sustainable social impact, as a means to demonstrate the value of the innovation and convince others to adopt it. The need to improve the processes by which social impact is achieved – while never abandoned – is likely to become a secondary concern at this point in the life of the social innovation. During the mainstreaming phase, social innovators are thus likely to invest in methods that demonstrate the net impact of the innovation such as experimental approaches. Alternatively, other approaches such as monetary metrics, by emphasizing avoided costs or financial benefits of the innovation, may also serve to enlist support for broader institutional adoption. Table 6.2 summarizes our contingency model.

Building upon our previous comments on the role of *legitimacy* in shaping social impact assessment practices, it is important to discuss here how legitimacy concerns may moderate our proposed framework. In particular, we argue that innovations, during the early stages of their life cycle, will lack legitimacy due to their newness (Singh et al., 1986; Stinchcombe, 2000). Innovators are therefore likely to want to display signs of appropriateness to important referents to gain the legitimacy required to garner support. We therefore contend that during the problem and business model stage, social innovators are quite likely to adopt (or pretend to adopt) the social impact assessment approaches prescribed by their major institutional referents, if such prescriptions exist, whether or not they match the social innovation's actual needs. As the innovations scale and mature, these pressures for legitimacy may decrease in intensity since the innovation is likely to have established a successful track record and rely on diversified sources of support. We therefore contend that in the later stages of the social innovation cycle, social innovators are more likely to adopt the methods that really suit their needs as opposed to the methods that are prescribed by powerful institutional referents.

Conditions related to the resources available to the innovator, the type of the innovation as well as the time spent in a given phase may further moderate our model. Our model relies on assumptions regarding *resources available* at each stage that are derived from general observations, but specific circumstances (founding conditions, specific support, and so on) may challenge these assumptions. High-profile initiatives that gain significant funding early on, for example, may find that this early funding accelerates expectations and the timeframe for proving impact, lest investors get restless. On the other hand, many innovations fail to gain significant outside support after the business model stage or lose support after early success, thus never making it to the scaling up phase. These innovations have little need to prove their impact to external groups as they bootstrap their success and may thus focus almost exclusively on assessments to improve their performance.

Our model further assumes a unique *type of innovation*, yet different types of innovations may generate specific impact assessment needs. Innovations that require regulatory approvals, such as medical-related innovations, will also need to focus on proving impact much more and earlier than products that do not require such approvals. Innovations where the benefit is relatively direct and immediate – such as low-cost eye surgeries that restore sight or innovations that enable new wage-earning opportunities, for example – may be able to avoid focusing on proving impact by simply using outputs and immediate outcomes as proxies. Innovations are likely to need to devote additional effort to proving impact where the link between outputs and ultimate impact benefits are more indirect and over longer timeframes. Correspondingly, "broad-but-shallow" innovations (providing small improvements in the lives of many) are likely to feel less of a burden in justifying the smaller levels of impact claimed, which often come relatively directly and immediately, than innovations that provide "deep-for-few" benefits.

Finally, the *time* spent in any particular development stage may also act as a moderator of our model. Many innovations never make it to the later stages of the social innovation cycle and may remain at the business model stage for extended periods. These groups may reach a performance ceiling within their current stage and become complacent regarding assessments that improve performance. They may focus on metrics to prove impact to maintain or acquire support. Conversely, they may even forgo their focus on formalized assessments, settling for current levels of performance and scale until the end of their innovation's life cycle.

A FUTURE RESEARCH AGENDA FOR SOCIAL IMPACT ASSESSMENT

How do we know when social innovation works? As highlighted in this chapter, we have seen, in the past decade, a proliferation of books and articles attempting to address that question, both in academic and practitioners' spheres (Lall, 2017). Whether they map existing approaches (Becker and Vanclay, 2003; Ebrahim et al., 2014; Grieco, 2015; Millar and Hall, 2013; Rawhouser et al., 2017) or propose new social impact assessment frameworks (Arvidson et al., 2013; Banerjee et al., 2011; Kroeger and Weber, 2014), these contributions have certainly enriched our understanding of social impact assessment, but have so far failed to provide innovators with clarity about how they should think about the assessment of the impact of their social innovations.

Towards Practice-driven Research

To better help innovators on the ground, we call for the development of future research that better takes into account the experience and insights of actors on the ground to develop practice-driven theories and frameworks. Molecke and Pinkse (2017) show the gap between social impact assessment theories and methods and how they are implemented (or not) on the ground: among the 22 small- to medium-sized social enterprises that they surveyed, they found that only two used a formal methodology to assess their impact. The other 20 expressed strong critical views about existing social impact assessment methodologies and relied on bricolage to craft ad hoc social impact assessment procedures that they felt would better serve their needs and interests. It is thus urgent that research on social impact assessment better takes into account the reality of social innovators facing the daunting challenges of the complexity of the process, the competing demands of important stakeholders (boards, funders, regulators, and so on) and the costs (both human and financial) associated with the practice.

Future research could further develop models that clarify which approaches are best suited for which type of actors, which type of business models, what type of objectives, and what types of resources. Various types of actors are involved in the use or prescription of social impact assessment: social innovators themselves, but also policy makers, multilateral agencies, and foundations. These various actors, although driven by a common motivation to solve the planet's grand challenges, have in fact very different interests in social impact assessment: for some, social impact assessment may be a matter of sound management and monitoring of their activities, for others, it may be a matter of control to ensure the efficient use of their funds, while for others, it may be a reputational or political issue to assess the performance of their policies.

They further operate at very different scales with very different levels of resources and power. While social innovators traditionally focus on the impact of their own activities and rely upon limited human and financial resources, large foundations or public agencies have access to skills and resources but seek to evaluate social impact at the level of a portfolio of programs or a large-scale policy. Furthermore, social impact evaluations are generally constructed to serve the interests of the innovators or their funders, overlooking how evaluations might provide accountability to beneficiaries themselves. It will be important for future research to better account for these specificities and constraints and explore how they shape the implementation and use of social impact assessment approaches. More broadly, a systematic review of the individual and organizational factors (in addition to life cycle change and purpose) that may influence actors in their use of social impact assessment would contribute to better inform its theory and practice.

Future research could further enrich this picture by qualitatively interviewing social innovators over the life cycle of their innovations to explore how social impact assessment needs and strategies change and evolve over the course of the innovation life cycle. We call upon researchers to capture the dynamic aspects behind how and why innovators implement specific assessment strategies and how these strategies change over time. Of particular interest is how innovators lead processes of change within their evaluation regimes to adapt to new demands and new stakeholders as they transition from one innovation stage to the next. These qualitative accounts could be complemented by quantitative studies that would draw a more accurate picture of how social impact assessment is currently experienced and implemented by social innovators on the ground. This valuable information could help scholars working on the development of social impact assessment methods to better understand the needs, constraints, interests, and strategies of social innovators on the ground.

To take into account recent evolutions in the social innovation space (Doherty et al., 2014), future research should also explore how the development of hybrid initiatives addressing social goals through commercial means (Battilana and Lee, 2014) challenges our current knowledge about social impact assessment. Assessing social impact in the context of these hybrid initiatives requires taking into account both their social and economic performance (Battilana et al., 2015) and may require the development of new hybrid approaches that account for these two dimensions while recognizing the contradictions and complementarities between them (Battilana et al., 2017; Ebrahim and Rangan, 2014). A recent study by André et al. (2018) provides a very valuable first step in that regard. They identify the key role of "compromising performance accounts" that form an arena for dialogue in a hybrid organization and bring together groups holding different evaluative principles. These processes subsequently yield metrics, which can be used to evaluate the social performance of the organization. More research is required to understand the specific social impact assessment requirements of these loci of social innovation.

From Normative to Pragmatic Approaches

Our call for practice-driven approaches further requires that practitioner-oriented studies as well as academic research evolve from a dominant normative stance to a more pragmatic one. As illustrated by the work of Molecke and Pinkse (2017), the various normative pressures put on social innovators to assess their impact have been largely inefficient to contribute to the development of rigorous social impact assessment practices.

Rigorous and systematic impact evaluations remain the privilege of large grant making organizations that have the expertise and resources to craft, implement, or outsource such approaches for their portfolio of grantees (Ebrahim and Rangan, 2014; Nicholls, 2009). Social innovators rely on a variety of pragmatic strategies that include relying on external consultants, resorting to bricolage to develop their own ad hoc assessment processes, symbolically embracing social impact assessment while actually not implementing it, or fully ignoring it (Desa and Basu, 2013; Di Domenico et al., 2010; Molecke and Pinkse, 2017). Future research needs to go beyond uniform normative prescriptions to uncover the obstacles to social impact assessment and to identify the factors that may drive the fruitful implementation of these practices. Such research may also recognize that formal social impact assessment procedures may not always be relevant or meaningful for social innovators and further identify the boundary conditions of the relevance of the practice.

Finally, we encourage future research to go beyond the question of "How to conduct social impact assessments?" to explore the much more challenging question of "What to do with the results of social impact assessment?" Whether it is used with the goal to prove the worth of the innovation towards external stakeholders or with the goal to improve the innovation process, social impact assessment is meant to provide meaningful information that various actors then need to act upon. If results are below expectations, measures could be taken to fix the value chain or reallocate resources, whereas if results are on or above expectations, measures may be taken to further maximize the impact. However, qualitative accounts suggest that actors don't always act upon the outcomes of the social assessments (Hendricks et al., 2008), either because they question their validity, because they may be faced with resistance to change, because they have nothing to compare their results to, or because they don't have the human and financial resources needed to implement the required changes. Future research may thus explore in a systematic fashion what social innovators, funders, or policy makers do with the results of social impact assessments and identify the factors that may influence their willingness and ability to act upon these results in order to enhance their social impact.

While there is no doubt that much progress has been made towards a better understanding of when and how social innovation works, much is left to be discovered to help social innovators deliver on the full promise of social impact. While early work in that space has focused on developing the tools and methods to measure the production of impact, it is important that future research pays more attention to when, how, and why existing methods can be used and how they can be more than rituals to actually serve the purpose of creating positive social change. We hope to have provided, with this chapter, a step, albeit modest, in this direction.

REFERENCES

Ali, I., Hatta, Z.A., Azman, A., and Islam, S. 2017. Microfinance as a development and poverty alleviation tool in rural Bangladesh: a critical assessment. *Asian Social Work and Policy Review*, 11(1), 4–15.

Altenburg, T., Lundvall, B., Joseph, K., Chaminade, C., and Vang, J. 2009. Building inclusive innovation systems in developing countries: challenges for IS research. In B.Å. Lundvall, K.J. Joseph, C. Chaminade and J. Vang (eds), *Handbook of Innovation Systems and Developing Countries: Building Domestic Capabilities in a Global Setting*, Cheltenham, UK and Northampton, MA, USA: Edward Elgar Publishing, pp. 33–56.

Anand, S. and Hanson, K. 1997. Disability-adjusted life years: a critical review. *Journal of Health Economics*, 16(6), 685–702.
Andersson, R., Eriksson, H., and Torstensson, H. 2006. Similarities and differences between TQM, six sigma and lean. *The TQM Magazine*, 18(3), 282–96.
André, K., Cho, C.H., and Laine, M. 2018. Reference points for measuring social performance: case study of a social business venture. *Journal of Business Venturing*, 33(5), 660–78.
Ansari, S. and Euske, K.J. 1987. Rational, rationalizing, and reifying uses of accounting data in organizations. *Accounting, Organizations and Society*, 12(6), 549–70.
Arvidson, M., Lyon, F., McKay, S., and Moro, D. 2013. Valuing the social? The nature and controversies of measuring social return on investment (SROI). *Voluntary Sector Review*, 4(1), 3–18.
Bakewell, O. and Garbutt, A. 2005. *The Use and Abuse of the Logical Framework Approach*. Stockholm: Sida.
Banerjee, A. and Duflo, E. 2012. *Poor Economics: A Radical Rethinking of the Way to Fight Global Poverty*. New York: Public Affairs.
Banerjee, A., Banerjee, A.V., and Duflo, E. 2011. *Poor Economics: A Radical Rethinking of the Way to Fight Global Poverty*. New York: PublicAffairs.
Barman, E. 2017. The social bases of philanthropy. *Annual Review of Sociology*, 43(1), 271–90.
Battilana, J. and Lee, M. 2014. Advancing research on hybrid organizing – insights from the study of social enterprises. *The Academy of Management Annals*, 8(1), 397–441.
Battilana, J., Sengul, M., Pache, A.-C., and Model, J. 2015. Harnessing productive tensions in hybrid organizations: the case of work integration social enterprises. *Academy of Management Journal*, 58(6), 1658–85.
Battilana, J., Besharov, M., and Mitzinneck, B. 2017. On hybrids and hybrid organizing: a review and roadmap for future research. In R. Greenwood, C. Oliver, T.B. Lawrence and R.E. Meyer (eds), *The SAGE Handbook of Organizational Institutionalism*, Vol. 2, Thousand Oaks, CA: SAGE, pp. 133–69.
Becker, H.A. and Vanclay, F. 2003. *The International Handbook of Social Impact Assessment: Conceptual and Methodological Advances*. Cheltenham, UK and Northampton, MA, USA: Edward Elgar Publishing.
Behn, R.D. 2003. Why measure performance? Different purposes require different measures. *Public Administration Review*, 63(5), 586–606.
Brest, P., Katz, S., Peeler, H., and Stangler, D. 2012. A decade of outcome-oriented philanthropy. *Stanford Social Innovation Review*, 10(2), 42–7.
Campbell, A., Converse, P.E., and Rodgers, W.L. 1976. *The Quality of American Life: Perceptions, Evaluations, and Satisfactions*. New York: Russell Sage Foundation.
Carson, R.T. and Hanemann, W.M. 2005. Contingent valuation. In K.-G. Maler and J.R. Vincent (eds), *Handbook of Environmental Economics*, Vol. 2, Amsterdam: Elsevier, pp. 821–936.
Chen, H.-T. and Rossi, P.H. 1983. Evaluating with sense the theory-driven approach. *Evaluation Review*, 7(3), 283–302.
Choi, N. and Majumdar, S. 2014. Social entrepreneurship as an essentially contested concept: opening a new avenue for systematic future research. *Journal of Business Venturing*, 29(3), 363–76.
Christensen, R.A. and Ebrahim, A. 2006. How does accountability affect mission? The case of a nonprofit serving immigrants and refugees. *Nonprofit Management and Leadership*, 17, 195–209.
Clark, C., Massarsky, C.W., Raben, T.S., and Worsham, E. 2012. Scaling social impact: a literature toolkit for funders. https://centers.fuqua.duke.edu/case/knowledge_items/scaling-social-impact-a-literature-toolkit-for-funders/ (accessed 23 February 2019).
Corbin, J. and Strauss, A. 2014. *Basics of Qualitative Research: Techniques and Procedures for Developing Grounded Theory*. Thousand Oaks, CA: SAGE.
Cozzens, S. and Sutz, J. 2012. Innovation in informal settings: a research agenda, March. Paper commissioned by IDRC Innovation for Inclusive Development Programme.
De Groot, R.S., Wilson, M.A., and Boumans, R.M. 2002. A typology for the classification, description and valuation of ecosystem functions, goods and services. *Ecological Economics*, 41(3), 393–408.
Desa, G. and Basu, S. 2013. Optimization or bricolage? Overcoming resource constraints in global social entrepreneurship. *Strategic Entrepreneurship Journal*, 7(1), 26–49.
Di Domenico, M., Haugh, H., and Tracey, P. 2010. Social bricolage: theorizing social value creation in social enterprises. *Entrepreneurship Theory and Practice*, 34(4), 681–703.
Dickert, S., Sagara, N., and Slovic, P. 2011. Affective motivations to help others: a two-stage model of donation decisions. *Journal of Behavioral Decision Making*, 24(4), 361–76.
DiMaggio, P. 2002. Measuring the impact of the nonprofit sector on society is probably impossible but possibly useful. In P. Flynn and V.A. Hodgkinson (eds), *Measuring the Impact of the Nonprofit Sector*, New York: Springer Science and Business Media, pp. 249–72.
DiMaggio, P. and Powell, W.W. 1983. The iron cage revisited: collective rationality and institutional isomorphism in organizational fields. *American Sociological Review*, 48(2), 147–60.
Doh, J.P., Howton, S.D., Howton, S.W., and Siegel, D.S. 2010. Does the market respond to an endorsement

of social responsibility? The role of institutions, information, and legitimacy. *Journal of Management*, 36(6), 1461–85.
Doherty, B., Haugh, H., and Lyon, F. 2014. Social enterprises as hybrid organizations: a review and research agenda. *International Journal of Management Reviews*, 16(4), 417–36.
Duflo, E. 2003. Grandmothers and granddaughters: old-age pensions and intrahousehold allocation in South Africa. *The World Bank Economic Review*, 17(1), 1–25.
Duflo, E., Banerjee, A., Glennerster, R., and Kinnan, C.G. 2013. *The Miracle of Microfinance? Evidence from a Randomized Evaluation*. Washington, DC: National Bureau of Economic Research.
Ebrahim, A. 2003. Accountability in practice: mechanisms for NGOs. *World Development*, 31(5), 813–29.
Ebrahim, A. 2005. Accountability myopia: losing sight of organizational learning. *Nonprofit and Voluntary Sector Quarterly*, 34, 56–87.
Ebrahim, A. and Rangan, V.K. 2014. What impact? A framework for measuring the scale & scope of social performance. *California Management Review*, 56(3), 118–41.
Ebrahim, A., Battilana, J., and Mair, J. 2014. The governance of social enterprises: mission drift and accountability challenges in hybrid organizations. *Research in Organizational Behavior*, 34, 81–100.
Eikenberry, A.M. and Kluver, J.D. 2004. The marketization of the nonprofit sector: civil society at risk? *Public Administration Review*, 64(2), 132–40.
Elkington, J., Hartigan, P., and Litovsky, A. 2010. From enterprise to ecosystem: rebooting the scale debate. In P. Bloom and E. Skloot (eds), *Scaling Social Impact*, New York: Springer, pp. 83–102.
Emerson, J. 2003. The blended value proposition: integrating social and financial returns. *California Management Review*, 45(4), 35–51.
Foster, C. and Heeks, R. 2013. Conceptualising inclusive innovation: modifying systems of innovation frameworks to understand diffusion of new technology to low-income consumers. *The European Journal of Development Research*, 25(3), 333–55.
Frumkin, P. 2008. *Strategic Giving: The Art and Science of Philanthropy*. Chicago, IL: University of Chicago Press.
Gafni, A. and Birch, S. 2006. Incremental cost-effectiveness ratios (ICERs): the silence of the lambda. *Social Science & Medicine*, 62(9), 2091–100.
George, G., McGahan, A.M., and Prabhu, J. 2012. Innovation for inclusive growth: towards a theoretical framework and a research agenda. *Journal of Management Studies*, 49(4), 661–83.
George, G., Howard-Grenville, J., Joshi, A., and Tihanyi, L. 2016. Understanding and tackling societal grand challenges through management research. *Academy of Management Journal*, 59(6), 1880–95.
GIIN. 2011. Data driven: a performance analysis for the impact investing industry. In *Impact Reporting and Investment Standards (IRIS)*, New York: Global Impact Investing Network, pp. 1–32.
Gray, R. 2001. Thirty years of social accounting, reporting and auditing: what (if anything) have we learnt? *Business Ethics: A European Review*, 10, 9–15.
Greiner, L.E. 1972. Evolution and revolution as organizations grow. In C. Bowman and D.C. Asch (eds) (1989), *Readings in Strategic Management*, London: Palgrave, pp. 373–87.
Grieco, C. 2015. *Assessing Social Impact of Social Enterprises: Does One Size Really Fit All?* Rome: Springer.
Hall, P.D. 2004. A historical perspective on evaluation in foundations. In M. Braverman, N. A. Constantine and J. Slater (eds), *Philanthropy and Evaluation: Contexts and Practices for Effective Philanthropy*, San Francisco, CA: John Wiley & Sons, pp. 27–50.
Hall, P.D. 2005. A solution is a product in search of a problem: a history of foundations and evaluation research. http://citeseerx.ist.psu.edu/view/download?doi=10.1.1.473.7085&rep=rep1&type=pdf (accessed 23 February 2019).
Hendricks, M., Plantz, M.C., and Pritchard, K.J. 2008. Measuring outcomes of United Way-funded programs: expectations and reality. *New Directions for Evaluation*, 119, 13–35.
Hubbard, G. 2009. Measuring organizational performance: beyond the triple bottom line. *Business Strategy and the Environment*, 18, 177–91.
Jo, H., Kim, H., and Park, K. 2015. Corporate environmental responsibility and firm performance in the financial services sector. *Journal of Business Ethics*, 131(2), 257–84.
Kaplan, R.S. and Norton, D.P. 1995. Putting the balanced scorecard to work. In D.G. Shaw, C.E. Schneider, R.W. Beatty and L.S. Baird (eds), *Performance Measurement, Management, and Appraisal Sourcebook*, Amherst, MA: Human Resource Development Press.
Kaplan, S. and Garrett, K. 2005. The use of logic models by community-based initiatives. *Evaluation and Program Planning*, 28(2), 167–72.
Kim, S.-Y., Lee, G., and Goldie, S.J. 2010. Economic evaluation of pneumococcal conjugate vaccination in The Gambia. *BMC Infectious Diseases*, 10(260), 1–18.
Kirk, R.E. 1982. *Experimental Design*. Wiley Online Library.
Kramer, M., Graves, R., Hirschhorn, J., and Fiske, L. 2007. From insight to action: new directions in foundation evaluation. https://www.fsg.org/publications/insight-action (accessed 23 February 2019).

Kroeger, A. and Weber, C. 2014. Developing a conceptual framework for comparing social value creation. *Academy of Management Review*, 39, 513–40.
Lall, S. 2017. Measuring to improve versus measuring to prove: understanding the adoption of social performance measurement practices in nascent social enterprises. *VOLUNTAS: International Journal of Voluntary and Nonprofit Organizations*, 28(6), 2633–57.
Lamont, M. 2012. Toward a comparative sociology of valuation and evaluation. *Annual Review of Sociology*, 38, 201–21.
Lowell, S., Trelstad, B., and Meehan, B. 2005. The ratings game. *Stanford Social Innovation Review*, 3(2), 38–45.
MacKeith, J. 2011. The development of the outcomes star: a participatory approach to assessment and outcome measurement. *Housing, Care and Support*, 14(3), 98–106.
Mair, J. and Marti, I. 2006. Social entrepreneurship research: a source of explanation, prediction, and delight. *Journal of World Business*, 41(1), 36–44.
Margolis, J.D., Elfenbein, H.A., and Walsh, J.P. 2007. Does it pay to be good? A meta-analysis and redirection of research on the relationship between corporate social and financial performance. *Ann Arbor*, unpublished Working Paper.
McKinley, T. 2010. Inclusive growth criteria and indicators: an inclusive growth index for diagnosis of country progress. ©Asian Development Bank. http://hdl.handle.net/11540/1405 (accessed 23 February 2019).
Meyer, J.W. and Rowan, B. 1977. Institutionalized organizations: formal structure as myth and ceremony. *American Journal of Sociology*, 83(2), 340–63.
Millar, R. and Hall, K. 2013. Social return on investment (SROI) and performance measurement: the opportunities and barriers for social enterprises in health and social care. *Public Management Review*, 15, 923–41.
Molecke, G. and Pinkse, J. 2017. Accountability for social impact: a bricolage perspective on impact measurement in social enterprises. *Journal of Business Venturing*, 32(5), 550–68.
Mulgan, G. 2006. The process of social innovation. *Innovations*, 1(2), 145–62.
Murray, R., Caulier-Grice, J., and Mulgan, G. 2010. *The Open Book of Social Innovation*. London: National Endowment for Science, Technology and the Arts.
Nicholls, A. 2009. "We do good things, don't we?": blended value accounting in social entrepreneurship. *Accounting, Organizations and Society*, 34, 755–69.
Nicholls, A. 2010. The legitimacy of social entrepreneurship: reflexive isomorphism in a pre-paradigmatic field. *Entrepreneurship Theory and Practice*, 34(4), 611–33.
Nussbaum, M.C. 2001. *Women and Human Development: The Capabilities Approach*. Cambridge, UK: Cambridge University Press.
Nussbaum, M. and Sen, A. 1993. *The Quality of Life*. Oxford, UK: Oxford University Press.
Parmenter, D. 2015. *Key Performance Indicators: Developing, Implementing, and Using Winning KPIs*. Hoboken, NJ: John Wiley & Sons.
Polonsky, M. and Grau, S.L. 2011. Assessing the social impact of charitable organizations – four alternative approaches. *International Journal of Nonprofit and Voluntary Sector Marketing*, 16, 195–211.
Power, M. 1997. *The Audit Society: Rituals of Verification*. Oxford: Oxford University Press.
Rawhouser, H., Cummings, M., and Newbert, S.L. 2017. Social impact measurement: current approaches and future directions for social entrepreneurship research. *Entrepreneurship Theory and Practice*, 43(1), 82–115.
Roche, C.J. 1999. *Impact Assessment for Development Agencies: Learning to Value Change*. Oxford: Oxfam.
Rogers, P.J. 2008. Using programme theory to evaluate complicated and complex aspects of interventions. *Evaluation*, 14(1), 29–48.
Rourke, B. 2014. Philanthropy and the limits of accountability. Philanthropy for Active Civic Engagement (PACE) and the Charles F. Kettering Foundation. https://www.kettering.org/catalog/product/philanthropy-and-limits-accountability-relationship-respect-and-clarity (accessed 23 February 2019).
Sachs, J.D. 2012. From Millennium Development Goals to sustainable development goals. *The Lancet*, 379(9832), 2206–11.
Santos, F.M. 2012. A positive theory of social entrepreneurship. *Journal of Business Ethics*, 111(3), 335–51.
Santos, F., Salvado, J.C., de Carvalho, I.L., and Schulte, U.G. 2013. The life cycle of social innovations. In O. Thomas and S. Rene (eds), *Social Innovation*, Heidelberg: Springer, pp. 183–95.
Schreiner, M. 2014. The PPI Manual: a comprehensive manual on using the Poverty Probability Index. http://www.povertyindex.org/learning-materials (accessed 23 February 2019).
Sen, A. 2001. *Development as Freedom*. Oxford: Oxford University Press.
Singh, J.V., Tucker, D.J., and House, R.J. 1986. Organizational legitimacy and the liability of newness. *Administrative Science Quarterly*, 31(2), 171–93.
Slovic, P. 2007. If I look at the mass I will never act: psychic numbing and genocide. *Judgment and Decision Making*, 2(2), 79–95.
Stievenart, E. and Pache, A.-C. 2014. Evaluer l'impact social d'une entreprise sociale: points de repère. *Revue internationale de l'économie sociale: Recma*, 331, 76–92.

Stinchcombe, A.L. 2000. Social structure and organizations. In J.A. Baum and F. Dobbin (eds), *Economics Meets Sociology in Strategic Management*, Bingley, UK: Emerald Group Publishing Ltd, pp. 229–59.

Sun, M., Nagata, K., and Onoda, H. 2011. The investigation of the current status of socially responsible investment indices. *Journal of Economics and International Finance*, 3(13), 676–84.

Taylor, S.J., Bogdan, R., and DeVault, M. 2015. *Introduction to Qualitative Research Methods: A Guidebook and Resource*. Hoboken, NJ: John Wiley & Sons.

Ura, K., Alkire, S., Zangmo, T., and Wangdi, K. 2012. A short guide to Gross National Happiness Index. https://www.gov.uk/dfid-research-outputs/a-short-guide-to-gross-national-happiness-index (accessed 23 February 2019).

Utz, A. and Dahlman, C. 2007. Promoting inclusive innovation. In M.A. Utz (ed.), *Unleashing India's Innovation: Towards Sustainable and Inclusive Growth*, Washington, DC: World Bank. https://openknowledge.worldbank.org/handle/10986/6856105-128 (accessed 23 February 2019).

Van de Ven, A.H. and Poole, M.S. 1995. Explaining development and change in organizations. *Academy of Management Review*, 20(3), 510–40.

Venkataraman, S. 1997. The distinctive domain of entrepreneurship research. *Advances in Entrepreneurship, Firm Emergence and Growth*, 3(1), 119–38.

W.K. Kellogg Foundation. 2006. W. K. Kellogg Foundation's logic model development guide. http://www.wkkf.org/resource-directory/resource/2006/02/wk-kellogg-foundation-logic-model-development-guide (accessed 23 February 2019).

Westley, F. and Antadze, N. 2010. Making a difference: strategies for scaling social innovation for greater impact. *Innovation Journal*, 15(2), 1–19.

Wood, D.J. 1991. Corporate social performance revisited. *Academy of Management Review*, 16(4), 691–718.

Wry, T. and Haugh, H. 2018. Brace for impact: uniting our diverse voices through a social impact frame. *Journal of Business Venturing*, 33(5), 566–74.

Zott, C. and Huy, Q.N. 2007. How entrepreneurs use symbolic management to acquire resources. *Administrative Science Quarterly*, 52(1), 70–105.

PART III

COMMUNITY AND PLACE

7. Indigenous social innovation: what is distinctive? And a research agenda

Ana María Peredo, Murdith McLean and Crystal Tremblay

In recent years, governments and non-governmental organizations, as well as universities, have come together in seeing "social innovation" as a way to address long-standing and deeply rooted social ills (Ayob et al., 2016). Our focus in this chapter is on the connection between the promise of social innovation and a particular population that is especially acquainted with the kinds of problems that social innovation is supposed to tackle: Indigenous peoples around the world.

Indigenous peoples are not one population, but a numerous and varied set of communities in many different localities. Typically, they face chronic social, cultural, economic and political challenges (Hall and Gandolfo, 2016; World Bank, 2011) as a consequence of colonization processes and racism, though their constellation and intensity vary from place to place. The many dimensions of poverty are evident in the striking differences that typify the contrast between these populations and their surrounding settler societies not only with respect to income, but also health and health care, education and employment, housing, living conditions and opportunities of many kinds. Given this background, it might seem the most obvious form of connection to be explored would be the way in which innovations not yet identified or attempted might be employed to address the difficulties faced by Indigenous peoples. We have a different question, or rather, set of questions. In this chapter, we raise the question of what specifically *Indigenous* social innovation (ISI) might look like, and whether something like that is already taking place. We ask further what we can learn from distinctively Indigenous social innovation that could inform our attack on social problems faced not only by the Indigenous but by other disadvantaged peoples and communities.

We begin with a brief exploration of the concept of social innovation. We proceed then to look at two main literature streams to inform our search for what is distinctive about ISI. These streams suggest three aspects in which we might expect ISI to be grounded: (1) traditional knowledge and practices; (2) distinct cosmology and culture; and (3) struggles for decolonization and Indigenous resurgence. We then consider a specific case of Indigenous innovation that illustrates how those distinctive aspects work in practice and the possibilities that opens for Indigenous communities. We conclude with a research agenda.

WHAT IS SOCIAL INNOVATION?

The concept of "social innovation" has become a heading for policy initiatives and focused scholarly attention only in recent years (Ayob et al., 2016), though the phenomena it refers to have arguably been with us throughout human civilization. As with any burgeoning subject area, the concept is subject to a variety of understandings and explications (Andrew and Klein, 2010; Ayob et al., 2016; Government of Canada, 2010; Mulgan et al., 2007; Phills et al., 2008; Westley, 2008). While there is general agreement on many paradigm cases – innovations such as "Fair Trade" products, micro-credit, co-operative housing, emissions trading, community kitchens and Meals on Wheels – and historical examples that are now part of life in many of our countries, such as trade unions, co-operatives, collective insurance, publicly funded health schemes and many more – there is disagreement both as to what makes social innovation, innovation and what makes it social.

Innovation

A considerable variety of things may be the carriers of social innovation. Phills et al. observe that "A social innovation can be a product, production process, or technology (much like innovation in general), but it can also be a principle, an idea, a piece of legislation, a social movement, an intervention, or some combination of them" (2008, p. 39). It is tautological to assert that innovation requires novelty, something new in any of the things that are properly called an innovation. It is open to question, however, how that novelty should be understood.

Practitioners and promoters of social innovation often speak of "new ideas" as characteristic of social innovation, but there is wide agreement among scholars that social innovation is frequently, perhaps usually, the adaptation and perhaps recombination of existing ideas. Phills et al. represent this view in stating that "innovations need not necessarily be original." All that is required, they suggest, is that "they must be new to the user, context or application" (2008, p. 37). Often what is new is the *combination* of items (Mulgan et al., 2007, p. 5). As a research brief produced for the Canadian Government puts it, "[social innovation] often involves novel applications (or recombinations) of existing ideas and/or their application to new areas" (Government of Canada, 2010, p. 1; see also Mulgan et al., 2007, p. 5). The concept of bricolage – the inventive combination of elements that are at hand but not generally recognized as resources – has been shown to illuminate the concepts of entrepreneurship (Baker and Nelson, 2005) and social entrepreneurship (Di Domenico et al., 2010). It seems fully applicable to social innovation.

There is a variety of opinion concerning not only the quality of novelty in social innovation, but also the magnitude of its impact. Mulgan (2006) and Westley (2008) represent many scholars who regard social innovation as bringing about a systemic change, addressing the underlying sources of social problems and not just their symptoms. From this point of view, social innovations are disruptive and large scale rather than incremental and context specific. Others, such as Phills et al. (2008), decline to make such a distinction, on the grounds that impact is essentially ranged on a continuum, with any attempt to draw a significant distinction based on subjective judgment.

For the purpose of this chapter, we will adopt a broad view of the character of novelty in social innovation. As mentioned, many different kinds of entities can count as innovative. Innovation with respect to any of them will often, perhaps typically, not be a total novelty but a recombination and/or reapplication of familiar ideas. We accept that the range of impact is a continuum, though we can see why research on social innovation focuses more on innovations that are relatively systemic and wide-ranging in their impact.

The magnitude of the problems that we face, the forces that sustain them, and the hope that we may address them in some long-term fashion seem to call for responses that go to the roots of the problems.

Social

The social element in social innovation has been interpreted in a variety of ways along two complementary paths: (1) What are the outcomes of the innovation? and (2) What are the innovators aiming at?

Regarding outcomes, Mulgan et al. state simply that social innovations "work in meeting social goals" (2007, p. 8). Phills et al. offer a similarly general suggestion. Social innovations, they say, are those "for which the value created accrues primarily to society as a whole rather than private individuals" (Phills et al., 2008, p. 36). Pol and Ville more cautiously stipulate that a social innovation "has the potential to improve either the quality or the quantity of life" (2009, p. 881).

A more focused idea of the target population emerges when researchers specify the objective of social innovation in terms of problems to be addressed. Westley expresses a commonly held view when she states that her interest is "in those social innovations that address seemingly intractable social problems – homelessness, poverty, and mental health" (2008, p. 2). No doubt it would be a mistake to rule out innovations that produce general improvements in the well-being of a society or some group within it, whether or not there is a clear sense of hardship. But what are recognized as urgent social problems, and those who suffer from them, do come in for special attention when social innovation is discussed.

A more radical approach to the social element in social innovation has been championed especially by Moulaert and Hillier (2009). For them, a fundamental aspect of the outcomes of social innovation is the transformation of social relations. Social innovation, they contend, leads to "a better inclusion of excluded groups and individuals into various spheres of society at various spatial scales" (Moulaert and Hillier, 2009, p. 4). Social innovation, on this view, entails an ethical priority of "social justice" (Moulaert and Hillier, 2009, p. 4).

A second strand in the social aspect literature of social innovation emphasizes that the social outcomes must be more than positive externalities. Mulgan et al., for example, define the term as "innovative activities and services that are motivated by the goal of meeting a social need and that are predominantly developed and diffused through organisations whose primary purposes are social" (2007, p. 8). One could object that motivation is hard to determine and generally mixed (Phills et al., 2008). But Mulgan et al.'s use of the idea of "primary purposes" suggests that what they have in mind is not really motivation, but objectives or intentions. Of course, intentions/objectives/goals are generally mixed as well, and the aim of producing socially desirable outcomes is often somewhere on a continuum between a minor goal and a totally dominant intention (Peredo and McLean, 2006). But the suggestion that socially valuable outcomes must result from an individual or organization's intentions, and not just accidental results of normal business activity, seems sound. We will assume that the goal of social benefit must be significant, but need not be the exclusive, or even primary, intentional aim.

The inclusion by Mulgan et al. of a requirement that social innovations "are predominantly developed and diffused through organisations whose primary purposes are social" (2007, p. 8) may seem to rule out profit-seeking organizations as potential agents of social innovation. That is surely too strong. In effect, this restriction seems to suggest that prosocial intentions should not only be strong determinants of the innovation, but almost exclusive. The existence of companies that aim to make money but also to benefit society is well recognized (Vogel, 2007). We will assume that if prosocial outcomes are prominent among the goals of an organization, even if they might not be "primary," they might well produce social innovations. It seems important, as well, to recognize that social innovation often occurs where business and government interact with third sector organizations in producing social benefit (Phills et al., 2008; Waddell, 1999). We take Mulgan's restriction to be just a way of underlining the requirement that the benefits of social innovation are deliberately sought, and are not merely positive externalities of regular, profit-seeking business activity. We welcome a special concern for inclusion and social justice as a vital element in social innovation, whether or not that is made part of its definition. In a nutshell, the social aspect of social innovation lies in the fact that some kind of social benefit is the outcome, and it is something intentionally sought out, and not the accidental byproduct of pursuing some other goal.

We have discussed what makes social innovation innovative, and what makes it social. For the purpose of this chapter, we propose the following definition: Social innovation is a novelty in some practice, product, technology or other phenomenon with social impact, where (a) that novelty is not necessarily a new invention but may be a combination/recombination/reapplication of existing factors; (b) it results in significant social benefit, especially amelioration of a significant social problem; and (c) that benefit is the intentional aim and not an accidental byproduct of the innovation. Our proposed definition is not precise and tidy; and that, we suggest, simply reflects the way that social innovation is in the real world. It is a phenomenon of great impact, but there are no sharp boundaries between the kinds of things that we will agree in recognizing as examples, and those we might not. We hold that there is wide enough agreement on paradigm cases, and on the general features that pick them out, to make the discussion of what we can learn from them and how to promote them very worthwhile. Our particular interest is how the concept applies to innovations taking place in the Indigenous world.

INDIGENOUS SOCIAL INNOVATION

Who are the Indigenous?

The United Nations estimates that the worldwide population of Indigenous peoples numbers more than 370 million, distributed over 70 countries worldwide (United Nations Permanent Forum on Indigenous Issues, 2017). Those engaged with Indigenous affairs generally agree in favoring a criterion that recognizes self-identification as a primary marker for Indigeneity, rather than a formal definition. At the same time, they converge on a broad agreement on the characteristics of Indigenous societies. Peredo et al. (2004) identify six features that are generally included in recognizing Indigenous society:

> (1) descent from inhabitants of a land prior to later inhabitants, (2) some form of domination by the later inhabitants, (3) maintenance of distinguishing socio-cultural norms and institutions

> by the indigenous group, (4) an attachment to ancestral lands and resources, (5) often, but not always, subsistence economic arrangements, and (6) an association with distinctive languages. (2004, p. 5)

They note that not all elements are present in all cases, but in most instances of modern Indigenous cultures, all six characteristics are present to at least some degree.

Underlying this list of characteristics is a lived history in which those features are blended in shared experience extending over many generations, shaping the identify of Indigenous peoples (Sigurdarson, 2009). To begin with, the descent from early inhabitants of the land is typically and vividly represented in traditions, stories, songs, art forms or other cultural expressions that link the Indigenous with their ancestors and their place. Second, distinct cultural norms and institutions – for example, collective forms of organization and economies based on reciprocity and gifts rather than markets – have also been part of what distinguishes Indigenous history. These have typically been dismissed by colonizers as alien and primitive, rather than rich and complex patterns of interaction embedded in distinct worldviews. Third, a sense of deep attachment to ancestral lands quite alien to European ideas of property or ownership (Bryan, 2000), sometimes embedded in a sense of being parented by it or kinship with it, is a fundamental characteristic of most Indigenous outlooks (Sigurdarson, 2009). Fourth, Indigenous cultures have often maintained themselves in those lands by means of economies that draw on the endowments of the environment in ways that require intimate knowledge of the nature of that environment and are embedded in a sense of stewardship and reciprocity in relation to it. Fifth, different languages embody different ways of constructing and perceiving reality (Athanasopoulos et al., 2015), and distinct languages are an obvious and vital marker of Indigenous identity, capturing and expressing the distinct worldviews, cultural patterns and traditional knowledge that make up Indigenous identity.

These interconnected indicators of indigeneity are all embedded in the remaining and transformational element listed above: domination by colonizing incomers. Traditional bearers of the links with ancestors – stories, songs, dances and so on – were precisely among the things meant to be suppressed by practices of assimilation, for example, Residential Schools in Canada (Miller and Marshall, 2017) and Aboriginal child removal in Australia (Krieken, 2004). Distinguishing socio-cultural norms and institutions were likewise meant to be extinguished by the colonial powers that meant to absorb Indigenous peoples into their "superior" cultures. The attachment to land had to give way to the need of incomers to find habitation, to subordinate the land to agricultural practices based on a different sense of relationship to the land, and along the way to turn land into something that could be exchanged in markets. In the drive to assimilation, languages were deliberately snuffed out as part of what was holding the Indigenous back from progress into "civilization," and the advancing extinction of Indigenous languages continues apace (Sigurdarson, 2009).

Indigenous scholar Taiaiaki asserts that this potent mix of Indigenous character, mingled with the experience of colonization, is the defining characteristic of the Indigenous identity. "It is this oppositional, place-based existence," he says, "along with the consciousness of being in struggle against the dispossessing and demeaning fact of colonization by foreign peoples, that fundamentally distinguishes Indigenous peoples from other peoples of the world" (Alfred, 2005, p. 597).

It is this shared experience of a rich heritage, marginalized and threatened with extinction, that provides the context in which ISI takes place.

A Working Definition, and What Might We Expect to be Distinctive about Indigenous Social Innovation?

This aspect of the chapter draws on three strands of scholarly literature. First, there is an emergent multidisciplinary body of literature that explicitly recognizes and discusses the concept and the practice of Indigenous innovation: for example, Alexiuk (2013), Drahos (2011), Drahos and Frankel (2012b), Huaman and Sriraman (2015), McCarthy et al. (2014), Tapsell and Woods (2008, 2010) and Volynets (2015). Second, there is a considerably larger literature that considers topics obviously bordering on and bound up with ISI: topics such as Indigenous economies, Indigenous entrepreneurship and Indigenous social enterprise. Prominent examples here are Anderson et al. (2006), Banerjee and Tedmanson (2010), Berkes and Adhikari (2006), Dana (2015), Hindle and Moroz (2010), Kuokkanen (2011), Nikolakis (2010), Peredo and Anderson (2006), Peredo et al. (2004) and Tapsell and Woods (2008). Third, there is a nascent and vital literature that has its own powerful implications for ISI: the literature on what has come to be known as "Indigenous resurgence." Alexiuk (2013), Alfred (2013), Alfred and Corntassel (2005), Corntassel (2012), Simpson (2008) and Turner (2007) illustrate this important voice in framing our study.

By "Indigenous social innovation (ISI)," we mean a novelty informed by ancestral knowledge and practices, in some product, practice, technology or other phenomenon with social and cultural impact, developed and implemented by the Indigenous in accordance with their worldviews. As mentioned earlier, (a) the novelty is not necessarily a new invention but may be a combination/recombination/reapplication of existing factors, including traditional teachings and practices; (b) it results in significant social benefit, especially improving the lives of Indigenous peoples and/or serving to reaffirm their Indigenous ways of life; and (c) its benefit is the intentional aim and not an accidental byproduct of the innovation in harmony with their distinct cosmology and culture. The fact that this form of innovation is developed and implemented by the Indigenous means first, we not considering the development and application of innovations by external governments, corporations or other exogenous agents to Indigenous communities, however valuable or important those externally derived innovations might be. Second, we are not counting the appropriation of items from Indigenous life and culture and their application to problem-solving in settler cultures, though that has been and continues to be a significant form of innovation (and raises important ethical and political questions). The question, for instance, of how Indigenous traditional knowledge should be respected in international regulation of intellectual property is of vital current concern (Drahos, 2011; Drahos and Frankel, 2012b), but is beyond the scope of our inquiry here.

Our focus is on the Indigenous as the agents of social innovations aimed at benefiting primarily, but not necessarily exclusively, their own communities, whether those communities are rural or urban, gathered or disbursed. There are open questions as to how to see innovations in a context where Indigenous peoples are engaging with settler peoples in a joint activity, such as extractive enterprise on land to which the Indigenous have a claim. We say that for these to be regarded as ISIs, there must be a clear recognition that the Indigenous contribution is a major component of the intervention, and that Indigenous interests are primary in determining the objective of the innovation. Decisions here will need to be on a case-by-case basis. As above, co-option of Indigenous ideas to serve non-Indigenous commercial interests does not count as ISI.

As mentioned above, we raise three large-scale questions concerning ISI: (1) What might we expect to be distinctive about ISI? (2) What examples are there of ISI already taking place? (3) What learnings might be gathered from those examples and applied not only to Indigenous but other societies and communities? These questions compose something like a tri-focal lens that can be used to identify interventions with significant potential for Indigenous and broader betterment, and to amplify their impact. In this chapter, we make only a preliminary attempt at answering the first and second questions, but we argue that the research agenda they entail opens the door to enormous potential.

The emergent fields of Indigenous entrepreneurship and Indigenous social enterprise have been facing questions similar to the one posed here about the distinctiveness of ISI. Culture is a dominant theme in research on Indigenous entrepreneurship and Indigenous social enterprise, and it is recognized as a potent force in defining goals and purposes of Indigenous enterprise. Scholars generally agree in seeing an inclination in Indigenous culture to collective orientation and a spiritual connection with land (Anderson et al., 2006; Berkes and Adhikari, 2006; Peredo and Anderson, 2006).

The Indigenous resurgence research stream has highlighted efforts of Indigenous communities to reactivate and reconnect with Indigenous knowledge and practices as a pathway toward decolonization (Alfred and Corntassel, 2005; Corntassel, 2012). Simpson (2008) refers to efforts to flourish from inside out. Indigenous decolonization movements go beyond inclusion and aim at garnering respect for Indigenous philosophies and knowledge (Alexiuk, 2013).

Consider now question one: where should we look for distinctively ISI? We propose three promising grounds: (1) traditional knowledge and practices; (2) distinct worldviews and resulting cultural norms; and (3) the struggle for recovery from colonization – recovering sovereignty.

Grounded in traditional knowledge and practices

Indigenous societies have typically inhabited their lands for eons, often thousands of years, before being colonized by settler populations. What Turner writes about the Indigenous people of the Pacific Northwest could be said of many, perhaps most Indigenous groups:

> If there is one overriding theme extending over time and space for human survival in this vast region, it is change – and adaptation to change. Being keen and vigilant observers, scientists in the broadest sense of the word, indigenous peoples have not only used the resources around them but maintained and enhanced them in various ways . . . [T]hey have found diverse means, through developing cultural institutions and protocols, to control their impacts on other species and to accommodate the changes that have occurred over millennia. (2008, p. 14)

This ability to survive and adapt is built on a vast store of "traditional Indigenous knowledge (TIK)" (Barnhardt, 2005). This knowledge, and the innovation it has given rise to in adaptation to changing conditions, is intensely place based (Drahos and Frankel, 2012a; Tomlins-Jahnke and Forster, 2015), reflecting the deep attachment to traditional lands and resources that is characteristic of Indigenous peoples.

TIK is frequently represented and transmitted in ways that are unfamiliar to Western conventions of representing and transmitting knowledge, in forms such as story-telling, songs, dreams, religious ritual, art, dance and other kinds of symbolic representation (Drahos and Frankel, 2012a, p. 21). Traditional knowledge is generally transmitted, usually orally, by one generation to another generation, with elders playing a fundamental role as the keepers of traditional knowledge who not only preserve the knowledge but determine who is fit to convey it. Herman (2018) notes that the tradition in her Indigenous background, of orally transmitted knowledge guarded by a particular "keeper," is often seen as discrediting that knowledge in the eyes of non-Indigenous. It is perhaps these unfamiliar forms of representation, as well as the cultural disdain that settler societies typically display toward Indigenous ways, that has led to widespread disregard for TIK in Western scientific circles (Turner, 2008, p. 4). There has, however, been a growing recognition of insights to be gained from TIK (Heyd, 1995). Scholars increasingly see potential in bringing TIK together with conventional "scientific" thinking (for example, Kawagley and Barnhardt, 1998; Turner, 2008), especially in areas such as ecology, environmental sustainability and natural resource management (Menzies, 2006; Moller et al., 2004; Ng'asike and Swadener, 2015). Chhetri and Chhetri (2015) propose the idea of "alternative imagination" as a way of bringing Indigenous knowledge systems together with non-Indigenous formats to produce fresh and innovative insights into the world around us. As Dudgeon and Berkes (2003) point out, TIK is not static, but evolves as people encounter new circumstances and ways of thinking. TIK thus functions as a central base from which Indigenous social innovations may spring in response to new challenges facing Indigenous communities. As a Maya leader put it, "it is the base from where we reach" (personal communication). TIK should therefore be regarded as a dynamic and relevant resource and not a fixed body of knowledge attached only to a specific time and set of circumstances. The Quechua of South America, for example, use ancient organizational practices to create and maintain community-based enterprises that engage with the evolving global market economy, where their ancient practices of mobilizing labor provide them with unique competitive advantages (Peredo, 2012). Canadian Indigenous leader and former judge, Murray Sinclair, captured this point in his comment to the Indigenous Innovation Summit of 2015: "Innovation isn't always about creating new things. Innovation sometimes means looking back at our old ways and bringing them forward to this new situation" (National Association of Friendship Centres, 2015, p. 4). The rich resources of traditional Indigenous knowledge are clearly a place where one can expect to find grounds for Indigenous social innovation.

Grounded in distinct cosmology and cultural norms: all my relations

TIK is embedded in a cosmology, or worldview. While Indigenous cosmologies differ fundamentally around the world, they typically see the world as a place where "human and non-humans and others-than humans all dance their world into continued existence" (Apffel-Marglin, 2012, p. 18). The large variety and diversity of Indigenous peoples brings with it a multiplicity of cultural patterns. One substantial similarity that recurs in this multiplicity, however, is a conception of the unity of all beings and a profound interdependence of human, non-human and spiritual beings.

Rist (2000) provides a compelling example in his outline of the way that the Indigenous of the Bolivian Andes construct their agricultural practices, their economic interaction and their models of governance out of a cosmology that locates them and their communities in something like a comprehensive kinship relationship with one another, the natural world and the spiritual forces that govern it. This is vividly represented in the words of a campesino: "For us, potatoes are living beings; everyone has its own potato family. If we mistreat them, they get angry and tired and some day they will abandon us" (Rist, 2000, p. 311). Drahos and Frankel relate this sense of connectedness with nature to the place-based quality of Māori knowledge: "Rights over resources, and obligations such as that of being *kaitiaki*, are made concrete by being part of a group that is related to a place and is itself integrated into a network with human and non-human members (for example, the plants, animals, rivers of that place)" (2012a, p. 13). Turner holds that the cosmological view of the Indigenous in the Canadian West is captured in a phrase that is translated "everything is one" (2008, p. 179).

This idea of the unity of all beings is borne out, for example, in the concept of *buen vivir* that has taken hold in Latin America as an alternative to "development" (Lennon, 2015; Peredo, 2019; Walsh, 2010) and an example of the Indigenous resurgence movement. These holistic outlooks emerge in traditions of reciprocity and respect that extend beyond kin and tribal members to other inhabitants of the natural and supernatural world in what anthropologists Kew and Griggs label an "ethic of reciprocity" (1991, p. 27).

This is evident not only in the way that Indigenous peoples interact with their natural environment, but also in their economic (in the broadest sense) arrangements. Strong co-operative traditions within communities and groups are a standard feature of Indigenous societies. Forms of exchange that puzzle the standard analysis of neoclassical economists arise out of a "community orientation" in which community members experience their membership as resembling participation in the life of an organism, where their status and well-being is a function of mutual contributions to and from community (Peredo and Chrisman, 2006, p. 313). This outlook is reflected in a variety of institutions and traditions that function to balance individual/family interests with those of the community in which they have their being (Peredo and Chrisman, 2006). The concept of "inclusiveness" is thus a fundamental feature of the worldviews characteristic of Indigenous societies.

One outcropping of this inclusive view of society is a distinct and congruent conception of wealth. Turner captures the outlook of the Indigenous in the Pacific Northwest in a way that represents the perspective of many Indigenous communities: "Rich are those people who balance the benefits they receive in life with the responsibilities they assume for themselves, their families and communities, and their environment" (2008, p. 24). Thus, markets may be governed more by rules of barter than supply and demand, and they are surrounded by gift economies based on need and social relations rather than profit-seeking (Rist, 2000). Polanyi's view that market societies, which are taken to be a natural outgrowth of human nature, are in fact a recent invention, and market exchange only one mechanism for producing and distributing livelihood (Polanyi, 1944 [2001]), is richly illustrated in such traditions as the potlach system of the Indigenous in the Pacific Northwest (Trosper, 2003). A current example, which illustrates clearly the pattern of innovation built on combining ancient traditions with modern technology, is the network of community freezers operated by Inuit communities in Canada's far north. Recalling a time when hunters would collect food and then store it in permafrost locations open to everyone in the community, communities now use freezers for that purpose, contributing to food security for their members (Aningmiuq and Sarazin, 2018).

Clearly, this complex of distinctive cosmologies in which aspects of reality, natural and non-natural are seen as intimately connected, and the ways of interacting with other community members as well as the natural environment that flow from these worldviews, must be recognized as fertile ground from which Indigenous social innovation may emerge.

Grounded in a struggle for recovery from colonization, recovered sovereignty

A focus on recovering self-determination, or "sovereignty," constitutes something like a movement in Indigenous communities around the world. The emphasis on self-determination arises in the context of the profound and varied experience of colonization that is now built into the Indigenous sense of identity (Alfred and Corntassel, 2005). One Indigenous researcher felt challenged by her Pueblo communities to see sovereignty as a foundation for cultural recovery and survival (Enos, 2015). The drive for sovereignty is a drive for decolonization. As Indigenous scholar Corntassel puts it, "Being Indigenous today means struggling to reclaim and regenerate one's relational, place-based existence by challenging the ongoing, destructive forces of colonization" (2012, p.88). This outlook has led some Indigenous scholars to characterize the movement to recovery of self-reliance and sovereignty as "Indigenous resurgence" (Alfred and Corntassel, 2005; Corntassel, 2012; Simpson, 2008; Turner, 2007), emphasizing the recovery of Indigenous worldviews and connections with the land as the basis for a postcolonial identity. The discussion of this drive toward decolonization and recovered sovereignty that frequently occurs in the context of Indigenous innovation clearly marks that drive as a third place to look for Indigenous social innovation.

EXEMPLAR: THE T'SOU-KE FIRST NATION

In the previous section, we proposed three areas of Indigenous life and experience as rich with potential for generating social innovation: (1) traditional Indigenous knowledge; (2) distinct cosmologies and cultural forms; and (3) the struggle for recovered sovereignty. It seems certain that these sources, and perhaps others, have already been employed in important Indigenous social innovations; but there has been little attempt to search out and identify ISI, let alone study its scope and impact. Before proposing a research agenda aimed at stimulating those inquiries, we consider what could be considered a prototypical case: a bundle of connected innovations introduced by a Canadian First Nation with the aim of bettering their community.

> If you have a culture that has been carried on from your elders, your ancestors, you're going to know how things were protected, and saved, or used in a good way, so that it's still there for all generations to come. You have to know your culture and how people managed all these things years ago and use those today. (Linda Bristol, elder, founding member and cultural advisor of T'Sou-ke Arts Group)

T'Sou-ke is a small, Canadian First Nation of approximately 250 members located on the southern tip of Vancouver Island, approximately 30 kilometers (19 miles) southwest of the city of Victoria. Following colonization, the nation was confined to a fraction of its traditional territory and its members fell back on fisheries and the timber industry, for which their location and history gave them some capacity. They have remained active in those industries, though overexploitation by the non-Indigenous has considerably depleted the resources and activities associated with them, and other forms of maintenance have been limited to competing in a marketplace governed by colonial rules and large commercial enterprises. Like many Canadian First Nations, the community suffered from insecure employment.

The community's response to shrinking traditional resources and employment opportunities was a process and a project that has attracted widespread recognition for innovative projects in community-based renewable energy and food security. The results of that project, which is still being developed, have placed it on a path quite different from where recent history seemed to be leading. Underlying their endeavors has been the revitalization of traditional values, cultural practices and language, and the deliberate integration of these in the foundation of innovative development projects. Chief Gordon Planes locates their originality in a traditional worldview: "What we are doing is something that I believe we all should be doing . . . and we all should take care of Mother Earth before we can assure a healthy community and if we do that Mother Earth will be able to provide for us for our future generations" (Indigenous and Northern Affairs Canada, 2015).

In addition to housing the largest community solar project in British Columbia, the Nation has launched a number of other innovations that are leading the community to zero emissions and self-sufficiency, including food production, aquaculture and a revitalization of arts and culture. All are grounded in, and revitalizing, traditional cosmology and inherited skills. Their work toward sustainability has made them an eco-tourism destination, attracting more than 2,000 visitors a year for solar tours and education workshops (Troian, 2017).

The Community Planning Process: Seven Generations Ahead

The process began with the T'Sou-ke Nation, assisted by a community development facilitator, engaging in a community visioning process, involving citizens of the Nation from elders to children in identifying a comprehensive development vision. Inspired by their ancestral values and practices, including the community visioning of looking ahead seven generations, the Nation anchored their new economy in a traditional view of their culture and spirituality: "We used to live sustainably, and only took what we needed from the land. We need to get back to that" (Tammemagi, 2013). The outcome of that process was a plan that rested on four pillars: energy autonomy, food self-sufficiency, cultural renaissance and economic development.

In the visioning process, each community member was asked, "If you had the power to improve your community, what would you do?" One of the first goals that emerged was to pursue an energy-secure future for their nation (Ozog, 2012). T'Sou-ke felt faced with a challenge that called for social innovation – dealing with the environmental effects of hydrocarbon consumption, but also a specifically Indigenous challenge – energy dependency and energy deprivation (Ravotti, 2017; White Hawk, 2016).

In 2009, the T'Sou-ke Nation developed a plan for a Solar Community Program, secured funding for it from a variety of public and private sources, and went on to complete the installation of the largest solar photovoltaic installation in British Columbia. The installation is estimated to have reduced community energy use by 75 percent (Dodge and Kinney, 2013). "Facing climate change and increasing global oil prices, we knew that we wanted to become energy self-sufficient, and to not have to rely on the grid for power for evermore," says Chief Planes (Ozog, 2012, p. 50). The drive toward energy self-sufficiency arose naturally from a reimmersion in the First Nation's experience of having to live sustainably in their environment. As Chief Planes put it:

> First Nations have lived for thousands of years on this continent without fossil fuels. It is appropriate that First Nations lead the way out of dependency and addiction to fossil fuels and to rely on the power of the elements, the sun, the wind and the sea once again. (T'Sou-ke First Nation, 2017)

Community engagement with the visioning process helped reawaken this awareness, and made the achievement of an energy-secure future a top priority (Ozog, 2012). But the desire for energy autonomy was also rooted in a sensed need to recover political and social autonomy. "Power is power," says the community facilitator, "and becoming independent of the outside power grid means recovering some of our independence from the settler society that keeps the First Nations in a dependent relationship" (personal communication).

A Renaissance of Culture, Self-sufficiency and Sustainability

The Solar Community Program has attracted attention from other Indigenous and non-Indigenous communities across Canada and abroad. The initiative included the installation of a comprehensive photovoltaic system with a capacity of 75 kilowatts of energy from approximately 550 solar panels. The energy generated provides electrical needs for the Nation's offices and community hall, which are now net-zero in energy consumption, with any excess sold back to the BC Hydro grid. The program also included installing hot water systems employing roof-mounted thermal panels on many homes on the reserve, and an extensive energy-saving program providing direct cost savings to individuals within the community (Newell and King, 2013). The youth-driven T'Sou-ke Smart Energy Group has also provided behavioral training to encourage residents to turn down thermostats and reduce light usage. The ongoing goal is to get all buildings to net-zero energy usage.

Training community members in solar energy technology was an important part of the program. T'Sou-ke partnered with Home Energy Solutions, a solar electric contractor, and First Power, a "cultural interface" between technology companies, renewable experts and First Nations, to deliver training and technological expertise to nine community members, who were the principle installers for the T'Sou-ke project and have since worked in other communities on panel installation. Local artist Mark Gauti designed and etched a solar symbol on to one of the T'Sou-ke panels, adding an emphatic expression of culture to the technology and underlining a sense of community ownership.

Although the energy program, with its impressive installation of solar panels, is the center of attention for government, academics, tourists and other First Nations, it is, as pointed out above, only a part of a program aimed at increased self-sufficiency. The visioning process outcome of priorities for "energy security, food security, cultural renaissance and economic self-sufficiency" (Petrescu, 2014) emerged in a diverse portfolio of community-based enterprises, all grounded in traditional values and supporting the goal of self-sufficiency.

A Community Garden and "Ladybug Garden" grew from the vision for financial and food security for the community. The community garden program produces enough food for weekly gatherings, celebratory events and a box program for the elderly in the community. In addition to building resilience and community well-being, the garden program provides employment opportunities for youth and other members of the community. In 2014, the Nation started yet another enterprise and built three 35-by-150 feet greenhouses to grow wasabi, a plant best known as a piquant condiment for sushi. The cultivation and export of this cash crop in particular has become an important economic venture for the Nation, producing 15,000 plants per harvest. The community paid off its start-up costs with their first harvest, which brought in $100,000 in revenue (Troian, 2017).

The Nation has also launched a thriving aquaculture enterprise off their shores. A 82-hectare oyster farm produces 3 million oysters per harvest but with the capacity to grow up to 24 million oysters per harvest, leading to a partnership with the Chinese Canadian Aboriginal Development Enterprise to research the feasibility of farming oysters (Troian, 2017). The Nation plans to expand its operations to include sea cucumbers, another valuable cash crop for export.

Closely linked with these food security initiatives are activities meant to recover and sustain the traditional links with local food and medicines. Youth are taken on walks conducted by elders that reacquaint them with traditional resources and time-honored means of harvesting them respectfully (T'Sou-ke First Nation, 2017). A concern for food security is thus embedded in traditions not only of sustainability but a cosmology that unites people with an environment that is not just material.

In 2009 the community created T'Sou-ke Arts Group (TAG), a collection of carvers, knitters, weavers and artists, with the intention of restoring, reviving and living their culture. Organized as a non-profit organization TAG runs a number of workshops in the local community, and holds an annual arts sale, showcasing and selling Indigenous arts and crafts. In the words of Linda Bristol, founding member and cultural advisor of TAG,

> in order to know who you are and where you're from you need to know your culture. You can't move forward if you don't know what your identity is, and where you come from, and your culture within this community and your family. Art is something that we can be involved in right from being a very young child to for the rest of your life. (Personal interview)

One vital element in the process that underlies all these activities is represented in a document prominently displayed on the main meeting hall on the reserve's central space. It is a copy of the 1850 treaty by which the extensive T'Sou-ke traditional territories, apart from a small sector constituting the present reserves, became "the entire property of the white people for ever" in exchange for forty-eight pounds, six shillings and eight pence (Ministry of Aboriginal Relations and Reconciliation, 2006). Visitors to the reserve cannot help seeing the document, and its significance for the renewal processes underway in the Nation is quite apparent.

A Model that Travels

The T'Sou-ke model of social innovation has had an impact on neighboring non-Indigenous communities as well as communities continents away (Petrescu, 2014). A 2009 economic and technical study of the T'Sou-ke solar project concluded that similar solar installations could be even more beneficial in remote areas not served by conventional electrical grids.

The Indigenous community of Skidegate, located in the Haida Gwaii region of British Columbia, resembled most remote Indigenous communities in its heavy dependence on diesel-fueled generators for energy. Hearing about the T'Sou-ke undertaking aroused interest in the community, and in partnership with T'Sou-ke, they succeeded in securing funding first to study the application of T'Sou-ke's model to Skidegate, and then to produce their own version of it (Ozog, 2012). August of 2017 saw a 385-panel switched on and supplying energy to the community's heritage center. It was far from making the community self-sufficient in energy, but in the view of the community opens the way to such a future.

The Nation regularly acts as a mentor and advisor to communities throughout North America and has engaged with a variety of external associations, public and private partnerships. Their leadership in mitigating climate change has also attracted partnerships in national research projects, such as Indigenous Climate Action (ICA), an Indigenous-led initiative, represented through a coalition of individuals from different organizations, communities and regions whose mission is to fill the gaps between lived experiences of Indigenous peoples and policies and strategies being developed to address climate change.

Challenges Faced By Innovating Indigenous Communities

Indigenous communities share with other small communities a number of recurring challenges, as well as a number of potential difficulties that a history of colonization and marginalization has presented especially to Indigenous peoples.

Small communities, for instance, abound in "social capital," the product of networks in which trust and reciprocity may flourish (Portes, 1998; Putnam, with Leonardi and Nanetti, 1993). But social capital can have its drawbacks. Including people in networks, for example, can mean actively excluding others (Portes, 1998). Cliques develop, with their special interests and a sense of togetherness that excludes others and may be transmitted through kin and connections. Achieving a sense of shared purpose broad enough to sustain novel initiatives in these circumstances requires special efforts, which T'Sou-ke has fortunately been able to accomplish.

Indigenous peoples face challenges on top of these. They characteristically inherit in their settler setting a dependent status, thought to require close supervision and regulation, usually embodied in specific legislation and limiting their opportunity for independent initiative. They have frequently had their customary forms of self-governance replaced by imposed forms derived from the patterns of their colonizers, and live with the community tensions created by the coexistence of traditional and imposed governance models (see, for example, Ladner, 2006).

Scarcity of funding even for basic community needs is a serious and chronic problem for many, perhaps most Indigenous communities. Securing resources for special initiatives involving novelty is even more challenging, especially given the collective nature of Indigenous governance and decision-making that is hard for non-Indigenous governments and authorities to recognize. T'Sou-ke has been particularly inventive in identifying and pursuing grant opportunities.

Engaging Indigenous youth is crucial. This is a significant challenge for many Indigenous communities as their youth encounter the relentless spread of surrounding consumer cultures, requiring efforts that connect young people with their communities and traditions in ways that keep them alive and relevant.

The T'Sou-ke Nation seems to have surmounted these challenges remarkably, but in considering Indigenous social innovation generally, these challenges must be recognized and reckoned with.

Summary on T'Sou-ke

It is easy to discern in T'Sou-ke's initiative the pattern of endogenous support we hypothesize for Indigenous social innovation. It is clearly based in applying traditional knowledge to solving problems encountered by an Indigenous community; it is embedded in a traditional worldview that binds its people with their surroundings in a deep interdependence; and it expresses a desire to recover an autonomy that colonization has deprived them of. T'Sou-ke has attracted considerable attention for its innovation; though arguably, its rootedness in Indigenous foundations of the kind we suggest is under-appreciated.

What is particularly striking about the T'Sou-ke program of innovation is the way it embodies and advances the concept of inclusiveness. In fact, it could be said that the program is inclusive on at least three different levels. To begin with, the family of innovations, from solar panels through community gardens to arts groups, is built on seeing the community as fundamentally included in their natural and social environment in a way that is often lost sight of in modern societies. The holistic sense that so often characterizes Indigenous worldviews is borne out in the way that the innovations, which themselves are seen as interconnected, recall the community to a sense of inclusion with the natural and social forces that sustain them through reciprocal action. Second, the pattern of innovation is intensely inclusive in the way that it arises from a community visioning exercise that intentionally draws all voices in the community into the discussion, and not just those of people in power or with special interests. Inclusive community visioning requires that the goals of innovation, and the means by which they are pursued, have inclusive commitment and serve an inclusive purpose in a way that innovation often fails to achieve. Third, the T'Sou-ke social innovation has the effect of including their community as full, autonomous members of the wider society, respected for their distinctiveness and strengths, rather than second-class dependents meant for assimilation as the forces of colonization constructed them. This inclusive effect is achieved not by initiatives of outsiders wishing to benefit them, but by the community itself.

This multifaceted concept of inclusiveness is something we suggest needs to be brought to the study of social innovation in general. Indeed, our claim is that the T'Sou-ke phenomenon is the tip of an iceberg that embodies profound and inclusive social innovation but has scarcely begun to be recognized let alone explored and analysed. The potential of this iceberg calls for an energetic research program.

INDIGENOUS SOCIAL INNOVATION: A HISTORICAL, MULTILEVEL AND COMMUNITY-ENGAGED RESEARCH AGENDA

There is a large knowledge gap in management studies regarding Indigenous peoples in general and social innovation in particular. The formation of a "Native Caucus" at the 2013 meetings of the Academy of Management by a group of Indigenous and non-Indigenous scholars is among a number of developments signaling a growing interest in addressing that gap.

Historical context, multilevel analysis and community-based research methodologies are essential elements in advancing our understanding the process of ISI. Social innovation is always located in a historical, political and social context, as suggested earlier; but this is especially true in ISI. Current social and political circumstances for Indigenous peoples combine with historical forces to form an especially rich mixture that meets and interacts with technological innovation to create a diversity of unique environments for social innovation.

Inclusion, social justice and transformation of social relations are, for several researchers on social innovation, of central importance (Moulaert and Hillier, 2009). In considering ISI, these are absolutely fundamental. These factors generate large-scale questions such as: How do Indigenous communities' efforts toward improving the lives of their communities result in increased inclusion and social justice for their communities? Do these innovations transform their relations with mainstream society, and if so, in what ways and by what means? What internal and external barriers do the initiators of social innovation face in their efforts at transformation with respect to these factors?

Research on ISI innovation calls for an imaginative variety in conceptual basis for analysis. We noted above, for example, the recognition of a collectivist inclination in the social organization and outlook of Indigenous communities, and the way this flows from a tendency to a holistic perspective in worldviews. The collective perspective entails an interplay among individuals, families and communities that has not been easy to recognize and operationalize by researchers, business organizations and policy makers. Research into ISI will have to be inventive in its recognition of these dynamics not generally taken into account in management studies of social innovation.

Research into ISI should consider at least three levels of analysis: macro level, meso level and micro level. Macro-level analysis, for instance, would function at regional and national levels, and could take into account the influence of large-scale historical and socio-political factors, as well as institutional elements such as land tenure policies and property regimes. Land tenure and property regimes have been especially contested issues for Indigenous peoples in many regions and the relation of collectively held traditional knowledge to evolving conventions of intellectual property is a hotly debated topic (Drahos, 2011; Drahos and Frankel, 2012a). Meso-level analysis would focus on particular language groups within regional and national territories, and their distinguishing features that seem relevant to social innovation. Micro-level studies would consider factors that are characteristic of particular sub-groups such as "bands" or particular geographical gatherings within linguistically defined groups, perhaps even considering the role of particular kin or family factors. Box 7.1 illustrates the range of topics and issues that can be considered for building a research agenda at these various levels.

Box 7.1 is meant only to illustrate topics and issues, and there may well be an overlap among the different levels of analysis. Research designs that take into account and establish relations between the different levels – macro, meso and micro – could be particularly productive in understanding ISI processes and in theory building. In this chapter, we have made use of the emergent literature concerning Indigenous economies, Indigenous social entrepreneurship and Indigenous resurgence. The applications of other management theories and findings to ISI could be rewarding in both directions, creating useful research

BOX 7.1 A MULTILEVEL RESEARCH AGENDA

Institutional

- **Property rights**: For example, what land tenure regimes are most consistent with traditional Indigenous cultural practices and likely to facilitate positive ISI? How can Indigenous traditional knowledge and worldviews be respected in national and international regulation of intellectual property?
- **Political environment and forms of sovereignty**: For example, are there forms of settler government (e.g., unity states or federations) and political institutions (e.g., unicameral, bicameral or multicameral legislatures, varieties in court systems and jurisdictions) that are particularly favorable to ISI within its area of influence? What kinds of Indigenous sovereignty understandings (e.g., nation within nation, recovery of original lands, language) are most fruitful for ISI?
- **New relations**: For example, what kinds of policies and reports can facilitate ISI and open new spaces for new intercultural relations between Indigenous peoples and non-Indigenous peoples, fostering inclusion and appropriately transformed social relations? Are there examples of policies that work, or do not work, that need to be recognized and examined?
- **Funding**: What forms of funding would be most useful in supporting ISI initiatives?

Organizational or Indigenous Community

- **Social Innovation and ISI**: What are the main characteristics of ISI, and in what way do these distinguish ISI from non-Indigenous social innovation?
- **Goals and motivation**: What are the triggers/motivations that appear to lead to ISI? What is the role of spiritual practices in ISI? How do Indigenous worldviews shape the vision, goals and implementation of ISI?
- **Maintenance**: What are the cultural mechanisms maintaining ISI? Do the youth and elders play a distinctive role? What Indigenous cultural practices aimed at decolonization have informed ISI?
- **Impact**: What are the outcomes/impact of ISI in the well-being and long-term sustainability of the community? Are there particular forms of impact at various levels of analysis that are distinctive of ISI?
- **Leadership**: Are there characteristic forms of leadership and political arrangements at various levels that influence the creation, implementation and sustainability of ISI?
- **Resources and location**: Do natural resource endowments make a difference in the ISI process? Do the Indigenous in small remote communities tend to engage more in ISI? What are the characteristics of ISI as it occurs in concentrated rural locations as compared with ISI in dispersed urban settings? Are there differences in the motivation and/or goals of ISI between poor and rich country contexts? Are decolonization efforts a significant factor for ISI in poor countries?
- **Decolonization and sustainability**: How can ISI practices based on Indigenous knowledge and cosmology inform large society around decolonization and large sustainability issues?
- **Roles**: What is/can be the role(s) of intermediaries and facilitators (e.g., consultants, NGOs, governments, universities, financial institutions) in facilitating ISI processes?
- **Intercultural relations**: How do government policies, initiatives and reports on Indigenous peoples' circumstances – for example, on reconciliation – change relations, increase understanding of Indigenous worldviews and create space for ISI?
- **Media**: What is the role of the media in fostering ISI? What is the influence of the media in changing social relations between Indigenous and non-Indigenous populations?
- **Participation and motivation**: What motivates individuals to participate in ISI processes? What roles do individuals and families play in ISI? Are there characteristic patterns of transmission of ISI from various levels of organization?

- **Cultural identity**: What is the relation between ISI in arts, healing, cultural identity and economic development? How does ISI in arts contribute to community healing and the Indigenous resurgence process?
- **New technology and youth**: How do youth make use of digital social networks to reinforce Indigenous identity and build new intercultural relationships between Indigenous and non-Indigenous youth?

questions and illuminating ISI, while enhancing and deepening prevailing management theories. Research streams from entrepreneurship, for instance (innovation, community-based entrepreneurship and place-based entrepreneurship), as well as organization theory (motivation, leadership, diversity, identity, culture), strategy (goal settings, impacts), critical management (colonial and postcolonial, alternative organizations) and sustainability (natural environment and business) are all promising resources for exploring ISI, resources that may well be enriched by their new context.

RESEARCHING SOCIAL INNOVATION IN AN INDIGENOUS CONTEXT: SOME CHALLENGES

"Social innovation" is a concept developed in the environment of academic social science, especially management literature, and the application of notions developed in that setting to Indigenous life and circumstances often brings with it distorting assumptions (Peredo and McLean, 2013). There are risks in applying the idea of social innovation to the Indigenous context (Alexiuk, 2013, pp. 63ff). Indigenous peoples themselves often express skepticism about attempts to mingle Indigenous with non-Indigenous thought-forms (for example, Simpson, 2008). Further, it is easy to see how a non-Indigenous observer may have difficulty telling whether an idea or a product or a practice or their application is really something new, or something of long-standing but striking to an outsider. Likewise, some novelty in practice or principle may go unnoticed by a person not immersed in a particular community. The idea of what is to count as a benefit aimed at in innovation is perhaps even more subject to misunderstanding. If, as we suggest below, for instance, some Indigenous innovation is directed toward the recovery of autonomy and sovereignty, even where that may bring some material loss, recognizing this as a genuine benefit may take at least some cultural empathy.

More fundamentally still, some "innovations" occur in a context where Indigenous people engage in collaborative activity with non-Indigenous organizations in extractive or other activities on Indigenous land (Alexiuk, 2013, p. 65). Relationships of power, notions of what constitutes knowledge and what should be considered as cultural appropriation are foremost among the considerations that may load the idea of Indigenous social innovation with cultural, colonizing presuppositions.

One way of addressing the risks of applying a concept from academic social science, recognizing novelty, and cultural and colonizing assumptions, is to make the research into Indigenous innovation a matter of co-production, involving scholars in respectful dialogue with Indigenous persons and communities. The case study outlined above is developed out of such a process, where inappropriate assumptions may be exposed and questioned, and perspectives introduced that may surprise and enlighten researchers. A process of this kind is an essential element in research into Indigenous social innovation.

The concept, and realities, of social innovation are full of promise. Nowhere is that promise more needed that in the world's Indigenous communities. Research that explores the places where distinctively Indigenous social innovation might be found, and helps us understand how to enhance that innovation and amplify its impact not only in Indigenous communities but everywhere, could be transformational.

REFERENCES

Alexiuk, E. (2013). Exploring the common ground between social innovation and Indigenous resurgence: two critical indigenist case studies in indigenous innovation in Ontario, Canada. Master's thesis in Environmental Studies, University of Waterloo.

Alfred, T. (2005). *Wasáse: Indigenous Pathways of Action and Freedom*. Toronto, ON: University of Toronto Press.

Alfred, T. (2013). Being and becoming Indigenous: resurgence against contemporary colonialism. https://taiaiake.net/2013/12/13/being-and-becoming-indigenous-resurgence-against-contemporary-colonialism/ (accessed 18 December 2017).

Alfred, T. and Corntassel, J. (2005). Being Indigenous: resurgences against contemporary colonialism. *Government and Opposition*, 40(4), 597–614.

Anderson, R.B., Dana, L.P. and Dana, T.E. (2006). Indigenous land rights, entrepreneurship, and economic development in Canada: "opting-in" to the global economy. *Journal of World Business*, 41(1), 45–55.

Andrew, C. and Klein, J.-L. (2010). *Social Innovation: What is It and Why is It Important to Understand It Better?* (Collection of Theoretical Studies). Toronto, ON: Centre for Research on Social Innovation (CRISES), Université du Québec a Montréal.

Aningmiuq, A. and Sarazin, T. (2018). A path to community driven food innovation. *Stanford Social Innovation Review*, Winter. ttps://ssir.org/articles/entry/a_path_to_community_driven_food_innovation (accessed 10 November 2018).

Apffel-Marglin, F. (2012). *Subversive Spiritualities: How Rituals Enact the World*. Oxford and New York: Oxford University Press.

Athanasopoulos, P., Bylund, E., Montero-Melis, G. et al. (2015). Two languages, two minds: flexible cognitive processing driven by language of operation. *Psychological Science*, 26(4), 518–26.

Ayob, N., Teasdale, S. and Fagan, K. (2016). How social innovation "came to be": tracing the evolution of a contested concept. *Journal of Social Policy*, 45(4), 1–19.

Baker, T. and Nelson, R.E. (2005). Creating something from nothing: resource construction through entrepreneurial bricolage. *Administrative Science Quarterly*, 50(3), 329–66.

Banerjee, S. and Tedmanson, D. (2010). Grass burning under our feet: Indigenous enterprise development in a political economy of whiteness. *Management Learning*, 41(2), 147–65.

Barnhardt, R. (2005). Indigenous knowledge systems and Alaska native ways of knowing. *Anthropology & Education Quarterly*, 36(1), 8–23.

Berkes, F. and Adhikari, T. (2006). Development and conservation: Indigenous businesses and UNDP equator initiative. *International Journal of Entrepreneurship and Small Business*, 3(6), 671–90.

Bryan, B. (2000). Property as ontology: on Aboriginal and English understandings of ownership. *Canadian Journal of Law and Jurisprudence*, 3, 3–31.

Chhetri, N. and Chhetri, N. (2015). Alternative imaginations. In E.S. Huaman and B. Sriraman (eds), *Indigenous Innovation: Universalities and Peculiarities* (pp. 11–23). Rotterdam: Sense Publishers.

Corntassel, J. (2012). Re-envisioning resurgence: Indigenous pathways to decolonization and sustainable self-determination. *Decolonization: Indigeneity, Education & Society*, 1(1), 86–101.

Dana, L.P. (2015). Indigenous entrepreneurship: an emerging field of research. *International Journal of Business and Globalisation*, 14(2), 158–69.

Di Domenico, M., Haugh, H. and Tracey, P. (2010). Social bricolage: theorizing social value creation in social enterprises. *Entrepreneurship Theory and Practice*, 34(4), 681–703.

Dodge, D. and Kinney, D. (2013). T'sou-ke First Nation goes all in on energy conservation and solar. http://www.greenenergyfutures.ca/episode/38-tsou-ke-first-nation-goes-all-energy-conservation-and-solar (accessed 3 October 2017).

Drahos, P. (2011). When cosmology meets property: Indigenous people's innovation and intellectual property. *Prometheus*, 29(3), 233–52. doi:10.1080/08109028.2011.638213

Drahos, P. and Frankel, S. (2012a). Indigenous peoples' innovation and intellectual property: the issues. In P. Drahos and S. Frankel (eds), *Indigenous Peoples' Innovation: Intellectual Property Pathways to Development* (pp. 1–28). Canberra: ANU E Press.
Drahos, P. and Frankel, S. (eds) (2012b). *Indigenous People's Innovation: Intellectual Property Pathways to Development*. Canberra: ANU E Press.
Dudgeon, R.C. and Berkes, F. (2003). Local understandings of the land: traditional ecological knowledge and Indigenous knowledge. In H. Selins (ed.), *Nature Across Cultures* (pp. 75–96). Dordrecht: Springer.
Enos, A.D. (2015). Deep sovereignty. In E.S. Huaman and B. Sriraman (eds), *Indigenous Innovation: Universalities and Peculiarities* (pp. 25–42). Rotterdam, Boston, MA and Taipei: Sense Publishers.
Government of Canada (2010). "Social innovation": What is it? Who does it? *Policy Research Initiative*. http://www.horizons.gc.ca/sites/default/files/Publication-alt-format/2010-0032-eng.pdf (accessed 18 October 2017).
Hall, G. and Gandolfo, A. (2016). Poverty and exclusion among Indigenous peoples: the global evidence. *Voices on Development*. https://blogs.worldbank.org/voices/poverty-and-exclusion-among-indigenous-peoples-global-evidence (accessed 23 November 2017).
Herman, M. (2018). The critical role of traditional knowledge in social innovation. *Stanford Social Innovation Review*, Winter.
Heyd, T. (1995). Indigenous knowledge, emancipation and alienation. *Knowledge and Policy*, 8(1), 63–73.
Hindle, K. and Moroz, P. (2010). Indigenous entrepreneurship as a research field: developing a definitional framework from the emerging canon. *International Entrepreneurship and Management Journal*, 6(4), 357–85.
Huaman, E.S. and Sriraman, B. (eds) (2015). *Indigenous Innovation: Universalities and Peculiarities*. Rotterdam, Boston, MA and Taipei: Sense Publishers.
Indigenous and Northern Affairs Canada (2015). T'sou-ke First Nation: a leader in the innovative use of renewable energy in Canada. https://www.aadnc-aandc.gc.ca/eng/1360179335542/1360179499959 (accessed 3 October 2017).
Kawagley, A.O. and Barnhardt, R. (1998). Education indigenous to place: Western science meets native reality. *Journal of Research in Science Teaching*, 35(2), 133–44.
Kew, M. and Griggs, J.R. (1991). Native Indians of the Fraser Basin: towards a model of sustainable resource use. In H.J. Dorsey (ed.), *Perspectives on Sustainable development in Water Management: Towards Agreement in the Fraser River Basin* (pp. 17–47). Vancouver, BC: Westwater Research Centre, University of British Columbia.
Krieken, R. (2004). Rethinking cultural genocide: Aboriginal child removal and settler-colonial state formation. *Oceania*, 75(2), 125–51.
Kuokkanen, R. (2011). From Indigenous economies to market-based self-governance: a feminist political economy analysis. *Canadian Journal of Political Science*, 44(2), 275–97.
Ladner, K.L. (2006). Indigenous governance: questioning the status and the possibilities for reconciliation with Canada's commitment to Aboriginal and treaty rights. National Centre for First Nations Governance. http://epub.sub.uni-hamburg.de/epub/volltexte/2012/12730/pdf/kiera_ladner.pdf (accessed 20 November 2017).
Lennon, K.M. (2015). Local knowledge, cultural economies. In E.S. Huaman and B. Sriraman (eds), *Indigenous Innovation: Universalities and Peculiarities* (pp. 57–79). Rotterdam, Boston, MA and Taipei: Sense Publishers.
McCarthy, D.D.P., Millen, M., Boyden, M. et al. (2014). A First Nations-led social innovation: a moose, a gold mining company, and a policy window. *Ecology and Society*, 19(4). doi:10.5751/ES06771190402
Menzies, C.R. (2006). *Traditional Ecological Knowledge and Natural Resource Management*. Lincoln, NE: University of Nebraska Press.
Miller, J.R. and Marshall, T. (2017). Residential schools. http://www.thecanadianencyclopedia.ca/en/article/residential-schools/ (accessed 21 December 2017).
Ministry of Aboriginal Relations and Reconciliation (2006). http://www.llbc.leg.bc.ca/public/pubdocs/bcdocs/406899/history_payment.pdf (accessed 2 January 2018).
Moller, H., Berkes, F., Lyver, P.O.B. and Kislalioglu, M. (2004). Combining science and traditional ecological knowledge: monitoring populations for co-management. *Ecology and Society*, 9(3).
Moulaert, F. and Hillier, J. (2009). What is social innovation? And why is it politically relevant? Paper presented at Social Innovation: An Opportunity for Europe?, Brussels. http://katarsis.ncl.ac.uk/ws/documents/Katarsispoliocybrief1-50ct2009.pdf (accessed 3 November 2017).
Mulgan, G. (2006). Cultivating the other invisible hand of social entrepreneurship: comparative advantage, public policy, and future research priorities. In A. Nicholls (ed.), *Social Entrepreneurship: New Paradigms of Sustainable Social Change* (pp. 74–95). Oxford: Oxford University Press.
Mulgan, G., Tucker, S., Ali, R. and Sanders, B. (2007). *Social Innovation: What It is, Why It Matters, and How It Can Be Accelerated*. London: The Young Foundation. http://eureka.sbs.ox.ac.uk/761/1/Social_Innovation.pdf (accessed 10 November 2017).
National Association of Friendship Centres (2015). *Indigenous Innovation Summit Report 2015*. http://nafc.ca/wp-content/themes/nafc_new/assets/summit2015/assets/pdf/NAFC_IISReport2015_Web.pdf (accessed 5 December 2017).

Newell, R. and King, L. (2013). T'sou-ke. http://www.mc-3.ca/tsou-ke

Ng'asike, J.T. and Swadener, B.B. (2015). Turkana Indigenous knowledge. In E.S. Huaman and B. Sriraman (eds), *Indigenous Innovation: Universalities and Peculiarities* (pp. 107–27). Rotterdam, Boston, MA and Taipei: Sense Publishers.

Nikolakis, W. (2010). Barriers to indigenous enterprise development on communally owned land. *Global Business and Economics Review*, 12(1), 85–99.

Ozog, S. (2012). *Towards First Nations Energy Self-sufficiency: Analyzing the Renewable Energy Partnership Between T'sou-ke Nation and Skidegate Nand.* Prince George, BC: University of Northern British Columbia.

Peredo, A.M. (2012). The difference culture makes: the competitive advantage of reciprocal, non-monetary exchange. In L. Mook, J. Quarter and S. Ryan (eds), *Businesses with a Difference: Balancing the Social and Economic* (pp. 87–110). Toronto, Buffalo and London: University of Toronto Press.

Peredo, A.M. (2019, in press). *El "buen vivir"*: notions of wellbeing among Indigenous peoples of South America. In M. Manning, C. Fleming and A. Miller (eds), *Routledge Handbook of Indigenous Wellbeing*. London: Routledge.

Peredo, A.M. and Anderson, R.B. (2006). Indigenous entrepreneurship research: themes and variations. In C.S. Galbraith and C.H. Stiles (eds), *Developmental Entrepreneurship: Adversity, Risk, and Isolation* (pp. 253–73). Oxford: Elsevier.

Peredo, A.M. and Chrisman, J.J. (2006). Toward a theory of community-based enterprise. *Academy of Management Review*, 31(2), 309–28.

Peredo, A.M. and McLean, M. (2006). Social entrepreneurship: a critical review of the concept. *Journal of World Business*, 41(1), 56–65. doi:10.1016/j.jwb.2005.10.007

Peredo, A.M. and McLean, M. (2013). Indigenous development and the cultural captivity of entrepreneurship. *Business & Society*, 52(4), 592–620. doi:10.1177/0007650309356201

Peredo, A.M., Anderson, R.B., Galbraith, C.S., Benson, H. and Dana, L.P. (2004). Towards a theory of Indigenous entrepreneurship. *International Journal of Entrepreneurship and Small Business*, 1(1/2), 1–20.

Petrescu, S. (2014). Island First Nation grasps potential of alternative power. *Times Colonist*, 5 January. http://www.timescolonist.com/news/local/island-first-nation-grasps-potential-of-alternative-power-1.779062

Phills, Jr, J.A., Deiglmeier, K. and Miller, D.T. (2008). Rediscovering social innovation. *Stanford Social Innovation Review*, Fall, 34–43.

Pol, E. and Ville, S. (2009). Social innovation: buzz word or enduring term? *The Journal of Socio-Economics*, 38(6), 878–85.

Polanyi, K. (1944). *The Great Transformation: The Political and Economic Origins of Our Time*. Reprinted in 2nd Beacon Paperback (2001). Boston, MA: Beacon Press.

Portes, A. (1998). Social capital: its origins and applications in modern sociology. *Annual Review of Sociology*, 24(1), 1–24.

Putnam, R.D., with Leonardi, R. and Nanetti, R. (1993). *Making Democracy Work: Civic Traditions in Modern Italy*. Princeton, NJ: Princeton University Press.

Ravotti, N.M. (2017). Access to energy in Indian country: the difficulties of self-determination in renewable energy development. *American Indian Law Review*, 41(2), 279–318.

Rist, S. (2000). Linking ethics and the market: campesino economic strategies in the Bolivian Andes. *Mountain Research and Development*, 20(4), 310–15.

Sigurdarson, B. (ed.) (2009). *The State of the World's Indigenous Peoples*. New York: United Nations.

Simpson, L. (2008). *Lighting the Eighth Fire: The Liberation, Resurgence, and Protection of Indigenous Nations*. Winnipeg, MB: Arbeiter Ring Publishing.

T'Sou-ke First Nation (2017). Ladybug garden & greenhouse. http://www.tsoukenation.com/ladybug-garden-greenhouse/ (accessed 15 October 2017).

Tammemagi, H. (2013). Old ways, new path: how the T'sou-ke nation is powering its cultural revitalization. http://www.alternativesjournal.ca/people-and-profiles/old-ways-new-path (accessed 18 December 2017).

Tapsell, P. and Woods, C. (2008). A spiral of innovation framework for social entrepreneurship: social innovation at the generational divide in an Indigenous context. *Emergence: Complexity and Organization*, 10(3), 25–34.

Tapsell, P. and Woods, C. (2010). Social entrepreneurship and innovation: self-organization in an indigenous context. *Entrepreneurship and Regional Development*, 22(6), 535–56.

Tomlins-Jahnke, H. and Forster, M. (2015). Waewaetakamiria. In E.S. Huaman and B. Sriraman (eds), *Indigenous Innovation: Universalities and Peculiarities* (pp. 43–55). Rotterdam, Boston and Taipei: Sense Publishers.

Troian, M. (2017). B.C. First nation leads with green technology, sustainability. http://www.cbc.ca/news/indigenous/tsou-ke-nation-green-energy-leaders-1.4067833 (accessed 18 December 2017).

Trosper, R. (2003). Resilience in pre-contact Pacific Northwest social ecological systems. *Conservation Ecology*, 7(3).

Turner, N.J. (2008). *The Earth's Blanket: Traditional Teachings for Sustainable Living*. Vancouver, BC: D & M Publishers.

Turner, T. (2007). Indigenous resurgence, anthropological theory, and the cunning of history. *Focaal*, 49, 118–23.
United Nations Permanent Forum on Indigenous Issues (2017). Who are Indigenous peoples? http://www.un.org/esa/socdev/unpfii/documents/5session_factsheet1.pdf (accessed 11 December 2017).
Vogel, D. (2007). *The Market for Virtue: The Potential and Limits of Corporate Social Responsibility*. Washington, DC: Brookings Institution Press.
Volynets, I. (2015). Social innovation and Aboriginal communities. http://uakn.org/wp-content/uploads/2015/11/UAKN-Social-Innovation-and-Aboriginal-Communities-Policy-Recommendations-March-20152.pdf (accessed 8 December 2017).
Waddell, S. (1999). Business–government–nonprofit collaborations as agents for social innovation and learning. Paper presented at the Academy of Management, Chicago.
Walsh, C. (2010). Development as buen vivir: institutional arrangements and (de) colonial entanglements. *Development*, 53(1), 15–21.
Westley, F. (2008). The social innovation dynamic. SiG@Waterloo working paper. http://sigeneration.ca/blog/wp-content/uploads/2010/07/TheSocialInnovationDynamic.pdf (accessed 24 October 2010).
White Hawk, R.M. (2016). Community-scale solar: watt's in it for Indian country. *Environs: Environmental Law & Policy Journal*, 40, 1–19.
World Bank (2011). Indigenous peoples policy brief: still among the poorest of the poor. http://siteresources.worldbank.org/EXTINDPEOPLE/Resources/407801-1271860301656/HDNEN_indigenous_clean_0421.pdf (accessed 10 November 2011).

8. Urban innovation: at the nexus of urban policy and entrepreneurship

Jeffrey A. Robinson, Amol M. Joshi, Lutisha Vickerie-Dearman and Todd Inouye

INTRODUCTION

In *Cities are Good For You: The Genius of the Metropolis* (2013), Leo Hollis describes society's love/hate relationship with cities. We love them because they are the amalgamation of our creativity, innovation, and entrepreneurship; we love them because of their role in education, economy, and culture. And, yet, we are also discouraged and discontented by the inequality, inequity, and incredible level of social problems and despair that coincide with the wealth and culture of the place.

Social innovators are making a difference by addressing social problems found within urban contexts and boosting the economy via new policy and governance approaches (Gerometta et al., 2005) and the use of new and innovative business models that create social value (Mueller et al., 2015; Robinson and Dougherty, 2014). Policymakers are attempting to catalyse and nurture social innovation in urban areas with entrepreneurship policies that provide incentives to foster new ventures tailored to advance social inclusion in the improvement of urban economies (Ham et al., 2011; Jones, 2007; Robinson, 2007). While there are a number of emerging success stories of social innovation, many efforts fall short or suffer from unintended systematic and structural challenges that result from competing political, social, and cultural processes along with misaligned economic incentives (Bondonio and Greenbaum, 2007; Busso et al., 2013; Freedman, 2013; Hanson, 2009; Joshi, 2014; Kolko et al., 2013; Ludwig et al., 2008; Neumark and Kolko, 2010). The deployment of relevant business models such as social enterprise (Kerlin, 2006), venture accelerators (Erikson, 2003), triple bottom line ventures (Magala et al., 2007), benefits corporations (Di Domenico et al., 2009), and technology parks (Lundström and Zhou, 2011) is a key aspect of addressing urban issues and problems. Therefore, urban innovation represents processes developed by and outcomes that result from the interplay of social inclusion and innovation. Our aim is to synthesize the current attempts to encourage social innovation from a policy perspective and to describe the various business models that are used to enact innovative solutions to urban challenges. Thus, the phenomenon we examine is social inclusion through urban innovation.

After defining what we mean by urban innovation, we take two steps towards explaining the types of critical actors and strategic actions in this space. First, we explore a range of urban entrepreneurship policies and public–private partnerships designed to support social inclusion in innovation in the United States, Europe, Asia, and Australia. Second, we categorize several types of business models that are used in the urban policy environments. As such, we highlight a balanced mix of vivid, contemporary examples of urban innovations and their underlying business models from urban policy experiments and social inclusion initiatives around the world.

We build upon recent studies in management, economics, sociology, law, and public policy to provide a framework for scholars, entrepreneurs, and policymakers to understand the theoretical underpinnings and practical implications of urban innovation (Borzaga and Bodini, 2014; Cajaiba-Santana, 2014; George et al., 2012; Joshi et al., 2018; Moulaert et al., 2007). We conclude by presenting some future research directions and advice for academic researchers and practitioners hoping to make a difference in urban areas.

DEFINING URBAN INNOVATION

To define urban innovation, we build on the Rockefeller Foundation's definition of innovation to create our definition of urban innovation:

> a break from previous practice, occurring when different points of view or existing practices are framed, imagined, or combined in new ways. Innovation succeeds when it creates new pathways for solving entrenched social problems, resulting in lasting transformation of the systems that most affect vulnerable populations and leave stronger social relationships in their wake. (Rodin, 2013, p. 2)

Therefore, we define urban innovation as *a break from common practice to develop long-lasting transformations in urban communities, neighborhoods, and cities.*

We would further add emphasis to this definition by highlighting two overarching principles that should drive impactful urban innovation – social inclusion and transformation. For an urban innovation to be impactful, it must be socially inclusive – meaning that the actors, activities, and main beneficiaries represent various parts of the economy and society (George et al., 2012). Inclusion allows for interaction across social groups and benefits society by reducing socio-economic separation through developing stronger, and even new, relationships in the community (Mulgan et al., 2007). By transformation, we mean that the purpose of urban innovation is to change the circumstances or outcomes of beneficiaries (Landry, 2012). Transformation does not imply surface change; it means deep-seated change that remodels the mindset and creates new change agents (Landry, 2012). Both of these principles allow us to separate innovative activities that are small and incremental from urban innovations that have the potential to impact the economy and society in major ways.

MAJOR THEMES OF INCLUSIVE URBAN INNOVATION

Major themes within the scholarly work on inclusive urban innovation center on processes and outcomes for fixing the negative externalities caused by unequal wealth and resource distribution in communities that are historically disenfranchised (George et al., 2012). Impactful frameworks provided by the research in the field reveal localized social inclusion issues through the dynamic effects of the inhabitants, attempting to move away from the past mechanical and ineffective solutions applied to grand structural challenges (Landry, 2012).

In the second edition of his widely cited book, Charles Landry (2012) focuses on how a creative milieu is essential to transforming cities through strategic urban planning and providing the platform for sustainable innovation. To achieve urban equilibrium in light of the socio-economic gaps that exist within the base of the pyramid communities, Landry positions "wealth creation and social cohesion . . . as two sides of the same coin" (Landry, 2012, p. 164). In disagreeing with the notion that successful cities arise from happenstance or geographical abundance of resources, Landry provides the following strategy-making process for crafting creative cities, which features five components:

> [The process features five components of] planning; establishing indicators; execution; assessment; and reporting back. Within each phase there are key analytical tools including preparation and planning, assessing potential, devising indicators, execution, communicating and disseminating. (Landry, 2012, p. 168)

The *cycle of urban creativity*, *cultural resource mapping*, and the *innovation matrix* are additional tools, amongst others, that Landry provides to distinguish his toolkit as being a sustainable, cyclical process that effectively builds upon past project experience. Additionally, Landry's open-minded and holistic toolkit and strategy-making process address current issues in the approaches used for redressing grand structural and local social challenges. Landry's (2012) holistic approach enables decision makers to craft inclusive environments for urban economic development that is person-centered and balances static and dynamic issues, economic and social concerns, nature and nurture human characteristics, and the effect of names and titles of agencies and departments providing social services.

Also taking a person-centered approach to social innovation in support of social change, Mulgan et al.'s (2007) work puts forth a social innovation theory based on "connected difference." The authors' theory capitalizes on the benefits of connecting differences through combinations of existing resources being enacted across various organizational units with differing disciplines. These combinations in resources and organizational units create "new social relationships between previously separate individuals and groups," enable sustainability of the innovation through diffusion and embedding into society and establish a cycle whereby innovations build upon one another and welcomes future innovations (Mulgan et al., 2007, p. 5). Similarly, looking primarily at innovations in personal relations within society, Moulaert et al.'s (2013) book connects societal needs with political empowerment and mobilization. The authors believe that the researchers and practitioners of social innovation need to connect more with policy and public funding for successful socially innovative actions and practices.

When building relative frameworks that can merge the processes and outcomes of social innovation and public policy, George et al.'s (2012, p. 661) review of inclusive social innovation research sets up four aspects to be considered: (1) "inequalities that arise in development and commercialization of innovations . . . and that may occur as a result of value creation and capture"; (2) process led by organizations that try to address the inequalities and disenfranchisement of individuals and communities using social innovation activities; (3) inclusive growth as an outcome; and (4) tests of true growth. Inclusive growth as an outcome looks at "improvements in social and economic well-being of communities that have structurally been denied access to resources, capabilities and opportunities" (George et al., 2012, p. 661). Tests of true growth ask how much the trade-offs between growth and inequality are diminished based on jobs, "customers, employees, owners, suppliers and community members" (George et al., 2012, p. 662).

These four works presented in this section inform the path to achieving transformation and building inclusivity. With these definitional points and scholarly perspectives in mind, in the next section we present a framework for doing just that and four types of business model innovations used in the urban context that are transformative and inclusive.

ACHIEVING URBAN INNOVATION

To achieve urban transformation, Blockson (2003; Blockson and Van Buren, 1999) notes that multi-sector approaches must be used to address the complex problems of urban areas. Therefore, the private sector, public sector, and social sector must all be engaged to address the challenges. Here, we present a useful framework for organizing the urban entrepreneurship policy innovations and then demonstrate how business models used by the private and social sector are utilized in these different policy contexts to urban innovation.

Innovations in Urban Entrepreneurship Policy

In an insightful paper about social innovation in urban governance, Gerometta et al. (2005, p. 2015) write about strategies to create a more inclusive city:

> New policy approaches, such as integrated area approaches to social urban development, may provide a "window of opportunity" to new groups to be brought into the institutional frame of the governance of place (Tarrow 1994). Social innovation in urban governance relations means the establishment of new links and new relations, crossing the emerging lines of fragmentations, where ties have been abandoned as a result of social exclusion processes.

Here, we argue that new policy approaches are also necessary in urban entrepreneurship policy. Previous research has indicated the importance of public entrepreneurship policy on urban development and urban innovation (Jones, 2007; Mueller et al., 2015; Robinson, 2007; Robinson and Dougherty, 2014). As Robinson (2007, p. 107) writes:

> The relevance of formal and informal community institutional structures is also overlooked by simplistic approaches to urban economic development. The influence that these structures have on the identification of business opportunity and the survival of these businesses underscores the complexity of the context.

Urban innovations in the policy arena can address the complexity of the urban context and incentivize the "right" economic activities. These urban policy innovations allow for the various business model innovations that are transformative and inclusive to exist and flourish. We categorize these policy-oriented innovations as *market creating*, *market integration*, and *market incentivizing* (Table 8.1) and highlight several urban policy initiatives within the categories. Frankly, these innovations in urban entrepreneurship policy have had varying levels of success. However, they have influenced how entrepreneurship is enacted in their cities and urban areas.

Table 8.1 Policy innovations and urban innovation business models

	Market Creating	Market Incentivizing	Market Integrating
Urban Policy Innovation	Policies that act as a catalyst to stimulate new venture creation and enable longevity of existing ventures to remain in or relocate to urban areas	Policies that provide companies with incentives to use innovative business models to address social, environmental, and economic issues simultaneously	Policies that encourage existing markets to (1) consider more than just economic returns when developing contract opportunities and (2) develop strategies to include groups that have historically been left out of economic opportunities and integrate them into the broader economy
Business Models Used for Urban Innovation	• Social Enterprise • Venture Accelerator (when focused on social and/ or environmental objectives)	• Sustainable Entrepreneurship • B-Corp/Benefits Corporation • Technology Innovation Park	• Social Enterprise • Micro-finance Organization • Venture Accelerators (when used to support under-represented entrepreneurs)

Market creating

Market creating policies act as a catalyst to stimulate new venture creation and enable longevity of existing ventures to remain in or relocate to urban areas. By providing attractive benefits for company operations, these policies ensure that urban areas can become areas of job creation and economic development. We offer three examples of this type of policy innovation.

HUBZone Program (US) Since 1997, the Historically Underutilized Business Zones (HUBZone) Program in the United States has provided eligible small businesses with preferential access to federal procurement. In order to be eligible, the company must be a small business by Small Business Administration (SBA) standards and be 51 percent or more owned by a US citizen, Community Development Corporation, agricultural cooperative, or Indian tribe. Of key importance is that the company's headquarters must be located in a HUBZone and that at least 35 percent of its employees must reside in a HUBZone (as noted on their website),[1] thus promoting local hiring in urban areas.

The Empowerment Zone/Enterprise Community Program (US) This federal policy was designed to address years of underinvestment and underutilization of urban areas in some of the largest cities of the United States. By directing funding, resources, and technical assistance to a specific urban area, the Empowerment Zone/Enterprise Community Program attempted to merge external capital with local expertise. In the most successful zones and communities, the combination yielded new businesses, new jobs, and economic growth. In the less successful areas, politics and power structures maintained the status quo and these cities struggled to see social and economic gains (Ham et al., 2011; Oakley and Tsao, 2006). Nevertheless, the urban innovation demonstrated by this program represents a change in the governmental approach to urban entrepreneurship policy (Bondonio and Greenbaum, 2007; Robinson, 2007).

URBACT (EU) This program is a European Union (EU)-wide policy for sustainable urban development. URBACT is supported by €100 million in funding and spans 550 cities in 30 countries and 7,000 active stakeholders.[2] URBACT's focus is on sharing and exchanging knowledge across participants to improve the delivery, design, and implementation of urban policies throughout Europe.[3] Given the vast differences in size, scope, and scale among EU member nations, URBACT's programmatic efforts range from reducing energy consumption in heavily industrialized areas (Lewis et al., 2013), to reforming property rights in economically blighted cities (Aunsborg, 2007), to catalysing digital innovation clusters in creative centers (van Winden and de Carvalho, 2015a), to promoting sustainable tourism to culturally significant destinations (van Winden and de Carvalho, 2015b).

In these three examples, the place-based, community investment approach to urban entrepreneurship policy (Robinson, 2007) opens the door to new and underserved markets. Businesses that are developed or that move into these areas can and often do create jobs and opportunities for local residents. Many business models can work in this context.

Market integration

A market integration approach encourages existing markets to (1) consider more than just economic returns when developing contract opportunities and (2) develop strategies to include groups that have historically been left out of economic opportunities and integrate them into the economy. We offer two examples of policies that fall into this category.

Social procurement policy (Australia) As defined in the national report on the subject, social procurement "relates to how the purchase of goods, services and works by organizations can generate positive social impacts" (Burkett, 2010, p. 10). In practice, this Australian policy allows government agencies to choose social enterprises and other sustainable businesses in the procurement process over other businesses because the practices of these businesses promote more significant societal benefit. In doing so, the procurement process of governmental agencies promotes inclusion and economic development. Therefore, social procurement is especially applicable in urban areas.

Supplier diversity programs (US) Such programs are designed to increase the number of socially disadvantaged businesses providing goods and services to large companies. These types of policies have existed for many years in the private sector to support ethnic minority-owned and woman-owned business enterprises. As described in Shah and Ram (2006), private sector companies are not required by law to have supplier diversity programs but in recent years have found there is an economic and social justice rationale for contracting with and purchasing from diverse suppliers. These initiatives take on many forms. In the United States, the National Supplier Diversity Council describes the purpose of its programs as "Certify, Develop, Connect, and Advocate."[4] They work in collaboration with corporate partners who have set supplier diversity goals. Most programs provide active capacity building, technical assistance and mentorship of the ethnic minority-owned and woman-owned businesses. It has been noted that many (but certainly not all) minority-owned business are in and around urban areas and also hire more minority employees than other firms (Fairchild, 2008; Fairchild and Robinson, 2008). Therefore, these policies can provide significant mechanisms for economic development.

In these two examples of market integrating urban policy innovations, it is clear that promoting more integration in society is the broad and important goal. By developing business models and business approaches that fit these goals, entrepreneurs can impact social and economic issues in urban areas.

Market incentivizing

Market incentivizing activities provide companies with incentives to use innovative business models to address social, environmental, and economic issues simultaneously. Urban innovation received a major boost when legislative bodies in the United States and United Kingdom began to change their corporate legal code to include various forms of social enterprises. Policymakers saw the need to provide legal methods that would allow businesses to consider business functions of benefit to non-shareholder stakeholders, such as the community-at-large (Brakman Reiser, 2014). These considerations are useful when having to make a decision for the company that may not maximize profit, but may maximize another social good.

New Markets Tax Credits (NMTC) program (US) As a US federal-level program, NMTC initiatives "aims to break [the] cycle of disinvestment by attracting the private investment necessary to reinvigorate struggling local economies." [5] It accomplishes this investment by incentivizing the market economy to make significant investments into mostly urban areas. These tax credits function as an incentive for equity investments, not grants or other charitable contributions. This is in line with Porter's (1995) assertion that market development in urban areas will lead to economic development.

Sustainable Business Tax Credit program (US) This local municipality program is available in the City of Philadelphia for "sustainable" businesses that operate in the city limits. It is facilitated by the Office of Sustainability and allows businesses to lower their liability for the Business Income and Receipts Tax. This tax credit "encourages sustainable business practices in Philadelphia and encourages the growth of the local clean economy."[6] Certified B-Corps and benefits corporations are automatically able to take advantage of the tax credits. If a business is not certified, then they first provide a document summarizing their business model, employee and community interactions, impact on the environment, governance, and transparency. Second, they must present how the core business purposes meet specific sustainability criteria. Once the business has been approved, they are eligible for a tax credit equal to the applicant's total Business Income and Receipts Tax liability.

In both of these examples, the policy innovation did not lead to the business models. The business models were already being utilized. These policies were developed to provide these business models with more flexibility to exist and incentivized the use of these business models towards broader societal goals.

Business models as outcomes or antecedents of policy innovation

Urban areas can be challenging places to operate in because of the extremes of inequality and social disorganization. In order to operate in these areas, policymakers have recognized and in some cases responded to the need to encourage business models that are effective at addressing social and economic issues, including inclusivity and transformation. These business models can be understood as tests of true inclusive growth, called for by George et al. (2012). We define three urban business model innovations and sub-types along with examples below. In some cases, the policy innovations are created after observing these business models in action. In other cases, the policy innovations resulted in new business models that address social and economic issues of urban areas.

Social entrepreneurship business models

We define social entrepreneurship broadly as a business model approach that incorporates social goals and economic objectives into its operations and activities (Mair et al., 2006; Robinson, 2006). There are variations on this business model that constitute innovative approaches to specific types of social issues and in this case urban problems. Sustainable entrepreneurship/businesses, micro-finance organizations, social enterprises, and Benefit Corporations are all examples of social entrepreneurship business models that have been successfully used in urban areas.

Sustainable entrepreneurship and triple bottom line ventures Sustainable entrepreneurship (Dean and McMullen, 2007, p. 58) is defined as "the process of discovering, evaluating, and exploiting economic opportunities that are present in market failures which detract from sustainability, including those that are environmentally relevant." The key feature of this definition is that sustainable entrepreneurship is identifying market failures and seeking to use economic approaches to address them. There are many market failures in the urban context (Porter, 1995). Those entrepreneurs who are able to see the unique assets of urban areas and figure out ways to combine these resources to address market failures will create jobs, address social and environmental problems, and build successful ventures. We also see these features in the business models of so-called "triple bottom line ventures" – companies created with an explicit desire to make a social impact and address environmental issues.

An example of a triple bottom line venture that functions in a *market incentivizing* policy environment is RecycleForce in Indianapolis, Indiana. RecycleForce is the rare enterprise that combines both an environmental sustainability business with a prison re-entry social service department, right at the outset. The sustainability certifications that RecycleForce has obtained incentivizes its use of an innovative business model to signal that its materials are "recycled with the highest standards for data privacy, environmental controls, employee health and safety and corporate responsibility."[7] RecycleForce offers non-traditional recycling services by specializing in electronic waste, in addition to other materials, while providing life-changing workforce training to formerly incarcerated individuals.

Micro-finance organizations Micro-finance is a poverty reduction strategy popularized by Nobel Prize winner Dr Mohammed Yunnus. A micro-finance organization provides small loans to borrowers "to alleviate financial constraints for the poor and support consumption choices that increase household welfare and/or provide avenues for future ongoing income" (Cobb et al., 2016, p. 2103). The core business model for these micro-finance organizations is to provide the loans to borrowers by charging them an interest rate that covers the administration, overhead, and services related to the micro-finance approach. This aspect of the micro-finance organization business model has come under criticism due to the high interest rates related to these loans.

Micro-finance organizations often operate in a *market integrating* policy environment. For example, Mission Asset Fund (MAF)[8] transforms the traditional way of lending in immigrant communities by using a unique technology platform to track and report financial transactions in community lending circles. MAF recognized that people in these communities have long established practices of lending and borrowing money with each other through lending circles without the benefit of building their mainstream financial credit history. MAF's modern spin on lending circles, in addition to other financial programs and services they offer that are based on community trust, help people obtain their path to the financial mainstream (Caplan, 2014). Specifically, this first-of-a-kind social loan program rapidly proved its ability to help people open bank accounts, avoid predatory lenders through access to affordable loans, and quickly and safely build their credit history. Working to help people build a more financially stable future, MAF's financial innovation not only builds credit scores, but also helps strengthen communities though integration.

Social enterprise The social enterprise model differs from the sustainable business model as it is mission-driven, often affiliated in some way with a non-profit organization or non-governmental organization (NGO). In some cases, these social enterprises are for-profit subsidiaries of not-for-profit organizations. In other cases, these social enterprises are run as sophisticated, earned income generating programs within existing non-profit organizations. Some have noted that these close affiliations with NGOs also mean that the mission takes priority over profits.

Café Reconcile[9] is an example of a social enterprise operating in a *market creating* policy environment. Café Reconcile is a restaurant in the Central City neighborhood of New Orleans, specifically located there to address the blight, lack of jobs, and youth development issues in Central City. Café Reconcile renovated a dilapidated building in the middle of a blighted neighborhood, established an on-the-job culinary training program, and recruited local troubled youth to it. The area where they established the restaurant had the highest murder rate in the city. This may have been the worst place to open a business. However, their business model included both social and economic goals and the poverty- and crime-stricken area has benefited with more than 400 jobs for youth in the first five years of existence.

An example of how a social enterprise can operate in a *market integration* policy environment is City Fresh Foods,[10] a catering company with a business model that seeks to employ the unemployed, underemployed, and the formerly incarcerated. Established in 1994, City Fresh Foods merges the for-profit operations of a food services business with social returns to bring economic opportunities to Dorchester, an inner-city area in Boston, Massachusetts. The employees are integrated into the company with access to the larger industry by taking on supervisory responsibilities within City Fresh Foods or taking their newly found job skills to other employers as they continue to expand and flourish.

Benefits Corporations/B-Corps This particular legal form of social entrepreneurship can see much variation across state regulations. However, there are three legal provisions for Benefit Corporations that are common amongst all states:

> a benefit corporation has: 1) a corporate purpose to create a material positive impact on society and the environment; 2) expanded fiduciary duties of directors which require consideration of non-financial interests; and 3) an obligation to report on its overall social and environmental performance as assessed against a comprehensive, credible, independent and transparent third-party standard. (Clark and Vranka, 2013, p. 15)

B-Corps preceded the Benefit Corporation legislation of various states. B-Corps are certified by B-Lab, an organization founded in 2006 to help "tens of thousands of businesses, investors, and institutions measure what matters by using the B-Impact Assessment and B-Analysis to manage their impact and the impact of the businesses with whom they work – with as much rigor as their profits." Certified B-Corps can use the "Circle B" on their products and/or websites as an indicator of their certification after scoring more than 80 percent on the B-Impact Assessment.

An example of how a social enterprise can work within a *market incentivizing* policy environment is Greyston Bakery.[11] Greyston Bakery uses an open hiring approach to employing local residents of Yonkers, New York, who have typically been difficult to hire. Open hiring "fills jobs without judging applicants or asking any questions."[12] Greyston Bakery is a $10 million industrial-scale bakery that provides all of the brownies for Ben and Jerry's Ice Cream. By promoting this type of inclusive and transformative thinking benefits corporation approach to urban social entrepreneurship Greyston Bakery is an urban innovation.

Technology and Innovation Parks: "Social Silicon Valleys"

Social innovation refers to "new ideas that work in meeting social goals . . . giving the relatively poor and powerless more control over their own lives and advancing social justice" (Mulgan et al., 2006, p. 9). From Santa Fe to Singapore to Spain, a new breed of technology and innovation parks described as "Social Silicon Valleys" (Mulgan et al., 2006, p. 9) has emerged to serve as local clusters for driving social innovation and capturing "social increasing returns to scale" (Bresnahan et al., 2001, p. 835). These parks differ from earlier public–private partnership efforts focused on urban development in three major ways. First, these parks are formed with the *primary goal of promoting social, rather than technological innovation*, and their progress is measured accordingly. Second, these parks concentrate on nurturing and supporting the *local process of social innovation* by leveraging regional and global networks of social capital. Third, these parks implement programs that *direct participants' expertise towards solving practical problems* that are embedded in their urban surroundings (Bresnahan et al., 2001).

As an example of how technology innovation parks can operate within a *market incentivizing* policy environment, the Santa Fe Innovation Park (SFIP)[13] in the desert of northern New Mexico utilizes the region as a living laboratory for experimenting with different approaches to managing water resources, preserving biodiversity, and adapting to climate change. SFIP brings together scientists, activists, and policymakers to spark innovation through the engineering of social systems.

Venture Accelerators

A venture accelerator is similar in purpose to a business incubator in that new businesses are selected for residence in shared work spaces with other new ventures. Most accelerators provide mentoring, technical assistance, and venture funding and limit the amount of time in residence to periods shorter than incubators. Not every venture accelerator would meet our additional criteria for urban innovation. Unless they are inclusive and designed to make a transformative difference in their community or region, we are not giving them consideration here.

Located in New Orleans, Louisiana, Camelback Ventures' (Camelback) overarching goal is to address the inequities of the schooling system for minority populations and low-income communities. As a venture accelerator, Camelback exists in a *market creation* policy environment. Camelback welcomes local leaders with ideas that address education or social impact issues within their local community into a six-month fellowship with $40,000 in seed funding, coaching, necessary business connections, experiential workshops, and three-day intensive summits.

A virtual accelerator and an example of how to operate within a *market integration* policy environment, the Cincinnati USA Regional Chamber Minority Business Accelerator (MBA)[14] enables the African-American and Hispanic-owned businesses in their investment fund portfolio to raise their visibility, credibility, and viability through technical assistance and consultation on growth obstacles. The Cincinnati MBA is focused on reducing disparity in the region's business community by driving economic activity through transformative programs such as the Goal Setting Initiative, where local corporations and non-profits of different sizes pledge to spend a certain amount of funds with minority businesses in the region. As of 2014 they had 40 Goal Setters that have taken the pledge. In 2013, they collectively pledged to spend a record $1.1 billion with local minority businesses.

IMPLICATIONS

Our purpose in writing this chapter is to provide a framework for understanding urban innovation related to both entrepreneurship and urban policy. We defined urban innovation as new approaches to develop long-lasting transformations in urban communities, neighborhoods, and cities. We made the case that urban innovations are essential for economic growth and social development in our cities as the world becomes more urbanized. Anecdotal evidence of the success in using these models and policies are well documented.

We have focused on the innovations in urban entrepreneurship policy and presented three types of urban innovations from a policy perspective. The market creating approach to policy identifies urban locations where underutilized physical assets, human resources, and social capital inside communities are linked to financial capital and local social capital from outside of the community to create new places for economic growth. The market incentivizing approach demonstrates how economic actors can be incentivized into activities that benefit society. The market integrating approach to policy develops avenues for government and the private sector to participate in building and sustaining a more integrated (and inclusive) economy.

We have presented three types of business models that work within these urban policy innovations. The most well known of these is social entrepreneurship, an approach that can support social and economic development in urban areas. We further categorized the social entrepreneurship business model into sustainable or triple bottom line businesses, social enterprises, micro-finance organizations, and benefits corporations/B-Corps. The examples presented in each of these sub-categories give some necessary texture to how these approaches leverage inclusion strategies and are transformative in nature.

The second business model is technology and innovation parks for social innovation. These models are important for developing new products, systems, and ideas for social good. The third business model is the venture accelerator. Seeing how this model is used in the urban context helps us to understand how these approaches cultivate and support the best new ideas for urban transformation.

Our framework (Table 8.1) brings these urban policy innovations and the business models together so that policymakers, social entrepreneurs, and other change makers can be more strategic about their approach to societal change. In the following, we present some future directions for practitioners and academic researchers.

Academic Research

We encourage more academic research about urban innovation because more than anecdotal evidence is needed. We believe there is limited research in this space because urban innovation clearly sits at the intersection of sociology, economics, urban public policy, social work, business, and entrepreneurship. At these intersections, it is often difficult to talk the same language about the phenomenon we are experiencing and translation is necessary (Robinson, 2007; Robinson and Dougherty, 2014). As noted by Gerometta et al. (2005), when interesting phenomena sit at such intersections, it is a challenge to bring the relevant fields together for discussion and an even steeper challenge to conduct research that is received well by these various audiences. While we realize the importance and relevance of urban innovation for society, we propose to the reader that in order to have useful studies of urban innovations, researchers will need to draw on all of these relevant fields in order to make a contribution. How can this cross-disciplinary and multi-disciplinary research be done? Here are three starting points for the journey.

Academic research can be useful to provide an evidence-based rationale for future actions. Therefore, one journey for research will investigate the consequences (intended or unintended) of deploying urban innovations to address social and economic issues. What are the implications of having these policies in place in urban areas or having these types of business models used alongside more traditional business models? This research would need to collect data about the types of urban innovation we have described in this chapter and understand the impact of these urban innovations on the beneficiaries and communities where they occur.

A second approach might explore why and where these types of urban innovation emerge as viable options for social and economic transformation. There is very little research on the origins of social innovation and none on urban innovation as noted earlier in this chapter (Mueller et al., 2015; Robinson and Dougherty, 2014). This would be invaluable work for the increasing number of mega-cities that have populations of more than 10 million. If we can foster, support, and encourage more urban innovation, then perhaps the largest challenges in society can be addressed.

Our third point for academic researchers interested in studying urban innovation is to go beyond traditional paradigms of research, as Burrell and Morgan (2017) and Jennings et al. (2005) remind us. Different styles and approaches to research on the same phenomenon will ask different questions in a variety of ways and the findings of such alternative perspectives will provide us with a more nuanced understanding of the phenomenon we call urban innovation.

Urban Innovation Practitioners

We believe that the examples we have presented in this chapter represent an important wave of pragmatic and important solutions for actors who want to see inclusive and transformative change in urban communities. We highlight four points of convergence with the theme of inclusive innovation that practitioners should be aware of as they undertake this work.

First, we highlight one of the insights from Table 8.1. If you are a policymaker who wants to encourage the establishment of social entrepreneurial ventures, technology innovation parks, and social venture accelerators, it is useful to create an appropriate urban policy environment for the types of entrepreneurship you want to encourage. Policymakers should consider how their policies fit into our framework of market creating, market integrating, and market incentivizing policy environments as they consider the possible implications of these types of changes. Social entrepreneurs and others seeking to create organizations and businesses that make positive social impacts should consider what places have the supportive policy environment that aligns with their work.

Second, applying urban innovations does not happen in a vacuum – context matters. Each of these urban innovations happens in a particular socio-economic and political context that should be understood before transferring them directly to a new context. For example, the urban innovations of the United States would need to be adapted to be used in China, Singapore, or South Africa. The basic principles would be important but the variation of social, economic, and institutional structures would require some modification from the original business model or policy. In fact, the act of moving these innovations from one context to another may lead to further urban innovations.

Third, using urban innovation requires building bridges and not erecting walls. Since urban innovation is inclusive and transformative, it will naturally be boundary spanning. The examples we have presented in this chapter demonstrate collaboration across sectors, utilization of networks, and co-production. And the practitioners of urban innovation are adept at building these bridges within and across communities.

Fourth, it should be acknowledged that practicing urban innovation in inclusive and transformative ways is challenging work. Therefore, it requires allies, partners who provide resources and support at the appropriate times. Many entrepreneurs and policymakers will agree that this type of work can be draining without the appropriate social support. It is our hope that the urban innovators reading this chapter will find others of like-mind that will partner with them for societal benefit because we believe that the future of our world will be determined by how well we practice urban innovation around the world.

NOTES

* All websites were last accessed on 12 July 2018.
1. https://www.sba.gov/contracting/government-contracting-programs/hubzone-program/understanding-hub zone-program
2. http://urbact.eu/who-we-are
3. http://urbact.eu/urbact-glance
4. http://www.NMSDC.org
5. https://www.cdfifund.gov/programs-training/Programs/new-markets-tax-credit/Pages/default.aspx
6. https://beta.phila.gov/departments/office-of-sustainability/program
7. http://www.RecycleForce.org
8. http://www.MissionAsseFund.org
9. http://www.CafeReconcile.org
10. http://www.CityFresh.com
11. http://www.greyston.org/bakery
12. https://greyston.org/the-center-for-open-hiring/
13. http:// www.SantaFeInnovate.org
14. http://www.cincinnatichamber.com/the-chamber-at-work/departments-staff/minority-business-accelerator)

REFERENCES

Aunsborg, C. 2007. National profile on land ownership in urban regeneration-Denmark. URBACT.

Blockson, L.C. 2003. Multisector approaches to societal issues management. *Business & Society*, 42(3), 381–90.

Blockson, L.C. and Van Buren, H.J. 1999. Strategic alliances among different institutions: an argument for multi-sector collaboration in addressing societal issues. *Crossing the Borders: Collaboration and Competition Among Nonprofits, Business and Government.* Washington, DC: Independent Sector Working Papers.

Bondonio, D. and Greenbaum, R.T. 2007. Do local tax incentives affect economic growth? What mean impacts miss in the analysis of enterprise zone policies. *Regional Science and Urban Economics*, 37(1), 121–36.

Borzaga, C. and Bodini, R. 2014. What to make of social innovation? Towards a framework for policy development. *Social Policy and Society*, 13(3), 411–21.

Brakman Reiser, D. 2014. Regulating social enterprise. *UC Davis Business Law Journal*, 14(2), 231–46.

Bresnahan, T., Gambardella, A. and Saxenian, A. 2001. "Old economy" inputs for "new economy" outcomes: cluster formation in the new Silicon Valleys. *Industrial and Corporate Change*, 10(4), 835–60.

Burkett, I. 2010. Social procurement in Australia. The Centre for Social Impact, University of New South Wales. https://www.csi.edu.au/media/uploads/Social_Procurement_in_Australia_Report_-_December_2010.pdf, accessed 12 July 2018.

Burrell, G. and Morgan, G. 2017. *Sociological Paradigms and Organisational Analysis: Elements of the Sociology of Corporate Life*. Abingdon, UK and New York: Routledge.

Busso, M., Gregory, J. and Kline, P. 2013. Assessing the incidence and efficiency of a prominent place based policy. *American Economic Review*, 103(2), 897–947.

Cajaiba-Santana, G. 2014. Social innovation: moving the field forward. A conceptual framework. *Technological Forecasting and Social Change*, 82, 42–51.

Caplan, M.A. 2014. Communities respond to predatory lending. *Social Work*, 59(2), 149–56.

Clark Jr, William H. and Vranka, L. 2013. The need and rationale for the benefit corporation: why it is the legal form that best addresses the needs of social entrepreneurs, investors, and, ultimately, the public. http://benefitcorp.net/sites/default/files/Benefit_Corporation_White_Paper.pdf, accessed 12 July 2018.

Cobb, J.A., Wry, T. and Zhao, E.Y. 2016. Funding financial inclusion: institutional logics and the contextual contingency of funding for microfinance organizations. *Academy of Management Journal*, 59(6), 2103–31.

Dean, T.J. and McMullen, J.S. 2007. Toward a theory of sustainable entrepreneurship: reducing environmental degradation through entrepreneurial action. *Journal of Business Venturing*, 22(1), 50–76.

Di Domenico, M., Tracey, P. and Haugh, H. 2009. The dialectic of social exchange: theorizing corporate–social enterprise collaboration. *Organization Studies*, 30(8), 887–907.

Erikson, T. 2003. Towards a taxonomy of entrepreneurial learning experiences among potential entrepreneurs. *Journal of Small Business and Enterprise Development*, 10(1), 106–12.

Fairchild, G.B. 2008. The influence of residential segregation and its correlates on ethnic enterprise in urban areas. *Journal of Business Venturing*, 23(5), 513–27.

Fairchild, G.B. and Robinson, J.A. 2008. Unlearned lessons from letter from Birmingham jail: the work begun, the progress made, and the task ahead. *Business & Society*, 47(4), 484–522.

Freedman, M. 2013. Targeted business incentives and local labor markets. *Journal of Human Resources*, 48(2), 311–44.
George, G., McGahan, A.M. and Prabhu, J. 2012. Innovation for inclusive growth: towards a theoretical framework and a research agenda. *Journal of Management Studies*, 49(4), 661–83.
Gerometta, J., Haussermann, H. and Longo, G. 2005. Social innovation and civil society in urban governance: strategies for an inclusive city. *Urban Studies*, 42(11), 2007–21.
Ham, J.C., Swenson, C., İmrohoroğlu, A. and Song, H. 2011. Government programs can improve local labor markets: evidence from state enterprise zones, federal empowerment zones and federal enterprise community. *Journal of Public Economics*, 95(7), 779–97.
Hanson, A. 2009. Local employment, poverty, and property value effects of geographically-targeted tax incentives: an instrumental variables approach. *Regional Science and Urban Economics*, 39(6), 721–31.
Hollis, L. 2013. *Cities are Good For You: The Genius of the Metropolis*. Indianapolis, IN: Bloomsbury.
Jennings, P.L., Perren, L. and Carter, S. 2005. Guest editors' introduction: alternative perspectives on entrepreneurship research. *Entrepreneurship Theory and Practice*, 29(2), 145–52.
Jones, S.R. 2007. Supporting urban entrepreneurs: law, policy, and the role of lawyers in small business development. *Western New England Law Review*, 30, 71–91.
Joshi, A.M. 2014. Innovation policy. In D.J. Teece and M. Augier (eds), *The Palgrave Encyclopedia of Strategic Management*, Vol. 5. Basingstoke: Palgrave Macmillan, pp. 1–6.
Joshi, A.M., Inouye, T.M. and Robinson, J.A. 2018. How does agency workforce diversity influence Federal R&D funding of minority and women technology entrepreneurs? An analysis of the SBIR and STTR programs, 2001–2011. *Small Business Economics*, 50(3), 499–519.
Kerlin, J.A. 2006. Social enterprise in the United States and Europe: understanding and learning from the differences. *Voluntas: International Journal of Voluntary and Nonprofit Organizations*, 17(3), 247–63.
Kolko, J., Neumark, D. and Mejia, M.C. 2013. What do business climate indexes teach us about state policy and economic growth? *Journal of Regional Science*, 53(2), 220–55.
Landry, C. 2012. *The Creative City: A Toolkit for Urban Innovators*. London: Earthscan.
Lewis, J.O., Ní Hógáin, S. and Borghi, A. 2013. Cities of tomorrow – action today. URBACT II Capitalisation. Building energy efficiency in European cities.
Ludwig, J., Liebman, J.B., Kling, J.R. et al. 2008. What can we learn about neighborhood effects from the moving to opportunity experiment? *American Journal of Sociology*, 114(1), 144–88.
Lundström, A. and Zhou, C. 2011. Promoting innovation based on social sciences and technologies: the prospect of a social innovation park. *Innovation: The European Journal of Social Science Research*, 24(1–2), 133–49.
Magala, S., Dixon, S.E. and Clifford, A. 2007. Ecopreneurship – a new approach to managing the triple bottom line. *Journal of Organizational Change Management*, 20(3), 326–45.
Mair, J., Robinson, J. and Hockerts, K. 2006. *Social Entrepreneurship*. London: Palgrave Macmilllan.
Moulaert, F., Martinelli, F., González, S. and Swyngedouw, E. 2007. Introduction: social innovation and governance in European cities: urban development between path dependency and radical innovation. *European Urban and Regional Studies*, 14(3), 195–209.
Moulaert, F., MacCallum, D., Mehmood, A. and Hamdouch, A. 2013. General introduction: the return of social innovation as a scientific concept and a social practice. In F. Moulaert, D. MacCallum, A. Mehmood and A. Hamdouch (eds), *The International Handbook on Social Innovation*. Cheltenham, UK and Northampton, MA, USA: Edward Elgar Publishing, pp. 1–6.
Mueller, S., D'Intino, R.S., Walske, J., Ehrenhard, M.L., Newbert, S.L., Robinson, J.A. and Senjem, J.C. 2015. What's holding back social entrepreneurship? Removing the impediments to theoretical advancement. *Journal of Social Entrepreneurship*, 6(3), 245–56.
Mulgan, G., Wilkie, N., Tucker, S., Ali, R., Davis, F. and Liptrot, T. 2006. Social Silicon Valleys: a manifesto for social innovation. Young Foundation.
Mulgan, G., Tucker, S., Ali, R. and Sanders, B. 2007. Social innovation: what it is, why it matters and how it can be accelerated, Skoll Centre for Social Entrepreneurship. http://eureka.sbs.ox.ac.uk/761/1/Social–Innovation.pdf, accessed 12 July 2018.
Neumark, D. and Kolko, J. 2010. Do enterprise zones create jobs? Evidence from California's enterprise zone program. *Journal of Urban Economics*, 68(1), 1–19.
Oakley, D. and Tsao, H.S. 2006. A new way of revitalizing distressed urban communities? Assessing the impact of the federal empowerment zone program. *Journal of Urban Affairs*, 28(5), 443–71.
Porter, M. 1995. The competitive advantage of the inner city. *Harvard Business Review*, 73(3), 55–71.
Robinson, J.A. 2006. Navigating social and institutional barriers to markets: how social entrepreneurs identify and evaluate opportunities. In J. Mair, J. Robinson and K. Hockerts (eds), *Social Entrepreneurship*. Basingstoke: Palgrave Macmillan, pp. 95–120.
Robinson, J.A. 2007. Urban entrepreneurship: patterns and policy. *Western New England Law Review*, 30, 103–118.

Robinson, J.A. and Dougherty, D. 2014. Bridging the gap between policy, practice and academia: unleashing social innovation and entrepreneurship for societal benefit. National Science Foundation/ Rutgers Business School. https://www.doi.org/10.13140/RG.2.2.32704.33284, accessed 12 July 2018.
Rodin, J. 2013. Innovation for the next 100 years. *Supplement to the Stanford Social Innovation Review*, 2–5.
Shah, M. and Ram, M. 2006. Supplier diversity and minority business enterprise development: case study experience of three US multinationals. *Supply Chain Management: An International Journal*, 11(1), 75–81.
Tarrow, S. 1994. *Power in Movement, Social Movements, Collective Action and Politics*. Cambridge: Cambridge University Press.
van Winden, W. and de Carvalho, L. 2015a. New style cluster policy: riding the waves of San Sebastian's emerging surf economy: case study. URBACT II capitalisation.
van Winden, W. and de Carvalho, L. 2015b. The open data economy: promoting digital innovation in Dublin. Saint-Denis: URBACT.

9. Community social innovation: taking a long view on community enterprise

Neil Stott, Michelle Fava and Natalie Slawinski

INTRODUCTION

Communities are increasingly turning to social innovation to address challenges that impact them such as climate change, deindustrialization (or industrialization in the global south) and exclusion due to poverty, race or gender. Social innovation – the 'creation and implementation of new solutions' to social problems (Tracey and Stott, 2017, p. 51) – refers to the use of novel organizational vehicles, activities and strategies to facilitate change. Place-based community enterprises (an organizational form predating social enterprise) have been engaged in social innovation for over a century. In this way, community enterprises have attempted to build organizational models that emphasize the inclusion of people and places excluded from opportunities, resources or power. In this chapter, we explore the role of community enterprise in social innovation.

Communities are an important field to study with regards to social innovation. While they are seeking to create solutions and wrestle a degree of control over their destinies, communities are being encouraged to engage in social innovation by policy makers, funding bodies and more socially oriented corporate organizations. Funders often attempt to fulfil their own social and economic inclusion agendas, believing community organizations can help achieve inclusion of the so-called 'hard to reach'. Community entrepreneurship is promoted as a means to preserve services or local assets, create wealth and to increase local resilience to global change through community control and ownership of capital (Peredo and Chrisman, 2006).

While community social innovation is promoted as a new idea, there is a long history of community organizations engaging in socio-economic change, through community economic development, that has largely been forgotten. Policy makers using communities as the proving grounds for strategy is hardly new; poor places in particular have seen waves of interventions that reflect government or foundations' changing agendas. Community entrepreneurship is not a new phenomenon; many community enterprises have a deeply rooted and sustained relationship with particular places and, we will suggest, act as 'anchor organizations' providing a degree of consistency in the face of socio-economic change.

One challenge for organizational scholars studying community social innovation is that 'community' is notoriously difficult to define. Contemporary definitions tend to make a distinction between geographic (place-based) and elective (choice or affiliation-based) communities (Almandoz et al., 2017). Geographic definitions emphasize the combination of strong membership ties, small scale and boundedness (Marquis and Battilana, 2009). Geographic communities may well have numerous elective communities within them, such as a sports club, as well as members being part of external elective communities such as faith networks. Increasingly, technology is enabling numerous elective/affiliation-based communities (Almandoz et al., 2017), which need not be geographically bounded. In this chapter, we refer specifically to geographic communities.

Despite their current role in social innovation, and their long history, scholarly interest in community enterprises has declined in recent years (exceptions include Peredo and Chrisman, 2006; Somerville and McElwee, 2011). We see much potential for reinvigorating research and practice in community social innovation. How community organizations succeed or fail as resources wax and wane can offer important insights. Their approaches to capital, inclusion, governance and how they manage institutional and organizational relationships are of particular interest to us.

We argue that community enterprises deserve renewed attention for the following reasons. First, they have been organizational precursors to social enterprise with a distinct role and history, and they experience similar organizational challenges and often survive for decades through the feast and famine of public policy attention. Second, as microsites of tenacious (if sometimes futile) resistance to macro change, they not only resist but proffer solutions. Third, as a consistent presence in many poor communities, they have substantial organizational memory and sensemaking capacity in the face of change. Finally, they support individual and collective action over generations. Taking a 'long view' offers 'a rich vein of research opportunities that could reinvigorate the practice and potential of social innovation in poor places' (Stott and Tracey, 2018, p. 8).

Our aim in this chapter is to reinvigorate scholarly interest in community social innovation and community enterprise. We begin by reviewing literature on community economic development, including neglected work from the late 1970s onwards, to highlight the key debates and outline a longer view of organizational practice. We outline themes and issues and then suggest a framework for theory building in community social innovation, drawing on our extensive experience of community development practice and that of participants in our recent fieldwork. We conclude with an agenda for future research.

COMMUNITY ENTERPRISE: THEORY AND PRACTICE

The Neglect of Community Enterprise in Social Innovation Research

Community social innovation can be understood as enacting social innovation at a micro, place-based level, to overcome social problems experienced by individuals or groups, many of whom are excluded. While interest in social innovation and enterprise has grown among contemporary organizational scholars, they have largely disregarded the extent to which this work happens in local communities (Stott and Tracey, 2018). Social innovation in communities has a long history that could provide researchers with a more nuanced perspective. Organizational and social enterprise researchers have paid sparse attention to the roles of local communities and places in social enterprise research (for exceptions, see Johnstone and Lionais, 2004; McKeever et al., 2015).

Organizational research has not only ignored the role of communities and community enterprises but has also neglected its history. Contemporary social innovation builds on generations of interventions aimed at improving the lives of people and their communities, yet organizational scholarship rarely engages with the vast historical literature on past approaches. Certain approaches are particularly persistent and resurface in the policy landscape. For instance, social pathology approaches frame the problem as 'diseases' (such as welfare dependence) within particular populations, with interventions including (or often swinging between) punishment and prevention. Social planning approaches aim at systemic interventions to social problems and are usually orchestrated by the state or philanthropic foundations. Such interventions have been 'done to' and sometimes 'done with' communities (Stott and Tracey, 2018). In contrast, 'done by' interventions privilege the role of community members. They stem from conflict or social confrontation approaches (Rubin and Rubin, 1992) aimed to resist or revolt against oppression, neglect or imposed change. Over time, radical traditions, such as community organizing and Black Power, of the 1960s USA morphed, by and large, into social compromise approaches such as community development (Immerwahr, 2015; Purnell, 2012). Community development attempts to empower groups and communities to take a degree of control by working within democratic processes.

Community social innovation also builds on generations of organizations which aimed to transform people and communities. Most places have a complex organizational environment. There are outposts of public agencies, non-governmental organizations (NGOs) and charities. Numerous organizations shape community life without a physical presence, such as foundations. There are also home-grown voluntary organizations, charities and not-for-profits. Most focus on providing advocacy or services and have traditionally raised income through public or philanthropic grants as well as donations or sponsorship. An alternative approach is to use grant or other income to invest in assets to deliver a sustained income through trading. In other words, this approach combines community, social and commercial logics to deliver community economic development. While community economic development and community enterprise are not the only ways to engage in community social innovation, these two approaches dominate the historical landscape, and are therefore our focus.

Theoretical Approaches to Community Economic Development

Community economic development can be characterized as a localized (micro) response to macro social and economic change (Imbroscio et al., 2003) which attempts to stabilize, rebuild and grow local economies by creating and anchoring wealth through community control and ownership of capital. While, as Soifer et al. suggest, consistent and concise definitions of community economic development are hard to find, and the 'field has been given short shrift in the academic literature' (2014, p. 4), it is a resilient idea which has shaped policy and practice since the 1960s. While this is a neglected field, there is some significant scholarly and practitioner literature from 1970 to 2000, substantial (if largely forgotten) work on the cooperative movement and a few significant recent contributions (Haugh, 2007). Most recent work suffers from what Cummings et al. call 'attention decay' – a focus on recent work and forgetting of earlier contributions (2017, p. 5) from which contemporary scholars and practitioners could learn. In this subsection we provide an overview of largely forgotten work.

Failure and opportunity

Debates on community economic development are frequently framed as a response to failure or opportunity. A failure focus views community economic development organizations as reacting to shortcomings of the state, market or particular social groups. Market and public sector perspectives focus on the 'the non-existence, withdrawal or failure' of private enterprise or public services, particularly in poor places (Spear et al., 2017, p. 42). For Giloth (1998), community crises caused by events such as factory closures are often triggers for interventions aiming to leverage social and physical capital in order to fill the gaps through trading rather than relying on philanthropy. Similarly, systemic economic shocks such as the 2008 financial crash have also acted as catalysts (Parés et al., 2017).

Another aspect of the failure focus is the tendency to view poor places, or particular groups within them, as a 'liability' with skill or resource deficits. This is a persistent theme in state place-based interventions such as regeneration schemes. In contrast, an opportunity focus emphasizes the impact of public or philanthropic investment on stimulating activity as well as the potential for social change from within communities. So, the 'liability' perspective is countered by the 'asset' or 'strengths' view, which emphasizes the latent skills and capital held within communities (Green and Haines, 2012; Perry, 1987).

The opportunity for social and economic change from within resonates across the political spectrum and, like the concept of community, offers something to everybody. Community economic development has been supported by communitarians, neoliberals and the utopian left alike (Amin et al., 2002). For the communitarian, it offers a self-reliant and 'democratically active' community, which acts as a bulwark against the centralizing state and the heterogeneity of corporate globalization. For the neoliberal, community economic development should engage local actors in the market by providing services for themselves, reducing over-reliance on the state. For the anti-capitalist utopian, it offers the potential for ownership of decision making and power to be held within communities, an important element of the solidarity economy.

Alternative and holistic perspectives

Finding a balance between 'commercial reality' and 'social idealism' has 'consumed considerable energy' (Pearce, 1993, p. 25) in community economic debates. We characterize two prominent perspectives as alternative and holistic. The strongest social idealist claims lie in the former, with roots in the radical groups of the English Civil War (1640–60). For example, the Diggers advocated absolute equality, asserting that the earth was a common treasury for all. They occupied, farmed and built homes on common land (Gurney, 2017). Social idealism is also rooted in the nineteenth-century cooperative movement. Robert Owen imagined villages of cooperation, a 'complete community ideal' producing goods to meet their own needs, supplanting the capitalist economy (Robertson, 2010, p. 2).

The call for self-reliant places also emerged in black communities in nineteenth-century America (Wallace, 1999), which informed later thinking on black nationalism and capitalism (Hill and Rabig, 2012). Community leaders in the 1960s began to see integration as a chimera and community economic development as 'a concrete expression of a renewed interest in an old idea in the African American community, that of separate development' (Halpern, 1995, p. 129). The idea of autonomous places built on the principles of mutual aid, direct governance and local production was also central to the social anarchism of Peter Kropotkin (1899 [1974]).

For Imbroscio, community economic development became 'part of a larger grass-roots protest effort', especially by marginalized groups who saw political conflict as integral to socio-economic change (1997, p. 99). Such activity was a 'challenge to the logic of capital accumulation' (Soifer, 1990, p. 250) and a means to achieve the 'social emancipation of land, labor and capital from the competitive market' (Bruyn, 1987, p. 8). This radical mode of organization departed from corporate capitalism and bureaucratic socialism. It was a 'blueprint for broad political-economic reconstruction' (Imbroscio, 1997, p. 98); in other words, 'reinventing capitalism' (Halpern, 1995, p. 142). Such ideas reappear in recent work on re-embedding economies within ecological systems, which argues that to sustain life, community economies that are ethical, sustainable and local need to replace capitalist economies (Gibson-Graham et al., 2013). The alternative perspective is also prevalent in recent social innovation literature, particularly in European and South American traditions of the social and solidarity economy – the creation of an alternative economy that fundamentally changes political, social and economic life (Laville, 2015).

The holistic perspective balances social idealism with commercial reality. It develops interventions to simultaneously tackle multiple problems. It presupposes a long-term relationship between organizations and communities, and the latent potential of the community to mobilize, organize and nurture assets. It evolved as nineteenth-century cooperators shifted from Owen's 'complete community ideal' into what they felt was a more pragmatic 'state within a state' or cooperative commonwealth model, whereby cooperators built self-supporting organizations within the capitalist system and therefore co-existed rather than posing a direct challenge (Robertson, 2010). This entails creating local institutions and buildings to provide employment, goods and services. The cooperative movement exemplified this approach and occupied 'a central position in community life' (Robertson, 2010, p. 3). Rubin (1993) found that community entrepreneurs saw themselves as 'activist community promoters' in which their mission was one of holistic change in which 'the equity consequences of development are as important as its profitability' (Rubin, 1993, p.431).

A holistic approach often privileges import substitution strategies; growing your own and expanding 'local production for local consumption' rather than purely exporting production or chasing inward investment (Persky et al., 1993, p. 28). 'Growing your own' includes housing, education and social service provision as well as training and employment; in other words, social-economic subsidiarity. Holism also includes political subsidiarity – decisions concerning the community being made by its members – advocating for devolution of power from the state to localities. Recently, the idea of holism has re-emerged with the concept of 'collective impact', a term which refers to broad cross-sector collaboration to tackle large-scale social change (Kania and Kramer, 2011).

Organizational approaches to community enterprise

Community enterprise, and the scholarship focused on it, has a long and largely forgotten history, which includes cooperatives, community business, Community Development Corporations (CDCs) and development trusts. In this subsection, we compare social and community enterprises, and then provide a historical overview.

Social enterprises are commonly defined as organizations that pursue a social mission using business activities to sustain their operations and mission. While social and community enterprises share characteristics (such as a social purpose and trading) there are a number of differences (Tracey et al., 2005), the most obvious being community enterprise's relationship to a specific location. Approaches to assets and profit also differ. Community enterprises generally hold assets in trust and commit to being 'not for private profit', while many social enterprises do not uphold these principles. Additionally, their approaches to community development and empowerment differ. While social enterprises may benefit disadvantaged groups, they do so 'often without prior roots in that community or constituency' (Pearce, 2009, p. 30). However, the distinctions are far from clear-cut. Many community enterprises position themselves as social enterprise. This is in part due to the legitimacy currently afforded to social enterprise business models.

What constitutes a community enterprise has changed over time. However, most definitions are built around three interconnected themes; place, intent and governance. Community enterprises aim to deliver social purpose through a combination of social, environmental, cultural and economic work. They tend to have grown from, and remain rooted in, a specific locality. Their purpose is to meet the needs and aspirations of a place, through sustaining the organization over time and actively involving the community in its governance. In doing so, they attempt to build and anchor community wealth, often through physical asset development. Community enterprises, therefore, are deeply embedded in place. This is especially the case for those enterprises based in rural or depleted communities, where traditional for-profit businesses do not find it beneficial to locate (Shrivastava and Kennelly, 2013). They are 'not for private profit' incorporating a non-distributive constraint, and surplus is retained to be reinvested for organizational development, resource acquisition or community investment such as grants (Haugh, 2007). As Hayton (1996) suggests, such criteria place an organizational 'big ask' – to be simultaneously economically credible, deliver social benefits and involve the community often in the most challenging contexts.

Early community enterprises

Historically, community enterprises – or, more broadly, social purpose organizations delivering social and commercial outcomes – have existed in different guises since the first retail cooperatives, experimental anarchist communities and Tolstoyan movement enterprises in the nineteenth century (Alston, 2013). Inspired by Kropotkin, trading anarchist colonies were established near Newcastle and Sheffield (Wyler, 2009). Tolstoyan communes set up multiple enterprises such as in electrical work and carpentry (Alston, 2013).

The early cooperatives provided a holistic solution to community needs for decades. They often focused on developing shops to provide working class communities with affordable and safe products. Many diversified into the production of goods and services (Robertson, 2010). For example, the Desborough Cooperative Society had farms, mines, brickmakers, homes, savings bank, sports and education facilities (Sanders et al., 1913).

The rise of community enterprise

Community businesses blossomed in Scotland from the 1970s, providing employment and training (McArthur, 1986). In England, community business has recently re-emerged. Swersky and Plunkett suggest there are three new types: public asset managers, who take control of former public assets; business savers, who take on business of particular value to a community; and community start-ups, which start from scratch (2015, p. 9). This new wave reflects the impact of public austerity and the withdrawal of the state from many services.

A holistic approach re-emerged in 1960s USA with CDCs and in the UK with development trusts – developing housing, ventures and social projects. The literature on CDCs, the 'central institution in the theory and practice of community economic development' (Simon, 2001, p. 119), highlights the dilemmas of the 'big ask' enshrined in definitions of community enterprise. Most were set up in communities with crumbling infrastructure, abject housing, poverty and crime. The intent was expressed through a philosophy of 'holistic development' and the 'logic of joining physical and social development' (Rubin, 1995, p. 146). Housing was seen as the 'economic engine' to create jobs, homes and ventures, as well as a means to democratize expertise and control. They 'positioned the neighbourhoods they represented as corporate entities, prepared to borrow money and finance professional housing and business development' (Rabig, 2012, p. 249).

Rubin saw CDCs as niche organizations which brokered links with capital and political power; bridging roles 'to reconcile commercial and ideological goals of bringing about community empowerment and local economic transformation' (1995, p. 128). While the first wave of CDCs was overtly political, often the practitioner arm of Black Power movements (Purnell, 2012), subsequent generations focused on building alliances to achieve their missions.

CDCs' legitimacy rested on community participation. This proved difficult and was 'always tempered by some measure of elite control' (Immerwahr, 2015, p. 162). They excelled in using the community participation requirements of other agencies to 'insert themselves forcefully' into decision making, by threatening to block development (2015, p. 162). CDCs rapidly became an agent of state welfare delivery. In doing so, they became third party bureaucracies and political actors. Their managers and board became accomplished lobbyists, exchanging votes for contracts (Marwell, 2007). In Boston, CDCs 'superseded elected local politicians' (Levine, 2016, p. 1268) as the legitimate representatives. They negotiated directly with state and national government. This constituted a clear challenge to local representative democracy.

Development trusts emerged through protest or regeneration schemes. In the UK, citizen campaigns led to the formation of iconic development trusts such as Westway (1971) and Coin Street Community Builders (1984). Westway leased land under the motorway that ripped their community apart. Coin Street Community Builders were gifted land on London's South Bank after they helped to prevent a hotel and office project.

CDCs and development trusts succeeded by building asset portfolios. Community ownership and management were seen as fundamental to anchoring wealth within poor places. Assets became independent sources of income and a means to cross-subsidize other projects. Much of the property acquired was marginal land and buildings, such as redundant public assets. It took ingenuity and perseverance to make them fit for purpose and financially viable. As CDCs and development trusts became proficient at managing asset portfolios, they increasingly raised capital to deliver complex projects such as housing refurbishment. The success of CDCs, like Bedford-Stuyvesant and development trusts like Coin Street, became powerful exemplars for the movement and, later, for government (Hart, 2010).

COMMUNITY ENTERPRISE: THEMES AND ISSUES

In this section, we outline two themes that emerged from our review of the literature. First, community enterprises are organizational precursors to social enterprise and so, a critical look at past literature can provide insights for contemporary research and practice. Second, collective action is an effective way of supporting the marginalized. Sustaining collective action over generations is challenging, but can have real benefit, albeit subject to the boom and bust of successive funding initiatives.

Learning from Past Community Enterprises

Myopia and sugar-coating

In creating a new category and persuading others of its validity, boundaries are demarcated (Jones et al., 2012). When a new category, such as social enterprise, is foregrounded, the potential learning from older categories can be overlooked. We suggest that such myopia infuses the history of community and social enterprises. While social enterprise research is relatively new (Battilana and Lee, 2014), the long history of *community* enterprise is rarely acknowledged. An instance of this 'myopia' can be seen in the supporters of early Scottish community business who rejected the cooperative model, believing it to privilege economic over social objectives (Hayton, 1983). However, they overlooked the fact that cooperative movements sustained themselves at scale, and delivered much more than economic benefits. Such myopia can lead to unnecessarily long learning curves and even organizational failure.

Social and community enterprise scholars have a tendency to be 'uncritically laudatory' (Loxley, 2007, p. 1) at best, 'weak in method, atheoretical, ahistorical' (McCulloch, 2000, p. 397) at worst. The problem seems to be that activists exaggerate potential and achievement. The word 'community' can be 'used as some sort of shield' and therefore community enterprise is held as 'above criticism' (Hayton, 1996, p. 18). Furthermore, the literature is 'produced by enthusiasts and is characterised by an absence of critical appraisal' (McArthur, 1993, p. 222).

Such myopia and sugar-coating has led to recent social and community enterprise literature privileging the role of the entrepreneur or the community (e.g., Haugh, 2007; Peredo and Chrisman, 2006). If we take a longer view, it becomes clear that the origins, and subsequent boom and bust, of successive generations of community enterprises are as much the result of political and philanthropic attention as they are of the efforts of individual enterprises or communities (see Immerwahr, 2015). Community enterprises' origin narratives often emphasize activist responses to events, particularly injustices or problems (e.g., Pearce, 2009). However, establishing a community enterprise is rarely a spontaneous event. It usually stems from decades of activism, as well as having been orchestrated by external actors such as the state, foundations and support organizations. For instance, the Bedford-Stuyvesant Restoration Corporation was built on the activism of a coalition of 90 community organizations, yet its launch was due to the alignment of the political and philanthropic objectives of Robert Kennedy and the Ford Foundation (Purnell, 2012).

The struggle for legitimacy and sustainability

Powerful stakeholders frame the expectations of community and social enterprises through their funding policies, which emphasize measurable impact. Therefore, there is the temptation to over-promise impact. Funders buy into the belief that social enterprise can deliver social, economic and environmental impact simultaneously. However, 'reality can be dramatically different than the ideal' (McArthur, 1993, p. 229). A central problem has been the weight of expectations around empowering the poorest communities while creating jobs, wealth and opportunity. In order to survive, many community businesses found niches that did not require much capital or expose start-ups to competition, but also did not deliver much return, therefore 'low pay was endemic' (Hayton, 1996, p. 15). While Hayton found that employees were positive, their situation was inherently precarious as many community businesses struggled to break even and relied on fresh injections of state support to survive. Both employees and the wider membership were rather passive. Managers talked the engagement talk, but sidestepped it in practice, as their energies went into trying to run viable businesses. Hayton concluded 'the fault may lie with those promulgating the concept [of community enterprise] rather than the businesses themselves' (1996, p. 8). The problem, therefore, can be linked to overblown expectations and the idea that hybrid organizations in poor places can deliver change alone.

The idea of social enterprises as hybrids, managing the tensions between commercial and social logics, is foreshadowed in the community enterprise literature (e.g., Wallace, 1999). Organizations that fail to achieve a balance compromise their legitimacy. Hayton's (1996) research illustrates the perils: too much emphasis on a social logic puts financial sustainability at risk; increased commercialism puts community relationships at risk. Rubin revealed 'economic and administrative fragility' as isomorphic pressures from funders led to value conflicts in balancing efficiency with empowerment; technical and financial dependence with autonomy; and the temptation of quick, top-down, neighborhood uplift with community participation (1995, p. 134). For Rubin, the issues began when CDCs chased funding or public contracts rather than the social problem (p. 134). Hayton suggests the only way to maintain autonomy and balance objectives is to include activities from which 'higher profits can be made, higher wages paid and more money spent on community projects' (1996, p. 18).

In lauding social and community enterprise, scholars have largely neglected organizational failure (Tracey and Jarvis, 2006). We can learn significant lessons from examples of operational and financial decline. Failure is often in the eye of the beholder, and it is important to acknowledge the differing measures of success of various stakeholders. As is often the case, in the Scottish 1980s evaluation reports, community businesses sustaining themselves with public funds were seen as failures (McArthur, 1993). Yet, they still provided key services to impoverished communities.

It could appear that community enterprises are destined to struggle, given the weight of expectations on them, including the imperative to build profitable businesses in poor places, where others have failed. Community businesses have tried to overcome this by creating niches which, unsurprisingly, return low profits, precipitating financial crises (McArthur, 1986). We can learn from the experiences of CDCs, which, in making niches viable, also made them attractive to the private sector, leading to competition and ultimately financial failure of the CDC venture (Halpern, 1995). Yet, if local people still received the goods or service, it could still be considered as a successful outcome, even if taken out of community ownership.

Funders and support agencies often advise on what 'works', and community enterprises mimic each other's 'successes'. Unfortunately, the business models promoted are often financially marginal from inception when operating in low income places. Until CDCs expanded their areas of benefit, building businesses in more affluent areas in order to survive (Halpern, 1995) – a strategy echoed by UK development trusts in the 2000s – financial survival without public or philanthropic support had often been an illusion.

Community enterprises need to achieve legitimacy within their communities. Often, the issues facing such places are so pressing, community enterprises feel beholden to confront the state and local elites. Yet 'legitimacy in the eyes of the state' can impact on organizational survival (Minkoff, 1993, p. 890). Minkoff found significant difference in the life chances of those who challenge the state (1993, p. 890). How community enterprises manage legitimacy across multiple domains is not well understood. Again, a long view can provide insight. For example, Rubin's (1995) research showed that while most early CDCs benefited from state support, they became increasingly confrontational as the pace of change seemed inadequate for the challenges they faced. In time, CDCs began to balance confrontation and conforming – the former to keep the 'change agenda alive' and latter to keep the 'organization alive' (Rubin, 1995, p. 139). They often undertook challenges in a 'veiled fashion' usually through coalitions (p. 140), which included 'campaigns of resistance' to funder pressure and 'preemptive campaigns' (p. 153).

The role of membership organizations, coalitions and networks has been neglected in recent community and social enterprise research. Ostensibly, such organizations provide peer support, technical support and promotion of the model to others. However, it is apparent that they also advocate, lobby and confront powerful institutions. We suggest they are also instrumental in creating, and building legitimacy in, concepts such as social enterprise. The cooperative movement was an exemplar of integrating action, education and promotion from the local to national level (Robertson, 2010). 'Cooperative missionaries' spread the message from town to town (Sanders et al., 1913). Cooperators traded with each other, built new enterprises collectively and provided support through funds, education, campaigns and, in the UK, creating a political party. Crucially, they built and sustained an environment in which cooperatives were seen as legitimate. Getting close to power can be advantageous. However, as many support organizations rely on state or foundation financial support – directly or through contracts – reliance can also lead to conflicts of interest or tensions between the needs of their members and funders.

Learning from Collective Action

Micro resistance to macro change

A central premise of community economic development is that micro action can make a difference in the face of macro changes, but to what degree this is achievable is contentious. Community enterprises are embedded in place, and action is enabled or constrained by local, national and global institutions. We lack a nuanced understanding of the microfoundations of place-based social action as well as the impact of different institutional contexts. We lack understanding of how place-based social action is enabled or resisted by more powerful actors, and the collective action required to overcome such resistance.

There are oft-repeated claims that community enterprise is effective in 'addressing exclusion problems in the most severely disadvantaged inner city areas' (Spear et al., 2017, p. 41) and has substantially tackled poverty at a local level. Yet, numerous studies have highlighted the marginal impact of community enterprise in alleviating poverty (e.g., Hayton, 1996). Even well-funded flagship community enterprises have been questioned. The Bedford-Stuyvesant Restoration Corporation, 'the nation's test case for creating private-public partnership to combat urban poverty failed to reduce poverty rates significantly' (Purnell, 2012, p. 236). Following experimentation with community enterprises in the UK, Community Development Projects came to the gloomy conclusion that local action was largely ineffective in the face of structural change in the poorest communities (CDP, 1977).

Some see community enterprise as a piecemeal, patchwork and particularistic approach rather than a universal solution (Amin et al., 2002; McCulloch, 2000). For Gunn and Gunn, it is simply a mismatched fight; and in confronting capital, communities 'do so on their knees' (1991, p. 2). Porter considers community entrepreneurs misguided, as they 'treated the inner city like an island isolated from the surrounding economy and subject to its own laws of competition' (1995, p. 55). There appear to be 'clear limits to what can be achieved at the local level' (Tabart et al., 2001, p. 14). The impact of community enterprise has been underwhelming and even overstated at times. This is, in part, due to the weight of expectations placed on such organizations and a proclivity to over-promise impact to secure funds. However, it is important to remember that, for many places, the 'fragile' strategies of community enterprises are vital (Halpern, 1995, p. 145). What critics often overlook is the ability of organizations to sustain communities through 'long, despairing decades' in 'neighbourhoods that had been abandoned and denigrated by others' (Rabig, 2012, p. 265). Impact that may appear negligible can, in fact, be preventing further community deterioration. Another problem is that most metrics are blunt instruments which fail to capture the everyday interactions between an organization and its community. Even small acts hidden from view can be hugely beneficial to those experiencing hardship.

Mobilizing resources

Community and social enterprises' ambitions to tackle social needs often outstrip their capacity to deliver. To overcome constraints, organizations attempt to leverage others' resources, from both within and external to the community (Perry, 1987). To mobilize resources, community enterprises adopt a variety of strategies, including: shared projects with external actors; building governance structures that include varied local constituencies; securing external political patrons; and maintaining strong social networks with beneficiaries (Vermeulen et al., 2016).

Balancing community needs with those of external actors can create significant legitimacy challenges as compromises are invariably made. Logan and Molotch described how early CDCs abandoned insurrection and were 'tamed' and 'incorporated' by powerful local elites (1987, p. 139). Moreover, they built 'turf and institutions' which they then defended (p. 139). But, as Simon (2001) argues, community economic development is designed to be defensive and remedial. CDCs also learned that direct confrontation usually hurt the organization more than the target. They recognized that protecting turf, at the expense of others with equally depleted environments, was counterproductive. To achieve their objectives they turned to creating coalitions within the community, between

CDCs and other advocacy organizations as well as building relationships at all levels of government (Perry, 1987).

CDCs and development trusts are often portrayed as 'community anchor organizations' which secure wealth and opportunity within localities (Henderson, 2014). Pearce (1993, 2003) envisaged 'core' community enterprises which would build and support other community groups and broker connections with the state and private sector. For Henderson and McWilliams, community anchor organizations build 'a viable organization and sector' while committed to 'sustaining an egalitarian, progressive social vision' and empowerment (2017, p. 11). Henderson argues that community anchor organizations can lead on 'highly localised' service design and delivery, and 'related local economic, social and democratic developments' (2015, p. 1).

The idea of community anchors increasingly resonates with community organizations and the state. The former seek legitimacy and resources, the latter aim to save resources and reduce liabilities. It is prominent in Scottish debates on the future of public services and may become a focus of social policy elsewhere. Yet the idea, practice and implications of community anchor organizations has not received much scholarly attention. While an attractive concept, we are concerned that such an all-encompassing notion of the community anchor organization can lead, once again, to unrealistic expectations.

Community enterprises that have survived for decades tend to have a land and property portfolio. Asset transfer and development have become integral to many community organizations' strategies, and are promoted by government. However, land and property are not necessarily assets. Many of the assets offered to today's community enterprises are ones which other organizations could not sustain. Location, cost of capital, the potential to generate income and external change can impact on viability. For example, Coin Street's success has been, in part, due to rising land and property values on London's South Bank. Westway made use of marginal land under a flyover and built a leisure complex, but financial success may well be due to gentrification of the surrounding area. There is a paucity of research on community enterprise asset portfolios' performance and the impact on organizational sustainability.

Cross-sectoral partnerships are perceived as essential in tackling complex problems, yet creating and sustaining them is an inherently difficult process (Bryson et al., 2006). Long-standing community enterprises have experienced the trials and tribulations of myriad partnerships, and 'partner disillusionment' when they fail (Le Ber and Branzei, 2010). In addition to this, 'community disillusionment' arises when promises are not delivered. External relationships and resource mobilization are clearly important for community enterprise. Therefore, we suggest that, to achieve sustainability, they must develop a repertoire of knowledge, practices and values for navigating the ever changing external landscape. There appears to be untapped knowledge within long-standing community enterprises that could provide insights for contemporary practice.

How community enterprises survive over time is not well understood. Sustainable revenue from assets is seen as crucial (Tracey et al., 2005). While assets are important, other factors emerge from our ongoing fieldwork: the patience and effort required to build and sustain relationships; rebuilding relationships among the changing external organizational landscape; and bringing partner projects to fruition (Stott et al., 2018). Some of our respondents demonstrate the ability to shrink to a sustainable core when resources are hard to find and remain poised to take advantage of opportunity. The significant factor is the ability to sustain collective action over time. To do so, community enterprises must maintain community and external legitimacy through feast and famine, pass the organizational torch from generation to generation and maintain a committed and resilient cadre of activists. Mature community enterprises exhibit a wealth of community and organizational knowledge and have developed the mechanisms to capture and communicate it over time.

A COMMUNITY SOCIAL INNOVATION TYPOLOGY

In this section, we adapt Tracey and Stott's (2017) framework for conceptualizing social innovation – social entrepreneurship, intrapreneurship and extrapreneurship – to *community* social innovation (Table 9.1). We draw on our current fieldwork with community enterprises to illustrate the concepts of community entrepreneurship, intrapreneurship and extrapreneurship. Through our fieldwork, we have witnessed the tenacity and creativity displayed by community enterprises, who need to adapt over time, with limited resources, in some of the most challenging places. We suggest that to overcome these challenges, community social innovation organizations must be simultaneously entrepreneurs, intrapreneurs and extrapreneurs.

Community Entrepreneurship

Community entrepreneurship is largely concerned with creating and sustaining community enterprises. What is clear from our fieldwork is that community enterprises, particularly long-standing ones, spend considerable time and effort in leveraging their

Table 9.1 A typology of community social innovation

	Community Entrepreneurship	Community Intrapreneurship	Community Extrapreneurship
Definition:	Process of creating and growing not for private profit ventures and projects, where the motivation of the entrepreneurs is to address challenges within a specific community	Process of addressing challenges with community partners, including community groups and organizations	Process of cross-sector work which facilitates alternative combinations of ideas, people, places and resources to address community challenges
Approach to social change:	Creates change through the founding, development and maintenance of community organizations	Creates change by leveraging the resources and capabilities of individuals, groups and organizations located within the community	Creates change through platforms that support collective effort and by partnering with organizations outside the community

Source: Adapted from Tracey and Stott (2017).

own resources and capabilities within a specific locality to make change and respond to shifting circumstances.

For example, the Shorefast Foundation operates social enterprises, including the Fogo Island Inn, in Newfoundland. Shorefast has found ways to draw on community traditions and assets to find what it calls 'new ways with old things' (Slawinski, 2016). Using asset-based community development, Shorefast discovered through extensive interactions with community members Fogo Island's most important assets and found novel ways to leverage them. Recognizing that quilt making and rug hooking were declining yet defining traditions, Shorefast decided to include locally made quilts and hooked rugs in every guestroom of the Inn. In addition to creating jobs, the Inn distributes its surpluses back into the community.

Community Intrapreneurship

Within organizations there is constant debate between stakeholders – staff, board and members – on what should and could be done. Social needs often outstrip organizational resources. Prioritization is a daunting process when up close and personal to the plight of community members. We suggest that, in delivering local action, community intrapreneurship – usually characterized as an internal process – also spills out of the organization, to leverage the resources and capabilities of other groups and organizations in the community. This could mean partnering with existing groups or organizations, or helping to create new ones. It also includes building relationships within the community to leverage expertise, time and commitment to the organization in other forums such as local political and governmental organizations.

For example, development trusts like Goodwin (Hull) and Central Halls (Glasgow) provide seed support to local people wishing to set up activities such as youth work. The Fogo Island Inn relies on supporting services such as eco-tourism products and local food producers. Shorefast started a micro-lending fund to incubate local businesses that could support tourism. Community intrapreneurship of this sort is now framed as 'community anchor' work by some practitioners, but appears to have a much longer history and is integral to the practice of community enterprise.

Community Extrapreneurship

Community extrapreneurship refers to the process of cross-sector work that facilitates alternative combinations of ideas, people, places and resources to address community challenges. It may be assumed that community enterprises lack the capacity to engage in extrapreneurship, but it appears to be 'integral to micro-organizational practices and vital to survival and impact'; those organizations which 'build complex relationships, influence, and power locally are likely to be most effective in addressing deep-rooted social problems' (Stott and Tracey, 2018, p. 12).

Shorefast has partnered with organizations outside the community to promote its social mission of 'cultural and economic resilience for Fogo Island'. For instance, the Fogo Island Shop, another of Shorefast's social enterprises, partnered with a design retailer in major centers to carry the Shop's line of high-end locally created furniture, and to promote Shorefast's Economic Nutrition Label which provides consumers with a breakdown of the impact they are having on the local economy. Five community enterprises in Glasgow have recently created a cooperative to collectively bid for city-wide contracts to improve employment prospects for their beneficiaries.

We see the typology as an analytical tool, with which to question, problematize and investigate the practices of community social innovation. The typology enables researchers to look separately at three strands of practice, understanding the role of each and how they contribute to the whole.

A RESEARCH AGENDA FOR COMMUNITY SOCIAL INNOVATION

In this section, we suggest avenues for future research. In particular, we look at how community enterprises can provide a useful context for extending social enterprise research and organizational theory more generally. We then examine methodological considerations for such research.

Moving the Research Agenda Forward

Building on the community social innovation typology

The framework above may be a useful way to take community social innovation research forward. Research on community entrepreneurship could be further developed. We would like to see more longitudinal and historical studies, to understand how enterprises form, adapt to, decline or weather external macro changes. Broad studies would also be useful to ascertain what constitutes success and failure from multiple stakeholders' perspectives. Further to this, most research has focused on the global north, yet community entrepreneurship is a worldwide phenomenon. There is therefore a need to examine community enterprise in other geographic and cultural contexts. Many questions remain. How do different contexts influence the emergence and spread of community enterprises, and how do they respond? When is community enterprise an expression of local needs and aspirations, and when is it imposed by the agendas of foundations, powerful international actors or self-interested funders? What difference does community enterprises make, and how do they function in situations of extreme poverty?

The other two types of community social innovation in our framework – intrapreneurship and entrepreneurship – have received less attention, and opportunities are ripe for research. More research around intrapreneurship would shed light on how enterprises partner with others in the community. In particular, it would be beneficial to look at how new organizations are created, and how they build effective and supportive ecosystems, especially in the context of specific communities facing resource constraints. For example, a recent study by Pret and Carter (2017) closely examined how niche entrepreneurs manage relationships with competitors in order to ensure the most value for their communities. A new area of research would be examining the role of community enterprise members in brokering relationships through their membership of other local organizations. Also, future research could examine how organizations perpetuate themselves over generations by nurturing future activists.

Finally, research on community extrapreneurship has been limited. Little is known about the processes involved in partnerships between community actors and outside actors, particularly across sectors. Yet, such partnerships are critical for attracting resources and for building legitimacy. Research on cross-sector work is a promising domain which has begun to examine practices that enhance collaboration and impediments such as goal conflict (Selsky and Parker, 2005). Further research on how community enterprises build and sustain trust, leadership and legitimacy (Bryson et al., 2006) through cross-sector work would be of great utility to practitioners.

Taking a long view

As this chapter has argued, organizational and social enterprise scholars have taken a rather myopic look at social and community enterprises, virtually ignoring the long history of community social innovation, and the role of community enterprises as precursors to today's social enterprises. Some of the gaps in the literature we discussed earlier may be addressed by taking a long view. Indeed, as Cummings et al. noted, 'more history rather than less could promote innovation' through generating a plurality of ideas, challenging assumptions and overcoming dominant logics (2017, p. 4). Taking a long view of community enterprise, including the institutional environments in which community and social enterprises emerged, changed or were maintained, may provide rich opportunities for research on hybrid organizing, institutional work and other areas of organizational theory. Given the longevity of some community enterprises, particularly cooperatives, one area that is ripe for future research is the wealth of organizational memory – community knowledge, history and collective sensemaking – in older organizational forms. There are rich opportunities to study cooperatives longitudinally, given their long histories and archival resources.

Taking a long view also exposes the numerous challenges faced by community enterprises over the past decades. In such research it remains important to maintain a critical perspective, to avoid sugar-coating the past. More work is needed to avoid the tendency in current research of being excessively laudatory. There is a need to temper the uncritical research produced by enthusiasts. A more balanced account of challenges and failures could also inform social enterprise practitioners, organizations and other institutional actors who support social enterprise.

The social innovation zeitgeist is embraced by the public, corporate and social sectors alike. However, there is a danger of overlooking the potential for resistance to arise when the social sector grows to a point at which it challenges the state or corporate sector. There are historical precedents for this. In the 1920s, the UK cooperative movement experienced significant resistance from business and political leaders. Cooperatives achieved financial success, captured local consumers and espoused the participation of working class people. Coops were then deemed to be undermining local competition and capitalism as a whole, and were seen as a harbinger of class conflict (Killingback, 1988). More recently, there have been examples in which strong partnerships between community enterprises and the central state have been seen as a threat to local government, perceived as undermining local democratic processes, as with CDCs (Levine, 2016). Further historical research on resistance to social change at micro and macro levels can provide salutary lessons for contemporary practice.

Understanding the role of place in organizational scholarship

Scholars have recognized that organizations are 'simultaneously embedded in multiple environments' (Marquis and Battilana, 2009, p. 295) including local, organizational and transnational fields. Research on community enterprise is an ideal context for studying the role of place in shaping organizations, and indeed to understand how communities are shaped by organizations, and vice versa (Elmes et al., 2012). Such research could extend the efforts of scholars who have argued that organizational research is lacking contextualization and who call for organizational research on place (e.g., Shrivastava and Kennelly, 2013).

Organizational scholars have recently taken a greater interest in studying grand challenges, such as climate change. These are often experienced more acutely in poor communities, who suffer the direct impacts. It is in these communities that we feel the most fruitful avenues of research lie, as they must deal with the immediate reality.

Methodological Considerations

The research agendas outlined above indicate a need for more detailed knowledge about the ways in which community enterprises engage in social innovation. Negotiating local power structures is a major challenge facing community organizations, particularly when dealing with large-scale or powerful stakeholders, and when there are conflicts of interest or differing measures of success.

The importance of taking a relational view

We propose that further research into inter-organizational relationship management can inform and support the practice of community and social entrepreneurs. Critical resources exist beyond organizational boundaries and are embedded in others' complementary capabilities and 'knowledge sharing routines' (Dyer and Singh, 1998). However, our knowledge of this 'relational view' is limited (Hampel et al., 2017).

Such relational dynamics are key to understanding the success and longevity of community organizations, but can prove slippery subject matter for researchers. Qualitative evidence in this arena contains much room for ambiguity and 'sugar-coating'. Learning from people's experiences is key, but there is likely to be a blurring of boundaries between the personal and professional lives of those who dedicate their lives to community development. Personal accounts can be very insightful, but also differ in regard to the same events. Participants may feel inhibited, omitting sensitive information or negative experiences. They might select episodes that paint their organization in a favourable light. This is especially true when contributing to case studies in which their organizations are to be named.

For these reasons, we anticipate a need to go beyond conventional modes of discovery in order to gain more nuanced understandings of the relational aspects of community enterprise. Doing this means acknowledging the varying ways in which communities, organizations, and those in their broader contexts, perceive themselves and each other. How multiple actors construe their own and each other's roles is key, as it can provide important insights, such as their differing measures of success. But this is enmeshed with how individuals *feel about* those roles and their performance: how roles fit (or do not fit) with their values (Lok et al., 2017). Recognizing the place of emotion in motivating individuals (Pinder, 2014) can help us understand organizations as complex 'emotional arenas' (Fineman, 2000) in which needs, values and aspirations influence choices and behaviors at every level. How something 'feels' to a certain group can be a valid inquiry for organizational research, for example, fear can play an important role in motivating employees to remain in unjust employment relationships (Fineman, 2000, p. 268).

Slow research

For the reasons outlined above, inter-organizational research becomes tricky subject matter for researchers as it strays beyond the realm of the factual and into the affective. It therefore requires a greater level of trust between researcher and participant, and benefits from a longer process of relationship building; a slower kind of engagement. Alternative modes of knowing – visual, arts based and dramaturgical – which are gaining popularity in organizational research (e.g., Clarke and Holt, 2017; Mullen, 2003) can embrace ambiguity and affective dimensions. They therefore offer useful ways of eliciting and analysing richer personal accounts, addressing the 'crucial need to undertake detailed observation' (Unsworth et al., 2011, p. 189), combined with approaches to '[m]ulling over the data in multiple ways to draw out meanings' (p. 186). Alternative modes of presentation (that rely less on lengthy texts) can also provide more engaging ways of presenting findings to stakeholders.

Participatory action research

One solution to the problem of participant inhibition can be for research to be conducted by stakeholders themselves, but this requires the additional skillset of research methodologies, and the problem of piecing together partial and ambiguous accounts remains. What is necessary is a re-imagining of the relationship between researchers and participants. This can be provided by participatory action research models, which entail an epistemological shift in which 'the asymmetrical subject–object relationships' between researcher and researched are intentionally shifted to a more equal subject–subject relationship (Fals-Borda, 1991, p. 152). Such research actively involves stakeholders, blurring boundaries between research and action. This model is particularly beneficial when seeking to understand bottom-up change.

A deeper sense of ownership of the research can lead participants to speak more candidly and to participate with a greater sense of purpose. Ideally, this would include shaping research agendas and questions. Likewise, with deep engagement it is expected that researchers involved become acutely aware of the challenges faced by those they study, and share the desire to actively participate in the development of the organizations. With mutual vested interest, it is easier for research partners to become critical friends.

CONCLUSION

Community enterprises offer rich opportunities for organizational research and great potential to inform practice. As precursors to social enterprises, community enterprises (and especially cooperatives) have a long history of addressing societal challenges at a local level, yet this history has been largely neglected. Researchers and practitioners have a tendency to embrace the emancipatory and entrepreneurial narratives surrounding community enterprise. However, this is sometimes over-emphasized to achieve organizational legitimacy in the eyes of stakeholders. Proposals may over-promise, while reports sugar-coat results. This is ultimately counterproductive, as it leads to disenchantment and loss of legitimacy.

We need authentic narratives of community enterprise which account for their own, context-dependent measures of success. These narratives should also include the important (and largely ignored) roles of the state and external support organizations in creating and sustaining community enterprises. Realistic perspectives on what local action can actually do in the face of macro change are also essential, and gaining this understanding will require thinking not only of community entrepreneurship but also how organizations enact intrapreneurship and extrapreneurship. It would be especially useful to reconsider the alluring concept of 'community anchor organization' with respect to the issues mentioned here, as we are in danger of repeating the 'big ask' on place-based organizations. While land and property are integral to long-term viability, we feel that patience and the capacity to sustain collective action over generations are equally important.

Taking a long view allows us to see the practices and processes involved in sustaining the benefits resulting from community social innovation, including how organizations survive lean times. To expose the practices and processes involved in this, we recommend that researchers consider alternative, slow and arts-based methods of data collection, analysis and dissemination. We also advocate participatory approaches which value the deep knowledge and expertise of community practitioners. In taking this approach we hope that future research can enrich the field of social innovation by harnessing the wealth of experience of community innovators to avoid myopia and repeating mistakes.

REFERENCES

Almandoz, J., Marquis, M. and Cheely, M. (2017), 'Drivers of community strength: an institutional logics perspective on geographical and affiliation based communities', in Royston Greenwood, Christine Oliver, Thomas B. Lawrence and Renate E. Meyer (eds), *The Sage Handbook of Organizational Institutionalism*, 2nd edn. London: Sage, pp. 190–213.

Alston, C. (2013), 'Britain and the International Tolstoyan Movement, 1890–1910', in B. Beasley and P.R. Bullock (eds), *Russia in Britain, 1880–1940: From Melodrama to Modernism.* Oxford: Oxford University Press, pp. 1–34.

Amin, A., Cameron, A. and Hudson, H. (2002), *Placing the Social Economy.* London: Routledge.

Battilana, J. and Lee, M. (2014). 'Advancing research on hybrid organizing – insights from the study of social enterprise', *The Academy of Management Annals*, **8** (1), 397–441.

Bruyn, S.T. (1987), 'Beyond the market and the state', in S.T. Bruyn and J. Meehan (eds), *Beyond the Market and the State: New Directions in Community Economic Development*. Philadelphia, PA: Temple University Press, pp. 3–27.

Bryson, J.M., Crosby, B.C. and Stone, M.M. (2006), 'The design and implementation of collaborations: propositions from the literature', *Public Administration Review*, **66**, 44–55.

CDP (1977), *Gilding the Ghetto: The State and the Poverty Experiment.* London: CDP Inter-Project Editorial Team.

Clarke, J. and Holt, R. (2017), 'Imagery of ad-venture: understanding entrepreneurial identity through metaphor and drawing', *Journal of Business Venturing*, **32** (5), 476–97.

Cummings, S., Bridgeman, T., Hassard, J. and Rowlinson, M. (2017), *A New History of Management.* Cambridge: Cambridge University Press.

Dyer, J.H. and Singh, H. (1998), 'The relational view: cooperative strategy and sources of interorganizational competitive advantage', *Academy of Management Review*, **23** (4), 660–79.

Elmes, M., Jiusto, S., Whiteman, G., Hersh, R. and Guthey, G. (2012), 'Teaching social entrepreneurship

and innovation from the perspective of place and place making', *Academy of Management Learning and Education*, **11** (4), 533–54.
Fals-Borda, O. (1991), 'Remaking knowledge', in O. Fals-Borda and M. Rahman (eds), *Action and Knowledge: Breaking the Monopoly With Participatory Action-Research*. New York: Apex Press, pp. 146–64.
Fineman, S. (ed.) (2000), *Emotion in Organizations*. Los Angeles, CA: Sage.
Gibson-Graham, J.K., Cameron, J. and Healy, S. (2013), *Take Back the Economy: An Ethical Guide for Transforming Our Economies*. Minnesota, MN: University of Minnesota Press.
Giloth, R.P. (1998), 'Jobs, wealth, or place: the faces of community economic development', *Journal of Community Practice*, **5** (1/2), 11–27.
Green, G.P. and Haines, A.L. (2012), *Asset Building and Community Development*, 3rd edn. London: Sage.
Gunn, C. and Gunn, H.D. (1991), *Reclaiming Capital: Democratic Initiatives and Community Development*. Ithaca, NY: Cornell University Press.
Gurney, J. (2017), 'Gerrard Winstanley and the left', *Past and Present*, **235** (1), 179–206.
Halpern, R. (1995), *Rebuilding the Inner City: A History of Neighbourhood Initiatives to Address Poverty in the United States*. New York: Columbia University Press.
Hampel, C., Lawrence, T.B. and Tracey, P. (2017), 'Institutional work: taking stock and making it matter', in R. Greenwood, C. Oliver, R. Suddaby and K. Sahlin-Andersson (eds), *The Sage Handbook of Organizational Institutionalism*, 2nd edn. London: Sage, pp. 558–90.
Hart, L. (2010), *To Have and to Hold*, 2nd edn. London: Development Trusts Association.
Haugh, H. (2007), 'Community-led social venture creation', *Entrepreneurship Theory and Practice*, **31**, 161–82.
Hayton, K. (1983), 'Employment creation in deprived areas: the local authority role in promoting community business', *Local Government Studies*, **9** (6), 39–55.
Hayton, K. (1996), 'A critical examination of the role of community business in urban regeneration', *The Town Planning Review*, **67** (1), 1–20.
Henderson, J. (2014), 'Towards a critical understanding of community anchors and a community sector theory and practice', Doctoral dissertation, Heriot-Watt University.
Henderson, J. (2015), *Community Anchors*. Edinburgh: What Works Scotland.
Henderson, J. and McWilliams, C. (2017), 'The UK community anchor model and its challenges for community sector theory and practice', *Urban Studies*, **54** (16), 1–17.
Hill, L.W. and Rabig, J. (2012), 'Towards a history of the Business of Black Power', in Laura Warren Hill and Julia Rabig (eds), *The Business of Black Power: Community Development, Capitalism and Corporate Responsibility in Postwar America*. New York: University of Rochester Press, pp. 15–42.
Imbroscio, D.L. (1997), *Reconstructing City Politics: Alternative Economic Development and Urban Regimes*. Thousand Oaks, CA: Sage.
Imbroscio, D.L., Williamson, T. and Alperovitz, G. (2003), 'Local policy responses to globalization: place-based ownership models of economic enterprise', *The Policy Studies Journal*, **3** (1), 31–52.
Immerwahr, D. (2015), *Thinking Small: The United States and the Lure of Community Development*. Boston, MA: Harvard University Press.
Johnstone, H. and Lionais, D. (2004), 'Depleted communities and community business entrepreneurship: revaluing space through place', *Entrepreneurship and Regional Development*, **16** (3), 217–33.
Jones, C., Maoret, M., Massa, F.G. and Svejenova, S. (2012), 'Rebels with a cause: formation, contestation and expansion of the de novo category "Modern Architecture," 1870–1975', *Organization Science*, **23** (6), 1523–45.
Kania, J. and Kramer, M. (2011), 'Collective impact', *Stanford Social Innovation Review*, Winter, 36–41.
Killingback, N. (1988), 'Limits to mutuality: economic and political attacks on co-operation during the 1920s and 1930s', in S. Yeo (ed.), *New Views of Co-operation*. London: Routledge, pp. 207–28.
Kropotkin, P. (1899), *Fields, Factories and Workshops Tomorrow*. Reprinted in Colin Ward (ed.) (1974). London: Allen and Unwin.
Laville, J. (2015), 'Social and solidarity economy in historical perspective', in Peter Utting (ed.), *Social and Solidarity Economy: Beyond the Fringe*. London: Zed Books, pp. 41–56.
Le Ber, M.J. and Branzei, O. (2010), '(Re)forming strategic cross-sector partnerships: relational processes of social innovation', *Business and Society*, **49**, 140–72.
Levine, J.R. (2016), 'The privatization of political representation: community based organizations as nonelected neighbourhood representatives', *American Sociological Review*, **81** (6), 1251–75.
Logan, J. and Molotch, H. (1987), *Urban Fortunes*. Berkeley, CA: University of California Press.
Lok, J., Crees, D., Dejordy, R. and Voronov, M. (2017), 'Living institutions: bringing emotions into organizational institutionalism', in R. Greenwood, C. Oliver, R. Suddaby and K. Sahlin-Andersson (eds), *The Sage Handbook of Organizational Institutionalism*, 2nd edn. London: Sage, pp. 591–620.
Loxley, J. (2007), 'Introduction', in John Loxley (ed.), *Transforming or Reforming Capitalism: Towards a Theory of Community Economic Development*. Halifax, Canada: Fernwood Publishing, pp. 1–6.
Marquis, C. and Battilana, J. (2009), 'Acting globally but thinking locally? The enduring influence of local communities on organizations', *Organizational Behaviour*, **29**, 283–302.

Marwell, N.P. (2007), *Bargaining for Brooklyn: Community Organizations in the Entrepreneurial City.* Chicago, IL: University of Chicago Press.
McArthur, A. (1986), 'An unconventional approach to economic development: the role of community business', *The Town Planning Review*, **57** (1), 87–100.
McArthur, A. (1993), 'An exploration of community business failure', *Policy and Politics*, **21** (3), 219–30.
McCulloch, A. (2000), 'Evaluations of a community regeneration project: case studies of Cruddas Park Development Trust, Newcastle upon Tyne', *Journal of Social Policy*, **29** (3), 397–419.
McKeever, E., Jack, S. and Anderson, A. (2015), 'Embedded entrepreneurship in the creative re-construction of place', *Journal of Business Venturing*, **30** (1), 50–65.
Minkoff, D.C. (1993), 'The organization of survival: women's racial-ethnic voluntarist and activist organizations, 1955–1985', *Social Forces*, **71**, 887–90.
Mullen, C.A. (2003), 'Guest editor's introduction: a self-fashioned gallery of aesthetic practice', *Qualitative Inquiry*, **9** (2), 165–81.
Parés, M., Ospina, S.M. and Subirats, J. (eds) (2017), *Social Innovation and Democratic Leadership: Communities and Social Change from Below*. Cheltenham, UK and Northampton, MA, USA: Edward Elgar Publishing.
Pearce, J. (1993), *At the Heart of the Community Economy: Community Enterprise in a Changing World.* London: Calouste Gulbenkian Foundation.
Pearce, J. (2003), *Social Enterprise in Anytown*. London: Calouste Gulbenkian Foundation.
Pearce, J. (2009), 'Social economy: engaging as a third system?', in Ash Amin (ed.), *The Social Economy: International Perspectives on Economic Solidarity*. London: Zed Books, pp. 22–33.
Peredo, A.M. and Chrisman, J.T. (2006), 'Towards a theory of community-based enterprise', *Academy of Management Review*, **31** (2), 309–28.
Perry, S.E. (1987), *Communities On the Way: Rebuilding Local Economies in the United States and Canada.* New York: State University of New York Press.
Persky, J., Ranney, D. and Wiewel, W. (1993), 'Import substitution and local economic development', *Economic Development Quarterly*, **7** (1), 18–29.
Pinder, C.C. (2014), *Work Motivation in Organizational Behavior*. New York: Psychology Press.
Porter, M.E. (1995), 'The competitive advantage of the inner city', *Harvard Business Review*, **73** (3), 55–71.
Pret, T. and Carter, S. (2017), 'The importance of "fitting in": collaboration and social value creation in response to community norms and expectations', *Entrepreneurship and Regional Development*, **29** (7–8), 639–67.
Purnell, B. (2012), 'What we need is brick and mortar: race, gender and early leadership of the Bedford-Stuyvesant Restoration Corporation', in Laura Warren Hill and Julia Rabig (eds), *The Business of Black Power: Community Development, Capitalism and Corporate Responsibility in Postwar America*. New York: University of Rochester Press, pp. 217–44.
Rabig, J. (2012), 'A fight and a question: community development corporations, machine politics and corporate philanthropy in the long urban crisis', in Laura Warren Hill and Julia Rabig (eds), *The Business of Black Power: Community Development, Capitalism and Corporate Responsibility in Postwar America*. New York: University of Rochester Press, pp. 245–73.
Robertson, N. (2010), *The Co-operative Movement and Communities in Britain, 1914–1960: Minding Their Own Business.* Surrey: Ashgate.
Rubin, H.J. (1993), 'Understanding the ethos of community-based development: ethnographic description for public administrators', *Public Administration Review*, **53** (5), 428–57.
Rubin, H.J. (1995), 'Renewing hope in the inner city: conversations with community-based development practitioners', *Administration & Society*, **27** (1), 127–60.
Rubin, H.J. and Rubin, I.S. (1992), *Community Organizing and Development*, 2nd edn. New York: Macmillan.
Sanders, R.M., Marlow, C. and Marlow, J. (1913), *Jubilee Souvenir of the Desborough Cooperative Society 1863–1913*. Desborough: Desborough Cooperative Society.
Selsky, J.W. and Parker, B. (2005), 'Cross-sector partnerships to address social issues: challenges to theory and practice', *Journal of Management*, **31** (6), 849–73.
Shrivastava, P. and Kennelly, J. (2013), 'Sustainability and place-based enterprise', *Organization and Environment*, **26** (1), 83–101.
Simon, W.H. (2001), *The Community Economic Development Movement: Law, Business and The New Social Policy*. Durham, NC: Duke University Press.
Slawinski, N. (2016), '(G)local philanthropy: local ideas, global potential – the Shorefast Foundation', in T. Jung, S. Phillips and J. Harrow (eds), *The Routledge Companion to Philanthropy*. London and New York: Routledge, pp. 37–41.
Soifer, S.D. (1990), 'The Burlington community land trust', *Journal of Urban Affairs*, **12**, 237–53.
Soifer, S.D., McNeely, J.B., Costa, C.L. and Pickering-Bernheim, N. (2014), *Community Economic Development in Social Work*. New York: Columbia University Press.
Somerville, P. and McElwee, G. (2011), 'Situating community enterprise: a theoretical exploration', *Entrepreneurship and Regional Development*, **23** (506), 317–30.

Spear, R., Teasdale, S., Lyon, F. et al. (2017), 'Social enterprise in the United Kingdom: models and trajectories', ICSEM Working Papers No. 40, International Comparative Social Enterprise Models Project.
Stott, N. and Tracey, P. (2018), 'Organizing and innovating in poor places', *Innovation: Organization and Management*, **20** (1), 1–17.
Stott, N., Fava, M., Tracey, P. and Claus, L. (2018), 'Playing well with others? Community cross-sector work in poor places'. Paper presented at the Re-thinking Cross-Sector Social Innovation Conference, 6–7 April, Social Innovation and Change Initiative, Harvard Kennedy School, Cambridge, MA.
Swersky, A. and Plunkett, J. (2015), 'What if we ran it ourselves?' Getting the measure of Britain's emerging community business sector', *Social Finance*, accessed 18 November 2017 at http://www.powertochange.org.uk/wp-content/uploads/2016/03/What-if-we-ran-it-ourselves-JAN2015.pdf
Tabart, T., Fulton, A. and Clark, R. (2001), 'Taking the future in their hands: local development practice around the world', *Rural Society*, **11** (1), 5–21.
Tracey, P. and Jarvis, O. (2006), 'An enterprising failure', *Stanford Social Innovation Review*, **4** (1), 66–70.
Tracey, P. and Stott, N. (2017), 'Social innovation: a window on alternative ways of organizing and innovating', *Innovation: Organization and Management*, **19** (1), 51–60.
Tracey, P., Phillips, N. and Haugh, H. (2005), 'Beyond philanthropy: community enterprise as a basis for corporate citizenship', *Journal of Business Ethics*, **58**, 327–44.
Unsworth, R., Ball, S., Bauman, I. et al. (2011), 'Building resilience and well-being in the margins within the city: changing perceptions, making connections, realising potential, plugging resources leaks', *City*, **15** (2), 181–203.
Vermeulen, F., Minkoff, D.C. and van der Meer, T. (2016), 'The local embedding of community-based organizations', *Nonprofit and Voluntary Sector Quarterly*, **45** (1), 23–44.
Wallace, S.L. (1999), 'Social entrepreneurship: the role of social purpose enterprises in facilitating community economic development', *Journal of Developmental Entrepreneurship*, **4** (2), 153–74.
Wyler, S. (2009), *A History of Community Asset Ownership*. London: Development Trusts Association.

10. Collective social innovation: leveraging custodianship, tradition and place on Fogo Island

M. Tina Dacin and Peter A. Dacin

We are a community of possibilities, not a community of problems. Community exists for the sake of belonging and takes its identity from the gifts, generosity, and accountability of its citizens. (Peter Block, *Community: The Structure of Belonging*)

INTRODUCTION

The concept of innovation is ubiquitous amongst scholars, practitioners and policy-makers. We focus on collective social innovation as a pathway for inclusive innovation. According to George et al. (2012), inclusive innovation is a process that involves the "development and implementation of new ideas which aspire to create social and economic wellbeing" (p. 663). In this regard, inclusive innovation is akin to the process of social innovation, which refers to innovative activities brought about to meet a social need (Mulgan, 2006, p. 146).

In this chapter we examine social innovation at the level of community and how the interplay of tradition and place serve as key resources to yield inclusive prosperity. We demonstrate how gaining an understanding of collective social innovation at the community level requires the need to identify both the needs of the community as well as the capacity or pool of valuable resources inherent in a community. We suggest that by examining phenomena at the community level introduces two other important concepts closely associated with community, the concepts of tradition and place. We view the interplay of tradition and place serving as key resources to yield community prosperity. As such, we also suggest a critical role for community members who are engaged together as vested custodians in enacting these resources and reviving, reinventing and renewing traditions.

Considering these concepts together, we then develop a framework that suggests that the building blocks of social innovation have roots in three key phenomena: place embeddedness, community identity and community character. Embeddedness in place and a shared history are a basis for developing belonging, attachment and shared fate among community members. Community identity is important for the relational ties or associations that it brings among community members, and community character, through cultural values and traditions, ascribes meaning to the community that is carried across time. While discussed separately in this chapter, it is clear that these three building blocks are inextricably intertwined through their rootedness in place. And it is these resources of community identity, as well as the valued, shared and unique historical knowledge and traditions embedded within place that custodians enact and protect for successful social innovation and inclusive communities.

We illustrate our ideas by focusing on the community of Fogo Island, a remote island off the coast of Newfoundland. As an island off an island (Newfoundland is also an island), places like Fogo are commonly known as outports. Outports are isolated communities and, as such, really interesting contexts to study the process and outcomes of innovation.

THEORETICAL OVERVIEW

We begin our overview with a discussion of social innovation. Following this we examine the characteristics of community and its relationship to place. We explore how a community's character is carried over time through its culture and traditions and how these traditions are revived, reinvented and renewed as a form of collective social innovation.

Social Innovation

A basic definition of social innovation is that it "refers to innovative activities and services that are motivated by the goal of meeting a social need" (Mulgan, 2006, p. 146). Expanding this basic definition, Westley (2008) adds that "social innovation is an initiative, product, process or program that profoundly changes the basic routines, resource and authority flows or beliefs of any social system." While these definitions provided a basic notion of social innovation, they did not explicitly discuss the importance of social innovation being targeted towards complex social problems or needs. Addressing this shortcoming, Phills et al. (2008, p. 36) refined the concept's definition by suggesting that social innovation is "a novel solution to a social problem that is more effective, efficient, sustainable, or just than existing solutions and for which the value created accrues primarily to society as a whole rather than private individuals." That is, Phills et al. (2008) suggest that beyond benefits accrued to any individual, the benefits and value emanating from social innovation should be considered, first and foremost, at a broader societal level. It is this societal-based approach that we take as a starting point in our examination of the practice and process of social innovation. Given this, we next explore the concept of social innovation at the community level of analysis.

Collective Social Innovation in Communities

An understanding of how local communities operate and sustain themselves is increasing in importance for academics, practitioners and policymakers. Fine (2012) refers to communities as "tiny publics" where social relations are organized by networks of affiliation vested in one another, promoting strength and cohesion through like-mindedness and shared understandings. In the broadest sense, communities are groupings that bring together individuals and their shared identity, expectations and interests (Storper, 2005).

Marquis et al. (2011) define communities as "collections of actors whose membership in the collective provides social and cultural resources that shape their action. Membership can result from a number of factors including propinquity, interest in a common goal or common identity" (p. xvi). In an influential paper, Marquis and Battilana (2009) examine the importance of community for organizing. For Marquis and Battilana, a community level of analysis is "a local level of analysis corresponding to the populations, organizations, and markets located in a geographic territory and sharing, as a result of their common location, elements of local culture, norms, identity, and laws" (Marquis and Battilana, 2009, p. 286).

In communities with little to no institutional arrangements such as developing contexts, rural communities or remote communities, we see the emergence of "commons" organizations (Meyer, 2017). For example, in rural communities lacking both economic resources and institutions typically found in urban contexts, institutional failures or voids lead to the emergence of community organizations which operate to complement or substitute for institutions. In this case, institutional voids may be a good thing as community members in rural and remote communities learn self-sufficiency and resilience independent from common regulative and policy apparatus.

Historically, development work tended to focus on community needs as problems of passive community recipients to be fixed from the outside. More recently, however, community development approaches (that is, Asset-Based Community Development) view community members as active producers of change as opposed to passive recipients (Kretzmann and McKnight, 1993). These more recent approaches explore how community members identify strengths and collectively use them to address issues that matter most to them and their communities. Building on ideas by Bollier and Helfrich (2012), Meyer's (2017) study of community development banks in Brazil finds four components inherently critical to the formation of commons in a community context. These include collective decision-making (community participation), community social control over key activities, servant leadership (altruism and compassion) and a desire for social change entailing a more inclusive and cooperative future. Furthermore, a collective action focus on community capacity lends to the process of forming new local institutions, resources and processes from within the community. This process of personally vesting in devoting their attention and assessing their capacity is a key building block for collective action and community custodianship.

In our view, collective social innovation is the outcome of inclusive community relationships, place embeddedness, and the cultural character of communities as well as a process of "the act of doing," of community members engaging together as custodians to fill needs and craft new opportunities. Communities are vast repositories of resources that can be bricolaged for innovation and social change (Di Domenico et al., 2010). Collective social innovation is an inclusive process that shifts both the routines and resource flows inside a community.

Social innovation at the community level suggests the need to identify both the needs of the community as well as the capacity or pool of valuable resources inherent in a community. Critical aspects of collective social innovation include the meaning taken from and character inherent in place, the relational ties or associations among community members that yield community identity, as well as the valued, shared and unique historical knowledge and traditions embedded within place. In the next subsections, we elaborate on each of these important characteristics underlying community social innovation.

Understanding place

In the early 1990s the field of economic geography began to take note of the importance of contextual settings in locational analysis. Labelled "the cultural turn" (Barnett, 1998; Scott, 2004), this refocusing of attention began a period in which economic geographers introduced and tried to understand "the role of culture in the eventuation of economic practices" (Scott, 2004, p. 483). Later, Barnes (2003), extending the work of Geertz (1983), argued that "knowledge is historically constrained, and produced within particular material settings that include, for example, individual geographical sites" (p. 73). This view opened up new ways of looking at place and social life as regional economic realities were now seen to result directly from local cultural forces (Barnes, 2003; Scott, 2004). That is, interest in locality studies from social and cultural geography introduced new perspectives on the formation of cultural identity in contemporary society and how it is constituted and reconstituted in place (Agnew, 1987; Cooke, 1989; Massey, 1991). To examine the increasingly complex nature of social interaction and cultural practices, place became a lens for analysis and researchers could no longer simply assert that "place matters" (Cresswell, 2004). Places became "dynamic arenas that are both socially constituted and constitutive of the social" (Dixon and Durrheim, 2000, p. 27).

Studies of place distinguish between space and place. Place is a complex, dynamic social and cultural construct while space tends to be detached from cultural interpretation (Gieryn, 2000; Hillier and Hanson, 1984). Sack (1997) identifies the dimensions of place as including nature, social relations and meaning and, as such, place mediates social life. Place requires human agency (Sack, 1988), and the ability to socially construct places is the result of our freedom to create meaning (Entrikin, 1991). In this view, place is continuously constructed through human practices and institutions, while it also helps shape those same practices and institutions (Giddens, 1984), simultaneously requiring both physical and semiotic (Bourdieu, 1990) approaches to understanding.

The rich nature of the term "place" unveils the geographical, architectural and social connotations of an environmental experience (Canter, 1977). Spaces can transform into places once they become "endowed with meaning" through various cultural processes (Cresswell, 2004; Gieryn, 2000; Low and Altman, 1992; Tuan, 1977). Tuan (1974, 1977), Relph (1976) and others emphasize how places are shaped through human involvement in activities and routines. These activities and routines, in turn, create both an emotional and a physical commitment to that place. Meaning may be endowed on a space and its physical features through such means as images, ideas and symbols (Pred, 1983; Williams, 1989). In this manner, places become repositories and contexts within which community relationships and ties are built; and it is to those social relationships and not "just to the place qua place, to which people are attached" (Low and Altman, 1992, p. 7).

According to Proshansky et al. (1983), attachment to place is embodied in an individual's "place identity" consisting of conceived cognitions about the physical world that represent memories, ideas, feelings, attitudes, values, preferences, meanings and the complexity of physical settings that define day-to-day existence. This view is analogous with Hummon's (1992) concept of environmental embeddedness, Tuan's affective ties to place or "topophilia" (1974), and Relph's (1976) "sense of place." Massey (1991), for example, suggests that each place is a particular constellation of social relations weaved together at a particular locus, thus creating a unique sense of place (Williams, 1985). Consequently, places are continuously dynamic and fluid (Martin, 2003) since "the same location may be interpreted through different senses of place" (Rose, 1995, p. 97).

As Schneekloth and Shibley (1995, p. 1, emphasis original) note, "placemaking is not just about the relationship of people to their places; it also creates relationships *among* people in places." Place creates valuable cultural attachments among place members and their goals (Beyer et al., 2000). Embedded in place leads to the formation of both place identity (attachment place) as well as attachment among community members (community identity). Community identities are important. For example, research demonstrates how identity in the form of regional sentiments influences investment and prosperity (Greenwood et al., 2010). As such, relationships among community members often transcend self-interest and result in a sense of belonging and goodwill (Almandoz et al., 2016).

Community members come together based on relational attributes of trust, loyalty, common sets of values and interest in each other's well-being (Brint, 2001). Citing Brint (2001), Almandoz et al. (2016) highlight the need for community members to value the community in its own right and/or for the positive impact in shaping a common set of values. Community members derive from community a sense of belonging, of who they are and why it matters. Building on the work of Giddens (1984) and others, Molotch et al. (2000, p. 794, emphasis added) discuss the role of community associations as linking devices that bring together heterogeneous actors as well as contain "*memory traces* through which . . . a social structure can transpose itself" over time or space. Marquis and Battilana (2009) also refer to the role of community social associations which serve to sustain community identities.

We now turn to a discussion of place and traditions. This literature allows us to explore the distinctiveness of places through the embodiment and practice of unique sets of traditions and practices in the characterization of community. Following this, we link traditions to collective social innovation in communities.

Place and Cultural Traditions

Molotch (2003) argues that the relationship between place and culture can be best understood as the "valorisation of milieu" (p. 679). This understanding then brings some clarity to how clusters or agglomerations of cultural industries can generate positive externalities by contributing to the quality of life and enhancing the image and prestige of a local area. In this manner, place-specific competitive advantage occurs because local cultural symbols and artefacts become congealed in a region's products, thus imbuing them with authentic character and value (Molotch, 2003). As such, mnemonic places (Zerubavel, 1997) that evoke memories and embody histories and relics of the past (such as monuments) become important cornerstones when building new cultural economies.

Work on cultural sustainability (Birkeland, 2008; Hawkes, 2001; Strange, 1999) greatly emphasizes roots and heritage. We also wish to highlight the importance of considering locality, community and place in sustainability of heritage. Sustainable communities can only be founded on commonalities and rootedness in place (Hay, 1998) and the desire for sustainability cannot be met without attention to the cultural and economic conditions that enable people to renew and reconnect their ties to place (Hay, 1998, 2005). Such a connection evolves out of the "real, active and natural participation in the life of the community . . . and is automatically brought about by place" and ultimately the need to be rooted in our social surroundings (Weil, 1952, p. 53).

Cultural elements play an important role in the economic revitalization of regions. In *The Death and Life of Great American Cities*, Jane Jacobs highlights the importance of unique cultural experiences to the vitality and economic viability of cities (Jacobs, 1961).

More recently, Zukin suggests that during the 1970s and 1980s a "symbolic economy" rose to prominence with almost every city deciding "to promote its art museums, and convert old railroad terminals and power stations to cultural complexes" in an attempt to capitalize on cultural amenities to promote the economy (Zukin, 1998, p. 833). In their examination of music in the Italian Piedmont, Mizzau and Montanari (2008) detail how new policy initiatives emerged to harness the power of culture to enhance the local economy.

Molotch et al. (2000) discuss the character of communities and how traditions carry the character of a place or community over time. They refer to the notion of "place distinctiveness" as an important underlying factor in how a place achieves and reproduces coherence over time. An understanding of the value of traditions embedded in place is important for community social innovation, as many innovations stem from the revitalization of traditional practices localized to a particular area. McGrath and Brennan (2011) address the maintenance of traditions through objects that symbolize experiences, often characterized by practices such as song, dance, story-telling and craft. The act of craft, in particular, combines traditional and new skills that are embedded in place and community (Blundel and Smith, 2013). Community members play important custodial roles in the maintenance of traditions by learning, practicing and teaching traditions so that they continue over time and do not fade into history. Intergenerational community relationships allow for the revitalization of traditions within more modern contexts. In the next subsection, we further explore the role of tradition for community social innovation. With an attachment to both community and place, community members take on the unique and important role of custodians. Custodians are actors (individual or collective) who seek to maintain institutionalized practices such as traditions (Dacin and Dacin, 2008; Soares, 1997).

Tradition and Collective Social Innovation

Traditions reside in place. We define traditions as living social arrangements in organizations infused with value and meaning derived from interpretations of the past (Dacin and Dacin, 2008; Soares, 1997). Molotch et al. (2000) suggest that traditions carry the character of communities over time. Much historical knowledge is embedded in local craft and tradition and is carried across time in the enactment of practices and sharing of information. McGrath and Brennan (2011) explore the role of tradition as a key means of stimulating community interaction as well as sharing collective and deeply embedded knowledge and the resultant impact on a community's well-being (p. 341). McGrath and Brennan's work is central to understanding the connection between tradition and community. Taking an "interactional" perspective, they address the centrality of local connections and capacity in the emergence of community among actors who share common territory. Common territory is comprised of shared history, traditions and culture (p. 341). For McGrath and Brennan (2011), intergenerational development and cultural preservation can be accomplished through work that promotes communication and interaction. Preserving community is crucial as loss of community translates into apathy (Brennan and Israel, 2008), but who cares for the culture and traditions of community and why do they care? In other words, why do community custodians enact and maintain some traditions while letting others wane?

Stinchcombe and March (1965) raise several issues concerned with the study of tradition by stating, "The problem is to specify who it is that carries 'tradition' and why they carry it, whose 'interests' become 'vested,' under what conditions, by what devices, whose 'folkways' cannot be changed by regulation, and why" (p. 167). For some, there is one actor, the custodian, that appears to serve a prominent role in creating, preserving and reshaping traditions (Shils, 1978; Soares, 1997). Giddens also suggests that the integrity of a tradition is not simply a function of time or persistence but rather stems more from individuals' abilities to capture the connections between the present and the past through "continuous work of interpretation" (Giddens, 1990, p. 64). Soares (1997) further argues that traditions may be viewed as resource warehouses that present strategic opportunities for custodians to enact in the course of their custodial activities. While not explicitly using the term custodian, Giddens (1990) suggests that guardians who are both emotionally vested agents and mediators hold the authority for this work of interpretation (see also DeJordy, 2010 for a more complete discussion of guardianship).

The importance of vestedness is crucial for custodianship. Without meaningfulness for custodians, a tradition may simply decay over time. Collective action in the form of custodianship will only take place if a tradition is important and meaningful for community members. In a study of the resurgence of collective identity, Howard-Grenville et al. (2013) propose that custodians facilitate the resurrection of past social arrangements by authenticating experiences, enrolling bystanders to identify with the tradition and modelling behaviors necessary to restore practices to new generations of the community. Interestingly, the important function of transmission in Howard-Grenville et al. (2013) was largely fulfilled by voluntary custodians working in unofficial roles who had emotional and aesthetic investment in reviving the collective identity. Custodians were not mandated to participate but elected to do so in a project to restore tradition.

We suggest that community members take custodianship for a community's most meaningful traditions and work to protect and preserve these traditions from decline. The work of maintaining traditions involves ongoing re-interpretation and while the core or essence of a tradition may remain intact, its periphery is reshaped and re-imagined to continue its inclusiveness, relevance and meaning (Dacin and Dacin, 2008). In doing so, the projects to sustain traditions very often create new processes and practices yielding social innovation at the level of community. In their study of quilters, Cheek and Piercy (2008) observed a diversity of needs fulfilled through the "practice" and maintenance of tradition including reifying connection to a community and solidifying a sense of community identity.

Our discussion above yields a number of important insights for understanding collective social innovation at the community level. First, it points to the importance of embeddedness in place in that a sense of shared place and history yields belonging, attachment, identity and shared fate. Second, culture and tradition serve as important resources as the foundation for a community's "sociobiographical memory" of place (Olick and Robbins, 1998), as carriers of history and knowledge through mnemonic places and memory traces (Molotch et al., 2000; Zerubavel, 1997). As noted by Molotch et al. (2000), a community's character is carried across time through its culture and traditions. Third, this points to the importance of exploring inclusiveness and the connective tissue and trust in the associational ties across community members (Marquis and Battilana, 2009; Molotch et al., 2000). Finally, collective social innovation is an inclusive process of routines, resources

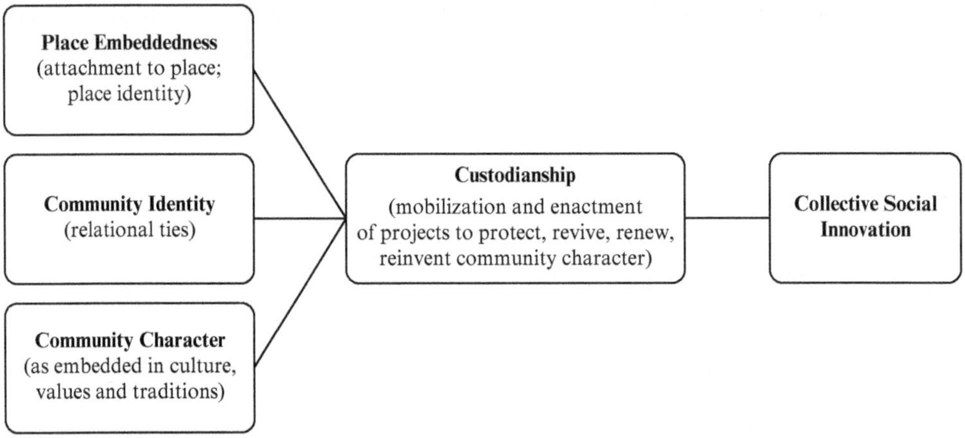

Figure 10.1 Building blocks of collective social innovation

and relationships in a community. It is the outcome of "collective custodianship" – community members engaging together as custodians in vested programs and projects. In Figure 10.1, we capture the building blocks of collective social innovation described above.

In the next section, we apply this thinking about collective social innovation to illustrate how a rural community on an island off the northeast coast of Newfoundland is reviving, renewing and reinventing tradition through projects that allow for custodianship.

COLLECTIVE SOCIAL INNOVATION: AN ILLUSTRATION

The context for our study is Fogo Island, a remote island off the coast of Newfoundland. As mentioned earlier, places like Fogo are commonly known as outports. During the 1960s Fogo Islanders experienced pressure from the Newfoundland government to relocate off Fogo to the main island of Newfoundland. During this time Fogo Islanders were also experiencing challenges resulting from a decline in the fishery on which they depended. Many left Fogo Island during this time and its population decreased by half from over 6,000 residents to under 3,000. For those who remained, the challenge became one of survival. However, Fogo Islanders are known for their ingenuity, resilience, persistence and love of place – their place.

Since the 1960s many social innovations occurred on Fogo Island, and we focus on one set in particular, those associated with the revival of craft traditions. Specifically, we examine how Fogo Islanders worked to revive and renew traditions, create new rituals and build a sense of collective custodianship of place. In particular, we focus on one social innovation, the renewal of punt boat building and its more recent connection to furniture making. In general, Fogo Island crafts are very much embedded in place and embodied in the making of place. Stemming from the revival of these crafts, a renewed sense of place coupled with social innovation at the community level built, and continues to build, a sense of shared prosperity and a vibrant future for Fogo Islanders.

Our theorizing of community, place and tradition as building blocks for collective social innovation is based upon a closer look at the rural and remote community of Fogo Island, Newfoundland. Newfoundland was the last province to join Canada in 1949. Comprised of numerous coastal communities, known as outports, and a few inland centres, the province holds a special connection to the sea. Throughout most of Newfoundland, the sea shapes everyday life from the fisheries to representation in culture. Fogo Island is an island community of 110 square miles situated in Notre Dame Bay off the northeastern coast of the island of Newfoundland. For centuries, outport communities sustained themselves through small-scale, inshore cod fisheries. However, as the cod fishery collapsed and the provincial government sought to enact resettlement programs, the decline of the Fogo Island community appeared inevitable. Social innovation is not new for Fogo Islanders. Community-level social innovations such as the Fogo Process and the formation of the Cooperative in the 1960s, described below, serve as the foundation for much of the innovation observed today. The current community collective action projects on Fogo Island are motivated in large part by the work of the Shorefast Foundation.

In the late 1960s, the Newfoundland government sought to relocate the population of much of Newfoundland's 1,000 or more rural, coastal outports to more centralized locations. A push towards modernization, a declining tax base and lack of a sustainable fishery are often reasons provided by policymakers for motivating changes in government policies. For decades before and afterwards, however, Newfoundland has had to address issues of poverty reduction. High levels of unemployment, the cod moratorium and the absence of vibrant and progressive policies led to sustained economic decline.

In the late 1960s, several communities on Fogo Island resisted resettlement as the community was involved in an innovative participatory filmmaking intervention known as "the Fogo Process." A partnership of the extension Service of Memorial University (MUN) and the National Film Board of Canada (NFB), three activist filmmaker/researchers sought to use film as a medium to generate dialogue and debate across Fogo's ten or more disparate communities previously divided by religious (Protestant versus Catholic) and spatial distance (Banoub, 2012). Donald Snowden and Fred Earle from MUN and Colin Low from the NFB made a series of 29 films in 1967 which gave locals much needed voice and input into the process of democracy. Fogo Island has a long and rich history of cooperative organizing beginning with the formation of the Fishermens' Protective Union in the early 1900s.

In 1967, during this time of resistance to resettlement, Fogo Islanders also formed a community-based hybrid enterprise known as the Fogo Island Cooperative. It is a hybrid enterprise because it represents the interests of fishers (producers) as well as fish plant workers (Haiven and Haiven, 2009). This Cooperative has mostly succeeded to this day. However, the fate of the inshore fishery was not a success. In 1992, the cod fishery off Newfoundland collapsed pushing the province into a severe economic crisis. The introduction of large factory trawler boats, overfishing and poor fisheries management by government regulators are largely blamed for the decline in fish stocks. Regulators placed an indefinite moratorium on fishing for cod and the livelihood of many in the inshore fishery on Fogo Island could have come to an end. In response, the fishers on Fogo Island were quick to adapt to other products such as shrimp, turbot, crab and herring. In doing so, the Cooperative was able to sustain itself over time (Haiven and Haiven, 2009).

As an early example of collective social innovation, the Fogo Island Cooperative foreshadowed many of the recent efforts of the Shorefast Foundation on Fogo Island. The Shorefast Foundation, a registered Canadian charity, was established by Zita Cobb and her two brothers, Tony and Alan Cobb in 2003 with the mandate to help secure a sustainable and resilient future for Fogo Islanders. The Foundation operates a number of social enterprises and initiatives in the arts, fishery, domestic craft and eco-luxury tourism. In 2013, the Foundation opened the Fogo Island Inn, a community held social enterprise with 29 rooms providing guests with an authentic and luxurious immersion into Fogo Island life and history. Through the work of the Shorefast Foundation and the momentum of community projects largely driven by Zita and her brothers, revival on Fogo Island is taking place. The Shorefast projects are simultaneously global, drawing in tourists and contemporary artists (for example, Fogo Island Arts; Fogo Island Inn), and local as they push the ethos of the local community out to the broader world (for example, Fogo Island Fish; Fogo Island Shop).

In the following section, we focus on a community project involving craft traditions and their embeddedness in community and place: punt boat building. This illustrative example demonstrates tradition as a carrier of community character and historical knowledge over time (Molotch et al., 2000). The craft of punt boat building serves to bridge the past with the present to craft a sustainable future for the island.

Leveraging Historical Knowledge, Tradition and Place on Fogo Island

The revival of craft traditions and their renewal into contemporary craft leverages centuries old knowledge held in the hearts and minds of Fogo Islanders. One example of leveraging historical knowledge involves punt boat building. In this boat-building example, we examine how the focus has largely been to preserve and protect historical knowledge embedded in time and place and how this knowledge has been translated or reinvented into more contemporary form. We look at this example as an illustration of a community custodial project and collective social innovation.

The Fogo Island Punt Boat

Newfoundland has a long and rich history in the craft of boat building (Taylor, 1982). Boats are an integral part of life in coastal communities. The punt is more than a boat. It is a boat that is the embodiment of centuries of hardship, resilience and creativity. Used for more than fishing, these boats were the key means of transportation between coastal communities. Typically used for inshore fishing when fishers are within sight of land, punts are usually no longer than 18 feet, undecked and square-backed boats.

The craft of wooden boat building is deeply embedded in local communities. The method of building punts is passed down through generations but this craft has been eroding in recent years. Master boat builders are revered for their expertise but, as with many other craft traditions, building punts is quite literally a dying art. Fogo Island is a community recognized for its boat-building heritage. Until recently, there were seven master boat builders on Fogo Island. As of 2017, there are six. Punts and their builders hold knowledge carried through time – an embodiment of human resilience, ingenuity and resourcefulness.

There is much more to building a punt than there is to simply making a boat. Produced by local master boat builders, traditional punts are between 13 and 18 feet in length. They are made of wood construction using the plank over the "timbers" framing method and the "half-model" or moulding (whole-moulding) method. Models of boats are passed down across generations and there is a technique to harvesting the right type of timber to build the boat and when to harvest the wood. Frank Combden, a master boat builder on Fogo Island, uses a three-piece mould to build the main frame for his boats. As described in the oral history of Frank Combden on Boats and Builders (a website dedicated to preserving knowledge about the craft of boat building, http://boatsandbuilders.com/boat-building/frank-combdens-punt), the shape of the stem of the boat is determined by the shape of the tree from which it was harvested (Figure 10.2).

In order to build a punt boat, the builder must utilize the natural curves of spruce and juniper trees and first be able to see the form of the boat represented in the trunk and

Photo provided by Wooden Boat Museum of Newfoundland and Labrador. Used with permission.

Figure 10.2 Frank Combden of Fogo Island and the stem of his punt boat

Photo by Patrice Halley. Photo provided courtesy of Shorefast. Used with permission.

Figure 10.3 A punt boat

stem of a tree (Hall, 2013). The tree's natural curves form the structural ribs of the punt. Centuries old knowledge of punt-building skills carried through time allow the boat builders to recognize potential trees for harvesting and doing so only when the time is right. Figure 10.3 is a picture of a punt boat under construction illustrating its structural ribs.

The community or social organization is essential in making and maintaining culture. As a key building block of collective social innovation, associational ties among community members are key for community identity. Reliance on fishing in small boats shaped the connections and forms of belonging among community members. Following the cod moratorium in 1992, coastal communities began the long struggle of redefining their identity (Sider, 2003). What is the role of tradition in maintaining and rebuilding community identity? How does this take place and who makes it happen?

Renewing Interest in Boats and Boat Building: The Great Fogo Island Punt Race

An early initiative of the Shorefast Foundation, the annual "Great Fogo Island Punt Boat Race" was introduced in 2007. Concerned that the craft of small boat building was disappearing and that the need for punts was disappearing, the annual race had multiple objectives. The first was to create a need for punts to be built. The second was to revitalize interest in the punt. Finally, it served as a means to bring the community together in a project around saving heritage. In doing so, the punt becomes an embodiment of place in addition to an embodiment of human resilience described above – a carrier of community character over time.

As stated on the Punt Race website:

> our greatest accomplishment by far has been the creation of many new punts resulting from our race, built or commissioned by competing rowers, which has helped to preserve our heritage. By

> creating a fun community event using the punt, an integral piece of our culture and history, we have been able to see the value of old ways and bring them into contemporary times. (http://www.tothereandback.org/wp2017/)

Two other initiatives also serve to preserve the traditional knowledge of building punts. The first was a limited time program named the Punt Boat Building School Program. In 2007, Shorefast collaborated with Fogo Island Central Academy, a local high school, to sponsor a punt boat-building course offered by two local master boat builders. The second initiative is the establishment of the Fogo Island Punt Centre. Set to open in 2019, the Punt Centre is a gathering space for education and practice. It will deliver programming inclusive of races but also provide a deeper connection with punts such as, but not limited to, boat-building classes and deep knowledge on the preservation of heritage punt boats. These initiatives provide opportunities for teaching and learning about wooden boat heritage across generations that is inherent to the traditional practice of craft and the maintenance of a community's character over time (Molotch et al., 2000). In doing so, Shorefast has been able to mobilize collective custodianship to preserve the historical knowledge and practices embedded in place.

Translating Historical Knowledge: Creating the Punt Chair

During the process of building the Fogo Island Inn, the Shorefast Foundation (now Shorefast) invited some of the best designers from the world to gather together on the island and engage in a series of Design Dialogues aimed at reviving, preserving, protecting and re-interpreting local knowledge. Élaine Fortin from Quebec, Canada, is the designer of the punt chair. Utilizing the same method of carefully harvesting the correct juniper and spruce timber used in building punt boats, the chair's legs and frame are built from the naturally curved roots of the trees with no steaming used in the building process (illustrated in Figure 10.4). Each punt chair is identified by location of where it was harvested and also by its producer.

The punt chair is now a carrier of hundreds of years of knowledge, craft skill and boat-building tradition. It is a reinvention of boat-building tradition but maintains the connection to place and to the craft skill of punt boat building. The designer, furniture makers and boat builders engaged in a process of collective social innovation as they served important custodial roles in preserving and translating the knowledge and skills of building punts. The translation of centuries old boat-building knowledge into the materiality and ethos of the punt chair exemplifies the innovative means by which knowledge is pulled from the past into the future.

DISCUSSION

Collective action in communities forms important pathways for social innovation that, in turn, build sustainability, success of community development projects, and revitalize shared prosperity in contexts where existing systems, practices and institutional arrangements have failed, do not exist or are no longer viable. Collective activities associated with placemaking serve an important role within the Fogo Island community. Fogo Islanders'

Photo by Mark Bennett. Photo provided courtesy of the Fogo Island Shop. Used with permission.

Figure 10.4 A punt chair

roles as custodians have resulted in the revitalization of practices that seek to save *and* celebrate place. In our chapter we sought to understand collective social innovation at the level of community. We drew on the literature on communities, place and tradition to better understand the provenance of innovation over time in the rural and remote context of Fogo Island, Newfoundland.

What mobilizes community members to engage in collective community action to protect, renew and reinvent traditions? We contend that custodianship of a community's traditions largely occurs when actors are vested in a number of ways. First, community members must know their strengths and resources embedded in place. In rural and remote communities, innovation arises from needs not wants. The resilience and ingenuity of community members to thrive in times of hardship builds great resolve.

Second, relational ties among community members yield a sense of shared fate. The practice of working and crafting together builds community bonds and connections beyond the act of production itself. Fogo Islanders have a long and rich history of working together and of "doing" (Z. Cobb, in personal conversation, 2018). Early initiatives such as the Fogo Process and the formation of the Fogo Island Cooperative were pivotal projects that allowed community members to engage in dialogue and debate.

Third, culture and traditions carry a community's character over time. The traditions or practices maintained by custodians are those that hold the most meaning for a community and its members. In the case of punt boat building, Fogo Island is known for its historical knowledge of this craft. This knowledge bestows a sense of pride in the community as master boat builders are known beyond a community's boundaries.

In our illustrative case we saw traditions *revived* (boat building), *renewed* (The Great Fogo Island Punt Race) and *reinvented* (from punt boat to punt chair). We suggest that the craft of punt boat building is a micro-institution, an institutionalized practice carried through time, brought forward in its traditional material form yet open to translation via embedded remnants of knowledge into a new aesthetic (Dacin and Dacin, 2008). The re-imagining of the boat to chair contemporizes the practice by innovating and moving the rooted and embodied knowledge across time and place. It is this ability to innovate with and upon historical knowledge buttressed by collective custodianship that yields shared prosperity and a sustainable future. As suggested by Zita Cobb, "it is in the act of doing" – of community members engaging together to fill needs and craft new opportunities through both their embeddedness in place and embodiment of place that yields social innovation.

Directions for Future Research

Our chapter provides several insights for inclusive innovation and for understanding collective social innovation at the community level. We highlight the role of community embeddedness in place and contend that a community's survival is dependent on the collective custodianship, reproduction and maintenance of its historical knowledge embodied in its craft skills and traditions (McGrath and Brennan, 2011). Below, we suggest a number of directions for scholars of community and inclusive innovation.

First, we suggest the need for more of a collective action perspective on social innovation pointing to the importance of exploring and strengthening associational ties across community members (Marquis and Battilana, 2009; Molotch et al., 2000). However, a caveat of this perspective is the need to account for diversity of community interests and, no matter how inclusive the innovation, solutions must often be sequenced, accepted and well understood.

Second, more work needs to be done to understand how a community can assess its core assets and resources. While some work has been done by practitioners of Asset-Based Community Development (Kretzmann and McKnight, 1993), this approach to mapping out a community's resources, skills and experiences has not been fully embraced by scholars and policymakers. An issue is that such approaches may have difficulty addressing systemic disenfranchisement and that a community's stock of social capital may be insufficient to revive the community.

Third, as communities engage in collective custodianship of their cultural knowledge and heritage, what are the processes by which inclusion is not only encouraged but ensured? Inclusive innovation must entail social justice, empowerment and democracy. Thus, additional questions for scholars to ask include: What is the role of power in custodianship? Whose voice matters most and why? Who are community elites and how do they come to matter? And what is the role of community elites in deciding what pathways will be pursued and which of these hold the most promise for sustained community resilience?

Innovation (social and inclusive) at the community level must ultimately address the social, cultural and economic viability of place. Thus, a final research direction to pursue is a stronger understanding of the variance in the focus of custodianship or custodial efforts across communities over time. Not everything is revived, renewed or maintained. Custodians decide what to maintain and what to let go. And letting go in one form may mean retaining or reinventing what matters in another form as in the case of the punt chair.

ACKNOWLEDGEMENT

The authors would like to acknowledge support from the Social Sciences and Humanities Research Council of Canada.

REFERENCES

Agnew, J. (1987), *Place and Politics: The Geographical Mediation of State and Society*, Boston, MA: Allen and Unwin.

Almandoz, J., C. Marquis, and M. Cheely (2016), *Drivers of Community Strength: An Institutional Logics Perspective on Geographical and Affiliation-based Communities*, New York: Sage.

Banoub, D. (2012), "Fogo Island arriving: 'an anti-essentialist reading of the production of place'", *Newfoundland and Labrador Studies*, **27**(1), 33–62.

Barnes, T. (2003), "The place of locational analysis: a selective and interpretive history", *Progress in Human Geography*, **27**(1), 69–95.

Barnett, C. (1998), "The cultural turn: fashion or progress in human geography?", *Antipode*, **30**(4), 379–94.

Beyer, J.M., D.R. Hannah, and L. Milton (2000), "Ties that bind: culture and attachments in organizations". In N. Ashkanasy, C. Wilderom, and M. Peterson (eds), *Handbook of Organizational Culture and Climate*, Thousand Oaks: CA: Sage, pp. 323–38.

Birkeland, I. (2008), "Cultural sustainability: industrialism, placelessness and the re-animation of place", *Ethics, Place & Environment*, **11**(3), 283–97.

Block, P. (2008), *Community: The Structure of Belonging*, San Francisco, CA: Berrett-Koehler.

Blundel, R.K. and D.J. Smith (2013), "Reinventing artisanal knowledge and practice: a critical review of innovation in a craft-based industry", *Prometheus*, **31**(1), 55–73.

Bollier, D., and S. Helfrich (eds) (2012), *The Wealth of the Commons: A World Beyond Market and State*, Amherst, MA: Levellers Press.

Bourdieu, P. (1990), *The Logic of Practice*, Stanford, CA: Stanford University Press.

Brennan, M.A. and G.D. Israel (2008), "The power of community", *Community Development*, **39**(1), 82–98.

Brint, S. (2001), "Gemeinschaft revisited: a critique and reconstruction of the community concept", *Sociological Theory*, **19**(1), 1–23.

Canter, D.V. (1977), *The Psychology of Place*, London: Architectural Press.

Cheek, C. and K.W. Piercy (2008), "Quilting as a tool in resolving Erikson's adult stage of human development", *Journal of Adult Development*, **15**(1), 13–24.

Cooke, P. (1989), "The contested terrain of locality studies", *Tijdschrift voor Econornische en Sociale Geografie*, **80**(1), 14–29.

Cresswell, T. (2004), *Place: A Short Introduction*, Oxford: Blackwell Publishing.

Dacin, M.T. and P.A. Dacin (2008), "Traditions as institutionalized practice: implications for deinstitutionalization". In R. Greenwood, C. Oliver, K. Sahlin, and R. Suddaby (eds), *The Sage Handbook of Organizational Institutionalism*, London: Sage, pp. 327–52.

DeJordy, R. (2010), *Institutional Guardianship: The Role of Agency in Preserving Threatened Institutional Arrangements*, Boston, MA: Boston College.

Di Domenico, M., H. Haugh, and P. Tracey (2010), "Social bricolage: theorizing social value creation in social enterprises", *Entrepreneurship Theory and Practice*, **34**(4), 681–703.

Dixon, J. and K. Durrheim (2000), "Displacing place-identity: a discursive approach to locating self and other", *British Journal of Social Psychology*, **39**(1), 27–44.

Entrikin, J.N. (1991), "The betweenness of place". In J.N. Entrikin (ed.), *The Betweenness of Place*, London: Palgrave, pp. 6–26.

Fine, G.A. (2012), *Tiny Publics: A Theory of Group Action and Culture*, New York: Russell Sage Foundation.

Geertz, C. (1983), *Local Knowledge: Further Essays in Interpretive Anthropology*, New York: Basic Books.

George, G., A.M. McGahan, and J. Prabhu (2012), "Innovation for inclusive growth: towards a theoretical framework and a research agenda", *Journal of Management Studies*, **49**(4), 661–83.
Giddens, A. (1984), *The Constitution of Society*, Cambridge: Polity Press.
Giddens, A. (1990), *Consequences of Modernity*, Stanford, CA: Stanford University Press.
Gieryn, T.F. (2000), "A space for place in sociology", *Annual Review of Sociology*, **26**, 463–96.
Greenwood, R., A.M. Diaz, S.X. Li, and J.C. Lorente (2010), "The multiplicity of institutional logics and the heterogeneity of organizational responses", *Organization Science*, **21**(2), 521–39.
Haiven, J. and L. Haiven (2009), "Do cooperatives protect workers' rights? Lessons from Canada". In *The Modernization of Labour Law and Industrial Relations in a Comparative Perspective*, the Netherlands: Kluwer Law International, pp. 459–71.
Hall, P. (2013), "Recruiting the visual: knowing our commonplace towards an encyclopedia of local knowledge". Doctoral dissertation, Memorial University of Newfoundland.
Hawkes, J. (2001), *The Fourth Pillar of Sustainability: Culture's Essential Role in Public Planning*, Melbourne: Common Ground Publishing and Cultural Development Network.
Hay, R. (1998), "A rooted sense of place in cross-cultural perspective", *The Canadian Geographer*, **42**(3), 245–66.
Hay, R. (2005), "Becoming ecosynchronous, part 1. The root causes of our unsustainable way of life", *Sustainable Development*, **13**(5), 311–25.
Hillier, B. and J. Hanson (1984), *The Social Logic of Space*, Cambridge: Cambridge University Press.
Howard-Grenville, J., M.L. Metzger, and A.D. Meyer (2013), "Rekindling the flame: processes of identity resurrection", *Academy of Management Journal*, **56**(1), 113–36.
Hummon, D.M. (1992), "Community attachment: local sentiment and sense of place". In I. Altman and S.M. Low (eds), *Place Attachment*, New York: Plenum Press, pp. 253–76.
Jacobs, J. (1961), *The Death and Life of Great American Cities*, New York: Random House.
Kretzmann, J.P. and J. McKnight (1993), *Building Communities from the Inside Out*, Evanston, IL: Center for Urban Affairs and Policy Research, Neighborhood Innovations Network, pp. 2–10.
Low, S.M. and I. Altman (1992), "Place attachment: a conceptual inquiry", *Human Behavior & Environment: Advances in Theory & Research*, **12**, 1–12.
Marquis, C. and J. Battilana (2009), "Acting globally but thinking locally? The enduring influence of local communities on organizations", *Research in Organizational Behavior*, **29**, 283–302.
Marquis, C., M. Lounsbury, and R. Greenwood (2011), "Introduction: community as an institutional order and a type of organizing". In *Communities and Organizations*, Bingley, UK: Emerald Group Publishing, pp. ix–xxvii.
Martin, D. (2003), "Place-framing as place-making: constituting a neighborhood for organizing and activism", *Annals of the Association of American Geographers*, **93**(3), 730–50.
Massey, D. (1991), "The political place of locality studies", *Environment and Planning*, **23**(2), 267–81.
McGrath, B. and M.A. Brennan (2011), "Tradition, cultures and communities: exploring the potentials of music and the arts for community development in Appalachia", *Community Development*, **42**(3), 340–58.
Meyer, C. (2017), "Building commons in community enterprises: the case of self-managed microfinance organizations in Brazil", *Academy of Management Proceedings 2017 – Best Conference Papers*. https://doi.org/10.5465/AMBPP.2017.43, 30 October, accessed 2 February 2018.
Mizzau, L. and F. Montanari (2008), "Cultural districts and the challenge of authenticity: the case of Piedmont, Italy", *Journal of Economic Geography*, **8**(5), 651–73.
Molotch, H. (2003), *Where Stuff Comes From: How Toasters, Toilets, Cars, Computers, and Many Other Things Come to Be*, London: Routledge.
Molotch, H., W. Freudenburg, and K.E. Paulsen (2000), "History repeats itself, but how? City character, urban tradition, and the accomplishment of place", *American Sociological Review*, **65**(6), 791–823.
Mulgan, G. (2006), "The process of social innovation", *Innovations: Technology, Governance, Globalization*, **1**(2), 145–62.
Olick, J. K. and J. Robbins (1998), "Social memory studies: from 'collective memory' to the historical sociology of mnemonic practices", *Annual Review of Sociology*, **24**(1), 105–40.
Phills, J.A., K. Deiglmeier, and D.T. Miller (2008), "Rediscovering social innovation", *Stanford Social Innovation Review*, **6**(4), 34–43.
Pred, A. (1983), "Structuration and place: on the becoming of sense of place and structure of feeling", *Journal for the Theory of Social Behavior*, **13**(1), 45–68.
Proshansky, H.M., A.K. Fabian, and R. Kaminoff (1983), "Place-identity: physical world socialization of the self", *Journal of Environmental Psychology*, **3**(1), 57–83.
Relph, E.C. (1976), *Place and Placelessness*, London: Pion.
Rose, G. (1995), "Place and identity: a sense of place". In D. Massey and P. Jess (eds), *A Place in the World? Places, Cultures and Globalization*, Oxford: Oxford University Press, pp. 87–132.
Sack, R.D. (1988), "The consumer's world: place as context", *Annals of the Association of American Geographers*, **78**(4), 642–64.
Sack, R.D. (1997), *Homo Geographicus*, Baltimore, MD: Johns Hopkins University Press.

Schneekloth, L.H. and R.G. Shibley (1995), *Placemaking: The Art and Practice of Building Communities*, New York: John Wiley & Sons.

Scott, A.J. (2004), "A perspective of economic geography", *Journal of Economic Geography*, **4**(5), 479–99.

Shils, E. (1978), "Roots – the sense of place and past: the cultural gains and losses of migration". In W.H. McNeil and R.S. Adams (eds), *Human Migration: Patterns and Policies*, Bloomington, IN: Indiana University Press, pp. 404–26.

Sider, G.M. (2003), *Between History and Tomorrow: Making and Breaking Everyday Life in Rural Newfoundland*, Vol. 1, Toronto: University of Toronto Press.

Soares, J.A. (1997), "A reformulation of the concept of tradition", *International Journal of Sociology and Social Policy*, **17**(6), 6–21.

Stinchcombe, A.L. and J.G. March (1965), "Social structure and organizations". In J.P. March (ed.), *Handbook of Organizations*, Chicago: Rand McNally, pp. 142–93.

Storper, M. (2005), "Society, community, and economic development", *Studies in Comparative International Development*, **39**(4), 30–57.

Strange, I. (1999), "Urban sustainability, globalization and the pursuit of the heritage aesthetic", *Planning Practice & Research*, **14**(3), 301–11.

Taylor, D.A. (1982), "Boat building in Winterton, Trinity Bay, Newfoundland". Master's thesis, Memorial University of Newfoundland.

The Great Fogo Island Punt Race. http://www.tothereandback.org/wp2017/ and http://www.fogoislandregatta.com/c_heritage.html, accessed 2 March 2019.

Tuan, Y.-f (1974), *Topophilia: A Study of Environmental Perception, Attitudes, and Values,* Englewood Cliffs, NJ: Prentice Hall.

Tuan, Y.-f. (1977), *Space and Place: The Perspective of Experience*, Minneapolis, MN: University of Minnesota Press.

Weil, S. (1952), *The Need for Roots*. London: Routledge and Kegan Paul.

Westley, F. (2008), "The social innovation dynamic", *Frances Westley, SiG@ Waterloo.*

Williams, R. (1985), *Keywords: A Vocabulary of Culture and Society*, Oxford: Oxford University Press.

Williams, R. (1989), *Resources of Hope: Culture, Democracy, Socialism*, New York: Verso.

Zerubavel, E. (1997), *Social Mindscapes: An Invitation to Cognitive Sociology*, Cambridge, MA: Harvard University Press.

Zukin, S. (1998), "Urban lifestyles: diversity and standardization in spaces of consumption", *Urban Studies*, **35**(5/6), 825–40.

PART IV

SYSTEMS, INSTITUTIONS AND INFRASTRUCTURE

11. Coordinating infrastructure changes to meet retiring baby boomers' needs

David Souder

INTRODUCTION

This chapter aims to illustrate how management scholarship plays a pivotal role in helping to achieve social inclusion innovations proposed by experts in other fields. Although I focus on one specific example – the development of inclusive residences for retiring baby boomers – my broader point is that the achievement of complex social goals depends on thoughtful application of the wide-angle lens and systems orientation that epitomize management scholarship (Dunne and Martin, 2006). Current generational challenges, such as flawed incentives in the health care payment system or the inconsistency of primary and secondary education quality, require innovation in social systems as well as technology. The expertise to address such challenges will come from many disciplines, and a management perspective can generate unique contributions by explaining how multiple trends affect each other and interact to influence an entire system toward change. In this example, the expertise of urban planners and architects can be complemented and enriched by the broad-based stakeholder coordination that distinguishes management scholars and practitioners from more specialized fields (Kotha et al., 2013).

Management scholars are often aware of the limitations of a generalist perspective, and only tentatively push insights into the public sphere. Admittedly, real world applications of social innovations will be imperfect and messy, and deployed in ways never intended. But social challenges will not solve themselves. They are important precisely because they require attention from multiple areas of expertise rather than just one. Just as businesses must often resolve tradeoffs in priorities between marketing and operations, or decide whether to expand sales efforts or the research lab, social challenges require both the science and art of managerial skills to develop innovations with broader support.

Specifically, stakeholder coordination enables efficiencies that allow new types of urban residences to include both retirees and young adults at prices that are simultaneously affordable for consumers and profitable for investors. As baby boomers reach retirement age, the number of Americans over 65 will nearly double – to 80 million – from 2010 to 2040 (West et al., 2014, p. 5). Many baby boomers have lived most of their lives in suburbs designed to meet the needs of child-rearing families, but unconducive for aging residents to access desired amenities (McIlwain, 2012). Consequently, the US sits on the verge of an unprecedented social challenge to include suburban retirees in active lifestyles despite declining mobility. Notwithstanding their population decline since 1950, most industrial cities retain the infrastructure for transportation and culture built to the scale of a more populous past. Urban planners have proposed reusing this existing infrastructure in the development of inclusive and walkable residential communities that offer improved "wealth, health, and sustainability" to residents (Speck, 2012, p. 16). Yet even though city living seems conducive to the desired lifestyle of many retirees (McIlwain, 2010, 2012), and walkability resonates with many young professionals, a majority of baby boomers express a preference to remain in suburban-style housing (Kotkin, 2015). As a result, developers have only cautiously pursued plans to reshape the physical layout of cities in retiree-friendly ways.

This chapter explains how management scholarship can be applied to facilitate the development of inclusive urban residences that will appeal to baby boomers at ages they have not yet reached, and the corresponding adjustments needed in civic priorities and funding flows. Done well, catering to the needs of baby boomers can jump-start demand and ultimately promote inclusion across age and income demographics, generating spillover benefits (George et al., 2012) and revitalizing city centers for generations to come.

DECLINING SOCIAL INCLUSION FOR SUBURBAN RETIREES AND THE OPPORTUNITY FOR CITY RESIDENCES

Baby Boomer Demographics

For over 60 years, the life cycle needs of baby boomers have disproportionately influenced economic trends and business output because their births altered the US population growth trajectory. Using data and projections from the US Census Bureau, each line on Figure 11.1 tracks the population over time for a different age range. As baby boomers enter each age range, the slope of each line becomes noticeably steeper, only to then revert to a more historical growth trajectory once boomers have exited the age range.

The development of US suburbia is one example of a phenomenon grounded in the life cycle needs of baby boomers. Popular suburbs offer nice yards, good schools, and neighbors with children – amenities that appeal to many families with young children (Messia, 2003). Accordingly, when boomers were children, the suburban population grew from 40 million in 1950 to 100 million in 1980. Once the boomers became parents themselves, suburbs continued expanding and became home to 51 percent of US residents – over 150 million people – by 2010 (Mather et al., 2011).

However, with baby boomers' children mostly grown, and as they prepare for retirement, suburban life becomes less conducive to their current and future needs. Spacious yards may be great for playtime, but they require manual upkeep that becomes increasingly burdensome with age. And while good schools are important to younger parents, they often impose high property taxes on empty-nesters. Zoning ordinances that separate commerce from residences make it easier to keep kids safe, but they also force the use of cars to buy groceries, visit doctors, or attend cultural activities. Even without such zoning, few suburban areas have sufficient population density to support a full array of retail activity within reasonable walking distance. In short, suburban life depends on automobiles (see Lindstrom and Bartling, 2003, p. xix).

Yet driving becomes increasingly difficult and dangerous as people age, impeding full societal inclusion and compromising safety. Many older drivers voluntarily reduce their time behind the wheel at night or in bad weather, but rarely give up their cars entirely. Line 19 of Table 11.1 shows that 90 percent of households headed by 65–74 year-olds possess a vehicle – virtually unchanged from the level observed for younger ages. Beyond

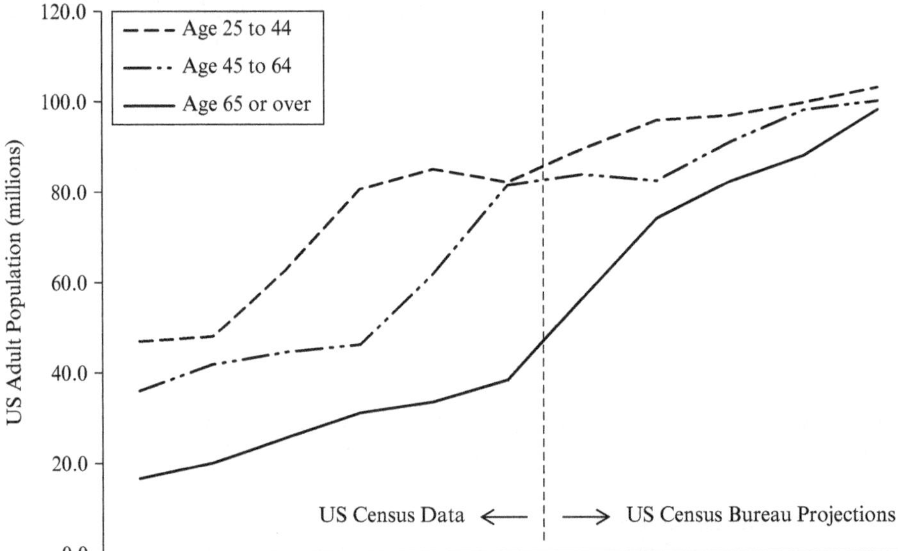

	1960	1970	1980	1990	2000	2010	2020	2030	2040	2050	2060
Age 25 to 44	46.9	48.0	62.7	80.6	85.0	82.1	89.5	95.8	96.9	99.7	103.0
Age 45 to 64	36.1	41.8	44.5	46.2	62.0	81.5	83.9	82.4	91.0	98.1	100.0
Age 65 or over	16.6	20.1	25.6	31.1	33.5	38.4	56.4	74.1	82.3	88.0	98.2

Source: US Census Bureau, actual data 1960–2010 and projections (as of 1 July) for 2020–2060.

Figure 11.1 US adult population by age, 1960–2060

age 75, car possession is noticeably lower; however, even then more than three-quarters of households still own at least one vehicle. Total vehicles per household declines at age 65 (see line 4), but the number of vehicles per person remains similar after accounting for the corresponding reduction in household size (line 2). Given that cars have come to symbolize the identities of suburban residents, many retirees are reluctant to give up their cars because it feels like they are giving up their freedom. Consequently, unless they move to residences that are not car-dependent, aging suburban baby boomers will either continue driving in less-than-safe conditions, or increasingly feel stranded in their homes and frustrated with the inability to function autonomously.

Meanwhile, suburban parents regularly drive to work and shuttle kids between after-school activities, but have limited time to attend cultural events. Once the children are grown, and especially after retirement, there is more time for leisure activities, as seen in cultural institutions' high concentration of patronage among older demographics. Cars remain essential to reach these events for suburbanites, and at some age, the hassle of driving home with limited night vision after an evening performance will become prohibitive. Suburban isolation already exists, but will become increasingly prevalent with the impending volume of retirees.

As the US population has more than doubled since 1950, the life cycle of baby boomers largely explains why such population growth has been overwhelmingly concentrated in suburbs rather than the cities they surround (Nelson, 1988). Only six of the 20 largest

Table 11.1 2010 Consumer unit characteristics by age of reference person

	Total US	Under 25	25 to 34	35 to 44	45 to 54	55 to 64	65 to 74	75 or over
Mean values:								
1 Before-tax income	$62481	$26881	$59613	$76128	$79589	$68906	$49711	$31782
2 Number of persons	2.5	2.0	2.9	3.3	2.8	2.2	1.9	1.6
3 Number of earners	1.3	1.2	1.5	1.6	1.6	1.3	0.7	0.2
4 Number of vehicles	1.9	1.1	1.7	2.0	2.3	2.2	1.9	1.3
5 After-tax income (per person)	$24285	$13389	$20192	$22465	$27238	$30278	$25576	$19774
6 Annual expenses (per person)	$19244	$13742	$16075	$16953	$20639	$23136	$21807	$19706
Expense categories (mean values):								
7 Food at home (per person)	$1450	$1099	$1151	$1289	$1560	$1673	$1691	$1652
8 Food away (per person)	$1002	$938	$949	$978	$1022	$1085	$1018	$769
9 Housing (per person)	$6623	$4777	$5809	$6073	$6750	$7579	$7589	$7138
10 Utilities (per person)	$1464	$909	$1113	$1235	$1505	$1809	$1918	$1956
11 Apparel (per person)	$680	$780	$720	$618	$702	$714	$624	$443
12 Transportation (per person)	$3071	$2346	$2838	$2655	$3305	$3687	$3203	$2680
13 Health care (per person)	$1263	$388	$621	$783	$1165	$1754	$2591	$2971
14 Entertainment (per person)	$1002	$611	$776	$927	$1103	$1220	$1232	$859
15 Education (per person)	$430	$953	$289	$292	$748	$417	$126	$88
Percentage of consumer units:								
16 Renting a residence	34	86	55	35	27	20	18	20
17 Owning residence with mortgage	41	9	39	56	55	45	29	13
18 Owning residence without mortgage	25	5	6	9	18	35	53	67
19 Possessing at least 1 vehicle	88	68	89	90	92	91	90	79

Note: "Consumer unit" generally refers to households; "reference person" refers to the head of household.

Source: 2010 Consumer Expenditure Survey, US Bureau of Labor Statistics; per person calculations performed by authors.

cities in the US increased population between 1950 and 2010, and for two of these six cities (Houston and Kansas City), land area grew so much that population *density* declined. Another two cities – New York and San Francisco – increased population by just 4 percent within approximately the same land area. Los Angeles and Seattle are the exceptions to the rule, with enough population growth to increase their population density by at least 10 percent.

Reusing City Infrastructure

Prior literature explains how migration to the suburbs contributed toward a variety of social and economic challenges that collectively produced "distressed cities" (Nelson, 1988). Recently, however, some authors have extolled the virtues of walkability and urban renewal (Cortright, 2009; Glaeser, 2011; Speck, 2012). As a byproduct of their historic role in bringing people together to exchange goods, services, information, and ideas (Glaeser, 2011), virtually every city and large town that thrived during the industrial era has a densely packed historic downtown with cultural institutions that remain in existence today. Libraries, art museums, performing arts centers, fine restaurants, and major or minor league sports facilities can be sources of pride for an entire metro area. Whereas retail shopping has largely followed young families in shifting away from cities to suburbs (Falk, 2013), few suburbs can support a full array of cultural institutions on their own, thus largely remaining located in population centers. Now underutilized because such infrastructure was built at the scale of a more populous past, these urban resources can help transform cities into inclusive residential centers offering a lifestyle featuring variety and autonomy with little need for cars.

Cultural infrastructure is more fun to discuss, but the same reasoning applies to functional infrastructure such as bus routes and sewage systems. Many cities have maintained this infrastructure at the larger scale of past population levels, and can therefore accommodate an influx of new residents. By contrast, initiatives to relocate cultural activities to the suburbs require new infrastructure expenses that are redundant with a nearby city center. Furthermore, aging suburbanites would still need to drive to these venues. City residences offer a more inclusive way to resolve the tension between driving and aging for retirees currently residing in the suburbs (McIlwain, 2012). Areas with high urban density are already popular with young professionals, because social inclusion can be achieved without cars through walkable access to groceries, drugstores, medical care, retail banks, restaurants, and cultural activities (Cortright, 2009; Glaeser, 2011; Speck, 2012). Relocating retirees to cities has the advantage of promoting social inclusion across generations, and avoiding the reluctance of many retirees to move into "senior communities" as they prefer to not be surrounded entirely by their generational peers and lose a daily connection to the vibrancy of youth (McIlwain, 2012). Neither retirees nor young professionals are primarily focused on child-rearing, and as a result, their discretionary spending overlaps considerably. Both are drawn to the same types of restaurants and retail stores – although not necessarily at the same times of day.

Making cities inclusive for retirees offers considerable spillover benefits. Experts have identified at least seven distinct social issues that would be influenced positively by shifting residents from suburban to urban living: (a) reduced carbon footprint from apartments versus single-family homes; (b) improved safety from a reduction in driving by retirees;

(c) promotion of investments in mass transit rather than new highway construction; (d) preservation of iconic cultural institutions; (e) greater proximity of families across generations; (f) facilitation of retiree exercise and proactive health management; and (g) rehabilitation of otherwise struggling industrial cities (Carlino et al., 2007; Coutts et al., 2007; Florida, 2009; Glaeser, 2011; Speck, 2012).

However, other experts contend that urban advocates have over-emphasized these spillover benefits and ignored a pertinent empirical finding: as individuals, many boomers express a preference to remain in their current homes or downsize within a suburban community (Kotkin, 2015). From this perspective, urban residences aimed at baby boomers will have disappointing occupancy rates, and it would make more sense to develop conducive housing in suburban settings. Where such age-based communities already exist, they often include features like wider lanes to make driving easier rather than eliminating the need for retirees to drive (McIlwain, 2012).

The efficiency behind reusing existing infrastructure rather than building anew offers a compelling argument in favor of emphasizing city residences for retiring baby boomers. Yet the willingness to embrace the benefits of urban living is constrained by the suburban American identity that has become dominant over the past 60 years. It is therefore important to identify the mix of attributes that can entice baby boomers to voluntarily move into former industrial cities. By analysing why boomers have made the choices they have, and carefully thinking about how those choices are likely to evolve in the years to come, it is possible to envision residential communities in former industrial cities that would – perhaps to their surprise – provide high levels of social inclusion to a large number of retiring boomers. Even though the social benefits of this approach provide good reasons for policy-makers to support efforts to create such residential communities, the argument does not require individual consumers to seek any of these social goods. All they need is a self-interested attraction to living in an inclusive urban setting at an affordable cost. The social innovation can thus be entrepreneurial, not bureaucratic.

Evolving consumer demand

Beyond the attributes of inclusive cities, it is important to anticipate the needs of baby boomers at the stage of life not yet reached: retirement. Management scholarship dating back more than 50 years (Simon, 1959) helps explain how and why people make challenging decisions that influence future consumer demand. Recall the 2010 Consumer Expenditure Survey, summarized in Table 11.1, which shows how income and spending patterns are similar – and different – across age ranges. Before-tax household income peaks for 45–54 year-olds (line 1), but when divided by the number of household members, per capita income is highest for 55–64 year-olds (line 5). Predictably, average income falls as people reach normal retirement age. Expenses also decline (line 6), but by less than the reduction in income. For households headed by someone 75 or older, expenses approximately equal income.

Demand for specific retail types can be anticipated by comparing expense categories for retirement-aged households against the patterns shown by younger households, especially those in the 55–64-year-old range (lines 7 through 15 in Table 11.1). Because household sizes vary significantly, all expenses are computed on a per-person basis. The cost for basic necessities, such as food prepared at home, stays almost constant from age 55 and up. Expenditures on meals away from home remain at high levels for 65–74 year-olds, but drop significantly (25 percent) for those over 75. Housing costs per person peak from ages 55–74, as many people remain in larger homes even after their children are grown, and only drop slightly (6 percent) from these levels beyond age 75. Utility costs per person are highest for the oldest age group, presumably due to greater temperature sensitivity. Predictably, expenses for apparel, transportation, and education all decline past retirement age, while health care expenses per person significantly rise across all age categories. Similar to meals away from home, entertainment expenses are at high levels for 65–74 year-olds but decline significantly after age 75. A closer analysis of the data shows that expenses for gasoline declined for older households but the cost for car insurance and maintenance rose – consistent with the idea that many retirees live in places requiring ownership of cars used with decreasing frequency. This also connects to a broader discussion about the high joint cost of housing and transportation (Lipman, 2006), which affects retirees as well as working families.

ANALYSING POPULATION CHANGES SINCE 1950

To better understand how the baby boomer era has influenced individual cities, I analysed population changes from 1950 to 2010 for the 100 largest cities in the US and surrounding metro areas. City centers that have declined in population since 1950 were built with urban density that became underutilized as society reorganized around personal vehicles. If retiring baby boomers find car-centric lives less conducive, it may be possible to reuse the old infrastructure from the very same cities that have lost population in recent decades. Based on changes in land area and population density since 1950, Table 11.2 describes seven qualitative categories of US cities.

Group A lists 19 cities that in 1950 had very high population density (generally defined as more than 5,000 residents per square mile), but had lost more than 33 percent of that population density since 2010. All of these cities occupy approximately the same land area as they had historically. Located mainly in the Northeast and Midwest regions of the US, these cities also retain many of the cultural institutions that signified their relative economic importance prior to World War II. Many are places where people say they do *not* want to live in retirement – for reasons that include cold weather, high taxes, and safety concerns. For example, Buffalo and Newark have been named on lists of the worst places to retire (Kim, 2015). Overcoming such perceptions will be necessary to attract retirees to reuse the infrastructure of these cities. Group B lists another 17 cities that also continue to occupy a similar land area and have experienced population decline, although not to the same extent as the cities in Group A. All of these cities continue to have population density that rounds to at least 5,000 residents per square mile, and could still accommodate an influx of retirees to approach historic population peaks.

Group C lists nine cities that have annexed a sizable amount of surrounding land to increase their square mileage by at least 60 percent. Consequently, these cities have also experienced significant reductions in population density even when nominal populations are higher (Norfolk and Grand Rapids). The population of the ten cities in Group D has increased modestly since 1950 within a similar land area, resulting in density that has maintained or increased from historic levels and an urban infrastructure that may not qualify as underutilized. On the other hand, their population growth implies an appeal

Table 11.2 100 most populous cities in the US in 1950

City	1950 Rank	Population		2010 Rank	Area (sq. miles)			Change in Area	Density (in 000s)			Change in Density
		1950	2010		1950		2010		1950		2010	
GROUP A: Cities with high historic density, little change in area, and density decline of at least 33%												
A1 Detroit, MI	5	1849568	713777	18	140	→	139	−1%	13.2	→	5.1	−61%
A2 Baltimore, MD	6	949708	620961	21	79	→	81	3%	12.1	→	7.7	−36%
A3 Cleveland, OH	7	914808	396815	45	75	→	78	4%	12.2	→	5.1	−58%
A4 St. Louis, MO	8	856796	319294	58	61	→	62	1%	14.0	→	5.2	−63%
A5 Pittsburgh, PA	12	676806	305704	59	54	→	55	2%	12.5	→	5.5	−56%
A6 Buffalo, NY	15	580132	261310	70	39	→	40	3%	14.7	→	6.5	−56%
A7 Cincinnati, OH	18	503998	296943	62	75	→	78	4%	6.7	→	3.8	−43%
A8 Newark, NJ	21	438776	277140	68	24	→	24	3%	18.6	→	11.5	−38%
A9 Rochester, NY	32	332488	210565	98	36	→	36	−1%	9.2	→	5.9	−36%
A10 Akron, OH	39	274605	199110	109	54	→	62	15%	5.1	→	3.2	−37%
A11 Syracuse, NY	47	220583	145170	166	25	→	25	−1%	8.7	→	5.8	−33%
A12 Youngstown, OH	57	168330	66982	300	33	→	34	4%	5.1	→	2.0	−62%
A13 Flint, MI	60	163143	99763	299	29	→	32	11%	5.6	→	3.1	−45%
A14 Albany, NY	69	134995	97856	300	19	→	21	13%	7.1	→	4.6	−36%
A15 Erie, PA	75	130803	101786	298	19	→	22	17%	7.0	→	4.6	−34%
A16 Trenton, NJ	80	128009	84913	300	7	→	8	6%	17.8	→	11.1	−38%
A17 Scranton, PA	83	125536	76089	300	25	→	25	1%	5.0	→	3.0	−40%
A18 Camden, NJ	86	124555	77344	300	9	→	9	4%	14.5	→	8.7	−40%
A19 Wilmington, DE	95	110356	70851	300	10	→	11	11%	11.3	→	6.5	−42%
GROUP B: Cities with high historic density, little change in area, and density decline less than 33%												
B1 Chicago, IL	2	3620962	2695598	3	208	→	228	10%	17.5	→	11.8	−32%
B2 Philadelphia, PA	3	2071605	1526006	5	127	→	134	5%	16.3	→	11.4	−30%
B3 Washington, DC	9	802178	601723	24	61	→	61	−1%	13.1	→	9.9	−24%
B4 Boston, MA	10	801444	617594	22	48	→	48	1%	16.8	→	12.8	−24%
B5 Minneapolis, MN	17	521718	382578	48	54	→	54	0%	9.7	→	7.1	−27%
B6 St. Paul, MN	35	311349	285068	67	52	→	52	0%	6.0	→	5.5	−8%
B7 Jersey City, NJ	37	299017	247597	75	13	→	15	14%	23.0	→	16.7	−27%
B8 Providence, RI	43	248674	178042	130	18	→	18	3%	13.9	→	9.7	−30%

Table 11.2 (continued)

City	1950 Rank	Population		2010 Rank	Area (sq. miles)			Change in Area	Density (in 000s)			Change in Density
		1950	2010		1950		2010		1950		2010	
B9 Worcester, MA	50	203 486	181 045	126	37	→	37	1%	5.5	→	4.8	−12%
B10 Hartford, CT	54	177 397	124 775	199	17	→	17	−1%	10.2	→	7.2	−29%
B11 New Haven, CT	59	164 443	129 779	188	18	→	20	12%	9.2	→	6.5	−30%
B12 Springfield, MA	61	162 399	153 060	154	32	→	32	1%	5.1	→	4.8	−7%
B13 Bridgeport, CT	63	158 709	144 229	167	15	→	16	10%	10.9	→	9.0	−17%
B14 Cambridge, MA	87	120 740	105 162	257	6	→	6	4%	19.5	→	16.4	−16%
B15 Berkeley, CA	91	113 805	112 580	230	10	→	10	10%	12.0	→	10.8	−10%
B16 Reading, PA	96	109 320	88 082	300	9	→	10	11%	12.4	→	9.0	−28%
B17 New Bedford, MA	97	109 189	95 072	300	19	→	20	5%	5.7	→	4.8	−17%
GROUP C: Cities with high historic density, area increase of at least 60%, and density decline												
C1 Milwaukee, WI	13	637 392	594 833	28	50	→	96	92%	12.7	→	6.2	−51%
C2 Toledo, OH	36	303 616	287 208	66	38	→	81	111%	7.9	→	3.6	−55%
C3 Dayton, OH	44	243 872	141 527	173	25	→	56	123%	9.8	→	2.5	−74%
C4 Richmond, VA	46	230 310	204 214	104	37	→	60	61%	6.2	→	3.4	−45%
C5 Norfolk, VA	48	213 513	242 803	78	28	→	54	92%	7.6	→	4.5	−41%
C6 Grand Rapids, MI	55	176 515	188 040	123	23	→	44	90%	7.5	→	4.2	−44%
C7 Evansville, IN	79	128 636	117 429	216	18	→	44	145%	7.1	→	2.7	−63%
C8 Canton, OH	89	116 912	73 007	300	14	→	25	81%	8.3	→	2.9	−65%
C9 South Bend, IN	90	115 911	101 166	269	20	→	41	105%	5.7	→	2.4	−57%
GROUP D: Cities that have maintained or increased density from historic levels												
D1 New York, NY	1	7 891 957	8 175 133	1	315	→	303	-4%	25.0	→	27.0	8%
D2 San Francisco, CA	11	775 357	805 235	13	45	→	47	5%	17.4	→	17.2	−1%
D3 Seattle, WA	19	467 591	608 660	23	71	→	84	19%	6.6	→	7.3	10%
D4 Oakland, CA	27	384 575	390 724	47	53	→	56	5%	7.3	→	7.0	−3%
D5 Miami, FL	42	249 276	417 650	44	34	→	36	5%	7.3	→	11.6	60%
D6 Yonkers, NY	64	152 798	195 976	114	17	→	18	5%	8.9	→	10.9	23%
D7 Paterson, NJ	66	139 336	146 199	163	8	→	8	4%	17.2	→	17.3	1%
D8 Arlington, VA	68	135 449	207 627	102	24	→	26	8%	5.6	→	8.0	41%
D9 Elizabeth, NJ	92	112 817	124 969	197	12	→	12	5%	9.6	→	10.1	5%
D10 Allentown, PA	100	106 756	118 032	214	16	→	18	12%	6.7	→	6.6	−1%

GROUP E: Cities with high historic density that expanded in area												
E1 Kansas City, MO	20	456 622	459 787	37	81	→	315	291%	5.7	→	1.5	−74%
E2 Indianapolis, IN	23	427 173	820 445	12	55	→	361	555%	7.7	→	2.3	−71%
E3 Denver, CO	24	415 786	600 158	26	67	→	153	129%	6.2	→	3.9	−37%
E4 San Antonio, TX	25	408 442	1 327 407	7	70	→	461	563%	5.9	→	2.9	−51%
E5 Columbus, OH	28	375 901	787 033	15	39	→	217	451%	9.5	→	3.6	−62%
E6 Portland, OR	29	373 628	583 776	29	64	→	133	108%	5.8	→	4.4	−25%
E7 Louisville, KY	30	369 129	597 337	27	40	→	325	715%	9.3	→	1.8	−80%
E8 Atlanta, GA	33	331 314	420 003	40	37	→	133	261%	9.0	→	3.2	−65%
E9 Omaha, NE	40	251 117	408 958	42	41	→	127	212%	6.2	→	3.2	−48%
E10 Long Beach, CA	41	250 767	464 257	36	35	→	50	45%	7.2	→	9.2	28%
E11 Jacksonville, FL	49	204 517	821 784	11	30	→	747	2374%	6.8	→	1.1	−84%
E12 Tulsa, OK	51	182 740	391 906	46	27	→	197	637%	6.8	→	2.0	−71%
E13 Nashville, TN	56	174 307	601 222	25	22	→	475	2060%	7.9	→	1.3	−84%
E14 Wichita, KS	58	168 279	382 368	49	26	→	159	520%	6.5	→	2.4	−63%
E15 Sacramento, CA	67	137 572	466 488	35	17	→	98	479%	8.1	→	4.8	−41%
E16 Fort Wayne, IN	72	133 607	253 691	74	19	→	111	488%	7.1	→	2.3	−68%
E17 El Paso, TX	76	130 485	649 121	19	26	→	255	897%	5.1	→	2.5	−50%
E18 Kansas City, KS	77	129 553	145 786	164	19	→	125	567%	6.9	→	1.2	−83%
E19 Mobile, AL	78	129 009	195 111	116	25	→	139	448%	5.1	→	1.4	−72%
E20 Shreveport, LA	81	127 206	199 311	108	24	→	105	339%	5.3	→	1.9	−64%
E21 Tampa, FL	85	124 681	335 709	55	19	→	113	497%	6.6	→	3.0	−55%
E22 Savannah, GA	88	119 638	136 286	181	15	→	103	606%	8.2	→	1.3	−84%
E23 Peoria, IL	94	111 856	115 007	225	13	→	48	272%	8.7	→	2.4	−72%
E24 Corpus Christi, TX	98	108 287	305 215	60	22	→	161	647%	5.0	→	1.9	−62%
E25 Phoenix, AZ	99	106 818	1 445 632	6	17	→	517	2922%	6.2	→	2.8	−55%

Table 11.2 (continued)

City	1950 Rank	Population		2010 Rank	Area (sq. miles)			Change in Area	Density (in 000s)			Change in Density
		1950	2010		1950		2010		1950		2010	
GROUP F: Cities with moderate density that more than doubled in population												
F1 Los Angeles, CA	4	1 970 358	3 792 621	2	451	→	469	4%	4.4	→	8.1	85%
F2 Houston, TX	14	596 163	2 100 263	4	160	→	600	275%	3.7	→	3.5	−6%
F3 Dallas, TX	22	434 462	1 197 816	9	112	→	341	204%	3.9	→	3.5	−9%
F4 San Diego, CA	31	334 387	1 307 402	8	99	→	325	227%	3.4	→	4.0	20%
F5 Fort Worth, TX	38	278 778	741 206	16	94	→	340	263%	3.0	→	2.2	−27%
F6 Oklahoma City, OK	45	243 504	579 999	31	51	→	606	1094%	4.8	→	1.0	−80%
F7 Charlotte, NC	70	134 042	731 424	17	30	→	298	892%	4.5	→	2.5	−45%
F8 Austin, TX	73	132 459	790 390	14	32	→	298	828%	4.1	→	2.7	−36%
GROUP G: Cities with moderate density and slow or negative population growth												
G1 New Orleans, LA	16	570 445	343 829	52	199	→	169	−15%	2.9	→	2.0	−29%
G2 Memphis, TN	26	396 000	646 889	20	104	→	315	202%	3.8	→	2.1	−46%
G3 Birmingham, AL	34	326 037	212 237	97	65	→	146	124%	5.0	→	1.5	−71%
G4 Salt Lake City, UT	52	182 121	186 440	124	54	→	111	106%	3.4	→	1.7	−50%
G5 Des Moines, IA	53	177 965	203 433	105	55	→	81	47%	3.2	→	2.5	−22%
G6 Spokane, WA	62	161 721	208 916	100	42	→	59	43%	3.9	→	3.5	−9%
G7 Tacoma, WA	65	143 673	198 397	110	48	→	50	4%	3.0	→	4.0	33%
G8 Gary, IN	71	133 911	80 294	300	42	→	57	37%	3.2	→	1.4	−56%
G9 Chattanooga, TN	74	131 041	167 674	138	28	→	137	390%	4.7	→	1.2	−74%
G10 Baton Rouge, LA	82	125 629	229 493	85	30	→	77	155%	4.2	→	3.0	−28%
G11 Knoxville, TN	84	124 769	178 874	129	25	→	99	288%	4.9	→	1.8	−63%
G12 Fall River, MA	93	111 963	88 857	300	34	→	40	19%	3.3	→	2.2	−33%

unmatched in most other central cities, as New York, San Francisco, Seattle, and Miami have reputations as desirable for all ages.

All of the cities in Groups E and F have expanded significantly both in land area and population, with most now having land areas notably larger than the cities in Group A. These cities are in a different phase of development, as most continue to expand their populations in suburban-style residential units within their vast city limits. Cities in Group E had a population density of more than 5,000 residents per square mile in 1950, and some of these cities may have pockets of underutilized urban resources that could be redeployed in the fashion described here. Group F features cities that started with lower density, having developed mainly in the car-centric era and having less long-standing infrastructure. Table 11.3 shows that these cities have a smaller percentage of baby boomers (under 30 percent of their population was 45–74 years old in 2010, compared to a range of 32–35 percent for all other groups), and thus Group F cities have a less pressing need to redesign themselves around the needs of retirees.

The 12 cities in Group G had only moderate population density (less than 5,000 residents per square mile) in 1950, and since then, population growth has been slow or negative. Whereas similar characteristics within the other groups enable general conclusions to be drawn, Group G cities are more idiosyncratic and defy easy analysis. However, because population density was never high in these cities, they are unlikely to be the most suitable places to reuse city infrastructure.

Going forward, the combination of factors that caused baby boomers to concentrate in the suburbs will likely unravel (Florida, 2009), but this unraveling will take time to develop. Suburbs will likely remain the top choice for many parents of school-aged children (Pinsker, 2015) – but will also be increasingly incompatible with the social inclusion needs of post-retirement baby boomers. Many of the cities analysed here, and especially those in Groups A, B, and C, have the capacity to accommodate a sizable number of these suburban retirees as residents. Now cities just need the inclusive residences to go along with it – plus the willingness of people to redefine their identities to accept urban living. After all, plenty of suburbanites who find the preceding arguments compelling often remain in their suburban homes. It will take a concerted effort to understand how the attributes of city living connect with the consumer needs of retirees.

The argument for transforming urban centers relies on proximity of residents to the retail and cultural activities they need. Proximity can be achieved horizontally – by having little space between residences, as in row houses – or vertically in high-rise residences. Urban advocates have pointed to the high walkability and social inclusion enabled by mixed-use construction that locates residences in high-rises above street and plaza-level retail activities (Glaeser, 2011). A cluster of high-rise buildings within a few city blocks has the ability to offer enough residents to support a full array of ground-floor retail activity – for example, a full supermarket as well as multiple restaurants, coffee vendors, clothing shops, and financial service providers. For residents with limited mobility, mixed-use high-rise construction has the added benefit of allowing residents to access the retail options in their own buildings autonomously with elevators.

It is hardly coincidental that this description conjures images of the largest cities in Group D (New York, San Francisco, Seattle, and Miami). Many other cities have sections that fit this image, and typically these are among the more desirable places to live. Of course, other factors contribute to the success of these cities, including legacies of location

Table 11.3 Average characteristics by group

Group	Aggregate City Population		City Area (sq. miles)		Change in City Area	Density (in 000s)		Change in Density	Aggregate Metro Area Population		Change in Population	Percent of Population Aged 45–74
	1950	2010	1950	2010		1950	2010		1950	2010		2010
A	8 683 995	4 422 373	812	843	4%	10.7	5.2	−51%	17 552 549	25 324 872	44%	34.8
B	9 996 435	7 667 990	743	780	5%	13.5	9.8	−27%	21 922 919	42 913 186	96%	33.4
C	2 166 677	1 950 227	254	502	97%	8.5	3.9	−54%	4 134 395	7 874 200	90%	34.3
D	10 415 912	11 190 205	595	608	2%	17.5	18.4	5%	19 072 728	38 514 880	102%	33.0
E	5 748 434	12 913 798	847	5 630	565%	6.8	2.3	−66%	14 106 912	50 567 804	258%	32.1
F	4 124 153	11 241 121	1 029	3 276	218%	4.0	3.4	−14%	8 870 865	39 253 282	342%	29.8
G	2 585 275	2 745 333	726	1 341	85%	3.6	2.0	−43%	4 415 753	10 047 779	128%	32.2
TOTAL	43 720 881	52 131 047	5 006	12 979	159%	8.7	4.0	−54%	90 076 121	214 496 003	138%	33.4

and weather. Vancouver, British Columbia, is often cited as an example where such neighborhoods were created by design. In contrast to the American embrace of suburban sprawl during the boomer era (Lindstrom and Bartling, 2003), Vancouver expanded its city population by focusing deliberately on well-spaced, mixed-use construction. Glaeser (2011, pp. 240–1) credits this "good planning" with attracting high-skilled human capital that enhances the city's prosperity. The Vancouver experiment can be imitated to jointly revitalize former industrial cities and provide better housing options for retirees currently living in their suburbs. Popular press articles suggest this has already begun in several cities in Groups A or B, including Detroit, Hartford, and Youngstown (Seay, 2015; Segal, 2013; Sowers, 2015).

A RESEARCH AGENDA FOR SOCIAL INNOVATIONS TO HELP BABY BOOMERS AND INDUSTRIAL CITIES

The Role of Management Scholarship

In order to transform the urban environment into an inclusive residential environment for retirees, new social and organizational systems need to be created that serve the needs of a broad array of stakeholders. These include retirees, urban land owners, city governments and existing residents, property developers, retail merchants, health care providers, and more. Management scholars have developed several theories that can speak directly to managing this process, especially stakeholder theory (Freeman, 1984) and shared value creation (Porter and Kramer, 2011). Other major research streams also provide useful insights. For example, agency theory stresses the importance of designing incentives and rules for stakeholder interactions based on knowledge of complex governance dynamics (Eisenhardt, 1989). Likewise, transaction cost economics helps explain how to balance market and non-market relationships (Williamson, 1979), and entrepreneurship research defines how to incubate and harness the power of innovation to achieve broad societal aims by motivating individual risk takers (Hitt et al., 2011).

Management scholars are often trained with the wide-angle and long-term perspectives that would facilitate progress in developing urban residences that promote social inclusion among baby boomers. This training should produce better forecasts or more innovative solutions than narrower disciplines employing a more limited set of analytical tools, but the academic field generally categorizes future-oriented policy work as consulting rather than research, and prefers its scholars to study innovation rather than initiate it. The field's opportunity to contribute toward a better world depends on a greater willingness to utilize management theory not only to explain events already observed, but also to propose social innovations for potential improvement. Some areas for proactive analysis related to retiring baby boomers and urban residences are described below.

Comprehensive upfront planning is needed so that the infrastructure provides adequate scale to promote social inclusion efficiently. Because of high asset specificity, market transactions alone will be inadequate to design efficient ways to reuse city centers that serve the needs of retiring baby boomers (Williamson, 1985). Hierarchical coordination will be needed to manage the logistics and internal operations for the entire community from the very beginning of the planning. Whereas developers have autonomy over the scale and usage of most construction projects based on initial sales projections, the broader scope of this initiative suggests a need to anticipate the eventual, long-range vision of an integrated, walkable environment. From this perspective, it is essential to have input from an ongoing management company focused on the flexibility to adapt to the changing needs of a resident population. Ongoing governance and internal management skills will be needed to achieve social inclusion not only within the communities that are created, but also between these innovative communities and established urban stakeholders.

Stakeholder coordination is vital to making a cluster of residences a commercial and social success. If the cluster has too few restaurants, it will lack appeal and residences will not fill – but if it has too many restaurants, some will lack viability. Thoughtful management should be able to price this accordingly, initially keeping retail rents at modest levels to obtain higher occupancy rates. Given that retirees often have flexible schedules, residents could be offered discounts to eat or use workout facilities at off-peak times when demand from working professionals is low. For locations with harsh weather conditions, the pedestrian plaza could include retractable coverings to ensure that residents could access all of these amenities year-round without needing to encounter severe weather.

Envisioning a mix of businesses promoting social inclusion entails both optimization and creativity. Such a transformation of industrial cities requires a high level of imagination that can be loosely compared to the product development for Apple's iPad, where market research was famously disregarded, and few consumers saw an immediate need for an iPad when it launched. However, the Apple design team had anticipated the variety of ways consumers would enjoy using a tablet computer after they saw its capabilities, and initial skeptics were won over by observing the usage of their early adopting friends. This created sufficient demand to justify Apple's high costs of product development. Similarly, although suburban baby boomers may initially react to industrial cities by saying, "I would never move there," well-conceived details will attract some early adopters who lead the way for other skeptics to see for themselves the better life for retirees that could be created.

Applying Research to Create Dynamic Cities that Attract Retirees (and Others)

In the spirit of stakeholder coordination, three facets of urban design have unique implications when making cities desirable to older residents. First, walkable clusters of mixed-use high-rises in central cities have an important advantage in ensuring a critical aspect of social inclusion relevant to inducing retirees to live in urban areas: safety. High pedestrian activity and good lighting are essential. Retail space at the plaza level would keep lights on at all times, keeping the region bright and walkable. Dense residential neighborhoods obviously have more foot traffic, and can also justify the employment of door attendants who help promote safety and cleanliness.

Many former industrial cities currently lack such walkability and need to follow the examples of New York and Vancouver in hiding their parking (Speck, 2012). Surface-level parking lots and concrete structures work against safety and walkability. These parking areas sit idle most of the time – full of parked cars during working hours and nearly empty otherwise. Whereas retail activity promotes social inclusion by bringing people together, parking lots divide people from each other and make it unpleasant to walk between locations. In a related vein, walking plazas help reduce congestion by allowing both pedestrians and automobiles to move more freely by traveling at different levels.

Second, no discussion of baby boomer needs can ignore the importance of medical facilities. Medical advances since 1950 have lifted US life expectancy at birth from 68 to 79 (Arias, 2014, p. 51), and also increased the need for retirees to have regular access to medical facilities. If medical services are only accessible by driving, sensible retirees will be reluctant to abandon their cars for urban living. This implies that appropriate medical facilities are essential to creating the social inclusion retirees need, and a cluster of walkable, high-rise residences should be designed to include a clinic.

While such a location for a clinic is unusual today, it is not difficult to imagine given the rapid expansion of medical offices in less traditional suburban locations. Meanwhile, an increasing number of health care organizations are migrating toward preventative maintenance – which features more frequent but less intense patient interactions – rather than responding to major health problems. If retirees remain in the suburbs, it would be counterproductive to build new facilities in cities, which will require not only driving but also parking structures that consume valuable space. However, if a community of frequent users were living within close proximity to the new medical facilities, the medical practice would be sustainable by providing routine medical services to residents within walking distance. Only those with more severe health problems will need to travel to a larger medical facility.

Third, urban residences can allow retirees to save money by giving up car ownership, but sometimes these retirees will still need the customized transportation they currently obtain in their own vehicles. As another opportunity for stakeholder coordination, high-rise residences could attract customers by offering free, personal transportation anywhere within a metro area. Building management could coordinate local transportation needs for all residents, with no ride-sharing or lengthy wait times. Providing such a service would be affordable if planned in advance, and promotes social inclusion while reducing the need for retirees to drive or park cars during long periods of little use. High-rise construction costs increase with the need for larger parking structures, and without guaranteed transportation, everyone will insist on keeping their own car – which again wastes space in the parking structure most of the time. Offering guaranteed transportation means that nobody needs a car. New business models offered by Zipcar, Uber, and Lyft illustrate how everyone's transportation demands can be met at a lower aggregate cost without individual car ownership (and storage) – and with fewer retirees behind the wheel.

Stakeholder coordination is therefore essential long past the initial construction of urban residences. Building management would be able to anticipate times of peak demand and ensure that additional vehicles show up. Good planners can be enticed to sign up early, and management can analyse data to prepare for the impetuous behavior of the poor planners. This task is akin to a permanent hotel concierge, with the entire enterprise existing to make residents (whether retirees or young professionals) included in the social fabric of an urban oasis that leaves behind the yardwork and driving of suburban life. It can be seen as a benevolent hierarchy centralizing activities not to exploit others, but rather to serve multiple constituencies effectively.

Ongoing stakeholder coordination opportunities go beyond the typical scope of a residential building. For example, most projections of future medical costs for retirees are onerous and likely to preclude other more productive uses of the same funds (Knickman and Snell, 2002). Two keys to reducing medical costs for retirees involve preventative care and attention to mental health (Counsell et al., 2006; Fries et al., 1993; Goetzel et al., 2002). If left up to individuals, neither of these activities will be done well, as many people prefer to "tough it out" rather than actively seek early intervention. But building management could partner with on-site clinics to form accountable care organizations, responsible for proactively managing the health of residents to reduce medical costs, with the opportunity to earn profits for achieving this goal.

Relatedly, a forward-thinking management company could fill positions that interact daily with residents – including reception workers, restaurant wait staff, and bartenders – with individuals possessing enough medical or psychology training to recognize developing medical or mental health issues. Such employees could simultaneously create social connections with residents, address minor problems before they become major ones, and reduce the cost of care – both by sharing helpful nudges directly with residents during ordinary daily exchanges and by recognizing patterns of symptoms quickly and reporting them so that medical staff could work to curtail diseases at an early stage. Clearly it will add cost to attract highly educated employees into roles that rarely place a premium on education, but these costs may be offset by addressing health issues before they advance and need costlier care.

Role of Individuals

In addition to the systemic considerations of stakeholder coordination, social change requires individual-level attention that can also form the basis of future research into the emotional and habitual changes to driving that need to be changed. For many suburban boomers, cars are not merely a tool – or means to an end – but have become an expression of individual identity that often defines the end goal itself. This car-based cultural identity builds on the notion of an American "pastoral ideal" that attracted the baby boomers and their parents to the suburbs (Marx, 1964), reinforced by depictions of homogeneous suburban consumption epitomized by the sitcoms of the 1950s and 1960s (Lindstrom and Bartling, 2003, p. xix). Cars empower people with the flexibility and autonomy to transport family members to whatever activities they select, often in the least possible time. For many people, especially working parents, such perceived time savings make cars a compelling mode of transportation.

Note that these time savings are defined narrowly at the level of the family and ignore the high costs to society of car transportation. Glaeser (2011) provides a list: (a) roads are expensive to build and maintain while impeding pedestrian movement; (b) cars use more fuel to transport people than equivalent trips by bus, train, or foot, consuming a high percentage of discretionary household income and contributing to climate change and geopolitical instability; and (c) congestion occurs when the demand for roads exceeds their supply, and stalled vehicles increase pollution, induce road rage, and waste people's time – an ironic contrast to the family-level time efficiency that motivates much car usage in the first place. Viewed from the perspective of society overall rather than families seeking travel autonomy, cars are notably *in*efficient. Reduced car usage would alleviate congestion while reduced aggregate fuel consumption would have economic, environmental, and geopolitical benefits.

Yet consumer decisions reflect individual concerns rather than societal ones, suggesting that a shift toward urban residences for retirees should emphasize voluntary transactions. Retirees would justifiably resent being told to live in cities for their own good (and the benefit of society). The iPad example remains salient. Nobody was forced to buy one, and yet Apple's first-year sales vastly exceeded expectations for a new and untested product (Paczkowski, 2011) because the company had done a good job of anticipating what people would want once it was available. By thinking carefully about the evolving needs for social connectivity among the growing number of retirees, future demand can be anticipated in a way that economizes on other costs (such as health care) and avoids crowding out other opportunities for productive growth.

Overall, retirees are good candidates for reducing automobile usage because they have less demands on their time, smaller household sizes, and increased difficulty operating cars safely and comfortably. However, unless they move, most suburban retirees cannot realistically stop driving and expect adequate access to the goods and services they want and need. Deciding to change residence is always disruptive, and moving into a city after a lifetime in the suburbs exacerbates this stress (Huy, 1999) – suggesting a further role for the expertise of management scholars in overcoming the resistance of people to change their routines (Pettigrew et al., 2001). The successful design of urban residential communities will likewise benefit from accommodating emotional aspects of the transition from one life phase to the next, such as settling into a new and unfamiliar location that requires identity transition (Conroy and O'Leary-Kelly, 2014).

For retiring baby boomers with a long history in the suburbs, the uncertainty surrounding their remaining lifespan will increase the perceived stakes of getting this decision right. In such cases, benefit and cost estimates of staying in the suburbs and moving to the city are difficult to fully evaluate, breeding doubt and paralysing decision making. Management scholarship can help specify the role of emotion in such decisions, including the need for a leap of faith (Kanter, 1983) and an emphasis on emotional connection more than rationality (Huy, 1999). By applying such management scholarship about the influence of emotional dynamics on the willingness to change, leaders of urban residential projects can take specific actions to enhance a person's receptivity to consider change.

Finally, the benefits of this social innovation go beyond the social inclusion of suburban retirees to incorporate potential identity resurrection for inner cities. Many cities were originally symbols of pride for their regions – lending their names to sports teams and hosting great cultural institutions. Suburbanization has diverted these positive city identities in the minds of many baby boomers (Nelson, 1988; Speck, 2012). Therefore, in addition to efforts at the individual level to help retiring baby boomers embrace the advantages of urban living, it is essential for any industrial city pursuing this approach to engage proactively in the process of identity resurrection (Howard-Grenville et al., 2013).

CONCLUSION

Now is the right time to be thinking about where retiring boomers will live to achieve social inclusion. The largest birth-year cohorts will retire during the 2020s, and we are now witnessing just the beginning of baby boomers contemplating how they want to live their golden years. Given the lead time to build, construct, and market high-rise buildings, construction must precede demand. New residential concepts will fail if developers and planners do not cater to the expectations of the target market segment. Broad thinking is just as important in this endeavor as narrow expertise. The generalist perspective of management scholars can help avoid the most obvious mistakes and pursue valuable connections across specialties.

ACKNOWLEDGMENTS

I greatly appreciate the many conversations and helpful suggestions provided on earlier versions of this chapter from Greg Reilly, Scott Johnson, Mary Caravella, John Elliott, Adam Kleinbaum, Norm Bowie, Myles Shaver, Kevin McMahon, Meg Warren, and Tim Folta.

REFERENCES

Arias, E. (2014), United States Life Tables, *2010 National Vital Statistics Reports*, 63(7), 1–62.

Carlino, G.A., S. Chatterjee, and R.M. Hunt (2007), Urban density and the rate of invention, *Journal of Urban Economics*, 61(3), 389–419.

Conroy, S.A. and A.M. O'Leary-Kelly (2014), Letting go and moving on: work-related identity loss and recovery, *Academy of Management Journal*, 39(1), 67–87.

Cortright, J. (2009), Walking the walk: how walkability raises home values in US cities. CEOs for Cities. https://community-wealth.org/content/walking-walk-how-walkability-raises-home-values-us-cities.

Counsell, S.R., C.M. Callahan, A.B. Buttar, D.O. Clark, and K.I. Frank (2006), Geriatric resources for assessment and care of elders (GRACE): a new model of primary care for low-income seniors, *Journal of the American Geriatrics Society*, 54(7), 1136–41.

Coutts, A.M., J. Beringer, and N.J. Tapper (2007), Impact of increasing urban density on local climate: spatial and temporal variations in the surface energy balance in Melbourne, Australia, *Journal of Applied Meteorology and Climatology*, 46(4), 477–93.

Dunne, D. and R. Martin (2006), Design thinking and how it will change management education: an interview and discussion, *Academy of Management Learning & Education*, 5(4), 512–23.

Eisenhardt, K.M. (1989), Agency theory: an assessment and review, *Academy of Management Review*, 14(1), 57–74.

Falk, G. (2013), *Twelve Inventions which Changed America: The Influence of Technology on American Culture*, Lanham, MD: Hamilton Books.

Florida, R. (2009), How the crash will reshape America, *The Atlantic*, March. https://www.theatlantic.com/magazine/archive/2009/03/how-the-crash-will-reshape-america/307293/.

Freeman, R.E. (1984), *Strategic Management: A Stakeholder Approach*, Boston, MA: Pitman.

Fries, J.F., C.E. Koop, C.E. Beadle et al. (1993), Reducing health care costs by reducing the need and demand for medical services, *New England Journal of Medicine*, 329(5), 321–5.

George, G., A.M. McGahan, and J. Prabhu (2012), Innovation for inclusive growth: towards a theoretical framework and research agenda, *Journal of Management Studies*, 49(4), 661–83.

Glaeser, E. (2011), *Triumph of the City: How Our Greatest Invention Makes Us Richer, Smarter, Greener, Healthier, and Happier*, New York: Penguin Group.

Goetzel, R.Z., R.J. Ozminkowski, L.I. Sederer, and T.L. Mark (2002), The business case for quality mental health services: why employers should care about the mental health and well-being of their employees, *Journal of Occupational and Environmental Medicine*, 44(4), 320–30.

Hitt, M.A., R.D. Ireland, D.G. Sirmon, and C.A. Trahms (2011), Strategic entrepreneurship: creating value for individuals, organizations, and society, *Academy of Management Perspectives*, 25(2), 57–75.

Howard-Grenville, J., M.L. Metzger, and A.D. Meyer (2013), Rekindling the flame: processes of identity resurrection, *Academy of Management Journal*, 56(1), 113–36.

Huy, Q.N. (1999), Emotional capability, emotional intelligence, and radical change, *Academy of Management Journal*, 24(2), 325–45.

Kanter, R.M. (1983), *The Change Masters*, New York: Simon & Schuster.

Kim, S. (2015), The best and worst US cities to retire in. http://abcnews.go.com/Business/best-worst-us-cities-retire/story?id=31610938 (accessed 15 July 2015).

Knickman, J.R. and E.K. Snell (2002), The 2030 problem: caring for aging baby boomers, *Health Services Research*, 37(4), 849–84.

Kotha, R., G. George, and K. Srikanth (2013), Bridging the mutual knowledge gap: coordination and the commercialization of university science, *Academy of Management Journal*, 56(2), 498–524.

Kotkin, J. (2015), Countering progressives' assault on suburbia, *Real Clear Politics*, 10 July.

Lindstrom, M.J. and H. Bartling (2003), *Suburban Sprawl: Culture, Theory, and Politics*, Lanham, MD: Rowman & Littlefield.

Lipman, B.J. (2006), *A Heavy Load: The Combined Housing and Transportation Burdens of Working Families*, Washington, DC: Center for Housing Policy.

Marx, L. (1964), *The Machine in the Garden: Technology and the Pastoral Ideal in America*, New York: Oxford University Press.

Mather, M., K. Pollard, and L.A. Jacobsen (2011), First results from the 2010 census, *Population Reference Bureau Reports on America*, July.

McIlwain, J.K. (2010), *Housing in America: The Next Decade*, Washington, DC: Urban Land Institute.

McIlwain, J.K. (2012), *Housing in America: The Baby Boomers Turn 65*, Washington, DC: Urban Land Institute.

Messia, R. (2003), Lawns as artifacts: the evolution of social and environmental implications of suburban residential land use. In M.J. Lindstrom and H. Bartling (eds), *Suburban Sprawl: Culture, Theory, and Politics*, Lanham, MD: Rowman & Littlefield, pp. 69–84.

Nelson, K.P. (1988), *Gentrification and Distressed Cities: An Assessment of Trends in Intrametropolitan Migration*, Madison, WI: University of Wisconsin Press.

Paczkowski, J. (2011), With iPad sales, Steve schools the street again, 20 January. http://allthingsd.com/20110120/with-ipad-sales-steve-schools-the-street-again/ (accessed July 2015).

Pettigrew, A.M., R.W. Woodman, and K.S. Cameron (2001), Studying organizational change and development: challenges for future research, *Academy of Management Journal*, 44(4), 697–713.

Pinsker, J. (2015), Young Americans: yearning for the suburbs, stuck in the city, *The Atlantic*, 27 January.

Porter, M.E. and M.R. Kramer (2011), Creating shared value, *Harvard Business Review*, 89(1/2), 62–77.

Seay, G. (2015), Amenities are magnets for Hartford's newest apartments, *Hartford Business Journal*, 27 July.

Segal, D. (2013), A missionary's quest to remake Motor City, *New York Times*, 13 April.

Simon, H.A. (1959), Theories of decision-making in economics and behavioral sciences, *American Economic Review*, 49(3), 253–83.

Sowers, S. (2015), An Ohio city reinvents its downtown, *New York Times*, 27 May, B4.

Speck, J. (2012), *Walkable City: How Downtown Can Save America, One Step at a Time*, New York: Farrar, Straus, and Giroux.

West, L.A., S. Cole, D. Goodkind, and W. He (2014), 65+ in the United States: 2010, *US Census Bureau Current Population Reports*.

Williamson, O.E. (1979), Transaction-cost economics: the governance of contractual relations, *Journal of Law and Economics*, 26(3), 377–96.

Williamson, O.E. (1985), *The Economic Institutions of Capitalism*, New York: The Free Press.

12. Sustainable technology-enabled innovations for ageing-in-place: the Singapore example

Hwee-Pink Tan and Hwee-Xian Tan

AGEING AND SUSTAINABLE DEVELOPMENT

The United Nations Sustainable Development Goals (SDG) are a global vision for humanity. They were adopted by all the world's governments in 2015, and will guide global development until the year 2030. The 2030 Agenda for Sustainable Development sets out a universal plan that ensures that the SDGs are met for all segments of society at all ages, with a particular focus on the most vulnerable – including older persons or seniors.

According to the 2017 study on "World Population Ageing" by the United Nations [1], 12.7 percent of the world's population today comprises older persons (aged 60 years and above), and this percentage is projected to increase to 16.4 percent and 21.3 percent by 2030 and 2050, respectively. Based on the same study, nearly one-fifth of the population in Singapore today is aged 60 and above, and this is estimated to increase to approximately 30 percent and 40 percent, respectively, by 2030 and 2050. In fact, 2018 marks the year that the proportion of seniors (aged 65 and above) in Singapore will match those younger than 15, for the first time [2]. With declining birth rates, there is a corresponding increase in the number of older persons who *live alone* [1].

As a result of increasing life expectancy, more seniors become frail, whereby they experience fatigue, unintended weight loss and diminished strength. Seniors who are frail tend to have higher fall risks, and gradually rely on mobility aids (such as rollators, walkers and wheelchairs) in their daily commute. At a societal level, this results in an increasing need for *barrier-free access*,[1] so that seniors can continue to travel within and beyond their community, with ease and convenience.

With global shortages and rising costs of institutionalized resources and facilities for healthcare and eldercare, it is necessary that seniors can *age-in-place*, where they can continue to live in their own home and community independently, safely and comfortably [3] without compromising their desire for independence, autonomy and privacy. This is especially challenging for seniors who live alone, as well as those who require barrier-free access. In the following, we outline the challenges that need to be addressed, and how technology can play a role, for these seniors to successfully age-in-place.

Needs for Seniors Living Alone

The proportion of seniors living alone is increasing. In 2017, 13 percent of older persons worldwide were living alone, as compared to 9 percent in 1990 and 12 percent in 2010. In Singapore, the proportion of seniors (aged 65 and above) living alone increased from 16.2 percent to 18.6 percent between 2005 and 2015 [4]. In super-aged Japan (where the proportion of the population aged 65 years and above passed 20 percent in 2006, and stood at 26.7 percent in October 2015), 16 percent of older persons were living alone in 2017.

The risks faced by seniors living alone are multifaceted, ranging from their safety and physical health, to their psychological wellbeing. Between 2007 and 2011, at least 50 seniors who had lived alone in Singapore passed away in their own homes, only to be discovered after a prolonged period [5]. Similarly, in Japan, *Kodokushi* incidents (the Japanese phenomena of people dying alone and remaining undiscovered for a long period of time) number 30,000 per year, and is expected to increase to 200,000 annually by 2040 [6].

According to the ten-year Singapore Longitudinal Ageing Studies [7], seniors who live alone have a 70 percent higher risk of dying prematurely as compared to their peers, and are twice as likely to feel depressed. In particular, those living in smaller apartments are at a higher risk than those who live in larger housing types. Based on a follow-up study [8], nearly 92 percent of seniors who are frail are single, divorced or widowed, with the primary causes of frailty being malnutrition, lack of exercise and presence of chronic diseases.

As seniors living alone often have a limited network of family and friends, they face higher risks of social deprivation, which can lead to pertinent issues such as depression, loneliness and social isolation. A study by Tai [9] reveals that feeling lonely raises one's risk of dying by 34 percent, compared to those who are neither lonely nor isolated. In another study by Shimada et al. [10], it was revealed that 31 percent of seniors living alone in urban Japan are socially isolated, compared to 24.1 percent for those living with family. In fact, loneliness and social isolation are often associated with various negative health repercussions, such as greater risk of cardiovascular disease [11] and cognitive impairment [12, 13], as well as worsened sleep quality [14]. Loneliness has also been found to be correlated with higher mortality rates among seniors [15, 16].

There is clearly a need to collect data to better understand the various risk factors of each vulnerable senior as well as leverage: (1) more abundantly available community resources (for example, community caregivers and volunteers) to offer timely assistance; and (2) domain experts who can ensure that the data are accurate and relevant, and who can subsequently introduce intervention plans to improve the quality of life of these seniors.

Accessibility for Independence and Mobility in Seniors

The Ministry of Health (MOH) in Singapore predicts that approximately three in ten residents will live for a decade more after they have suffered a disability [17]. Given that many seniors have to rely on mobility aids due to their disabilities and/or increasing frailty, the physical environment of the neighborhood has to be elderly-friendly and barrier-free. This enables seniors to have safe, independent and unhindered access to public amenities, communal and recreational facilities, as well as the public transport system, allowing them to participate in activities outside of their residential homes, so that they can age successfully.

However, existing codes on barrier-free accessibility that are imposed on buildings only apply to the approach and common spaces within the building. Barrier-free accessibility requirements are not imposed on the *interconnections* between adjacent buildings and infrastructures, and there is often little incentive to do so, especially if they are not part of the same development. The problem of barrier-free *inaccessibility* is exacerbated at the interconnections [18] between new developments and existing spaces, due to the lack of clear division of responsibilities for implementing accessibility provisions. In fact, it may take a wheelchair-bound person 30 minutes for a last-mile journey from an underground MRT[2] station to a building above, in contrast to just 2 minutes for able-bodied individuals [19]. This struggle in last-mile travel is not isolated, as a study by the National Council of Social Services [20] reveals that seven out of ten respondents with disability(s) desire improved levels of independence and mobility. According to other research that was conducted in Australia by Withers [21], four out of five people in wheelchairs had not been to anywhere new in the previous year.

There is clearly a need for accessibility data to be captured, such that gaps in interconnections can be uncovered, to support the end-to-end route planning for wheelchair users. Furthermore, barrier-free accessibility in the neighborhoods can be instrumental in facilitating seniors in utilizing amenities in the community and participating in community activities, thereby minimizing the likelihood of social deprivation.

Technologies for Community Dwelling Seniors to Age-in-Place

Fortunately, the maturing of sensor, communication and computing technologies, as well as data science, enables (1) continuous and passive monitoring of day-to-day activities of seniors, both within and out of the home; (2) sense-making for intelligent detection and notification of anomalous events; and (3) collaborative decision support for seniors living alone and those who require barrier-free access (that is, in wheelchairs), to age-in-place. However, their widespread adoption and deployment remain elusive due to seniors' unfamiliarity with technology and perception of privacy invasion. In the following, we broadly classify recent innovations to address the needs of these vulnerable[3] seniors.

Technologies for community care of seniors living alone

Technologies for seniors living alone to age-in-place have a strong focus on passive in-home monitoring, without the need for active participation by the seniors [22, 23]. Data from unobtrusive devices such as motion sensors and door contact sensors can be collaboratively analysed to measure levels of activities, or to identify changes in daily functioning at home, so as to trigger targeted care.

Since 2004, the Oregon Center for Ageing and Technology has conducted research studies and pilot testing of in-home technologies for health monitoring, intervention and support of independent living for 30 community dwelling seniors [24]. In addition to passive monitoring using sensors, each participant receives a desktop computer and Internet broadband services, along with computer training based on their computer literacy. Subsequently, participants receive a weekly online health questionnaire about behaviors that may affect activity patterns. The participants are also expected to self-report changes to the home environment.

The CSIRO Smarter Safer Homes platform [25], comprising the sensor-based in-home monitoring system, cloud computing server, an iPad application, family/carer portal and clinical portal, has been piloted in 26 homes in Australia for durations between 3 to 12 months since 2013. These pilots were used to validate the usability and acceptability of the platform, ability to extract knowledge on daily functions and its impact on delivery of care services.

City4Age [26], a European project funded under the Horizon 2020 Framework Programme for Research and Innovation, focuses on the use of smart city data to support active and healthy ageing among seniors. In particular, data from in-home sensors, smartphones and wearables will be used to capture the lifestyle of seniors living in cities, in order to detect signs of frailty or mild cognitive impairment. Subsequently, intervention plans will be developed to stimulate improvement in the quality of life of individuals, by interacting with them through mobile phones, TV displays, home robots or messaging devices. Selected groups of about 20 seniors over 70 years old will be monitored in cities including Athens, Montpellier, Singapore, Lecce and Birmingham.

In Singapore, 500 homes of seniors living alone were fitted with an emergency help device, motion sensors and door contact sensors in 2013 [27], with Lions Befrienders Service Association (LBSA)[4] as the care responder to meet the safety needs of seniors. In 2015, the Housing & Development Board (HDB)[5] completed the trial of a similar system with 12 flats [28], targeting the next-of-kin as the care responder. Although the trial was extended for up to 3,200 households [29], the actual take-up and status of the trial remains unclear.

Technologies for barrier-free access for seniors in wheelchairs

While innovations for in-home monitoring have been driven in a *top-down* manner, the collection/reporting of accessibility data for wheelchair users has largely followed a *bottom-up* approach and relies on *crowdsourcing*[6] – whereby the public can contribute information relevant to a given cause. AllGoEasy [30] is a voluntary initiative started by a wheelchair user [19] to help disabled friends who are often frustrated by the lack of sufficient information on accessibility. It crowdsources accurate, reliable and detailed location-specific accessibility information from the public, so as to instill confidence for wheelchair users to go out and explore Singapore. Wheelmap [31] is a similar initiative that provides an online, worldwide map for finding and marking wheelchair-accessible places, and rating them according to a simple traffic light system.

In December 2016, Google Maps, the top route planning application in the market, began to add accessibility details to annotate if a particular location (such as a restaurant or public building) is wheelchair accessible [32]. In July 2017, it started to crowdsource a larger set of accessibility options to almost seven million places around the world [33]. In March 2018, Google Maps launched a "wheelchair-accessible" option for route planning in six major cities: London, New York, Tokyo, Mexico City, Boston and Sydney [34].

In Singapore, several infrastructural enhancements are also underway to provide seniors with safe and unhindered travel passage – via accessible elevators, walkways and transport pick-up points, and complemented by a user-friendly transportation system to their destinations [18]. More recently [35], through the Green Man+ scheme, a senior can explicitly extend the time allocation for a particular traffic crossing, by tapping her travel concession card at the corresponding traffic pole. The Silver Zone program, on the other hand, involves the installation of senior-friendly road safety features, such as narrowing of roads and two-stage crossings, in residential areas with high senior resident populations, relatively higher accident rates involving seniors and closer proximity to senior amenities.

In the following section, we summarize the key learnings and gaps of existing innovations in the literature, and propose a collaborative framework for sustainable and scalable technology-enabled innovations for ageing-in-place. We describe some instantiations of this framework in the third section, and conclude with a research agenda in the final section.

COLLABORATIVE FRAMEWORK FOR SUSTAINABLE AND SCALABLE TECHNOLOGY-ENABLED SOCIAL INNOVATIONS

Key Learnings and Gaps Identified in Existing Technology-enabled Ageing-in-Place Innovations

We first define the intended objectives and outcomes of sustainable technology-enabled ageing-in-place. The supporting technological platform must be scalable and highly reliable, and replicated with ease across vast numbers of seniors. It must be cost-effective and manageable with a sustainable business model. Next, as the needs of vulnerable seniors may differ from one another, the technological platform must be able to capture relevant static and dynamic contextual information which will be essential for sense-making, in order to trigger personalized and actionable wisdom for care and intervention. Finally, beyond the beneficiaries, the system must be able to support a large and dynamic ecosystem of stakeholders (which may include people, public as well as private entities), with varying (and potentially conflicting) roles and priorities.

We summarize the key learnings and gaps of existing innovations in the literature in the following subsections.

Clinically/technology-led initiatives

For seniors living alone, clinically-led initiatives [24] focus on linking sensor-derived features (for example, average time spent in the bedroom) with measurable clinical outcomes (such as cognitive level and physical frailty). As the scale of deployment is relatively small (a few dozen homes), there is limited focus on the dependability and extensibility of the technology system, which are necessary considerations for a system operator,[7] for large-scale rollouts. On the other hand, technology-led initiatives [25] focus primarily on usability and acceptance of the deployed systems, and are typically also deployed in relatively small scales. Without a direct link with clinical outcomes, such systems are unable to inform personalized care, thus reducing their value in providing better quality of lives for seniors. In addition, the lack of engagement with community (non-health) care resources can limit the ability for such innovations to scale.

For wheelchair users, existing innovations [30–34] focus on crowdsourcing for pervasive collection of accessibility data. However, these systems rely on manual inputs by contributors, which may result in user fatigue. Moreover, the data collected may be subjective and do not contain rich context (for example, manual versus electric wheelchair, gradient of ramp, bumpiness and so on), and contributors who are not wheelchair users may provide inaccurate or irrelevant data.

Another obvious gap is the lack of engagement with policy makers and funders, who provide the necessary support and intervention (financial and/or infrastructure enhancement) for these vulnerable seniors.

Government- and community-led initiatives

Government and community organizations play an important role in seeding social inclusion and innovation. The notion of technology-enabled ageing-in-place is relatively new, in terms of technology readiness, social acceptance and business models. As such, it is important that the government and other partners in the eldercare ecosystem adopt a *living lab* concept to support large-scale private–public pilot initiatives to cushion the risks involved. While various pilots have been initiated in Singapore [27–29] and Europe [26], there is a need for a *Whole-of-Government* and public–private collaborative approach to engage all the key stakeholders, to ensure that these pilots can eventually scale and attain the intended reach in a sustainable manner.

Proposed Framework for Sustainable Social Innovation

Although technology plays a key role in solving social problems, the application of emerging technologies such as Internet of Things[8] (IoT), Artificial Intelligence (AI)[9] and crowdsourcing to tackle social problems is still in its infancy. In fact, technology alone cannot solve social problems – it is most effective when supported by underlying human forces. As illustrated above, siloed approaches for technological innovations for ageing-in-place tend to achieve only depth (either on clinical or technological fronts); they have to be complemented with sufficient breadth, which can only be attained through collaborative efforts with the relevant stakeholders.

We hypothesize that collaboration is key for technology-enabled social innovations to be sustainable, and that this collaboration needs to happen at various levels. In the following subsections, we describe the context of such innovations for vulnerable seniors to age-in-place in greater detail.

Collaborative stakeholders

An effective collaborative ecosystem of enabling partners can take place only if the needs of each stakeholder (in terms of their expectations from the innovation) is well understood, from the design thinking perspective. It should be noted that the needs of different stakeholders may sometimes be conflicting.

Below, we enumerate the stakeholders that are relevant for vulnerable seniors in Singapore, and articulate each of their needs:

- "Can non-intrusive technologies be used to better enable person-centric care for me to age-in-place?" Mr Lim, 73 years old, living alone (beneficiary).
- "Can non-intrusive technologies be used to direct me to travel independently from one place to another in a hassle-free manner?" Ms Tan, 60 years old, wheelchair user (beneficiary and user).
- "Can I be notified when I need to provide care for a senior (who can be a family member), including information on his specific needs and wellbeing status, so that the care can be targeted?" Ms Koh, 45 years old, caregiver (user).
- "Is the innovation sufficiently reliable so that there is minimal need for maintenance? Can I extract maximum value from the innovation that can be translated into benefits for other stakeholders, and thus revenue for business sustainability?" Mr Ong, 43 years old, CTO, Tech4Elderly Pte Ltd.

- "Is there evidence that the innovation can improve the wellbeing of vulnerable seniors?" Dr Ho, 50 years old, Ageing Planning Office, Ministry of Health.
- "Can insights derived from the innovation serve as an accurate proxy for a specific medical condition, for instance, cognitive impairment, to trigger intervention?" Dr Surendra, Senior Consultant, Geriatric Psychiatrist.
- "Is it economically viable and useful to have technologies in the homes that can improve the safety and wellbeing of seniors living alone?" Mr Yap, 40 years old, Technology Research, Housing Development Board.
- "Does the innovation result in improved age-friendliness in our housing estates, so that vulnerable seniors can remain physically, socially and mentally well, and safe?" Ms Lee, 35 years old, Urban Planner, Urban Redevelopment Authority.

The concerns of the above stakeholders constitute a needs analysis that represent important inputs to the innovation to maximize its value to each stakeholder.

Collaborative technologies and infrastructure

Technological innovations can quickly become obsolete when incumbent technologies are replaced with newer and better ones. In the case of emergent technologies such as IoT, AI and crowdsourcing, it is essential to design such technology-based systems with *modularity*, *extensibility* and *interoperability*[10] in mind. In fact, technological innovations thrive on open standards, protocols and architectures for interoperability.

We observe two key approaches: (1) *fully proprietary*, which includes building all components of the solution in-house; and (2) *integrative*, which allows for various integration points in the end-to-end system. While the former approach may lead to more reliable stand-alone systems, the latter approach is advocated as it promotes a competitive, healthy and innovative environment for technology innovations, which can result in increased reliability and affordability, and hence increased user adoption rates.

In addition to *modularity*, *extensibility* and *interoperability*, another key aspect of collaborative/cooperative technologies is that they should contain features that are friendly to the beneficiaries, users and/or operators, so as to attain acceptance and sustained usage. For instance, senior-friendly interfaces typically exhibit large fonts and contrasting colors for actionables. An iterative approach to interaction design and prototyping, whereby user feedback is continuously sought and incorporated into the final product, is strongly advocated.

Finally, the supporting infrastructure for sustainable social innovation should follow a collaborative approach to allow for scalability and resource sharing. The conventional siloed approach for infrastructure does not facilitate resource sharing among different technological/service providers. A collaborative infrastructure, along with the necessary management and access control in place, is not only cost-efficient but can also enhance the value to different stakeholders.

Collaborative sense-making

For the innovation to benefit each vulnerable senior, it is necessary to have: (1) multi-type, multi-source data; (2) multi-disciplinary data; and (3) analysis and presentation of data that is relevant and beneficial to each stakeholder.

In the longer term, community eldercare to meet the holistic (including health and social) needs of seniors requires the reliable assessment of behavioral, physical and clinical status across multiple interrelated spectrums (cognitive, social, physiological and environmental). Conventional ethnographic methods, including periodic surveys and assessments, are costly and labor-intensive. Moreover, these ad hoc assessment tools are unable to detect and identify events that rarely or infrequently occur, as well as those that evolve slowly over time, and lack a clear initial onset. Therefore, the multimodal, multi-disciplinary data collection required for such assessments should include the following:

- *Continuous (that is, round-the-clock) objective data* from passive and unobtrusive monitoring that can help us understand the activity levels of the senior at home. Examples include infrastructured devices such as motion sensors, door contact sensors, smart plugs and bed sensors.
- *Intermittent objective data* (through participation and interaction). Examples include *in-home* wireless-enabled weighing scales and blood pressure devices, and *wearables* such as fitness trackers, smart watch proximity beacons (which can be attached to personal belongings such as wallets and keychains) and other devices to capture out-of-home accessibility information. The frequency of these data readings may range from a few times a day to a few times a month, as they may require human participation and/or interaction.
- *Periodic subjective assessment*. These include psychosocial surveys, which can either be self-assessed or administered by a third party. The surveys include widely accepted scales that are linked to wellbeing indicators, such as satisfaction with life, sleep quality, depression, cognition and mobility status. As surveys are generally labor-intensive and time-consuming to administer/complete, they are usually carried out on a quarterly or half-yearly basis. Results from the surveys can be used to understand the seniors' subjective wellbeing.
- *Ad hoc subjective observations*. These are typically unstructured data, and can be derived from visual observations of, and conversations with, the seniors. The observations can be effective in picking up unusual events, such as hospital visits and falls. Other types of data that may be captured through such means include service provision and utilization data from caregiving partners. These data can often be used to explain outliers or anomalies in certain features and patterns derived from objective data. For example, a senior may go out less frequently than usual soon after he is discharged from hospital.

Ideally, the above data sources should be collected and analysed in an integrative and interdisciplinary manner, in collaboration with domain experts such as geriatric professionals, in order to derive general as well as specific actionable insights to improve the wellbeing of seniors.

INSTANTIATIONS OF THE PROPOSED FRAMEWORK

With its globally recognized excellence in integrating computing, management and social science, the Singapore Management University (SMU) is well poised to achieve multidisciplinary excellence in creating smart city[11] solutions across multiple domains – such as ageing and healthcare management, as well as urban management and sustainability. SMU's state of the art city campus in Singapore makes it ideal for piloting such citizen-centric solutions in partnership with both the public and private sectors. In this section, we discuss our experience in two exemplary instantiations of the proposed collaborative framework for technology-based social innovation to benefit vulnerable seniors in Singapore.

Technology-enabled Ageing-in-Place for Seniors Living Alone

Since late 2014, SMU has played a key role in various interdisciplinary projects, seeded by the SHINESeniors project [36], to study the use of sensor-enabled homes to enable senior Singaporeans who live alone to age-in-place in the community. It represents a holistic study that builds upon existing work to address: (1) the immediate and personal safety needs of the senior (*reactive care*); (2) long-term health and social needs of the senior (*preventive care*); and (3) technology-centric and care-centric challenges for sustainable technology-enabled community eldercare.

Collaborative stakeholders

The enabling partnership ecosystem of the various projects, which is key to its sustainability, comprises: (1) key agencies in the Singapore Inter-Ministerial Committee on Ageing, including the Ministry of Health (MOH), Housing & Development Board (HDB) and Urban Redevelopment Authority (URA), to ensure that the projects remain relevant and aligned to the national agenda; (2) representative and supportive community (social) eldercare organizations, which provide the necessary first-level caregiver response and support, and are key to the successful recruitment of senior participants; (3) regional health groups, one which advises on the appropriate care model, and provides round-the-clock call center services to seniors who require social chats, and the other with expertise in geriatric psychiatry and access to senior participants for the study of sensor-enabled homes for mild cognitive impairment in seniors; (4) research and technology partners, including A*STAR[12] and Tata Consultancy Services, to ensure usability and value to seniors and their caregivers, scientific rigor, as well as commercial viability to the technology platform; (5) seniors themselves, who are primary beneficiaries of the project and provide valuable inputs to improve the user experience of the system; and (6) Next-Of-Kin (NOK) of the seniors to complement the first-level caregiver support and response team.

Collaborative technologies and infrastructure

The technology platform [37–39] encompasses three main components: (1) a modular and extensible IoT platform that enables the acquisition of sensor data to understand the seniors' living patterns at home; (2) cloud-based servers for storage, processing and needs-driven analytics; and (3) user interfaces for caregiver notification and response.

Typical smart home[13]-based solutions that are provided by vendors are proprietary systems that are unable to scale with the evolving needs of the project. This can result in: (1) exorbitant costs for the integration efforts of new devices that are required; and/or (2) multiple aggregation devices at the home if the new devices cannot be integrated into the existing system, which translate to higher costs.

To circumvent these issues, the team has focused on the design, implementation and deployment of a modular and extensible IoT platform that is based on open standards.[14] The IoT platform supports the sensor-enabled home, whereby COTS (commercial off-the-shelf) wireless sensor devices are integrated with a mains-powered gateway.[15] Multimodal sensor devices used in the basic setup [37] include motion sensors in each zone of the home (for example, living room, each bathroom, each bedroom, kitchen), a contact sensor at the main door, a Bluetooth-based beacon[16] that is attached to the keychain of the seniors, a sensorized medication box [38] that captures the inferred medication consumption behavior of the seniors (by tracking the opening of the box), as well as a help button that is attached to a lanyard. The gateway, which is equipped with standard wireless interfaces that support existing and future in-home devices beyond the basic setup, aggregates the data from these sensor devices and transmits these to the cloud-based servers via the Internet. The IoT platform is designed to be extensible so that additional sensor devices [39] can be easily integrated.

Data from the IoT platform are aggregated and further analysed at the backend, based on the varying requirements of the stakeholders – in particular, the seniors themselves and the caregivers. Personalized alerts are then pushed to the caregivers (who may either be NOKs or community caregivers), for the appropriate care interventions to the seniors, through a collaborative caregiving platform that has been designed for both usability and community care. In particular, only actionable alerts are triggered to the caregivers, to reduce alert fatigue from information overload. Rich contextual information that is helpful for the caregiver to provide prompt and targeted interventions, such as the last known location of the senior, is included in the alert message. The platform also supports a collaborative many-to-many care model, whereby many community caregivers take care of many seniors, by allowing the same alert to be reliably transmitted and updated to multiple caregivers in real-time. Furthermore, the collaborative caregiving platform enables the logging of care and intervention activities, which are automatically captured at the backend servers for further analysis on the effectiveness of care.

For sustainability beyond the research phase, it is of paramount importance that the technologies are reliable and require low maintenance, to ensure business viability by the system operator by minimizing the operational costs. A quantitative comparison of system reliability (as measured by the uptime of the gateway and the individual sensor devices) was conducted for vendor solutions [40] for ten homes between September 2016 and March 2017; it was revealed that reliability levels were between 92 percent and 96 percent. Reactive system maintenance with partial system information resulted in prolonged system downtimes, rendering the system non-dependable which is clearly unacceptable. To ensure sustainability from the perspective of system operators, the team put into place full system monitoring capabilities, coupled with proactive notifications of targeted and prioritized maintenance needs (actionable insights) through a collaborative user interface (similar to the way that the caregivers receive notifications for alerts), resulting in a consistent average performance of more than 99 percent in system uptime.

Collaborative sense-making

In addition to continuous objective IoT data from multimodal sensors, baseline and quarterly follow-up psychosocial surveys and assessments are conducted with the seniors. Through regular monthly visits to the seniors' homes, ad hoc observational data (such as health and mobility status of the senior, and environmental state of the home), as well as unusual events (such as hospitalizations and falls) as verbalized by the seniors are captured, and also used for collaborative sense-making.

One important requirement of the study is to detect and react to events of distress at home (such as falls or unconsciousness), which result in prolonged inactivity[17] in the home. While such events should be detected as soon as they occur – so that timely help can be rendered to the senior, it is also important to minimize false positives (that could arise due to prolonged napping of seniors). By applying intelligent algorithms on the data collected from each senior [41], we were able to detect and notify caregivers of real events of distress within 5–6 hours, while keeping false positives to levels deemed acceptable by our caregiving partners.

Beyond reactive care, we perform extensive feature engineering on the continuous objective IoT data, followed by correlation analysis with subjective wellbeing scores computed from the psychosocial surveys. This allows us to determine the set of IoT-derived features that are linked to specific wellbeing. For example, based on data obtained over six months from 50 seniors, risk of depression [42] can be detected by the amount of "room-level movement" and "going out," while risk of social loneliness [43] is associated with day-time napping duration, time spent in the living room and "going out" behavior.

Collaborative sense-making may also be used to trigger targeted interventions by the caregivers to improve senior wellbeing. By studying the inferred medication adherence of the seniors (based on usage of the sensorized medication box), we are able to distinguish seniors who have regular medication patterns versus those who do not (in terms of daily intake timing and/or intake frequency) [38]. With feedback from the seniors and caregivers, we are able to iteratively improvise and improve the usability of the system [44], as well as demonstrate improvements in medication regularity in some of the senior participants, following data-driven intervention.

In another collaboration with the Lions Befrienders Service Association (LBSA), with data from in-home monitoring systems installed in 50 homes [27], we identified and rectified the root causes of system performance issues that had resulted in caregiver fatigue. Despite the lower data resolution, we achieved online (timely) detection of behavioral changes in the seniors [45] to trigger care, while eliminating false positives due to system faults that are typically observed in real deployment environments. In addition, although LBSA collects a multitude of data related to the seniors' wellbeing and the services they provide, caregivers do not have insights to: (1) the overall effectiveness of their services; and (2) what caregiving approaches work best for seniors. Through applying AI techniques on the amalgamated data from various sources, useful insights were derived for LBSA's caregivers to: (1) identify specific seniors who require specialized care; and (2) design personalized interventions to improve the effectiveness of their services [46].

In an observational pilot study led by the National University Health System, we aim to use sensor-derived features to distinguish seniors clinically assessed with mild cognitive impairment (MCI) versus those who are cognitively healthy (HC). The primary hypothesis that continuous and non-continuous data obtained from a multitude of low-cost sensors over two months will differ between both groups was evaluated over seven blocks of 55 seniors over 14 months. In [39], we share key lessons learned from deploying the sensor system which was extended from the basic IoT platform, together with the solutions implemented to improve system reliability. Preliminary analysis [47, 48] indicates differences in sensor-obtained activity patterns between the HC and MCI groups. In addition, qualitative feedback from research participants was positive, and there was enthusiasm for the system to be fine-tuned to support more seniors living alone.

The above results hold promise for the further application of IoT and AI for online detection of deterioration in the wellbeing of community dwelling seniors living alone. This allows for early intervention to take place, and increases the value of the innovation to various stakeholders.

Technology-enabled Ageing-in-Place for Wheelchair Users

As seniors age, their mobility status tends to deteriorate, thus increasing their dependence on mobility aids (such as rollators and wheelchairs) for their daily commute. This dependence on mobility aids, coupled with lack of information on accessible paths, can potentially inhibit seniors from venturing out of their homes, and lead to social isolation [43] and depression [42].

The SmartBFA (Smart Mobility and Accessibility for Barrier-Free Access) project [49] aims to find barrier-free access routes between destinations, through the use of passive, crowdsourced sensor data from wheelchair volunteers. In SmartBFA, sensors are retrofitted onto the wheelchairs of volunteers to collect data on the condition (such as ramps, slopes, bumpiness and rain shelter) of roads that have been traversed. Subsequently, the sensor data are analysed to derive features of road conditions, as well as accessibility metrics. Such information can be displayed on existing mapping applications [30–34] to enable barrier-free access users to find wheelchair-friendly paths to their destinations.

Collaborative stakeholders

The ecosystem for a barrier-free access Singapore requires the collaborative support of several key stakeholders, comprising: (1) government agencies such as the Land Transport Authority and the Building and Construction Authority, which are responsible for the planning and regulation of streets and buildings, respectively; (2) community care partners and organizations that are affiliated with persons with disabilities, such as the Holland-Bukit Panjang Town Council, Handicaps Welfare Association and Singapore National Paralympic Council, which are instrumental in helping to recruit wheelchair participants for the data collection phase; (3) private organizations, such as property developers, which may be potential consumers of (and thus attribute value to) the accessibility information; and (4) wheelchair users themselves, who are the main beneficiaries of the system.

Collaborative technologies and infrastructure

The SmartBFA technology platform comprises: (1) the IoT sensor platform, which measures road environmental conditions through multimodal sensors retrofitted on wheelchairs of participants, and transmits such data automatically to the backend platform; (2) scalable backend platform and data analysis engine; and (3) user interface for visualization and action by end users.

The multimodal sensor devices include accelerometers, gyroscopes and location-based sensors such as the Global Positioning System (GPS). Instead of consuming the volunteers' data plan (which may be a deterrence to volunteer), the data are *only* transmitted to the backend whenever there is WiFi connectivity. The backend data analysis engine converts the raw sensor signal into accessibility indices for different road segments. The user visualization component displays the annotated accessibility indices on a map when a wheelchair user searches for a route from the source to the destination.

Collaborative sense-making

In addition to continuous and objective sensor data on road conditions, periodic surveys are administered to the research participants. From these surveys, we aim to have a better understanding of the participants' general travel patterns, wheelchair travel patterns, as well as the impact of their disabilities on their social, family, community and economic life, so that appropriate measures can be undertaken by the relevant stakeholders to improve the quality of their lives.

While the research is still in its infancy stage, it is envisioned that the actionable insights generated will be valuable to different stakeholders. For instance, wheelchair users and their immediate caregivers will be able to use the processed data to find barrier-free paths to their intended destinations. On the other hand, planning agencies can use the data to identify places with poor barrier-free interconnectivity, and subsequently improve the accessibility of these places.

ENSURING SUSTAINABILITY OF TECHNOLOGY-ENABLED AGEING-IN-PLACE: FUTURE RESEARCH

Existing siloed innovations (see first section) for technology-enabled ageing-in-place for community dwelling seniors focus primarily on: (1) usability and value creation of sensor-enabled homes for seniors living alone through targeting specific needs, such as physical safety (reactive care) and wellbeing (preventive care); and (2) manual crowdsourcing of accessibility data by the general public for the environment beyond the home to maximize barrier-free access for wheelchair users.

In the second section, we proposed a collaborative framework to ensure the sustainability of technology-enabled social innovations. We explained the framework in the context of ageing-in-place for vulnerable community dwelling seniors, and described two examples of how aspects of this framework have been instantiated (third section). To date, through this framework, we have engaged five public entities and three technology partners. Furthermore, our innovations have collectively benefited more than 200 vulnerable seniors and five caregiving organizations, laying the foundation for sustainability. In the following, we outline future research areas within the collaborative framework that can bring our innovations closer to sustainability.

Collaborative Stakeholders

Beyond the stakeholders considered, future research can look into collaboration with the partners outlined in the following subsections.

Institutional care partners

Our existing technological innovation to trigger community care for seniors living alone relies primarily on formal caregivers, community volunteers and next of kin to deliver care. This is typically best effort, given the very high beneficiary-to-staff ratio, and other day-to-day office hour obligations. As round-the-clock care service providers become increasingly available [50, 51] and are important for scalability, community care models that can exploit a wider network of care partners should be investigated.

Community partners

Seniors are commonly regarded as consumers of services, and community caregivers and volunteers as producers of services, where the value of such services is often quantified in economic or altruistic terms. While technology innovation can alleviate the productivity crunch, there is still a dire need for community resources to support caregiving, as well as basic maintenance of the deployed systems.

The concept of time banking [52] has the potential to bridge the gap between consumers and producers of services. With time banking, credits are earned for every hour of service provided, and these credits can be used in turn to purchase an hour's worth of services provided by others. In technology-enabled community eldercare, younger and more-abled seniors in the community can earn credits by contributing their time for both the technology (basic maintenance) and social (befriending, cooking, sewing and so on) aspects, and redeem them in the future. Similarly, wheelchair users, both young and old, can earn credits by contributing to accessibility data, and redeem care services as and when needed.

Another potentially sustainable source of community resources are youth volunteers, as many high school and college students around the world are obliged to complete mandatory community service prior to graduation.

Non-for-profit partners

In the preceding sections, we described partnerships that are essential to support the technological innovations when deployed at scale. While such economies of scale can result in cost reduction and demonstrate social impact, it is unlikely that vulnerable seniors will be willing or are able to pay for such innovations, or the services enabled. While it is commonplace for the government and philanthropic organizations to provide subsidies for healthcare and social services, such subsidies for technology-enabled social innovations and services are far and few.

However, with the recent push for digital inclusion, schemes such as the Home Access Programme [53] were launched in April 2017 to help close the digital divide by providing an affordable broadband bundle package to low-income households in Singapore. Under the same umbrella – the Digital Innovation fund – the Social Innovation Programme will support voluntary welfare organizations by encouraging the adoption of IT solutions to better improve help to their end-beneficiaries. Recently, Temasek Foundation Cares,[18] in partnership with Careline [50], hopes to connect with lonely seniors using free smartphones that are preinstalled with custom mobile applications. These initiatives hold promise for the proposed technology-enabled social innovations to benefit from the subsidies.

For-profit partners

Insurance companies such as AIA and Manulife already offer wellness programs (such as AIA Vitality [54] and ManulifeMOVE [55]) where consumers can purchase wearables at discounts, and clock points if they meet certain steps, heart rate and calories scores, which can be used for benefits such as retail discounts and reductions in annual premium. By extending the service to track activity levels through passive monitoring, risk factors on various aspects of an individual's wellbeing can be inferred (see the fourth section), which can be used to recommend self-care through persuasive technology.

With increasing demand for food delivery services, we are seeing a rise in the use of personal mobility devices for food delivery. In Singapore, the Workplace Safety and Health Council recently introduced new safe riding guides to keep Singapore's food delivery riders safe. To this end, companies such as Deliveroo, Foodpanda and GrabFood can benefit by integrating accessibility information onto their existing mobile applications in order to guide their food delivery riders along more accessible (and thus safer) routes.

Collaborative Technologies and Infrastructure

Thus far, our technological innovations for sensor-enabled homes and wheelchair accessibility focus on collection of data from myriad sources, and making sense of them with cross-disciplinary teams, to understand the needs of vulnerable seniors so that a third party, for example, community caregivers and public agencies, can provide care and infrastructural enhancements, respectively.

As smartphones and other wearable devices become more pervasive, they can be augmented with additional sensor data to provide granular information about the seniors' activities out of the home – through both passive inputs and manual inputs. For example, this provides a quantitative means to evaluate if community amenities such as therapy gardens and exercise corners are well utilized. Beyond serving as a natural means of data collection, smartphones are key enablers of *persuasive technology* – defined as technology designed to change attitudes or behaviors of the users through persuasion and social influence, but not through coercion. In the case of vulnerable seniors, this may translate into self-care, thus alleviating the perception of coercion from community care.

Recently, Singapore saw the official launch of its first '*retirement village*' at Admiralty [56], which integrates housing for seniors with a medical center, eldercare and childcare centers, a community park, vegetable farm, as well as a 900-seat food center and nearly 20 dining and retail outlets. Another ambitious project is underway to equip all 110,000 lamp posts in Singapore with various capabilities to improve urban planning – serving to be more than just a light source [57]. As part of Singapore's Smart Nation Sensor Platform project, these lamp posts can be fitted with a network of wireless sensors to transform them into "smart lamp posts." For example, environmental sensors can monitor rainfall, humidity and temperature, and noise sensors can detect unusually loud sounds, such as a person screaming or a car crash. It will be interesting to study how new community sensing technologies can complement such new typologies and infrastructural enhancements for dense, urban mixed-use developments to benefit vulnerable seniors.

Collaborative Sense-making

Apart from cognitive decline and decline in social wellbeing, the onset of other chronic conditions – such as physical frailty and lower urinary tract symptoms (LUTS) – can also be manifested in the activity levels of the seniors. For example, frequent night-time toileting (which can be detected by in-home sensors) is a common symptom of LUTS, while reduced frequency of going out is common with deteriorating physical frailty. With early detection – such as via continuous monitoring through unobtrusive technology – physical, nutritional and cognitive interventional approaches are effective in reversing frailty and LUTS. This can be achieved by extending cross-disciplinary collaborations to a broader group of healthcare professionals for collaborative sense-making.

NOTES

1. Barrier-free access refers to the concept of designing a living environment for the use of every individual, irrespective of age, ability and status in life. In the context of this chapter, we will focus on wheelchair users.
2. The MRT, or Mass Rapid Transit, is a rapid transit system forming the major component of the railway system in Singapore, spanning most of the city-state.
3 Henceforth, vulnerable seniors will refer to community dwelling seniors who either live alone or are wheelchair users, or both.
4. LBSA is a social service organization which was formed in 1995 by the Lions Club of Singapore and a Lions District Project. Its mission is to provide friendship and care for seniors to age-in-place with community participation, enabling them to enjoy meaningful and enriching lives.
5. The HDB is the statutory board of the Ministry of National Development responsible for public housing in Singapore.
6. Crowdsourcing is the practice of engaging a crowd or group for a common goal – often innovation, problem solving or efficiency, and is powered by new technologies.
7. The system operator refers to a private business entity that will operate and maintain the technological platform after the research phase.
8. Internet of Things is the network of day-to-day objects embedded with sensors, and connectivity, so that real-time and anticipatory decisions can be made.
9. When applied to Internet of Things, Artificial Intelligence enables the detection of patterns in data so that it can learn from these patterns to adjust the ways in which it then analyses that data.
10. Interoperability of technologies refers to the ability for technologies to work and co-exist.
11. A smart city is a municipality that uses digital technologies to increase operational efficiency, share information with the public and improve both the quality of government services and citizen welfare.
12. The Agency for Science, Technology and Research (A*STAR) is a statutory board under the Ministry of Trade and Industry of Singapore. The agency supports research and development that is aligned to areas of competitive advantage and national needs for Singapore.
13. A smart home typically refers to a residence that has appliances, lighting, heating, air conditioning and so on that can communicate with one another, and can be controlled remotely.
14. Open standards are standards made available to the general public and are approved and maintained via a collaborative and consensus-driven process.
15. An analogy for the gateway would be the thalamus, a structure of the brain that receives signals from the sensory organs (sensors) and passes them along to the appropriate area of the cerebral cortex (backend) to be processed.
16. The beacon periodically announces its presence to the gateway; if it is too far from the gateway, it will not be detected, and we can infer that the senior is out of the home.
17. Prolonged inactivity at home can be deduced, for example, by collectively analysing data from the motion sensors, the door contact sensor and the beacon.
18. Temasek Foundation Cares is a Singapore-based non-profit philanthropic organization that funds and supports meaningful and innovative community-based programs for the benefit of Singaporeans.

REFERENCES

[1] United Nations, Department of Economic and Social Affairs, Population Division (2017), "World Population Ageing 2017".

[2] F. Mokhtar (2017), "Singapore's demographic time bomb starts ticking next year: UOB report", accessed 2 June 2018 at https://www.todayonline/singapore/spores-demographic-time-bomb-starts-ticking-next-year-uob-report.

[3] N. Farber, Douglas Shinkle, Jana Lynott, Wendy Fox-Grage and Rodney Harrell (2011), "Aging in place:

A state survey of livability policies and practices", Paper presented at the National Conference of State Legislatures, AARP Public Policy Institute, December.

[4] Department of Statistics, Ministry of Trade & Industry, Singapore (2018), "Population Trends".

[5] J. Tai (2015), "Old and home alone in Singapore", accessed 29 May 2018 at https://www.straitstimes.com/singapore/old-and-home-alone-in-singapore.

[6] Kawai (2016), "Kodokushi – dying alone in Japan", accessed 29 May 2018 at https://hubpages.com/health/Kodokushi-Dying-alone-in-Japan.

[7] T.P. Ng, A. Jin, L. Feng et al. (2015), "Mortality of older persons living alone: Singapore Longitudinal Ageing Studies", *BMC Geriatrics*, **15** (126), 1–9.

[8] K. Wei, M.S.Z. Nyunt, Q. Gao, S.L. Wee and T.P. Ng (2017), "Frailty and malnutrition: related and distinct syndrome prevalence and association among community-dwelling older adults: Singapore Longitudinal Ageing Studies", *Journal of the American Medical Directors Association (JAMDA)*, **18** (12), 1019–28.

[9] J. Tai (2015), "More seniors in Singapore taking own lives", accessed 29 May 2018 at https://www.straitstimes.com/singapore/more-seniors-in-singapore-taking-own-lives.

[10] K. Shimada, S. Yamazaki, K. Nakano and S. Yasumura (2014), "Prevalence of social isolation in community-dwelling elderly by differences in household composition and related factors: from a social network perspective in urban Japan", *Journal of Aging and Health*, **26** (5).

[11] I. Kawachi, G.A. Colditz, A. Ascherio et al. (1996), "A prospective study of social networks in relation to total mortality and cardiovascular disease in men in the USA", *Journal of Epidemiology and Community Health*, **50** (3), 245–51.

[12] C.O. Luanaigh and B.A. Lawlor (2008), "Loneliness and the health of older people", *International Journal of Geriatric Psychiatry*, **23** (12), 1213–321.

[13] J.T. Cacioppo and L.C. Hawkley (2009), "Perceived social isolation and cognition", *Trends in Cognitive Sciences*, **13** (10), 447–54.

[14] J.T. Cacioppo and L.C. Hawkley (2003), "Social isolation and health, with an emphasis on underlying mechanisms", *Perspectives in Biology and Medicine*, **46** (3), 39–52.

[15] A.C. Patterson and G. Veenstra (2010), "Loneliness and risk of mortality: a longitudinal investigation in Alameda County, California", *Social Science and Medicine*, **71** (1), 181–6.

[16] S. Shiovitz-Ezra and L. Ayalon (2010), "Situational versus chronic loneliness as risk factors for all-cause mortality", *International Psychogeriatrics*, **22** (3), 455–62.

[17] L. Tang (2018), "ElderShield to be renamed CareShield Life with higher, lifetime payouts from 2020", accessed 2 June 2018 at https://www.todayonline.com/singapore/eldershield-be-renamed-careshield-life-higher-and-lifetime-payouts-kick-2020.

[18] B. Sadasivan, Mohamad Maliki Osman and Halimah Yacob (2006), *Report of the Committee on Ageing Issues, 2006*, accessed 29 May 2018 at https://www.msf.gov.sg/publications/Pages/Report-of-the-Committee-on-Ageing-Issues-2006.aspx.

[19] A. Chia (2014), "Teams in the running to win seed funding for apps that help people with disabilities", accessed 29 May 2018 at https://www.todayonline.com/singapore/teams-running-win-seed-funding-apps-help-people-disabilities.

[20] National Council of Social Services (2018), "Understanding the Quality of Life of Adults with Disabilities", accessed 29 May 2018 at https://www.ncss.gov.sg/Press-Room/Publications/Detail-Page?id=Understanding-the-Quality-of-Life-of-Adults-with-D.

[21] S. Withers (2017), "NSW startup developing navigation for wheelchair users", accessed 29 May 2018 at https://www.bit.com.au/news/nsw-startup-developing-navigation-for-wheelchair-users-480261.

[22] M. Larizza, Ingrid Zukerman, Fabian Bohnert et al. (2012), "Studies to determine user requirements regarding in-home monitoring systems", in J. Masthoff, B. Mobasher, M.C. Desmarais and R. Nkambou (eds), *Lecture Notes in Computer Science*, Berlin, Heidelberg: Springer, **7379**, pp. 139–50.

[23] M.C. Pol, S. Poerbodipoero, S. Robben et al. (2013), "Sensor monitoring to measure and support daily functioning for independently living older people: a systematic review and roadmap for further development", *Journal of the American Geriatrics Society*, **61** (12), 2219–27.

[24] J.A. Kaye, Shoshana A. Maxwell and Nora Mattek (2011), "Intelligent systems for assessing aging changes: home-based, unobtrusive, and continuous assessment of aging", *Journals of Gerontology: Series B*, **66B** (1).

[25] D. Bradford, Zhang Qing and Mohan Karunanithi (2016), "The Smarter Safer Homes Project: extending independence for the elderly", accessed 29 May 2018 at https://publications.csiro.au/rpr/pub?pid=csiro:EP159306.

[26] L. Mainetti, L. Patrono and P. Rametta (2016), "Capturing behavioral changes of elderly people through unobtrusive sensing technologies", Paper presented at the International Conference on Software, Telecommunications and Computer Networks (SoftCOM), Split, Croatia, 22 September.

[27] D. Nathan (2015), "TNP at 27: presenting the hardware and heartware of Project Helping Hands",

accessed 29 May 2018 at https://www.tnp.sg/news/singapore-news/tnp-27-presenting-hardware-and-heartware-project-helping-hands.
[28] V. Koh (2015), "HDB completes trial of smart elderly monitoring and alert system", accessed 29 May 2018 at https://www.todayonline.com/singapore/hdb-completes-semas-test-bed.
[29] C.J. Loh (2016), "Smart devices trial extended to 3,200 households in Yuhua", accessed 29 May 2018 at https://www.channelnewsasia.com/news/singapore/smart-devices-trial-extended-to-3-200-households-in-yuhua-8086356.
[30] T. Zhu (2014), "Allgoeasy", Facebook Referencing Group, 21 March, accessed 29 May 2018 at https://www.facebook.com/AllGoEasy.
[31] R. Krauthausen (2010), "Wheelmap", accessed 29 May 2018 at https://en.wikipedia.org/wiki/Wheelmap.org.
[32] M. Petronzio (2016), "Google Maps now finally tells you when a business is wheelchair accessible", accessed 29 May 2018 at https://mashable.com/2016/12/16/google-maps-wheelchair-accessible-locations/#xZ6qo8ZSSOqi.
[33] B. Heater (2017), "Google Maps now lets users add wheelchair accessibility details for locations", accessed 29 May 2018 at https://techcrunch.com/2017/07/08/google-maps-now-lets-users-add-wheelchair-accessibility-details-for-locations/.
[34] J. Vanian (2018), "Google debuts wheelchair accessible routes in Google Maps", accessed 29 May 2018 at http://fortune.com/2018/03/15/google-maps-wheelchair-accessible-routes/.
[35] K.Y. Gan (2016), "I feel young in my Singapore! Action plan for successful ageing", accessed 29 May 2018 at https//www.moh.gov.sg/content/moh_web/ifeelyoungsg/about-the-action-plan/what-is-the-plan-about.html.
[36] L. Bai, A. Gavino, P. Lee et al. (2015), "SHINESeniors: personalized services for active ageing-in-place", Paper presented at the IEEE Smart Cities Conference, Guadalajara, Mexico, 25 October.
[37] A.C. Valera, Pius Lee, H.P. Tan, H.X. Tan and H. Liang (2018), "Real-world large-scale IoT systems for community eldercare: experiences and lessons learned", in D.L. Nielsen (ed.), *Elderly Care: Options, Challenges and Trends*, New York: Nova Science Publishers, pp. 53–80.
[38] X. Toh, H.X. Tan, H. Liang and H.P. Tan (2016), "Elderly medication adherence monitoring with the Internet of Things", Paper presented at the IEEE PerCom Workshops, Sydney, 18 March.
[39] B.T. Ng, H.P. Tan and H.X. Tan (2017), "Managing sensor systems for early detection of mild cognitive impairment in community elderly: lessons learnt and future work", Paper presented at the IRC Conference on Science, Engineering and Technology, Singapore, 10 August.
[40] H.P. Tan and A. Zhang (2018), "Real-world large-scale IoT systems for community eldercare: a comparative study on system dependability", Paper presented at the IEEE International Conference on Information Networking, Chiang Mai, Thailand, 12 January.
[41] A.C. Valera, H.P. Tan and L. Bai (2016), "Improving the sensitivity of unobtrusive inactivity detection in sensor-enabled homes for the elderly", Paper presented at the IEEE PerCom Workshops, Sydney, 18 March.
[42] N.P.S. Huynh, H.P. Tan and Y. Lee (2017), "Towards unobtrusive mental well-being monitoring for independent-living elderly", Paper presented at the International Workshop on Physical Analytics (WPA), Niagara Falls, New York, 19 June.
[43] N. Goonawardene, X. Toh and H.P. Tan (2017), "Sensor-driven detection of social isolation in community-dwelling elderly", in J. Zhou and G. Salvendy (eds), *Lecture Notes in Computer Science*, Berlin, Heidelberg: Springer, **10298**, pp. 378–92.
[44] H.X. Tan, H.P. Tan and H. Liang (2018), "Technology-enabled medication adherence for seniors living in the community: experiences, lessons, and the road ahead", Paper presented at the HCI International, Las Vegas, CA, 19 July.
[45] T.T. La, A. Valera, H.P. Tan and C. Koh (2016), "Online detection of behavioral change using unobtrusive eldercare monitoring system", Paper presented at the International Conference on Queueing Theory and Network Applications (QTNA), Wellington, 13 December.
[46] M. Huang, C. Koh, N. Goonawardene, H.P. Tan and J. Teo (2017), "Employing in-home sensor technology to explore elderly needs and community participation: implications on personalizing community elder care", Paper presented at the APRU Population Aging Conference, Singapore, 13 October.
[47] H.X. Tan and H.P. Tan (2018), "Early detection of mild cognitive impairment in elderly through IoT: preliminary findings", Paper presented at the IEEE World Forum on Internet of Things, Singapore, 8 February.
[48] I. Rawtaer, Rathi Mahendran and E.H. Kua (2018), "In-home sensors for assessment of cognitive and psychological health of older adults: a pilot study", Paper presented at the World Psychiatric Association Thematic Congress, Melbourne, 28 February.
[49] W. Wong (2018), "App identifying barrier-free routes for wheelchair users in the works", accessed 2 June

2018 at https://www.channelnewsasia.com/news/singapore/app-identifying-barrier-free-routes-for-wheel chair-users-in-the-9947668.

[50] L. Lai (2017), "Round-the-clock hotline service to give patients a listening ear", accessed 2 June 2018 at https://www.straitstimes.com/singapore/health/round-the-clock-hotline-service-to-give-patients-a-listening-ear.

[51] Certis Cisco, "Certis OK! Home Monitoring and Response Services", accessed 1 June 2018 at https://sg.certissecurity.com/certis-ok.

[52] E.S. Cahn and C. Gray (2015), "The time bank solution", accessed 2 June 2018 at https://ssir.org/articles/entry/the_time_bank_solution.

[53] S. Lo (2018), "Will IMDA reconsider extending Home Access Programme for low-income households", accessed 1 June 2018 at https://www.todayonline.com/voices/will-imda-reconsider-extending-home-access-programme-low-income-households.

[54] L. Tan (2017), "Staying healthy can be a rewarding exercise", accessed 2 June 2018 at https://www.straitstimes.com/singapore/health/every-step-counts-for-vitality-members.

[55] E. Natalia (2018), "ManulifeMOVE gives you cash to move more", accessed 1 June 2018 at https://www.runsociety.com/news/manulifemove-gives-you-cash-to-move-more/.

[56] W.L. Toh (2017), "Woodlands modern kampung first to integrate active ageing hub and childcare centre", accessed 2 June 2018 at https://www.straitstimes.com/singapore/woodlands-retirement-kampung-one-of-15-projects-to-win-ministers-team-awards-2017.

[57] A. Khan (2018), "'Smart lamp posts' in Singapore won't shine light into people's lives", accessed 1 June 2018 at https://www.channelnewsasia.com/news/singapore/smart-lampposts-singapore-wont-shine-light-peoples-lives-10229804.

13. How firms bring social innovation and efficiency to the global effort to recover from national uncertainty shocks

Luis Ballesteros

> . . . Everything disappeared . . . The government was absent for days after the disaster . . . And when they arrived, they did not know exactly what to do, how to coordinate the aid, what functions to perform . . . We coped with it with our own resources and with a lot of help from the private sector. (Municipal official, aftermath of the earthquake and tsunami in 2010 in Maule, Chile) (Polanco, 2012, p. 32)

"There was no time for sitting and making big plans and budgets. We needed to act in urgency." Felipe Purcell, Vice President for Corporate Affairs at the mining company Anglo American, reflected on his company's response to the earthquake and resulting tsunami that devastated the coast of Chile in 2010. It was indeed a challenging time for orchestrating a humanitarian response. A new federal administration was taking office in a few days and many functions at the local level were already missing coordination. "The municipal government disappeared, and the national government was absent for days after the disaster," a municipal official in Chile's Maule region stated. "And when the [government officials] arrived, they did not know exactly what to do, how to coordinate the aid, what functions to perform."

Purcell and his team traveled from Santiago to two of the most devastated regions to pinpoint where their help could best be leveraged. Anglo American had turned to the mining ministry for further guidance, which had asked the company to support the immediate national priority of reopening all the nation's schools within six weeks. To avoid bureaucratic delays, the government urged Anglo American to move through its own channels, and Purcell concurred.

Though Anglo American had no special history with building schools, it did have plenty of large-scale construction know-how for quickly assembling structures. Mobile buildings and temporary encampments were its life-blood. Purcell and his team contacted the makers of mobile structures with which his company had long contracted, and they were soon delivering state-of-the-art buildings that might have rimmed a copper mine but were now for towns without a functioning schoolhouse. The company specified that the materials and designs for the new schools were to be resistant to seismic shocks, waterproof, and temperature impervious for at least a decade.

By collaborating with the local community, in less than 90 days, Anglo American built six schools from scratch for more than 4,500 students in four communities, including one massive 80,000-square foot building for 2,000 students. And it did so by the President's deadline of having all Chile's children back in school just weeks after the earthquake. The buildings, which came equipped with computer labs, food services, and curricular materials, received several international awards and were adopted as a model for the reconstruction. Chile's President Piñera personally joined the inauguration of some of the schools built by Anglo American (Useem et al., 2015).

The actions of Anglo American point to the capacity of for-profit organizations to bring innovation and efficiency to the provision of public goods, traditionally known as corporate pro-social behavior or corporate social responsibility (CSR). Here we emphasize the firm's intervention when societies experience uncertainty shocks – that is, exogenous and unpredictable hazards that significantly disrupt the welfare of a geographical area, such as natural disasters, terrorist attacks, technological accidents, pandemics, and episodes of violent crime – and governments lack the means to meet social needs (Baker and Bloom, 2013; Ballesteros et al., 2017; Bloom, 2009; Kunreuther and Useem, 2018). With technical know-how, reconfigurable resources, and quick-building financial capacity, firms often step forward to supplement aid from traditional providers, such as national governments and multilateral agencies.

AN ERA OF GLOBAL UNCERTAINTY SHOCKS

The history of economic and social development has been, in part, a function of how societies deal with calamity, and disaster uncertainty is tightly connected with human evolution. Since the turn of the twenty-first century, however, there has been something new about managing uncertainty shocks: the traditional public network of assistance is now largely insufficient to fund disaster management (Ballesteros and Kunreuther, 2018).

In this sense, the central tenet of this chapter is that the social implications of the engagement of firms in the provision of public goods in the aftermath of uncertainty shocks is higher than ever – an outcome of two connected factors. First, processes of urbanization, environmental degradation, and economic integration have dramatically increased the cost of providing critical public goods in the context of low-probability, high-magnitude shocks. For instance, the average annual inflation-adjusted economic loss associated with earthquakes, floods, hurricanes, and other natural calamities sextupled from $54 billion in the 1980s to $314 billion in the 2010s (Munich Re, 2013; Useem et al., 2015). Since the 1980s, the aggregate economic loss increased almost threefold to reach $1.2 trillion in the 2000s. The financial commitment to recover and rebuild is sometimes larger than the size of the affected national economy. That was the case of the earthquake that destroyed Port-au-Prince in 2010 with an economic cost of 117 percent of Haiti's gross domestic product (GDP), and Nepal's earthquake in 2015, for which cost estimates have ranged from 50 to more than 100 percent of its GDP (Ballesteros et al., 2017).

Large disasters cause, on average, significant drops in economic growth for at least a decade after the shock and this vulnerability is not necessarily associated with a pre-existing level of economic development (E. Cavallo et al., 2013). Given the accumulation of capital, the rise in the economic costs of these phenomena has been particularly steep in richer economies. For instance, the economic loss of Hurricane Harvey in 2017 is projected to be enormous and as high as $190 billion. The disaster in Texas may thus become one of the costliest natural disasters in American history, potentially exceeding Hurricane Katrina's cost of $108 billion.

The aftermath of Japan's Tōhoku disaster in 2011 revealed, for instance, that even high-income countries are at risk and face grave financial shortfalls. The earthquake, tsunami, and meltdown of nuclear reactors at Fukushima hit Japan at a moment when public indebtedness had already ballooned to twice the size of its economy, and that proved an albatross on the government's capacity to cope with the crisis. Japanese policy makers created an emergency relief budget, for example, but the outlay proved woefully inadequate, and the earthquake destruction soon morphed into the largest economic crisis for Japan since World War II. Producer numbers plummeted, the stock market plunged, and trade deficits soared; foreign markets linked to Japanese manufacturing suffered significant drops in industrial output as well (Blaikie et al., 2014; A. Cavallo et al., 2013; Olcott and Oliver, 2014).

We have seen similar scenarios in Italy, after the L'Aquila earthquake in 2009; in New Zealand, after the Christchurch earthquake in 2011; and in the US, after Superstorm Sandy in 2012. All three were developed nations that most experts assumed could self-finance their recovery, yet each suffered deeply when disaster struck and outstripped its state capacities.[1]

The second factor fueling the social value of the corporate provision of public goods in the responses to disasters is the drop in the relative financial capacity of traditional funding sources of relief and recovery. The nominal annual value of international aid coming from governments, multilateral agencies, non-profit organizations, and individual charity increased by $6 billion from 1990 to 2011 or 1.9 percent of the real increase in the costs of natural disasters during the same period. As a result, the real value of international aid for disaster financing has declined in recent years (Kellett and Caravani, 2013). While international aid covered over 4 percent of disaster costs worldwide in 2000, that figure dropped to about 3 percent in 2010. Overall, a 10 percent increase in disaster costs during the past four decades has been followed by a mere 0.7 percent average increase in international aid. Between 1980 and 2012, the median value of international assistance is estimated to have covered just 5 percent of the affected nations' economic losses, and for high-income countries, that fraction drops to less than 1 percent (Becerra et al., 2014; Munich Re, 2015).

This skew is because the international aid channel provides modestly to medium- and high-income countries, where the costliest disasters occur. In recent years, low-income countries have received 89 percent of the United Nations' (UN) humanitarian assistance. By contrast, the UN directed only 8 percent of its relief to medium-income countries such as Chile and Mexico, and less than 3 percent to high-income countries, such as Japan. The Organisation for Economic Co-operation and Development's Official Development Assistance, the UN's Office for the Coordination of Humanitarian Affairs, and other multilateral organizations traditionally issue appeals for aid when disasters have hit low-income but not higher-income countries. As a result, a relatively large absolute and per capita share of multilateral public aid goes to low-income economies. Given that slant, the uncovered economic vulnerability to disasters may grow proportionally with the income level of the economy (Becerra et al., 2014).

On the other hand, commercial insurance practices have not proven sufficient to cover fat-tail disaster losses, particularly in large markets. Nowadays, insurance covers some 25 percent of disaster losses in high-income countries, such as Canada and Germany, and less than 4 percent in low- and medium-income countries (Kellett and Caravani, 2013; Noy, 2012; Weitzman, 2011). Costly disasters such as Hurricane Katrina and Hurricane Andrew have exposed the financial limitations of the insurance industry in higher-income countries to hedge low-probability, high-magnitude disasters. For example, 13 insurance companies declared bankruptcy after Hurricane Andrew. For Hurricane Katrina, insurance covered just 46 percent of the destruction, and for Harvey in 2017, a comparable fraction has been calculated. In Japan, only 20 percent of the damage by the 2011 earthquake and tsunami was insured. Overall, the annual growth rate of disaster losses worldwide during the last 40 years has outpaced the growth of commercial insurance by five percentage points (Bevere et al., 2015; Cummins and Mahul, 2009).

Hence, large disasters have been outstripping traditional public and market-based mechanisms for relief and recovery. As a result, many nations have increasingly struggled to finance the rising price of responding and recovering after low-probability, high-consequence shocks. The UN reported in 2016 that traditional disaster financing has never "been so insufficient" because the annual funding gap of large crises is increasing year by year and estimated a gap of $15 billion for 2015. The agency urged to "stimulate innovation" and "improve the efficiency" of how the global community responds to large shocks (Blaikie et al., 2014; Cohen and Werker, 2008; Kellett and Caravani, 2013; OCHA, 2016; United Nations, 2016).

THE INCREASING ROLE OF BUSINESS ORGANIZATIONS IN FINANCING UNCERTAINTY SHOCKS

Given the growing costs of disasters, business organizations are increasingly being asked to make up for the funding gap of large disasters, and many have stepped forward. Reports of firms funding social and economic infrastructure – such as educational facilities, roads, and water sanitation plants – and/or services, such as telemedicine and technical training – date back to the 1800s (Alessi, 1975; Douty, 1972). Since the turn of the twenty-first century, however, the frequency and magnitude of the corporate provision of public goods in the aftermath of disasters have experienced unprecedented growth (Ballesteros et al., 2017). Between 1999 and 2015, for instance, the fraction of the 10,000 largest firms at the international level engaging in this behavior went from 15 percent to over 70 percent and their average donation increased by 1,800 percent.

In some instances, business largesse has exceeded the contributions of all traditional responders including foreign governments, international agencies, and non-profit organizations and individual charity combined. In the aftermath of Chile's earthquake and tsunami in 2010, for example, 55 percent of all international aid came from corporations. Similarly, in the aftermath of the 2011 Tōhoku disaster and the 2013 Typhoon Haiyan in the Philippines, firms accounted for 68 percent and 52 percent of the total international aid flow, respectively (OCHA, 2016).

One indicator of business' new and now prominent place at the table is the increasing inclusion of representatives of firms at multilateral forums, where governmental and non-governmental agencies attempt to stimulate business action and shape it into a less ad hoc and more disciplined flow. An example is the Fourth Session of the Global Platform for Disaster Risk Reduction – "the world's foremost gathering of stakeholders committed to reducing disaster risk and building the resilience of communities and nations" – whose agenda focused on the role of the business sector in helping build disaster-resilient societies (Figure 13.1).[2]

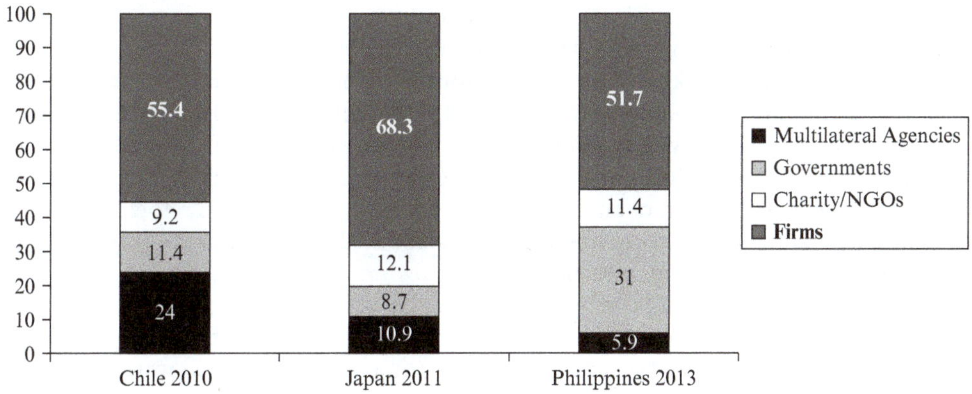

Figure 13.1 The rise of corporate disaster giving

A report on the management of the disaster caused by the 2017 Hurricane Maria in Puerto Rico states that victims had received more efficient aid from firms than from the federal government.[3] One reason for that is the capacity of firms with local operations to mobilize resources and reach emergency areas, which has been a problem for the Federal Emergency Management Agency (FEMA). Finally, the provision of relief to victims of the earthquake of 9 September that devastated Mexico City has been led by civil society and business organizations. Aid coming from the Mexican government has been limited by political factors and administrative obstacles.[4]

ARE FIRMS BRINGING SOCIAL INNOVATION AND MEETING THE SOCIAL NEED?

In the context of the rising level of the corporate provision of public goods in the wake of national disasters, a pertinent question is the social implications for affected communities. Unfortunately, systematic study of the social implications of CSR has not kept pace with the phenomenon. Studies have observed that firms are facing calls to not only engage in traditional forms of CSR, but also to adopt responsibilities that have historically fallen to aid agencies, governments, and non-governmental organizations. Firms are increasingly developing self-standards to substitute for regulations that governments are unable or unwilling to enforce or engaging in the provision of public goods by building and managing hospitals, schools, and community projects (Ballesteros et al., 2017; Matten and Crane, 2005; Ostrom, 2000; Potoski and Prakash, 2005; United Nations, 2016). Based on the observation of these unique forms of CSR, scholars have begun to develop frameworks to describe and predict CSR and examine how firms benefit from these practices (Ballesteros, 2017; Ballesteros and Gatignon, 2018; Henisz et al., 2014; Madsen and Rodgers, 2015; Marquis and Tilcsik, 2016; Marquis et al., 2007; Muller et al., 2014; Scherer and Palazzo, 2007). As with the broader CSR literature, though, we know very little about societal outcomes and opinions are divided as to whether or not social welfare benefits should be expected (Margolis et al., 2007). Similarly, the empirical literature has largely concentrated on the business case for, and drivers of, such behavior, rather than on its social value (cf. Aguinis and Glavas, 2012; Mellahi et al., 2016).

Hence, the idea that stakeholders benefit from the firm's intervention has generally been assumed rather than empirically evaluated (Kaul and Luo, 2018). Moreover, the topic has been subject to significant tension in the literature. Recent work, for instance, has shown how CSR initiatives often focus more on firm goals than stakeholder interests, symbolically addressing them but not genuinely responding to them. Therefore, the social value of corporate disaster giving has not been established and remains actively debated (Cuypers et al., 2015; Marquis and Qian, 2013).

On the surface, corporate disaster giving might appear to be an unmitigated social good given that uncertainty shocks may be a significant constraint on economic growth. Yet its social value depends to a large extent on how companies actually allocate their aid. If corporate donations are misdirected for strategic considerations or by other business logics away from the most pressing social needs, corporate giving may be a costly misallocation of scarce resources and socially suboptimal, whatever benefits may be adding to the firm (Barro, 2007; Taleb, 2010).

One aggregate statistic suggests that we should not be optimistic about corporate disaster giving bringing social innovation and meeting social needs. More than 85 percent of business disaster aid goes to medium- and high-income economies, even though more than 90 percent of the deaths associated with natural disasters occur in lower-income countries. On first glance, hence, that allocation might appear suboptimal (Becerra et al., 2012; EM-DAT, 2014; Guha-Sapir et al., 2004). We see, for instance, company contributions going disproportionately to some types of countries. Take the case of Nepal that was more physically devastated by a 7.8-magnitude earthquake in 2015 than was Japan by its Tōhoku earthquake. While Japan lost one inhabitant for every 10,000 residents, Nepal lost one for every 3,000. Nevertheless, by contrast with the vast business outpouring for Japan's recovery, less than 5 percent of the international aid coming into Nepal came from business. Similarly, firms gave five times less to the 2010 earthquake in Haiti than to the earthquake in Chile the same year; even though the death toll was over 400 times greater. Typhoon Bopha in the Philippines in 2012 killed more than ten times as many as did Hurricane Sandy in the US, but firms worldwide gave ten times more to American that Philippine relief.

One argument for explaining the lesser corporate giving to country disasters involving greater losses of life may be that company executives are voluntarily neglecting evident human needs in deference to their firm's private calculus. Another argument may be that they are erring in underappreciating the humanitarian needs and are thus miscalculating the efficient allocation of their resources. In either case, the result would be a suboptimal allocation of scarce economic resources for social welfare, at least by this criterion. Following this line of argument, firms may be sacrificing the *doing good* part of the corporate-philanthropy formula in pursuit of the *doing well*, if they are indeed securing direct business benefits such as preferred treatment by regulators or indirect benefits such as reputational gains.[5]

However, a recent study offers evidence of an alternative and perhaps surprising claim. The study uses systematic analyses of aid for all the major natural disasters that affected the world between 2003 and 2013 with a database of all donations (from individuals, firms, non-profit organizations, governments, and multilateral agencies) reported in electronic media. Using the total value of government funds, formal insurance, and international aid at the time of a disaster, the study calculates a nation's financial capacity to respond. It then ranks the 3,115 major disasters that occurred worldwide between 2003 and 2013 according to the size of the gap between this capacity and the cost of a disaster. The outcome of this procedure defies commonly held assumptions on the financial vulnerability to large disasters: 87 percent of the 150 disasters with the largest financial gap occurred in medium- and high-income countries.

Subsequently, the statistical analyses reveal that corporate giving is more likely to be allocated to countries whose government is less able to supply essential goods following fat-tail calamities. These states have high financial fragility, but in many cases do not receive significant aid from traditional sources because of their relative affluence. That is, company dollars are in fact going to the countries that are most financially vulnerable in the wake of a large disaster (Ballesteros et al., 2017).

This suggests that the corporate provision of collective goods is helping to satisfy a social need that traditional sources of disaster financing are not meeting. Since countries highly vulnerable to calamities cannot expect aid inflows from international disaster aid programs to cover a significant proportion of the economic toll imposed by large shocks, the need is high for complementary sources of financing.

One argument to explain why company aid better targets financial gaps in the wake of disasters than traditional aid is the economic purpose of the firm. Disasters are most likely to attract managers' attention when they disrupt market welfare and, consequently, their firms' performance. The larger the share of a company's income from a given market, the larger the managerial attention on an event disrupting the market's status quo. Hence, business managers' concern with the economic consequences of disasters should be directly proportional to their firms' economic reliance on disaster-exposed markets (Gavetti et al., 2007; Hoffman and Ocasio, 2001; Lampel et al., 2009).

Because of their interest in economic processes that affect the market demand and the supply chain, business managers may also receive better market signals regarding the distress of an affected nation and its financial capacity to comeback than do traditional external donors. Thus, firms are likely to become active providers of public goods after a disaster when managers believe that the economic magnitude of a disaster may exceed the three main sources for a country's relief and recovery financing. By focusing their giving on disasters with the largest market consequences, firms in effect help cushion their own financial shocks (Alessi, 1975; Ang et al., 2014; Friedman, 1970; Hirshleifer, 1963; Husted et al., 2012; Khan and Kumar, 1997; White and Lang, 2012).

The foreign entities that comprise the traditional international aid structure base an evaluation of the capacity to recover on static measures such as GDP that constrain their ability to capture the dynamic and extreme nature of large disasters. Many of these models build on assumptions that key institutional and economic variables (for example, trade) are fixed, even though they are themselves among the setbacks brought on by large-scale disasters. Suboptimal decision frameworks among policy makers may be at fault as well. Disasters in higher-income countries, such as Hurricane Katrina, the Tōhoku disaster, and Superstorm Sandy, show that cognitive biases often lead public leaders to underestimate the scope of a crisis and overestimate their ability to respond (Cavallo and Frankel, 2008; Kahneman, 2011; Kunreuther et al., 2002; Saiia et al., 2003; Schwab, 2014; Taleb, 2010; Wokutch et al., 2013).

This focus of firms on financial effects is in line with a theoretical expectation that pro-social behavior becomes strategic when it not only helps society but also the company itself, reducing the real cost of philanthropy to the firm. In other words, although corporate disaster giving may be driven by social preferences, such as altruism and reciprocity (Muller et al., 2014), business managers strategically are likely to focus their pro-social behavior in disaster-affected nations where the direct and indirect business implications for the firms are greatest (Chamlee-Wright and Storr, 2009; Sandler, 2013). The self-interested premise that a firm's performance may be weakened if the market is not soon restored may thus have the unintended effect of driving a firm to invest private resources where the gap in international aid is largest (cf. Godfrey, 2005; Porter and Kramer, 2002; Saiia et al., 2003; Wokutch et al., 2013).

Given these arguments, the recent rise of corporate disaster giving may be fueled by the internationalization of capital and economic interdependencies. Of note, during the last 30 years, the number of firms with multinational operations and the number of foreign affiliates among the world's 10,000 largest firms grew threefold and tenfold, respectively. Given that the exposure to disasters is higher for the average multinational enterprise than for the single-country firm, this internationalization of economic activity has likely increased management attention on the effects of large disasters and the allocation of firm resources on relief and recovery.

The ongoing globalization of economic activities has thus led businesses to become more dependent on people, services, and suppliers from around the world. Global supply chains face risks from myriad disruptions such as political coups, natural disasters, and terrorist attacks. Making market operation and distribution less vulnerable depends upon the actions of many actors. A shock in one region of the globe can have significant impacts on the operations of firms in other parts of the world. This high degree of interdependency means that the risks faced by any one firm are not solely due to its own activities and choices, but can be caused by others, possibly far from its headquarters.

Consider the historical flood event that occurred in Thailand in 2011. Only after the disaster did many multinational firms realize that their suppliers had located their factories in flood-prone areas that had not invested in disaster prevention and mitigation. The severe floods damaged or destroyed the assets of more than 14,000 firms in a country that produces over 30 percent of the world's hard-disk drives and serves as the Asian production hub for Japanese car makers.

As a result, Western Digital Corp., the world's largest maker of hard-disk drives, posted a quarterly loss and its production would not return to normal for months. Apple announced a setback supply of components used in Mac computers. Toyota was forced to suspend its automobile production due to lack of parts. Ford, which assembles one of its cars in Thailand, suspended its production. In addition to the internationalization of capital, this case highlights the role that increased urbanization and the concentration of production play in disaster risk.[6, 7]

In consequence, a strategic definition of non-market behavior will tend to focus firms' giving on countries where they have a high proportion of market interest. In other words, while decision makers in public and multilateral agencies generally focus on nations with the greatest human losses associated with disasters because of their humanitarian missions, business managers generally focus on nations where they are most economically reliant because of their financial objectives.

This specialization helps explain the allocation of corporate disaster giving internationally where we see a strong skew toward middle- and higher-income countries where disaster costs tend to be high and where traditional aid tends to be low (Cummins and Mahul, 2009). Accordingly, corporate giving may be a more optimally distributed resource for funding economic recovery from disasters than traditional international aid, particularly when human loss is not highly correlated with economic damage (Fink and Redaelli, 2011; United Nations, 2016).

Does Corporate Giving Complement or Substitute International Aid?

Of importance, the social consequences of the company provision of public goods depends on its effects on aid from traditional providers. Put differently, if the rise in corporate giving in recent decades has crowded out and substituted perfectly multilateral aid, the net social benefit could be nil. In a recent study (Ballesteros, 2017), I have tested this argument and found support for the argument that corporate disaster giving is a complementary good to traditional sources of international aid. A 1 percent increase in the dollar amount of corporate disaster giving would yield a 0.018 percent increase in the magnitude of financing coming from foreign governments and multilateral agencies. This finding bears on theories that analyse the crowding-out effect of public investment and private philanthropy, and we extend previous studies by suggesting that firms furnish essential disaster relief to become a Pareto-improvement resource in affected countries where traditional entities do not direct sufficient funding for relief and recovery (Andreoni, 1993; Hochman and Rodgers, 1969; Roberts, 1984). Taken together, these results suggest that business organizations often act as a stop-loss mechanism for costly disasters. More specifically, business donations focus on the gap between the financing provided by the traditional sources of international aid and the economic hardship resulting from a disaster.

DO FIRMS MEET THE SOCIAL NEEDS CREATED BY LARGE SHOCKS MORE EFFICIENTLY?

The UN reports that, given the widening financial gap that societies face when responding to national shocks, the goal is not only supplying more resources but supplying them more efficiently. The UN report notes:

> A group of experts appointed by the UN Secretary-General "concurs with a widely shared view among stakeholders that systemic change in humanitarian aid delivery is needed in order to raise new money and use it more effectively. Greater efficiency will create a virtuous circle by drawing in more funding . . . As part of (a new) agreement, donors would not simply give more but give better, by being more flexible, and aid organizations would reciprocate with greater transparency." (United Nations, 2016, p. vi)

In this tenor, the social value of corporate disaster giving depends not only on whether it helps reduce the funding gap of disasters but also on whether society is better off with the corporate intervention than with a higher level of international public and multilateral assistance. And critics have warned that the corporate engagement in the provision of public goods may crowd out more productive forms of aid from traditional providers and that it is better for specialized agencies, like FEMA and the Red Cross, to direct relief since they bring expertise in precisely that (Barro, 2007; Friedman, 1970; Gao, 2011; Godfrey et al., 2009; Lev et al., 2010; Muller and Kräussl, 2011; Weitzman, 2011; Wokutch et al., 2013).

Hence, the second pertinent question, given the rise of corporate disaster giving, refers to whether the firm, an entity not created for disaster aid, might nonetheless help restore social welfare in a more efficient fashion than traditional sources of aid. That is, we want to identify the mechanisms and conditions under which firms have a comparative advantage to satisfy humanitarian needs vis-à-vis other suppliers of public goods.

Do Firms Help Countries to Receive Emergency Relief Faster?

But what determines efficiency in disaster response? Studies on social risk management suggest that whether a disruption morphs into a full-fledged disaster depends largely on the speed of the response to the emergency. Extreme disruptions spur short-lived crisis moments during which an immediate inflow of monetary and in-kind donations to supply essential goods is important. The tardy and then inadequate US reaction to the impact of Hurricane Katrina on New Orleans is a case in point, as federal and local officials' disorganized management of the catastrophe overshadowed the storm's physical destruction. Regarding the provision of relief during the emergency, experts concur that essential goods include food and water, housing, medical attention, and the restoration of the staples of the country's social and economic infrastructure, such as communication and transportation (Benjamin et al., 2011; Day et al., 2009; Day et al., 2012).

In a series of analyses employing a quasi-experimental design (Ballesteros et al., 2017), Wharton Professors Michael Useem, Tyler Wry, and I found that, for the countries affected by natural disasters between 2003 and 2013, aid arrived significantly faster when the share of aid from companies with local operations in the affected country was greater. Nations where firms with local operations provided at least 7.7 percent of total aid received almost 92 percent more aid during the first four weeks after the disaster than counterfactual countries. The difference increased to 158 percent when firms with local operations accounted for more than 23.8 percent of aid, and almost 200 percent when such firms provided over 44.4 percent of aid. In other words, the marginal effect on relief speed increases with the share of corporate giving.

Do Firms Help Countries Recover Greater?

The studies above suggest that firms that have operations in an affected country may be strategically and better positioned than traditional donors to efficiently supply disaster goods to that market (Ballesteros et al., 2017). A firm's unique resources, by virtue of its local presence, result in a comparative advantage for the provision of relief and recovery. This advantage centers on (1) understanding the local needs of those impacted by the disaster; (2) reallocating funds, goods, and services from other locations; and (3) delivering relief and recovery expeditiously. Complementarities between a company's philanthropy and its market operation drive efficiency in the provision of collective goods. Firms economically connected to a disaster-stricken country draw on their global and local routines and market-based competences to deliver disaster relief in a timely fashion.

First, in the aftermath of disasters, business managers' identification of local needs is informed by the destruction of public goods that are instrumental to their firm's financial performance. Public managers by contrast must consider a wide range of competing needs and demands. We know, for instance, that electoral factors can affect presidential disaster declarations and political considerations may explain as much as 50 percent of the variation in the allocation of federal disaster relief within the US. Foreign governments are found to favor oil-exporting countries and countries with similar political systems. Government officials are also reported to respond more favorably to requests for disaster aid when the disasters are widely reported in the media. Traditional public aid is thus subject to political and special-interest factors that can hamper effective allocation, and the same is likely to characterize multilateral agency giving as well (Cohen and Werker, 2008; Eisensee and Strömberg, 2007; Fink and Redaelli, 2011; Franks, 2013; Garrett and Sobel, 2004; Platt, 2012; Reeves, 2011).

Another factor favoring the comparative advantage of business giving is associated with its method for evaluating the local relief and recovery needs. Foreign government officials generally operate with a top-down approach, while business managers may draw on their country operations for a bottom-up identification of local needs. Company managers can draw on their local grassroots relationships, networks of affiliates, and partner organizations for granular guidance on where assistance is most essential. They can also directly work with disaster victims and other local stakeholders to identify the best actions for restoring economic activity while also better appreciating the preferences of affected communities (Useem et al., 2015).

Local company managers, for instance, sometimes even assume the role of local disaster task-force coordinator or serve as their firm's main liaison among headquarters, local affiliates, the community, and government authorities. That network centrality is a unique resource that gives the corporation a close-up view of the scale of the emergency and local response that foreign governments and multilateral agencies do not have (Twigg, 2001).

In the aftermath of the 2010 Chilean disaster, for example, the multinational mining company, Anglo American, relied on its local managers to assess the situation. Just hours after the earthquake, Anglo American's London-based headquarters received information on the destruction and approved what became one of the first major donations for relief and recovery from any source. Among other actions, the company quickly dispatched a fleet of heavy equipment, normally used in its mining operations, to gather street debris and remove rockslides, and it worked directly with displaced residents to erect emergency housing.

The second factor favoring the comparative advantage of corporate giving is related to the need for the rapid reallocation of resources. The delivery of international public and multilateral aid often faces deep-rooted bureaucratic constraints that militate against quick deployment. Hence, when the magnitude of a disaster's hardship requires donors to swiftly ramp-up their engagement, firms face fewer restraints and are likely to be able to respond more rapidly than foreign governments and multilateral agencies. By way of one illustration, nearly 40 percent of the pledges by international public and multilateral agencies for recovery from the 2010 earthquake in Haiti were still outstanding in 2013 – but 100 percent of the corporate pledges had been disbursed (Ballesteros, 2017; Becerra et al., 2013; Cohen and Werker, 2008; Franks, 2013; Lipscy and Takinami, 2013; OCHA, 2016; White and Lang, 2012).

Additionally, firms also benefit from synergies when transferring fungible resources across their network of corporate affiliates. Company managers can mobilize resources that have few capacity constraints and are scalable across markets. When Sri Lanka was hit by the 2004 Indian Ocean tsunami, for instance, Coca-Cola converted its soft-drink production lines to bottle drinking water and delivered it to victims using its own distribution system. Additionally, market internationalization helps business managers diversify their geographically based risks and thereby improve their ability to rapidly focus their giving in a way that traditional providers often cannot. Consequently, firms can provide disaster response at a lower cost than traditional donors (Anderson et al., 1974; Barney, 1991; Kaul and Luo, 2018; Oetzel and Oh, 2014; Penrose, 1959; Thomas and Fritz, 2004; Whiteman et al., 2005).

Third, regarding the provision of disaster relief and recovery, given the narrowly defined objective function of business enterprise, corporate intervention can better target areas for relief and recovery that facilitate a faster restitution of market status quo than can public and multilateral agencies. Corporate giving of firms that depend on a stricken market is more likely to go to disaster goods with direct economic payoffs than official aid. This argument is supported by empirical work on public economics showing that private investment often has greater positive effect on growth than does public investment.[8] Governments often carry out costly public investments that are politically appealing, but have negative social surplus (Cavallo and Daude, 2008; Day et al., 2012; Khan and Kumar, 1997; Khan and Reinhart, 1990; Robinson and Torvik, 2005).

Firms, for example, aim at restoring market distribution when rebuilding roads and bridges, mitigating variance in employee productivity when rebuilding health facilities, and improving consumers' purchasing power through direct transferences to victims. In this process, companies achieve greater cost advantages than traditional public and multilateral agencies since they can draw upon their organizational routines and market-based competences to inform and innovatively address relief and recovery needs. In the aftermath of the Indian Ocean tsunami, for instance, manufacture companies helped rebuild schools by drawing on their country-specific experience in large-engineering projects.

Finally, business managers often bring greater expertise than traditional donors for evaluating the cost–benefit impact of relief and recovery initiatives, building actions on business competences, and as a result delivering relief and recovery goods more efficiently than traditional sources. When the logistics company TNT assisted the UN in redesigning relief warehouses in Italy, for example, TNT applied its operating experience to optimize warehouse storage and train personnel in inventory management, saving the UN agency an estimated $450,000 annually. In sum, companies economically connected to an affected country can base their disaster response actions on their business competences, providing disaster goods more efficiently, and having a more positive implication on social welfare than traditional sources (Hart, 1995; Khan and Kumar, 1997; Khan and Reinhart, 1990; Tomasini and Van Wassenhove, 2009; Wassenhove et al., 2008).

In the econometric analyses described above, we found that firms with local operations have helped countries obtain aid resources rapidly, thereby meeting a critical goal of disaster response: providing fast relief. But is company aid also more efficient to meet the longer-run goal of disaster recovery? Our analyses report a significant difference between the annual growth rate as measured by the Human Development Index (HDI)[9] of disaster-

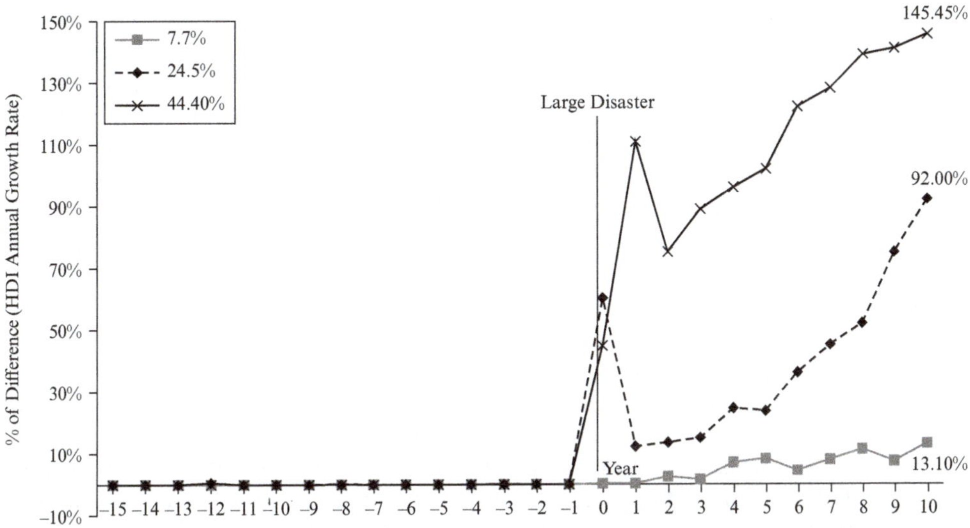

Note: The figure shows the difference in HDI growth rate between treatment nations and correspondent synthetic controls for 15 years before the disaster and 10 years after the disaster. Period (0) is the disaster year. No sizeable effects before the disaster year suggest that the synthetic control method has generated efficient control nations. Treated are disaster countries with a substantial share of disaster giving coming from firms economically active in the affected country (as defined by the 7.7 percent, 24.5 percent, and 44.4 percent cutoff points). The total sample of country-year disasters in the period 2003–13 is 464.

Figure 13.2 The effect of giving from locally active firms on disaster recovery

stricken countries that received a significant proportion of disaster aid from firms with local operations and similar countries that received less aid from such firms. According to the HDI, the level of recovery after ten years is notably higher for countries that received at least 24.5 percent of disaster aid from firms with local operations. On average, the annual growth rate of HDI for such nations is 92 percent higher than for counterfactual nations. The difference increases to 145 percent when disaster-hit countries received at least 44.4 percent of international aid from firms with local operations (Figure 13.2).

How the Overlap Between Pro-social Behavior and Market Operation Affects the Efficiency of the Company Action

The comparative advantage of corporate disaster giving is also likely to vary among firms and across time. A plausible argument is that the greater the overlap between a firm's market operation and the social need, the greater the business manager's capacity in the non-market sphere. In this way, the firm is able to use its routines and core competences to supply disaster goods with even greater efficiency than public and multilateral entities. The express-delivery company, DHL, for instance, has often assumed a lead role in coordinating the reception of relief supplies and their distribution after a disaster, drawing on its competences in inventory control and rapid dispatch. When that has occurred, fewer donated goods have gone to waste and less airport congestion has resulted than during other disaster-response operations (Wassenhove et al., 2008).

Moreover, a pre-existing relatedness between market and non-market choices increases the economic efficiency of corporate disaster giving since firms can economize in their allocation of relief resources. Firms face relatively low costs in reconfiguring or reallocating their own products and services, further adding to the net social benefit, as could be seen in Ericsson's provision of mobile phones to humanitarian workers in the aftermath of the 2004 Indian Ocean tsunami or FedEx's delivery of relief goods in the 2008 floods in Mexico (Ballesteros, 2017; McWilliams et al., 2006; Porter and Kramer, 2006).

Corporate disaster giving that is strongly associated with the organization's core business operation is thus likely to optimize the allocating of its largesse. Also, in line with an argument in the literature on non-market strategy, when corporate giving is consistent with business objectives, we can expect it to be more disciplined in delivery (cf. Porter and Kramer, 2002; Saiia et al., 2003; Wokutch et al., 2013).

In the study mentioned above, published in the *Academy of Management Journal* in 2017, we observe that affected countries received aid faster when the giving from firms is related with their core operation. Thus, when the share of corporate giving is at least 24.5 percent of total international aid, and such donation is at least 7.7 percent connected with the corporate donors' market operation, treated nations receive aid 170 percent faster than counterfactual nations. The difference in speed of relief increases to 260 percent for cases where at least 44.4 percent of international aid comes from firms with local operations and 42.4 percent of such giving is related to the donors' core operations. In other words, the marginal effect on relief speed increases with the share of corporate giving that is connected with firms' market operations.

We also found evidence of statistically and economically significant effects of the overlap between pro-social behavior and market operation on long-run disaster recovery and, thus, on the comparative advantage of corporate disaster giving. For instance, countries that received at least 44.4 percent of disaster aid from firms and at least 42.4 percent of such donations relates with firms' core operations observed an annual growth rate of Human Development Index of about 190 percent greater than counterfactual countries at the end of the tenth post-disaster year (Figure 13.3). This suggests that when disaster giving is arguably a cost-efficient option for the firm – the economically reliant company is able to connect its giving to its core business operations – the size of the positive social effect is significantly larger.

FUTURE RESEARCH

In 1998, Debraj Ray pointed that "The story of economic (development) is, in many ways, a story of how (innovative,) imaginative institutions replace the formal constructs we are accustomed to" (Ray, 1998, p. 4). This chapter narrates how for-profit organizations are bringing innovation and creativity to help communities around the world meet an increasing social challenge. The effects of low-probability, high-consequence disasters on economic development have risen dramatically faster and greater than the aid resources provided by individual charity, public, multilateral, and non-profit organizations in the aftermath of large disasters.

This narrative focuses on arguments and recent evidence of the organizational mechanisms and environmental conditions under which firms hold a comparative advantage in

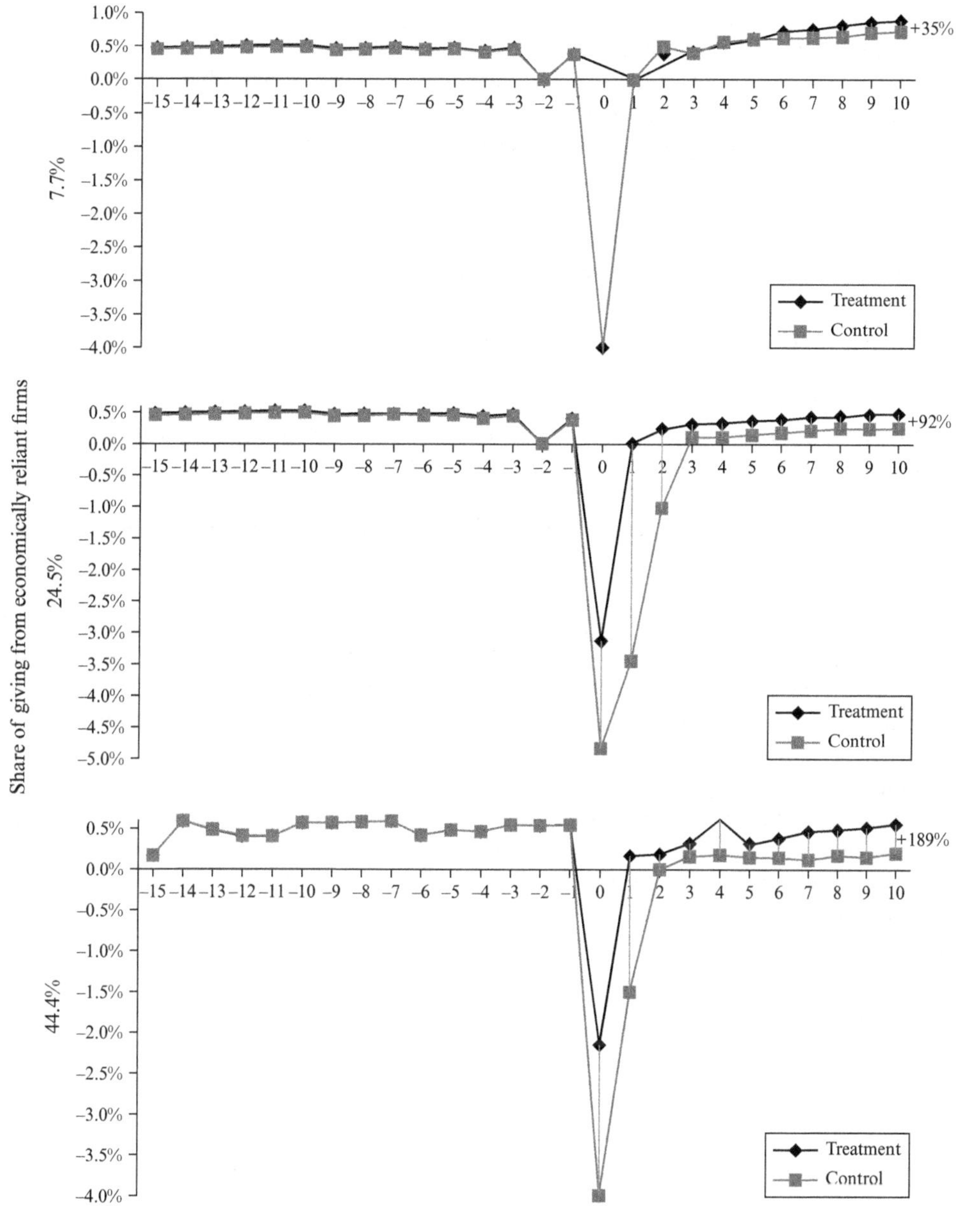

Note: The outcome variable is the annual growth rate of HDI. Treated are disaster countries with at least 42.4 percent of in-kind giving that is related to the donor's core operation coming from firms economically active in the affected country (as defined by the 7.7 percent, 24.5 percent, and 44.4 percent cutoff points). Each figure shows the difference between the annual growth rates of HDI for treated and control nations 15 years before the disaster and 10 years after the disaster. The total sample of country-year disasters in the period 2003–13 is 464.

Figure 13.3 The effect of relatedness in the relationship between disaster giving from locally active firms and disaster recovery

disaster relief and recovery vis-à-vis traditional suppliers such as public and multilateral agencies. A local presence enhances the efficiency of corporate provision of collective goods and an overlap between a firm's business operation and its pro-social behavior enhances the comparative advantages of the firm in non-market strategy – resulting in social innovation and efficiency. Companies that are economically connected to the disaster-stricken country are in an advantageous position to help drive timely delivery of disaster assistance, thereby lessening the adverse impact of natural disasters on social welfare.

I identify potential reasons behind firms' focus on economically costly disasters that can disrupt the financial performance of the corporation – those extreme events that hit countries where the firm has economic interdependencies and where there is a significant gap in the traditional public and multilateral sources of funding for relief and recovery. Resources coming from firms that have operations in the affected country constitute a complementary good to traditional international aid and they help mitigate a local government's incapacity to finance disaster relief and recovery, particularly in nations traditionally deprived of the latter.

How to Structure and Organize the Role of Firms in Helping Countries Respond to Large Shocks?

A relevant inquiry in light of the rapid rise of firms' engagement in disaster relief and recovery centers on the ideal level of participation in such social endeavor. This is important because, recently, the share of business largesse in disaster response has exceeded the relative participation of other entities. Based on research on public economics, one can argue that the marginal productivity of corporate giving will decrease as its magnitude increases because such productivity is partly a product of complementarities with public investment (Cavallo and Daude, 2008; Khan and Kumar, 1997). Private giving, for instance, may well stimulate public intervention in areas or on a scale that firms are not willing or able to fully achieve themselves. Moreover, philanthropy requires an institutional framework that is difficult to substitute through private mechanisms or externalize via markets. That is, a lack of public goods may make the costs of supplying disaster relief and recovery unbearable for any average firm. Finally, it is likely that some of the strategic factors that motivate corporate philanthropy may be only salient when there is also an opportunity for enhancing business–government relations. Managers may expect to bolster corporate legitimacy in the local market by giving to disasters, but that depends on a parallel interest by traditional donors.

A cornerstone of the ideas presented in this chapter is that the effect of aid on disaster relief and recovery is not only a matter of the availability of resources, but also the efficiency of those resources to address the social need, which includes how fast those resources get to the victims. Therefore, an important inquiry concerns the relationship among efficiency in aid, economic growth, and institutional development. Recalling that low-income nations also tend to have relatively low institutional capacities, an interesting paradox arises. Corporate disaster giving constitutes a scarcer resource in low-income countries, hence its marginal value should be higher than in high-income countries. At the same time, lower levels of local institutional capacities may result in a lower marginal productivity of business giving. For instance, high levels of corruption increase the inefficiency of recovery funding since governments are less likely to enforce building codes and infrastructure quality, and more likely to engage in rent seeking. Hence, from the perspective of global welfare, is it efficient to allocate private giving to lower-income countries that may have a higher marginal utility for their victims but lower utility for productivity? Further empirical work may help clarify this paradox (Kahn, 2005).

By looking at the systematic evaluation of the social consequences of corporate disaster giving, I suggest that the greater focus of company giving on economic recovery and the greater focus of public and multilateral giving on human relief is socially efficient – a socially innovative solution. The lower economic footprint of corporations in some countries makes corporate giving more a function of social preferences, such as altruism, and given the argument on the conditions for a comparative advantage of the firm, a less impactful resource on social welfare.

Hence, the fact that traditional international aid concentrates on countries such as Nepal and Myanmar and corporate aid on countries such as Chile and Japan is an appropriate allocation of global resources. The rise of corporate disaster giving is a Pareto-improvement mechanism in disaster countries lacking enough international aid for disaster funding. Moreover, if corporate donors obtain private benefits from such giving and the private gains are not misdirected from business purposes (for example, philanthropy is not subject to moral hazard), the effect is to enhance shareholder value and no other sector of society is worse off, and corporate disaster giving can thus be seen as a Pareto-optimal choice – a subject worthy of empirical exploration.

Extending the Comparative Advantage of Firms to Other Social Areas

There is no one answer to the complex problem of responding to large social risks. But it is clear that the corporate community has an increasingly vital role to play. On 1 February 2016 the World Health Organization declared the Zika virus to be a public health emergency. Initially centered in Brazil, the outbreak spread to more than 20 other countries. "We need a coordinated international response," said Margaret Chan, the executive director of WHO.[10] WHO's emergency announcement was intended to help coordinate immediate actions by health agencies around the world to research and prevent further spread of the virus. This chapter presents arguments to consider the business community as first responders in similar crises. It suggests that a socially efficient way to fuel efficiency in responding to humanitarian crises is by fostering corporations to intervene directly. These firms will do the most good by donating to areas where they have operations, and by tailoring aid to leverage existing competencies and resources.

For national or international crises, businesses can effectively complement the traditional sources of international disaster relief – filling in where those sources and local governments lack the capacity or the will. Partnerships between corporate donors and agencies in recipient countries can help ensure that the business assistance is directed to where it is most needed. And those partnerships can be either de facto, with each informally complementing the other, or more formal, with each explicitly coordinating with the other. Both forms are to be encouraged.

For the value of a de facto partnership, consider Lawson, Japan's second largest convenience store franchise with more than 10,000 outlets. It has a long-standing practice of working to remain open in disaster zones, no easy task given Japan's perch along the Pacific ring-of-fire. Lawson created a protocol for keeping its stores staffed and stocked in even the most calamitous moments, with twice-annual drills to field-test its practicalities. Then, just five minutes after Japan's earthquake in 2011, Lawson executives invoked the emergency protocol among their convenience stores in the affected region. Of Lawson's more than 900 stores in the area, some 60 percent managed to remain open, and 90 percent of the rest reopened within six weeks. The company proactively delivered food and water to evacuation centers. Even then, many roads were still impassable, and Lawson sent in truckloads of motorcycles to deliver its supplies. When motor fuel could not be obtained, it dispatched a gasoline truck to deliver them.

In the wake of the Ebola outbreak in West Africa in 2014, other companies did much the same on their own. Henry Schein, Inc., a supplier of healthcare products, for instance, gave $1 million in masks, gloves, gowns, coveralls, sanitizers, and other protective gear to thwart the epidemic's spread. It also joined the Ebola Private Sector Mobilization Group, a coalition of more than 40 large corporations organized by steel-maker ArcelorMittal. ArcelorMittal itself constructed new Ebola treatment centers. Firestone built a treatment center when a nearby hospital would not accept Ebola patients; Unilever gave several millions of bars of soap; Coca-Cola used its distribution network to deliver medical supplies; and Federal Express delivered urgently required medical supplies and protective equipment.

It is necessary to conclude this chapter with a reflection on the public policy and managerial implications of the rise of the company provision of public goods in the aftermath of disasters. First, decision makers in public and multilateral agencies may want to make greater effort to focus the attention of business leaders on where the greatest disaster funding gap exists. They may also want to draw upon the presented research on the comparative advantages of the firm to guide their decisions on how best to stimulate and coordinate corporate disaster giving in a socially optimal fashion.

For policy makers, this argument would imply to consider ways to, on the one hand, facilitate the participation of the business community in more challenging environments. Arguably, a potentially efficient structure is to reorganize the specialization of entities in international aid. With the specialization of business organizations in crises in more developed countries, multilateral agencies, foreign governments, and other non-profit organizations may focus on poorer countries.

Recent disasters offer validation for this idea. In August 2017, record monsoon rains hit Bangladesh, India, and Nepal at the same time as Hurricane Harvey wreaked destruction on the Gulf Coast in the US. A vice-president of international services at the Red Cross explained that despite the similar nature of the disasters, the task of providing disaster relief to each region differed dramatically due to differences in the quality of institutions and resulting support systems.[11] The level of response in Asia versus that in more developed nations such as the US supports the argument that the greater focus of corporate giving on economic recovery and the greater focus of public and multilateral giving on human relief is a win–win from the standpoint of global welfare. The lower economic footprint of corporations in Nepal than in the US makes corporate giving a less socially impactful resource, given the argument of the local presence of the firm as one of the conditions for a comparative advantage of the firm.

CONCLUSION

This chapter summarizes the evidence of how business organizations are indeed bringing social innovation to the way communities cope with and recover from the consequences of uncertainty shocks. The economic hardships associated with natural disasters, terrorist attacks, technological accidents, pandemics, and episodes of violent crime are expected to continue to grow because of expanding human settlement in risk-prone regions, environmental degradation, and the internationalization of supply chains, which fuels economic interdependencies. If governments, multilateral agencies, and other traditional funding sources of disaster relief and recovery continue to be insufficient, the social value of corporate disaster giving is thus likely to rise over time regardless of the level of development of the national economy. Here we offer some ideas to formalize and organize the increasing participation of the business community in helping societies manage uncertainty shocks around the world.

NOTES

1. http://www.nytimes.com/2009/04/07/world/europe/07italy.html?_r=0, accessed 2 February 2019; http://www.nytimes.com/2012/10/31/us/hurricane-sandy-barrels-region-leaving-battered-path.html?pagewanted=all, accessed 2 February 2019; http://www.nytimes.com/2011/02/23/world/asia/23zealand.html, accessed 2 February 2019.
2. http://www.preventionweb.net/globalplatform/2013/home, accessed 2 February 2019.
3. https://www.wnyc.org/story/puerto-ricos-never-ending-emergency/, accessed 2 February 2019.
4. https://www.nytimes.com/2017/09/20/world/americas/mexico-earthquake-aid.html, accessed 2 February 2019; https://yaledailynews.com/blog/2017/09/29/earthquake-apocalypse-civil-society-vs-the-mexican-state-by-carlos-hernandez/, accessed 2 February 2019.
5. Wins from disaster giving.
6. Chester Dawson and Yoshio Takahashi, Thai floods force Toyota to suspend US production. *Wall Street Journal*, 28 October 2011. http://www.wsj.com/articles/SB10001424052970203554104577000691656368920, accessed 2 February 2019.
7. http://www.bloomberg.com/news/articles/2011-10-20/worst-thai-floods-in-50-years-hit-apple-toyota-supply-chains, accessed 2 February 2019.
8. Khan and Reinhart (1990), for example, found in a sample of 24 countries that, while the contribution of public investment is negative, private investment contributes 43 percent to average economic growth.
9. The Human Development Index (HDI) is a measure of aggregate social welfare. HDI is calculated annually by the United Nations Development Programme and tracks a nation's level of health and longevity, knowledge and education, and standard of living (Anand and Sen, 2000).
10. Sabrina Tavernise and Donald G. McNeil, Jr, Global health emergency declared over zika virus. *New York Times*, 2 February 2016; World Health Organization, 1 February 2016. http://www.who.int/mediacentre/news/statements/2016/emergency-committee-zika-microcephaly/en, accessed 2 February 2019.
11. http://www.npr.org/sections/goatsandsoda/2017/08/29/547002884/epic-floods-not-just-in-texas-are-a-challenge-for-aid-groups), accessed 2 February 2019.

REFERENCES

Aguinis, H. and Glavas, A. 2012. What we know and don't know about corporate social responsibility: a review and research agenda. *Journal of Management*, 38(4), 932–68.

Alessi, L. De. 1975. Toward an analysis of postdisaster cooperation. *American Economic Review*. http://www.jstor.org/stable/1806401, accessed 2 February 2019.

Anand, S. and Sen, A. 2000. The income component of the Human Development Index. *Journal of Human Development*, 1(1), 83–106.

Anderson, C.R., Hellriegel, D., and Slocum, J.W. 1974. Managerial response to environmental stress. *Academy of Management Proceedings*, 1, 56.

Andreoni, J. 1993. An experimental test of the public-goods crowding-out hypothesis. *American Economic Review*, 83(5), 1317–27.

Ang, S.H., Benischke, M.H., and Doh, J.P. 2014. The interactions of institutions on foreign market entry mode. *Strategic Management Journal*, 36.10(2015), 1536–53.

Baker, S. and Bloom, N. 2013. Does uncertainty reduce growth? Using disasters as natural experiments. NBER Working Papers. https://doi.org/10.3386/w19475, accessed 2 February 2019.

Ballesteros, L. 2017. Firm's economic reliance to national markets and the corporate provision of public goods. Working Paper 56. *The Wharton School Research Series*.

Ballesteros, L. and Gatignon, A. 2019. The relative value of firm and nonprofit experience: tackling large-scale social issues across institutional contexts. *Strategic Management Journal*, https://doi.org/10.1002/smj.2968.

Ballesteros, L. and Kunreuther, H. 2018. Organizational decision making under uncertainty shocks (no. w24924). National Bureau of Economic Research.

Ballesteros, L., Useem, M., and Wry, T. 2017. Masters of disasters? An empirical analysis of how societies benefit from corporate disaster aid. *Academy of Management Journal*, 60(5), 1682–708.

Barney, J. 1991. Firm resources and sustained competitive advantage. *Journal of Management*, 17(1), 99–120.

Barro, R.J. 2007. Rare disasters, asset prices, and welfare costs. *American Economic Review*, 99(1), 243–64.

Becerra, O., Cavallo, E., and Noy, I. 2012. Foreign aid in the aftermath of large natural disasters. http://www.iadb.org/intal/intalcdi/PE/2012/10593.pdf, accessed 2 February 2019.

Becerra, O., Cavallo, E., and Noy, I. 2013. Where is the money ? Post-disaster foreign aid flows. *Environment and Development Economics*, 20(5), 561–86.

Becerra, O., Cavallo, E., and Noy, I. 2014. Foreign aid in the aftermath of large natural disasters. *Review of Development Economics*, 18(3), 445–60.

Benjamin, E., Bassily-Marcus, A.M., Babu, E., Silver, L., and Martin, M.L. 2011. Principles and practice of disaster relief: lessons from Haiti. *Mount Sinai Journal of Medicine: A Journal of Translational and Personalized Medicine*, 78(3), 306–18.

Bevere, L., Orwig, K., and Sharan, R. 2015. Natural catastrophes and man-made disasters in 2014: Convective and winter storms generate most losses. Sigma 2 (2015), 2015.

Blaikie, P., Cannon, T., Davis, I., and Wisner, B. 2014. *At Risk: Natural Hazards, People's Vulnerability and Disasters*. London: Routledge.

Bloom, N. 2009. The impact of uncertainty shocks. *Econometrica*, 77(3), 623–85.

Cavallo, A., Cavallo, E., and Rigobon, R. 2013. Prices and supply disruptions during natural disasters. http://www.nber.org/papers/w19474.

Cavallo, E. and Daude, C. 2008. Public investment in developing countries : a blessing or a curse? *Development*, 39, October, 65–81.

Cavallo, E.A. and Frankel, J.A. 2008. Does openness to trade make countries more vulnerable to sudden stops, or less? Using gravity to establish causality. *Journal of International Money and Finance*, 27(8), 1430–52.

Cavallo, E., Galiani, S., Noy, I., and Pantano, J. 2013. Catastrophic natural disasters and economic growth. *Review of Economics and Statistics*, 95(5), 1549–61.

Chamlee-Wright, E. and Storr, V.H. 2009. Club goods and post-disaster community return. *Rationality and Society*, 21(4), 429–58.

Cohen, C. and Werker, E.D. 2008. The political economy of "natural" disasters. *Journal of Conflict Resolution*, 52(6), 795–819.

Cummins, J.D. and Mahul, O. 2009. *Catastrophe Risk Financing in Developing Countries: Principles for Public Intervention*. Washington, DC: World Bank.

Cuypers, I.R., Koh, P.S., and Wang, H. 2015. Sincerity in corporate philanthropy, stakeholder perceptions and firm value. *Organization Science*, 27(1), 173–88.

Day, J.M., Junglas, I., and Silva, L. 2009. Information flow impediments in disaster relief supply chains. *Journal of the Association for Information Systems*, 10(8), 1.

Day, J.M., Melnyk, S.A., Larson, P.D., Davis, E.W., and Whybark, D.C. 2012. Humanitarian and disaster relief supply chains: a matter of life and death. *Journal of Supply Chain Management*, 48(2), 21–36.

Douty, C.M. 1972. Disasters and charity: some aspects of cooperative economic behavior. *American Economic Review*, 62(4), 580–90.

Eisensee, T. and Strömberg, D. 2007. News droughts, news floods, and US disaster relief. *Quarterly Journal of Economics*, 22(2), 693–728.

EM-DAT. 2014. The OFDA/CRED International Disaster Database. Université catholique. http://www.emdat.be.

Fink, G. and Redaelli, S. 2011. Determinants of international emergency aid – humanitarian need only? *World Development*, 39(5), 741–57.

Franks, S. 2013. *Reporting Disasters: Famine, Aid, Politics and the Media*. London: Hurst Publishers.

Friedman, M. 1970. The social responsibility of business is to increase its profits. *New York Times Magazine*, 32, September, 13.
Gao, Y. 2011. Philanthropic disaster relief giving as a response to institutional pressure: evidence from China. *Journal of Business Research*, 64(12), 1377–82.
Garrett, T.A. and Sobel, R.S. 2004. *The Political Economy of FEMA Disaster Payments*. New York: Springer.
Gavetti, G., Levinthal, D., and Ocasio, W. 2007. Perspective – Neo-Carnegie: the Carnegie School's past, present, and reconstructing for the future. *Organization Science*, 18(3), 523–36.
Godfrey, P.C. 2005. The relationship between corporate philanthropy and shareholder wealth: a risk management perspective. *Academy of Management Review*, 30(4), 777–98.
Godfrey, P.C., Merrill, C.B., and Hansen, J.M. 2009. The relationship between corporate social responsibility and shareholder value: an empirical test of the risk management hypothesis. *Strategic Management Journal*, 30, December, 425–45.
Guha-Sapir, D., Hargitt, D., and Hoyois, P. 2004. *Thirty Years of Natural Disasters 1974–2003: The Numbers*. Louvain-la-Neuve: Presses universitaires de Louvain.
Hart, S. 1995. A natural resource based view of the firm. *Academy of Management Review*, 20(4), 986–1014.
Henisz, W.J., Dorobantu, S., and Nartey, L.J. 2014. Spinning gold: the financial returns to stakeholder engagement. *Strategic Management Journal*, 35(12), 1727–48.
Hirshleifer, J. 1963. *Disaster and Recovery: A Historical Survey*. DTIC Document.
Hochman, H.M. and Rodgers, J.D. 1969. Pareto optimal redistribution. *American Economic Review*, 59(4), 542–57.
Hoffman, A.J. and Ocasio, W. 2001. Not all events are attended equally: toward a middle-range theory of industry attention to external events. *Organization Science*, 12(4), 414–34.
Husted, B.W., Jamali, D., and Saffar, W. 2012. Location, clusters, and CSR engagement: the role of information asymmetry and knowledge spillovers. *Academy of Management Proceedings*, 2012(1).
Kahn, M.E. 2005. The death toll from natural disasters: the role of income, geography, and institutions. *Review of Economics and Statistics*, 87(2), 271–84.
Kahneman, D. 2011. *Thinking, Fast and Slow* (Vol. 1). New York: Farrar, Straus and Giroux.
Kaul, A. and Luo, J. 2018. An economic case for CSR: the comparative efficiency of for-profit firms in meeting consumer demand for social goods. *Strategic Management Journal*, 39(6), 1650–77.
Kellett, J. and Caravani, A. 2013. Financing disaster risk reduction: a 20 year story of international aid. http://www.odi.org/sites/odi.org.uk/files/odi-assets/publications-opinion-files/8574.pdf, accessed 2 February 2019.
Khan, M.S. and Kumar, M.S. 1997. Public and private investment and the growth process in developing countries. *Oxford Bulletin of Economics and Statistics*, 59(1), 69–88.
Khan, M.S. and Reinhart, C.M. 1990. Private investment and economic growth in developing countries. *World Development*, 18(1), 19–27.
Kunreuther, H. and Useem, M. 2018. *Mastering Catastrophic Risk: How Companies are Coping with Disruption*. New York: Oxford University Press.
Kunreuther, H., Meyer, R., Zeckhauser, R., Slovic, P., Schwartz, B., Schade, C., . . . and Hogarth, R. 2002. High stakes decision making: normative, descriptive and prescriptive considerations. *Marketing Letters*, 13(3), 259–68.
Lampel, J., Shamsie, J., and Shapira, Z. 2009. Experiencing the improbable: rare events and organizational learning. *Organization Science*, 20(5), 835–45.
Lev, B., Petrovits, C., and Radhakrishnan, S. 2010. Is doing good good for you? How corporate charitable contributions enhance revenue growth. *Strategic Management Journal*, 31, 182–200.
Lipscy, P.Y. and Takinami, H. 2013. The politics of financial crisis response in Japan and the United States. *Japanese Journal of Political Science*, 14(3), 321–53.
Madsen, P.M. and Rodgers, Z.J. 2015. Looking good by doing good: the antecedents and consequences of stakeholder attention to corporate disaster relief. *Strategic Management Journal*, 36(5), 776–94.
Margolis, J.D., Elfenbein, H.A., and Walsh, J.P. 2007. Does it pay to be good? A meta-analysis and redirection of research on the relationship between corporate social and financial performance. *Ann Arbor*, 1001, 48109–234.
Marquis, C. and Qian, C. 2013. Corporate social responsibility reporting in China: symbol or substance? *Organization Science*, 25(1), 127–48. http://pubsonline.informs.org/doi/abs/10.1287/orsc.2013.0837, accessed 2 February 2019.
Marquis, C. and Tilcsik, A. 2016. Institutional equivalence: how industry and community peers influence corporate philanthropy. *Organization Science*, 7039, 1–17.
Marquis, C., Glynn, M.A., and Davis, G.F. 2007. Community isomorphism and corporate social action. *Academy of Management Review*, 32(3), 925–45.
Matten, D. and Crane, A. 2005. Corporate citizenship: toward an extended theoretical conceptualization. *Academy of Management Review*, 30(1), 166–79.
McWilliams, A., Siegel, D.S., and Wright, P.M. 2006. Corporate social responsibility: strategic implications. *Journal of Management Studies*, 43(1), 1–18.

Mellahi, K., Frynas, J.G., Sun, P., and Siegel, D. 2016. A review of the nonmarket strategy literature: toward a multi-theoretical integration. *Journal of Management*, 42(1), 143–71.

Muller, A. and Kräussl, R. 2011. Doing good deeds in times of need: a strategic perspective on disaster donation. *Strategic Management Journal*, 32, January, 911–29.

Muller, A.R., Pfarrer, M.D., and Little, L.M. 2014. A theory of collective empathy in corporate philanthropy decisions. *Academy of Management Review*, 39(1), 1–21.

Munich Re. 2013. *Significant Natural Catastrophes 1980–2012*. NatCatSERVICE.

Munich Re. 2015. Loss events worldwide 1980–2014: 10 costliest events ordered by overall losses. MunichRe, NatCatSERVICE. http://www.munichre.com/site/corporate/get/documents_E-567437233/mr/assetpool.shared/Documents/5_Touch/_NatCatService/Significant-Natural-Catastrophes/2014/10-costliest-events-ordered by-overall-losses.pdf, accessed 12 February 2017.

Noy, I. 2012. Investing in disaster risk reduction: a global fund. SEF Working Paper. 14/2012, August.

OCHA, UN. 2016. United Nations Office for the Coordination of Humanitarian Affairs. Financial Tracking Service (FTS), https://fts.unocha.org/pageloader.aspx?page=contact-ContactUs&select=3, accessed 30 June 2015.

Oetzel, J.M. and Oh, C.H. 2014. Learning to carry the cat by the tail: firm experience, disasters, and multinational subsidiary entry and expansion. *Organization Science*, 25(3), 732–56.

Olcott, G. and Oliver, N. 2014. Social capital, sensemaking, and recovery: Japanese companies and the 2011 earthquake. *California Management Review*, 56(2), 5–22.

Ostrom, E. 2000. Collective action and the evolution of social norms. *The Journal of Economic Perspectives*, 14(3), 137–58.

Penrose, E.T. 1959. *The Theory of the Growth of the Firm*. Cambridge: Basil Blackwell and Mott Ltd.

Platt, R.H. 2012. *Disasters and Democracy: The Politics of Extreme Natural Events*. Washington, DC: Island Press.

Polanco, M.M. 2012. Efectos sociales del terremoto en Chile y Gestión Política de la reconstrucción durante el gobierno de Sebastián Piñera (2010–2011). *Revista Enfoques*, X(16), 19–46.

Porter, M.E. and Kramer, M.R. 2002. The competitive advantage of corporate philanthropy. *Harvard Business Review*, 80(12), 56–68, 133.

Porter, M.E. and Kramer, M.R. 2006. The link between competitive advantage and corporate social responsibility. *Harvard Business Review*, 84(12), 78–92.

Potoski, M. and Prakash, A. 2005. Green clubs and voluntary governance: ISO 14001 and firms' regulatory compliance. *American Journal of Political Science*, 49(2), 235–48.

Ray, D. 1998. *Development Economics*. Princeton, NJ: Princeton University Press.

Reeves, A. 2011. Political disaster: unilateral powers, electoral incentives, and presidential disaster declarations. *Journal of Politics*, 73(4), 1142–51.

Roberts, R.D. 1984. A positive model of private charity and public transfers. *Journal of Political Economy*, 92(1), 136–48.

Robinson, J.A. and Torvik, R. 2005. White elephants. *Journal of Public Economics*, 89(2–3), 197–210.

Saiia, D.H., Carroll, A.B., and Buchholtz, A.K. 2003. Philanthropy as strategy when corporate charity "begins at home." *Business and Society*, 42(2), 169–201.

Sandler, T. 2013. Buchanan clubs. *Constitutional Political Economy*, 24(4), 265–84.

Scherer, A.G. and Palazzo, G. 2007. Toward a political conception of corporate responsibility: business and society seen from a Habermasian perspective. *Academy of Management Review*, 32(4), 1096–1120.

Schwab, K. 2014. *The Global Competitiveness Report 2013–2014*. Geneva: World Economic Forum.

Taleb, N.N. 2010. *The Black Swan: The Impact of the Highly Improbable Fragility*, Vol. 2. New York: Random House.

Thomas, A. and Fritz, L. 2004. Disaster Relief, Inc. *Harvard Business Review*, 84(11), 114.

Tomasini, R. and Van Wassenhove, L. 2009. *Humanitarian Logistics*. New York: Springer.

Twigg, J. 2001. Corporate social responsibility and disaster reduction: a global overview. http://drr.upeace.org/english/documents/References/Topic 7-Preparedness- Early Warning, Planning, Monitoring and Evaluation/Twigg 2001 CSR and disaster management.pdf, accessed 2 February 2019.

United Nations. 2016. High-Level Panel on Humanitarian Financing. Too important to fail – addressing the humanitarian financing gap. https://reliefweb.int/sites/reliefweb.int/files/resources/%5BHLP%20Report%5D%20Too%20important%20to%20fail%E2%80%94addressing%20the%20humanitarian%20financing%20gap.pdf.

Useem, M., Kunreuther, H., and Michel-Kerjan, E. 2015. *Leadership Dispatches: Chile's Extraordinary Comeback from Disaster*. Stanford, CA: Stanford University Press.

Wassenhove, L.N., Tomasini, R.M., and Stapleton, O. 2008. Corporate responses to humanitarian disasters: the mutual benefits of private-humanitarian cooperation. Conference Board. https://www.conference-board.org/publications/publicationdetail.cfm?publicationid=1469.

Weitzman, M.L. 2011. Fat-tailed uncertainty in the economics of catastrophic climate change. *Review of Environmental Economics and Policy*, 5(2), 275–92.

White, S. and Lang, H. 2012. Corporate engagement in natural disaster response. Center for Strategic and International Studies. http://csis.org/files/publication/120117_White_CorporateEngagement_Web.pdf, accessed 10 May 2012.

Whiteman, G., Muller, A., van der Voort, J., van Wijk, J., Meijs, L.C., and Pique, C. 2005. The tsunami's CSR effect: MNEs and philanthropic responses to the disaster. *ERIM Report Series Reference No. ERS-2005-062-ORG*.

Wokutch, R.E., Singal, M., Poria, Y., and Hong, M. 2013. Crisis situations and role of strategic CSR in decision-making. *Academy of Management Proceedings*, 2013(1), 16136.

14. The lack of public goods in emergent economies: a call for research and a case study of an innovative organisational design

Nuno Gil

INTRODUCTION

The problem motivating this call for research is the lack of public goods in emergent economies – institutional environments that lack efficient markets, well-defined property rights, contract-enforcing mechanisms, basic infrastructure and the codified, enacted and enforced rule of law (George et al., 2012; Khanna and Palepu, 1997). To navigate these 'institutional voids' organisations work towards their goals, by using intermediaries – agents that broker relationships, bringing about activities between two or more parties that could not readily happen otherwise (Mair et al., 2012; McDermott et al., 2009). Institutional intermediaries are those agents that help to create and develop institutions, thus helping create the prescriptions that people use to organise all forms of interaction (North, 1990; Ostrom, 1990). The shortfall of institutions makes it a grand challenge to build other public goods, which makes this problem so complex, uncertain and difficult to resolve that it seems intractable, like ending global hunger or eradicating extreme poverty (Colquitt and George, 2011; Ferraro et al., 2015; Grodal and O'Mahony, 2017).

Extraordinarily, the focus of management scholarship on institutionally underdeveloped environments has been on how private actors can navigate institutional voids, and thus navigate the lack of public goods, in order to create and appropriate value. Thus, this literature has focused on how multinational firms and entrepreneurs use intermediaries like business incubators, science parks and development agencies to enter in emergent markets. This literature shows that intermediaries help private firms access public resources, and acquire capabilities, certification and informal resources. Some intermediaries act as closed-system agents, only seeking to create benefits for the restricted set of system participants; others act as open-system agents, seeking to create benefits for parties beyond the participants and to improve the general institutional environment (Dutt et al., 2016).

This body of literature is instructive, but neglects how the state itself can develop institutions and other public goods, and thus how intermediaries can help the state fill institutional voids. And yet, there is a vast group of intermediaries that are ready to help struggling governments access much needed finance, human capital and other resources to produce public goods: multilateral organisations and development banks, charitable donors, and development agencies owned by both advanced economies and emerging economies. This development assistance, though, comes with strings attached that constrain the architecture of the inter-organisational contexts that are formed to produce public goods. In other words, the intermediaries act as organisational designers by influencing choice on the system components, on their relationships to each other and the environment, and on the principles and widely held shared rules by which the organisational system evolves and orchestrates complementary resources (Fjeldstad et al., 2012; Simon, 1962).

The role of intermediaries as organisational designers is particularly salient in the inter-organisational contexts formed to develop capital-intensive public goods like utility networks, transportation and other basic infrastructure technology, for example, hospitals, schools and affordable housing. Infrastructure is a class of public goods that is a prerequisite to economic growth and sustainable development. Yet a conflation of factors, including population growth, climate change and rapid urbanisation is exacerbating the infrastructure gap in emergent economies. The challenge to bridge this gap is colossal: for example, with 90 per cent of urban growth occurring in the developing world, the number of slum dwellers is projected to reach 2 billion by 2023 – about a fourth of the world's population (UN-Habitat, 2008). In Africa alone, whose population is expected to reach *40 per cent* of the world's population in this century, less than half of the people have access to electricity; water scarcity and lack of infrastructure to deal with extreme weather, such as the Cape Town drought, present other pressing problems (IEA, 2016; UN, 2017, 2018).

Strikingly, the intermediaries presently assisting the emergent economies to build basic infrastructure differ sharply in their approach to navigating institutional voids. These differences are rooted in the emerging global order, as China rises to become the world's biggest economy and the share of the global economy of the advanced economies, hobbled by fiscal pressures and populism, shrinks. Development assistance disbursed by traditional intermediaries occurs mostly in the form of grants and loans that are conditional on western principles of good governance – transparency, stakeholder engagement, accountability, equity, and rule of law (Burnside and Dollar, 2000; Hermes and Lensink, 2001). As a result, the organisational contexts enabled by traditional intermediaries cannot grow until the intermediaries first help the authorities to build managerial capacity in the public sector, and legal and policy frameworks for budgeting and public expenditure management. In other words, filling the institutional voids is as much a part of the system-level goal as is building basic public infrastructure.

In marked contrast, Chinese development finance comes with limited conditionality. Rather than 'aid', Chinese finance provided by, for example, the Exim Bank of China or the China Development Bank are basically export credits more akin to syndicated loans from European commercial banks or US export credits. Accordingly, the Chinese intermediaries take the institutional environment as a given. Their focus is to build the capital-intensive infrastructure first and to develop institutions (if any) second. Furthermore, Chinese finance is tied to purchasing and importing from China as much technology and services as possible, a model pioneered by Japan decades earlier (Brautigam, 2009, 2011). To create opportunities for Chinese firms to work abroad quickly, these networks exploit institutional voids or artfully manoeuvre around them. These differences notwithstanding, both forms of organising to pursue development merit research, as they complement one another. In Africa, for example, Chinese finance towards development is about to exceed finance from the World Bank, and already dwarfs finance from the 'West'; for example, from 2000 to 2015, $63 billion was disbursed by the Export-Import Bank of China against $1.7 billion by the US Eximbank (Eom et al., 2017).

Recently, Gil et al. (2019) argue that this situation is suggestive of a fundamental organisational duality. Design dualities exist when organisations wish to pursue two jointly desirable objectives, but struggle to reconcile the two because the attributes underlying one pole of the duality tend to be incompatible with those that underlie the other pole, for example, to exploit or explore; to integrate or differentiate (Evans and Doz, 1989; Lawrence and Lorsch, 1967). Faced with difficulties to design organisations to pursue dualities, the organisation architects choose instead to focus on one of the poles of the duality, as opposed to doing both; in other words, they choose 'gains from focus' in detriment of 'gains from ambidexterity' (Birkinshaw and Gibson, 2004; Smith and Tushman, 2005). In the grand challenge that is filling the gap in basic infrastructure, a duality arises because the objectives of building the infrastructure and the institutions quickly are both desirable. Failure to build robust institutions and local capabilities compromises the long-term sustainability of the technological outcomes. But failure is also not to build basic infrastructure *quickly* considering the urgent need to equip societies to cope with population growth, urban migration, and climate change. Still, designing organisational contexts that reconcile both objectives is hard because they tend to have incompatible attributes, which raises the question if more ambidextrous and thus more effective systems cannot be designed – the core question underlying this research call.

The remainder of this call for research is organised as follows. I first draw on organisational design literature to formulate a research agenda informed by the challenge of developing the emergent economies' infrastructure. I then illustrate opportunities for management scholarship with evidence from innovative forms of organising set up to upgrade the informal settlements in Cairo, the world's fastest-growing city.[1] I conclude with considerations on opportunities and challenges for inputting this research agenda into action.

BUILDING PUBLIC GOODS IN EMERGING ECONOMIES

In recent years, China's economic rise has given governments of emerging economies agency to choose between two very different approaches to pursue development. This phenomenon has exacerbated a duality in designing organisational systems to build capital-intensive public goods. This duality is the subject of an unresolved debate in the development literature, which is summarised below, before laying out a research agenda for management scholarship. To put this debate in perspective, it is worth noting that China has pledged $1 trillion over the coming decades to build the emergent economies' infrastructure through the Belt and Road Initiative – China's cooperative development strategy launched in 2013, whose scope ranges from building a new capital city for Egypt to railways, hospitals and dams in sub-Saharan Africa, ports and power stations in Asia, and gas pipelines in Eurasia.

On one side of the debate is the idea that western finance is dogmatic and inflexible, that good governance principles increase transaction costs too much and that the impact of western aid on growth has been negligible (Hirchman, 1967; Moyo, 2009; Tan-Mullins et al., 2010). Accordingly, China is seen as providing much needed investment in basic public infrastructure; bringing technical and commercial know-how and widening market access; and getting infrastructure done quickly without tiresome 'strings' attached (Henderson, 2008; Hernandez, 2017). Yet other scholars claim that Chinese finance is nothing more than 'rogue aid', serving an opaque clique of interests dominated by informal and personal relationships (Naim, 2007). They also claim that China is allowing profligate states to build up unsustainable levels of debt, retain weak financial, economic and political governance, and occasionally infringe human and civil rights (Dreher and Fuchs, 2011).

Yet, as the allure of the Chinese centralised, state-led approach grows in emerging economies and hope wanes on more inclusive, market-oriented approaches espoused by advanced economies, more research is needed to understand what exactly is going on here. I contend that one cognitive lens relevant to illuminate this phenomenon is organisation design. We know that organisational design choice is contingent on the institutional environment to which the organisation must relate (Lawrence and Lorsch, 1967; Scott, 1981; Thompson, 1967). We also know that institutions are more than just background conditions – they directly influence strategic choices available to an organisation, and organisations are known to achieve and sustain competitive advantage through strategies that overcome, shape and capitalise on the nature of their institutional environments (Henisz, 2002; Khanna and Palepu, 1997, 2010; Khanna and Rivkin, 2001). Furthermore, the actor-networks enabled by development finance are but instantiations of 'meta-organisations', that is, networks of autonomous actors which are unified by an identifiable system-level goal (Gulati et al., 2012). So, a choice between intermediaries that espouse differing principles to navigate institutional voids is a choice between different forms of (meta)-organising. And this raises the question as to how the designed structures and processes across the two forms of organising enable the participants and the environmental stakeholders to create and appropriate value.

Importantly, we should not necessarily expect to find in the Chinese-enabled forms of organising highly innovative structures and processes to resolve the problems of collaboration and coordination to integrating effort. On the contrary, numerous accounts suggest that Chinese-enabled organisational systems tend to centralise decision-making authority in the hands of a tight-knit coalition restricted to the Chinese actors (lender, main contractor) and the recipient state (Gil et al., 2019). This coalition is governed by contracts, but does not operate under pressures for accountability, stakeholder engagement and transparency. Hence, the deals between the participants are opaque, key stakeholders are excluded from the decision-making process, and suppliers are not selected through competitive markets. To resolve coordination problems, this form of organising relies on authoritarian political leaders and top bureaucrats with the power to mandate subordinates to provide the necessary information – a design suggestive of Demsetz's (1988) idea of coordination by 'direction'. At odds with calls for cooperative forms of organising, these closed and stratified networks may not rule out the use of coercion to acquire private resources that lie outside the system, for example, to acquire private land; rumours, often corroborated by evidence, are rife on the use of informal inducements in the form of bribes, kickbacks and other illegal activity to facilitate cooperation. And as characteristic of highly hierarchical systems, there is tight control over the right of the participants to speak on behalf of the actor-network (Zuckerman, 2010).

And yet, there is conflicting evidence on the performance of this closed, stratified and opaque forms of organising. On the one hand, evidence points to remarkable achievements, such as the rapid developments of Addis Ababa's light rail transit, the first in Sub-Saharan Africa, and the railway connecting Kenya's capital city to the port city of Mombasa – two infrastructures with potential for creation of broad social value. Then, on the other hand, there are accounts of organisational failures due to underestimation of the strength of the institutions protecting property rights, often a legacy of the colonial period, and customary rights; the case, for example, of Chinese railway investments in Nigeria (Gil et al., 2019). This conflicting evidence raises interesting questions:

- Is the effectiveness of Chinese-enabled forms of organising contingent on particular attributes of the institutional environment?
- Is the use of informal inducements a prerequisite for this form of organising to work?
- Do its chances of effectiveness rely on particular attributes of the focal problem?
- And what does effectiveness mean in this context?

This last question is particularly hard to address, when not only information flows on costs and benefits are covert, but also the outcomes are long-lived and so data on the creation of social value takes decades to assemble. This is the case, for example, of the Tazara railway, a route for bulk trade from Zambia's copper belt to the Tanzanian port of Dar es Salaam, built in the 1970s with Chinese finance. This railway has struggled to create social value since its opening, but the option is still open. Relatedly, recent accounts suggest that the design of Chinese-enabled organisational systems to build infrastructure is itself evolving. For example, the Belt and Road Initiative is creating opportunities for western companies to work with Chinese partners.[2] And a China–International Monetary Fund (IMF) capacity development centre was established in 2018 to train Chinese officials to work abroad – collaborations with potential to catalyse innovative forms of organising.

Interesting and relevant as these questions might be, gaining access to the inner workings of Chinese-financed organisational contexts is not easy, due to their own approach to navigating institutional voids. But this difficulty is a useful backdrop for thinking about alternative questions to ask. The first question revolves around setting organisational boundaries under good governance constraints. These constraints are rooted in decades of western scholarship on the contribution of strong institutions and a shared belief in the rule of law to economic growth. This body of work posits the value of separating policy from the personal interests of the elites; of the rules governing economic exchange and governing how these rules are enforced and may be changed, and of the capacity of the state to commit credibly to upholding property rights (North and Weingast, 1989; North et al., 2009).

To meet these good governance constraints, the organisational leaders are expected to share decision rights with key sovereign stakeholders outside the value chain, for example, environmental agencies, local governments, and other public agencies. Further, they are expected to 'co-opt' (Lawrence and Lorsch, 1967) other stakeholders, trading access to their resources for a loss of decision-making autonomy. Any decision to locate decision rights is an organisational design choice (Aghion and Tirole, 1997). Hence, good governance constraints are about setting organisational boundaries. This does not mean that the leading participants in an organisational context enabled by traditional intermediaries are prohibited from making unilateral decisions. They can; but these organisational contexts must follow the rule of law and respect property rights to attend to distributional concerns on value creation. Further, these contexts are also expected to help develop institutions and capabilities, for example, legislation for budgeting and managing public expenditure, structures to arbitrate disputes and management capacity of public agencies. These constraints exacerbate their interdependency with the institutionally underdeveloped environment – a source of uncertainty that threatens their survival.

Importantly, good governance constraints do not advocate flat organisational systems with equal members. They also do not advocate that the systems need to be open to any actor wanting to join in. On the contrary, inter-organisational contexts enabled by traditional intermediaries remain stratified and closed, with the lender and the state sharing the 'gatekeeper' role (Rothaermel and Boeker, 2008). But collective action costs increase with efforts to enfranchise key sovereign stakeholders, and to engage with other stakeholders; further to design contracts to govern resource exchanges and to develop surrounding institutions also leads to high transaction costs. Changing institutional regimes is particularly time-consuming and costly because of information asymmetries, incompatible interests and equity concerns (Libecap, 1989). This raises the question of how, under the shadow of good governance, organisational boundaries can be manipulated to *simultaneously* economise on transaction costs, encourage cooperation and accelerate growth.

A second broad research question, triggered by the loss of allure in the inter-organisational contexts enabled by traditional intermediaries, relates to the role of the informal organisation. Organisational design choices matter because they mandate interactions for exchanging and mobilising resources in the pursuit of collective goals (Gulati and Puranam, 2009). In other words, designed structures and processes are what both constrain and enable collective action. But researching connections between organisational design and social networks is also critical to further our understanding of organisational performance (Van de Ven et al., 2013). We know that dispute resolution ultimately hinges on the interplay between formal and informal mechanisms. And we also know that informal mechanisms can compensate for the formal organisation by encouraging individuals to behave in certain ways that can add value, even if the formal organisation does not reward or emphasise those behaviours (Gulati and Puranam, 2009). Furthermore, in institutionally underdeveloped and resource-constrained environments, organisations are more effective if they have the capacity to mobilise informal resources like local know-how, networks of trust, and traditional technologies (George et al., 2016).

The idea that inconsistencies between the formal and informal organisation can be leveraged to create ambidextrous inter-organisational contexts seems particularly relevant to tackle the grand challenge motivating this call for research. Perrow's (1986) study of complex systems shows that management by direct controls is unreliable and expensive. And paraphrasing Perrow, he went further, stating that the vast proportion of the activity in organisations goes on without personal directives and supervision, and even without written rules. Our focal challenge suggests a duality in organisational design: we need quick action to build infrastructure *and* to build institutions. Yet empirical evidence shows that the two objectives are hard to reconcile. For instance, for more than a decade the World Bank has worked with the government of Kampala, Uganda's capital, to upgrade its network of colonial-era roads. The Bank claims that Kampala is a 'city in transformation'. But the achievements on the ground have been limited and way outpaced by the rapid growth of Kampala's population. This sense of frustration is even greater in Lagos, Nigeria, which will soon become Africa's largest city by population: 15 years after the World Bank helped set up a transportation agency, Lagos still lacks very basic public transportation (Gil et al., 2019).

So it is worth exploring ways by which the informal organisation can compensate for the slowness of the formal organisation enabled by traditional intermediaries. Evidence from systems enabled by Chinese finance suggests that their rapid achievements can be traced in part to cooperation facilitated by informal private gains. The role of a powerful informal organisation is also documented in accounts of the nineteenth-century US infrastructure boom (Chandler, 1977; Levy, 2014). But of course, the idea of a compensatory fit by which the informal organisation pushes in a direction away from good governance is unsettling; turning a blind eye to bribery, corruption and other illegal activities goes against the principle of accountability that pressures organisations to credibly commit to follow promised and/or reasonable procedures (Freeland and Zuckerman, 2018). It is more reassuring to think of complementarities in terms of supplementary fit, in which the informal and formal organisations push in the same direction (Kogut and Zander, 1996; Milgrom and Roberts, 1990; Siggelkow, 2002). But Perrow (1986) argues it is not unusual for activity in complex organisations to go on in permitted violation of the rules. And even if we accept that there might be value in complementarities in terms of a compensatory fit, practical problems and lack of understanding of boundary conditions suggest an opportunity to build new theory.

Crucially, evidence suggests that traditional intermediaries are trying to improve the effectiveness of development assistance through innovative forms of organising. The merits of researching these efforts are better evaluated by considering the evidence from the following case of an innovative form of organising set up to upgrade the informal settlements of Cairo.

INNOVATIVE ORGANISING TO UPGRADE CAIRO'S GARBAGE CITIES

Cairo, the world's fastest-growing city, is a suitable setting to research new forms of organising to build public goods whilst navigating institutional voids for three reasons. First, about two-thirds of its over 22 million people are already trapped in slums and informal settlements with alarming life conditions: limited access to basic infrastructure, no property rights, ramshackle houses and threat of forced evictions (Sims, 2010). Second, as a gateway for migratory flows into Europe, Cairo has been at the forefront of western donor efforts to improve informal settlements. Under pressure from the international community, the Egyptian state has recognised that informal areas are not totally clandestine, but rather outcomes of policies of negligence and laissez-faire (Khalifa, 2015); the state has also set up a public agency, the Informal Settlement Development Facility, to tackle the problem. And third, the very same authoritarian state has, for decades, attempted to tackle this problem through centralised initiatives that are akin to the models espoused by the Chinese funders. Efforts to evict the poor from inner-city areas and relocate them in new satellite cities in the desert have nonetheless failed because the poor cannot afford to live far away from the city (Sims, 2015). But now, illustrating the duality at the core of this call for research, the Egyptian state is in advanced talks with Chinese funders to build, in five to seven years, New Cairo. This scheme to build a £30 billion purpose-built capital in the desert is seen as a massive gamble by urban planners.[3] Accessing data on New Cairo is virtually impossible, which shifts our focus to the efforts of the western agencies to upgrade informal settlements; central to their approach to organising is the participatory development policy.

THE PARTICIPATORY DEVELOPMENT POLICY

Participatory approaches are a response of western actors to a widely felt need for a power reversal between the development agencies and the poor – the beneficiaries (Chambers, 1983). The basic idea is to see the poor as development partners, or as Chambers (1983, p. 150) says, 'to put the last first'. So a participatory approach allows the poor to directly influence decisions on capital allocation. This idea has been institutionalised as follows:

> the empowerment of the people to effectively involve themselves in creating the structures and, in designing policies and programmes that serve the interests of all, as well as to effectively contribute to the development process and share equitably in its benefits.[4]

A participatory approach assumes that the risks of organisational failure are higher if the poor are left out of a formal, deliberative decision-making process. By enfranchising the poor, a participatory approach seeks to encourage the poor to cooperate and voluntarily contribute resources under their direct control, for example, know-how, networks of trust, time, labour and even cash. But a participatory approach does not seek to use contracts to formalise the resource exchanges. Instead, the idea is to build a temporary, informal organisation not dissimilar to the informal organisations formed in emergent situations (Majchrzak et al., 2007). This informality can belie the organisational goal to resolve ill-defined property rights and formalise informal economic activity. But a participatory approach recognises that building a formal temporary organisation would lead to unaffordable transaction costs, such as the costs of bargaining, delays, information measurement, supervision, enforcement and political action (Williamson, 1979).

Numerous accounts suggest that a participatory approach works better than a top-down approach at encouraging voluntary resource contributions from the poor; it also works better at attracting good maintenance for the outcomes (Baiocchi, 2003; Osmani, 2008). Other accounts, though, show that a participatory approach is not easy to implement because the poor tend to mistrust the authorities, lack the skills to collaborate, and may not see how the benefits of participating outweigh the costs (Osmani, 2008). Other issues are the risks of local elites capturing the participatory activities to solidify previous inequalities and of the poor feeling incentivised to distort information (Platteau and Abraham, 2002; Rigon, 2014). There is also a risk that a participatory approach becomes merely a rhetorical discourse in order to masquerade a consultation process (Cooke and Kothari, 2001; Kumar and Corbridge, 2002).

The idea of supplementing contract governance with an informal organisation involving actors with ill-defined property rights resonates with Williamson's (1979) idea of combining simple contracts with complex governance structures reserved for complex relations. Still, this hybrid governance structure remains underexplored. We turn now to illustrate how this idea was put into action to upgrade Cairo's garbage cities before discussing this form of organising.

UPGRADING CAIRO'S GARBAGE CITIES

The case focuses on a project that won an award for urban innovation[5] to upgrade the Zabbaleen ('garbage people' in Arabic) cities of Cairo. It is an 'extreme case' for inductive research (Siggelkow, 2007) in that the project succeeded in quickly building much needed infrastructure whilst changing surrounding institutions. The Zabbaleen are a community of 60–70,000 families who live in informal settlements and handle about a third of the waste generated daily in Greater Cairo.[6] The men collect garbage manually and transport it using donkey and motorised carts; the women and children sort and recycle waste manually for their families, or against a low daily wage for others in makeshift workshops and households, separating paper, plastic, glass and food in bags ready to be sold for recycling.

Informal waste pickers – the 'poorest of the poor' – represent considerable savings for developing economies, both for picking up the waste left uncollected by the public and private sectors and for recycling substantially more waste, thus reducing the need for landfills. But waste pickers, estimated to be about 10 per cent of the inhabitants in slums around the world (Wilson et al., 2006), live surrounded by potentially infectious, disease-ridden garbage. In Cairo, a centralised attempt by the Egyptian state to address the solid waste management problem by privatising waste collection in the early 2000s had failed. Due to lack of local know-how, the contractors overlooked the difficulties of serving Cairo's narrow streets and alleys with their modern trucks; they also struggled to recruit staff because of the social stigma of being a garbage collector. Complicating matters, the cash-strapped Municipalities[7] struggled to pay the contractors and meet their contractual obligations to provide basic infrastructure for the contractors to handle the waste. This made it hard for the contractors to meet their own performance targets, which triggered fees that the contractors refused to pay (Scheinberg et al., 2010). The residents themselves continued to prefer paying the Zabbaleen to collect their garbage unofficially from their door, as opposed to taking the garbage out and putting it into the contractors' large bins. And the residents were also frustrated that they had to pay a 'cleaning' fee for the contractors' services. Attempts by the contractors to hire the Zabbaleen fell flat, since most Zabbaleen found it more lucrative to stay in the informal sector. Occasionally, the Zabbaleen sought to sabotage the private contractors' work by collecting waste before the contractors could come to collect.

When the Egyptian state asked the World Bank and the United Nations for help in 2010, both multilaterals advised the state to integrate the Zabbaleen in a new solid waste management policy; such an inclusive approach would also tackle the inhumane and undignified conditions in these garbage cities. Because upgrades of informal settlements rarely generate revenues, they are suitable for charitable aid. But foreign donors cannot offer a grant unless the sovereign state that is the recipient of the funds agrees to be aided. Facilitating resource exchanges between donors and the host state are the implementation agencies that play a role akin to the institutional intermediaries of private enterprises. Seeing opportunity for funding, GIZ, an implementation agency fully owned by Germany, proposed to the Egyptian state a pilot project as part of its Participatory Development Program (PDP) – a bilateral collaboration to attract foreign funds. I turn now to examine how a participatory approach led to a hybrid inter-organisational context.

DEVELOPING A 'NEXUS' OF CONTRACTS

A 'nexus' of contracts was at the core of the architecture of the inter-organisational context designed to upgrade the garbage cities. First, there was the 2004 agreement of bilateral cooperation by which the Egyptian state allowed GIZ to engage with local authorities, civil society actors and the Cairenes. As part of this agreement, GIZ co-located an operational team in the Ministry of Planning facilities, and committed to a schedule of monthly meetings and reports of its plans and activities. One level down, GIZ entered into a contract with the Qalyubera Governorate, an administrative entity overseeing over 5 million people with delegated authority from the state to implement the national solid waste policy in the 11 towns under its jurisdiction. This authority was further delegated to the Municipalities (town governments), which were mandated to monitor the activities of the waste contractors and the Zabbaleen, pay the waste contractors and levy and collect fees. In exchange for cost-free investment and capability-building, the Governorate committed to contribute land so GIZ could go ahead and build solid waste management facilities. The Governorate also authorised GIZ to work with two Municipalities, each one hosting a garbage city.

Agreements with the authorities notwithstanding, GIZ lacked funds to finance the upgrades of the two Zabbaleen cities and was constrained by good governance requirements that required using costly international tenders to select suppliers. A solution for the financial bottleneck emerged when the Bill and Melinda Gates Foundation announced plans to fund projects to fight urban poverty. This donor was interested to find out if there was a 'silver bullet . . . something that could be transformative', as one consultant noted. In full alignment with the goal of GIZ, the Gates Foundation wanted to support solutions that would enable engagement 'with the poor . . . turn them from being beneficiaries into partners', as Melinda Gates said.[8] The reputation of the GIZ PDP programme in Egypt, the oldest GIZ development programme worldwide, reassured the donor that their money would be put to good use. In turn, GIZ welcomed aid from the Gates Foundation, since it was unclear when aid from the European Union would arrive. The $5 million grant from the Gates Foundation came with a formal commitment to a participatory approach, a fixed budget and timescale, and reporting and monitoring requirements.

This nexus of contracts between GIZ, the state, the local authorities and the donor enabled the set up of an organisational system that was unified by the goal of upgrading the Zabbaleen garbage cities and economy formalising their economic activities. The resource exchanges between these participants were not difficult to decompose into contractible transactions because the resources were measurable, and did not involve high degrees of reciprocal interdependence (Baldwin, 2007). Instead, it was more about pooling resources (work permits, knowledge, networks of trust, and finance) in the hands of GIZ to enable the agency to get on with the job. Even so, these contracts left this organisational system constrained by sub-goals, targets and a commitment to a participatory approach. We turn now to examine how this last commitment translated into adding a collective-action structure.

COLLECTIVE ACTION UNDER THE SHADOW OF CONTRACTUAL GOVERNANCE

A participatory approach allows the poor to directly influence the decisions that affect their lives in exchange for their cooperation. Still, enfranchising the Zabbaleen was a risky choice because of conflicting interests and a lack of mutual trust between the poor and the local authorities. In other words, the GIZ expected significant rivalry in the choices that would need to be made to allocate the capital resources. But after the Zabbaleen were granted decision rights, the shadow of contractual governance made it costly for the contracting partners to renege on this pledge and violate the terms of the bargain. So, in other words, by sharing decision rights with the poor, the GIZ created a collective-action structure where some of the capital that was available became a common resource, conflating high rivalry with low excludability (Ostrom, 1990).

To implement their participatory approach, the GIZ planned one year of regular face-to-face meetings. The emphasis was to get the Zabbaleen groups representing the interests of women, the young and businesses, as well as of the Municipalities and local popular councils, to search for common ground on shared problems, potential solutions and corresponding capital allocation plans. The risk of failure was high because at any point one party could choose to free ride and make demands disproportional to what that party was willing to contribute to an equitable solution. Another risk was that participants might refuse to share private information. The Zabbaleen worried about the authorities coming to evict them, and sell the land of the garbage cities to real-estate projects; wary of more fines, the Zabbaleen were also reluctant to reveal their revenues; the places where they were picking up, recycling and dumping waste, and their collection routes; the local popular councils, too, were concerned about being punished by the local authorities if they complained too much. In turn, the Governorate did not want to disclose the budget for solid waste management as they were concerned that the Zabbaleen could exploit this information if they were to bid for contracts; and the Municipalities did not want to reveal how much money was being officially collected in fines on the waste pickers and the contractors, as there could be bribes involved, and were pushing instead for stricter regulation of the Zabbaleen activity.

To encourage the parties to share private information, the GIZ presented itself as a facilitator without private interest – 'There wasn't a sense that GIZ was leading, they were supporting, but never branding it as a western donor pushing their agenda', said one respondent. For each planning workshop, which could last several hours, the Zabbaleen were free to choose the venue, time and who would represent them. In total, around 1,000 Zabbaleen participated in the workshops; GIZ also met weekly with seven committees of 10–12 residents to discuss the problems, solutions and get feedback. In addition, if one party was reluctant to share information in a multilateral meeting, the GIZ would meet first just with that party to allay their fears that by sharing information their interests could be harmed:

> We've procedures to get to consensus: When we say to community groups, 'you've to pay more' that is a financial loss for them. But if they don't pay more they don't get proper waste management; the same for the informal sector. If you formalise, you've more scrutiny, pay taxes, but also get a contract, more security. For the Municipality, if you improve waste management you get less anger even if in the short-term you've to pay a bit more.

Over time, a sense of trust emerged between the Zabbaleen, the residents and the authorities that enabled open discussion of alternative solutions. The core set of contracts gave the GIZ the authority and the money to offer inducements for the poor and others to cooperate in the implementation of whatever solution all the parties agreed upon. But the GIZ was not in a position to force upon the participants a solution; the solution needed to emerge by consensus to avoid one of the parties defecting from the collective-action arena.

THE PERFORMANCE OF THIS HYBRID FORM OF ORGANISING

To examine the performance of this inter-organisational context we investigated the extent to which the two objectives of the aforementioned duality were met: building infrastructure and changing the institutions. The findings suggest that in about three years, a quick achievement in the development aid sector, the project succeeded both in building basic infrastructure that dignified the living and working conditions of the Zabbaleen and in building institutions to formalise the Zabbaleen economic activities.

The solution agreed upon involved compromise and reciprocation. First, the Governorate received a cost-free $1.5 million investment on a waste recovery centre and a transfer station in exchange for making public land available to build the facilities; the location of the facilities was agreed by consensus after the Zabbaleen complained the initial plans made it too costly for them to travel to sort and unload the waste that lacked value. Second, the Zabbaleen received motorised carts and saw their workshops upgraded in terms of health and safety conditions at no cost to them. The Municipalities were also equipped, at no cost to them, with technology to monitor the Zabbaleen and improve waste collection routes. In exchange, the activities of 200 waste pickers were formalised into four legal entities; these entities were awarded contracts from the Municipalities through competitive tendering for 80 per cent of the waste produced daily. The Zabbaleen women were also organised in a legal entity. They were trained to separate waste which was highly combustible and not recycled, and awarded a contract with Lafarge, a cement manufacturer, who committed to buy that solid waste to use as additional fuel.[9] Importantly, the nexus of contracts proved flexible enough to cope with the costs of collective action. For example, the GIZ was allowed to re-tender the waste transfer centre domestically after bids from an international tender turned out to be unaffordable; the donor allowed money reallocations to avoid no-cost extensions; and the bilateral agreement of cooperation with the Egyptian state proved resilient enough to cope with a shift of the Egyptian state towards further centralisation of power after 2014.

More challenging was to leverage the local outcomes to impact national policy. The initial reaction of the government was good, and a test run started to create more Zabbaleen-run companies in Cairo.[10] In addition, the government set up an inter-ministerial unit of participatory development, and even invited the Zabbaleen to discuss a new national solid waste management policy. This warm reaction was linked to the arrival to government of Laila Iskander, a civil society actor passionate about helping the Zabbaleen – 'I've no fear for the Zabbaleen. They are unbeatable', said Laila. But as the Egyptian state became increasingly centralised, Laila left, and without a political sponsor, an application to the World Bank for a loan to integrate more Zabbaleen communities was dropped.[11] In sum, this hybrid form of organising built infrastructure quickly whilst changing the institutions. But institutional shifts at the field level have, for now at least, constrained the diffusion of this organisational innovation within Egypt.

DISCUSSION

This case illuminates exciting opportunities for management scholarship through looking at public goods provision in emergent economies. The findings suggest an inclusive form of (meta)-organising that is hardly explored in the literature. The basic idea is to supplement a nexus of contracts with a collective-action structure in order to orchestrate all the complementary resources needed to achieve the system-level goal in an institutionally underdeveloped context. The main attribute of this organisational 'contraption' is the way in which it combines contractual governance (Williamson, 1979) with collective-action governance (Hardin, 1968; Libecap, 1989; Ostrom, 1990) to navigate institutional voids.

Underlying this organisational design choice is a fundamental trade-off: incur the costs of consensus building and the risk of a tragedy of the commons (Hardin, 1968) to economise on the transaction costs that would otherwise be incurred to acquire resources that exist in a regime of ill-defined property rights and inefficient markets. So, where the resources are measurable and there is no high degree of reciprocal interdependency, this form of organising uses contracts to govern resource exchanges. Where the resources are hard to measure, there is a high degree of reciprocal interdependency, the markets are inefficient and property rights are ill-defined, a collective-action structure is instead employed to encourage cooperation and voluntary contributions of informal resources (know-how, networks of trust).[12] The way by which the nexus of contracts allows for informal resource exchanges with the poor creates a hybrid system to navigate the institutional voids. This organisational design choice may seem unnecessarily complicated and inefficient, as with any man-made 'contraption', but the findings suggest that this form of organising can be a useful social artefact to tackle grand societal challenges when there is a shortfall of institutions in the environment.

Of course, as a stand-alone governance structure, collective action has long been a subject of attention by theorists (Hardin, 1968; Olson, 1965; Ostrom, 1990). The high transaction costs of transforming collective action into contractual governance, that is, the costs of contracting *for* property rights (Libecap, 1989), have also been extensively theorised. But the idea of combining contractual and collective-action governance, that is, contracting 'for' collective action, is underexplored. Nonetheless, our findings suggest that there is value in so doing. The nexus of contracts is in agreement with the idea that when the transaction costs are negligible, the organisations lack incentives to bring activities in-house (Williamson, 1979, 1985). Furthermore, resource exchanges that do not involve high levels of reciprocal interdependency are not difficult to decompose into contractible transactions (Baldwin, 2007). The choice to build a nexus of contracts does not assume the contracting process needs to be complete, but assumes that through political negotiations, with reasonable costs, the parties can reach sufficient alignment of interests *ex ante* of the contract agreement, and that safeguards can also be devised to deter opportunistic behaviour *ex post* (Macneil, 1978; Williamson, 1985). Thus, the nexus of contracts leverages the advantages of a legal framework to unify a group of actors under a shared goal albeit the shortfall of institutions in the environment.

However, this nexus of contracts is insufficient to ensure that the inter-organisational context can be effective and survive. The crux of the problem is its reciprocal interdependency with the poor, and the weak institutions in which the poor are enmeshed. This interdependency creates uncertainty around what can be done and how, and the extent to which the outcomes are legitimate and sustainable. Forging a contract with the poor *ex ante* would also be very costly and time-consuming. The Zabbaleen may live in a regime of ill-defined property rights that is unsuitable to prevent common losses. But as the failure to privatise solid waste management shows, attempts to change institutional regimes are costly, especially if the number of participants is high, information asymmetries are sharp, the interests are competing, and the redistribution of economic benefits is involved (Libecap, 1989). To overcome this problem, the organisational designers make a judgement that it can be more advantageous to share decision rights with the poor than to leave them outside the organisational boundaries.

By giving the poor direct influence on some capital allocation decisions, competitive preferences emerge on the priorities and how to solve the problems. Rivalry yields conflict, but once decision rights are granted to the poor, it is not easy for the contracting parties to withdraw them. First, because a participatory approach is a contractual commitment that restricts the ability of the contracting parties to renege on their promise. In other words, the shadow of contractual governance makes it costly not to maintain the bargain. And second, excluding the poor could cause the whole organisational context to fail: if the poor see no legitimacy in the system, they would lack incentives to share know-how. Turning against the poor could also incentivise them to try to sabotage the organisational activities – as the Zabbaleen did when they were excluded from the privatisation decision. Hence, a participatory approach effectively transforms some – but not all – organisational resources into Ostrom's (1990) common-pool resources, that is, resources that are rivalrous in consumption by many actors, all of which are costly to exclude (Gil and Pinto, 2018; Gil et al., 2015). In so doing, the organisational designers incur the risk of underutilisation of shared resources and concomitant failure to provide a public good (Hardin, 1968; Libecap, 1989; Olson, 1965). This risk of failure is especially high in collective-action structures of the type created by a participatory approach where a few actors control most of the resources – if the poor claimants do not perceive any threat by the resourceful actors to defect to be credible, they may try to exploit the resourceful claimants (Olson, 1965).

And yet on balance, our findings show the organisational designers judge that it is better to bring collective-action and concomitant social dilemmas inside the organisational boundaries than to incur transaction costs to resolve the ill-defined property rights *ex ante*. This judgement is informed first by the hope that intrinsic motivation to identify and solve shared problems will encourage the poor to join the collective-action structure – in the same way that strangers join informal organisations to tackle emergent situations (Majchrzak et al., 2007); and second, that face-to-face interaction and rewards to cooperate can encourage mutual trust and a shared goal and potentially identity to emerge – albeit with the lack of a centralised authority to control voice rights (Freeland and Zuckerman, 2018). This organisational choice creates a complex form of organising. But what makes this organisational 'contraption' attractive is the opportunity it creates to orchestrate complementary resources whilst navigating the institutional voids. And another advantage that should not be overlooked is a greater sense of ownership and responsibility for the sustainability of the co-produced solutions.

CONCLUSION

Building public goods, notably capital-intensive infrastructure, in emergent economies requires extensive coordinated collective action towards a shared goal, albeit a shortfall of institutions in the environment – a problem that challenges boundary conditions in management scholarship (George et al., 2012). This need to assemble vast networks of autonomous actors is a recurring pattern that explains the complexity and uncertainty of the task structure for tackling grand challenges. In other words, grand challenges require both a high degree of differentiation among the participants to attend to the different facets of the task structure and a high degree of integration to achieve desirable outcomes (Knudsen and Srikanth, 2014). Amplifying this complexity in emergent economies is the need to navigate the institutional voids.

In agreement with these ideas, this chapter calls for more management research on the inter-organisational contexts formed to produce public goods in emergent economies. I ground this call on a great challenge of our times – the increasing infrastructure gap observed in the developing world. Drawing from organisation design theory, I propose a research agenda focused on a duality of objectives that are difficult to reconcile: do things quickly whilst changing institutions to create sustainable outcomes – a duality that gains more significance as the Chinese economy continues to rise whilst doubts grow in the advanced economies on their own models of democracy, individual freedom and market economy.

Admittedly, it is difficult to negotiate access to inter-organisational contexts enabled by Chinese finance. But this should not deter us from investigating this grand challenge. Rather, we should see in this difficulty a source of ideas to interrogate the organisational designs that are constrained by western requirements. Two areas to create more ambidextrous forms of organising seem promising: the manipulation of organisational boundaries and the interplay between the formal and informal organisation. To this point, I offer evidence of an innovative form of organising that allows for collective action under the shadow of contractual governance. This insight suggests exciting opportunities for building management theory, and influencing existing organisational theory for those who venture to research this grand challenge.

NOTES

1. For this account, I build on a detailed account of this case presented in Gil and Macaulay (2019).
2. T. Hancock, 2017. China encircles the world with One Belt, One Road strategy. *Financial Times*, 4 May.
3. P. Kingsley, 2015. A New Cairo: Egypt plans £30bn purpose-built capital in desert. *Guardian*, Monday 16 March.
4. African Charter on Popular Participation in Development and Transformation.
5. 2016 Guangzhou International Award for Urban Innovation.
6. *National Solid Waste Management Programme Egypt – Main Report. Egypt*, 2011; National Strategic Directives for Solid Waste Management in Egypt, 2014. National Solid Waste Management Programme, Ministry of the Environment, November.
7. Greater Cairo was administratively organised in three governorates (Giza, Cairo and Qalyubera) which collectively oversaw 35 Municipalities or town governments.
8. M. Walker, 2012. 'Voices of change': a trip through Dharavi. January Impatient Optimists, Bill & Melinda Gates Foundation.
9. D. Perilli, 2015. Lafarge tackles hurdles to refuse-derived fuels production in Egypt. Global Cement, 3 June.
10. S. El Wardany, 2015. Why Cairo recycles better than NYC in waste-picking tale: cities. Bloomberg, 20 January.
11. Cairo Municipal Solid Waste Management Project (P152961), 2014. Project Information Document. Concept Stage, World Bank.
12. Informal resources are difficult to acquire through market transactions, and thus it is better to transfer them within organisational boundaries (Kogut and Zander, 1996). Our findings do not contradict this idea, but our boundaries are the boundaries of the inter-organisational system, not the bound.

REFERENCES

Aghion, P. and Tirole, J. 1997. Formal and real authority in organisations. *Journal of Political Economy*, 105(1), 1–29.

Baiocchi, G. 2003. Participation, activism and politics: the Porto Alegre experiment. In Archon Fung and Erik Olin Wright (eds), *Deepening Democracy: Institutional Innovations in Empowered Participatory Governance*. London and New York: Verso, pp. 47–85.

Baldwin, C.Y. 2007. Where do transactions come from? Modularity, transactions, and the boundaries of firms. *Industrial and Corporate Change*, 17, 155–95.

Birkinshaw, J. and Gibson, C. 2004. Building ambidexterity into an organisation. *MIT Sloan Management Review*, 45(4), 47–55.

Brautigam, D. 2009. *The Dragon's Gift: The Real Story of China in Africa*. New York: Oxford University Press.

Brautigam, D. 2011. Aid 'with Chinese characteristics': Chinese foreign aid and development finance meet the OECD-DAC aid regime. *Journal of International Development*, 23, 752–64.

Burnside, C. and Dollar, D. 2000. Aid, policies, and growth. *American Economic Review*, 90(4), 847–68.

Chambers, R. 1983. *Rural Development: Putting the Last First*. London: Longman.

Chandler, A.D., Jr. 1977. *The Visible Hand: The Managerial Revolution in American Business*. Cambridge, MA: The Belknap Press of Harvard University Press.

Colquitt, J.A. and George, G. 2011. Publishing in AMJ: topic choice. *Academy of Management Journal*, 54, 432–5.

Cooke, B. and Kothari, U. 2001. *Participation: The New Tyranny?* London and New York: Zed Books.

Demsetz, H. 1988. The theory of the firm revisited. *Journal of Law, Economics, and Organisation*, 4, 141–61.

Dreher, A. and Fuchs, A. 2011. Rogue aid? The determinants of China's aid allocation. Courant Research Centre 'Poverty, Equity and Growth' Discussion Paper 93, University of Goettingen.

Dutt, N., Hawn, O., Vidal, E., Chatterji, A., McGahan, A. and Mitchell, W. 2016. How open system intermediaries fill voids in market-based institutions: the case of business incubators in emerging markets. *Academy of Management Journal*, 59(3), 818–40.

Eom, J., Hwang, J., Atkins, L., Chen, Y. and Zhou, S. 2017. China Africa Research Initiative. School of Advanced International Studies Policy Brief No. 18, Johns Hopkins University.

Evans, P.A.L. and Doz, Y. 1989. The dualistic organisation. In P.A.L. Evans, Y. Doz and A. Laurent (eds), *Human Resource Management in International Firms: Change, Globalization, Innovation*. London: Palgrave Macmillan, Chapter 12, pp. 219–42.

Ferraro, F., Etzion, D. and Gehman, J. 2015. Tackling grand challenges pragmatically: robust action revisited. *Organisation Studies*, 36, 363–90.

Fjeldstad, Ø.D., Snow, C.C., Miles, R.E. and Lettl, C. 2012. The architecture of collaboration. *Strategic Management Journal*, 33(6), 734–50.
Freeland, R.F. and Zuckerman, E.S. 2018. The problems and promise of hierarchy: voice rights and the firm. *Sociological Science*, 5, 143–81.
George, G., McGahan, A.M. and Prabhu, J. 2012. Innovation for inclusive growth: towards a theoretical framework and a research agenda. *Journal of Management Studies*, 49, 661–83.
George, G., Corbishley, C., Khayesi, J.N.O., Haas, M.R. and Tihanyi, L. 2016. Bringing Africa in: promising directions for management research. *Academy of Management Journal*, 59(2), 377–93.
Gil, N. and Macaulay, S. 2019. Collective action under the shadow of contractual governance: the case of a participatory approach to upgrade Cairo's 'Garbage Cities'. In Nuno Gil, Anne Stafford and Innocent Musounda (eds), *Duality by Design: The Global Race to Build Africa's Infrastructure*. Cambridge, UK: Cambridge University Press, Chapter 10.
Gil, N. and Pinto, J. 2018. Polycentric organising and performance: a contingency model and evidence from megaproject planning in the UK. *Research Policy*, 47(4), 717–34.
Gil, N., Biesek, G. and Freeman, J. 2015. Interorganisational development of flexible capital designs: the case of future-proofing infrastructure. *IEEE Transactions in Engineering Management*, 62(3), 335–50.
Gil, N., Stafford, A. and Musonda, I. 2019. Introduction. In Nuno Gil, Anne Stafford and Innocent Musounda (eds), *Duality by Design: The Global Race to Build Africa's Infrastructure*. Cambridge, UK: Cambridge University Press, Chapter 1.
Grodal, S. and O'Mahony, S. 2017. How does a grand challenge become displaced? Explaining the duality of field mobilization. *Academy of Management Journal*, 60(5), 1801–27.
Gulati, R. and Puranam, P. 2009. Renewal through reorganisation: the value of inconsistencies between formal and informal organisation. *Organisation Science*, 20(2), 422–40.
Gulati, R., Puranam, P. and Tushman, M. 2012. Meta-organisation design: rethinking design in interorganisational and community contexts. *Strategic Management Journal*, 33(6), 571–86.
Hardin, G. 1968. The tragedy of the commons. *Science*, 162(3859), 1243–8.
Henderson, J. 2008. China and global development: towards a global-Asian Era? *Contemporary Politics*, 14(4), 375–92.
Henisz, W.J. 2002. The institutional environment for infrastructure investment. *Industrial and Corporate Change*, 11(2), 355–89.
Hermes, N. and Lensink, R. 2001. *Changing the Conditions for Development Aid. A New Paradigm* (ed. N. Hermes and R. Lensink). London: Frank Cass.
Hernandez, D. 2017. Are 'new' donors challenging World Bank conditionality? *World Development*, 96, August, 529–49.
Hirchman, A.O. 1967. *Development Projects Observed*. Washington, DC: Brookings Institution.
IEA. 2016. *World Energy Outlook 2016*. Paris: International Energy Agency.
Khalifa, M.A. 2015. Evolution of informal settlements upgrading policies in Egypt: from negligence to participatory development. *Ain Shams Engineering Journal*, 6, 1151–9.
Khanna, T. and Palepu, K.G. 1997. Why focused strategies may be wrong for emerging markets. *Harvard Business Review*, 75(4), 41–51.
Khanna, T. and Palepu, K.G. 2010. *Winning in Emerging Markets. A Road Map for Strategy and Execution*. Boston: Harvard Business Press.
Khanna, T. and Rivkin, J. 2001. Estimating the performance effects of business groups in emerging markets. *Strategic Management Journal*, 22(1), 45–74.
Knudsen, T. and Srikanth, K. 2014. Coordinated exploration: organising joint search by multiple specialists to overcome mutual confusion and joint myopia. *Administrative Science Quarterly*, 59, 409–41.
Kogut, B. and Zander, U. 1996. What firms do? Coordination, identity, and learning. *Organisation Science*, 7(5), 502–18.
Kumar, S. and Corbridge, S. 2002, Programmed to fail? Development projects and the politics of participation. *Journal of Development Studies*, 39(2), 73–103.
Lawrence, P.R. and Lorsch, J.W. 1967. Differentiation and integration in complex organisations. *Administrative Science Quarterly*, 12, 1–47.
Levy, B. 2014. *Working with the Grain: Integrating Governance and Growth in Development Strategies*. New York: Oxford University Press.
Libecap, G.D. 1989. *Contracting for Property Rights. Political Economy of Institutions and Decisions*. New York: Cambridge University Press.
Macneil, R. 1978, Contracts: adjustments of long-term economic relations under classical, neoclassical, and relational contract law. *Northwestern University Law Review*, 72, 854–906.
Mair, J., Marti, I. and Ventresca, M.J. 2012. Building inclusive markets in rural Bangladesh: how intermediaries work institutional voids. *Academy of Management Journal*, 55(4), 819–50.

Majchrzak, A., Sirkka, L.J. and Hollingshead, A.B. 2007. Coordinating expertise among emergent groups responding to disasters. *Organisation Science*, 18, 147–61.

McDermott, G.A., Corredoira, R.A. and Kruse, G. 2009. Public–private institutions as catalysts of upgrading in emerging market societies. *Academy of Management Journal*, 52(6), 1270–96.

Milgrom, P. and Roberts, J. 1990. Complementarities and fit: strategy, structure, and organisational change in manufacturing. *Journal of Accounting & Economics*, 19(2/3), 179–208.

Moyo, D. 2009. *Dead Aid: Why Aid is Not Working and How There is a Better Way for Africa*. London: Allen Lane.

Naim, M. 2007. Rogue aid. *Foreign Policy*, 159, 95–6.

North, D. 1990. *Institutions, Institutional Change, and Economic Performance*. Cambridge: Cambridge University Press.

North, D.C. and Weingast, B.R. 1989. Constitutions and commitment: the evolution of institutions governing public choice in seventeenth-century England. *Journal of Economic History*, 49(4), 803–32.

North, D.C., Wallis, J. and Weingast, B. 2009. *Violence and Social Order: A Conceptual Framework for Interpreting Recorded Human History*. Cambridge: Cambridge University Press.

Olson, M. 1965. *The Logic of Collective Action: Public Goods and the Theory of Groups*. Cambridge, MA: Harvard University Press.

Osmani, S. 2008. Participatory governance: an overview of issues and evidence. In *Participatory Governance and the Millennium Development Goals (MDGs)*. Publication based on the Expert Group Meeting on Engaged Governance: Citizen Participation in the Implementation of the Developmental Goals including the Millennium Development Goals (MDGs), 1–2 November 2006, New York: United Nations, pp. 1–48.

Ostrom, E. 1990. *Governing the Commons: The Evolution of Institutions for Collective Action*. Cambridge: Cambridge University Press.

Perrow, C. 1986. *Complex Organisations: A Critical Essay*, 3rd edn. New York: Random House.

Platteau, J.P. and Abraham, A. 2002. Participatory development in the presence of endogenous community imperfections. *Journal of Development Studies*, 39(2), 104–36.

Puranam, P., Alexy, O. and Reitzig, M. 2014. What's 'new' about new forms of organising? *Academy of Management Review*, 39(2), 162–80.

Rigon, A. 2014. Building local governance: participation and elite capture in slum-upgrading in Kenya. *Development and Change*, 45, 257–83.

Rothaermel, F.T. and Boeker, W. 2008. Old technology meets new technology: complementarities, similarities, and alliance formation. *Strategic Management Journal*, 29(1), 47–77.

Scheinberg, A., Simpson, M.H., Gupt, Y. et al. 2010. *Economic Aspects of the Informal Sector in Solid Waste*. Eschborn, Germany: German Technical Cooperation (GTZ).

Scott, W.R. 1981. *Organisations: Rational, Natural, and Open Systems*. Englewood Cliffs, NJ: Prentice Hall.

Siggelkow, N. 2002. Misperceiving interactions among complements and substitutes: organisational consequences. *Management Science*, 48(7), 900–916.

Siggelkow, N. 2007. Persuasion with case studies. *Academy of Management Journal*, 50(1), 20–24.

Simon, H.A. 1962. The architecture of complexity. *Proceedings of the American Philosophical Society*, 156, 467–82.

Sims, D. 2010. *Understanding Cairo: The Logic of a City Out of Control*. Cairo: American University in Cairo Press.

Sims, D. 2015. *Egypt's Desert Dreams. Development or Disaster?* Cairo: American University in Cairo Press.

Smith, W.K. and Tushman, M.L. 2005. Managing strategic contradictions: a top management model for managing innovation streams. *Organisation Science*, 16(5), 522–36.

Tan-Mullins, M., Mohan, G. and Power, M. 2010. Redefining 'aid' in the China–Africa context. *Development and Change*, 41, 857–81.

Thompson, J.D. 1967. *Organisations in Action*. New York: McGraw-Hill.

UN. 2017. *World Population Prospects: The 2017 Revision*. New York: Department of Economic and Social Affairs, Population Division, United Nations.

UN. 2018. *The United Nations World Water Development Report*. UN-Water.

UN-Habitat. 2008. *State of the World's Cities 2008/2009 Harmonious Cities*. London: Earthscan.

Van de Ven, A.H., Ganco, M. and Hinings, C.R. 2013. Returning to the frontier of contingency theory of organisational and institutional designs. *The Academy of Management Annals*, 7(1), 393–440.

Williamson, O.E. 1979. Transaction-cost economics: the governance of contractual relations. *Journal of Law and Economics*, 22(2), 233–61.

Williamson, O.E. 1985. *The Economic Institutions of Capitalism*. New York: Free Press.

Wilson, D., Velis, C. and Cheeseman, C. 2006. Role of informal sector recycling in waste management in developing countries. *Habitat International*, 30, 797–808.

Zuckerman, Ezra A. 2010. Speaking with one voice: a 'Stanford School' approach to organisational hierarchy. In Claudia Bird Schoonhoven and Frank Dobbin (eds), *Stanford's Organisation Theory Renaissance, 1970–2000* (Research in the Sociology of Organisations), Vol. 28. Bingley, UK: Emerald Group Publishing, pp. 289–307.

15. An institutional framework to the scaling up of inclusive social innovations: the case of La Salada

Silvia Dorado and Pablo D. Fernández

INTRODUCTION

In a classic paper on the challenges we face to address social problems, Rittel and Webber (1973) declared that the "relatively easy [social] problems have been dealt with," and it was time to turn "our attention to others that are much more stubborn" (p. 156). Stubborn problems are not just complicated, they are "wickedly" complex because they are defined by qualities including durability, circular causality, and redistribution implications likely to be resented and resisted by incumbent actors (Dorado and Ventresca, 2013; Rayner, 2006).

Across the world, we can find individuals engaged in advancing all sort of "social innovations" with the potential to alleviate these wickedly complex problems (Westley and Antadze, 2010). They include technological innovations (solar power), novel processes (distribution of mosquito screens), or policy approaches (local participation). Most of what we know about social innovation derives from research on these entrepreneurial (Rindova et al., 2009) and compassionate efforts (Kanter, 2010; Miller et al., 2012; Mulgan et al., 2007). Explorations of these efforts have furthered our understanding of the profile of social innovators and entrepreneurs (Leadbeater, 1997; Miller et al., 2012; York et al., 2016) and the opportunities for social innovation (Mair and Marti, 2009). Research has also considered whether for-profit organizations should be expected to engage in social innovation (Bansal and Roth, 2000; Campbell, 2007; Crane et al., 2014; Margolis and Walsh, 2003; O'Toole and Vogel, 2011; Porter and Kramer, 2011), and, more broadly, whether the pursuing of social goals should be combined with profit goals (Battilana and Dorado, 2010; Pache and Santos, 2012; York et al., 2015). This research has also furthered our understanding on our ability to measure the effectiveness of these efforts (Bansal and Roth, 2000; Santos et al., 2015). Nevertheless, we know less about the question explored in this chapter, namely, the challenges and opportunities for the scaling up of social innovations. As we argue in this chapter, scaling up of social innovations involves their institutionalization – that is, their diffusion from time-to-time and from place-to-place. Only those social innovations that institutionalize will scale up and out and thereby have the type of lasting or revolutionary impact required to make inroads into the alleviation of wickedly complex problems.

The institutionalization of social innovations cannot be taken for granted and, like for-profit innovations, depends only partially on the value they create (Hargadon and Douglas, 2001). Consider, for example, Garud and colleagues' exploration of the cochlear implants technology (Garud, 2008; Garud and Rappa, 1994). They show how, after many years of working to bring this innovation to the market, the actors involved found – to their surprise – that this technology, which they thought everyone would appreciate as having great social value (bringing hearing to deaf people), was negatively valued by people in the deaf community (Garud, 2008; Garud and Rappa, 1994). Nevertheless, most of what we know about scaling has disregarded the challenges to scaling brought about by such disagreements and focused only on issues associated with the availability of resources to support the growth and diffusion that founders see as worthy of support (Brest and Born, 2013; Höchstädter and Scheck, 2015; Milligan and Schöning, 2011). The question of resources is, of course, a central one (see, for example, Murray et al., 2010) for all innovations, regardless of the degree of agreement on their social value. But as suggested in recent scholarship, the availability of resources to support the scaling up of social innovations cannot be understood without considering challenges to the emergence of widespread agreement about their value that is required for their institutionalization (Cajaiba-Santana, 2014; Van Wijk et al., forthcoming; Westley et al., 2013). Institutionalization describes a process through which social innovations both diffuse and gain increasing degrees of self-replication and resilience (Berger and Luckmann, 1991; Tolbert and Zucker, 1996; Zucker, 1977). Moreover, as Schumpeter (2003) reminded us, such institutionalization processes are likely to be accompanied by the erosion and undermining of institutionalized structures, with redistributive implications, most likely, resented by incumbents.

A thorough review of the institutional literature suggests that the institutionalization of social innovations is subject to two forces, namely, justification and cooptation. These two forces define both the likelihood for social innovations to gain acceptance and thereby access the necessary support to preserve their essential qualities and the likelihood of modifications to these qualities and thereby the risk of the erosion of those qualities that allow them to alleviate wickedly complex problems.

Justification follows from regulatory arguments, normative explanations, and cognitive narratives (Boltanski and Thévenot, 2006; Thornton et al., 2012) that actors use to frame and gain support for innovations (Lounsbury and Glynn, 2001; Powell and Rerup, 2016). It is rooted in actors' interpretations of the possible and defines how actors gain awareness and make sense of ideas new to the world (Ocasio, 1997) by reflecting on how they relate to the rules, norms, and practices that shape their thinking (Douglas, 1986). Justification also defines, of course, how new ideas are translated from one context to another (Czarniawska-Joerges and Sevón 2005; Smets et al., 2011). Justification can hinder necessary access to support and acceptance; it can also bring about expected and unexpected changes and reinterpretations. For example, pioneers of microfinance defined this social innovation by highlighting the small size of loans and acceptance of unusual local collaterals (for example, group guarantee) and emphasizing the need to involve loan officers to sell, evaluate, and collect on loans so as not to over-indebt the poor (Otero and Rhyne, 1994). However, in its diffusion, the involvement of loan officers lost relevance and was abandoned, particularly by for-profit banks. This is not surprising since loan officers' wages was the costlier component of a microfinance loan (*The Economist*, 2005; Battilana et al., 2009; Dorado, 2015). In short, the qualities that define the social value of innovations are not intrinsic to the new object, process, or policy. These qualities are but partially controlled by innovator pioneers and are subject to changes depending on how these qualities are appreciated through the lenses of justification (pre-existing and well-accepted understandings of what is possible and desirable). In the case of cochlear implants, the challenge emerged as this technology was seen as disputing an understanding embraced in the deaf community – deafness understood as a human condition which should be embraced, not cured or remediated, because it is not dissimilar from the many other attributes that are distinguishable among people (race, gender, sexual orientation, and so on). In the case of microfinance, the challenge followed from emerging trends in banking that prioritize the use of scoring instead of the costly labor-intensive engagement of loan officers.

Actors can willfully partake in and steer justification forces, at least partially (Hargadon and Douglas, 2001; Rao, 1998), but the outcomes of their efforts are still likely to be unexpected. For example, research on rationalization – a specific type of justification associated with the logic of capitalism (Weber, 1952, 1978) – has shown how justification dynamics can redefine the outcomes of social innovations by prioritizing the need to measure and track performance over other goals (Quattrone, 2015; Weber, 1952, 1978). This follows from codification and standardization practices which by increasing the degree of abstraction in the transmission of knowledge can hide crucial causalities between actions and outcomes (Alexander, 1988). One example of how rationalization-based justification dynamics endangered the scaling of social innovations is provided by the New Lanark Mill (see O'Toole and Vogel, 2011).

In the late nineteenth century, Robert Owen, one of the New Lanark Mill's owners, embraced an unheard of approach to worker relations. He offered workers benefits such as relatively short working hours, a grievance procedure, guaranteed employment during economic downturns, and contributory health, disability, and retirement plans. Workers were also given access to clean, decent housing, a preschool, daycare, and adult night school. Interestingly, following these reforms, New Lanark became "the world's most productive and profitable textile mill" (O'Toole and Vogel, 2011, p. 63). However, Lanark co-owners failed to see the connection between these novel practices and productivity, and pressed to eliminate them in the search for increased efficiencies and thereby profits. Although likely never acknowledged by the other owners, the elimination of workers' benefits did little to increase profitability and may have instead contributed to losses that caused the mill to close soon afterward.

Cooptation stands as a related but ontologically different force defining the growth and diffusion of social innovations (Hirsch and Lounsbury, 1997; Selznick, 1996). Cooptation forces are associated with the stalling, and deviations in the original purpose, of an innovation depending on how incumbents appreciate its potential to serve or undermine their interests (Selznick, 1949, 1996). The term emphasizes the power dynamics (Pfeffer, 1973) that frame the negotiations required for a social innovation to gain permanency and diffuse. Cooptation moderates the social innovation's impact or reshapes it to advance private interests (Barley, 1986). Cooptation is engendered in actors' perceptions about the potential for the social innovation to either undermine incumbent resource distributions or be influenced by actors wishing to advance interests unrelated to those of their innovator pioneers (Lawrence et al., 2002; Leblebici et al., 1991; Oliver, 1992; Selznick, 1949; Zietsma and Lawrence, 2010). For example, the actors more likely to de-emphasize the need for loan officers in microfinance were for-profit banks, which viewed microfinance as a new venue for profits instead of a way to support poverty alleviation. Incumbent actors are likely to use their privileged position to hinder the institutionalization of the innovation (Wijen, 2014), they can also coopt those elements of the innovation that undermine their interests (Selznick, 1949), and even steer its institutionalization to support features which may not be those that explain its social value, as in the example of the combustion engine (Rao, 1998).

Selznick's (1949) study of the Tennessee Valley Authority (TVA) illustrates how cooptation can bring about the erosion of the social value expected or desired by its promoters. The TVA was created in 1933 to manage waterways connected issues in the Tennessee Valley, including navigation, flood control, and electricity generation. An essential element of this innovation was a democratic styled governance. This governance style, designed to give voice to all actors impacted by the changes, was eventually undermined by local elites, who advanced decision-making models that favored their interests.

This chapter explores these two forces: justification and cooptation. It does so with a framework that articulates their impact on the institutional carriers of social innovations – symbolic systems, relational systems, practices, and artifacts. Our interest is on inclusive social innovations, that is, those innovations associated with "improvements in the social and economic wellbeing of communities that have structurally been denied access to resources, capabilities, and opportunities" (George et al., 2012, p. 661). These innovations are of particular interest since, as argued, they are the most likely to be challenged by incumbents because their redistributive implications are, in most cases, explicit (Amis et al., 2017). The chapter illustrates the value of the framework offered to explain the scaling up of inclusive innovations by considering the example of La Salada, a "paraformal" market located in Buenos Aires, Argentina, that has served as an entrepreneurial staircase for the poor. The chapter ends with a discussion of the research implications.

INSTITUTIONAL CARRIERS AND THE IMPACT OF JUSTIFICATION AND COOPTATION FORCES ON SCALING

Following institutional theory, the first step in the growth and diffusion of social innovations involves the work of talented entrepreneurs willing and able to frame innovations in ways that make them appear socially acceptable and desirable (Aldrich and Fiol, 1994; Lounsbury and Glynn, 2001). For example, Rao (1998) traces the emergence of consumer protection agencies to the framing work of talented actors he describes as institutional entrepreneurs (Dorado, 2005). Other processes of knowledge transmission follow this first step. These processes are known as translation (Czarniawska, 1997) and involve the packaging and formulation of novel information within specific narratives that explain and justify its value (Wedlin and Sahlin, 2017). Both these framing and translation processes expose social innovation to justification and cooptation forces with the potential to erode their social value, that is, their ability to alleviate wicked problems. This potential is well illustrated by the initial role played by Mohamed Yunus in the framing of microfinance and the subsequent collective translation of this novel practice as it diffused into mainstream banking. As discussed later, these forces may challenge social innovations but these innovations may still preserve their essential qualities. On occasion, they can also have a positive effect in fueling their diffusion. This is illustrated by the rapid diffusion of cellular telephony worldwide.

Mohamed Yunus framed the value of microfinance through an imagery of the poor as self-starters and entrepreneurs. This imagery convincingly justified the need to support microfinance but was probably detached from the reality of most microfinance clients.

The consequences of such detachment have proven to be detrimental to the social valuation of microfinance in the long run. Fundamentally, this imagery created the expectation of microfinance as a tool to create wealth and employment. However, as many pioneers suspected and careful research has subsequently shown, the clearest effect of microfinance is not that of creating wealth and employment (see, for example, Banerjee et al., 2009), but of increasing the degree of financial self-reliance of the poor. The latter is a valuable social outcome but one which appears, in comparison, to be of less value than that of creating wealth and employment. The result has been an underserved tarnishing of microfinance (Roodman, 2012).

Moreover, as mentioned earlier, the diffusion of microfinance into mainstream banking brought about an unexpected reinterpretation of one of its core features, namely, the reliance on loan officers to sell, evaluate, and collect on loans as perhaps too costly and unnecessary (Battilana et al., 2009). This reinterpretation has engendered a dilution of the responsibility of microfinance organizations to give loans only to those who can repay, something which has the potential to critically erode the social value of microfinance. Unfortunately, there are already examples of such erosion. Most dramatically, the decision by borrowers of SKS (a well-known microfinance organization located in Andhra Pradesh, India) to commit suicide when faced with the prospect of defaulting on loans taken to pay for things such as a wedding or a funeral that, it should have been clear to SKS's loan officers, these borrowers could never pay back.

In short, justification and cooptation forces encroach on the value of social innovations by defining the framing and translation required for their growth and diffusion. Next, we further explore their impact as forces eroding, preserving, and on occasion fueling social innovations by considering the four arenas for, or carriers of, these framing and translation processes (see Scott, 2003). These are symbolic systems (Kennedy, 2008; Kennedy and Fiss, 2013), relational systems (Glynn, 2008), practices (Ventresca and Kaghan, 2008), and artifacts (Rafaeli and Pratt, 2013).

Symbolic systems are, of course, central to any process of information transmission. Transmission can occur within informal systems and, organically, through interpersonal communication (Powell and Rerup, 2016). Research on institutional entrepreneurship has explored these dynamics when considering the framing processes that allow new social structures to gain initial support (Lounsbury and Glynn, 2001; Rao, 1998). In addition, there is a substantial body of research exploring the role of formal systems, including media outlets (Kennedy, 2008) and theorization reports in professional (Reay and Hinings, 2005; Strang and Meyer, 1993) and educational settings (Dunn and Jones, 2010).

These formal systems are riddled with opportunities for actors to intervene and modify the content of social innovation and, in fact, their content is unlikely to diffuse without modifications. Justification dynamics will define the format and content of these narratives emphasizing the coherent ordering of beliefs and actions, the elimination of inconsistencies, and/or the reduction of all individual instances, whatever their diversity, to the status of general classes (Shils, 1980). In turn, incumbent actors can use narratives to justify and coopt innovations so that they advance their interests. As illustrated later, in our discussion of La Salada, actors will advance arguments about the need to hinder the diffusion of the social innovation or to bring modifications which both unexpectedly and predictably encroach on the most radical elements of the innovation. In the case of inclusive innovations that are likely to run against dominant distributions of resources

(Selznick, 1949) and mainstream institutional logics (Thornton et al., 2012), such encroachments are likely to bring about an erosion of the social value of the innovation. But this does not necessarily need to be the case.

The diffusion of social innovations follows not only from the way that information is packaged but also from who is involved (Czarniawska-Joerges, 1996; Rovik, 1998). *Relational systems* are thus central arenas for framing and translation processes, paving the scaling up of social innovations. Relational systems include the connections that exist among actors, including individuals and organizations. They can take a plurality of templates (Morris et al., 2008). Most research on framing and translation, with its focus on symbolic systems, has assumed away variances in the process created by the relational template linking actors. This is not surprising when we consider that most of what we know about transmission of new social structures, through informal interpersonal channels, derives from research on framing. In this research, the only relevant relational templates are reciprocity based because they have been shown to allow actors to gain support for inventions to bring about their scaling even when this may involve drastic institutional change (Aldrich and Fiol, 1994; Dorado, 2013; Hampel et al., 2017; Padgett and McLean, 2006). However, systems with other relational templates (Morris et al., 2008) also play a role in the dynamics of framing and translation of social innovations. This is important because framing and translation within bureaucratic, conflictive, or competition-based relational templates may make social innovations more vulnerable to erosion and manipulation associated with justification and cooptation forces (Tönnies, 1955). This is nicely illustrated by the case of La Salada, whose origins are connected with trust-based relational templates combined in desirable and undesirable ways with alternative relational templates, for example, conflictive, that defined its outcomes in dramatic ways.

Scholars have also convincingly pointed to the role of *practices* as a vehicle for the transmission of social structures. The role of practices as carriers is particularly relevant if and when they become patterned into habitualized routines (Berger and Luckmann, 1991; Bourdieu, 1990; Giddens, 1984), microfounded (Powell and Colyvas, 2008) on symbolic rules of thumb (Powell and Rerup, 2016) and connected to the tacit knowledge (Scott, 2003) that actors develop as they interact in the course of their activities. Practices exist in the local (Hallett and Ventresca, 2006). They feed and are fed and supported by symbolic (Maguire and Hardy, 2009; Wedlin and Sahlin, 2017) and relational systems (Padgett and McLean, 2006). Their vulnerability to the influence of cooptation and justification has been well explored in studies of bureaucracy (see, for example, Allison, 1971). La Salada also highlights their value in creating space for the preservation of the essential qualities of inclusive innovations.

Finally, *artifacts* are a recent focus of institutional research but there is an extensive literature on their role in the innovation literature (Carlile, 2002). In addition, institutional scholars have also recently begun to explore the role of objects not considered in the innovation literature, namely, buildings (Jones, 2013), which, as La Salada will help to illustrate, can play a central role on how a social innovation becomes grounded and, thereby, more likely to help preserve desirable qualities.

The innovation literature has discussed the role of artifacts as boundary objects (Carlile, 2002), exploring how their materiality facilitates the transmission of ideas crossing the language boundaries that separate symbolic systems grounded in disconnected

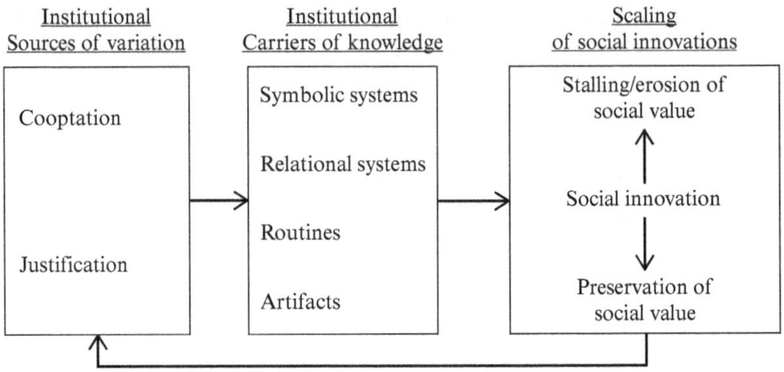

Figure 15.1 Scaling up of social innovation: an institutional framework

institutional logics. It has also highlighted their role as a source of variance bringing about unpredictability on what gets transmitted in processes of translation (Czarniawska-Joerges, 1996; Czarniawska-Joerges and Sevón, 2005; Sahlin and Wedlin, 2008). But the nature of objects as inherently polysemous (Carlile et al., 2013) also sets them aside from the other three carriers as particularly prone to translations that depart from the original meaning of their creators. Because of their polysemy, social innovations that rely on objects may be particularly prone to dynamics of cooptation and justification redefining their original content, especially those that threaten the status quo. But this same quality can help them escape these forces. This appears to have been the case in La Salada.

In short, from an institutional perspective the scaling of social innovations involves their framing and translation which occurs through four different knowledge transmission carriers – symbolic, relational, practices, and artifacts. These carriers stand as arenas where justification and cooptation forces can encroach on the institutionalization of social innovation. They mediate, that is, create and limit, the risk for cooptation and justification and can then bring about erosion, preservation, and even enhancement of the social value expected from social innovations. Figure 15.1 provides a graphic summary of the institutional theory-inspired model of scaling (that is, institutionalization) of social innovations advanced in the chapter.

The next section illustrates this model with the example of La Salada, a paraformal market which in its 30-year life-span has grown, diffused, and changed in substantial ways. To date, it has retained a quality that grants it the label of inclusive social innovation, namely, its stand as an entrepreneurial staircase for the poor to create, develop, and grow their businesses from backroom workshops to legal or paralegal establishments.

LA SALADA: THE SCALING OF A CONTESTED SOCIAL INNOVATION

La Salada is now a 20-hectare market located in a rather dodgy area of Lomas de Zamora, a municipality in the periphery of Buenos Aires. This market attracts producers and wholesale buyers of garments, apparel goods, and shoes. Some buyers are local; many others visit from distant places in Argentina and neighboring Brazil and Paraguay. There are also an increasing number of cookie cutter replicas (Saladitas), 600 according to one account (Girón, 2017), across Argentina.

La Salada's origins trace back to the late 1980s as a social gathering of Bolivian immigrant families after their Monday visits to Buenos Aires' central market (the city's fruits and vegetables wholesale market). In a rather unorganized way, some of them started to offer clothes produced in small family workshops. Demand was overwhelming and fueled the market's relocation to its current site, where shady promoters built three central buildings that house it: Urkupiña (1991), Ocean (1995), and Punta Mogote (1999). Subsequently, street vendors began to locate to the periphery of the main buildings, in an area referred to as La Ribera, but stalls there are still today periodically dismantled by the police (street vending is illegal in Buenos Aires). There is also a growing number of buildings filling up what used to be open spaces between them.

La Salada forms an unparalleled paraformal market (Mörtenböck and Mooshammer, 2015). While numbers vary widely, conservative estimates place the number of visitors at 30,000 for every opening day and daily sales anywhere between US$3.2 million to US$20 million. It is even difficult to know the number of stalls constituting the market. Some place the number at 7,000 while others count as many as 30,000 stalls. The large discrepancy responds to the large number occupying the surrounding streets of the market. In 2010, a 4-square meter central place was sold for US$100,000.

Informality, fake products, tax evasion, and unregistered labor are some of the defining qualities of La Salada. Our characterization of this massive market as a social innovation for inclusive growth (George et al., 2012) follows not from its illegality but from its role, preserved over the years, as an entrepreneurial staircase for poor entrepreneurs such as Carmela and Jose Quispe (pseudonyms), a Bolivian couple we interviewed in their workshop in 2017.

Carmela had left Bolivia with the promise of a permanent job at a garment factory. The job she obtained was a far cry from what she expected. She ended up living and working in a small room with six more Bolivian immigrants; two of them were a young couple with a child from Cochabamba, and the rest were Paceños like her. She and her coworkers worked long hours, sometimes more than 16 hours a day. They seldom went out, warned about immigration and police officers looking for illegal people like them to be deported. Therefore, they spent their days sewing, also motivated by exploitative piecework payment arrangements. She met Jose, and together they decided to break away on their own. With a little money they had saved, they bought a sewing machine and the material for a short run of jeans. They brought them to La Salada, and within a couple of hours, they sold out. Encouraged by their success, they reinvested their money in the business to buy more material.

Eventually, Carmela called her relatives back in Bolivia to join them and announced on the Bolivian community radio that they were hiring sewers. It took some time to gather the money to buy two other sewing machines, but eventually they managed to set up a workshop by their house, giving shelter to family members. Every Wednesday evening Jose traveled by bus to La Salada carrying a black sack with the products of the week. He paid US$30 for the use of a stall in Ocean; normally, in four or five hours all the products were sold. Jose followed the same routine for a couple of years. The workshop grew as they added more machines and workers, and even started designing clothes under their own brand. The couple then moved out of La Salada, having developed a list of clients that bought from them direct, increasing predictability and eliminating the need to have a stall.

At the time of writing, La Salada has grown and diffused well beyond what its initial founders ever expected. Cooptation and justification forces have shaped its evolution. These forces have also eroded to a certain extent its value as an entrepreneurial staircase for the poor.

Symbolic Systems

The transition of La Salada from a transient informal market into a multi-building complex follows first from the talents of some controversial individuals (for example, Enrique Antequera, Gonzalo Rojas Paz, Jorge Castillo) with great framing talent. These individuals were able to combine vendors to put money upfront and contribute quotas for the purchase and erecting of buildings. They were able to negotiate with the local authorities both to turn a blind eye to their activities and to provide them with some legal guarantees to scaffold their real estate deals. Much of the social value that has been eroded from this innovation has been coopted by these politically savvy individuals for their own benefit. It was not easy and reports connect a plurality of violence and death events to these dynamics.

Formal symbolic transmission systems including media coverage (see Hacher, 2011), professional reports (D'Ovidio et al., 2007; Kestelboim, 2008), and academic studies (see Dewey, 2017; Lieutier, 2010; Ossona, 2010) have helped to preserve the social value of La Salada by increasing its visibility, which has brought more customers and favored its diffusion. Media coverage, however, arrived only once the market had taken a stronghold and has been mostly negative, reflective of the social unease this market generates. The coverage is less than flattering, focused on its illegality and suggestive of the complicity of police and local politicians turning a blind eye to its operations.

Professional reports by the European Union and the US State Department are supportive of this media coverage and focus particularly on the large amount of counterfeit merchandise sold in the market. Garment industry groups claim the amount to be as high as 70 percent of what is sold; our visits to the market suggests this may be an exaggeration.

These reports have been countered in the media by one rather outspoken leader, Jorge Castillo, the majority owner of Punta Mogote.[1] He has argued that the market creates employment for local producers and democratizes access to goods for those who cannot pay the prices charged in local shopping centers and malls.

Finally, by and large, academic reports have explored La Salada as an expression of a period steep in neoliberal ideologies that have defined economic policies in Argentina since the 1980s (Dewey, 2017; Lieutier, 2010). In the 1990s, these policies brought about trade liberalization which fueled the move of garment manufacturing from factories to sweatshops and the tailoring of retail outlets to the needs of high-income consumers, leaving a huge part of the population unattended (Dewey, 2017).

Relational Systems

La Salada emerged out of a community effort and was defined by a solidarity relational template which has not been considered in the institutional literature. Members of the

Bolivian immigrant community had begun trading foods and goods that they produced or smuggled at a weekly fair, rather successfully to the surprise of all. Through their weekly gatherings, joint efforts to find suitable locations, and frequent confrontations with the police, they began forming a community of convenience made stronger because of its roots in a common ethnic background and migrant experience (Corbalán, 2003).

Its original solidarity relational template slipped within a few years. This transition is not surprising and follows from the *cooptation* of these initial communitarian efforts by opportunistic profit-seeking, and rather ruthless, individuals. These exchanges bred several Mafioso-type networks feuding for control of the most profitable part, that is, rentals of stall space. Interestingly, competition among these mafioso networks has brought both physical and legal security and stability to La Salada, even if only in a limited way. These outcomes have followed from their justification work to gain legitimacy for their networks and, in the process, these mafioso-type networks contributed to the preservation and growth of La Salada. For example, through clarification of property rights and also from their embracing, even if in a limited way, legal requirements such as taxation even if only through the *monotributo*, a tributary innovation that facilitates the collection of taxes from small businesses in Argentina.

In fact, it appears that La Salada has grown and expanded geographically because of competition among these Mafioso networks to gain the favor of the many poor entrepreneurs who have found an opportunity to get out of poverty in the market. It has done so against the commercial interests of mainstream corporations that see it as a threat to the value of their intellectual property; and the blind eye approval of policymakers.

Practices

While symbolic and relational systems have, over the years, yielded a number of threats to the survival of La Salada, its fairs have weathered them and continue to grow. This degree of stability derives from practices which are the result of dynamic forces. Once set in motion, these forces become unstoppable. There is a clear demand for La Salada's products and there are many suppliers willing to rent a stall for a day or a few hours to sell their produce. Some of the producers that make up these suppliers are new; others pre-date La Salada as workers in workshops and sweatshops – as many as 30,000, scattered across the metropolitan area of Buenos Aires. Like before, these individuals work in semi-slavery conditions, often in confinement or under threat (Arcos, 2013; INTI, 2011; Lieutier, 2010), but La Salada has allowed many to partake of the profits.

Practices specific to La Salada have supported its preservation and growth, for example, formalized opening hours and days, per day stall rentals, parking facilities, and the many locals offering the ancillary services required for smooth trading: transport services, buyers' tours, intermediaries, private security agencies, collectors, moneylenders, and so on. Others have continued to support its social purpose. One example of such a practice is the sub-rental of stalls. A producer arrives before opening time to rent a stall, sells his or her products, and then offers the space to another vendor, who will pay for the remaining hours. This cycle ends when there are no more customers. Sub-rental arrangements are practical because traders may only need to use the stall for the few hours required to sell their products. They are valuable because they permit cost sharing, allowing for even the smallest producers to sell their products.

Artifacts

The practices that have helped to preserve and grow La Salada follow from the stability afforded by the contruction of the three buildings that form it. The history behind the construction of these buildings illustrates particularly well the role that cooptation and justification forces have had on both the erosion and preservation of the social value of La Salada.

Selling on the streets is forbidden under Argentinian laws, which explains why, from its inception, the trading in La Salada attracted the unfavorable attention of local authorities. After several evictions and relocations, the largely Bolivian traders organized their relations with public officials by naming two representatives. These two "representatives" collected money from traders and led negotiations on behalf of the collective. To serve their own interests, as much as those of the collective, they identified a permanent location for the fair. Initially, they were the only owners of one of the buildings (Urkupiña). But the success of this initial building attracted the attention of other investors to finance the purchase and renovation of the other two buildings (Ocean and Punta Mogote) that make up La Salada.

The architecture of the buildings matches their original function. They are flanked by a plurality of side entrances on all sides forming a mesh of corridors. There is also a large space allotted for parking to facilitate the arrival of large vehicles. Today, parking in La Salada allows for more than 600 buses bringing shopping tours from every corner of Argentina and other neighboring countries. The buildings allow the formalization of trading and define its character as a wholesale market.

RESEARCH AGENDA

In this chapter, we have explored the scaling of social innovations as a process of institutionalization. We have argued that the scaling of social innovations cannot be taken for granted because their institutionalization can stall and also be subject to variations that can erode their social value. As suggested in the literature, knowing where variations are likely to emerge helps to minimize the risk of erosion (Chowdhury and Santos, 2010; Winter and Szulanski, 2001). As suggested in this chapter, it is also important to consider not only the source of the variation (justification or cooptation) but also the type of carrier (symbolic, relational, practice, artifact) channeling it. The framework proposed points to the relevance of exploring the scaling up of social innovations through considering each of their carriers and attending to their interplay. Let's review them in order.

As widely established in the literature, symbolic systems play a central role in the transmission of knowledge and will, thereby, be central to variations in the scaling up of social innovations. Following the framework advanced here, central questions should address the erosion risk presented by cooptation and justification forces. Two questions emerge as particularly relevant. First, the focus of social innovation research has been centered on their potential to alleviate a complex social problem. Attention to this framework highlights the need for research that considers differences in risk erosion depending on how much the social innovation departs from mainstream institutional logics and/or threatens legitimate incumbent interests (Zietsma and Lawrence, 2010). As illustrated in the example of La Salada, symbolic systems are likely to bring visibility to contested social innovations, and even support for their diffusion, but can undermine their potential for legitimacy. In fact, it could be that a potential solution fits well with existing logics and that the increased visibility brought about by symbolic carriers may speed and spread the innovation beyond what was initially expected. One example of such an innovation is wireless technologies. These technologies are well supported by a capitalist logic that allows entrepreneurs to realize the win–win, double bottom line proposition involved in increasing the reach of wireless systems so that they can serve populations that were previously disconnected.

Second, future research should also consider conflicts in the symbolic systems relevant to the transmission of social innovations. A particularly relevant question may be the following: How can the man-bites-dog logic, which defines media coverage (that is, what gets published by the media is not what is ordinary and routine but what is unusual and surprising), lead to the misrepresentation of social innovations? It is also important to consider the impact (erosion, preservation, and – as in the case of wireless technology – support) that the logics that frame not only media coverage, but also the theorization of innovations can have on social innovations.

Questions that consider the role of symbolic systems may be particularly relevant in explorations of the scaling up of social innovations for inclusive growth (George et al., 2012). The reason, this chapter contends, is that it is more likely for this profile of innovation to run against the grain of dominant logics and incumbent interests.

The role of relational systems provides another relevant research direction. As suggested in the literature, relational systems bring support to innovations besides symbolic systems. But the fundamental insight from this research is that actors may be willing to support innovations because of reasons associated with the social capital of the individual (or organization) asking them (Brown and Ashman, 1996; Coleman, 1990; Putnam et al., 1994), including their reputation or a prior history of reciprocal interactions (Aldrich and Fiol, 1994). This support may allow for social innovations to progress even when they threaten mainstream logics. It is also true, however, that reliance on relational systems can expose social innovations to the risk of cooptation by vested interests. It can also generate, as in the case of La Salada, a high degree of instability as the social networks advance conflicting interests.

Interesting research questions should explore differences in the risk of cooptation considering, at least, three different avenues. Researchers need to consider the degree to which relational and symbolic systems are supportive of one another. Zietsma and Lawrence's (2010) study of the interplay between practice and boundary work provides a relevant theoretical framework for such exploration.

Researchers may also want to explore relational systems other than the reciprocal ones considered in the literature. There are alternative relational templates that can bring about support to social innovations that have been disregarded so far. For example, La Salada points to the role of solidarity links among individuals based on kinship and a shared immigration experience. At some point in time, these templates may make social innovations vulnerable to abuse because of the challenges associated with collective action but can also provide them with the initial fuel required to operate against the grain of established practices (Putnam et al., 1994).

Our framework also points to the value of researching the critical role played by practices. This vehicle may be of particular interest because it highlights the different dynamics involved in the self-replication in time and the diffusion in space of social innovations. Self-replication in time follows the routinization of existing practices (Giddens, 1984). Diffusion in space also requires routinization but is likely accompanied by processes of translation (Sahlin and Wedlin, 2008), which the literature suggests are not possible without adjustments to local conditions. The incorporation of local conditions makes routinization of social innovations vulnerable to losing its critical elements (Chowdhury and Santos, 2010). It will be interesting to explore the interaction of these two processes (self-replication and diffusion) depending on variables such as cultural or geographical distance among the sites of diffusion, or the degree of self-replication of social innovations prior to their diffusion.

Another important avenue of research is to consider the connection between processes of routinization and those framing the transmission of social innovations via symbolic and relational systems. As suggested by La Salada, practices can become routinized and diffuse against the grain of highly critical media coverage and against the protest by representatives of legitimate incumbent interests. However, this lack of alignment may not always occur. It is important then to explore the influence on the scaling of social innovations that can emerge from differences in the degree of alignment between practices and formal symbolic systems as well as practices and relational systems. It may be that these differences influence in meaningful ways the speed or difficulty with which social innovations scale up.

Finally, there is much need for research on the role of artifacts. There is a wealth of evidence pointing to artifacts as central in processes of knowledge transfer (Carlile, 2002). However, there is little on their value to bring about the self-replication and/or diffusion of social innovations. This lack of attention is unwarranted considering the central role that artifacts play in the definition of practices (Barley, 1986; Leonard-Barton, 1988). As the case of La Salada illustrates, sometimes practices developed because of the physical attributes of an artifact (in the case of La Salada, the central market-shaped buildings) become the core vehicle framing the routinization of the social innovation.

Besides the influence that artifacts can have in the development and routinization of practices, there is also a need to consider how they define and are defined by symbolic and relational systems. The interactive relation with symbolic systems has been explored by other scholars (see, for example, Jones, 2013) but, to our knowledge, scholars have yet to explore how specific relational systems make more or less likely the emergence of artifacts, for example, the constructions of buildings, that increase the likelihood for social innovations to self-replicate and diffuse. Moreover, considering the centrality of artifacts, it will be important to explore how justification and cooptation forces frame their development broadly given their interplay with the other three institutional carriers that define the self-replication and diffusion of social innovations.

In addition, the framework advanced puts center stage a question suggested by social innovation scholars (Westley and Antadze, 2010) that has received less attention than desirable, namely, concerning differences between the scaling up or growth of social innovations and their scaling out or diffusion to settings other than its context of origin. Scaling up occurs over time as social innovations grow and gain permanency. The dynamics of knowledge transmission associated with such a process will be rather different than those associated with their scaling out to geographical locations outside its original context. Fundamentally, knowledge transmission in a process involving scaling out is more likely to require more radical forms of translation, because of the larger degree of variance between contexts than those with a shared history (Granovetter, 1992; Harrington and Fine, 2006).

In conclusion, the growth and expansion of social innovations cannot be taken for granted. This is particularly true for inclusive social innovations because of their explicit redistributive implications. In this chapter, we have explored the challenges generated by justification and cooptation, two institutional forces that impact on the symbolic and relational systems, practices and artifacts involved in the framing and translation of innovations from time-to-time and place-to-place. We have presented a model that articulates such impact and offered an institutional theory-based research agenda on the growth and diffusion of inclusive social innovations.

NOTE

1. Punta Mogote has a radio and TV channel and Jorge Castillo is a skilled communicator.

REFERENCES

Aldrich, H.E. and Fiol, C.M. (1994). Fools rush in? The institutional context of industry creation. *Academy of Management Review*, 19(4), 645–70.

Alexander, J.C. (1988). *Action and its Environments: Toward a New Synthesis*. New York: Columbia University Press.

Allison, G.T. (1971). *Essence of Decision: Explaining the Cuban Missile Crisis*. Boston, MA: Little, Brown and Company.

Amis, J., Munir, K.A., Mair, J. et al. (2017). Institutions and economic inequality. In R. Greenwood, C. Oliver, T. Lawrence, and M. Meyer (eds), *The SAGE Handbook of Organizational Institutionalism*, 2nd edn. London: Sage, pp. 705–36.

Arcos, M.A. (2013). "Talleres clandestinos": el traspatio de las "grandes marcas". Organización del trabajo dentro de la industria de la indumentaria. *Cuadernos de Antropología*, 10, Julio–Diciembre, 333–51.

Banerjee, A.V., Duflo, E., Glennerster, R., and Kinnan, C. (2009). *The Miracle of Microfinance?: Evidence from a Randomized Evaluation*. IFMR Research, Centre for Micro Finance, NBER, Cambridge, MA.

Bansal, P. and Roth, K. (2000). Why companies go green: a model of ecological responsiveness. *Academy of Management Journal*, 43(4), 717–36.

Barley, S.R. (1986). Technology as an occasion for structuring: evidence from observations of CT scanners and the social order of radiology departments. *Administrative Science Quarterly*, 31(1), 78–108.

Battilana, J. and Dorado, S. (2010). Building sustainable hybrid organizations: the case of commercial microfinance organizations. *Academy of Management Journal*, 53(6), 1419–40.

Battilana, J., Leca, B., and Boxenbaum, E. (2009). How actors change institutions: towards a theory of institutional entrepreneurship. *Academy of Management Annals*, 3(1), 65–107.

Berger, P.L. and Luckmann, T. (1991). *The Social Construction of Reality: A Treatise in the Sociology of Knowledge*. London: Penguin.

Boltanski, L. and Thévenot, L. (2006). *On Justification: Economies of Worth*. Princeton, NJ: Princeton University Press.

Bourdieu, P. (1990). *The Logic of Practice*. Stanford, CA: Stanford University Press.

Brest, P. and Born, K. (2013). When can impact investing create real impact? *Stanford Social Innovation Review*, 11(4), 22–31.

Brown, L.D. and Ashman, D. (1996). Participation, social capital, and intersectoral problem solving: African and Asian cases. *World Development*, 24(9), 1467–79.

Cajaiba-Santana, G. (2014). Social innovation: moving the field forward. A conceptual framework. *Technological Forecasting and Social Change*, 82, 42–51.

Campbell, J.L. (2007). Why would corporations behave in socially responsible ways? An institutional theory of corporate social responsibility. *Academy of Management Review*, 32(3), 946–67.

Carlile, P.R. (2002). A pragmatic view of knowledge and boundaries: boundary objects in new product development. *Organization Science*, 13(4), 442–55.
Carlile, P.R., Nicolini, D., Langley, A., and Tsoukas, H. (2013). *How Matter Matters: Objects, Artifacts, and Materiality in Organization Studies*. Oxford: Oxford University Press.
Chowdhury, I. and Santos, F. (2010). Scaling social innovations: the case of Gram Vikas. In P.N. Bloom and E. Skloot (eds), *Scaling Social Impact*. London: Palgrave Macmillan, pp. 147–66.
Coleman, J.S. (1990). *Foundations of Social Theory*. Cambridge, MA: Belknap-Harvard University Press.
Corbalán, Mauricio (2003). Lectura de Economías étnicas de Michel de Certeau (1986). In F. Álvarez, M. Di Peco, N. Muñoa, and M. Zuccon (eds), *Desayunando Lecturas*. Buenos Aires: Fundación Start, pp. 35–44.
Crane, A., Palazzo, G., Spence, L.J., and Matten, D. (2014). Contesting the value of the shared value concept. *California Management Review*, 56(2), 130–53.
Czarniawska, B. (1997). *Narrating the Organization. Dramas of Institutional Identity*. Chicago, IL: University of Chicago Press.
Czarniawska-Joerges, B. (1996). *Travels of Ideas*. Gothenburg: School of Economics and Commercial Law, University of Gothenburg, and Gothenburg Research Institute, pp. 13–48.
Czarniawska-Joerges, B. and Sevón, G. (2005). *Global Ideas: How Ideas, Objects and Practices Travel in a Global Economy*, Vol. 13. Copenhagen: Copenhagen Business School Press.
D'Ovidio, María, Malamud, L., Cremona, M., Martelletti, L., and Peña, J. (2007). *Quién es quién en la cadena de valor del sector de indumentaria textil. Hacia una solución conjunta del sector*. Buenos Aires: Fundación El Otro.
Dewey, M. (2017). Domestic obstacles to labor standards: law enforcement and informal institutions in Argentina's garment industry. *Socio-Economic Review*, 16(3), 567–86.
Dorado, S. (2005). Institutional entrepreneurship, partaking, and convening. *Organization Studies*, 26(3), 385–414.
Dorado, S. (2013). Small groups as context for institutional entrepreneurship: an exploration of the emergence of commercial microfinance in Bolivia. *Organization Studies*, 34(4), 533–57.
Dorado, S. (2015). Microfinance re-imagined: personal banking for the poor. In T. Baker and F. Welter (eds), *Routledge Companion to Entrepreneurship*. New York: Routledge, pp. 179–92.
Dorado, S. and Ventresca, M.J. (2013). Crescive entrepreneurship in complex social problems: institutional conditions for entrepreneurial engagement. *Journal of Business Venturing*, 28, 69–82.
Douglas, M. (1986). *How Institutions Think*. Syracuse, NY: Syracuse University Press.
Dunn, M. and Jones, C. (2010). Institutional logics and institutional pluralism: the contestation of care and science logics in medical education, 1967–2005. *Administrative Science Quarterly*, 55(1), 114–49.
Garud, R. (2008). Conferences as venues for the configuration of emerging organizational fields: the case of cochlear implants. *Journal of Management Studies*, 45(6), 1061–88.
Garud, R. and Rappa, M.A. (1994). A socio-cognitive model of technology evolution: the case of cochlear implants. *Organization Science*, 5(3), 344–62.
George, G., McGahan, A.M., and Prabhu, J. (2012). Innovation for inclusive growth: towards a theoretical framework and a research agenda. *Journal of Management Studies*, 49(4), 661–83.
Giddens, A. (1984). *The Constitution of Society: Outline of the Theory of Structuration*. Berkeley, CA: University of California Press.
Girón, N. (2017). *La Salada: radiografía de la feria más polémica de Latinoamérica*. Buenos Aires: Planeta Argentina.
Glynn, M.A. (2008). Configuring the field of play: how hosting the Olympic Games impacts civic community. *Journal of Management Studies*, 45(6), 1117–46.
Granovetter, M. (1992). Problems of explanation in economic sociology. In Nitin Nohria and Robert Eccles (eds), *Networks and Organizations: Structure, Form, and Action*. Boston, MA: Harvard Business School Press, pp. 25–56.
Hacher, S. (2011). Sangre salada. *Una Feria En Los Márgenes. Buenos Aires, Marea Editorial.*
Hallett, T. and Ventresca, M.J. (2006). Inhabited institutions: social interactions and organizational forms in Gouldner's patterns of industrial bureaucracy. *Theory and Society*, 35(2), 213–36.
Hampel, C.E., Lawrence, T.B., and Tracey, P. (2017). Institutional work: taking stock and making it matter. In R. Greenwood, C. Oliver, T. Lawrence, and M. Meyer (eds), *The SAGE Handbook of Organizational Institutionalism*. London: Sage, pp. 558–90.
Hargadon, A.B. and Douglas, Y. (2001). When innovations meet institutions: Edison and the design of the electric light. *Administrative Science Quarterly*, 46(3), 476–501.
Harrington, B. and Fine, G.A. (2006). Where the action is: small groups and recent developments in sociological theory. *Small Group Research*, 37(1), 4–19.
Hirsch, P.M. and Lounsbury, M. (1997). Ending the family quarrel: toward a reconciliation of "old" and "new" institutionalisms. *American Behavioral Scientist*, 40(4), 406–18.
Höchstädter, A.K. and Scheck, B. (2015). What's in a name: an analysis of impact investing understandings by academics and practitioners. *Journal of Business Ethics*, 132(2), 449–75.

INTI (2011), Diseño de indumentaria de autor en Argentina: diagnóstico productivo e impacto económico basado en la Encuesta Nacional de Diseño de Indumentaria de Autor 2011, INTI.
Jones, M.R. (2013). Untangling sociomateriality. In P. Carlile, D. Nicolini, D. Langley, and H. Tsoukas (eds), *How Matter Matters: Objects, Artifacts and Materiality in Organization Studies*. Oxford, UK: Oxford University Press, pp. 197–226.
Kanter, R.M. (2010). From spare change to real change: the social sector as beta site for business innovation. *Harvard Business Review*, 77, 122–32.
Kennedy, M.T. (2008). Getting counted: markets, media, and reality. *American Sociological Review*, 73(2), 270–95.
Kennedy, M.T. and Fiss, P.C. (2013). An ontological turn in categories research: from standards of legitimacy to evidence of actuality. *Journal of Management Studies*, 50(6), 1138–54.
Kestelboim, M. (2008). Estimación del tamaño del mercado de indumentaria y de textiles para el hogar de la Argentina. Fundación Protejer.
Lawrence, T.B., Hardy, C., and Phillips, N. (2002). Institutional effects of interorganizational collaboration: the emergence of proto-institutions. *Academy of Management Journal*, 45(1), 281–90.
Leadbeater, C. (1997). *The Rise of the Social Entrepreneur*. London: Demos.
Leblebici, H., Salancik, G.R., Copay, A., and King, T. (1991). Institutional change and the transformation of interorganizational fields: an organizational history of the US radio broadcasting industry. *Administrative Science Quarterly*, 36(3), 333–63.
Leonard-Barton, D. (1988). Implementation as mutual adaptation of technology and organization. *Research Policy*, 17(5), 251–67.
Lieutier, Ariel (2010). *Esclavos: Los trabajadores costureros en la ciudad de buenos aires*. Buenos Aires: Retórica Ediciones.
Lounsbury, M. and Glynn, M.A. (2001). Cultural entrepreneurship: stories, legitimacy, and the acquisition of resources. *Strategic Management Journal*, 22(6–7), 545–64.
Maguire, S. and Hardy, C. (2009). Discourse and deinstitutionalization: the decline of DDT. *Academy of Management Journal*, 52(1), 148–78.
Mair, J. and Marti, I. (2009). Entrepreneurship in and around institutional voids: a case study from Bangladesh. *Journal of Business Venturing*, 24(5), 419–35.
Margolis, J.D. and Walsh, J.P. (2003). Misery loves companies: rethinking social initiatives by business. *Administrative Science Quarterly*, 48(2), 268–305.
McKague, K., Zietsma, C., and Oliver, C. (2015). Building the social structure of a market. *Organization Studies*, doi: 0170840615580011.
Miller, T., Grimes, M., McMullen, J., and Vogus, T. (2012). Venturing for others with heart and head: how compassion encourages social entrepreneurship. *Academy of Management Review*, 37(4), 616–40.
Milligan, K. and Schöning, M. (2011). Taking a realistic approach to impact investing: observations from the World Economic Forum's Global Agenda Council on Social Innovation. *Innovations: Technology, Governance, Globalization*, 6(3), 155–66.
Morris, M.W., Podolny, J., and Sullivan, B.N. (2008). Culture and coworker relations: interpersonal patterns in American, Chinese, German, and Spanish divisions of a global retail bank. *Organization Science*, 19(4), 517–32.
Mörtenböck, P. and Mooshammer, H. (2015). *Informal Market Worlds Atlas. The Architecture of Economic Pressure*. Rotterdam: NA1010 Publisher.
Mulgan, G., Tucker, S., Ali, R., and Sanders, B. (2007). *Social Innovation: What It is, Why It Matters and How It Can be Accelerated*. London: The Basingstoke Press.
Murray, R., Caulier-Grice, J., and Mulgan, G. (2010). *The Open Book of Social Innovation*. London: The Young Foundation.
O'Toole, J. and Vogel, D. (2011). Two and a half cheers for conscious capitalism. *California Management Review*, 53(3), 60–76.
Ocasio, W. (1997). Towards an attention-based view of the firm. *Strategic Management Journal*, 18(S1), 187–206.
Oliver, C. (1992). The antecedents of deinstitutionalization. *Organization Studies*, 13(4), 563–88.
Ossona, J.L. (2010). El shopping de los pobres: Anatomía y fisiología socioeconómica y política de La Salada. Documento presentado en VI Congreso del CEISAL "Independencias-Dependencias-Interdependencias" en l'Université de Toulouse-Le Mirail, Francia.
Otero, M. and Rhyne, E. (1994), *The New World of Microenterprise Finance*. West Hartford, CT: Kumarian Press.
Pache, A. and Santos, F. (2012). Inside the hybrid organization: selective coupling to conflicting institutional logics. *Academy of Management Journal*, 56, 972–1001.
Padgett, J.F. and McLean, P.D. (2006). Organizational invention and elite transformation: the birth of partnership systems in Renaissance Florence. *American Journal of Sociology*, 111(5), 1463–568.

Pfeffer, J. (1973). Size, composition, and function of hospital boards of directors: a study of organization–environment linkage. *Administrative Science Quarterly*, 18, 349–64.
Porter, M. and Kramer, M.R. (2011). Creating shared value. *Harvard Business Review*, 89(1/2), 62–77.
Powell, W.W. and Colyvas, J.A. (2008). Microfoundations of institutional theory. In R. Greenwood, C. Oliver, K. Sahlin, and R. Suddaby (eds), *The Sage Handbook of Organizational Institutionalism*. London: Sage, pp. 276–98.
Powell, W.W. and Rerup, C. (2016). Opening the black box: the microfoundations of institutions. In R. Greenwood, C. Oliver, T. Lawrence, and M. Meyer (eds), *The SAGE Handbook of Organizational Institutionalism*, 2nd edn. London: Sage, pp. 311–37.
Putnam, R.D., Leonardi, R., and Nanetti, R.Y. (1994). *Making Democracy Work: Civic Traditions in Modern Italy*. Princeton, NJ: Princeton University Press.
Quattrone, P. (2015). Governing social orders, unfolding rationality, and Jesuit accounting practices: a procedural approach to institutional logics. *Administrative Science Quarterly*, 60(3), 411–45.
Rafaeli, A. and Pratt, M.G. (2013). *Artifacts and Organizations: Beyond Mere Symbolism*. London: Psychology Press.
Rao, H. (1998). Caveat emptor: the construction of nonprofit consumer watchdog organizations. *American Journal of Sociology*, 103(4), 912–61.
Rayner, S. (2006). Wicked problems: clumsy solutions – diagnoses and prescriptions for environmental ills. Jack Beale Memorial Lecture on Global Environment, James Martin Institute for Science and Civilization.
Reay, T. and Hinings, C.B. (2005). The recomposition of an organizational field: health care in Alberta. *Organization Studies*, 26(3), 351–84.
Rindova, V., Barry, D., and Ketchen, D.J. (2009). Entrepreneuring as emancipation. *Academy of Management Review*, 34(3), 477–91.
Rittel, H.W. and Webber, M.M. (1973). Dilemmas in a general theory of planning. *Policy Sciences*, 4(2), 155–69.
Roodman, D. (2012). *Due Diligence: An Impertinent Inquiry into Microfinance*. Washington, DC: Brookings Institution.
Rovik, K-A. (1998). *Moderne organisasjoner: trender i organisasjonstenkningen ved tusenårsskiftet*. Bergen, Norway: Fagbokforlaget.
Sahlin, K. and Wedlin, L. (2008). Circulating ideas: imitation, translation and editing. In R. Greenwood, C. Oliver, K. Sahlin, and R. Suddaby (eds), *The SAGE Handbook of Organizational Institutionalism*. London: Sage, pp. 218–42.
Santos, F., Pache, A.-C., and Birkholz, C. (2015). Making hybrids work. *California Management Review*, 57(3), 36–58.
Schumpeter, J.A. (2003). *Capitalism, Socialism and Democracy*. E-library: Taylor and Francis.
Scott, W.R. (2003). Institutional carriers: reviewing modes of transporting ideas over time and space and considering their consequences. *Industrial and Corporate Change*, 12(4), 879–94.
Selznick, P. (1949). *TVA and the Grass Roots: A Study in the Sociology of Formal Organization*, Vol. 3. Los Angeles, CA: University of California Press.
Selznick, P. (1996). Institutionalism "old" and "new". *Administrative Science Quarterly*, 41, 270–77.
Shils, E. (1980). *The Selected Papers of Edward Shils, Volume 3: The Calling of Sociology and Other Essays on the Pursuit of Learning* (Vol. 3). Chicago, IL: University of Chicago Press.
Smets, M., Morris, T., and Greenwood, R. (2011). From practice to field: a multi-level model of practice-driven institutional change. *Academy of Management Journal*, 55, 877–904.
Strang, D. and Meyer, J.W. (1993). Institutional conditions for diffusion. *Theory and Society*, 22(4), 487–511.
The Economist (2005). Special report: microfinance. Micro no more. 5 November, accessed 25 July 2013 at http://www.economist.com/node/5079360.
Thornton, P.H., Ocasio, W., and Lounsbury, M. (2012). *The Institutional Logics Perspective: Foundations, Research, and Theoretical Elaboration*. Oxford: Oxford University Press.
Tolbert, P. and Zucker, L.G. (1996). Institutionalization of institutional theory. In S. Clegg, C. Hardy, and W. Nord (eds), *Handbook of Organization Studies*. London: Sage, pp. 175–90.
Tönnies, F. (1955). *Community and Association: (Gemeinschaft und gesellschaft)*. London: Routledge and Kegan Paul.
Van Wijk, J., Zietsma, C., Dorado, S., de Bakker, F., and Marti, I. (forthcoming). Social innovation: integrating micro, meso and macro level insights from institutional theory. *Business & Society*.
Ventresca, M.L. and Kaghan, W. (2008). Routines, "going concerns", and innovation: towards an evolutionary economic sociology. In J. Beckert (ed.), *Handbook of Organizational Routines*. Cheltenham, UK and Northampton, MA, USA: Edward Elgar Publishing, pp. 52–8.
Weber, M. (1952). The essentials of bureaucratic organization: an ideal-type construction. *Reader in Bureaucracy*, 19, 19–21.

Weber, M. (1978). Economy and society: an outline of interpretive sociology. *Readings in Economic Sociology*, 3(3), 24–37.
Wedlin, L. and Sahlin, K. (2017). The imitation and translation of management ideas. In R. Greenwood, C. Oliver, T. Lawrence, and M. Meyer (eds), *The SAGE Handbook of Organizational Institutionalism*. London: Sage, pp. 102–27.
Westley, F. and Antadze, N. (2010). Strategies for scaling social innovation for greater impact. *The Innovation Journal: The Public Sector Innovation Journal*, 15(2).
Westley, F.R., Tjornbo, O., Schultz, L. et al. (2013). A theory of transformative agency in linked social-ecological systems. *Ecology and Society*, 18(3), 27.
Wijen, F. (2014). Means versus ends in opaque institutional fields: trading off compliance and achievement in sustainability standard adoption. *Academy of Management Review*, 39(3), 302–23.
Winter, S.G. and Szulanski, G. (2001). Replication as strategy. *Organization Science*, 12(6), 730–43.
York, J., Hargrave, T., and Pacheco, D. (2015). Converging winds: logic hybridization in the Colorado wind energy field. *Academy of Management Journal*. doi:10.5465/amj.2013.0657
York, J.G., O'Neil, I., and Sarasvathy, S.D. (2016). Exploring environmental entrepreneurship: identity coupling, venture goals, and stakeholder incentives. *Journal of Management Studies*, 53(5), 695–737.
Zietsma, C. and Lawrence, T.B. (2010). Institutional work in the transformation of an organizational field: the interplay of boundary work and practice work. *Administrative Science Quarterly*, 55(2), 189–221.
Zucker, L.G. (1977). The role of institutionalization in cultural persistence. *American Sociological Review*, 42(5), 726–43.

16. Social innovation as institutional work

Warren Nilsson

THE SOCIAL INNOVATION MOVEMENT

As the social innovation movement grows larger and more ambitious, it must also become humbler and more intimate. In the early 2000s, the social innovation conversation was comfortingly workmanlike, cast in the language of 'problems' with 'solutions' waiting patiently to be discovered (Mulgan, 2006; Phills et al., 2008). It framed the world as somewhat askew machinery, and seemed to call for inspired tinkerers and craftsmen to set things right, one problem at a time.

More recently, the conversation has run wider, becoming increasingly infused with the language of systems thinking and complexity. In this light, the most profound social innovations are not solutions to discrete problems. They are disruptions to fundamental social practices and relationships – the regulative, normative, and cultural structures that inscribe systems (Heiskala, 2007; Howaldt and Schwarz, 2010; Howaldt et al., 2014; Murray et al., 2010; Westley and Antadze, 2010). Put simply, social innovation is social change (Cajaiba-Santana, 2014).

So twenty-first-century social innovation cannot be disconnected from the longer arc of social critique and social movement. Certainly, something like social innovation can be discerned throughout history, whenever human beings have wrestled consciously with the social structures that they inhabit and that inhabit them. But perhaps there *is* something fresh in the dispersion of the current call. Social movements typically focus on specific issues, ideologies, and end goals. But social innovation now postulates a kind of creative agency that is omnidirectional and radically distributed. It is concerned with the remarkable everydayness of the who, what, and where of ongoing social change. It is less about a particular issue in a particular time and place than about the consistent expansion of everyone's capacity to reimagine the world on Monday. And to do it again on Tuesday.

Thus, Heiskala (2007) sees the distinguishing valence of social innovation as an increase in collective learning and collective power, a way to enhance system reflexivity and nourish new realms of co-creative torque. Unger (2013) puts it best. He explicitly calls social innovation a movement and proposes that the work of this movement is 'to resist and subvert the dictatorship of no alternatives . . . in the direction of an enhancement of agency in all domains of social life of the capacity for invention and self-direction' (p. 2). He is confident that the necessary conditions for global transformation are already in place, and detects a 'kind of ceaseless Brownian motion that we can discern throughout the world' whose 'unifying spirit' is not a particular utopian structure or ideology but 'radical experimentalism' itself (p. 4). And because this experimentalism is invoked 'in all domains of social life,' the social innovation movement necessarily positions itself as fully inclusive. If no domain of social life can be excluded from collaborative social reconstruction, then logically no group or class of persons can be excluded either. To exclude any social category of people is to leave out the social domains and sub-domains that those people uniquely delimit and express.

GRAND CHALLENGES AND INSTITUTIONAL WORK

This hopeful and all-compassing incantation of reflexive agency leaves social innovation theory searching for new ways to make sense of systemic intervention through localized platforms. If the large, consolidated movement is not the primary transformation mechanism of social innovation, how do we take up grand challenges? How do we effectively link macro-system dynamics to the expanded micro-agency happening on the ground? How can true system change be nourished by all of those eager living labs, eccentric community organizations, nervy public agencies, untamed networks, and thirsty, headlong schools, clinics, churches, mosques, temples, gardens, and prisons – for that is where social innovation is happening?

By posing questions like these, the social innovation movement offers a powerful way to reinvigorate structure-agency questions from the perspective of grand challenge praxis. Cajaiba-Santana (2014) argues, however, that the structural and agentic schools of social innovation scholarship proper have rarely conversed. But there are glimmerings. Westley and colleagues have devoted considerable attention to the relationships between strategic agency, macro social change, and systemic resilience through a social innovation lens. Drawing on complexity theories (for example, Stacey, 1995) and resilience theories in ecology (for example, Holling, 2001), they emphasize cross-scale interaction, particularly via agentic communication between the niche and landscape levels of a given system. Social innovators are individuals, organizations, initiatives, and networks that enable and convene that cross-scale interaction (McGowan and Westley, 2015; Moore and Tjornbo, 2012; Moore and Westley, 2011; Moore et al., 2014; Westley et al., 2013). This approach tills rich ground for a number of practice-based insights. And it is consonant with Senge et al.'s (2015) framing of system leadership, which also emphasizes distributed agency expressed through actors who are skilled at seeing the system, fostering systemic reflection, and helping other actors shift from a reactive, problem-solving form of agency to a more proactive, co-creative, aspirational form of agency.

Other researchers point to institutional theory in sociology and organization studies (Scott, 2001) as a promising but underused lens for developing structure-agency perspectives of social innovation (for example, Cajaiba-Santana, 2014; Dacin et al., 2011; Heiskala, 2007; Nilsson, 2015). Institutional theory offers one explanation of how practices are instantiated and reproduced across social space and time at multiple scales (Berger and Luckmann, 1967; DiMaggio and Powell, 1991; Giddens, 1984; Jepperson, 1991). It is less a theory of social structure per se than a theory of structural inertia – how institutions develop regulative, normative, and cultural legitimacy (Scott, 2001) over time and how institutions interweave to form broader logics and fields that are very difficult to change. But institutions do change, of course. At one time, institutional theory emphasized institutional change via strategic agency at the field level, highlighting entrepreneurial actors using specific skills to forward discrete projects (for example, DiMaggio, 1988; Fligstein, 1997). But increasingly, institutional researchers study more diffuse, nonlinear, distributed dynamics of social transformation involving multiple modes of agency over a wide range of intentional (though not necessarily strategic) actors and interactions (for example, Dorado, 2005). This latter perspective has been developed and given coherence under the umbrella term 'institutional work' (Lawrence and Suddaby, 2006).

Institutional work scholarship begins with the presumption that both the angel and devil are in the details. Since institutions only exist through their enactment, actors regularly express reflexive agency in all institutionalized environments. Institutional work research uses a practice lens to explore how this agency is brought to bear at the micro level in the ongoing interplay between institutional creation, disruption, and maintenance (Lawrence et al., 2009, 2011). The new emphasis on the rich micro-agency involved in even the most stable, implacable macro-institutions has been particularly revealing. It turns out that, despite the apparently conclusive evidence of our daily experiences, institutions don't maintain themselves; we maintain them. Institutional researchers are not glib about this insight, however. They reject both 'determinism' and 'heroism,' recognizing the oppressive rigidity of many institutions while also acknowledging 'the potential for emancipation from some of those structures some of the time' (Lawrence et al., 2011, p. 56).

Institutional theory offers an especially practical social innovation lens through its key insight that institutions are performative (Lounsbury and Crumley, 2007). Institutions are not living in the ether somewhere. They do not exist separately from their enactment (performance) and from our memories of them (Giddens, 1984). Even the largest macro-institutions, like the international monetary system or global gender regimes, are performed through countless micro-interactions. Certainly, there are superstructural rules and norms and mechanisms in place, but they only have force insofar as they are enacted – by ministers during meetings, administrators during processing, the person on the street who uses 'money' for a 'transaction' to acquire 'ownership' of a particular 'good,' or the pair of friends who reenact gender stereotypes. The force of institutions – for good and bad – lies in how unthinkingly most of us go along with most rules, norms, and beliefs, most of the time.

Institutional work research demonstrates, however, that this ritualized, seemingly automatic reproduction of institutions is deceptive. Because institutions never completely delimit our interactions in every detail, and because the symbolic orders we maintain in our minds are not 'perfectly shared,' social structuring is not a given; it is a 'practical organizational accomplishment' (DiMaggio and Powell, 1991, p. 20). Institutional work scholarship builds on this insight by recognizing the highly leveraged systemic power of the mundane. Institutional work involves:

> the efforts of individuals and collective actors to cope with, keep up with, shore up, tear down, tinker with, transform, or create anew the institutional structures within which they live, work, and play, and which give them their roles, relationships, resources, and routines. (Lawrence et al., 2011, p. 53)

Put crudely, the raw material for system transformation is right there before us all of the time. We are swimming in it. We are (re)creating it. Becoming more conscious of this gift – this peril – can help social innovation actors see their systems more clearly and work with them more creatively, enhancing overall agency and potentially accelerating impact. An institutional work lens makes clear the entanglement of macro-structures with micro-interactions in the day-to-day.

A HEURISTIC FOR SOCIAL INNOVATION AS INSTITUTIONAL WORK

In summary, the question at the heart of the social innovation movement is how to effectively connect macro-systemic grand challenges to micro-praxis in the pursuit of enhanced systemic reflexive agency. An institutional work lens offers a number of theoretical and practical advantages for exploring this question. Its performative framing takes the micro and the macro to be mutually constitutive, a duality rather than a binary (Giddens, 1984). Its emphasis on practice shows institutional agency to be accessible to individual and small-group actors. Its emphasis on distributed action shows institutional agency to be accessible to a wide variety of actors across all subject positions (with relative but not absolute limitations). And finally, theories of institutional work recognize the interpenetration of multiple institutions at the micro level (Friedland and Alford, 1991). The whole system is alive and before us no matter how we attempt to bracket it in our organizations. We may tell ourselves that we are working in the field of food security, or healthcare, or human rights. Indeed, the individual logics of those fields may feel overwhelming and dominant to the professionalized actors who grow up in them. But institutional work itself cannot be so neatly domesticated.

> [It] demand[s] a more holistic account of institutional action that moves beyond simple dyadic relationships and discrete logics, toward the assumption that actors, at any given time, are subject to pressures from many different institutions and are often responding locally, creatively, incrementally, and more or less reflexively. (Lawrence et al., 2011, p. 57)

That is, even while we work furiously *on* a particular issue by offering someone a meal, say, or revising the next revolutionary app, we are working *with* and *through* a much broader system of institutional dynamics.

Taken together, these features of institutional work theory offer a radical vision of social innovation, revealing how actors can work on the complex roots of a system, rather than merely on its symptomatic effects. Consider Heeks et al.'s (2013) ladder of inclusive innovation, which describes six levels of inclusion: intention, consumption, impact, process, structure, and post-structure. The first three describe a kind of inclusion offering little or no agency for the target groups of the innovation process. The latter three are more agentic and leveraged, including previously marginalized groups in the processes, strategies, and framings of the institutional spaces in question. The first three categories rearrange the institutional system, the second three disrupt and remake the institutional system at a more fundamental level. By definition, they involve institutional work.

Despite the potentially fruitful links between institutional work scholarship and social innovation, there are few examples of empirical institutional work research with an explicit social innovation focus (for a counter example, see Lawrence and Dover, 2015). A number of institutional work studies have explored social purpose organizations and projects (for example, Battilana and Dorado, 2010; Creed et al., 2010; Maguire et al., 2004; Mair et al., 2012), but they have generally not invoked social innovation research or attempted to derive broad-based social innovation theory (Nilsson, 2015). This may be one reason that institutional work research is still only scratching the surface in terms of its potential real-world impact (Dover and Lawrence, 2010). Hampel et al. (2017) identify three important gaps in the institutional work literature to date. First, research has focused mostly on middle-range institutions rather than on large-scale institutions that are 'more complex and distal than the simpler, more proximal institutions located in fields and organizations' (p. 567). Yet it is precisely these 'societal institutions' (for example, financial systems, class systems, human rights regimes, social-ecological relationship patterns) that are most fully implicated in grand challenges. Second, institutional work research has yet to explore 'collaborative work of heterogeneous networks of actors' (p. 560), emphasizing instead more unitary collective actors like organizations, professional associations, and interest groups. Even the smallest-scale social innovators, however, find themselves enmeshed in multiple fields and multiple networks confronting a dynamic heterogeneity on a daily basis. Third, research has prioritized symbolic forms of institutional work over material and relational forms. Social innovation work, on the other hand, requires a rich interaction between symbol, substance, and relationship. Overall, it is clear that current gaps in the institutional work and social innovation literatures are mutually implicated.

If social innovation research is to take up the institutional work challenge (and/or vice versa), how can it keep its intimacy? How can it invoke societal institutions without falling prey to high-level abstraction and to the assumption that systemic work necessarily involves scale? These are the very tendencies that have made it difficult for institutional theory to be applied in practice by the average social innovator. One possibly useful strategy for researchers and practitioners alike might be to develop heuristics that reveal the systemic, performative nature of seemingly local innovations. An institutional work heuristic could suggest strategies for increasing a given social innovation's impact in the problem domain it is addressing. But it could also reveal the innovation's potential contribution to the broader social innovation movement goal outlined above: increasing systemic reflexive agency.

The following five performative dimensions may be a useful starting point toward such a heuristic: roles, social identities, resource flows, authority processes, and meanings. They are not intended to be exhaustive, but they do represent important analytical lenses in the wider institutional theory literature. Each of these dimensions involves a mode of structural enactment critical to holding a given institution together. To engage in social innovation with a systemic eye is to disrupt and reimagine at least one of these modes. The dimensions are not mutually exclusive. Meanings are implicated in roles are implicated in authority processes are implicated in resources flows, and so on. For example, authority processes may be rooted in functional roles (chief executive officers (CEOs), presidents) or in social identities (classes, castes, privileged ethnicities). Nevertheless, it is useful to bracket the dimensions as each provides a different sort of doorway into action.

In the following sub-sections, I shall briefly describe the five dimensions and flesh them out with examples from social innovation practice. The examples are illustrative not superlative. They are not offered as best practices, and I make no claims about their ultimate effectiveness. Here the focus is on how a given innovation challenges the performative dimension in question, not whether or to what degree the innovation is achieving social impact (though many of these projects have had a clear impact).

As these examples will illustrate, there are at least two broad areas of institutional work cutting across a wide variety of social innovation initiatives. The first centers around a kind of *value inclusion*, expanding the value matrix of a given field by valorizing previously underrepresented people, resources, relationships patterns, and/or modes of knowledge. The second involves enhancing a field's capacity for *structural experimentalism*, increasing the structural flexibility of the field by making its linkages less rigid and its boundaries more plastic. Both of these forms of institutional work contribute to overall system reflexivity and distributed agency in a variety of ways, as I begin to tease out below. I offer them tentatively, as a rough hypothesis of what it is that might bind social innovation together as a movement in practice.

Roles: Who Does What

Roles are arguably the primary structuring feature of institutional fields, inscribing who does what and how. Roles are an outgrowth of the division of labor. They arise from the reciprocal typification of habitualized actions and actors and this typification happens to such a degree that a given function (hunting, accounting, managing) comes to be seen as separate from the person who happens to be inhabiting it at the moment (Berger and Luckmann, 1967). 'Elizabeth who is hunting' becomes, simply, 'a hunter.' The rules, norms, and beliefs (Scott, 2001) undergirding legitimated practices in any institutional field are salient only when the appropriate category of person acts them out in some way. 'To say, then, that roles represent institutions is to say that roles make it possible for institutions to exist, ever again, as a real presence in the experience of living individuals' (Berger and Luckmann, 1967, p. 92). Consequently, role disruption is one of the most powerful and potentially far-reaching forms of social innovation work.

There are two key modes of role disruption prevalent in social innovation. The first involves creating new roles within existing institutional fields by *valorizing previously excluded forms of knowledge*. Consider the healthcare initiative mothers2mothers. Working in several countries in southern Africa, the organization has dramatically lowered mother-to-child HIV transmission rates in newborns (Schweer and Strang, 2012). Its primary innovation is the inclusion of a new role in the healthcare system: the mentor mother. Mentor mothers are HIV-positive women who have themselves successfully managed the protocols for preventing transmission to their newborns. In turn, they are integrated into local healthcare facilities as paid, professional healthcare workers. They educate, counsel, and support women through pregnancy and the early days after delivery.

What might seem like a simple programmatic strategy is in fact a stark challenge to the existing role configurations of institutionalized healthcare. Training and certification structures are deeply embedded and highly formalized and professionalized across all levels of the health system. The pathways to becoming a healthcare worker are long and narrow, contingent on the acquisition of scientific knowledge and ritualized technical practice.

Mentor mothers, in contrast, qualify relatively quickly, with just a small amount of formal training. From the perspective of the typical healthcare knowledge system, their journey is short. But their expertise is of a different order: it is cultural and experiential, developed over the long arc of a life in community, in family, in body. It is no less hard won than a doctor's or nurse's nor is it less critical for effective healthcare delivery, as mothers2mothers' results have borne out.

Boston Uncornered (Day, 2018), an initiative that enables former gang members to pursue university education full-time, adopts a similar strategy. The student journey is supported by 'college readiness advisors' who are themselves former gang members. This pattern of role disruption is visible in many social innovations. It involves constructing new roles (or widening old ones) to integrate types of knowledge that are marginalized by existing institutions. Often that knowledge is experiential, drawing on wide biographical swaths of social practice. It may also be cultural-historical, embedded in knowledge traditions generally excluded from dominant industrial, bureaucratic, and Cartesian logics. Professionalized institutional fields can have a difficult time making sense of such knowledge. It is complex. It is contextual. It is difficult to measure and impossible to control. But it is essential to the generation and diffusion of social innovation. This kind of role disruption and creation has the potential to increase system reflexivity by integrating wider bands of system knowledge.

The second prevalent pattern of role disruption in social innovation involves *deconstructing roles, making their components available for inclusive role bricolage*. Most institutional logics presuppose a rigid association between roles and complexes of functions and routines. Social innovation work often challenges that association. For example, at Lumiar schools in Brazil (Downie, 2004), the traditionally institutionalized role of teacher is deconstructed into two roles: tutors, who serve as developmental mentors, and masters, who are content experts. Masters are often practitioners in their own fields – architects, engineers, artists, scientists. They are brought in ad hoc, as the content structure of the curriculum flexes in response to individual needs and participatory decisions.

More generally, social innovation often relies on simplifying various aspects of the role structures that currently dominate a given field. While professionalization promotes disciplinary depth, it can be accompanied by a kind of mystification, making even rudimentary functions associated with the profession seem opaque to the uninitiated. Social innovation work challenges this opacity, revealing many sub-functions that can be pursued by the non-legitimated. This role deconstruction does not obviate the need for professionals, but it places them in a looser, more co-creative relationship with other actors.

The resulting role bricolage opens the way for many forms of social innovation. The Green Belt movement (Muthuki, 2006) has turned many residents of rural communities in Kenya into tree cultivators and micro-entrepreneurs. Sentencing circles in Canada (LaPrairie, 1995) draw on indigenous traditions to engage victims, perpetrators, and community members essentially as collaborative judges; they use dialogue to arrive at a consensus around a formal sentence informed by restorative justice. PRECE in Brazil (Lessa et al., 2016) is a network of self-organized 'cells' through which rural students who don't have good geographic access to schools create their own learning spaces and teach each other. Prisoners in the Sustainability in Prisons program in the US (Straus, 2013) act as ecologists, working to preserve endangered species. In each case a role is being deconstructed, and an aspect of that role is being carried out by an unlikely group of actors, who often themselves occupy an altogether different set of roles. The deconstruction and simplification of roles allows agency to be more distributed across more kinds of actors. And by providing more accessible raw material for role bricolage, it also offers opportunities for the invention of new modes of agency altogether.

Social Identities: Who Belongs to What

Institutional fields are also structured through social identities, the categories of identity that define and separate groups. Social identities structure who belongs to what. Social identity researchers offer social-psychological explanations of how people come to associate themselves in and with groups. Whenever a person perceives herself to be part of a particular group, she begins to experience group characteristics, however they might be defined, as an essential part of who she is (her fundamental nature, her place in the world, and so on). Being a woman, or a Zimbabwean, or a Latina, say, becomes a central lens through which the self is understood (Hogg et al., 1995; Stets and Burke, 2000).

Institutional scholars recognize the institutional salience of social identities. Institutions are partially constructed through patterns of emotional solidarity and 'feelings of comembership or antagonism' (DiMaggio and Powell, 1991, p. 26). But again, institutional theorists understand social identity not as a structural state or a personal commitment, but as an ongoing, relational practice (Bourdieu, 1977, 1985; Collins, 2004; Giddens, 1984). Social identities have varying degrees of closure, and not all potential or even actual identities play a strong structuring role in a given field. Gender, race, ethnicity, religion, geography, and so on are often major social identities. But other, more localized identities may emerge as specific to different cultural and economic contexts.

Social identities do not imply a status hierarchy in and of themselves, but the vertical instinct in most social systems is strong. Even in unstructured situations, people quickly form groups and begin contrasting their own group with others in terms favorable to themselves (Hogg and Terry, 2000; Tajfel, 1970; Turner, 1999). In this way, social identities often become social classes or status groups, defining not only who belongs to what but who is better than whom. Thus, social identities typically lead to fragmentation and stratification (Bourdieu, 1985; Collins, 2004).

Roles may take on aspects of social identities and vice versa. For example, 'lawyer' is a functional role. It defines and bundles certain types of activities and prescribes how to do them. But it may also serve as a social identity, if people who are lawyers don't just perform tasks but also connect strongly to the very idea of being a lawyer and associate themselves more closely with lawyers than with other 'kinds of people.' This identity is reinforced if society at large also sees lawyers as a different category of person with important and distinct personality traits and cultural similarities. Thus 'lawyer' becomes not only a particular type of work but also a social class and kind of ethnicity or geography. Similarly, a social identity like 'woman' may become strongly associated with specific functional roles like 'childcare' or 'nursing' in certain social systems.

Social innovation rarely tries to erase or transcend social identities. Indeed, it often elevates them, working to increase dignity and agency by *valorizing previously oppressed or suppressed identities*. Social identities are not seen as fixed categorical realities but as meaningful constructions worthy of care and interest and nourishment.

From this perspective social movements have often played a key social innovation role. The black consciousness movement in South Africa wrestled with fixed frameworks around the worth and meaning of being black. It rejected the geometry of whiteness as a central identity against which blackness needed to be defined and instead sought to explore black identity on its own terms, thereby strengthening modes of agency that eventually brought down apartheid (Hirschmann, 1990). Third wave feminism both invigorates and challenges the category of 'woman' or 'female' itself by seeing in it an abundance of identities and expressions. It explores the value and power of multiple spectrums of gender identity and also highlights the intersectionality of gender with other oppressed identity expressions including sexual orientation, race, and economic class.

And in some ways it disrupts the very idea of identity by celebrating the fecundity and irreducibility of personal identity expressions (Snyder, 2008).

The valorization of social identities can also be one dimension of broader social innovation work to address grand challenges. In Nunatsiavut, a self-governing Inuit region in Canada, communities are combatting food insecurity by re-connecting to traditional culture. From communal freezers to hunting apprenticeships, social innovators are integrating indigenous skills and modes of organizing with contemporary practices and technologies to enhance the region's food resilience (Aningmiuq and Sarazin, 2018).

In all of these cases, agency is enhanced by recognition of multiple 'worths' in diversity. Agency then is not the province of a particular category of people, but something inherent in all identities, though each will give that agency its own particular expression. This kind of existential valorization, often disguised (and decried) as identity politics, is in fact a meta-challenge to the overall institutional instinct toward class, a disruption of the vertical dimension itself, though of course structures of oppression can always be reinvented. This meta-challenge works to foster distributed system agency by increasing the number and types of actors who can participate in a meaningful way in different aspects of the system.

Another important dimension of social identity work in social innovation focuses on increasing structural flexibility by *convening cross-identity interaction*. Individual social identities are celebrated but not isolated. Humanitas in the Netherlands (Jansen, 2015), for example, bridges generational divides between the social identities 'seniors' and 'youth' in order to tackle housing and aging challenges. University students, faced with critical housing shortages, come to live in a nursing home for free in exchange for a commitment to volunteer a certain number of hours per month in the home. Living side by side with senior residents, they are able to build real, long-term, intergenerational relationships. The project also lowers staffing and cost pressures on the nursing home itself.

In Boston, The Food Project (Fisman, 2007), like many similar initiatives, brings youth together from different racial, geographic, and economic contexts to engage directly with food security and sustainability issues. Young people from urban, mostly black, mostly lower-income communities and from suburban, mostly white, mostly higher-income communities work together at the organization's rural and urban farming sites. The experience is a significant cross-cultural shock and an accelerated developmental journey for most participants, with respect to both how they connect to other social identities and how they understand their own. Ultimately, this kind of convening work increases system reflexivity by cross-pollinating the different forms of system knowledge (histories, cultures, experiences, technologies, and so on) held by individual identity groups.

Resource Flows: Who Gets What

Social innovation is often concerned with resource flows – the institutional dynamics that control who has access to what kinds of resources. Giddens (1984, p. 33) emphasizes the materiality of allocative resources: 'Allocative resources refer to capabilities – or, more accurately, to forms of transformative capacity – generating command over objects, goods or material phenomena.' Friedland and Alford (1991, p. 234) also differentiate the material and ideal dimensions of institutions, but they approach materiality somewhat more broadly as 'supraorganizational patterns of human activity by which individuals and organizations produce and reproduce their material subsistence and organize time and space.' Here again the focus is not on material goods per se but on the flows of goods through institutional enactment. Resource flows are structured through complex arrays of property rights, physical and relational infrastructure, and assumptions about what roles and classes of people should have access to what types of information. For the purpose of our institutional work heuristic, then, we'll include flows of money, material goods, intangible goods like intellectual property, relational (social) capital, information, and time.

Many social innovations have a primary motivation of making specific resource flows more inclusive in the face of endemic poverty and/or historical inequality. One powerful form of socially innovative institutional work is the *valorization of hidden and discounted resources*. This kind of work involves recognizing and leveraging previously overlooked value or potential value. For example, the general practice of Asset Based Community Development (Mathie and Cunningham, 2003, 2005) helps residents look at community resources with an appreciative eye, rather than simply through the lens of what seems to be lacking. Boarded up buildings, proximity to nature, and access to key transportation routes, say, might be seen as valuable real estate with development implications. Taken-for-granted historical and cultural features can be recognized for their current contributions to wellbeing and for their generative potential. People and networks are assessed not only for their needs and deficits but also for the social and cultural capital they can bring to bear on any type of community development project.

More specifically, Lakheni in South Africa (Schiller, 2015) leverages the often obscured social capital inherent in crèches and other community-based organizations to develop consumer networks for low-cost group purchases of staple goods and services. The community-based organizations serve as key marketing and distribution partners in the networks. Lumkani (Eastaugh, 2017), also in South Africa, uses a similar strategy, enabling smart-networked fire prevention in informal communities by valuing and tapping into existing neighborhood collaborative relationships. Tangible resources are also frequently undervalued. The Empty Shops Network in the UK (Dixon et al., n.d.) identifies empty or underused retail spaces and uses them as temporary museums or other kinds of artistic venues. Much of the institutional work around projects like these involves convening and communicating so that these hidden forms of value become recognized by field members, from community residents themselves to broader commercial and political actors. The overall resource base of a given field is thus increased. Perhaps more tellingly, the kinds of value revealed and created tend to have been previously hidden precisely because they are associated with marginalized people and communities that have been excluded from mainstream institutions. Revaluing these resources provides not only a boost in the 'raw material' immediately available for change but also an increase in system reflexivity as this clearer understanding of available resources becomes part of the shared image of what the system is and what it has to offer.

Decentralizing distributive infrastructure is institutional work that contributes to the development or redesign of resource distribution channels so that a given resource flow becomes more locally responsive, customizable, multifocal, interactive, and/or participatory. Decentralizing infrastructure may involve any combination of technology innovation, political advocacy, relationship building, and the development of technical instruments and legal forms. It often requires new types of actors and new information platforms.

Zipline in Rwanda (Murphy, 2017) uses drones to deliver critical, time-sensitive supplies like blood and pharmaceuticals to remote healthcare facilities with limited access to major roads. Local healthcare providers enter their requests real-time through an app, and the average delivery time is 20 minutes. A less obvious example is the Hole in the Wall project (Wilby, 2016), which disrupts educational infrastructure in India by placing unrestricted computers in open, easily accessible, non-school locations.

The intangible infrastructure of social finance is also regularly the subject of innovative institutional work. Social impact bonds (Warner, 2013) reconfigure the flows of social service funding through government agencies, service providers, investors, and donors. Crowdfunding platforms (Belleflamme et al., 2015) like Kickstarter, Indiegogo, and Patreon offer major departures from traditional finance infrastructure. And local currencies (Dittmer, 2013) attempt to build community connectivity and resilience by re-localizing resource exchange, as the currencies cannot be used beyond their catchment areas.

A number of social innovations focus on broadcasting information that was previously narrow-channel or completely inaccessible. Broadcasting may include developing new infrastructure. But it may also simply use existing informational infrastructure for new purposes. Information is a critical resource in any institutional field, and access to information has a particularly strong influence on human rights, economic justice, and environmental sustainability. For example, the 'I Paid a Bribe' project (Ang, 2014), provides an online platform for crowdsourcing information on bribery patterns in India. The outdoor clothing and equipment manufacturer Patagonia uses their 'Footprint Chronicles Initiative' (Mainwaring, 2011) to update customers on the details of the environmental impact of a given product's supply chain. The company's reporting includes both positive steps toward more sustainable practices and the negative impacts that they have still not been able to overcome. And there are a variety of mobile farming applications developed from a social innovation perspective (Social App Hub, 2018). These apps keep small-scale farmers up-to-date on things like local market pricing, weather, agricultural inputs and techniques, new technologies, and additional sources of funding and support.

The general effect of decentralized infrastructure is to increase distributed agency as previously excluded actors are given new access to productive tangible and intangible resources that they can use to act entrepreneurially, developmentally, and/or politically.

Authority Processes: Who Decides What

Authority processes in institutional fields structure who decides what. Institutions both constrain and enable choice (Beckert, 1999; Giddens, 1984), and the rules, norms, and beliefs about who gets to choose and how those choices are made determine relative levels of freedom and creative agency across the system. In the institutional theory literature, agency is often associated less with control and domination (Lawrence, 2008) (though these factors present their own social innovation problems) than with the ability to get things done (Giddens, 1984), to influence the actions of other agents (Giddens, 1984; Lawrence, 2008), thereby having the capability to maintain, change, or depart from the institution itself (Berger and Luckmann, 1967; Jepperson, 1991)

Many social innovations don't, in fact, challenge deep power structures, but those that do typically move in the direction of increasing local autonomy by *valorizing local knowledge.*

Participatory budgeting (Baiocchi and Ganuza, 2014), for example – a social innovation pioneered in Brazil that has now spread to some 1,500 municipalities worldwide – shifts budget decisions into open, deliberative citizen forums. Participatory budgeting processes are not merely consultative. Citizens propose projects and then make decisions together on which of them to fund. Valorizing local knowledge often requires disintermediation, enhancing direct connections between those affected by a decision (citizens, residents, employees, users, and so on) and the power structures that drive that decision.

Another mode of institutional work often taken up by social innovators concerned with authority processes is *convening relational (dialogic) decision-making processes.* Disintermediation in and of itself does not foster dialogue, since disintermediation might be accomplished by any mechanism invoking direct choice. There is little dialogue involved in most crowdsourcing platforms, for example. And something like direct citizen budgeting might be accomplished via citizen referenda through traditional structures (polling places) or new aggregators (for example, voting apps) without requiring face-to-face interaction. But many social innovations go farther, convening structures that allow people not just to indicate yes or no on a particular decision but to dialogue about the benefits, risks, and fundamental values embedded in that decision. The dialogic character of participatory budgeting engages people from across the social spectrum with each other in potentially co-creative ways.

In this vein, social innovation often moves away from decisions vested in individual roles (for example, CEO, operations manager, city councilor) toward decisions that arise out of thick conversation. The relationship becomes the site of agency rather than the role. Consequently, decisions become less binary, shifting away from simplified yes/no choices and toward a multivalent interrogation of foundational institutional questions and frames. Social innovation, however haltingly, trends toward a meta-institutional shift in the character of work and public life. It invokes something like Arendt's 'action' (1958), Freire's 'dialogue' (2000), or Habermas's 'communicative action' (1984), a distributed mode of political and creative agency realized through collaborative reflection and inquiry rooted in profoundly shared reflexivity.

Meanings: Who Signifies What

Meanings are the 'substances' of institutions, 'the unobservable, but essential, "value" anchoring an institutional logic' (Friedland, 2013, p. 34). The institutional logics perspective (Friedland and Alford, 1991; Thornton and Ocasio, 2008) argues that even core constructs that we might take for granted as foundational and trans-institutional, like rationality, interests, and power, are in fact institutionally constructed and thus specific to particular logics, not to all logics. Institutional logics give the root metaphor, basis of strategy, and sources of legitimacy, authority, and identity to an institutional order (Thornton et al., 2012). Shared meanings also provide institutional justification; they are how we explain to ourselves why things are the way they are (Berger and Luckmann, 1967). And thus they also structure our motivations, the 'overall plans or programmes' that help us explain what we do, not least to ourselves (Giddens, 1984, p. 5). They propose explicit or implicit answers to the deep 'why' questions: Why are we doing this? What is it all for? Why should we do it this way rather than another? At first glance, institutional meanings might seem more fixed than performative. But like all institutional dimensions, they only have structuring power when they are enacted. People speak meanings. They defend them. They use them as orientation points for strategy and process.

One of the most radical (root) forms of institutional work is to challenge an institution's fundamental purpose within its day-to-day enactment. A form of this challenge prevalent in social innovation work is to expand an institution's core meanings by *valorizing holistic purposes.* This kind of work often focuses on moving an institution away from a narrowly defined functional purpose and seeking to make it more responsive to the 'whole person' and more reflexive about the needs and opportunities in the 'whole system.'

Democratic free schools (Morrison, 2008), for example, challenge the prevailing orientation in modern, industrial schooling that schools are primarily a feeder into the job market. They do not reject the idea that people should have jobs. But they orient themselves around the development of cooperative citizenship skills and personal growth through intrinsic guidance and motivation. Core rules and practices generally include school governance by all students and staff (one person/one vote) via regular forums and self-directed learning in which each student defines his or her own content needs and learning approach up to and including no classroom attendance or 'assignments' whatsoever.

Similar expansions of purpose can be found in many other areas of social innovation. At the global and national levels, for example, measures of overall wellbeing like the Genuine Progress Indicator, the Human Development Index, and Gross National Happiness challenge the heavily institutionalized emphasis on economic growth, measured by gross domestic product, as the chief orientation of policy. Similarly, new business models like the B-Corp (Wilburn and Wilburn, 2014) attempt to develop alternative incorporation and governance frameworks that change the strategic orientations and fiduciary obligations of businesses toward consideration of social and environmental as well as economic goals.

Social innovations like these not only provoke system reflexivity by expanding the dialogue around purpose but they also typically enhance distributed agency via the structuring implications of the values they are promoting (for example, whole personhood, democratic participation, co-responsibility for community and planetary stewardship, and co-creation of evolving institutions). Inherent in almost any sort of meaning work in a social innovation context is an ethical *interrogation of the participatory dynamics* of the current system and a move toward freer, more inclusive, more collaborative institutional fields.

Table 16.1 summarizes the heuristic presented above. The kind of institutional analysis represented by this heuristic can help social innovation practitioners think and act more fully as agents of system change. It can also enable them to connect more explicitly to the idea of social innovation as a movement. Strategic questions might include:

- What specific forms of institutional work have been the most effective for us?
- Could we deepen our institutional work in a dimension where we are already quite innovative?
- Could we begin pursuing institutional work in institutional dimensions where we are not currently innovating?
- Are there institutional dimensions where we are currently reinforcing a negative status quo, thereby impeding our ultimate social innovation goals?
- Are there institutional dimensions we deliberately want to avoid disrupting in order not to provoke resistance greater than we could respond to right now?

Table 16.1 An institutional work heuristic for social innovation

Performative Institutional Dimension	Institutional Work: Value Inclusion	Institutional Work: Structural Experimentalism
Roles *who does what*	Valorizing experiential and cultural expertise as a credential	Deconstructing roles to foster role bricolage
Social Identities *who belongs to what*	Valorizing marginalized or oppressed identities	Making social identity boundaries permeable
Resource Flows *who gets what*	Valorizing hidden and discounted resources	Decentralizing distributive infrastructure
Authority Flows *who decides what*	Valorizing local knowledge as power	Convening relational decision-making
Meanings *who signifies what*	Valorizing holistic purposes	Interrogating participatory dynamics

FUTURE RESEARCH DIRECTIONS

Exploring the ways that social innovation engages with various performative dimensions of institutional work offers a number of potential directions for future research. I will highlight four that seem to me especially generative.

Taking the Practice Turn

Institutional work scholarship has brought to institutional theory a renewed emphasis on practice (Lawrence et al., 2011). Practices are 'embodied, materially mediated arrays of human activity centrally organized around shared practical understanding' (Schatzki, 2001a, p. 11). Practices are neither objective nor subjective; they are intersubjective, constituted across social fields through interaction. They are rooted in 'shared embodied know-how' (Schatzki, 2001a, p. 12) or 'practical consciousness' (Giddens, 1984), the experiential knowledge we co-construct about how to move through and negotiate a given institutional space. Practices are experiential. They include visible behaviors or expressions, but they also have a 'teleoaffective' dimension (Schatzki, 2001b). That is, they include what we do, how we understand what we do, why we do it (teleo), and how we feel while doing it (affective).

Suddaby et al. (2013, p. 329) describe three areas of expanding common ground between strategy-as-practice research and institutional theory: 'a focus on what actors actually do, their shared cognitions, and the role of language in creating shared meanings.' Social innovation theory has spent little time developing a practice perspective. There are many case studies of specific social innovations and many overarching attempts to define the field, but there hasn't been an emphasis on rich categorizations of practice per se that reveal the dynamics of day-to-day practice and the broader macro-institutional implications thereof.

Two overarching research questions suggest themselves. First, how do social innovation actors actually experience the work of social innovation and what are the patterns in these experiences? This kind of research would need to go beyond the 'hero's journey' approach to social innovation storytelling, which focuses on the visible social entrepreneur or founder. Instead, it would have to approach the experiential dimension in a distributed way – looking at the experiential patterns of practice across multiple kinds of stakeholders.

Second, the institutional work of social innovation with respect to the performative dimensions outlined above could be explored in a much more fine-grained way. For example, mothers2mothers disrupted the role structure of the formal healthcare system by valorizing the experiential knowledge of HIV-positive mothers who had successfully gone through mother-to-child transmission prevention protocols. Valorizing experiential knowledge is a broad category of institutional work. But how is that work constituted in practice? What kinds of actions, language, rationales, emotions, and so on were involved? How were mentor mothers introduced into the system? How was their knowledge presented and legitimated in various forums? What was the mentor mother experience of this new role? How did patients, professional staff, and other stakeholders react? Any case of performative disruption can be examined from a practice perspective, thereby revealing much needed sub-categories of institutional work that might be theorized across different institutional dimensions and problem domains.

Social Innovation as Institutional Array

All social innovations interact with multiple institutional dimensions. They may be disrupting a dimension, transforming it, or reproducing it. The scholarly and practice focus tends to be on the particular dimension where the innovation is clearest. An energy project, say, might be explicitly aimed at shifting resource flows by installing renewable microgeneration systems. The 'story' of this innovation would typically emphasize the ecological and economic benefits of the resource shift. But research interrogating additional dimensions like authority processes or social identity could yield important information in a number of directions, painting a much richer picture and providing insight into broader research questions. How are certain institutional dimensions selected for action while others are avoided? Are there particular organizational structures or strategies relevant to specific institutional dimensions or combinations thereof?

And if we are interested in the contributions of specific social innovations toward broader system change, this kind of interrogation might be especially important. Analytical lenses that reveal how a given innovation might actually be reinforcing more problematic dimensions of a social system, even while making headway in certain dimensions, could help bring more ethical critique to social innovation scholarship. Given the often hagiographic tone of many popular social innovation case studies, such critique would be tonic. For example, Baiocchi and Ganuza (2014) reviewed participatory budgeting processes across a wide range of contexts. They examined two aspects of these processes: the communicative dimension, which involves convening neighbors across social identities and shifting informational resource flows; and the empowerment dimension, which has to do with the broader structures of municipal authority processes related to technical decision-making, funding sources, capital budgeting, and the links between various aspects of the bureaucracy. They found that most participatory budgeting processes have been genuinely innovative with respect to the communicative dimension, but the empowerment dimension is less clear, even though citizen empowerment is generally understood to be a foundational goal of participatory budgeting initiatives. They conclude:

> [T]he veneer of radical democracy can coexist with quite conservative policies. One of the lessons for critical scholars is probably that agnosticism, rather than what anthropologists call 'ontological complicity,' might be a better stance from which to evaluate participatory processes. (p. 34)

More multi-dimensional institutional work analyses like this might help us understand how, why, and when social innovation contributes to social transformation and how, why, and when it doesn't.

Social Innovation as Institutional Maintenance

Social innovation theory and practice is about changing institutions. But the values driving most social innovations – like equality, dignity, wellbeing, sustainability, and so on – also depend upon the *maintenance* of many key institutions. From a social innovation perspective, institutions are not bad; they are required. They create many of the conditions necessary for social agency, such as trust, coordination, specialization, and predictability.

Institutional work scholarship has brought institutional maintenance to the forefront. Lawrence and Suddaby (2006) argue that institutional maintenance requires 'considerable effort' (p. 234). If institutional work is 'intelligent, situated, institutional action' (p. 219), then there is indeed much work in 'supporting, repairing or recreating the social mechanisms that ensure compliance' (p. 230). Even the most stable institutions are challenged continually by institutional multiplicity (Clemens and Cook, 1999; Friedland and Alford, 1991), internal contradictions (Beckert, 1999; Seo and Creed, 2002), and cultural, technological, and political changes in the wider environment (Lawrence and Suddaby, 2006, p. 234). And yet, institutional maintenance remains the least understood and least studied aspect of institutional work (Lawrence and Suddaby, 2006; Lawrence et al., 2009).

How do social innovators identify and work to support the key institutional dimensions that are most important to their goals? For example, an organization working to disrupt roles and meanings related to experimental schooling might simultaneously want to preserve the basic public funding resource flows of the current system. An ecological organization might work to challenge authority processes by engaging local communities in decision-making, but might also wish to preserve the institutionalized role structure of scientific knowledge creation around climate change. A human rights group might simultaneously work to enhance the perceived value of local identity groups and to preserve existing global connections across identity groups. Can the idea of 'innovation' be applied to this kind of preservation and defense work? Can we discover innovative ways to fight the erosion of democratic authority processes that are already working or to maintain resource distributions in contexts that are understood to be relatively equitable?

Institutional maintenance might be the purview of the social innovation scholars in other ways. Institutional maintenance research has largely focused on the dominant actors in a field. 'Little attention has been paid to how less powerful and poorly resourced actors initiate or contribute to institutional change or maintenance' (Marti and Mair, 2009, p. 96). Social innovation is often driven by less powerful actors. Maintenance may also play an overlooked role in early-stage social innovation. Zietsma and McKnight (2009) found that institutional innovators worked with maintenance dynamics in proto-institutions:

> The final form of institutional co-creation work we found focused on constructing institutional maintenance mechanisms to facilitate the persistence of proto-institutions. Starting at initial creation, each of the proto-institutions studied included planned or actual mechanisms for their own maintenance both to ensure the proto-institution 'stuck' among early adopters and to stabilize the proto-institution once it became more widely adopted. The mechanisms worked by reinforcing the regulative, cognitive, and normative pillars of the proto-institution. (p. 164)

Finally, there is an important institutional maintenance role to be played in upholding the key narratives that sustain social innovation. Zilber (2009, p. 205) defines this kind of symbolic maintenance 'as the travel of institutional stories across social levels' and demonstrates that narrative maintenance work involves translation of 'societal meta-narratives into organizations and the lives of individuals.' Researchers could explore institutional narrative maintenance work in the context of various foundational social innovation narratives like democracy, human rights, social justice, planetary boundaries, and social ecological resilience.

Social Innovation as a Social Movement

There has been little formal scholarship connecting social innovation to social movement theories. If social innovation is indeed a movement, there is good reason to suspect that it is not altogether like previous movements. What kind of a movement is it, and how does it work? The broadest definitions of social movements do seem to make room for something like social innovation, for example:

> Social movements can be defined as the mobilized attempt of groups, organizations, and individuals, acting in some coordinated way to change policies, social structures, and the concrete distribution of goods and services. (Zald, 2004, p. 26)

Scholars have explored movements from several sustained perspectives including: political opportunities, mobilizing structures, collective action frames, and repertoires of contention (McAdam et al., 2001). More recently, McAdam and colleagues (2001) have offered a different framework, 'the dynamics of contention,' which deconstructs 'episodes' into mechanisms ('classes of events that alter relations among specified sets of elements') and meso-level processes (families of mechanisms). This approach is fine-grained and contextually specific, but it also leads to more generalizable conclusions about how social movements are constructed, arranged, and pursued in different types of context.

Something like this approach might be helpful for developing social innovation empirical work and theory building, but social movements have been studied and theorized largely in the context of explicit contention (McAdam et al., 2001). Social innovation does sometimes mobilize through contention, but more frequently it does not. An institutional work lens could help differentiate traditional social movement mechanisms, processes, and repertoires from social innovation mechanisms, processes, and repertoires. For example, in terms of resource flows, traditional social movements might revolve around claims, identities, property rights, the responsibilities of nation states, and so on. Much social innovation resource work is – for good or ill – focused on technological innovation and the development of distributed platforms that expand information access and create new production links. Similarly, in terms of role innovation, traditional social movements have often focused on using (or disrupting) formal political role structures like legislatures. Social innovation seems more frequently to have focused on disrupting professional and bureaucratic role structures. How do these differences play into the foundational mechanisms of the social innovation movement?

CONCLUSION

In some sense, the purpose of social innovation is social innovation. That is, apart from any specific problem we may be trying to solve, the deeper goal of social innovation is to breed more social innovation – so that the world's generative capacity might dramatically increase. There are both moral and practical reasons that the social innovation movement, in the end, should be about radically distributed, reflexive agency.

Institutional work scholarship offers a useful conceptual terrain for exploring concrete modes of social innovation. But it can also help reinforce the challenging idea that immediate impact, though welcome and even urgent, is not social innovation's lifeblood. The institutional work lens privileges the unsalvageable mess of people trying to claim agency in a fiercely complex world.

> The point where a focus on institutional work departs from traditional concerns is in its rejection of the notion that the only agency of interest is that associated with 'successful' instances of institutional change . . . Missing from such grand accounts of institutions and agency are the myriad, day-to-day equivocal instances of agency that, although aimed at affecting the institutional order, represent a complex mélange of forms of agency – successful and not, simultaneously radical and conservative, strategic and emotional, full of compromises, and rife with unintended consequences. (Lawrence et al., 2011, p. 52)

These 'equivocal instances of agency,' far from being social innovation failures, are the nourishment for enhanced resilience and continued experimentation. Which is not to say that the immediate, concrete goals of social innovation don't matter. Surely nothing matters more than health, justice, or sustainability to the people or systems currently denied those things. But what will sustain global wellbeing in the long run is not a particular set of solutions concocted in the first decades of the twenty-first century but the accelerating spread of the resilient experimental daring that social innovation is meant to breed.

REFERENCES

Ang, Y.Y. (2014), 'Authoritarian restraints on online activism revisited: why "I-Paid-A-Bribe" worked in India but failed in China', *Comparative Politics*, **47** (1), 21–40.

Aningmiuq, A. and T. Sarazin (2018), 'A path to community-driven food innovation', *Stanford Social Innovation Review*, **16** (1), 7.

Arendt, H. (1958), *The Human Condition*, Chicago, IL: University of Chicago Press.

Baiocchi, G. and E. Ganuza (2014), 'Participatory budgeting as if emancipation mattered', *Politics & Society*, **42** (1), 29–50.

Battilana, J. and S. Dorado (2010), 'Building sustainable hybrid organizations: the case of commercial microfinance organizations', *Academy of Management Journal*, **53** (6), 1419–40.

Beckert, J. (1999), 'Agency, entrepreneurs, and institutional change: the role of strategic choice and institutionalized practices in organizations', *Organization Studies*, **20** (5), 777–99.

Belleflamme, P., N. Omrani and M. Peitz (2015), 'The economics of crowdfunding platforms', *Information Economics and Policy*, **33** (December), 11–28.
Berger, P.L. and T. Luckmann (1967), *The Social Construction of Reality: A Treatise in the Sociology of Knowledge*, New York: Anchor.
Bourdieu, P. (1977), *Outline of a Theory of Practice*, Cambridge: Cambridge University Press.
Bourdieu, P. (1985), 'The social space and the genesis of groups', *Theory and Society*, **14** (6), 723–44.
Cajaiba-Santana, G. (2014), 'Social innovation: moving the field forward. A conceptual framework', *Technological Forecasting and Social Change*, **82** (February), 42–51.
Clemens, E.S. and J.M. Cook (1999), 'Politics and institutionalism: explaining durability and change', *Annual Review of Sociology*, **25**, 441–66.
Collins, R. (2004), *Interaction Ritual Chains*, Princeton, NJ: Princeton University Press.
Creed, W.E.D., R. DeJordy and J. Lok (2010), 'Being the change: resolving institutional contradiction through identity work', *Academy of Management Journal*, **53** (6), 1336–64.
Dacin, M.T., P.A. Dacin and P. Tracey (2011), 'Social entrepreneurship: A critique and future directions', *Organization Science*, **22** (5), 1203–13.
Day, A. (2018), 'From prison back to school', *Stanford Social Innovation Review*, **16** (1), 7–8.
DiMaggio, P.J. (1988), 'Interest and agency in institutional theory', in L.G. Zucker (ed.), *Institutional Patterns and Organizations*, Cambridge, MA: Ballinger, pp. 3–22.
DiMaggio, P.J. and W.W. Powell (1991), 'Introduction', in W.W. Powell and P.J. DiMaggio (eds), *The New Institutionalism in Organizational Analysis*, Chicago, IL: University of Chicago Press, pp. 1–38.
Dittmer, K. (2013), 'Local currencies for purposive degrowth? A quality check of some proposals for changing money-as-usual', *Journal of Cleaner Production*, **54**, 3–13.
Dixon, T., G. Allinson and M. Smith (n.d.), *The Social and Economic Impact of Innovation in the Arts*, London: Digital Innovation Fund for the Arts in Wales.
Dorado, S. (2005), 'Institutional entrepreneurship, partaking, and convening', *Organization Studies*, **26** (3), 385–414.
Dover, G. and T.B. Lawrence (2010), 'A gap year for institutional theory: integrating the study of institutional work and participatory action research', *Journal of Management Inquiry*, **19** (4), 305–16.
Downie, A. (2004), 'Learn what you want', *The Telegraph*, 9 February, accessed 26 December 2017 at http://www.telegraph.co.uk/education/educationnews/3326447/Learn-what-you-want.html.
Eastaugh, S. (2017), 'Lumkani: the little blue box that can save lives in slums', accessed 18 February 2018 at http://edition.cnn.com/2016/08/23/africa/lumkani-fire-detector-south-africa-2/index.html.
Fisman, L. (2007), Sowing a sense of place: an in-depth case study of changing youths' sense of places, PhD Thesis, Massachusetts Institute of Technology, Boston.
Fligstein, N. (1997), 'Social skill and institutional theory', *American Behavioral Scientist*, **40** (4), 397–405.
Freire, P. (2000), *Pedagogy of the Oppressed*, London: Bloombsbury Academic.
Friedland, R. (2013), 'God, love, and other good reasons for practice: thinking through institutional logics', in M. Lounsbury and E. Boxenbaum (eds), *Institutional Logics in Action, Part A*, Bingley, UK: Emerald, pp. 25–50.
Friedland, R. and R.R. Alford (1991), 'Bringing society back in: symbols, practices and institutional contradictions', in W.W. Powell and P.J. DiMaggio (eds), *The New Institutionalism in Organizational Analysis*, Chicago, IL: University of Chicago Press, pp. 232–63.
Giddens, A. (1984), *The Constitution of Society*, Berkeley, CA: University of California Press.
Habermas, J. (1984), *The Theory of Communicative Action Vol 1: Reason and the Rationalization of Society*, Boston, MA: Beacon Press.
Hampel, C.E., T.B. Lawrence and P. Tracey (2017), 'Institutional work: taking stock and making it matter', in R. Greenwood, C. Oliver, T.B. Lawrence and R. Meyer (eds), *SAGE Handbook of Organizational Institutionalism*, London: Sage, pp. 558–90.
Heeks, R., M. Amalia, R. Kintu and N. Shah (2013), 'Inclusive innovation: definition, conceptualization, and future research priorities', Working Paper No. 153, Centre for Development Informatics, University of Manchester.
Heiskala, R. (2007), 'Social innovations: structural and power perspectives', in T.J. Hämäläinen and R. Heiskala (eds), *Institutional Change and Economic Performance: Making Sense of Structural Adjustment Processes in Industrial Sectors, Regions, and Societies*, Cheltenham, UK and Northampton, MA, USA: Edward Elgar Publishing, pp. 52–79.
Hirschmann, D. (1990), 'The black consciousness movement in South Africa', *The Journal of Modern African Studies*, **28** (1), 1–22.
Hogg, M.A. and D.J. Terry (2000), 'Social identity and self-categorization processes in organizational contexts', *Academy of Management Review*, **25** (1), 121–40.
Hogg, M.A., D.J. Terry and K.M. White (1995), 'A tale of two theories: a critical comparison of identity theory with social identity theory', *Social Psychology Quarterly*, **58** (4), 255–69.

Holling, C.S. (2001), 'Understanding the complexity of economic, ecological, and social systems', *Ecosystems*, **4** (5), 390–405.

Howaldt, J. and M. Schwarz (2010), 'Social innovation: concepts, research fields and international trends', accessed at http://www.internationalmonitoring.com, accessed 5 March 2019 at http://www.sfs-dortmund.de/odb/Repository/Publication/Doc%5C1289%5CIMO_Trendstudie_Howaldt_Schwarz_englische_Version.pdf.

Howaldt, J., A. Butzin, D. Domanski and C. Kaletka (2014), *Theoretical Approaches to Social Innovation: A Critical Literature Review*, Dortmund: Sozialforschungsstelle.

Jansen, T.R. (2015), 'The nursing home that's also a dorm', accessed 31 January 2018 at https://www.citylab.com/equity/2015/10/the-nursing-home-thats-also-a-dorm/408424/.

Jepperson, R.L. (1991), 'Unpacking institutional arguments', in W.W. Powell and P.J. DiMaggio (eds), *The New Institutionalism in Organizational Analysis*, Chicago, IL: University of Chicago Press, pp. 143–63.

LaPrairie, C. (1995), 'Altering course: new directions in criminal justice – sentencing circles and family group conferences', *Australian and New Zealand Journal of Criminology*, **28** (1), 78–99.

Lawrence, T.B. (2008), 'Power, institutions, and organizations', in R. Greenwood, C. Oliver, K. Sahlin and R. Suddaby (eds), *The SAGE Handbook of Organizational Institutionalism*, London: Sage, pp. 170–97.

Lawrence, T.B. and G. Dover (2015), 'Place and institutional work: creating housing for the hard-to-house', *Administrative Science Quarterly*, **60** (3), 371–410.

Lawrence, T.B. and R. Suddaby (2006), 'Institutions and institutional work', in S.R. Clegg, C. Hardy, T.B. Lawrence and W.R. Nord (eds), *The SAGE Handbook of Organization Studies*, 2nd edn, London: Sage, pp. 215–54.

Lawrence, T.B., R. Suddaby and B. Leca (2009), 'Introduction: theorizing and studying institutional work', in T.B. Lawrence, R. Suddaby and B. Leca (eds), *Institutional Work: Actors and Agency in Institutional Studies of Organization*, New York: Cambridge University Press, pp. 1–28.

Lawrence, T.B., R. Suddaby and B. Leca (2011), 'Institutional work: refocusing institutional studies of organization', *Journal of Management Inquiry*, **20** (1), 52–8.

Lessa, B. de S., A.C.A.A. Souza and J.C.L. da Silva-Filho (2016), 'Education in cooperative cells as a social innovation: a case study in the Brazilian semiarid', *RAI Revista de Administração e Inovação*, **13** (3), 166–75.

Lounsbury, M. and E.T. Crumley (2007), 'New practice creation: an institutional perspective on innovation', *Organization Studies*, **28** (7), 993–1012.

Maguire, S., C. Hardy and T.B. Lawrence (2004), 'Institutional entrepreneurship in emerging fields: HIV/AIDS treatment advocacy in Canada', *Academy of Management Journal*, **47** (5), 657–79.

Mainwaring, S. (2011), 'Patagonia: the power of brand transparency', accessed 30 January 2018 at https://www.fastcompany.com/1749656/patagonia-power-brand-transparency.

Mair, J., I. Marti and M.J. Ventresca (2012), 'Building inclusive markets in rural Bangladesh: how intermediaries work institutional voids', *Academy of Management Journal*, **55** (4), 819–50.

Marti, I. and J. Mair (2009), 'Bringing change into the lives of the poor: entrepreneurship outside traditional boundaries', in T.B. Lawrence, R. Suddaby and B. Leca (eds), *Institutional Work: Actors and Agency in Institutional Studies of Organization*, New York: Cambridge University Press, pp. 92–119.

Mathie, A. and G. Cunningham (2003), 'From clients to citizens: Asset-based Community Development as a strategy for community-driven development', *Development in Practice*, **13** (5), 474–86.

Mathie, A. and G. Cunningham (2005), 'Who is driving development?: reflections on the transformative potential of Asset-Based Community Development', *Canadian Journal of Development Studies*, **26** (1), 175–86.

McAdam, D., S. Tarrow and C. Tilly (2001), *Dynamics of Contention*, Cambridge: Cambridge University Press.

McGowan, K. and F. Westley (2015), 'At the root of change: the history of social innovation', in A. Nicholls, J. Simon and M. Gabriel (eds), *New Frontiers in Social Innovation Research*, London: Palgrave Macmillan, pp. 52–68.

Moore, M.-L. and O. Tjornbo (2012), 'From coastal timber supply area to Great Bear Rainforest: exploring power in a social-ecological governance innovation', *Ecology and Society*, **17** (4), 26.

Moore, M.-L. and F. Westley (2011), 'Surmountable chasms: networks and social innovation for resilient systems', *Ecology and Society*, **16** (1), 5.

Moore, M.-L., O. Tjornbo, E. Enfors et al. (2014), 'Studying the complexity of change: toward an analytical framework for understanding deliberate social-ecological transformations', *Ecology and Society*, **19** (4), 54.

Morrison, K.A. (2008), 'Democratic classrooms: promises and challenges of student voice and choice, Part one', *Educational Horizons*, **87** (1), 50–60.

Mulgan, G. (2006), 'The process of social innovation', *Innovations*, Spring, 145–62.

Murphy, M. (2017), 'If you want to see how delivery drones should work, look at Africa', accessed 20 November 2017 at https://qz.com/1060756/if-you-want-to-see-how-delivery-drones-should-work-look-at-africa/.

Murray, R., J. Caulier-Grice and G. Mulgan (2010), *The Open Book of Social Innovation*, London: Young Foundation.

Muthuki, J. (2006), 'Challenging patriarchal structures: Wangari Maathai and the Green Belt movement in Kenya', *Agenda*, **20** (69), 83–91.

Nilsson, W. (2015), 'Positive institutional work: exploring institutional work through the lens of positive organizational scholarship', *Academy of Management Review*, **40** (3), 370–98.
Phills, J.A., Jr, K. Deiglmeier and D.T. Miller (2008), 'Rediscovering social innovation', *Stanford Social Innovation Review*, **6** (4), 34–43.
Schatzki, T.R. (2001a), 'Introduction: practice theory', in T.R. Schatzki, K. Knorr-Cetina and E. Von Savigny (eds), *The Practice Turn in Contemporary Theory*, London: Routledge, pp. 1–14.
Schatzki, T.R. (2001b), 'Practice mind-ed orders', in T.R. Schatzki, K. Knorr-Cetina and E. Von Savigny (eds), *The Practice Turn in Contemporary Theory*, London: Routledge, pp. 50–63.
Schiller, B. (2015), 'In South Africa's poor townships, social entrepreneurs are creating a food delivery service', accessed 18 February 2018 at https://www.fastcompany.com/3050378/in-south-africas-poor-townships-social-entrepreneurs-are-creating-a-food-delivery-service.
Schweer, C. and R. Strang (2012), *Mothers2mothers – Scaling Social Innovation in the Public Sector (Teaching Case)*, Oxford: University of Oxford Skoll Centre for Social Entrepreneurship.
Scott, W.R. (2001), *Institutions and Organizations*, Thousand Oaks, CA: Sage.
Senge, P., H. Hamilton and J. Kania (2015), 'The dawn of system leadership', *Stanford Social Innovation Review*, **13** (1), 27–33.
Seo, M.G. and W.E.D. Creed (2002), 'Institutional contradictions, praxis, and institutional change: a dialectical perspective', *Academy of Management Review*, **27** (2), 222–47.
Snyder, R.C. (2008), 'What is third-wave feminism? A new directions essay', *Signs: Journal of Women in Culture and Society*, **34** (1), 175–96.
Social App Hub (2018), 'Top 5 next-gen farming aid apps', accessed 30 January 2018 at https://www.socialaphub.com/article/top-5-next-gen-farming-aid-apps.
Stacey, R.D. (1995), 'The science of complexity: an alternative perspective for strategic change processes', *Strategic Management Journal*, **16** (6), 477–95.
Stets, J.E. and P. Burke (2000), 'Identity theory and social identity theory', *Social Psychology Quarterly*, **63** (3), 224–37.
Straus, T. (2013), 'Environmentalists in prison', *Stanford Social Innovation Review*, **11** (1), 72.
Suddaby, R., D. Seidl and J.K. Lê (2013), 'Strategy-as-practice meets neo-institutional theory', *Strategic Organization*, **11** (3), 329–44.
Tajfel, H. (1970), 'Experiments in intergroup discrimination', *Scientific American*, **223** (5), 96–103.
Thornton, P.H. and W. Ocasio (2008), 'Institutional logics', in R. Greenwood, C. Oliver, K. Sahlin and R. Suddaby (eds), *The Sage Handbook of Organizational Institutionalism*, London: Sage, pp. 99–128.
Thornton, P.H., W. Ocasio and M. Lounsbury (2012), *The Institutional Logics Perspective: A New Approach to Culture, Structure, and Process*, Oxford: Oxford University Press.
Turner, J.C. (1999), 'Some current issues in research on social identity and self-categorization theories', in N. Ellemers, R. Spears and B. Doosje (eds), *Social Identity: Context, Commitment, Content*, Oxford: Blackwell, pp. 6–34.
Unger, R. (2013), 'The task of the social innovation movement', Paper presented at Social Frontiers: The Next Edge of Social Innovation Research (Nesta Conference), London, accessed 10 December 2013 at http://www.nesta.org.uk/sites/default/files/professor_unger_social_frontiers_transcript.pdf.
Warner, M.E. (2013), 'Private finance for public goods: social impact bonds', *Journal of Economic Policy Reform*, **16** (4), 303–19.
Westley, F. and N. Antadze (2010), 'Making a difference: strategies for scaling social innovation for greater impact', *Innovation Journal*, **15** (2), article 2.
Westley, F., O. Tjornbo, L. Schultz et al. (2013), 'A theory of transformative agency in linked social-ecological systems', *Ecology and Society*, **18** (3), 27–42.
Wilburn, K. and R. Wilburn (2014), 'The double bottom line: profit and social benefit', *Business Horizons*, **57** (1), 11–20.
Wilby, P. (2016), 'Sugata Mitra – the professor with his head in the cloud', accessed 30 January 2018 at https://www.theguardian.com/education/2016/jun/07/sugata-mitra-professor-school-in-cloud.
Zald, M.N. (2004), 'Making change: why does the social sector need social movements?', *Stanford Social Innovation Review*, **2** (3), 25–34.
Zietsma, C. and B. McKnight (2009), 'Building the iron cage: institutional creation work in the context of competing proto-institutions', in T.B. Lawrence, R. Suddaby and B. Leca (eds), *Institutional Work: Actors and Agency in Institutional Studies of Organization*, New York: Cambridge University Press, pp. 143–77.
Zilber, T.B. (2009), 'Institutional maintenance as narrative acts', in T.B. Lawrence, R. Suddaby and B. Leca (eds), *Institutional Work: Actors and Agency in Institutional Studies of Organization*, New York: Cambridge University Press, pp. 205–35.

17. Challenges for global supply chains and opportunities for social innovation

Yong H. Kim and Gerald F. Davis

INTRODUCTION: NIKEFICATION OF THE ECONOMY

Since the 1980s, supply chains have become increasingly dispersed. Ford Motor Company's all-encompassing River Rouge plant with its 100,000 employees was once deemed the prototypical facility of production. However, the combination of a massive wave of bust-up takeovers and outsourcing movements pushed companies to change their corporate structures and operations to mimic those of Nike: a vertical disintegration model in which the company owning the brand focuses on the high-value tasks of design and marketing, and contracts out the production and distribution of its goods (Davis, 2013a). Products are now routinely produced and sold having never been touched by employees of the company named on the label; such "Nikefication" can be observed in almost all industries (Davis, 2013b). Apple iPhones, Gap clothing, and Nestlé Purina cat food are all manufactured by distant, unknown contractors, not by the brand-name company most consumers can easily recognize.

In our modern economy, effective supply chain strategy can make a significant difference. In fact, some of the most popular products on the market are sold by companies that barely engage in the manufacturing process. In 2010, California-based Vizio became the best-selling US television brand with only 200 employees, surpassing both Samsung and Sony. Excelling in its supply chain capabilities, Vizio became American consumers' low-cost producer of choice. Flip was the best-selling portable video camera in 2009, with a 22 percent market share and only 100 employees. The actual components necessary for making these products were readily available off the shelf, the designs were relatively straightforward, and, thus, the manufacturing process could be contracted out.

Although dispersed supply chains can significantly reduce firms' cost structures, they also limit their ability to monitor and control critical processes, thus creating many challenges around sustainability and social responsibility. One major issue with globally dispersed supply chains is that such dispersion makes detecting the identity of suppliers extremely difficult. In 2013, Bangladesh's Rana Plaza collapsed, killing over 1,100 garment workers. In the aftermath of the Rana Plaza disaster, authorities in Dhaka could not even determine the number of factories that fell under their jurisdiction, and some global brands reported their products were being produced by unauthorized subcontractors. Although some evidence suggests working conditions at first-tier suppliers are getting better, even car manufacturers, which rely heavily on their supply chains, have difficulty identifying their fourth- or fifth-tier suppliers.

Another major issue with globally dispersed supply chains is that they make implementing sustainability policies challenging for firms. One study found that in 2009, only six firms out of the Fortune 500 were able to disclose full information on greenhouse gas emissions across their entire value chain (Jackson, 2011). Indeed, more than half of a typical corporation's carbon emissions comes from its supply chain rather than within its own boundaries (AT Kearney, 2011). Companies are now forced to care about issues occurring in places where they are not operating but their suppliers are. However, assessing overall environmental or social risks requires engagement with suppliers several steps back that are often invisible to firms. For example, even household-name companies such as Apple and Hewlett-Packard have had to spend extra effort to vet their supply chains and clean their products from the use of conflict materials.

The lack of visibility into sub-tier suppliers also severely limits firms' ability to assess the size of supply chain risk and therefore their ability to take direct and effective actions to mitigate it. As supply chains are increasingly becoming longer, more dispersed, and more complex, firms are also increasingly exposed to high-impact, low-probability discrete events along their supply chains. However, firms do not normally have direct business relationships with their sub-tier suppliers despite the significant role these suppliers play in the production process. According to Wang et al. (2015), about one in five tier-2 suppliers in the high-tech industries are shared by the same tier-1 suppliers. When many tier-1 suppliers share a common tier-2 supplier, the supply base potentially has a single point of failure.

Yet the very conditions that spurred the vertically integrated corporation to be supplanted by disaggregated global supply chains across many industries also provide various opportunities for social innovation. The fact that firms can be successful by virtue of outsourcing the production process means social entrepreneurs can enter the scene without necessarily owning massive resources. The development in technologies for producing, communicating, and organizing reduces the importance of pursuing the economies of scale, quite contrary to Chandler's (1977 [1993]) observation of American business empires. At the same time, global supply chains also transmit and amplify the impact of social innovations due to their dispersed and complex nature. A natural disaster affecting select firms in one region may reveal the substantial risks originating from previously unnoticed complexity and interdependencies within globally dispersed supply chains. By the same token, the impact of small-scale innovative activities and services with social purposes may be transferred to different parts of global supply chains due to the complexity and interdependencies among the related companies.

EXTANT RESEARCH ON GLOBAL SUPPLY CHAINS

Broadly speaking, the literature on supply chain management examines how firms manage the total flow of goods and services from the supplier to the ultimate customer (Ellram, 1990). Prior research on supply chains generally hails from the field of operations management. Starting from research on inventory theory (Clark and Scarf, 1960), operations scholars contributed to a large body of research on global supply chain issues ranging from supply contracts to supply chain coordination (Lee et al., 1997) and, more recently, operational issues arising from the sharing economy (Cachon et al., 2017; Lee and Tang, 2018). For example, according to Web of Science's Core Collection data, among 31,179 supply chain-related articles published from 1990 to 2017, about two-thirds of them (n = 20,565; 64.7 percent) were from two research areas: "engineering" and "operations research management science."[1]

The objective of supply chain management is to "integrate and manage the sourcing, flow, and control of materials using a total systems perspective across multiple functions and multiple tiers of suppliers" (Mentzer et al., 2001, p. 6). Key processes that need to meet customers' demand within a supply chain range from customer relationship management, customer service management, demand management, order fulfillment, manufacturing flow management, and product development and commercialization (Lambert et al., 1998).

The three main themes of extant research on supply chain management, although beyond the scope of this chapter, are efficiency, coordination, and reliability (Anupindi et al., 1999). Classical logistics research comprises the study of management of inventory, transportation, and distribution, as well as issues in network design. Particularly in traditional supply chain management research, a heavy emphasis is placed on minimizing materials costs, transportation costs, manufacturing costs, and inventory costs (Simchi-Levi et al., 1999). In addition to studying how to save on production costs, scholars study how to design and manage supply chains that are responsive – not necessarily responsible – to manage variety. In the domain of supply chain coordination, the literature revolves around considerations of when to outsource or offshore production, and how to achieve effective intra-firm and inter-firm coordination (for example, contracts, incentives, synchronization, and so on). Finally, researchers have long recognized that extended supply chains are exposed to significant risks, and study how firms might deal with supply chain risk. Here the attention is given to various organizational, technological, and process capabilities firms need to build resilient supply chains.

The idea that the research in supply chain management and supply chain contracts is becoming saturated and stagnant is a growing concern (Lariviere, 2016). Some researchers have issued a call for the research community to pay closer attention to emerging trends and forces in the global economy through focusing on research that is more relevant to the business community and society at large, and more impactful by improving profits, changing lives, and creating a better world (Lee and Tang, 2018).

Studies within the supply chain research community used to pay little attention to accountability or sustainability issues. Yet, in the seemingly saturated field of supply chain management, research on social or environmental aspects of supply chains and sustainability has been rapidly growing in the past decade. From 2013 to 2017, about one in eight (or 1,899 out of 15,665) published supply chain-related articles had a social, environmental, or sustainability angle. From 2008 to 2012, about one in 13 (or 702 out of 9,328) articles shared this interest. From 2003 to 2007, about one in 25 (or 175 out of 4,228) did. The growing interest over the years is undeniable (Figure 17.1).

Despite the increasing interest in terms of the number of articles, research on supply chain sustainability has been dominated by case-based and anecdotal empirical studies. Brammer et al. (2011) provided a systematic review about the literature on sustainable supply chain management in an international context. They found a preponderance of case-based and anecdotal empirical studies in the literature, where only two out of 194 sampled articles provided any type of quantifiable estimates of the size and direction of the relationship between involvement with sustainable supply chain management and financial and operational performance indicators.

Aside from the lack of diversity in methodological approach, diversity in subject and theoretical focus is also lacking. The pressure on businesses to pay more attention to the

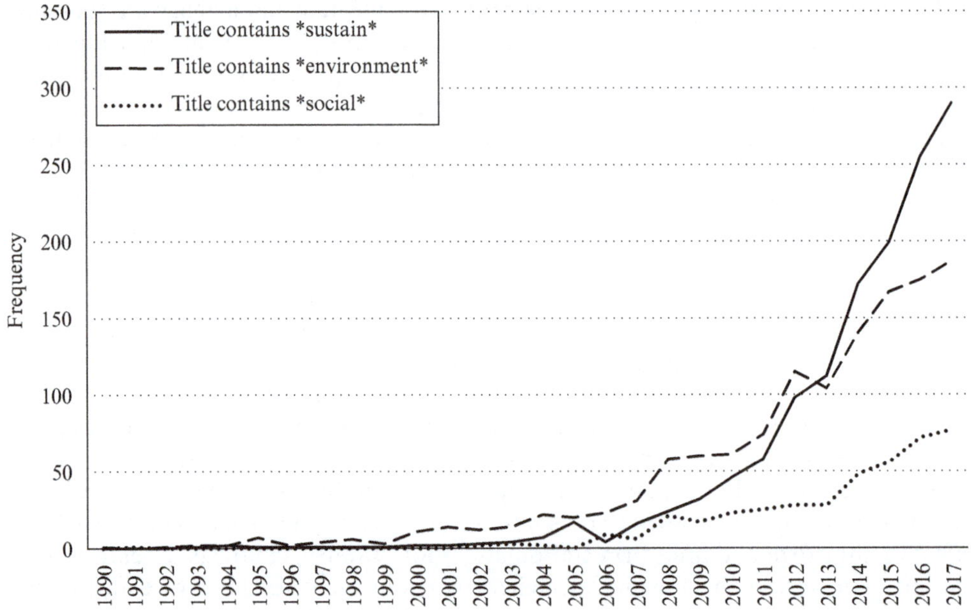

Source: Web of Science (http://www.webofknowledge.com).

*Figure 17.1 Number of supply chain-related articles published from 1990 to 2017 that contain *sustain*, *environment*, and *social* in their titles*

environmental and resource consequences of the products and services they offer and the processes they deploy has increased, but the notion of sustainable development is often reduced to just environmental improvements. The movement toward triple-bottom-line reporting (3BL) concerning the relationship between profit, people, and the planet has yielded a growing body of research about integrating environmental, health, and safety concerns with green-product design, lean and green operations, and closed-loop supply chains (Kleindorfer et al., 2005). Identifying and managing the environmental impact throughout the supply chain has become an established, mainstream topic of operations research (for example, Corbett and DeCroix, 2001; Klassen and Vachon, 2003).

On the other hand, as partially reflected in Figure 17.1 (that is, a slower increase in *social* supply chain-related articles), few researchers have focused on people (that is, social) issues in particular and the interrelation of issues concerning profit, people, and the planet. An article title by no means captures the entirety of the research. Nonetheless, strikingly, no article indexed in the Web of Science Database had "social innovation," the very subject of this edited volume, and "supply chain" together in the title. A similar Google Scholar search also yields only three articles that satisfy this simple Boolean query.[2] Consequently, the understanding of sustainable development is fragmented and mostly one-dimensional: environmentally based (Seuring and Müller, 2008). With limited methodological and substantive foci, the fact that a strong theoretical background is often missing, both within supply chain or operations management, as well as from a wider perspective, such as new institutional economics or strategic management (Seuring and

Müller, 2008), is not surprising. With the key interest in supply chain research shifting from minimizing costs to creating value, the research community is also shifting from separate disciplines to a multidisciplinary approach (Kleindorfer et al., 2005), inviting organization theory and strategy researchers to contribute and collaborate.

CORE PROBLEMS FOR ORGANIZATIONAL THEORY AND STRATEGY RESEARCH

The Economics of Supply Chains

The traditional approach to understanding firm boundaries is informed by transaction-cost economics. Scholars have pondered the question of the boundary of a firm ever since Coase's seminal article in 1937. A firm's decision to "make" or "buy" has implications for the firm's ability to monitor and control decisions within its boundaries. Transactions within a firm's boundaries can be monitored and controlled by management, but at a cost. Taking a transaction out of the market and organizing it internally creates additional bureaucratic costs. Therefore, internal organization is usefully thought of as the organization form of last resort: try markets, try hybrids, and have recourse to the firm only when all else fails (Williamson, 2008). Some generic goods and services can be obtained through simple market exchange in a cost-effective fashion. On the other hand, assets that are specific to a given transaction (that is, high asset specificity) can only be redeployed to alternative uses and/or users at a loss of productive value, and therefore preserving governance for such a transaction is important for firms. Subsequently, the firm boundaries resulting from the make-or-buy decision are drawn in a way to accomplish a transaction-cost-economizing result (Williamson, 1981).

So how does the make-or-buy problem look different now? In the transaction-cost economics tradition, the boundary of the firm issue treats a firm's "core technology" as given and examines whether the focal firm should integrate backwards into raw materials, laterally into components, or forward into distribution (Williamson, 1985). Also, implicit in the transaction-cost economics framework is that the goods and services to be provided have reached an advanced if not mature stage of development (Williamson, 2008, p. 11). In the past several decades, the vast improvements in information and communication technologies, low-cost shipping, and trade liberalization have shifted the cost balance from "make" to "buy" in many cases. Starting an enterprise has become trivially easy, ranging from creating a legal structure to hire temporary employees to contracting out for production and distribution. Production has become modular across nearly every industry, allowing both large and small firms to contract out the manufacturing and distribution of physical goods. In many industries, every piece of the product can be obtained from any off-the-shelf sheet materials and assembled with basic, readily available machine or low-skilled human beings. Under these circumstances, focusing on design and brand management and outsourcing the entire production process makes sense for a firm (Davis, 2013a, 2016). The economies of scale that made corporations indispensable have now shifted against corporations themselves. In addition to making corporations and long-term employment obsolete, however, extensive outsourcing – or a heavy reliance on supply chains – has important consequences, particularly related to environmental issues and social/human rights problems.

Environmental and Social Consequences of Outsourcing

The traditional view is that firms would chase the lowest environmental standards. Recognizing the significant costs associated with compliance with environmental standards, firms may avoid environmental regulations through offshoring, abandoning the market, or ignoring the regulations (Drake and Just, 2016; Walley and Whitehead, 1994). This so-called pollution haven hypothesis predicts that environmental regulations will move polluting activities for tradable products to poorer countries. Richer countries tend to have a stronger demand for environmental quality, and thus trade liberalization will make poorer countries a pollution haven (Copeland and Taylor, 1994, 2004). For example, using a sample of over 12,000 Japanese manufacturing firms, Cole et al. (2014) found that firms that undertake environmental activities are more likely to outsource internationally to abate high regulation costs associated with strict environmental regulations. Furthermore, in addition to the relocation or displacement of the entire production processes of firms, firms tend to relocate just the dirtier parts of the production process in response to increases in domestic regulations in their headquarter countries. The environment of developed countries is exploited for the profit of foreign multinational enterprises.

The pollution haven logic has also been extended to discussions of human rights, ethical labor practices, and product safety (Korten, 1995). The primary reason that firms in the United States and other developed economies have been outsourcing manufacturing to developing countries is to benefit from low labor costs. Leading multinational enterprises would subcontract manufacturing components to suppliers that would manufacture in low-wage factories, which tend to have poorer and less safe working conditions to ensure low production costs (Clott, 2004). With more firms relying on globally dispersed supply chains, they may take advantage of their geographically dispersed organizational structure to circumvent institutional pressure from countries with higher human rights and employment standards. For example, Surroca et al. (2013) found that in response to mounting pressures from their home country's stakeholders, some multinational enterprises transfer their socially irresponsible practices to their overseas subsidiaries. The preferred target becomes subsidiaries that appear independent from the focal enterprise in order to reduce the possibility that challenges to the subsidiary's legitimacy may spill over to the focal enterprise itself. Similar transfers could conceivably occur with respect to buyer–supplier relationships.

Race to the Bottom or First Step Toward Industrialization?

The perspective that firms will engage in arbitrage behavior, which is exploiting differences in environmental, safety, and labor regulations across different countries by strategically choosing countries with lax regulatory standards, leads to the fear of a "race to the bottom." Operating in a stringent regulatory environment means a firm needs to bear high regulation costs during the production process. These expenses put firms that are not outsourcing production to countries with loose standards at a cost disadvantage vis-à-vis their competitors that are cutting costs more aggressively. Firms' preference for a lax regulatory environment forces governments to lower the stringency of regulatory standards to attract firm investment, which in turn leads to environmental degradation and poorer working conditions.

In theory, regulatory competition between countries may result in either a "race to the top" or a "race to the bottom" in terms of regulatory stringency. If jurisdictions value environmental preservation more than they value investment by polluting firms, they may engage in a race to the top, each setting strict environmental regulations in an attempt to drive polluting firms from their borders. On the other hand, if a jurisdiction's policy makers value investment more than environmental quality, they may engage in a race to the bottom in environmental standards (Bernauer and Caduff, 2004; Murphy, 2004a, 2004b).

Existing studies find limited evidence about whether firms outsource the dirtier parts of production to minimize domestic environmental regulation costs (for example, Eskeland and Harrison, 2003; Levinson, 1996). The lack of clear empirical evidence is due to the fact that a firm's past experience and capabilities partially dictate how the firm will deal with the stringency of a country's environmental regulations in its decision to invest in that country (Hart, 1995; Madsen, 2009). For example, given that regulatory scrutiny is costly, some firms can go beyond current regulations and/or beyond compliance, and try to use environmentally sustainable production processes as a competitive advantage. Doing so may reduce the costs of changing technologies and operating policies to comply with new regulations in the future (Delmas, 2001; Van Woensel et al., 2001).

When it comes to the human and social side of supply chains (for example, safe working conditions, labor rights protection), Richard Locke's work on Nike's supply chains deserves attention (Locke, 2003, 2013; Locke et al., 2007). His work reveals that outsourcing is a double-edged sword. On the one hand, global outsourcing has allowed Nike to manufacture at a lower cost. On the other hand, it has created problematic supply chain issues. In the 1980s, critics rebuked Nike for sourcing its products in factories and countries where wages were low, working conditions were poor, and human rights abuses were rampant. In the 1990s, cases involving under-paid workers in Indonesia, child labor in Cambodia and Pakistan, and poor working conditions in China and Vietnam continued to damage Nike's reputation. Nike responded to these criticisms with several initiatives – developing a code of conduct for suppliers, increasing monitoring and inspection of its suppliers, creating an internal corporate social responsibility (CSR) department, and working with various international and non-profit organizations to help improve working conditions for workers in various developing countries. These initiatives have produced some positive changes among Nike's suppliers. For example, due to increased monitoring and inspection, Nike has been able to nearly eliminate the use of petroleum-based chemicals in its footwear production.

How can firms make their supply chains more humane and socially accountable? Firms have two options in terms of engaging with their suppliers: compliance with requirements and capacity building (Ciliberti et al., 2008). The first approach involves buyers setting standards for suppliers and incentivizing compliance via a strict monitoring program. The second approach involves building up supplier's own capacity for addressing sustainability issues. Again, Richard Locke's research strongly predicts the latter is better. First, private auditing and monitoring systems incur substantial costs but are unable to deliver a stable, significant improvement in the working conditions in supply chains, such as the protection of freedom of association or the reduction in excessive working hours. Second, real improvement in labor conditions can be achieved by a capacity-building approach wherein suppliers are not seen as immoral agents but rather as willing partners who lack certain organizational skills for effective code-of-conduct enforcement.

POLICY IMPLICATIONS AND NEW FRONTIERS FOR SOCIAL INNOVATION

Challenges for Visualizing Globally Dispersed Supply Chains

The core problem for effectively implementing social innovation in today's global supply chains is the challenge of visualizing the supply chains. According to a study conducted by BBMG (2014), 91 percent of consumers could not state where their favorite brands' clothing was manufactured. Depressing anecdotes from the Rana Plaza disaster imply firms may be in much the same situation as consumers. In this regard, studies of conflict minerals provide a rare opportunity to examine how organizational factors, including corporate structure and prior efforts at accountability, shape a company's ability to visualize and vet its supply chain. In 2010, Section 1502 of the Dodd-Frank Act was issued, giving companies over three years to determine and report on whether their products contained "conflict minerals" from the Democratic Republic of Congo (DRC) and its nine adjoining countries. Conflict minerals (tungsten, tantalum, tin, and gold, or 3TG) are essential in the production of a variety of devices, including consumer electronics such as mobile phones and laptops. The Dodd-Frank Act was an effort to reduce human rights violations by armed militant and rebel groups in the DRC region that have profited from the mining and sale of conflict minerals. Over 1,300 corporations submitted a conflict minerals report to the Securities and Exchange Commission. Kim and Davis's (2016) analysis revealed that almost 80 percent of corporations admitted they were unable to determine the country of origin of such materials. Alarmingly, the authors found that only 1 percent could certify themselves conflict-free with certainty beyond reasonable doubt. Furthermore, the more complex firms' supply chains were, the less able they were to understand their supply chains. For instance, the authors found that internationally diversified firms, and those with larger and more dispersed supply chains, were less likely to declare their products conflict-free. In short, the widespread practice of outsourcing may have reduced corporations' capacity to fully understand and account for their production process.

The pressure to advance firms' ability to fully understand their production process and vet their globally dispersed supply chains can come from various sources: regulatory actions, consumer demands, voluntary coordination among industry participants, activism by social entrepreneurs, employee pressures, and shareholder pressures.

Regulatory Actions and Industry Responses

In terms of regulation, a number of rules passed in the 2010s explicitly require companies to visualize their complete supply chains. In addition to Section 1502 of the Dodd-Frank Wall Street Reform and Consumer Protection Act ("conflict minerals act"), which was passed in December 2010, a lot of US-based companies had to comply with the California Transparency in Supply Chains Act, which was passed in September 2010. The latter requires all retailers and manufacturers with annual global revenues of more than $100 million that do business in the state of California to disclose information about their efforts to eradicate slavery and human trafficking from their direct supply chains when they make tangible goods for sale. The main goal of the Act was to improve corporate responsibility practices, refine traceability technologies, and create more informed and discerning consumer preferences (Pickles and Zhu, 2013), partially through extending the liability of firms for human rights issues even outside their boundaries (Barrientos, 2013). In May 2017, the European Union passed the final version of its Conflict Minerals Regulation with a broader range of reporting obligations and coverage of the regulation than its US counterpart.

Unless a firm deems to operate completely outside of the American and European markets, these rules force firms to spend more time and energy understanding their supply base and disclosing more information about their supply chains. For example, in the case of identifying conflict-free suppliers, companies jointly spent a total of $709 million (which amounts to about half a million US dollars for each company) and 6 million hours of manpower to prepare their conflict minerals reports (Bayer, 2014). Large corporations may have the resource slack to bear such expenses, but smaller firms are typically constrained in their ability to do the same. Indeed, the Securities and Exchange Commission initially predicted 6,000 issuers would file a Form SD, but only a quarter actually did. Non-filers were significantly smaller than filers in terms of total revenue, employee count, total assets, market capitalization, and sales (Kim and Davis, 2016). As a result, industry groups such as EICC, GeSI, and AIAG have also made substantial progress in identifying conflict-free smelters in the region, which enables their suppliers to shift to these smelters and reduces the financial burden of having to monitor their supplier base by themselves. These efforts are paying off: according to the Enough Project (2017), more than 70 percent of the world's smelters for the four minerals have now passed conflict-free audits, which is a vast improvement since 2010.

One unlikely source of pressure is the resurgence of nationalism. From Europe to the United States, 2016 was the year that saw a backlash against globalization and a resurgence of nationalism around the world (*The Economist*, 2016). In the era of President Trump and Brexit, the consequences of corporations' outsourcing practices on national unemployment have been brought to the spotlight. A huge part of Trump's appeal to his supporters was his promise of an "America First" trade policy that would end outsourcing and bring jobs back from places such as China and Mexico. In efforts to reduce costs, US companies had sent many well-paying, steady, manufacturing jobs overseas. For instance, the decline of the automobile industry led to a loss of almost half of Michigan's manufacturing jobs, and Detroit alone lost 150,000 auto industry jobs between 2000 and 2008 (Atkinson et al., 2012). Trump's victory in the 2016 presidential elections was propelled by voters throughout America's industrial heartland. Communities that suffered the loss of manufacturing jobs due to low-cost Chinese imports experienced political polarization, leading to the election of Donald Trump (Autor et al., 2016). After experiencing years of manufacturing decline, many of Trump's supporters are now hopeful about his promise to return manufacturing jobs and revitalize their economy. Bringing jobs back to America became a cornerstone of Trump's election campaign, leading a number of multinational enterprises – such as Amazon, Bayer, Carrier, Ford, General Motors, Lockheed Martin, and IBM – to announce new US jobs in the first year of Trump's presidency.

Of course, others have argued that it is not only outsourcing practices that have destroyed manufacturing jobs; robotics and high-tech automation are the main culprits of the loss of jobs. For example, Frey and Osborne (2017) estimate that 47 percent of all jobs in the United States are at risk of "computerization," meaning that associated occupations are potentially automatable in a decade or two. The larger supply chain issue brought up by the resurgence of nationalism, at least in the United States, would more likely involve the easing of environmental regulations such as focusing on fossil fuels, shrinking the role of the Environmental Protection Agency, and annulling the Paris climate accord. Despite growing nationalistic sentiments, outsourcing and the sustainability challenges associated with outsourcing are likely here to stay, if not exacerbated.

Consumer and Stakeholder Pressures

In recent years, market researchers have witnessed a growing demand from consumers for companies to address social and environmental issues. For example, a study of consumers from nine of the largest countries in the world by gross domestic product (GDP) found that 84 percent of consumers globally report that they seek out responsible products whenever they can (Sustainable Brands, 2015). Four in five are willing to consume or purchase fewer products to preserve natural resources or buy a product from an unknown brand if it has strong CSR commitments. The rising demand for supply chain accountability and transparency has resulted in a groundswell of new social innovations from entrepreneurs. In particular, millennials are among the most passionate about CSR. More than nine in ten millennials reported they would switch brands to one associated with a social or environmental cause. More than four in ten millennials also reported they would be willing to take a pay cut to work for a responsible company (Cone Communications, 2015).

Sometimes consumers and other stakeholders manifest their demand for responsible supply chains through boycotts, with a desire to make a difference and reduce the consumption for the target's products or services (Klein et al., 2004). Major companies such as Nike, Nintendo, and Apple have faced consumer pressure to establish supply chain governance systems to prevent labor abuses by their overseas contractors. Boycotts disrupt an organization's performance by reducing demand for its products or services, making such protests harmful for the targeted firm's financial performance (King and Soule, 2007). For example, Rock's (2003) research on the garment industry found that each news article about firms' sweatshop practices translated into an average loss of $70 million in market capitalization. Recognizing such a financial impact, boycotted firms are more likely to increase their prosocial-claims activity after a boycott is announced when the boycott event receives more media attention (McDonnell and King, 2013).

AVENUES FOR GLOBAL SUPPLY CHAIN SOCIAL INNOVATIONS

In part due to pressures from multiple sources, firms are now spending more resources and time to identify and monitor each step of their supplier base. To illustrate the growing interest, we downloaded the sustainability metrics of all companies that have a global company key (GVKEY) from Bloomberg ESG platform, which resulted in 13,872 unique firms. Bloomberg reports the Environmental Disclosure Score (that is, degree of transparency on environmental metrics) alongside the Social Disclosure Score (that is, degree of transparency on social metrics). About one in five sampled companies (2,709 out of 13,872) had a valid disclosure score. Figure 17.2 shows the median-spline plots of environmental

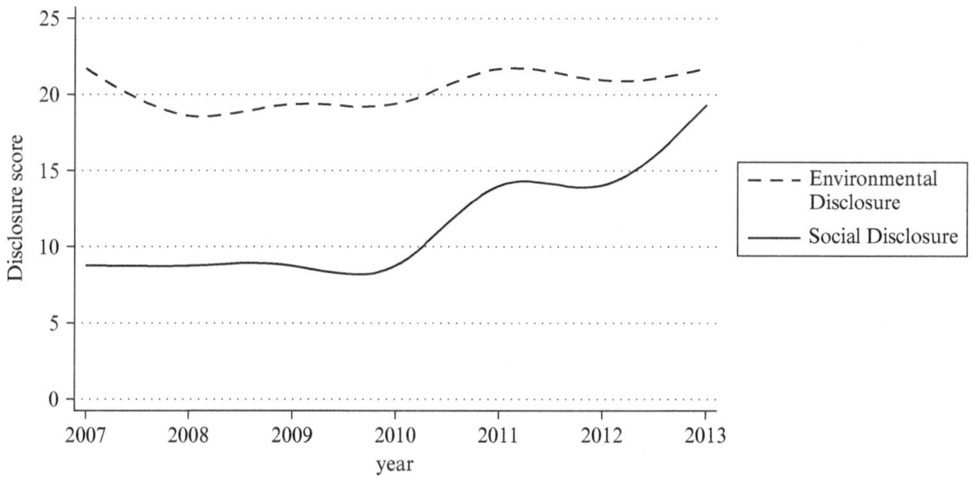

Source: Bloomberg Environment, Social and Governance (ESG) Database, extracted on 29 April 2015.

Figure 17.2 Trend in environmental and social disclosure, 2007–13

disclosure and social disclosure from 2007 to 2013. Companies are paying attention to sustainability issues, both social and environmental. In particular, social disclosure is gaining interest. Both disclosure scores remained stable despite the Great Recession, which occurred during this period. This finding is also consistent with Nollet et al. (2016), who traced S&P500 firms' corporate social performance during the 2007–11 period.

The demand for the market for virtue is evident. The primary challenge for firms to regard their businesses both as a vehicle to make money and as a means to improve society, according to Vogel (2005), is the substantial costs of socially responsible business behavior. Consumers, too, are slow to change their behavior even when they support a boycott's ideals (Miller and Sturdivant, 1977). Yet the rising demand for supply chain accountability and transparency, coupled with the vast improvements in information and communication technologies, have resulted in a groundswell of new social innovations from entrepreneurs.

Opportunities abound for future research on social innovation in global supply chains. A particularly promising direction for future research are the implications for entrepreneurial opportunities that put improving supply chain visibility at the core of their business model. For example, Fairphone is a social enterprise company that creates smartphones that are ethically sourced and manufactured according to principles of social and environmental responsibility. Based in the Netherlands, Fairphone hopes to develop mobile phone devices that are conflict-free, create fair labor conditions for workers along its supply chain, as well as help consumers use their mobile phones for a longer time period. The social entrepreneurs behind Fairphone should be applauded for their efforts to lead the charge in the mobile phone industry toward more sustainable practices. In fact, with growing consumer demand for responsible products, mobile phone manufacturers have been developing a variety of RFID readers that, in addition to allowing customers to pay for an item by simply swiping the phone over the tag, will allow them to link to data about the product's origin, certifications, and trajectory through the chain.

In the fashion industry as well, an upsurge of social innovations from entrepreneurs has occurred. US-based Everlane sells apparel, accessories, and shoes, and prioritizes transparency. The company spends months finding the best factories around the world, and builds strong personal relationships with the factory owners to ensure ethical practices at every step of the production process. At Everlane, customers have detailed information about the factory and production stories behind every product. For instance, before customers decide to purchase one of Everlane's bestsellers, the Silk Square Shirt, they can click on a link to find more information about the factory where the shirt was produced – a silk factory in Hangzhou, China, which was established in 2003, and hires 240 employees. They are told the factory is "located near a small river in Hangzhou" and has "three floors with expansive ceilings and well-kept grounds." Beyond text descriptions, customers are shown more than a dozen high-resolution photographs of the factory interiors and factory employees at work.

Large corporations are increasingly motivated to avoid potential bad press arising from social risks in their supply chain and to fend off growing regulatory auditing and reporting pressures. Technology-driven startups have been rushing to address these concerns. For instance, LaborVoices uses crowd-sourcing technology to instantly poll factory workers based all over the world on the safety and working conditions of the factories in which they work. Workers can use their mobile phones to anonymously call into a free hotline and answer a series of questions about abuse, wages, health, safety conditions, and child labor. The data collected by LaborVoices from workers provide factory-specific risk metrics about factories across countries and regions. Large corporations have used the information to identify low-risk, model factories and hedge against problematic factories. Similarly, Verité is a non-profit that has developed mapping technology that shows geographically where labor exploitation may be taking place. Major corporations, such as Patagonia, have used the tools and technologies provided by Verité to identify potential risks in their supply chain.

Driven by growing calls for transparency, firms such as Wal-Mart, Tesco, and Kroger are beginning to use new technologies to provide provenance data to the marketplace (New, 2010). Many companies are now using sophisticated ways to track the manufacturing trajectory of their products and share that information with consumers. Product labeling has evolved to include minuscule electronic devices and new types of bar codes that can be read with standard mobile phones. For example, Switcher is a Swiss apparel company that labels each of its products with a code consumers can enter at the website Respect-code.org to retrieve information about the firms and factories along the supply chain, as well as from ISO 14000 environmental performance certificates. Similarly, Anvil, a clothing brand, works with TrackmyT.com to provide multimedia information about the route of its products from raw materials to finished item. Blankiet Estate in Napa Valley, California, applies a special security seal called a Bubble Tag to each of its wine bottles. These tags carry a reference number consumers can enter at the website prooftag.com to ensure authenticity.

Further research opportunities exist to explore the interplay between different social innovators in the supply chain context. Is social innovation likely to come from large incumbent firms with high market share, or small new entrants with low market share? Scholars have suggested social innovations to deal with sustainability issues are likely to emerge from both incumbents and new entrants (Hockerts and Wüstenhagen, 2010), although they likely differ in how they pursue social innovations. Social innovation startups tend to adopt a more value-based approach in terms of their commitment to addressing social and environmental issues. Their innovative potential comes from being unencumbered by previous routines, organizational practices, or investments. Incumbents, on the other hand, tend to engage in social innovation as a reaction to pressure from stakeholders concerned about sustainability. Although they might be more anchored in traditional practices, their large market power, financial resources, and process innovation capabilities give them the ability to adopt social innovation practices. Some scholars argue that incumbents and new entrants may differ in the type of social innovations they pursue. Rigid routines constrain large incumbents, limiting them to incremental innovation, whereas small startups are in a better position to pursue radical innovation (Klepper, 1996; Utterback, 1994). For example, in the automotive industry, incremental social innovations, such as cars with lower petrol consumption, have mainly emerged from large incumbents, and radical social innovations, such as electric cars, have been mainly developed by new entrants, such as Tesla Motors (Schaltegger and Wagner, 2011). Similarly, industry incumbents and new entrants play mutually reinforcing roles in bringing about social innovation in supply chains. Up-and-coming social enterprises use new technologies to create applications and tools that provide rich data about conditions along the supply chain. Large corporations use these innovative applications and tools to clean up their supply chains. Without a doubt, both large corporations and small social enterprises play indispensable roles in addressing the challenges of transparency and accountability in global supply chains.

Finally, one promising line of future research would be validating if "going local" is a viable model for social innovation when more and more manufacturers are outsourcing entire systems. Given the social and environmental risks associated with globally dispersed supply chains, some have claimed the future of manufacturing is local. For example, Shuman's *Going Local* (2013) proposes that a key player in the transformation of the economy from global to local is the "community corporation," a business that is owned by residents of the community, the local government, or the community as a whole. Community corporations use local resources sustainably, employ local workers at decent wages, and serve the needs of their community. The "Buy Local" movement is at an all-time high, changing the way small businesses exist in their communities. Since 2010, "Small Business Saturday" has been celebrated the Saturday after US Thanksgiving, to encourage shoppers to patronize small, local business where they live. In particular, large American cities such as San Francisco and New York City have seen an unprecedented emergence of local manufacturers across various industries such as clothing, fashion accessories, furniture, food, and beer. Made In NYC is an initiative of the Pratt Center for Community Development, created to support local manufacturing in New York City. For Made In NYC, local manufacturing is seen as essential to an environmentally sustainable city. The initiative's strategy is to encourage consumers to shop locally, and to get companies to buy from each other to reinforce local supply chains. Similarly, SFMade is a non-profit organization that aims to support a vibrant local manufacturing sector in San Francisco. Having emerged from a grassroots movement, SFMade not only allows local manufacturers to connect and share resources, but also provides training and guidance on topics relevant to local manufacturers. The organization's vision is to create a more diverse and sustainable local economy, where companies that design and manufacture products locally flourish and, in turn, create jobs for citizens who contribute to the overall economic and social vibrancy of the city. This trend of turning inward by localizing manufacturing may be one form of social innovation that has emerged in recent years, representing a U-turn away from the unrelenting outward direction of global sourcing.

NOTES

1. To identify whether an article was related to supply chains, we used Web of Science's topic terms (that is, field tag "TS" on the platform) and searched instances of the phrase "supply chain" appearing in the article's title, abstract, and keywords. Web of Science applies lemmatization and stemming to its text corpus to effectively capture plurals and variant spellings of a word(s). As an aside, we found 36 published articles in Web of Science related to "social innovation" using the same criteria.
2. https://scholar.google.com/scholar?as_q=%22social+innovation%22+%22supply+chain%22&as_occt=title (accessed 11 November 2017).

REFERENCES

Anupindi, R., Chopra, S., Deshmukh, S.D., Van Mieghem, J.A. and Zemel, E. (1999), *Managing Business Process Flows*, Upper Saddle River, NJ and London: Prentice Hall and Prentice-Hall International.

AT Kearney (2011), *Carbon Disclosure Project: Supply Chain Report 2011*, London: CDP.

Atkinson, R.D., Stewart, L.A., Andes, S. and Ezell, S. (2012), *Worse than the Great Depression: What Experts are Missing about American Manufacturing Decline*, Washington, DC: Information Technology and Innovation Foundation.

Autor, D., Dorn, D., Hanson, G. and Majlesi, K. (2016), "Importing political polarization? The electoral consequences of rising trade exposure", National Bureau of Economic Research Working Paper Series No. 22637, Washington, DC, accessed February 2019 at https://www.nber.org/papers/w22637.

Barrientos, S.W. (2013), "'Labour chains': analysing the role of labour contractors in global production networks", *Journal of Development Studies*, **49**(8), 1058–71.

Bayer, C.N. (2014), "Dodd-Frank Section 1502: post-filing survey 2014", 1 October, accessed 10 August 2015 at http://www.payson.tulane.edu/sites/default/files/content/files/TulanePaysonS1502PostFilingSurvey.pdf.

BBMG (2014), "One year after Rana Plaza collapse consumer habits remain unchanged", 16 April, accessed 3 October 2014 at http://bbmg.com/news/bangladesh-title/.

Bernauer, T. and Caduff, L. (2004), "In whose interest? Pressure group politics, economic competition and environmental regulation", *Journal of Public Policy*, **24**(1), 99–126.

Brammer, S., Hoejmose, S. and Millington, A. (2011), *Managing Sustainable Global Supply Chain: Framework and Best Practices*, Ontario and London: Network for Business Sustainability, accessed 14 July 2015 at http://nbs.net/wp-content/uploads/nbs-systematic-review-supply-chains.pdf.

Cachon, G.P., Daniels, K.M. and Lobel, R. (2017), "The role of surge pricing on a service platform with self-scheduling capacity", *Manufacturing & Service Operations Management*, **19**(3), 368–84.

Chandler, A.D., Jr (1977), *The Visible Hand: The Managerial Revolution in American Business*, reprinted in 1993, Cambridge, MA: Harvard University Press.

Ciliberti, F., Pontrandolfo, P. and Scozzi, B. (2008), "Investigating corporate social responsibility in supply chains: a SME perspective", *Journal of Cleaner Production*, **16**(15), 1579–88.

Clark, A.J. and Scarf, H. (1960), "Optimal policies for a multi-echelon inventory problem", *Management Science*, **6**(4), 475–90.

Clott, C.B. (2004), "Perspectives on global outsourcing and the changing nature of work", *Business and Society Review*, **109**(2), 153–70.

Coase, R.H. (1937), "The nature of the firm", *Economica*, **4**(16), 386–405.

Cole, M.A., Elliott, R.J.R. and Okubo, T. (2014), "International environmental outsourcing", *Review of World Economics*, **150**(4), 639–64.

Cone Communications (2015), "New Cone Communications research confirms millennials as America's most ardent CSR supporters, but marked differences revealed among this diverse generation", 23 September, accessed 5 April 2017 at http://www.conecomm.com/research-blog/2015-cone-communications-millennial-csr-study.

Copeland, B.R. and Taylor, M.S. (1994), "North–south trade and the environment", *Quarterly Journal of Economics*, **109**(3), 755–87.

Copeland, B.R. and Taylor, M.S. (2004), "Trade, growth, and the environment", *Journal of Economic Literature*, **42**(1), 7–71.
Corbett, C.J. and DeCroix, G.A. (2001), "Shared-savings contracts for indirect materials in supply chains: channel profits and environmental impacts", *Management Science*, **47**(7), 881–93.
Davis, G.F. (2013a), "After the corporation", *Politics & Society*, **41**(2), 283–308.
Davis, G.F. (2013b), "Can global supply chains be accountable?", *Yale Global Online*, 16 May, accessed 18 May 2013 at http://yaleglobal.yale.edu/content/can-global-supply-chains-be-accountable.
Davis, G.F. (2016), *The Vanishing American Corporation: Navigating the Hazards of a New Economy*, Oakland, CA: Berrett-Koehler Publishers.
Delmas, M. (2001), "Stakeholders and competitive advantage: the case of ISO 14001", *Production and Operations Management*, **10**(3), 343–58.
Drake, D.F. and Just, R.L. (2016), "Ignore, avoid, abandon, and embrace: what drives firm responses to environmental regulation?", in A. Atasu (ed.), *Environmentally Responsible Supply Chains*, Cham, Switzerland: Springer International Publishing, pp. 199–222.
Ellram, L.M. (1990), "The supplier selection decision in strategic partnerships", *Journal of Purchasing and Materials Management*, **26**(4), 8–14.
Enough Project (2017), "Progress and challenges on conflict minerals: facts on Dodd-Frank 1502", June, accessed 14 July 2017 at http://enoughproject.org/special-topics/progress-and-challenges-conflict-minerals-facts-dodd-frank-1502.
Eskeland, G.S. and Harrison, A.E. (2003), "Moving to greener pastures? Multinationals and the pollution haven hypothesis", *Journal of Development Economics*, **70**(1), 1–23.
Frey, C.B. and Osborne, M.A. (2017), "The future of employment: how susceptible are jobs to computerisation?", *Technological Forecasting and Social Change*, **114**(Suppl C), 254–80.
Hart, S.L. (1995), "A natural-resource-based view of the firm", *Academy of Management Review*, **20**(4), 986–1014.
Hockerts, K. and Wüstenhagen, R. (2010), "Greening Goliaths versus emerging Davids – theorizing about the role of incumbents and new entrants in sustainable entrepreneurship", *Journal of Business Venturing*, **25**(5), 481–92.
Jackson, R. (2011), "Low-carbon's missing link", *Accountancy Futures*, **3**, 42–3.
Kim, Y.H. and Davis, G.F. (2016), "Challenges for global supply chain sustainability: evidence from conflict minerals reports", *Academy of Management Journal*, **59**(6), 1896–916.
King, B.G. and Soule, S.A. (2007), "Social movements as extra-institutional entrepreneurs: the effect of protests on stock price returns", *Administrative Science Quarterly*, **52**(3), 413–42.
Klassen, R.D. and Vachon, S. (2003), "Collaboration and evaluation in the supply chain: the impact on plant-level environmental investment", *Production and Operations Management*, **12**(3), 336–52.
Klein, J.G., Smith, N.C. and John, A. (2004), "Why we boycott: consumer motivations for boycott participation", *Journal of Marketing*, **68**(3), 92–109.
Kleindorfer, P.R., Singhal, K. and Van Wassenhove, L.N. (2005), "Sustainable operations management", *Production and Operations Management*, **14**(4), 482–92.
Klepper, S. (1996), "Entry, exit, growth, and innovation over the product life cycle", *American Economic Review*, **86**(3), 562–83.
Korten, D.C. (1995), *When Corporations Rule the World*, San Francisco, CA: Berrett-Koehler.
Lambert, D.M., Stock, J.R. and Ellram, L.M. (1998), *Fundamentals of Logistics Management*, Boston, MA: McGraw-Hill/Irwin.
Lariviere, M.A. (2016), "OM Forum – supply chain contracting: doughnuts to bubbles", *Manufacturing & Service Operations Management*, **18**(3), 309–13.
Lee, H.L. and Tang, C.S. (2018), "Socially and environmentally responsible value chain innovations: new operations management research opportunities", *Management Science*, **64**(3), 983–96.
Lee, H.L., Padmanabhan, V. and Whang, S. (1997), "Information distortion in a supply chain: the bullwhip effect", *Management Science*, **43**(4), 546–58.
Levinson, A. (1996), "Environmental regulations and manufacturers' location choices: evidence from the Census of Manufactures", *Journal of Public Economics*, **62**(1), 5–29.
Locke, R.M. (2003), "The promise and perils of globalization: the case of Nike", in T.A. Kochan and R. Schmalensee (eds), *Management: Inventing and Delivering its Future*, Cambridge, MA: MIT Press, pp. 39–70.
Locke, R.M. (2013), *The Promise and Limits of Private Power: Promoting Labor Standards in a Global Economy*, New York: Cambridge University Press.
Locke, R.M., Qin, F. and Brause, A. (2007), "Does monitoring improve labor standards? Lessons from Nike", *ILR Review*, **61**(1), 3–31.
Madsen, P.M. (2009), "Does corporate investment drive a 'race to the bottom' in environmental protection? A reexamination of the effect of environmental regulation on investment", *Academy of Management Journal*, **52**(6), 1297–318.

McDonnell, M.-H. and King, B. (2013), "Keeping up appearances: reputational threat and impression management after social movement boycotts", *Administrative Science Quarterly*, **58**(3), 387–419.

Mentzer, J.T., DeWitt, W., Keebler, J.S. et al. (2001), "Defining supply chain management", *Journal of Business Logistics*, **22**(2), 1–25.

Miller, K.E. and Sturdivant, F.D. (1977), "Consumer responses to socially questionable corporate behavior: an empirical test", *Journal of Consumer Research*, **4**(1), 1–7.

Murphy, D.D. (2004a), *The Business Dynamics of Global Regulatory Competition*, Berkeley and Los Angeles, CA: University of California Press.

Murphy, D.D. (2004b), *The Structure of Regulatory Competition: Corporations and Public Policies in a Global Economy*, New York: Oxford University Press.

New, S. (2010), "The transparent supply chain", *Harvard Business Review*, **88**, 1–5.

Nollet, J., Filis, G. and Mitrokostas, E. (2016), "Corporate social responsibility and financial performance: a non-linear and disaggregated approach", *Economic Modelling*, **52**, Part B, 400–7.

Pickles, J. and Zhu, S. (2013), "The California transparency in supply chains act", Capturing the Gains Working Paper No. 15, 23 March, accessed 11 August 2017 at http://ssrn.com/abstract=2237437.

Rock, M.T. (2003), "Public disclosure of the sweatshop practices of American multinational garment/shoe makers/retailers: impacts on their stock prices", *Competition & Change*, **7**(1), 23–38.

Schaltegger, S. and Wagner, M. (2011), "Sustainable entrepreneurship and sustainability innovation: categories and interactions", *Business Strategy and the Environment*, **20**(4), 222–37.

Seuring, S. and Müller, M. (2008), "From a literature review to a conceptual framework for sustainable supply chain management", *Journal of Cleaner Production*, **16**(15), 1699–710.

Shuman, M. (2013), *Going Local: Creating Self-Reliant Communities in a Global Age*, New York: Routledge.

Simchi-Levi, D., Simchi-Levi, E. and Kaminsky, P. (1999), *Designing and Managing the Supply Chain: Concepts, Strategies, and Cases*, New York: McGraw-Hill/Irwin.

Surroca, J., Tribó, J.A. and Zahra, S.A. (2013), "Stakeholder pressure on MNEs and the transfer of socially irresponsible practices to subsidiaries", *Academy of Management Journal*, **56**(2), 549–72.

Sustainable Brands (2015), "Study: 81% of consumers say they will make personal sacrifices to address social, environmental issues", 27 May, accessed 14 July 2016 at http://www.sustainablebrands.com/news_and_views/stakeholder_trends_insights/sustainable_brands/study_81_consumers_say_they_will_make_.

The Economist (2016), "Globalisation backlash 2.0", 26 July, accessed 5 April 2017 at http://www.economist.com/blogs/buttonwood/2016/07/economics-and-politics-0.

Utterback, J. (1994), *Mastering the Dynamics of Innovation: How Companies Can Seize Opportunities in the Face of Technological Change*, Boston, MA: Harvard Business School Press.

Van Woensel, T.O.M., Creten, R. and Vandaele, N. (2001), "Managing the environmental externalities of traffic logistics: the issue of emissions", *Production and Operations Management*, **10**(2), 207–23.

Vogel, D. (2005), *The Market for Virtue: The Potential and Limits of Corporate Social Responsibility*, Washington, DC: Brookings Institution Press.

Walley, N. and Whitehead, B. (1994), "It's not easy being green", *Harvard Business Review*, **72**(3), 46–51.

Wang, Y., Li, J. and Anupindi, R. (2015), "Risky suppliers or risky supply chains? An empirical analysis of sub-tier supply network structure on firm performance in the high-tech sector", Ross School of Business Working Paper Series No. 1297, University of Michigan, Ann Arbor, MI, accessed February 2019 at https://ssrn.com/abstract=2705654.

Williamson, O.E. (1981), "The economics of organization: the transaction cost approach", *American Journal of Sociology*, **87**(3), 548–77.

Williamson, O.E. (1985), *The Economic Intstitutions of Capitalism*, New York: Free Press.

Williamson, O.E. (2008), "Outsourcing: transaction cost economics and supply chain management", *Journal of Supply Chain Management*, **44**(2), 5–16.

PART V

INDIVIDUALS, ORGANIZATIONS AND ORGANIZING

18. Emotions as the glue, the fuel and the rust of social innovation

Charlene Zietsma and Madeline Toubiana

Increasingly, management scholars are turning to the grand challenges facing society and beginning to explore the processes by which social innovations are created and maintained (Ferraro et al., 2015). Social innovation has been described as 'the broad range of organizational and inter-organizational activity that is ostensibly designed to address the most deep-rooted "problems" of society' (Tracey and Stott, 2017, p. 51; see also Mulgan, 2006, 2012; Phills et al., 2008; Westley and Antadze, 2010). A focus on 'grand challenge' problems adds to the definition of social innovation, the idea that solving important societal problems would have 'a high likelihood of global impact through widespread implementation' (George et al., 2016, p. 1881). Examples of grand challenges in need of social innovation include various aspects of social inclusion, such as addressing income inequality, women's equal participation in markets and society, discrimination based on race, caste or sexual orientation, and other shared challenges including climate change, pandemics, social dislocation due to war, famine or persecution and other problems. Such challenges require coordinated, collaborative efforts (George et al., 2016) and distributed experimentation among multiple heterogeneous stakeholders with divergent conceptions of value, under conditions of complexity and radical uncertainty (Ferraro et al., 2015). In other words, addressing such challenges is an inherently relational activity under very difficult circumstances. As such, emotions come into play in multiple ways.

In this chapter we seek to explore the emergent literature on social innovation and make ties to the affective underpinnings of these activities. Although frequently left out of macro-organizational scholarship, emotions drive social activity and institutional processes (Fineman, 2000; Lok et al., 2017; Voronov and Vince, 2012), and as Jasper warned, 'all the cultural models and concepts in use . . . are mis-specified if they do not include explicit emotional causal mechanisms' (Jasper, 2011, p. 286). While emotions are important to all social activity, we argue they are particularly important to social innovation. They can motivate people to engage in social innovation (Cardon et al., 2017; Goss, 2005; Martí and Fernández, 2015; Miller et al., 2012; Qureshi et al., 2016; Yitshaki and Kropp, 2016), and can engage or mobilize others to support such social innovations (Grodal et al., 2015; Paulin et al., 2014). They can lead people working with others of different perspectives to common-ground, but also to battle-ground (see, for example, Fan and Zietsma, 2017; Toubiana and Zietsma, 2017). In this way, emotions can also stall or slow down social innovation, especially if such innovation threatens existing institutions and the logics with which embedded people identify. Accordingly, we suggest that understanding the role of emotions in social innovation is crucial in developing a theoretically rich and accurate account of social innovation processes. While disparate studies emerging in the literature have begun to provide us with hints of the roles emotions may play in social innovation, in this chapter we reach across these studies to more thoroughly theorize the effects of emotions, and to develop a research agenda going forward.

First, we describe a typology of social innovation developed by Tracey and Stott (2017), outlining three major types of social innovation: social entrepreneurship, social intrapreneurship and social extrapreneurship (which encompass three subtypes: social movements, cross-sector partnerships and non-governmental and development organizations). We then draw on three metaphors to examine the role of emotions in social innovation: emotions as fuel, emotions as glue and emotions as rust. We develop these metaphors theoretically, then apply them to the social innovation typology outlined by Tracey and Stott to examine existing literature that elaborates the metaphors. We then use the metaphors to derive a research agenda for each type of social innovation. We conclude the chapter with a call for future work in this important domain of scholarship and justification for how such work will add value to what we know about social innovation.

WHAT IS SOCIAL INNOVATION AND WHY DO EMOTIONS MATTER TO IT?

Tracey and Stott's (2017) recent typology of organizational and inter-organizational approaches to addressing societal problems described three different approaches to social innovation: social entrepreneurship, social intrapreneurship and social extrapreneurship.

Social entrepreneurship involves the founding of a venture where 'the social mission is explicit and central' (Dees, 1998, p. 2; Kickul and Lyons, 2016). Key to the process of engaging in social entrepreneurship is (a) 'adopting a mission to create and sustain social value'; (b) 'recognizing and relentlessly pursuing new opportunities to serve that mission'; and (c) 'engaging in a process of continuous innovation, adaptation, and learning value' (Dees, 1998, p. 4). In essence, social entrepreneurship is a social innovation that is generated through the formation of a venture with a specific social purpose. Social entrepreneurship has been seen as a crucially important type of social innovation, and especially so for addressing issues of inclusiveness. For example, social entrepreneurship has been used to help integrate disadvantaged people into the workforce (Alter, 2006; Pache and Santos, 2012; Tracey et al., 2011), such as an industrial cleaning company that employs homeless individuals,[1] or a skincare line using honey that employs previously incarcerated people to work with bees and make the product.[2] Thus, social entrepreneurship is by definition about social innovation, but also often about social inclusion.

Social intrapreneurship is a form of social innovation that takes place within an existing firm and leverages 'the resources and capabilities of established organizations' (Tracey and Stott, 2017, p. 53). Social intrapreneurship is often led by internal activists or 'tempered radicals' (Briscoe and Gupta, 2016; Meyerson, 2001; Meyerson and Scully, 1993), who advance a social or environmental outcome without formal authority, yet which may 'align with core business objectives' (Davis and White, 2015, p. 212). It may also be led by top managers (Tracey and Stott, 2017). The social innovations made by these actors can involve changes to practices and policies, like the adoption of same-sex domestic partner benefits (Briscoe and Safford, 2008) or recycling practices (Lounsbury, 2001), the creation of new product lines, like low emission cars (Davis and White, 2015), or a new spin-off business from within the larger organization such as MPESA from Vodafone (Grayson et al., 2017).

Social extrapreneurship, according to Tracey and Stott (2017, p. 55), involves 'the process of inter-organizational action that facilitates alternative combinations of ideas, people, places and resources to address social challenges and make social change'. It includes activities by *cross-sector partnerships* of public, private and third sector actors working together to address social and environmental problems, such as the Roundtable on Sustainable Palm Oil, which seeks to address environmental and social issues associated with palm oil production.[3] It also includes *social movements*, which often work in more conflictual ways to promote change in business, government and social practices, such as activism for more sustainable forest practices (Zietsma and Lawrence, 2010), or activism for domestic partner benefits (Briscoe and Safford, 2008). Finally, it can also include *non-governmental and development organizations* who typically work with and on behalf of disadvantaged groups for improvements in social inclusion, such as enabling market participation for women and fighting poverty in developing countries (for example, Mair et al., 2012).[4]

These approaches to social innovation are significantly different. Yet, in all cases, social innovation is aimed at creating societal benefits, often increasing social inclusion, social justice or the long-term sustainability of society. Nonetheless, it is important to point out that, even with the best of intentions, not all social innovations will have a positive impact. Social innovation is sometimes subject to opportunism, implementation problems and unintended consequences. Given radical uncertainty and complexity (Ferraro et al., 2015), it is often difficult to predict what the consequences of social innovation will be. Thus, while we present these approaches as forms of possible social innovation, we do not suggest that they will always be successful or positive for all involved.

Despite (and because of) these issues, the idea that emotions are involved in social innovation processes is incontrovertible. As Turner and Stets (2005, p. 2) have claimed:

> Emotions are the 'glue' binding people together and generating commitments to large-scale social and cultural structures; in fact, emotions are what make social structures and systems of cultural symbols viable. Conversely, emotions are also what can drive people apart and push them to tear down social structures and to challenge cultural traditions.

Yet, theoretical development of how emotions matter to social innovation is lacking. Based on our engagement with the literature and our own research, we present a threefold conceptualization of the role emotions may play in social innovation, using the metaphors of emotions as glue, fuel and rust.

THE THREEFOLD ROLE OF EMOTIONS IN SOCIAL INNOVATION: EMOTIONS AS GLUE, FUEL AND RUST

We present our view of the role of emotions in Figure 18.1, and describe the components of the model in line with the three roles for emotions we propose.

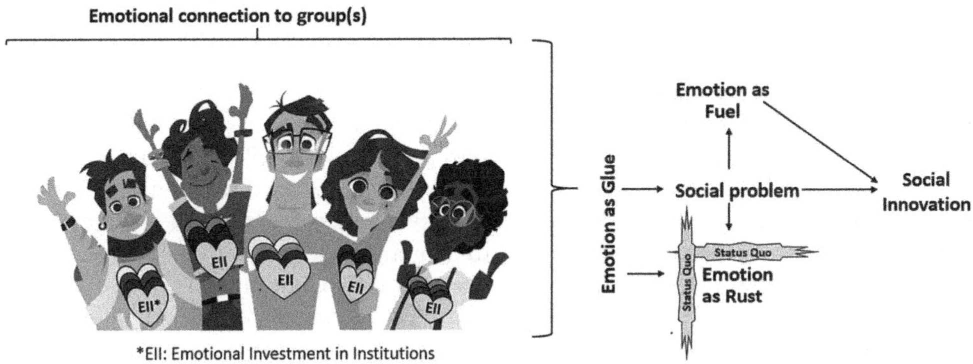

Figure 18.1 Role of emotions in social innovation

Emotions as Glue

Emotions are the social 'glue' (Turner and Stets, 2005) that connects 'human beings to each other and the world around them' (Goodwin et al., 2001, p. 10). People can become emotionally invested in their social groups and their institutional frameworks (Creed et al., 2014; Voronov and Vince, 2012).

> Emotions connect people to the institutional structures they inhabit, and are part and parcel of the institutionalization process: institutions come to be valued . . . (Selznick, 1957) by people who care about them, and feel a visceral, emotional connection to them (Bourdieu, 2000; Friedland, 2018) . . ..(Zietsma and Toubiana, 2018, p. 429)

As we show in Figure 18.1, we conceive of emotions operating as glue in several ways. First, emotions can act as the glue that connects us to the institutional norms, values, beliefs, practices and structures we are embedded within or surrounded by. That is, our emotional investment in institutions, which we depict as the heart in each person in the model, acts as glue binding us to particular institutions. As Voronov and Weber (2016, p. 456) noted, 'emotions are central to the very constitution of people as competent institutional actors', and institutions are inscribed in us through our very emotional commitments to them (Zietsma and Toubiana, 2018). Second, emotions are the glue that connects us to social groups – most commonly, this may be to the groups that we are connected to through our embeddedness within the same institutions, though this is not always the case and we may also become emotionally connected with other groups across and beyond one's home institutions (Fan and Zietsma, 2017; Ruebottom and Auster, 2018). People can become emotionally invested in and committed to social groups and this can act as glue emotionally binding people to particular social groups. Third, we can also become glued to particular social problems and/or the groups that they are associated with. This may be because we are seeking to enact our beliefs and values, by for example, fighting poverty in Africa or fighting for animal rights or environmental protection. Or it may be because we feel compassion for (Grimes et al., 2013) or connection to a particular group, such as children or victims of domestic violence. In this way, emotional investments can act as glue that can bond us to institutions, people or social problems.

Emotions as glue in social entrepreneurship

Social entrepreneurship as a type of social innovation requires more than motivation to realize. It is a process that involves people, resources and opportunity (Kickul and Lyons, 2016) and it is shaped by the institutional environment actors operate within (Gundry et al., 2011; Tracey et al., 2011). Emotions are important in this regard as they can cement and energize actors' collective commitment to a venture and act as the glue that holds the venture together when faced with challenge or threat (Cardon et al., 2017). Tracey and Phillips (2016) studied a social enterprise in the UK which became stigmatized in its community for the work it did in helping new migrant workers – this stigma led to an image crisis for the social enterprise. Its response to this crisis was to strengthen its organizational identity by emphasizing the care it had for all marginalized groups and by instilling pride in members for the work they did. What this study highlights is that because social innovation is often complex, it can become contested as multiple interest groups or institutional lenses are applied to the work conducted. For social entrepreneurship to thrive, ventures need to be able to leverage the emotions that glue employees and other stakeholders together so that they can maintain their purpose despite external threats. Emotions that bond us to social groups, institutions and social problems can be used to 'glue' us to social innovation processes, making us feel deeply invested in their enactment. For example, in the Japanese social enterprise, the Seikatsu Club, housewives formed close communities in which they explored and enacted their values as a group to improve life in Japan for their families. They were connected to and emotionally invested in their *hans* (local groups of neighbors), the values of the Club, and the economic, political and social problems of Japanese society, and this bonded them to their shared values and social innovation activities with the Seikatsu Club despite the challenges they faced (Leung et al., 2014).

Emotions as glue in social intrapreneurship

Social intrapreneurship is likely the least studied form of social innovation of those we mention in terms of emotions, yet, despite this, there is still strong evidence that emotions can also act as glue in this domain.

Gutierrez et al. (2010) provide a salient example of how this is the case. In their paper they describe a case of unlikely internal activism by members of the Catholic Church. While Church members were outraged by public reports of pedophile priests and the Church's suppression of their transgressions, instead of exiting, they chose to band together and attempt to make a change to the governance of the Catholic Church, to ensure the Church was more inclusive in caring for *all* of its members. Past work has shown that membership and identification with groups has 'emotional significance' (Pratt, 2000; Tajfel, 1978, p. 63, 1982) that can often not easily be discarded (Toubiana, 2014). These emotional investments to organizations and/or groups can act as the glue that ties actors together within them and leads them to work for social change internally rather than exit.

This emotional investment to groups can also be highlighted by recent actions of Starbucks' chief executive officer (CEO). Starbucks expressed its support for same-sex marriage legislation with the following statement:[5]

> Starbucks is proud to join other leading Northwest employers in support of Washington State legislation recognizing marriage equality for same-sex couples. Starbucks strives to create a company culture that puts our partners first, and our company has a lengthy history of leading and supporting policies that promote equality and inclusion . . . It is core to who we are and what we value as a company.

When investors at Starbucks' annual general meeting complained that the company was hurting its economic interests because of a boycott related to this support, CEO Howard Schultz responded by emphasizing his emotional investment in these social bonds: 'It is not an economic decision to me. The lens in which we are making that decision is through the lens of our people. We employ over 200,000 people in this company, and we want to embrace diversity. Of all kinds.'[6] Emotions bond us to groups, institutions and problems, and in doing so enable and support social intrapreneurship by driving change internally for these groups. In this way, emotions as glue are influential in social intrapreneurship, but just as clearly, this area is under-researched and we encourage further work to explore this topic.

Emotions as glue in social extrapreneurship

Emotional investment in the collective identity of a social movement is an important factor that bonds members to social movements, impacting movement retention and mobilizing capacity (Polletta and Jasper, 2001), and helping to smooth over conflict over movement ideology (Castello et al., 2013). Movements are held together by affective commitments and investments, without which their success in achieving social innovation would be limited (Goodwin et al., 2001).

Emotions are also important as glue in cross-sector partnerships. Such partnerships are difficult because of the heterogeneous groups involved, each with their own values and norms or institutional logics. Fan and Zietsma (2017) studied a cross-sector council formed to find a way to allocate water resources among stakeholders that shared the Okanagan Basin of lakes and rivers in the Okanagan Valley, British Columbia, Canada. These authors found that shared moral purpose and initial respect, trust and liking among groups with heterogeneous logics enabled iterative cycles of increasingly positive moral and social emotions that fostered members' engagement in the project. This was because it brought these people together and built emotional investment in the group and project, and this made it possible for members with distinct logics to come together under a shared water governance logic that enabled integrative solutions for managing water allocation. Emotions served as glue that held the partnership together and fostered innovation. However, the innovation began to decay when emotions were damaged in a breach of trust, showing how emotions serving as glue can be undermined, and, thus, must be actively maintained in processes of social innovation.

Emotions as glue are also quite important when non-governmental organizations (NGOs) and development organizations work with their local partners. These organizations 'tend to enjoy greater public trust' (Teegen et al., 2004, p. 468) than public or private sector organizations when working with disadvantaged populations, and without the trust of local partners, NGOs and development organizations would likely have very limited influence. Further, a significant part of the efforts of development organizations involve building trust and compassion among stakeholders in the context. As several studies have shown (Bardy et al., 2013; McKague et al., 2015; Tobias et al., 2013), social structure interventions (involving building emotional glue among local groups) and economic structure interventions go hand-in-hand, and Mair et al. (2012) showed how norms of caring could be used to facilitate the economic inclusion of women in Bangladesh. Emotions can serve as glue enabling these types of partnerships and innovation. However, emotions have been given limited attention in the management literature dealing with NGOs and development organizations, and future research is needed.

Emotions as Fuel

While emotions acting as glue tie people to institutions, social groups and social problems, emotions acting as fuel are often the impetus and sustenance for people engaging in social innovation. Emotions can motivate us and provide emotional energy (Collins, 2004) for action, inspiring us to enact values and institutional work (Gray et al., 2015; Voronov and Vince, 2012). We see this as being relevant across all forms of social innovation.

Emotions fueling social entrepreneurship

Emotions have been shown to play an important role in fueling all entrepreneurial activity (Cardon et al., 2009; Cardon et al., 2017; Goss, 2005; Goss et al., 2011; Jennings et al., 2015; Ndinguri et al., 2014). However, the emotions that fuel social entrepreneurship may not be the same as those that fuel traditional entrepreneurship. Miller and colleagues (Grimes et al., 2013; Miller et al., 2012) have theorized compassion as a key motivator for social entrepreneurship.

> Compassion is characterized by its other orientation and emotional connection linking an individual to a suffering community (Goetz, Keltner, and Simon-Thomas, 2010; Lazarus, 1991; Nussbaum, 1996, 2001). Compassion serves as a powerful motivator of action, compelling individuals to alleviate others' suffering (Batson and Shaw, 1991; Omoto, Maisch, and Barraza, 2009). (Miller et al., 2012, p. 617)

Specifically, they argue that compassion leads to 'increases in integrative thinking' pushing people to find solutions that benefit the collective and 'increases an individual's ability to make broad and creative associations' (Miller et al., 2012, p. 623). Compassion also shapes the traditional cost–benefit analysis entrepreneurs undertake when considering venture creation, and enables a more prosocial interpretation 'increasing the perceived benefits of acting to alleviate others' suffering' (2012, p. 623). In this way, compassion can act as fuel motivating and increasing the likelihood that a given individual may engage in social entrepreneurship.

Consider this example: a young women's father became paralysed and she watched him suffer, but then, over time, she saw him discover ways to live an independent life. When she met others facing similar challenges, she began to mentor them using the strategies her father had learned. Doing so, she realized how much suffering could be alleviated by mentoring and she founded i-bility, an Internet-based mentoring platform for people affected by disabilities (Bloom and Pirson, 2010). Care, empathy and compassion for others' suffering can motivate social innovation. These emotions can serve to draw your attention to suffering, how it might be alleviated and, ultimately, motivate action.

Emotions fueling social intrapreneurship

Why change-makers of any type are motivated to act has been a long-standing question in existing scholarship. The answer, of course, is complicated and can include a variety of factors that range from their particular interests to the identities that they hold dear (Rowley and Moldoveanu, 2003). We argue that emotions can serve as fuel that feeds social intrapreneurship activities.

Consider the work of Dutton and Dukerich (1991) on the response of the Port Authority of New York and New Jersey to the issue of homelessness. The Port Authority found itself confronted with problems in the delivery of its services due to the rising number of homeless people at its facilities. While initially in response to this issue the Port Authority claimed it was an issue for the police and that they were not in the business of social service, ultimately the Port Authority became part of designing innovative solutions to homelessness in the region. What triggered this internal shift that ultimately enabled social innovation? Dutton and Dukerich explain how negative press coverage of the Port Authority became prevalent as the issue of homelessness came under public scrutiny. This coverage sought to 'embarrass' Port Authority managers and painted them as 'Scrooge to Jersey City's poor' (p. 535). The negative coverage began to spill over and negatively influence those working for the Port Authority, and, as a result, they began to feel hurt and distressed at the characterizations of themselves and the organization. In sum, embarrassment and other negative emotions surfaced in response to how the organization's image was being perceived. Ultimately, while the belief continued that working on the issue of homelessness was not the job of the Port Authority, the Port Authority took action on the issue nonetheless and made adaptations within the organization, funding and supporting social innovation to provide services to the homeless. In sum, this case study provides evidence of how negative emotions such as embarrassment and guilt can emerge in response to negative perceptions of one's organization, and if these negative organizational images do not line up with these actors' understanding of the organization's identity, such emotions may fuel efforts to take innovative action to shift image back in line with identity. While this social intrapreneurship effort may have emerged in a bottom-up fashion, it required top management support in order to be implemented, and there are many examples of organization members advocating within their organizations for something they are passionate about (Briscoe and Safford, 2008; Lounsbury, 2001) or something they have been angered by and for which they want their organization to change its response (Toubiana and Zietsma, 2017).

One of the most well-known examples of top-down social intrapreneurship comes from the carpet company, Interface. As described on the company's website, emotion stimulated the company founder to challenge his company 'to become the first name in industrial ecology, a corporation that cherishes nature and restores the environment', through attention to 'people, process, product, place and profits':

> In 1994, while preparing remarks on Interface's environmental vision for a company task force meeting, Interface founder and Chairman, Ray Anderson, experienced a fundamental perspective change. Seeking inspiration for his speech, Ray read Paul Hawken's 'The Ecology of Commerce' and was deeply moved – an experience he has described as an epiphany. It awakened Ray to the urgent need to set a new course for Interface toward sustainability.[7]

Ray Anderson's emotional epiphany, which fueled his (and Interface's) subsequent actions toward sustainability, was indeed fuel for changes within the company.

Emotions as fuel in social extrapreneurship

Emotions have also been shown to be the motivating fuel in social extrapreneurship. The social movement literature has been most advanced in this respect, identifying that a movement's collective action frame (Benford and Snow, 2000) must resonate not only cognitively with audiences, but also emotionally (Bröer and Duyvendak, 2009; Giorgi, 2017; Jasper and Poulsen, 1995; Schrock et al., 2004) in order to mobilize potential activists. For example, Zietsma and Lawrence (2010) studied the boundary and practice work of activists advocating for more sustainable forest practices, and those of their forest company and forestry worker opponents. Activists used highly emotive language, referring to existing clearcutting practices as 'earth rape' perpetrated by forest company 'criminals' and their 'eco-leper' workers, destroying the 'indescribably lovely, magical, mystical, irreplaceable expression of nature that is an intact old-growth rain forest' (Zietsma and Lawrence, 2010, pp. 202, 205). Awe, love and rage seemed to combine to motivate their own participation, and were used to attempt to recruit others and gain media attention. Forest companies and forest workers disdainfully referred to the activists as 'eco-terrorists' and liars, and felt they were 'guilty of treason' for going against Canadian interests. Each side expressed moral indignation regarding the other, which seemed to fuel both their institutional work and their resistance to the work of their opponents. People's engagement in collective action may also be motivated by the chance to express and take pride in their identities, particularly those that have been stigmatized, such as both Christian conservatives (Stein, 2001) and gay rights activists (Kenney and Craig, 2012).

Social movement scholars have also expressed the importance of emotional energy as a fuel for activism, defined as 'the positive and energizing feeling that comes from participating in a high-intensity interaction ritual', the result of when 'copresent individuals become caught up in a common emotional rhythm' (Collins, 1993, p. 208). While emotional energy in Collins's terms seems to be created by physical presence, part of the 'common emotional rhythm' is often associated with shared moral emotions and purpose (Fan and Zietsma, 2017). Ruebottom and Auster (2018), for example, described how 'Me to We', a social movement organization, stimulated emotional energy and a moral purpose to fuel social change among youth through exciting interaction rituals involving music, light, sound and narratives of people who the youth could relate to and be inspired by. Bail (2012) showed that emotional energy can also have amplifying effects through media, showing that anti-Muslim fringe organizations that expressed fear and anger were disproportionately picked up by the media, creating a 'gravitational pull' that eventually altered the mainstream discourse itself. Emotions are often a resource that those seeking to mobilize social innovation via movements can draw on and use to enhance their objectives.

Less work has focused on emotions in fueling cross-sector partnerships and the work of NGOs and development organizations with their local partners. However, we can expect that emotions may factor into these collaborations just as they do with social entrepreneurship and social movements. Emotional appeals may serve to bring actors together, and shared emotions like compassion may fuel efforts to continue the work despite the difficulties of these partnerships across different institutional worlds. Thus, while often corporate/public sector members are driven by instrumental business/political cases, we suggest that they may also be fueled by feelings of moral responsibility or by emotionally resonant frames and ideologies. Indeed, however, much work remains to be done in this area of study.

Emotions as Rust

The flip side to emotions as fuel and glue for social innovation is that emotions can also actually stall and slow innovation processes (Calhoun, 2001), acting as rust (with potentially corrosive properties!). While emotions can motivate and glue people to innovations, they can also lead people to feel threatened by them and defensive of their institutions and social groups. When a proposed social innovation threatens those institutions or groups people are emotionally invested within, it can inspire virulent and even violent responses (Gill and Burrow, 2018; Toubiana and Zietsma, 2017). Furthermore, emotions like fear and shame may have the reverse effect of compassion, stalling or paralysing social innovation instead of inspiring it (Gould, 2009; Moon, 2013; Wijaya and Heugens, 2018). Finally, because social innovation usually involves working with heterogeneous groups with very different emotional investments, conflicts are likely. If groups remain rusted into their own emotional investments, without developing new 'glue' to connect them to the people, problems and institutions that are also connected to the social innovation process, social innovation is likely to stall.

Emotions as rust in social entrepreneurship

In a study of microfinance social enterprises in Bolivia, Battilana and Dorado (2010) found that between different employees who were 'steeped in their respective logics of reference' there emerged 'an intractable identity conflict that reached crisis proportions in mid-1996, when the impasse made it impossible to operate effectively' (p. 1427). We suggest this example highlights one of the ways in which emotions can act as rust to social innovation – emotional investment in one logic can slow down or sabotage social innovation that requires the adoption of dual or hybrid logics (Pache and Santos, 2013; Toubiana, 2014; Toubiana and Zietsma, 2017). Another social enterprise Battilana and Dorado (2010) studied was more successful because it hired people without strong emotional investment in banking or developing logics, allowing it to develop a strong organizational identity that glued all staff to the hybridized mission. In this way, emotions can stall social innovation if they lead social entrepreneurs or important stakeholders to resist change initiatives due to their emotional attachment to the status quo.

Discrete emotions may also act as rust for social innovation. Doern and Goss (2014) showed how the negative emotions of shame, humiliation and anger experienced by entrepreneurs in their attempts to appease Russian government officials corroded the entrepreneurs' motivation to grow. While the negative impact of shame and humiliation are linked in this study to traditional entrepreneurship, we predict that other negative social emotions can similarly act as rust to social entrepreneurs' social innovation efforts, but suggest we need further research to tease out which emotions might be the more corrosive on the social innovation process.

Emotions as rust in social intrapreneurship

While some emotions (such as compassion, excitement, pride or shame) can lead actors to engage in innovative social change within organizations, other emotions may stop them from doing so. Specifically, we suggest that fear and denial can corrode social intrapreneurship efforts. Wijaya and Heugens (2018) provide compelling evidence of stalled attempts at social change efforts within organizations, providing an interesting contrast to the work of Gutierrez and colleagues (Gutierrez et al., 2010). They outline how members of churches in urban Java, who were motivated to promote greater inclusiveness in membership, eventually stopped their efforts, paralysed by fears of their superiors despite their moral sense that existing practices were unjust. Where the legitimacy of leadership in the Catholic Church had been seemingly undermined by the press coverage of sexual abuse in Gutierrez and colleagues' study, no external or public legitimacy challenges to the leaders existed in Wijaya and Heugens's study. The power and authority of these leaders instilled fear into members and prevented them from acting on the social innovations they desired. Fear or other negative emotions such as denial can also lead actors 'to look away' and deny issues of concern that may emerge or avoid taking action on them, preventing change (Delmestri and Goodrick, 2016).

Emotions as rust in social extrapreneurship

Again, social movement research has had the most to say about the role of emotions as rust. Gould (2009) has described how shame prevented gay men from asserting their rights and demanding social inclusion with respect to the treatment of AIDS. Indeed, Moon (2013, p. 261) has suggested that emotions are mechanisms of social power used 'to silence, to incite discipline' and to keep people 'paralyzed and unable to act'. Social movements, when working in conflict against firms, can also incite angry responses and moral indignation among their targets, solidifying their resistance to social innovation (Zietsma and Lawrence, 2010). In this way, certain negative emotions can stall social innovation, and other emotions can lock people into defending the status quo. In both cases, emotions act as rust rather than fuel.

We can expect similar issues in cross-sector partnerships where members have become unable to compromise, or where there has been a breach of trust, stimulating negative emotions (Fan and Zietsma, 2017), or where negotiations of shared purpose have broken down due to conflicts and negative emotional reactions among members, potentially leading to social innovation failure (Ackermann et al., 2005; Eden and Huxham, 2001). Organizations with emotionally incompatible cultures or registers can also see failures of innovation processes as communications and social bonds break down (cf. Toubiana and Zietsma, 2017). Similarly, if development organizations lose (or fail to gain) the trust of their partners or aid targets, resistance to their change efforts can be expected, and continuing commitment to status quo institutional structures is more likely than social innovation.

DISCUSSION AND DIRECTIONS FOR FUTURE RESEARCH

As the literature has amply illustrated, social innovation is an emotion-laden process, and to be successful, social innovators of all types should be taking emotions into account. We have presented a model outlining the role of emotions as glue, fuel and rust in social innovation processes. We feel the metaphors of glue, fuel and rust are generative for thinking more deeply about what work remains to be done in researching emotions in social innovation processes.

In Table 18.1, we present a series of research questions that are aligned with the three metaphors we present, considering them across each type and subtype of social innovation. We draw attention to questions associated with the role of glue in social entrepreneurship

Table 18.1 Possible research questions associated with emotions as glue, fuel and rust in social innovation processes

	Glue	Fuel	Rust
Social Entrepreneurship	How can social entrepreneurs build new affective connections to support social innovations and new ways of operating? Are some social entrepreneurial ventures more likely to be successful than others based on the emotional investment that they are able to stimulate in their audiences (i.e., innovations for children rather than previously incarcerated men)? How can social entrepreneurs build emotional experiences into collaboration, experimentation and sharing to begin to legitimize their innovations and embed audiences in supportive social communities? How can social entrepreneurs foster emotional investment to build stronger glue for the innovation?	How might social entrepreneurs use emotions to make others passionate about their projects? How can social entrepreneurs moralize and/or energize social innovations in groups with different values? How do social entrepreneurs adapt their offerings to fit alternate institutional contexts without losing emotional energy? Does 'mission drift' result in lost emotional energy? What factors sustain emotional energy in the venture?	When social entrepreneurs' innovations are resisted emotionally, what strategies can be used to counter those negative emotions? What discrete emotions are most likely to act as rust for social entrepreneurs? What factors can transform shame and anger from paralysing emotions to mobilizing ones?
Social Intrapreneurship	How do social intrapreneurs build organizational buy-in by generating emotional investment using emotions? What strategies are more or less successful in helping intrapreneurs glue stakeholders to their initiatives? How can existing emotional registers or culture within an organization be used to deepen bonds for innovation?	What emotions are implicated in the emergence, sustenance and success of social innovation initiatives in firms? Under what conditions are emotional appeals vs. business-case pitches more effective for gaining corporate support for social innovations led by employees?	How do organizational values and cultural prescriptions generate emotions that can stall social innovation processes? Are there organizational cultures in which emotional appeals will be less successful in generating support for social innovations?

Table 18.1 (continued)

	Glue	Fuel	Rust
	Are social change initiatives led by employees or the CEO most likely to generate strong emotional investments? What are the limits to emotional investment's effectiveness in tying actors to social change? Does it start to wane or grow over time? Is it supportive of communities within the organization that value the social innovation?	How do social change initiators (whether employees or top management) build and generate emotional energy for social innovation? Does it differ depending on whether the initiative is top-down or bottom-up? Does social innovation impact existing emotional rules and registers within an organization? Does compassion motivate social intrapreneurs the same way as entrepreneurs or are other emotions involved?	While fear of failure has long been something technology companies have been working to eradicate to ensure innovation is fostered, what other emotions and/or types of fears may be stalling social intrapreneurship? How do legitimacy concerns and stakeholder evaluations impact the social innovation process? What specific emotions play a role in these dynamics? Under what conditions do employees come to value or resent top-down social innovations?
Social Extrapreneurship *Social movements*	Which types of mobilizing activities are best able to leverage existing emotional investments? Are solutions that result from collaboration, experimentation and sharing more likely to be substantively implemented vs. those that are negotiated or imposed (based on the emotional glue they generate)? Are solutions that come from collaborative processes less innovative than those that come from conflict or competitive negotiation?	How might the goals and values of social movements trigger distinct emotions? How might these distinct emotions have differing effects on the mobilizing efforts of the social movements? When social movements must speak to multiple audiences publicly, how can they manage their emotional framing strategies? How do online social movements generate emotional energy without physical co-presence? Is this energy more or less powerful than the traditional emotional energy generated in protests and physical gatherings?	When new strategies are called for, how do social movements move members beyond anger-fueled conflict to hope-fueled collaboration? Do social movements associated with anger and fear generate more funds than those associated with hope and collaboration? In what ways might fostering anger in social movements backfire? How can movements undo or reverse feelings of shame or fear that may be paralysing those interested in their social innovations?

Cross-sector partnerships	How can cross-sector partnerships negotiate and foster desired emotional investment outcomes when their institutionalized values differ? What activities create common ground for partners to invest emotionally?	Under what conditions does emotional energy wax and wane in cross-sector partnerships? What emotions seem to fuel cross-sector partnerships into fruition, and what emotions might fuel continued investment within them despite difficulties?	Under what conditions do cross-sector partnerships suffer from members' inflexible adherence to their own agendas? What role do emotions play? Are there strategies for combatting negative emotions and fostering positive ones for cross-sector partnerships?
NGOs, development organizations	How can NGOs and development organizations use emotional investment in social communities and networks to help them sustainably embed their innovations in new contexts?	How can NGOs and development organizations generate passionate support for social innovations that have no basis (or negative associations) in the institutional context of intervention? In what ways can NGOs and development organizations use existing emotional rules or registers in a given region to support and fuel their efforts?	How can NGOs and development organizations overcome the emotional threat innovation triggers in some stakeholders? Can positive emotions around experimentation be used to build trial and acceptance of innovations? What strategies can turn emotions from rust into glue and/or fuel?

by asking how social entrepreneurs can forge new affective connections to support their social innovations. For example, creating affective relationships with specialist social movement organization members could ensure that clean energy entrepreneurs get support in building their ventures and creating a conducive regulatory context (Pacheco et al., 2014). Or building on the understanding of consumer 'evangelists' (Massa et al., 2017), how can social ventures develop evangelists who can help to promote their ventures? Or can they build strong emotional investment in the venture among employees by emphasizing the social mission, similar to the zookeepers who saw their work as a deeply meaningful calling (Bunderson and Thompson, 2009)? Similarly, how can social entrepreneurs build glue between their products/services and their target audiences? Work by Purtik and Arenas (forthcoming) and Cartel et al. (2019) suggest the importance of embodied emotional experiences in experimentation and collaboration with new, socially innovative products and services, and there is certainly room to build on Collins's (2004) ideas of interaction rituals to glue key audiences to social ventures (see Ruebottom and Auster, 2018).

These questions are also relevant to social intrapreneurs looking to build glue between key stakeholder audiences and the social innovations they pursue. In addition, social intrapreneurs can consider the existing emotional register or culture within their organizations: Does it fit with their social innovation process? Can it be used to deepen bonds for innovation? Under what conditions do social innovation processes deepen the bonds between employees and (a) the social innovation and (b) the organization itself?

Social extrapreneurship can also benefit from more emotion-as-glue-focused studies. For example, while some social movements use conflictual processes, others use relationship-building cross-sector partnerships (see, for example, Bertels et al., 2014; Van Wijk et al., 2013). Can different outcomes be expected in social innovation processes that entail developing positive affective relationships versus those that are based in conflict? Relatedly, because social extrapreneurship efforts of all types involve working closely with others that hold disparate emotional investments in norms, beliefs, values and social groups, how can cross-sector partnerships create emotional investments in the partnership to glue partners to the common aims and communities associated with the social innovation? How can NGOs and development organizations build glue between themselves and their often seriously marginalized or disadvantaged target populations? How does the presence of glue affect the sustainability of social innovations in disadvantaged contexts? In this way, we encourage research to further examine the glue that bonds people to social innovations and the ways in which it can be strengthened or undermined.

A different set of questions can be raised when considering emotions as fuel. Social entrepreneurs and intrapreneurs, for example, might learn from social movement scholars how to mobilize and fuel action by using emotional frames, moral shocks, affective loyalties and interaction rituals. To do so, they will likely need to appeal to groups of different values. How can they build emotional investments in their target audiences when they, and their social innovations, are based in different value systems? How can social intrapreneurs and entrepreneurs maintain their own emotional energy when they are required to adapt their offerings to fit local contexts, or when they face mission drift because of the exigencies of making the business case (Jay, 2013)? How can social intrapreneurs build emotional energy among organization members to pursue social innovation projects, and how can they sustain it over time?

While social movement research has done a better job studying emotions in mobilization processes, further questions can also be asked in this domain. As web-based activism becomes more prevalent, new issues arise. How can social movements use emotional framing to different audiences, when all their online 'talk' is transparently available? How can social movement organizations build emotional investment on the web, when there is no physical co-presence of activists? How can emotional energy be built among online activists, and is it as effective as offline energy in stirring action that moves social innovation along, or is it mere slacktivism? How can such energy be maintained over time?

Similarly, in cross-sector partnerships and NGO/development organizations, how can emotional energy be maintained over time, particularly if emotions as rust are blocking social innovation processes? How can cross-sector partnerships and NGO/development organizations use emotional investments in existing institutions to anchor new beliefs, values and behaviors onto them, providing the possibilities for social innovation (Mair et al., 2012; Vaccaro and Palazzo, 2015).

Finally, the idea of emotions as rust also raises new research questions. For example, further investigations into discrete emotions such as shame, fear and anger could help to identify when such emotions act as rust (for example, Doern and Goss, 2014; Wijaya and Heugens, 2018) and when they act as fuel (Dutton and Dukerich, 1991) in social entrepreneurship and social intrapreneurship processes. We might also ask, what factors can transform these emotions from rust to fuel? In social intrapreneurship processes, what factors associated with organizational culture affect employees' emotional investments in social innovation processes, or the rust that makes them maintain the status quo? Does fear of failure suppress social innovation effort? Do affective loyalties to particular organizational stakeholders act as rust or fuel, and under what conditions?

In social extrapreneurship, similar questions can be raised. Rust factors may be embedded in culture and associated with partners, aid targets or state, village or religious governance organizations that have the potential to block social innovations, rather than merely in organizational cultures. When facing such rust factors, how can social extrapreneurs use emotions to turn threats into opportunities? We also may want to consider when emotions are corrosive and damaging to the social fabric of society? In cross-sector partnerships, are there strategies that can be used to foster emotional investment in the partnership and in the social innovation project? How can rust-filled interactions be converted into more positive, reflexive and open interactions through emotional processes (Fan and Zietsma, 2017)? Of course, there are many additional questions which may be raised. See Table 18.1 for additional examples.

While we have used glue, fuel and rust as discrete metaphors, they are of course, highly related. The emotional investment that glues people to institutions, groups and social problems may be necessary for emotions to act as fuel, and may also be that which leads emotions to act as rust. We have some indications in the literature that attachments to new social groups can result in reducing the emotional investment in one institutional domain (sanding the rust off, to use the metaphor), and increasing emotional investments in new institutions (Fan and Zietsma, 2017; Ruebottom and Auster, 2018), smoothing the way forward for social innovation. Emotions thus have multiple interrelated roles, and emotional investment may be central to all of this.

We suggest that much research is needed in this domain. While we have highlighted many important pieces of work in this chapter, in many of these papers, emotions were not central to the theorizing, although present in the data. As more and more papers focusing on emotions in social innovation processes emerge, however, we argue that it is important to look beyond individual effects to think more broadly about emotions' interrelationships both with each other, and with key aspects of the social innovation process. More explicit inclusion and theorizing of emotions in social innovation studies thus may reveal further insights and opportunities for the literature.

NOTES

1. http://cmngd.com/ (accessed 5 December 2017).
2. http://www.beelovebuzz.com/about-us/ (accessed 5 December 2017).
3. http://www.abc.net.au/news/2016-07-29/palm-oil-what-you-need-to-know-about-push-to-make-it-sustainable/7672312 (accessed 5 December 2017).
4. While Tracey and Stott include institutional entrepreneurs in this category, we have chosen to leave them out, as our reading of the literature suggests that actors in all categories of social innovation have been described as institutional entrepreneurs.
5. http://www.dumpstarbucks.com/documents/memo.pdf (accessed 5 December 2017).
6. https://www.bizjournals.com/seattle/video/c1eDBjYTo4LXS3IoL7s_pSdNyONvOFwF?autoplay=1 (accessed 5 December 2017).
7. http://www.interfaceglobal (accessed 5 December 2017).

REFERENCES

Ackermann, F., L.A. Franco, B. Gallupe and M. Parent (2005), 'GSS for multi-organizational collaboration: reflections on process and content', *Group Decision and Negotiation*, **14**(4), 307–31.
Alter, S.K. (2006), 'Social enterprise models and their mission and money relationships', in A. Nicholls (ed.), *Social Entrepreneurship: New Models of Sustainable Social Change*, Oxford: Oxford University Press, pp. 205–32.
Bail, C.A. (2012), 'The fringe effect: civil society organizations and the evolution of media discourse about Islam since the September 11th attacks', *American Sociological Review*, **77**(6), 855–79.
Bardy, R., A. Rubens and G. Jackson (2013), 'Contributing to changes of social order in emerging nations: the spillover effect of foreign direct investment', *Journal of International Management Studies*, **8**, 47–58.
Batson, C.D. and L.L. Shaw (1991), 'Evidence for altruism: toward a pluralism of prosocial motives', *Psychological Inquiry*, **2**(2), 107–22.
Battilana, J. and S. Dorado (2010), 'Building sustainable hybrid organizations: the case of commercial microfinance organizations', *Academy of Management Journal*, **53**(6), 1419–40.
Benford, R.D. and D.A. Snow (2000), 'Framing processes and social movements: an overview and assessment', *Annual Review of Sociology*, **26**(1), 611–39.
Bertels, S., A.J. Hoffman and R. DeJordy (2014), 'The varied work of challenger movements: identifying challenger roles in the US environmental movement', *Organization Studies*, **35**(8), 1171–210.
Bloom, G. and M. Pirson (2010), 'Supporting social change agents through the classroom: the SE lab model', *Journal of Corporate Citizenship*, **39**, 103–11.
Bourdieu, P. (2000), *Pascalian Meditations*, trans. R. Nice, Stanford, CA: Stanford University Press.
Briscoe, F. and A. Gupta (2016), 'Social activism in and around organizations', *Academy of Management Annals*, **10**(1), 671–727.
Briscoe, F. and S. Safford (2008), 'The Nixon-in-China effect: activism, imitation and the institutionalization of contentious practices', *Administrative Science Quarterly*, **53**(3), 460–91.
Bröer, C. and J. Duyvendak (2009), 'Discursive opportunities, feeling rules, and the rise of protests against aircraft noise', *Mobilization: An International Quarterly*, **14**(3), 337–56.
Bunderson, J.S. and J.A. Thompson (2009), 'The call of the wild: zookeepers, callings, and the double-edged sword of deeply meaningful work', *Administrative Science Quarterly*, **54**(1), 32–57.
Calhoun, C. (2001), 'Putting emotions in their place', in J. Goodwin, J.M. Jasper and F. Polletta (eds), *Passionate Politics: Emotions and Social Movements*, Chicago, IL: University of Chicago Press, pp. 45–57.
Cardon, M.S., J. Wincent, J. Singh and M. Drnovsek (2009), 'The nature and experience of entrepreneurial passion', *Academy of Management Review*, **34**(3), 511–32.

Cardon, M.S., C. Post and W.R. Forster (2017), 'Team entrepreneurial passion: its emergence and influence in new venture teams', *Academy of Management Review*, **42**(2), 283–305.

Cartel, M., E. Boxenbaum and F. Aggeri (2019), 'Just for fun! How experimental spaces stimulate innovation in institutionalized fields', *Organization Studies*, **40**(1), 65–92.

Castello, I., D. Barbera and C. Zietsma (2013), 'Intentional field creation: the case of an anti-plastic pollution social movement', in *Academy of Management Proceedings* (Vol. 2013, No. 1), Briarcliff Manor, NY: Academy of Management, p. 15951.

Collins, R. (1993), 'Emotional energy as the common denominator of rational action', *Rationality and Society*, **5**(2), 203–30.

Collins, R. (2004), *Interaction Ritual Chains*, Princeton, NJ: Princeton University Press.

Creed, W.D., B.A. Hudson, G.A. Okhuysen and K. Smith-Crowe (2014), 'Swimming in a sea of shame: incorporating emotion into explanations of institutional reproduction and change', *Academy of Management Review*, **39**(3), 275–301.

Davis, G. and C.J. White (2015), *Changing Your Company from Inside Out: A Guide for Social Intrapreneurs*, Boston, MA: Harvard Business Review Press.

Dees, J.G. (1998), *The Meaning of 'Social Entrepreneurship'*, Palo Alto, CA: Stanford University Press.

Delmestri, G. and E. Goodrick (2016), 'Looking away: denial and emotions in institutional stability and change', in J. Gehman, M. Lounsbury and R. Greenwood (eds), *How Institutions Matter! Research in the Sociology of Organizations*, Vol. 48A, Bingley, UK: Emerald Group Publishing, pp. 235–74.

Doern, R. and D. Goss (2014), 'The role of negative emotions in the social processes of entrepreneurship: power rituals and shame-related appeasement behaviors', *Entrepreneurship Theory and Practice*, **38**(4), 863–90.

Dutton, J.E. and J.M. Dukerich (1991), 'Keeping an eye on the mirror: image and identity in organizational adaptation', *Academy of Management Journal*, **34**(3), 517–54.

Eden, C. and C. Huxham (2001), 'The negotiation of purpose in multi-organizational collaborative groups', *Journal of Management Studies*, **38**(3), 373–91.

Fan, G. and C. Zietsma (2017), 'Constructing a shared governance logic: the role of emotions in enabling dually embedded agency', *Academy of Management Journal*, **60**, 2321–51.

Ferraro, F., D. Etzion and J. Gehman (2015), 'Tackling grand challenges pragmatically: robust action revisited', *Organization Studies*, **36**(3), 363–90.

Fineman, S. (ed.) (2000), *Emotions in Organizations*, London: Sage.

Friedland, R. (2018), 'Moving institutional logics forward: emotion and meaningful material practice', *Organization Studies*, **39**(4), 515–42.

George, G., J. Howard-Grenville, A. Joshi and L. Tihanyi (2016), 'Understanding and tackling societal grand challenges through management research', *Academy of Management Journal*, **59**(6), 1880–95.

Gill, M. and R. Burrow (2018), 'The function of fear in institutional maintenance: feeling frightened as an essential ingredient in haute cuisine', *Organization Studies*, **39**(4), 445–65.

Giorgi, S. (2017), 'The mind and heart of resonance: the role of cognition and emotions in frame effectiveness', *Journal of Management Studies*, **54**, 711–38.

Goetz, J.L., D. Keltner and E. Simon-Thomas (2010), 'Compassion: an evolutionary analysis and empirical review', *Psychological Bulletin*, **136**, 351–74.

Goodwin, J., J.M. Jasper and F. Polletta (2001), *Passionate Politics: Emotions and Social Movements*, Chicago, IL: University of Chicago Press.

Goss, D. (2005), 'Entrepreneurship and "the social": towards a deference-emotion theory', *Human Relations*, **58**(5), 617–736.

Goss, D., R. Jones, M. Betta and J. Latham (2011), 'Power as practice: a micro-sociological analysis of the dynamics of emancipatory entrepreneurship', *Organization Studies*, **32**(2), 211–29.

Gould, D.B. (2009), *Moving Politics: Emotion and ACT UP's Fight Against AIDS*, Chicago, IL: University of Chicago Press.

Gray, B., J.M. Purdy and S. Ansari (2015), 'From interactions to institutions: microprocesses of framing and mechanisms for the structuring of institutional fields', *Academy of Management Review*, **40**(1), 115–43.

Grayson, D., M. McLaren and H. Spitzeck (2017), *Social Intrapreneurism and All That Jazz: How Business Innovators are Helping to Build a More Sustainable World*, New York: Routledge.

Grimes, M.G., J.S. McMullen, T.J. Vogus and T.L. Miller (2013), 'Studying the origins of social entrepreneurship: compassion and the role of embedded agency', *Academy of Management Review*, **38**(3), 460–3.

Grodal, S., A. Nelson and R. Siino (2015), 'Help-seeking and help-giving as an organizational routine: continual engagement in innovative work', *Academy of Management Journal*, **28**(1), 136–68.

Gundry, L.K., J.R. Kickul, M.D. Griffiths and S.C. Bacq (2011), 'Creating social change out of nothing: the role of entrepreneurial bricolage in social entrepreneurs' catalytic innovations', *Advances in Entrepreneurship, Firm Emergence and Growth*, **13**, 1–24.

Gutierrez, B., J. Howard-Grenville and M.A. Scully (2010), 'The faithful rise up: split identification and an unlikely change effort', *Academy of Management Journal*, **53**(4), 673–700.

Jasper, J.M. (2011), 'Emotions and social movements: twenty years of theory and research', *Annual Review of Sociology*, **37**, 285–303.
Jasper, J.M. and J.D. Poulsen (1995), 'Recruiting strangers and friends – moral shocks and social networks in animal rights and antinuclear protests', *Social Problems*, **42**, 493–512.
Jay, J. (2013), 'Navigating paradox as a mechanism of change and innovation in hybrid organizations', *Academy of Management Journal*, **56**(1), 137–59.
Jennings, J.E., T. Edwards, P. Jennings and R. Delbridge (2015), 'Emotional arousal and entrepreneurial outcomes: combining qualitative methods to elaborate theory', *Journal of Business Venturing*, **30**(1), 113–30.
Kenney, J.S. and A. Craig (2012), 'Illegitimate pain: introducing a concept and a research agenda', in A. Hunt, K. Walby and D. Spencer (eds), *Emotions Matter: A Relational Approach to Emotions*, Toronto: University of Toronto Press, pp. 86–101.
Kickul, J. and T.S. Lyons (2016), *Understanding Social Entrepreneurship*, 2nd edn, New York: Routledge.
Lazarus, R.S. (1991), 'Progress on a cognitive-motivational relational theory of emotion', *American Psychologist*, **46**, 819–34.
Leung, A., C. Zietsma and A.M. Peredo (2014), 'Revolution of the middle-class housewives: identity work as a process for embedded change', *Organization Studies*, **35**(3), 423–50.
Lok, J., W.D. Creed, R. DeJordy and M. Voronov (2017), 'Living institutions: bringing emotions into organizational institutionalism', in R. Greenwood, C. Oliver, R. Meyer and T.B. Lawrence (eds), *Sage Handbook of Organizational Insitutionalism*, 2nd edn, London: Sage, pp. 591–620.
Lounsbury, M. (2001), 'Institutional sources of practice variation: staffing college and university recycling programs', *Administrative Science Quarterly*, **46**(1), 29–56.
Mair, J., I. Martí and M.J. Ventresca (2012), 'Building inclusive markets in rural Bangladesh: how intermediaries work institutional voids', *Academy of Management Journal*, **55**(4), 819–50.
Martí, I. and P. Fernández (2015), 'Entrepreneurship, togetherness and emotions', *Journal of Management Inquiry*, **24**(4), 424–8.
Massa, F.G., W.S. Helms, M. Voronov and L. Wang (2017), 'Emotions uncorked: inspiring evangelism for the emerging practice of cool-climate winemaking in Ontario', *Academy of Management Journal*, **60**(2), 461–99.
McKague, K., C. Zietsma and C. Oliver (2015), 'Building the social structure of a market', *Organization Studies*, **36**(8), 1063–93.
Meyerson, D.E. (2001), 'Radical change, the quiet way', *Harvard Business Review*, **79**(9), 92–100.
Meyerson, D. and M. Scully (1993), 'Tempered radicalism and the politics of ambivalence: personal alignment and radical change within traditional organizations', *Organization Science*, **6**(5), 585–600.
Miller, T.L., M.G. Grimes, J.S. McMullen and T.J. Vogus (2012), 'Venturing for others with heart and head: how compassion encourages social entrepreneurship', *Academy of Management Review*, **37**(4), 616–40.
Moon, D. (2013), 'Powerful emotions: symbolic power and the (productive and punitive) force of collective feeling', *Theory and Society*, **42**, 261–94.
Mulgan, G. (2006), 'The process of social innovation', *Innovations: Technology, Governance, Globalization*, **1**(2), 145–62.
Mulgan, G. (2012), 'The theoretical foundations of social innovation', in A. Nicholls and A. Murdock (eds), *Social Innovation*, London: Palgrave Macmillan, pp. 33–65.
Ndinguri, E., S.T.A. Phipps and L.C. Prieto (2014), 'Predictors of entrepreneurial venture exploitation tendencies: role of gender, emotion, motivation and role model accessibility', *Academy of Entrepreneurship Journal*, **20**(1), 23–36.
Nussbaum, M. (1996), 'Compassion: the basic social emotion', *Social Philosophy and Policy*, **13**, 27–58.
Nussbaum, M.C. (2001), *Upheavals of Thought: The Intelligence of Emotions*, Cambridge: Cambridge University Press.
Omoto, A.M., A.M. Maisch and J.A. Barraza (2009), 'Compassionate acts: motivations for and correlates of volunteerism among older adults', in B. Fehr, S. Sprecher and L.G. Underwood (eds), *The Science of Compassionate Love: Theory, Research, and Applications*, Chichester, UK: Blackwell, pp. 257–82.
Pache, A.-C. and F. Santos (2012), 'Inside the hybrid organization: selective coupling as a reponse to conflicting institutional logics', *Academy of Management Journal*, **56**(4), 972–1001.
Pache, A.-C. and F. Santos (2013), 'Embedded in hybrid contexts: how individuals in organizations respond to competing institutional logics', in M. Lounsbury and E. Boxenbaum (eds), *Research in the Sociology of Organizations: Institutional Logics in Action, Part B*, Vol. 39B, Bingley, UK: Emerald Group Publishing, pp. 3–35.
Pacheco, D.F., J.G. York and T.J. Hargrave (2014), 'The coevolution of industries, social movements, and institutions: wind power in the United States', *Organization Science*, **25**(6), 1609–32.
Paulin, M., R.J. Ferguson, K. Schattke and N. Jost (2014), 'Millennials, social media, prosocial emotions and charitable causes: the paradox of gender differences', *Journal of Nonprofit and Public Sector Marketing*, **26**(4), 335–53.

Phills, J.A., K. Deiglmeier and D.T. Miller (2008), 'Rediscovering social innovation', *Stanford Social Innovation Review*, **6**(4), 34–43.
Polletta, F. and J.M. Jasper (2001), 'Collective identity and social movements', *Annual Review of Sociology*, **27**, 283–305.
Pratt, M.G. (2000), 'The good, the bad and the ambivalent: managing identification among Amway distributors', *Administrative Science Quarterly*, **45**(3), 456–93.
Purtik, H. and D. Arenas (forthcoming), 'Embedding social innovation: shaping societal norms and behaviors throughout the innovation process', *Business and Society*. https://doi.org/10.1177/0007650318758329.
Qureshi, I., G.M. Kistruck and B. Bhatt (2016), 'The enabling and constraining effects of social ties in the process of institutional entrepreneurship', *Organization Studies*, **37**(3), 425–47.
Rowley, T.J. and M. Moldoveanu (2003), 'When will stakeholder groups act? An interest- and identity-based model of stakeholder group mobilization', *Academy of Management Review*, **28**(2), 204–19.
Ruebottom, T. and E.R. Auster (2018), 'Reflexive dis/embedding: personal narratives, empowerment and the emotional dynamics of interstitial events', *Organization Studies*, **39**(4), 467–90.
Schrock, D., D. Holden and L. Reid (2004), 'Creating emotional resonance: interpersonal emotion work and motivational framing in a transgender community', *Social Problems*, **51**, 61–81.
Selznick, P. (1957), *Leadership in Administration: A Sociological Interpretation*, New York: Harper and Row.
Stein, A. (2001), 'Revenge of the shamed: Christian right's emotional culture war', in J. Goodwin, J.M. Jasper and F. Polletta (eds), *Passionate Politics: Emotions and Social Movements*, Chicago, IL: University of Chicago Press, pp. 115–31.
Tajfel, H. (1978), *Differentiation Between Social Groups*, London: Academic Press.
Tajfel, H. (ed.) (1982), *Social Identity and Inter-Group Relations*, Cambridge: Cambridge University Press.
Teegen, H., J.P. Doh and S. Vachani (2004), 'The importance of nongovernmental organizations (NGOs) in global governance and value creation: an international business research agenda', *Journal of International Business Studies*, **35**(6), 463–83.
Tobias, J.M., J. Mair and C. Barbosa-Leiker (2013), 'Toward a theory of transformative entrepreneuring: poverty reduction and conflict resolution in Rwanda's entrepreneurial coffee sector', *Journal of Business Venturing*, **28**, 728–42.
Toubiana, M. (2014), *Once in Orange Always in Orange? The Cognitive, Emotional and Material Elements of De-identification and Logic Resilience*, York: Schulich School of Business, York University.
Toubiana, M. and C. Zietsma (2017), 'The message is on the wall? Emotions, social media and the dynamics of institutional complexity', *Academy of Management Journal*, **60**(3), 1–32.
Tracey, P. and N. Phillips (2016), 'Managing the consequences of organizational stigmatization: identity work in a social enterprise', *Academy of Management Journal*, **59**(3), 740–65.
Tracey, P. and N. Stott (2017), 'Social innovation: a window on alternate ways of organizing and innovating', *Innovation: Organization and Management*, **19**, 51–60.
Tracey, P., N. Phillips and O. Jarvis (2011), 'Bridging institutional entrepreneurship and the creation of new organizational forms: a multilevel model', *Organization Science*, **22**(1), 60–80.
Turner, J.H. and J.E. Stets (2005), *The Sociology of Emotions*, Cambridge: Cambridge University Press.
Vaccaro, A. and G. Palazzo (2015), 'Values against violence: institutional change in societies dominated by organized crime', *Academy of Management Journal*, **58**(4), 1075–101.
Van Wijk, J., W. Stam, T. Elfring, C. Zietsma and F. Hond (2013), 'Activists and incumbents structuring change: the interplay of agency, culture and networks in field evolution', *Academy of Management Journal*, **56**, 358–86.
Voronov, M. and R. Vince (2012), 'Integrating emotions into the analysis of institutional work', *Academy of Management Review*, **37**(1), 58–81.
Voronov, M. and K. Weber (2016), 'The heart of institutions: emotional competence and institutional actorhood', *Academy of Management Review*, **41**(3), 456–78.
Westley, F. and N. Antadze (2010), 'Making a difference: strategies for scaling social innovation for greater impact', *Innovation Journal*, **15**(2). https://www.innovation.cc/scholarly-style/2010_15_2_2_westley-antadze_social-innovate.pdf
Wijaya, H. and P. Heugens (2018), 'Give me a hallelujah! Amen! Institutional reproduction in the presence of moral perturbation and the dynamics of emotional investment', *Organization Studies*, **39**(4), 491–514.
Yitshaki, R. and F. Kropp (2016), 'Entrepreneurial passions and identities in different contexts: a comparison between high-tech and social entrepreneurs', *Entrepreneurship and Regional Development*, **28**(3/4), 206–33.
Zietsma, C. and T. Lawrence (2010), 'Institutional work in the transformation of an organizational field: the interplay of boundary work and practice work', *Administrative Science Quarterly*, **55**, 189–221.
Zietsma, C. and M. Toubiana (2018), 'The valuable, the constitutive and the energetic: exploring the impact and importance of studying emotions and institutions', *Organization Studies*, **39**(4), 427–43.

19. Income inequality: consequences and implications for social innovation

Xiang Zhou and Jason D. Shaw

Inequality is increasing throughout the world, including in the world's dominant economies such as the United States, Germany, China, and India (Alderson and Nielsen, 2002; Hung and Kucinskas, 2011; Ravallion, 2014). Wage premiums for skilled workers, globalization, and technological change are among the many work- and technology-based explanations for growing income disparities (Atkinson, 2016), but other factors such as greed may also play a role. In this chapter, we focus primarily on the outcomes of income inequality, the social consequences, and social innovations that alleviate certain disparities. First, we briefly discuss the definitions and measurements of income inequality. We then review commonly associated consequences and discuss proposed social innovations for ameliorating negative inequality. We conclude by suggesting several future research directions.

DEFINITIONS AND MEASUREMENTS OF INCOME INEQUALITY

Income inequality is defined as "the degree to which income in a given geographic area is distributed equally or unequally" (Eckenrode et al., 2014, p. 455). Although income equality can be measured within and between continents, geographic regions, or economic regions (for example, Heshmati, 2006; Ravallion, 2014), researchers most commonly study within-organization and within- and between-country inequality, typically referring to pay or wage disparities, spreads, or ranges (Shaw, 2014). In recent years, average within-country income inequality has been increasing, but between-country inequality has been decreasing (Hung and Kucinskas, 2011). In this chapter, we focus on two of the most studied income inequalities – within organizations and within countries. Other types of income inequality are beyond the scope of this chapter.

To operationalize income inequality, researchers have focused on wages, household income, or family income. Cowell (2011) provides a detailed discussion of inequality measurements, the most common being the Gini coefficient, the Theil index, the Robin Hood index, 90/10 family income ratio, coefficient of variation, and range. The literature's most dominant approach may be the Gini coefficient in which researchers observe "half of the arithmetic average of the absolute differences between all pairs of incomes in a population, the total then being normalized on mean income" (Subramanian and Kawachi, 2004, p. 78). The Gini index varies from 0, indicating perfect equality where everyone has an equal share of the aggregate income to 1, indicating perfect inequality where one person has all the income and the rest have none. Different measures of income inequality have distinct properties, but all operationalizations have strong intercorrelations and yield similar results (Evans et al., 2004; Shaw et al., 2002).

OUTCOMES OF INCOME INEQUALITY

In this chapter, we selectively review research in sociology, economics, and management disciplines, and summarize outcomes regarding within-organization and within-country income inequalities. For within-organization income inequality, the focus of management scholars, we concentrate on the frequently investigated behavioral and attitudinal outcomes. For within-nation income inequality, the purview of sociology and economics researchers, we review six commonly investigated outcomes associated with income inequality – health, crime, education, politics, social relations, and economic growth. The literature has identified other outcomes such as carbon emissions (Jorgenson et al., 2017).

Income Inequality Within Organizations

Within-organization income inequality usually occurs through unequal pay or wage dispersion, defined as "differences in pay levels between individuals within (i.e. horizontal or lateral dispersion) or across (i.e. vertical dispersion) jobs or organizational levels" (Shaw, 2014, p. 522). Management researchers have shown that pay and wage dispersion affects employee behaviors and attitudes, as indicated in outcomes such as performance and turnover.

Historically, the pay or wage dispersion literature has offered competing theories regarding positive and negative effects of pay dispersion on employee outcomes. Psychological theories of motivation suggest that highly dispersed pay motivates employees to perform well because they perceive that good performance leads to positive organizational outcomes (Lawler, 1971; Shaw, 2014). Higher pay dispersion is thought to sort superior from inferior performers and applicants (Lazear, 1999). Tournament theory also indicates that higher pay dispersion generates effort and performance. Alternatively, highly dispersed pay is thought to undermine cohesion and cooperation (Pfeffer and Langton, 1993).

A theory of explained and unexplained variation from Shaw et al. (2002) mostly resolves the competing perspectives. That is, the degree of dispersion or compression should be considered against whether pay differences can be explained with normatively acceptable reasons. For example, when employees are paid for individual performance, they react more positively to higher pay dispersion. Alternatively, when individual contributions do not explain pay variations, employees do not accept high dispersion. The theory also suggests that employees react negatively when income equality or pay compression are illegitimately dispensed. For example, employees will perceive non-differentiated pay as unfair when they work in low interdependence situations or when they are presumably paid for performance. Support for the general theory is found in numerous alternative contexts (for example, Shaw, 2015; Trevor et al., 2012) and in contexts outside of pay decisions (Garg et al., 2018).

Unsurprisingly, the explained dispersion theory has caused researchers to find generally weak to moderate main effect on the relationship between horizontal or vertical pay dispersion and organizational outcomes, as shown in the meta-analytic evidence (Song and Shaw, 2018). Despite extensive negative publicity about the ills of dispersed pay, researchers generally find positive although unsubstantial relationships between pay dispersion and dimensions of organizational performance. For example, across all types of organizational performance, vertical dispersion, in which pay is spread between the lowest and highest organizational levels, is related to performance (ρ = 0.08), and the difference significantly diverges from zero. Horizontal dispersion, in contrast, correlates with performance only at 0.01. The relationships are also weak in performance facets such as quality and productivity. Only turnover rates are moderately associated with pay dispersion (ρ = 0.17). Given that explained dispersion theory has predictive ability (Shaw et al., 2002), vertical and horizontal dispersions are expected to have limited direct effects. Consequently, research must advance beyond testing of explained pay dispersion to further determine whether variation has stable effects on outcomes.

Beyond common performance outcomes, the management literature offers little guidance in terms of other outcomes such as safety, well-being, and citizenship behaviors. In a rare study, Drago and Garvey (1998) examined pay dispersion effects on employees' helping behaviors and found support for the tournament, or contest, model. That is, promotion-based incentives were related to increased individual effort and decreased helping effort.

Similarly, only two studies have observed how within-organization income inequity relates to attitudes (Shaw, 2014). Using social comparison theory, Trevor and Wazeter (2006) found pay dispersion to be negatively related to pay equity perceptions in a large sample of public school teachers, but only for teachers with low internal pay standing. Analysing a sample of Danish employees, Clark et al. (2009) examined how comparative pay dispersion influenced job satisfaction. They found that employees feel relatively deprived when they compare earnings with higher-paid coworkers or feel hopeful in that higher coworker pay signals chances for higher future pay. Signaling effects outweighed status effects for predicting attitudes. Furthermore, within-occupation pay dispersion was negatively related to job satisfaction, while across-occupation pay dispersion was positively related to job satisfaction.

Pay dispersion has been associated with employee attitudes. Harris et al. (2008) studied the relationship between income comparisons and pay level satisfaction and found satisfaction became lower when pay fell below upward comparison pay levels but became higher when pay level moved closer to upward comparison pay levels. Perceptions of pay fairness may further influence life satisfaction, health outcomes, and job search intentions (Shaw and Gupta, 2001). Thus, when normatively accepted factors of performance, seniority, skill, longevity, and rank fail to explain highly dispersed pay variations, unfavorable social comparisons are likely. Consequently, attitudes may serve to mediate between explained versus unexplained dispersion and more distal organizational outcomes.

Income Inequality Within Nations

Health and well-being

Various theories and some robust evidence indicate that income and societal inequality are associated with poorer population health and well-being, but the conceptualizations differ dramatically from within-organization conceptualizations (Subramanian and Kawachi, 2004). In societies where wealth is highly concentrated at high levels, large groups live at or near abject poverty, with limited access to quality food and medical care. Consequently, wealthier groups may suffer spillover effects in that the unfavorable health conditions of the poor can erode social cohesion and increase psychological stress (Kondo et al., 2009). Another possibility is that income inequality damages public health through localized environmental pollution (Cushing et al., 2015) and increased mortality (Kennedy et al., 1996).

Going beyond sociological and epidemiological factors, Shaw et al. (2002) offered the explainable outcome theory arguing that psychological and attitudinal factors are causal mechanisms. In particular, excessive disparities often belie reasoning or logic, thus leading to widespread conclusions that they are illegitimate. Thus, high income inequality generates social comparisons that instigate feelings of unfairness, lack of trust, and reduced subjective well-being (Cheung and Lucas, 2016; Oishi et al., 2011). For example, using general social survey data, Oishi et al. (2011) found that perceived unfairness and lack of trust mediated the negative relationship between income inequality and happiness.

Despite the lack of large-scale empirical summary studies, a small meta-analysis of 19 cross-sectional studies revealed that income inequality is negatively related to self-rated health (Kondo et al., 2009). With conceptual variables at such a high level of analysis, it is difficult to draw causal conclusions. Clearly, most studies find that income inequality is negatively associated with population health (Wilkinson and Pickett, 2006).

Crime

Inequality has complex, multi-perspective relationships with criminal behavior. Societal unfairness may cause those who feel relatively deprived to perceive crime as a way to even the score (Stack, 1984). Wealth and power convey unequal structural advantages and opportunities, which may lead to criminal deviancy (Merton, 1968). Social disorganization theory argues that poverty and income inequality weaken community control (Shaw and McKay, 1942). Economists consider that crime involves opportunity costs and apprehension penalties (Becker, 1968).

The literature offers consistent although dated evidence supporting the general conclusion that economic inequality is positively associated with homicide (for example, Blau and Blau, 1982). Using cross-country time-series data, Fajnzylber et al. (2002) found that income inequality (Gini index) and GDP growth were the most robust and significant determinants of homicide or robbery. In a meta-analysis of 34 aggregate studies, Hsieh and Pugh (1993) found that poverty and income inequality were positively associated with violent crime. Pratt and Cullen (2005) conducted a meta-analysis and found that economic inequality was one of the strongest predictors of crime, with an overall mean effect size of 0.21. Using a dataset on urban counties, Kelly (2000) found support that social disorganization theory, strain theory, and economic theory all explain crime. Specifically, economic theory most strongly explained property crime; strain and social disorganization theory best explained violent crime.

Education

Low- and high-income families tend to vary in their parenting practices (Hoff et al., 2002), time use (Phillips, 2011), and educational expenditures (Kaushal et al., 2011), all factors associated with or contributing to gaps in educational achievement (Bailey and Dynarski, 2011; Reardon, 2011). For example, Phillips (2011) demonstrated that children in high-income families tend to be exposed to more adult speech and more books, contributing to superior academic performance. In an analysis of data from the US census and national longitudinal surveys, Bailey and Dynarski (2011) found that children from high-income families show higher college completion rates, while children from lower-income families show rather stable completion rates (Bailey and Dynarski, 2011). Even kindergarteners show gaps between family income and achievement (Chetty et al., 2014; Reardon, 2011). Differential access to private education (Besley and Coate, 1991) has disproportionate effects on later opportunities and mobility (Bailey and Dynarski, 2011; Neckerman and Torche, 2007).

Politics

Political scientists have historically contended that median voters are essential to political victories (Meltzer and Richard, 1981). However, as income disparity rises, median voters have less relative income and less political force, so that policies begin to diverge from the interests of those at the median and below. Although the literature has given mixed support to the median voter view (Lenz, 2004), some studies find evidence that higher income equality negatively affects those at lower ends. For example, Moene and Wallerstein (2001, 2003) found income inequality to be negatively associated with welfare spending for the unemployed and positively associated with welfare spending for the employed. The median voter model fails to consider that voting participation decreases as income decreases (Leighley and Nagler, 2013) so that public opinion becomes more focused on the needs of the privileged (Erikson, 2015). Therefore, income inequality may increase the low-income population but not the voting population (Lenz, 2004). Using cross-nation datasets, Solt (2008) found that as income inequality increases, the rich gain more power and influence, and political processes are more relevant to their interests. Gilens (2012) also argued that income disparity is associated with representational and political inequality. Besides political engagement and policymaking, You and Khagram (2005) argued and found that corruption increases when income inequality increases, perhaps because the rich use resources and motivation to secure current advantages, while the poor lack both material and normative resources to monitor and stop such processes.

Social relations

Another side effect of rising income inequality is residential segregation of rich and poor neighborhoods (Jargowsky 1996; Mayer, 2001; Reardon and Bischoff, 2011). The sociological and psychological literature (Neckerman and Torche, 2007) and the endogenous stratification view (Durlauf, 1996) explain the effects in terms of homophily. That is, higher-income individuals form homogeneous communities that have better-funded community support programs, facilities, and infrastructure. Thus, very few people enjoy disproportional motivation and resources to live in restricted communities (Benabou, 1996; Durlauf, 1996). As a result, low-income and high-income families form segregated communities.

Income inequality also appears to negatively affect collective social capital. Alesina and La Ferrara (2000) argued that population heterogeneity combining with homophily preferences prevents mixed income groups from associating with one another. They found support for their predictions that income inequality, ethnic fragmentation, and racial fragmentation are negatively related to participation in social activities. Leana and Meuris (2015) argued that under high income inequality, income is a social cue to infer and predict attitudes and behavior, which reduces interpersonal and collective trust. DiMaggio and Garip (2012) argued that networks aggravate intergroup inequality: members of homogeneous networks benefit one another and protect one another from harm.

Economic growth

Economists have offered alternative theories regarding income inequality's long-term impacts on economic growth. Persson and Tabellini (1994) combined the theories of endogenous growth and endogenous policy and used cross-sectional and panel data to show that public policies emphasizing regulation and redistribution impair production incentives and impede economic growth. In contrast, Foellmi and Zweimüller (2006) showed that the price effect motivates innovators to pursue high profits from the wealthy, but the market-size effect demotivates innovators because the market for new products becomes narrower. To explain why Korea and the Philippines have different growth rates, Benabou (1996) reviewed several theories regarding inequality and economic growth and hypothesized that credit constraints impede human capital accumulations. That is, credit constraints prevent the poor from making efficient amounts of investments. However, redistribution can allow them to earn higher returns, leading to higher growth rates (Benabou, 1996). Thus, *in toto*, the relationship between income inequality and economic growth remains unsettled.

Taking stock

The literature provides diverse and nuanced views of the relationships between income inequality and organizational and societal outcomes. At the organizational level, pay disparities have no consistent main effects on outcomes, but legitimate dispersion-creating practices and policies have several beneficial effects on performance and turnover patterns (Shaw, 2014). In contrast, only a few researchers have shown that nation-level inequality has consistent positive outcomes (Foellmi and Zweimüller, 2006). Although qualitative assessments can be nettlesome and quantitative summaries are needed, the literature is replete with empirical findings showing that income inequality has negative social, economic, physical, and psychological outcomes, such as educational inequality, crime, mortality, and substance abuse (Burdick-Will et al., 2011; Harding et al., 2010; Pebley and Sastry, 2004).

Causal directions between inequality and consequences are clearly multidirectional. For example, Beramendi and Rueda (2014) acknowledged that inequality shapes political involvement, constitution, and polarization, and that redistribution policies along with other factors explain patterns of income inequality (for example, Goñi et al., 2011). Some researchers argue that deeply intertwined governmental and economic policies constitute winner-take-all politics that produce winner-take-all economies (Hacker and Pierson, 2010).

FUTURE RESEARCH ON INCOME INEQUALITY AND SOCIAL INNOVATIONS

Many actions and interventions that could assuage the negative effects of income inequality fall under the general umbrella of social innovation – "organizational and inter-organizational activity that is ostensibly desired to address the most deep-rooted 'problems' of society" (Tracey and Stott, 2017, p. 51). For decades, scholars have studied conventional social solutions involving educational, fiscal, and other forms of redistribution. Some studies support redistribution (for example, Cooper, 1998); others do not (for example, Mulligan, 1995). Government-level social innovations include programs such as the Moving to Opportunity social experiment in the United States, which tested whether housing vouchers would improve housing, earnings, and education-based outcomes (Ludwig et al., 2013). Next, we summarize some social-innovation-based actions that organizations and governments may take to address income inequality. We also outline suggestions for future research on income inequality.

Governments often try to alleviate the problems associated with income inequalities. Autor (2014) argued that governments can most effectively reduce inequality by cultivating skills, such as through labor legislations ensuring safe working environments and through programs ensuring that children of all socioeconomic backgrounds have access to postsecondary education, good nutrition, and public health. For example, the US government instituted the Temporary Assistance for Needy Families Program to provide financial assistance to low-income families and the Supplemental Nutrition Assistance Program to provide food coupons for low-income families and individuals. The Moving to Opportunity experiment improved physical health and well-being in low-income families (Katz et al., 2001; Leventhal and Brooks-Gunn, 2003). Housing vouchers allowing relocation improved earnings and education (Chetty et al., 2016). The UK government offered the Working Tax Credit Programme providing tax benefits for low-income workers.

Atkinson (2016) suggested that when governments make policies and allocate research funds, they should invest in technological changes that favor labor to enhance employment and address other social urgencies. Rather than funding robotic research and driverless cars, governments should create demand for more care providers by promoting technologies that help the elderly stay in their homes. That is, properly constructed efforts to reduce income inequality would not impair economic performance and may instead boost it.

Some non-profit organizations are successfully using social innovation interventions to address inequality. For-profit organizations might use their models as well. Volunteers for LIFT, a US organization, provide holistic solutions such as personal well-being, social connections, and financial strength to help poor families break poverty cycles (LIFT, 2017a). LIFT recently reported that volunteers have helped poor families increase their average savings by $950 and decrease their average debts by $2,000 (LIFT, 2017b).

In a review of the working poor, Meuris and Leana (2015) suggested that organizations can alleviate income inequality and scarcity issues by (1) increasing wages for low-income employees; (2) redesigning jobs to develop knowledge and skills, reduce uncertainty, and provide autonomy; and (3) provide employee benefits that promote savings, support family responsibilities, and offer health and wellness programs.

Income inequality has practical and scholarly importance, but the literature lacks systematic data and research integration. We have offered some broad directions for future research on income inequality and social innovation. We suggest that income alone fails to capture complete gains. Instead, alternative measurements would more fully depict income inequality and possible solutions, such as the rarely studied measurement of non-monetary work returns (for example, Hamermesh, 1999), a particularly important issue because non-wage inequality may rise equally as fast or faster than income disparity (Pierce, 2001). Cumulative wage inequality is another recommended alternative measure (Bowlus and Robin, 2004; Evans et al., 2004; Flinn, 2002).

We call for future research to more rigorously test theories used in the literature. For example, relative deprivation theory suggests that people have increased stress, negative attitudes, and negative behavior when they compare themselves with better-off others (Stack, 1984). Consumption is more observable than income (Evans et al., 2004). Thus, consumption inequality, which is generally lower than income inequality, may be a better test of some theories (Cutler and Katz, 1992; Krueger and Perri, 2006). This perhaps could explain why the literature finds weaker than anticipated finding regarding relative deprivation. Scholars should also assess comparison targets and comparison frequencies to determine how income relates to outcomes.

Scholars have made many proposals for obtaining relative equality, but few high-quality papers have examined the success of such policies (Exworthy et al., 2006). Although evidence of success is essential, Bleich et al. (2012) identified several reasons for the lack of research on policy effects, such as the time lag between policy implementation and observed effects, the difficulty of addressing the confounding effects of race and income, and the lack of systematic reports and data. Therefore, we suggest that scholars should conduct more rigorously designed social experiments or use systematic, time-lagged data to examine the effects of policies in eliminating income inequality.

Managerial researchers have largely avoided income inequality research (Beal and Astakhova, 2017). Although theory generally agrees that organizations can benefit from income dispersion (Shaw, 2014; Shaw et al., 2002), empirical evidence remains somewhat nascent. However, managerial scholars can contribute significantly to the income inequality literature by considering the role of organizational context (Beal and Astakhova, 2017).

Organizational researchers have studied issues such as performance appraisals and turnover mainly using middle- to high-income "textbook workers" as study participants rather than poor and low-status workers (Leana et al., 2012). Only scattered and scant research has focused on employee compensation (Gupta and Shaw, 2014), so that organizational behavior and human resource management scholars know little about the implications of increasing wages for the working poor (Meuris and Leana, 2015). We call for managerial scholars to join economist-led policy discussions to study income inequality and poverty issues in organizations if we are to understand effects on all workers and increase the generalizability of organizational research. For example, Leana and Meuris (2015) have called for more research on income inequality effects on teams, leaders, groups, and organizations.

Income inequality at one level may influence outcomes at other levels. Lemieux et al. (2009) showed that performance pay schemes contribute to wage inequalities. Beal and Astakhova (2017) suggested developing and examining multilevel models that link individual-level behaviors, organizational-level actions, and national- or even societal-level income inequality trends. Future research should use multilevel analyses to probe into "bottom-up" or "trickle-down" processes that generate or eliminate income inequality.

Sociology, economics, and public health disciplines have focused much attention on income inequality. The organizational behavior field could gain greater understandings of poverty and income inequality by combining those unique perspectives. Although research tends to be constrained by its boundaries and to avoid integrating information, it is essential to bridge and integrate disciplines to provide insights into inequality issues, inspire new research, and create new ways of seeing.

REFERENCES

Alderson, A. and F. Nielsen (2002), "Globalization and the great U-turn: income inequality trends in 16 OECD countries", *American Journal of Sociology*, **107** (5), 1244–99.

Alesina, A. and E. La Ferrara (2000), "Participation in heterogeneous communities", *Quarterly Journal of Economics*, **115** (3), 847–904.

Atkinson, A. (2016), "How to spread the wealth practical policies for reducing inequality", *Foreign Affairs*, **95** (1), 29–33.

Autor, D. (2014), "Skills, education, and the rise of earnings inequality among the 'other 99 percent'", *Science*, **344** (6186), 843–51.

Bailey, M.J. and Susan M. Dynarski (2011), "Inequality in postsecondary education", in G.J. Duncan and R.J. Murnane (eds), *Whither Opportunity? Rising Inequality, Schools, and Children's Life Chances*, New York and Chicago, IL: Russell Sage Foundation and Spencer Foundation, pp. 117–32.

Beal, B. and M. Astakhova (2017), "Management and income inequality: a review and conceptual framework", *Journal of Business Ethics*, **142** (1), 1–23.

Becker, G.S. (1968), "Crime and punishment: an economic approach", *Journal of Political Economy*, **76** (2), 169–217.

Benabou, R. (1996), "Inequality and growth", *NBER Macroeconomics Annual*, **11**, 11–74.

Beramendi, P. and D. Rueda (2014), "Inequality and institutions: the case of economic coordination", *Annual Review of Political Science*, **17**, 251–71.

Besley, T. and S. Coate (1991), "Public provision of private goods and the redistribution of income", *American Economic Review*, **81** (4), 979–84.

Blau, J.R. and P.M. Blau (1982), "The cost of inequality: metropolitan structure and violent crime", *American Sociological Review*, **47** (1), 114–29.

Bleich, S., M. Jarlenski, C. Bell and T. LaVeist (2012), "Health inequalities: trends, progress, and policy", *Annual Review of Public Health*, **33**, 7–40.

Bowlus, A.J. and J.-M. Robin (2004), "Twenty years of rising inequality in US lifetime labour income values", *Review of Economic Studies*, **71** (3), 709–42.

Burdick-Will, J., J. Ludwig, S.W. Raudenbush, R.J. Sampson, L. Sanbonmatsu and P. Sharkey (2011), "Converging evidence for neighborhood effects on children's test scores: an experimental, quasi-experimental, and observational comparison", in G.J. Duncan and R.J. Murnane (eds), *Whither Opportunity? Rising Inequality, Schools, and Children's Life Chances*, New York: Russell Sage Foundation, pp. 255–76.

Chetty, R., N. Hendren, P. Kline, E. Saez and N. Turner (2014), "Is the United States still a land of opportunity? Recent trends in intergenerational mobility", *American Economic Review*, **104** (5), 141–7.

Chetty, R., N. Hendren and L.F. Katz (2016), "The effects of exposure to better neighborhoods on children: new evidence from the Moving to Opportunity experiment", *American Economic Review*, **106** (4), 855–902.

Cheung, F. and R. Lucas (2016), "Income inequality is associated with stronger social comparison effects: the effect of relative income on life satisfaction", *Journal of Personality and Social Psychology*, **110** (2), 332–41.

Clark, A.E., N. Kristensen and N. Westergård-Nielsen (2009), "Job satisfaction and co-worker wages: status or signal?", *The Economic Journal*, **119** (536), 430–47.

Cooper, S.J. (1998), *Redistribution and the Persistence of Income Inequality*, Cambridge, MA: John F. Kennedy School of Government, Harvard University.

Cowell, F. (2011), *Measuring Inequality*, Oxford: Oxford University Press.

Cushing, L., R. Morello-Frosch, M. Wander and M. Pastor (2015), "The haves, the have-nots, and the health of everyone: the relationship between social inequality and environmental quality", *Annual Review of Public Health*, **36**, 193–209.

Cutler, D.M. and L.F. Katz (1992), "Rising inequality? Changes in the distribution of income and consumption in the 1980s", *American Economic Review*, **82** (2), 546–51.

DiMaggio, P. and F. Garip (2012), "Network effects and social inequality", *Annual Review of Sociology*, **38**, 93–118.

Drago, R. and G.T. Garvey (1998), "Incentives for helping on the job: theory and evidence", *Journal of Labor Economics*, **16** (1), 1–25.

Durlauf, S.N. (1996), "A theory of persistent income inequality", *Journal of Economic Growth*, **1** (1), 75–93.

Eckenrode, J., E. Smith, M. McCarthy and M. Dineen (2014), "Income inequality and child maltreatment in the United States", *Pediatrics*, **133** (3), 454–61.

Erikson, R. (2015), "Income inequality and policy responsiveness", *Annual Review of Political Science*, **18**, 11–29.

Evans, W.N., M. Hout and S.E. Mayer (2004), "Assessing the effect of economic inequality", in K. Neckerman (ed.), *Social Inequality*, New York: Russell Sage Foundation, pp. 933–68.

Exworthy, M., A. Bindman, H. Davies and A.E. Washington (2006), "Evidence into policy and practice?

Measuring the progress of US and UK policies to tackle disparities and inequalities in US and UK health and health care", *The Milbank Quarterly*, **84** (1), 75–109.
Fajnzylber, P., D. Lederman and N. Loayza (2002), "Inequality and violent crime", *Journal of Law & Economics*, **45** (1), 1–40.
Flinn, C.J. (2002), "Labour market structure and inequality: a comparison of Italy and the US", *Review of Economic Studies*, **69** (3), 611–45.
Foellmi, R. and J. Zweimüller (2006), "Income distribution and demand-induced innovations", *Review of Economic Studies*, **73** (4), 941–60.
Garg, S., Q. Li and J. Shaw (2018), "Undervaluation of directors in the board hierarchy: impact on turnover of directors (and CEOs) in newly public firms", *Strategic Management Journal*, **39** (2), 429–57.
Gilens, M. (2012), *Affluence and Influence: Economic Inequality and Political Power in America*, Princeton, NJ: Princeton University Press.
Goñi, E., J. Humberto López and L. Servén (2011), "Fiscal redistribution and income inequality in Latin America", *World Development*, **39** (9), 1558–69.
Gupta, N. and J. Shaw (2014), "Employee compensation: the neglected area of HRM research", *Human Resource Management Review*, **24** (1), 1–4.
Hacker, J.S. and P. Pierson (2010), *Winner-Take-All Politics: How Washington Made the Rich Richer – and Turned Its Back on the Middle Class*, New York: Simon & Schuster.
Hamermesh, D.S. (1999), "Changing inequality in markets for workplace amenities", *Quarterly Journal of Economics*, **114** (4), 1085–123.
Harding, D.J., L. Gennetian, C. Winship, L. Sanbonmatsu, J.R. Kling and National Bureau of Economic Research (2010), "Unpacking neighborhood influences on education outcomes: setting the stage for future research", NBER Working Paper No. 16055, National Bureau of Economic Research.
Harris, M.M., F. Anseel and F. Lievens (2008), "Keeping up with the Joneses: a field study of the relationships among upward, lateral, and downward comparisons and pay level satisfaction", *Journal of Applied Psychology*, **93** (3), 665–73.
Heshmati, A. (2006), "The world distribution of income and income inequality: a review of the economics literature", *Journal of World-Systems Research*, **12** (1), 61–107.
Hoff, E., B. Laursen and T. Tardif (2002), "Socioeconomic status and parenting", in M.H. Bornstein (ed.), *Handbook of Parenting*, second edn, Mahwah, NJ: Lawrence Erlbaum Associates, pp. 231–52.
Hsieh, C.-C. and M. Pugh (1993), "Poverty, income inequality, and violent crime: a meta-analysis of recent aggregate data studies", *Criminal Justice Review*, **18** (2), 182–202.
Hung, H. and J. Kucinskas (2011), "Globalization and global inequality: assessing the impact of the rise of China and India, 1980–2005", *American Journal of Sociology*, **116** (5), 1478–513.
Jargowsky, P.A. (1996), "Take the money and run: economic segregation in US metropolitan areas", *American Sociological Review*, **61** (6), 984–98.
Jorgenson, A., J. Schor and X. Huang (2017), "Income inequality and carbon emissions in the United States: a state-level analysis, 1997–2012", *Ecological Economics*, **134**, 40–8.
Katz, L.F., J.R. Kling and J.B. Liebman (2001), "Moving to Opportunity in Boston: early results of a randomized mobility experiment", *Quarterly Journal of Economics*, **116** (2), 607–54.
Kaushal, N., K. Magnuson and J. Waldfogel (2011), "How is family income related to investments in children's learning?", in G.J. Duncan and R. Murnane (eds), *Whither Opportunity? Rising Inequality, Schools, and Children's Life Chances*, New York: Russell Sage Foundation, pp. 187–206.
Kelly, M. (2000), "Inequality and crime", *Review of Economics and Statistics*, **82** (4), 530–9.
Kennedy, B.P., I. Kawachi and D. Prothrow-Stith (1996), "Income distribution and mortality: cross sectional ecological study of the Robin Hood index in the United States", *British Medical Journal*, **312** (7037), 1004–7.
Kondo, N., G. Sembajwe, I. Kawachi, R.M. van Dam, S.V. Subramanian and Z. Yamagata (2009), "Income inequality, mortality, and self-rated health: meta-analysis of multilevel studies", *British Medical Journal*, **339** (7731), 1178–81.
Krueger, D. and F. Perri (2006), "Does income inequality lead to consumption inequality? Evidence and theory", *Review of Economic Studies*, **73** (1), 163–93.
Lawler, E.E. (1971), *Pay and Organization Effectiveness: A Psychological View*, New York: McGraw-Hill.
Lazear, E.P. (1999), "Personnel economics: past lessons and future directions", *Journal of Labor Economics*, **17** (2), 199–236.
Leana, C. and J. Meuris (2015), "Living to work and working to live: income as a driver of organizational behavior", *Academy of Management Annals*, **9** (1), 55–95.
Leana, C.R., V. Mittal and E. Stiehl (2012), "Perspective – organizational behavior and the working poor", *Organization Science*, **23** (3), 888–906.
Leighley, J.E. and J. Nagler (2013), *Who Votes Now? Demographics, Issues, Inequality, and Turnout in the United States*, Princeton, NJ: Princeton University Press.

Lemieux, T., W.B. Macleod and D. Parent (2009), "Performance pay and wage inequality", *Quarterly Journal of Economics*, **124** (1), 1–49.
Lenz, G.S. (2004), "The consequences of income inequality for redistributive policy in the United States", in K. Neckerman (ed.), *Social Inequality*, New York: Russell Sage Foundation, pp. 797–820.
Leventhal, T. and J. Brooks-Gunn (2003), "Moving to opportunity: an experimental study of neighborhood effects on mental health", *American Journal of Public Health*, **93** (9), 1576–82.
LIFT (2017a), *Our Solution – LIFT*, accessed 1 February 2018 at https://www.liftcommunities.org/why-lift/our-solution/.
LIFT (2017b), *Annual Report 2017 – LIFT*, accessed 1 February 2018 at https://www.liftcommunities.org/annual-report/.
Ludwig, J., G.J. Duncan, L.A. Gennetian et al. (2013), "Long-term neighborhood effects on low-income families: evidence from Moving to Opportunity", *American Economic Review*, **103** (3), 226–31.
Mayer, S. (2001), "How did the increase in economic inequality between 1970 and 1990 affect children's educational attainment?", *American Journal of Sociology*, **107** (1), 1–32.
Meltzer, A.H. and S.F. Richard (1981), "A rational theory of the size of government", *Journal of Political Economy*, **89** (5), 914–27.
Merton, R.K. (1968), *Social Theory and Social Structure*, enlarged edn, New York: Free Press.
Meuris, J. and C. Leana (2015), "The high cost of low wages: economic scarcity effects in organizations", *Research in Organizational Behavior*, **35**, 143–58.
Moene, K. and M. Wallerstein (2001), "Inequality, social insurance, and redistribution", *American Political Science Review*, **95** (4), 859–74.
Moene, K. and M. Wallerstein (2003), "Earnings inequality and welfare spending – a disaggregated analysis", *World Politics*, **55** (4), 485–516.
Mulligan, C. (1995), *Some Evidence on the Role of Imperfect Markets for the Transmission of Inequality*, Chicago, IL: University of Chicago Press.
Neckerman, K. and F. Torche (2007), "Inequality: causes and consequences", *Annual Review of Sociology*, **33**, 335–57.
Oishi, S., S. Kesebir and E. Diener (2011), "Income inequality and happiness", *Psychological Science*, **22** (9), 1095–100.
Pebley, A.R. and N. Sastry (2004), "Neighborhoods, poverty, and children's well-being", in K. Neckerman (ed.), *Social Inequality*, New York: Russell Sage Foundation, pp. 119–45.
Persson, T. and G. Tabellini (1994), "Is inequality harmful for growth?", *American Economic Review*, **84** (3), 600–21.
Pfeffer, J. and N. Langton (1993), "The effect of wage dispersion on satisfaction, productivity, and working collaboratively: evidence from college and university faculty", *Administrative Science Quarterly*, **38** (3), 382–407.
Phillips, M. (2011), "Parenting, time use, and disparities in academic outcomes", in G.J. Duncan and R. Murnane (eds), *Whither Opportunity? Rising Inequality, Schools, and Children's Life Chances*, New York: Russell Sage Foundation, pp. 207–28.
Pierce, B. (2001), "Compensation inequality", *Quarterly Journal of Economics*, **116** (4), 1493–525.
Pratt, T. and F. Cullen (2005), "Assessing macro-level predictors and theories of crime: a meta-analysis", *Crime and Justice*, **32**, 373–450.
Ravallion, M. (2014), "Income inequality in the developing world", *Science*, **344** (6186), 851–5.
Reardon, S.F. (2011), "The widening academic achievement gap between the rich and the poor: new evidence and possible explanations", in G.J. Duncan and R. Murnane (eds), *Whither Opportunity? Rising Inequality, Schools, and Children's Life Chances*, New York: Russell Sage Foundation, pp. 91–116.
Reardon, S. and K. Bischoff (2011), "Income inequality and income segregation", *American Journal of Sociology*, **116** (4), 1092–153.
Shaw, C.R. and H.D. McKay (1942), *Juvenile Delinquency and Urban Areas*, Chicago, IL: University of Chicago Press.
Shaw, J. (2014), "Pay dispersion", *Annual Review of Organizational Psychology and Organizational Behavior*, **1**, 521–44.
Shaw, J. (2015), "Pay dispersion, sorting, and organizational performance", *Academy of Management Discoveries*, **1** (2), 165–79.
Shaw, J. and N. Gupta (2001), "Pay fairness and employee outcomes: exacerbation and attenuation effects of financial need", *Journal of Occupational and Organizational Psychology*, **74** (3), 299–320.
Shaw, J., N. Gupta and J. Delery (2002), "Pay dispersion and workforce performance: moderating effects of incentives and interdependence", *Strategic Management Journal*, **23** (6), 491–512.
Solt, F. (2008), "Economic inequality and democratic political engagement", *American Journal of Political Science*, **52** (1), 48–60.
Song, P. and J. Shaw (2018), "The effects of pay dispersion: quantitative review and theory extension", Working Paper, Vanderbilt University, Nashville, TN.

Stack, S. (1984), "Income inequality and property crime", *Criminology*, **22** (2), 229–56.
Subramanian, S. and I. Kawachi (2004), "Income inequality and health: what have we learned so far?", *Epidemiologic Reviews*, **26** (1), 78–91.
Tracey, P. and N. Stott (2017), "Social innovation: a window on alternative ways of organizing and innovating", *Innovation-Management Policy & Practice*, **19** (1), 51–60.
Trevor, C.O. and D.L. Wazeter (2006), "A contingent view of reactions to objective pay conditions: interdependence among pay structure characteristics and pay relative to internal and external referents", *Journal of Applied Psychology*, **91** (6), 1260–75.
Trevor, C., G. Reilly and B. Gerhart (2012), "Reconsidering pay dispersion's effect on the performance of interdependent work: reconciling sorting and pay inequality", *Academy of Management Journal*, **55** (3), 585–610.
Wilkinson, R.G. and K.E. Pickett (2006), "Income inequality and population health: a review and explanation of the evidence", *Social Science & Medicine*, **62** (7), 1768–84.
You, J.-S. and S. Khagram (2005), "A comparative study of inequality and corruption", *American Sociological Review*, **70** (1), 136–57.

20. Frugal innovation and social innovation: linked paths to achieving inclusion sustainably

Yasser Bhatti and Jaideep Prabhu

INTRODUCTION TO LITERATURE

Social innovation has as its focus the provision of new solutions to address social problems and enhance social inclusion. As such, research on social innovation has the potential to address local problems as well as more systemic and structural issues, namely, the 'Grand Challenges' of our time. A question remains, however, about how, in practical terms, social innovation can meet the needs of large numbers of people without creating negative externalities such as environmental collapse or financial overreach. In the face of rising costs, resource constraints and growing demand, we argue that frugal innovation offers a practical way of tackling the Grand Challenges that social innovation sets out to solve. Specifically, we argue that the ability of social innovation to achieve greater inclusion can be enhanced if considered in conjunction with evolving models of innovation such as frugal innovation.

To do so, we begin by examining in greater detail these two types of innovation – frugal and social innovation – alongside a third type of pro-social innovation that is related to and links both, namely, inclusive innovation (see Table 20.1 for details).

Inclusive innovation is defined as 'the development and implementation of new ideas which aspire to create opportunities that enhance social and economic wellbeing for disenfranchised members of society' (George et al., 2012, p. 663). According to Nijhof et al. (2002), inclusive innovation refers to the 'inclusion of fundamental social responsibilities in both strategy and operations management in organizations' (p. 84). Nijhof et al.'s project on inclusive innovation seeks to develop a label for the integration of social responsibility and universal human rights within organizations. More recently, though, the term has been used to denote inclusive innovation systems that take into account context-specific issues, obstacles and needs in developing countries such as underserved low-income markets and informal institutions (Altenburg, 2011). The emphasis here is to better address the needs of the poor by lowering the cost of goods and services, or creating income earning opportunities for the poor, and improving knowledge creation and absorption effects most relevant for the poor (Dutz, 2007). George et al. (2012, p. 662) warn that 'The field is in a state of infancy – particularly with regard to theory that deals satisfactorily with inequality and with the implications of inequality for innovation.' Overall, however, inclusive innovation is about fostering growth and equality for underserved or disenfranchised people – though the means by which this is done or achieved remains unclear (George et al., 2012).

Social innovation is defined as 'the transformation of social systems in ways that both address social problems in a practical sense and shift our ways of thinking about these problems' (Lawrence et al., 2012, p. 321). Nicholls and Murdock (2012, p. 2), in a review

Table 20.1 Definitions of inclusive, social and frugal innovation

Inclusive Innovation	
'Inclusive innovation is the means by which new goods and services are developed for and/or by the billions living on lowest incomes'	Foster and Heeks, 2013, p. 333
'the development and implementation of new ideas which aspire to create opportunities that enhance social and economic wellbeing for disenfranchised members of society'	George et al., 2012, p. 663
'Innovations are inclusive if they benefit the poor in terms of additional income and employment'	Altenburg, 2011, p. 50
'by promoting more formal R&D efforts for poor people and more creative grassroots efforts by them, and by improving the ability of informal enterprises to exploit existing knowledge'	Dutz, 2007, p. xviii
'inclusion of fundamental social responsibilities in both strategy and operations management in organizations'	Nijhof et al., 2002, p. 84
Social Innovation	
'The term "social innovation" is used to describe a broad range of organizational and inter-organizational activity that is ostensibly designed to address the most deep-rooted "problems" of society, such as poverty, inequality and environmental degradation'	Tracey and Stott, 2017, p. 51
'the transformation of social systems in ways that both address social problems in a practical sense and shift our ways of thinking about these problems'	Lawrence et al., 2012, p. 321
'systems and processes of change in social relations' at one extreme and 'innovation in the conceptualisation, design and production of goods and services that address social and environmental needs and market failures' at the other	Nicholls and Murdock, 2012, p. 2
'A novel solution to a social problem that is more effective, efficient, sustainable, or just than existing solutions and for which the value created accrues primarily to society as a whole rather than private individuals'	Phills et al., 2008, p. 34
'Social innovation refers to new ideas that work in meeting social goals'	Mulgan et al., 2007, p. 8
Frugal Innovation	
'Frugal innovation – the creation of faster, better and cheaper solutions for more people that employ minimal resources'	Prabhu, 2017, p. 1
'Frugal innovation is the ability to "do more with less"'	Radjou and Prabhu, 2015, p. xvii
'means and ends to do more with less for many'	Bhatti, 2014, p. 296
'a design innovation process that properly considers the needs and context of citizens in the developing world is necessary in order to develop appropriate, adaptable, affordable, and accessible solutions, products and services'	Basu et al., 2013, p. 63
'innovative, low-cost and high-quality products and business models originating in developing countries and exportable to other developing countries or even the developed world'	George et al., 2012, p. 662
'"good-enough," affordable products that meet the needs of resource-constrained consumers'	Zeschky et al., 2011, p. 38

of the literature, state that social innovation research can be understood as focusing on 'systems and processes of change in social relations' at one extreme and 'innovation in the conceptualisation, design and production of goods and services that address social and environmental needs and market failures' at the other. In leaning towards the latter, Gundry et al. (2011) posit that if social entrepreneurs are primarily concerned with the development of innovative solutions to society's problems, then the act of doing so would be social innovation. Thus, social entrepreneurs provide innovative leadership in social enterprises (Dees, 1998) and the role of innovation in a social entrepreneurial organization is key (Borins, 2000). Such social entrepreneur traditions emphasized the social innovation, entrepreneurial activist and frame-breaking approaches to non-profit management (Benford and Snow, 2000; Dart, 2004). The stream of the social innovation literature that this work builds upon describes social innovation as the work of social entrepreneurs, emphasizing the role of individuals in developing innovative solutions for difficult social challenges (Bornstein, 2004; Bornstein and Davis, 2010; Dees and Anderson, 2006; Goldsmith, 2010; Hartigan and Elkington, 2008; Hoogendoorn et al., 2010). Consequently, social innovation is a practice-led field which is contextually based; most work has been on successful case studies rather than on understanding patterns and stages of social innovation (The Young Foundation, 2012). Further, much of the literature on social innovation has focused on the process perspective of social innovation, touching upon more practical concerns on how to develop and implement programmes and strategies. Consequently, there remain many opportunities to contribute to conceptual models of social innovation. For instance, Cajaiba-Santana (2014) has brought together the polarized view of social innovation between agentic and structuralist approaches to propose a new conceptual framework to investigate social innovation as a driver of social change.

Frugal innovation is commonly associated with increased affordability and low-cost solutions (Radjou and Prabhu, 2015; Woolridge, 2010). George et al. (2012, p. 662) define frugal innovation as 'innovative, low-cost and high-quality products and business models originating in developing countries and exportable to other developing countries or even the developed world'. Others call such innovations 'toned down' and 'good enough products' (cf. Hang et al., 2010; Zeschky et al., 2011), or low-cost products (Ramamurti, 2012). Frugal innovation is also often conflated with terms such as value-based design (DePasse et al., 2016), reverse innovation (Govindarajan and Trimble, 2012) and *jugaad* innovation (Radjou et al., 2012) due to similarities between their meanings and the contexts in which they are applied or studied. In contrast to the perception that frugal innovation may engender inferior quality, Bhatti (2014) finds that frugal innovations commonly exhibit superior quality and performance compared to alternatives. Many frugal innovations stem from emerging markets (Radjou and Prabhu, 2015) and from challenging contexts marked by resource constraints and institutional voids (Bhatti, 2014; Prabhu et al., 2017). Typical examples of frugal innovation include those where inputs and outputs are less costly but also where things are done more efficiently or where innovations provide wider access to larger populations through their scalability (Bhatti and Ventresca, 2012). Prahalad (2006) in his scholarly work and Basu in her practical work at the Frugal Innovation Lab (Basu et al., 2013; Bhatti et al., 2018) focus on the bottom of the pyramid – the largest and poorest socio-economic segment of the population. Prahalad's description of innovation as frugal calls for a shift away from innovation based on affluence and abundance. Innovators in seeking to serve these underserved market segments or challenging contexts embrace constraints and develop a mindset and skill set that is more suited for frugal innovation (Radjou et al., 2012).

ISSUES, THEMES, QUESTIONS

Scholars have argued that despite the gains reaped from the globalization of trade, the most important systemic problem which the global economy faces is its social inequality (Sen, 2001; Suter, 2010). Individually and collectively, we have been unable to cope with this challenge because of market failure in the private sector, silos in the public sector, and fragmentation and the lack of scalability in the civil sector (The Young Foundation, 2012). Consequently, a renewed focus in innovation on affordability is supported by civil society, governments, multinationals and entrepreneurs worldwide (Bhatti and Ventresca, 2012; Koh and Prabhu, 2016; Radjou and Prabhu, 2015). With growing concern about inequality, myriad actors are innovating in new ways to provide for more marginalized and underserved market segments globally. In the process of doing so, they have also challenged long-held assumptions and practices of innovation. Social innovation deals with social problems often precipitated as a result of market failure (Mulgan, 2006). And the emerging trend of frugal innovation suggests that poverty does not have to mean deprivation or reliance on handouts (Hart and Prahalad, 2002); the lack of resources and institutional voids, rather than presenting obstacles, offer opportunities for the development of new products, services and business models (Bhatti, 2012; Prabhu et al., 2017). What began as grassroots efforts to solve local problems, social and frugal innovation have both evolved to increasingly address Grand Challenges – more substantive, systemic and structural issues around economic and environmental sustainability as well as social inclusion worldwide.

The rising popularity of social innovation is associated with growing social, environmental and demographic challenges (The Young Foundation, 2012; Prabhu, 2017). These challenges are exacerbated due to the ambitions of the modern welfare state, the limitations of conventional market capitalism, deepening climate change, ever-increasing and ageing populations, and the impact of globalization and mass urbanization (The Young Foundation, 2012). With so many issues, themes and concerns facing social equality and well-being, it is not difficult to delineate social innovation as almost any type of innovation that transforms societal practices (Kesselring, 2009). Anything from a sect (Cornwell, 2007), the eBook (Cavalli, 2007) or even scientific management (Mumford and Moertl, 2003) could be classified as social innovation. Roth (2009) contends that even economic innovations are one type of social innovation since most are the outcome of societal efforts (Barré, 2001; Nowotny et al., 2001) or the result of the co-evolution of both economic and non-economic systems of society (Etzkowitz and Leydesdorff, 2000; Leydesdorff, 2005).

Our previous work (for example, Bhatti, 2014; Bhatti et al., 2018; Prabhu, 2017; Prabhu et al., 2017) suggests that frugal innovation deals with, makes use of, or overcomes resource constraints and institutional voids to create social value as well as profit generation, the former to improve lives, and the latter to make solutions sustainable. Frugal innovation has been studied in terms of new product development strategies (Zeschky et al., 2011), international business (Radjou and Prabhu, 2015), social entrepreneurship (Bhatti, 2014), engineering and design (Sharma and Iyer, 2012) and sustainability (Levänen et al., 2016). With so many facets to frugal innovation, it is also seen as a hybrid of different existing types of innovation, but mainly technological innovation, social innovation and institutional innovation (Bhatti, 2012). Examples of frugal innovations are diverse, ranging from advanced technology and manufacturing such as 3D printing or additive manufacturing, the Tata Nano Car, a startup Miroculous which seeks to diagnose diseases using RNA sequencing, to less technology-intensive social enterprises involving microfinance and affordable housing projects that strive for greater social inclusion.

The growing sophistication of managers who have arisen from backgrounds of poverty has played a key role in heightening awareness of the many disconnects of globalization (Stiglitz, 2007, 2015). Perhaps as a result, many companies are beginning to aspire to a 'shared value' philosophy (Porter and Kramer, 2011), by which they can create economic and social value by addressing the unmet needs of underserved populations (Prahalad, 2006). Cappelli et al. (2010) contend that this new managerial philosophy, or management approach from the edge (Gulati, 2010), is people. They label Indian companies as a 'compelling example of a model that succeeds financially while succeeding socially' (p. 22). Similarly, Prahalad and Mashelkar (2010, p. 2) argue that 'learning to do more with less for more people, we believe, should be the innovator's dream'. A member of the team that developed the GE MAC 400, a highly touted frugal medical device, says frugal innovation 'requires a shift in mind-set from value for money to value for many' (Govindarajan and Trimble, 2012, p. 150).

With so many different yet related notions of what innovation is (see Chandy and Prabhu, 2011 for a review and typology), we rely on two criteria to help us identify innovations, whether process or outcome based (Phills et al., 2008). First, the phenomenon must be novel. It may not be completely original, but it must be new to the user, use, application or context. The novelty associated with the innovation does not have to be universal, but can be new to the unit of adoption such as specific user, firm or market (Chandy and Prabhu, 2011; Rogers, 2003). Van de Ven (1986) too views innovation as a new idea or recombination of old ideas that to the people involved is perceived as new, even if to others it seems to be an imitation of something that exists elsewhere. Second, the innovation should entail improvement by being either more effective or more efficient relative to existing solutions (Chandy and Prabhu, 2011; Phills et al., 2008). Innovation may involve sophisticated and often capital-intensive research and development (R&D) by industrial organizations as well as incremental improvements to existing technology and business models brought about by anyone, by producers or consumers.

March and Simon (1958) argued that innovations often transpire by borrowing from other innovations rather than through *ab initio* invention. In this sense, both social innovation and frugal innovation draw from various other forms of innovation, such as technological, economic and institutional innovation, to offer something at least incrementally new to the user, use, application or context. And while individually the two constructs of social and frugal innovation have gained much prominence in practice and research, our core argument is that we may theoretically link the two in order to help increase our understanding of how to better achieve inclusive markets and societies both locally and globally. In focusing on addressing Grand Challenges, Table 20.2 lists several salient questions that, if taken up by scholars, could help connect social and frugal innovation in ways that make the sum greater than the parts. The table lists the substantive,

Table 20.2 List of sample research questions

Substantive Issues	Conceptual/Theoretical Issues	Empirical/Methodological Issues
What kind of innovation in terms of process, product or policy can have most impact on inclusive outcomes?	Which theories and models help us to relate frugal and social innovation to each other and other related concepts such as inclusion?	What can a grounded, theory-building research tell us about how entrepreneurs and for-profit and non-profit firms overcome resource constraints and institutional voids to develop highly affordable solutions for large numbers of citizens across geographical and sectoral contexts?
Which types of frugal and social innovations may enhance the competitiveness of for-profit and non-profit organizations and their sustainability?	How can we connect concepts and theories drawn from the management of technology and strategy with social and frugal innovation, and vice versa?	What can ethnographic approaches tell us about actors around the world and the strategies they employ over time to achieve their social objectives while remaining financially viable?
What constitutes social innovation as distinct from changing social behaviours and practices?	How can we define frugal and social innovation in such a way that helps to link them to each other?	What can quantitative research tell us about which innovations for underserved consumers are created and what is the impact of these markets on social and economic inclusion around the world?
How can a frugal innovation approach be a business opportunity in European and non-European markets for greater social inclusion?	What are the ways in which frugal and social innovations are similar and different from each other?	What natural experiments can help us to understand how regulatory or technological shocks impact social and frugal innovation and inclusion?
How can we assess the potential for 'reverse innovation' from developing to developed countries?	How does a static and dynamic, process view of the relevant relationships compare?	How can we conduct longitudinal field experiments that examine how such innovations impact social and economic inclusion?
Who, entrepreneurs or large firms, might be best suited to instituting frugal innovations, capturing value from them, and who benefits?	How can the new product development process be reconceptualized in light of the need for social impact and scalability?	Can we combine qualitative and quantitative techniques in understanding how institutions and human agents (managers, entrepreneurs and policy makers) interact in developing social and frugal innovations to promote social inclusion?
What strategies do innovators practise in pursuing frugal innovation for social purposes?	What is the role of experimentation and variations in contexts, processes and outcomes of these types of innovation?	How can techniques from computer science such as natural language processing and big data be combined to understand how social and frugal innovation is done at scale and how they bring about institutional change and social inclusion?
What are the obstacles and risks to unlocking the creative and business potential for frugal innovators in achieving inclusivity (e.g., technical, legal or regulatory, geographic, financial, cultural or others)?	What are the challenges and opportunities posed by managing the design and production of new products and services for sustainability?	
Which policy area(s) and at which level can help address and support use of frugal and social innovation together?	How do various actors focus on new forms and types of frugal and social mindsets, processes, outcomes, or impact in diverse geographical and institutional contexts?	
What are the similarities and differences between how social and frugal innovation are practised in emerging markets versus developed markets?	What is the role of institutions in helping or hindering the cause of social and frugal innovation in achieving social inclusion?	

Table 20.2 (continued)

Substantive Issues	Conceptual/Theoretical Issues	Empirical/Methodological Issues
What is the role of entrepreneurs relative to large firms, governments and non-governmental organizations as a source for propagating and practising social and frugal innovation?	What is the role of resource constraints and the use of bricolage and other processes to overcome resource scarcity? What forms of intellectual property can promote the scalability and sustainability of frugal and social innovations that in the end benefit the triple bottom line?	How do hybrid organizations that seek to balance social and financial goals operate and how should they be regulated? To what extent can frugal and social innovations be relied upon to help remove economic and social inequalities?

conceptual and empirical issues that link frugal and social innovation through inclusion for both economic and social concerns.

Under *substantive issues*, there are three types of unanswered questions worth addressing. First, what kind of innovation – process, product or policy – is most powerful in bringing about outcomes that reflect inclusive societies? Although a combination of all three types of innovation will probably be needed to address different types of and levels of Grand Challenges (such as provision of clean water, universal health coverage, climate change, humanitarian relief, and economic, cultural and gender equality), it would benefit innovators and leaders to understand which type to focus on to tackle these different problems. Second, important questions remain about the distinctive nature of social and frugal innovation in for-profit versus non-profit organizations, in entrepreneurial versus large firms, in social versus commercial enterprises, and in developing versus developed markets. Finally, questions remain about which of these forms, types or regions are promoting inclusive and sustainable growth and how can innovations be diffused from one to the other?

Under *conceptual or theoretical issues*, there is potential to draw upon mainstream theories and models to hypothesize the link between frugal and social innovation and other related concepts such as inclusion and sustainability. Conceptual frameworks that draw upon organizational behaviour, strategy and political economy can then be used to assess the similarities and differences between frugal and social innovation. These analytical insights may be further used to evaluate and reconceptualize innovation activity, such as the new product development process and how it may better take into account system-wide use of scarce resources. With the expectation that frugal and social innovations will benefit the triple bottom line – people, planet and profits – what types of intellectual property regimes can make frugal and social innovations attractive for investment as well as for scalability and sustainability?

Under *empirical or methodological issues*, many of the substantive and conceptual questions need to be assessed by gathering evidence using a range of qualitative, quantitative, cross-sectional, longitudinal and novel approaches such as natural experiments and real-time use of big data. The world is going through dynamic changes that reflect complex systems, and a broad mix of methodological approaches and methods would be needed to provide glimpses into both the positive and negative effects of evolving forms of innovation and hybrid organizations (Battilana and Dorado, 2010). All these issues can shed light on how frugal and social innovation together may improve economic and social inclusion as well as organizational, societal and environmental sustainability. We invite scholars to take up these questions if the promise of frugal and social innovation is to be realized to their full potential for inclusivity and sustainability. We support this invitation by presenting a conceptual framework to help us consider the power of frugal and social innovation together in better tackling the issues that underpin Grand Challenges.

Role of Social Innovation in Inclusion

Social innovations are seen as solutions to 'wicked problems' such as endemic poverty, rising healthcare costs, lack of affordable quality education, catastrophic disasters, neglected elderly and environmental degradation – complex issues that involve several different constituents, many of which have conflicting or competing objectives (Bates, 2011; Bocken et al., 2016; Karamchandani et al., 2009; Prabhu, 2017). Mulgan et al. (2007, p. 8) refer to social innovation as 'new ideas that work in meeting social goals'. They make a distinction between the social needs of society as a whole versus those of the individual based on 'merely personal needs or demands'. The real potential of innovation is in fact in its social dimension (cf. Pot and Vaas, 2008; Roth, 2009).

Although innovation studies are dominated by a focus on technical innovation (Roth, 2009), there is evidence that the notion of social innovation is present in the early works of economists such as Joseph Schumpeter and Nikolai Kondratiev (Kesselring, 2009). Schumpeter, for instance, distinguished between product, process, procedural and organizational innovations to tap into new markets. However, in order to assure the economic efficacy of technical innovations, Schumpeter emphasized the importance of social innovation in the economic arena as well as in culture, politics and a society's way of life (Howaldt and Schwarz, 2010; Tellis et al., 2009). In fact, the trajectory of technological innovation, economic performance and consequently social change predates Schumpeter in the works of classical sociologists like Karl Marx and political economists like Adam Smith. Around the same time as Schumpeter, the sociologist Ogburn (1937) was one of the first to distinguish technology and social innovation, but he still assumed the primacy of technology as a precursor and driver of social change (Howaldt and Schwarz, 2010).

For most of the second half of the twentieth century, however, the focus of innovation studies has almost exclusively been on technology innovation. Indeed, since Schumpeter, attention to social innovation in the literature is rare and marginal (cf. Moulaert et al., 2005). Specifically, in contrast to the dominant focus on business and technology innovation, there has been little systematic analysis of the design and diffusion of and support for social innovation (The Young Foundation, 2012). Only in the last two decades has social innovation gradually enjoyed a surge in interest. Desa's dissertation (2009) was one of the few and substantive works that helped to bridge the dominant focus on technology and the secondary focus on social innovation by exclusively studying technology ventures engaged in social innovation. Desa's subsequent work (2011) provides insights into how technology is used directly to address social problems in an economically sustainable manner. Even so, social innovation is presented as a secondary phenomenon which ensues as social change resulting from technological and economic innovation, a view still dominant today (Roth, 2009). For instance, Moulaert et al. (2005) comment that in the field of urban planning an overly technological focus paved the way for greater support for social innovation to theorize human development, empowerment and local development strategies (cf. The Young Foundation, 2012; Gerometta et al., 2005).

When we look beyond a technological focus, we begin to see social innovation as embodying a variety of actors and missions. Murray et al. (2010) stress not only new ideas including products, services and models, but also the creation of new social relationships or collaborations in the process of meeting social needs. A report on social innovation by The Young Foundation (2012), commissioned by the European Commission, finds that social innovation cuts across different private, public and civil sector actors even though most literature on social innovation tends to study it within a specific sector. Indeed, the literature shows that social innovation takes place in all three sectors, and often at the intersections of these sectors. More specifically, social ventures are deemed to operate at the nexus of economic, public and community sectors (Dees, 1996, 1998; Mair and Martí, 2006) or at the intersection of multiple institutions such as the market, government and the community (Desa, 2009; Shaw and Carter, 2007). Research has examined the role of governance, empowerment and capacity building in driving the dynamics of the relationships between different actors and the skills, competencies, assets and social capital that they bring to the table (The Young Foundation, 2012). The organizations engaged in social innovation are often able to span the intersection of various sectors – thereby becoming 'hybrid' organizations and potentially making it possible to be more inclusive (see Bocken et al., 2016). One type of this 'hybrid' organization is the social enterprise.

Perrini and Vurro (2006) argue that the nature of social innovation is multidimensional and operates throughout the social entrepreneurial process. However, much like social entrepreneurship, the notion of social innovation has been developed without clear definitions, boundaries and meaning (The Young Foundation, 2012). In fact, social innovation has received much less attention than social entrepreneurship has; the latter has benefited from greater traction with relatively well-defined definitions and analyses (cf. Mair and Martí, 2009; Nicholls and Murdock, 2012). Moreover, The Young Foundation (2012) contends that social innovation is far broader than social entrepreneurship, and that it poses both opportunities and challenges for knowledge discovery and use. According to a review of the literature in the same report, Hämäläinen and Heiskala (2007) identify five types of innovation: technological, economic, regulative, normative and cultural; taken together, these form the sphere of social innovations.

In contrast to the phenomenon of social innovation sometimes presented in the current literature, Bhatti's (2014) extensive study of social entrepreneurs finds that frugal and social innovators adopt a mix of technology, social and institutional innovations to overcome resource and affordability constraints and institutional voids (see also Bhatti et al., 2018). The findings further support Perrini and Vurro's (2006) claim that innovation among social entrepreneurs is viewed as a disparate range of concepts that stem from varied motivations, means and outcomes. These motivations and means draw from social concerns but also user, efficiency and challenge concerns for solving big and bold problems – the latter being particularly of interest to this chapter and book.

Social innovation is increasingly seen as spanning different actors and different types of innovation. Public discourse is also increasingly focused on social and economic problems prompting a call for more extensive social innovation (Howaldt and Schwarz, 2010). Despite this growth in attention to social innovation, the concept remains elusive with regard to terminology, concept and content (Howaldt and Schwarz, 2010). Consequently, 'the field of social innovation remains relatively undeveloped' (Mulgan et al., 2007, p. 3). The *Guardian* newspaper observes that 'Social innovation is the new global obsession. It might be a nebulous idea but it has huge potential . . . The language around social innovation easily slides into smoke and mirrors' (Roberts, 2008).

Role of Frugal Innovation in Inclusion

As business leaders wrestle with the problem of how to improve competitiveness while simultaneously reducing costs and improving quality, the idea of adopting 'frugal innovations' as a way of tackling these challenges is gaining in prominence (Bhatti, 2014; Bhatti et al., 2018; Prabhu, 2017; Radjou and Prabhu, 2015; Woolridge, 2010 and many others). Many of these innovations have originated in low- and middle-income countries where, in the absence of funding and basic infrastructure, multinationals, entrepreneurs and civil society are compelled to improvise and innovate to solve local problems (Bhatti and Ventresca, 2012; Prabhu and Jain, 2015). And especially since the promotion of the Sustainable Development Goals (SDGs) by the United Nations' General Assembly, a geographically dispersed and interdisciplinary mix of researchers and practitioners is looking at worldwide innovation strategies to solve some of the world's most pressing issues on water, sanitation, energy, housing, transportation, education and healthcare (Prabhu, 2017).

Frugal innovation has been touted in many diverse sectors such as: transportation, with the $2,500 TATA Nano car (Radjou et al., 2012); housing, with the $300 house (Bhatti, 2014); affordable solar energy and lighting (Koh and Prabhu, 2016; Miller, 2009); and telecommunications, with mobile banking (Bhatti, 2014; Radjou et al., 2012). Some of the most iconic examples stem from healthcare, such as GE's MAC 400, a $800 portable ECG machine (Immelt et al., 2009), Narayana Hrudayalaya's $1,500 cardiac surgery and Aravind's $30 cataract surgery (Chaudhary et al., 2012; Rangan, 2009). The MAC 400 as a product has been reverse innovated from India to the US and Narayana and Aravind as processes are also being reverse innovated elsewhere such as in a joint venture between Narayana and Ascension Health in the Cayman Islands (Bhatti et al., 2017a). Escalating demand and constrained resources, as reflected in the Grand Challenges of our time and outlined in the SDGs, are paving the way for affordable and quality solutions for the socially and economically disenfranchised, but also at more sustainable levels for the socially and economically well-off. By solving the needs for both poor and rich, frugal innovation, much like social innovation, is helping to close the inequality gap towards greater inclusion (Bhatti, 2014; Bhatti et al., 2018).

Examples abound of why frugal innovation is crucial to social innovation including inclusivity. Take the case of mobile phone banking in emerging markets. M-Pesa in Kenya, Telenor EasyPaisa in Pakistan and EKO in India have all employed frugal innovation techniques to innovate at the frontier of technology and institutions (Bhatti, 2014; Bhatti et al., 2018). They all help connect the large, underserved segment of poor 'unbanked' consumers to existing financial institutions and formal markets by leveraging the ubiquity of mobile technology. Even in the West, new businesses like Airbnb, BlaBla Car, eBay and E-Trade have used asset-light internet business models to enable people to trade with each other or in markets they were otherwise excluded from (Radjou and Prabhu,

2015). Some of these businesses, like Airbnb and eBay, began as grassroots solutions to personal problems faced by the founders but scaled because those problems were shared across the world.

Sustainably solving shared problems and providing basic services to all citizens around the world is challenging and ambitious (Munk, 2013; Sachs, 2005; Stiglitz, 2007). Global financial liquidity is low, public spending budgets have been slashed, state debt is at peak levels, natural resources are scarce, and consumers are spending less. The 2013 US Census found that 45 million (15 per cent) Americans live in poverty and almost 50 million (16 per cent) do not have health insurance (US Census Bureau, 2014). This puts 'scarcity on the agenda for Western companies, forcing them to find frugal ways to grow with less' (Radjou et al., 2012, p. 14). Firms adopt frugality at times of reduced recessionary revenues or competitiveness induced by squeezed profits. Governments across Europe and North America too have been emphasizing frugal innovation in the public sector as a way to cope with reduced public spending and increased focus on transparency and performance (Singh et al., 2012).

As the means to do more with less for more (Bhatti, 2014; Prabhu, 2017; Prahalad and Mashelkar, 2010), frugal innovations entail inputs and outputs that are more affordable and do so in order to have impact at a global scale. But this impact does not have to be detrimental to the planet and people. Indeed, sustainability is also an important element of frugal innovations (Levänen et al., 2016; Prabhu, 2017). Frugal thinking encourages the redesign of products into those that can be built with limited resources, and have maximum use with fewer inputs, leaving a minimal carbon footprint on the environment (Radjou and Prabhu, 2015). Existing business models that reflect the over-consumptive nature of existing top-of-the-pyramid strategies (Hart, 1997) could not conceivably fulfil the needs of 4–5 billion people at the bottom without increasing the rate of depletion of limited global resources (Hammond et al., 2007).

Frugally innovative services partly stem from doing good, but also from meeting unmet gaps in the market (Woolridge, 2010). To reach the 'the next three billion', as Ernst & Young (2011; see also Hammond et al., 2007) dubs this opportunity, it is necessary for companies to think differently about every stage in the new product development process so as to create entirely new products and services to fulfil the unmet needs of the three billion people worldwide who live at the bottom of the pyramid. In a survey of over 547 executives from around the world, Ernst & Young (2011) found that more than 75 per cent thought that adopting frugal innovation to create products and services was a major opportunity while 81 per cent agreed that frugal innovation is a concept that has as much relevance to developed as it does to rapidly growing emerging markets. Finally, more than one-third of executives surveyed said they were already benefiting from a more frugal approach to innovation, while a further 40 per cent planned to do so.

For instance, GE is trying to disrupt itself by departing from a glocalization strategy to one of reverse innovation which employs frugal innovation first in emerging markets and then in the West (Christensen, 2013; Immelt et al., 2009). By shifting from a strategy where products come first and countries come second, GE is trying to create new markets first in emerging countries and then import them into developed countries for new applications or new segments (Immelt et al., 2009).

Linking Social and Frugal Innovation through Inclusion

Social and frugal innovations have independently attracted the attention of practitioners, policy makers and academics for their potential to separately offer inclusive solutions for people around the world. We believe, however, that taken together these two types of innovation offer synergies that can produce a greater impact on the intended beneficiaries. Their joint effect also has implications for cooperation between different types of actors in the real world as well as among scholars who study innovation through various lenses. Specifically, we argue that social and frugal innovation can jointly be conceptualized as complementary approaches to improve local and global inclusion. In other words, inclusion can act as a bridge that links frugal innovation by mainstream commercial entrepreneurs and firms to social innovation by social entrepreneurs and enterprises. But linking the two types of innovation also showcases the challenges that social and commercial entrepreneurs face in trying to achieve inclusion: namely, merging two ostensibly contradictory organizational goals, that is, social value creation and profit generation. It can be tough to simultaneously achieve both these objectives, particularly in environments where even basic institutional infrastructure may not exist (Bhatti, 2014; Miller et al., 2012; Prabhu et al., 2017).

THEORETICAL FRAMEWORK

Taken together, social and frugal innovation could offer new theoretical and practical insights into improving inclusion by solving social issues. Social issues refer to concerns such as poverty, illiteracy and unemployment which are 'putative condition or situation that is labelled a problem in the arenas of public discourse and action' (Hilgartner and Bosk, 1988, p. 55). When social issues are resolved in a way that 'achieves an equivalent social benefit with fewer dollars or creates greater social benefit for comparable cost' (Porter and Kramer, 1999, p. 126), this process can be called social value creation (Miller et al., 2012). Although the proceeds of social benefit go mainly to society, as opposed to an individual or specific organization (Thompson, 2002), we also must acknowledge the need for financial surplus that stems from market-based activities to help make solutions sustainable. We are interested here in entrepreneurs and innovators who embrace inclusion to create both economic and social value by addressing the unmet needs of underserved populations. These may in turn be social entrepreneurs who look to serve underserved users whose needs are not sufficiently addressed (McMullen, 2011) or commercial entrepreneurs who adopt a 'shared value' approach in their business models (Porter and Kramer, 2011).

Social entrepreneurship and social innovation have often been intertwined to the extent that it can be hard to distinguish the two. Tracey and Jarvis (2007) claim that social entrepreneurship is often defined as innovation that leads to positive social change. This is perhaps due to the fact that the notion of trading for a social purpose is at the core of social entrepreneurship (Travis and Jarvis, 2007). A prevalent understanding of social entrepreneurs is that their primary objective is to create social value while a secondary but necessary objective is also to create economic value and ensure financial viability (Mair and Martí, 2006). The broad claim about social entrepreneurial activity is that it is market-based innovation focused on societal change (Nicholls, 2006; Nicholls and Murdock, 2012). Social enterprises are deemed to be a unique hybrid of organizations that exist somewhere between the 'purely philanthropic' at one end and the 'purely commercial' at the other (Dees, 1998).

With a focus on commercial market activity by social entrepreneurs to create social value alongside economic value, social entrepreneurship has its roots in the study of non-profit organizations. The adoption of business practices in non-profit organizations resonates with the literature on social entrepreneur traditions (see Dart, 2004 who cites examples by Dees et al., 2001; Emerson and Twersky, 1996). A focus on the financial bottom line was traditionally atypical or uncommon in the non-profit funding and service environment (Dart, 2004). But a greater focus on commercial activity by non-profits has brought about more attention to market-based approaches that focus on the financial bottom line, efficiency, reduced cost structures and market-focused social innovations (for example, Austin, 2000; Brinckerhoff, 2000; Dees et al., 2001; Emerson and Twersky, 1996).

Social enterprises often seek to create social value (Peredo and McLean, 2006; Shaw and Carter, 2007) through commercial market-based models (Hartigan, 2006; Hockerts, 2006; Lasprogata and Cotten, 2003; Thompson, 2002). Social entrepreneurs are committed to serving society (Austin et al., 2006; Brooks, 2008; Hartigan and Elkington, 2008; Nicholls, 2006) while mainstream commercial entrepreneurs primarily seek to create economic value (Austin et al., 2006). Another way to look at social entrepreneurship is to understand that benefits accrue primarily to targeted beneficiaries as opposed to owners (Alvord et al., 2004; Austin et al., 2006; Mair and Martí, 2006). Nevertheless, in this process of trading, social entrepreneurs have to exploit market opportunities, assemble resources, and develop products and/or services that help achieve 'entrepreneurial profit' (Schumpeter, 1934). Unlike purely commercial entrepreneurs who have an ultimate goal of financial return, and unlike purely non-profit entrepreneurs who have an ultimate goal of social philanthropy, social entrepreneurs and indeed many socially conscious commercial entrepreneurs have the dual goals of providing both mission-related social outcomes as well as market-based outcomes (Desa, 2011).

Building on this range of market activity, Bhatti (2014) connected the perspective of social entrepreneurs carrying out social and purposeful innovation with the perspective of commercial entrepreneurs or firms carrying out frugal and purposeful innovation. From a study of a large sample of social entrepreneurs, he found a common cross-cutting theme, namely, the focus on resolving the needs or aspirations of the disadvantaged, disenfranchised or marginalized segments of society, such as those at the base of the pyramid. Bhatti et al. (2018) find in terms of organizational boundaries, social entrepreneurs are seen as mainly social innovators and business entrepreneurs and firms are seen as mainly technological innovators. However, through a common focus on serving the underserved, whether for profit or social improvement, both types of organizations, that is, social entrepreneurs and mainstream businesses, are adopting notions of inclusion through social and/or frugal innovation (cf. Bhatti et al., 2013; Govindarajan and Trimble, 2012; Radjou et al., 2012).

The common, market-based activities of social innovators and frugal innovators suggest that this can serve as a bridge between the two. Therefore, there is a common ground that transcends and reconciles the different motivations and approaches between these two communities. While social innovation is seen as one facet by which to achieve

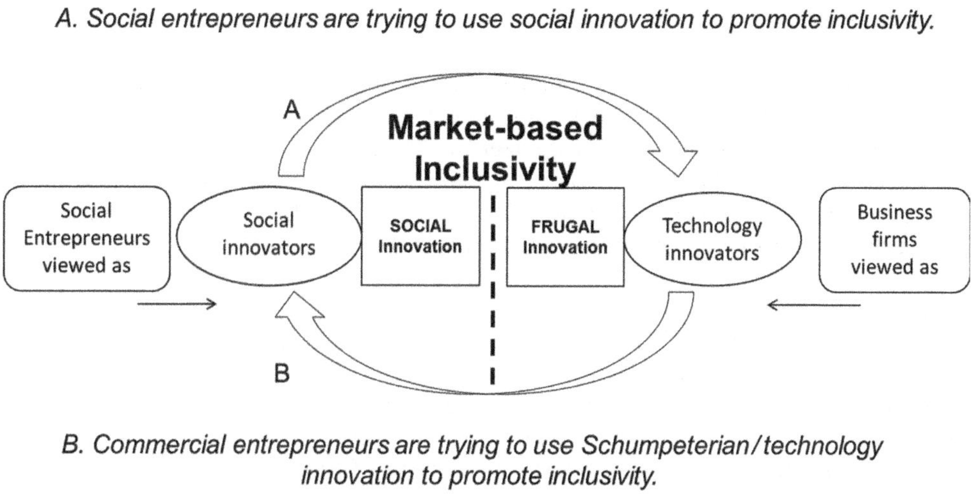

Figure 20.1 Connecting social and frugal innovation through inclusion

inclusion by social entrepreneurs, frugal innovation is the other facet by which to achieve inclusion by commercial entrepreneurs or large firms (Figure 20.1). Inclusion serves as a bridge to bring business into the activities of social entrepreneurs (for example, Mohammad Yunus and Grameen) and to bring social into the activities of corporations (for example, GE and Tata).

In other words, inclusion can be thought of as a boundary object that is helping to bridge traditional practices with alternative ones through different actors. What brings them together is the common drive to overcome inequality. This may have come about as a result of market, government or technology failure. Though civil society, social movements, academic researchers, government departments and commercial enterprises may all have their own agendas for taking part in the market for frugal innovations (Bhatti 2014; Bhatti and Ventresca, 2012; Bhatti et al., 2018), we argue that the main goal for each – social and frugal innovation – is the same, that is, to innovate in a way that promotes inclusive market participation and in a way that lessens social inequality in a sustainable way.

With increasing interest among researchers and practitioners regarding market-based solutions to social issues (Miller et al., 2012), we now outline some research opportunities for greater inclusion based on our theoretical model.

RESEARCH AGENDA

This chapter and our theoretical framework suggest several opportunities for future research in business in general as well as more specific sub-disciplines such as organizational theory, corporate strategy, policy, marketing, entrepreneurship and finance. We now turn to a discussion of the substantive, conceptual and methodological implications of this chapter for future research.

Substantive Issues

The main claim here is that a better understanding of how to embed frugal and social innovation in products, practices and attitudes within organizations can expedite the development of high-impact and cost-effective solutions that address the global challenges of burgeoning budgets, financial accountability, growing inequality and finite resources. But to do so, a great deal more theoretical and empirical research is needed on both social and frugal innovation as innovation approaches in their own right (Kesselring, 2009).

Future research must distinguish the *what, how and why* of frugal innovation along the lines of Fagerberg et al.'s (2005) categorization of 'how innovation differs', 'the systemic nature of innovation', 'innovation in the making' and 'innovation and performance'. Doing so would result in an improved understanding of how frugal innovation can be understood in terms of process, product or policy. Once these fundamental questions are addressed, scholars may be able to identify which types of frugal innovations can enhance the competitiveness of for-profit and non-profit organizations and their sustainability.

Similarly, the concept of social innovation has yet to become properly established in the academic literature in business (Aderhold, 2005). For instance, Kesselring's study of social innovation attempts to distinguish social innovation from social change by arguing that social change may ensue following concerted efforts to innovate. However, on this view, anything that constitutes social change may equally be labelled social innovation. Future research needs to be able to delineate what constitutes social innovation as distinct from changing social behaviours and practices. Research can also better examine the link between social movements and social innovation (Hensmans, 2003) – does one lead to the other and under what circumstances?

An improved understanding of social and frugal innovation individually and together can help policy makers who are interested in using and managing advanced social indicators of innovation (Moris et al., 2008) and developing new policy (Soete, 2007). The European Union (EU), for instance, is looking at advancing its innovation agenda through the lens of both social and frugal innovation with a particular focus on sustainability, the circular economy, energy efficiency and job creation among its member countries (European Commission, 2017; von Jacobi et al., 2017). (For further information, please see European Commission sponsored projects 'Frugal Innovation and the Re-Engineering of Traditional Techniques' and 'Creating Economic Space for Social Innovation'.) Keeping in mind the financial crisis and its aftermath, policy makers in the EU are seeking to promote competitiveness for more sustainable growth, stimulate employment, reduce poverty and improve social inclusion. To this end, the EU has sought to make recommendations to European companies and research centres on how a frugal innovation approach can be a business opportunity in European and non-European markets. This line of inquiry can help to determine how such business opportunities could be conducive for greater social inclusion.

Leveraging frugal innovation for social inclusion, however, poses many challenges. Particularly in affluent societies, but also ironically among lower income groups in developing countries as well, there is a tendency to equate frugality with poor quality and this makes the diffusion of frugal innovations challenging. Moreover, the direction of travel for innovation has always been from developed to emerging markets and the bias therefore, in research and practice alike, is against seeking inspiration for innovative ideas from resource-constrained environments and emerging markets (Bhatti et al., 2017a; Harris et al., 2016, 2017a, 2017b). Precisely for this reason, however, the study of frugal innovation in emerging markets provides a key opportunity to reassess underlying assumptions regarding innovation, such as the potential for 'reverse innovation' from developing to developed countries (cf. Bhatti et al., 2017a, 2017b; Prime et al., 2016, 2018) as well as who, entrepreneurs or large firms, might be best suited to instituting this strategy, protecting it and benefiting from it.

Conceptual/Theoretical Issues

This chapter and our theoretical framework offer many opportunities for future research to advance our theoretical understanding of social and frugal innovation and their links to inclusion. Both concepts of social and frugal innovation have gained increasing popularity in the academic and practitioner literature. However, there is a need to integrate diverse perspectives and situate arguments conceptually and theoretically.

First, we need holistic definitions for each of these two types of innovation in such a way that help to link them to each other. At the same time, we need a better understanding of how the two are similar and different from each other. Second, we need better theories and models of how they relate to each other and other related concepts such as inclusion. Further, these theories and models should go beyond a static understanding of the links to include a dynamic, process view of the relevant relationships. For instance, it is possible that for social innovation as an overarching concept to work, it needs frugal innovation along with other types of innovation (for example, technological innovation, bricolage, organizational innovation, business model innovation) at various points on the journey. Specifically, from a dynamic point of view, for a social innovation to be successful it might involve bricolage at the start of the journey (experimentation phase), followed by frugal innovation (scaling phase), and then eventually inclusive innovation (consolidation and expansion phase) (see Bocken et al. 2016; Koh and Prabhu, 2016).

Future research in international management should focus on developing three related areas: (a) connecting concepts and theories drawn from the management of technology and innovation with social and frugal innovation, and vice versa; (b) examining how the management of the new product development process must be reconceptualized in light of the need for social impact and scalability; and (c) studying the role of experimentation and variations in contexts, processes and outcomes of these types of innovation. Specifically, future research can look to the challenges and opportunities posed by managing the design and production of new products and services in emerging markets (Gupta and Wang, 2009; Tracey and Phillips, 2011). It can also study how various actors focus on new forms and types of innovation mindsets, processes, outcomes or impact in diverse geographical and institutional contexts. Future research can also examine the role of and link between different types of innovators and entrepreneurs and how hybrid organizations that seek to balance social and financial goals operate (see Bocken et al., 2016; Prabhu, 2017). Finally, future research should also examine the role of institutions in helping or hindering the cause of social and frugal innovation in achieving social inclusion (Koh and Prabhu, 2016; Prabhu et al., 2017).

In the entrepreneurship area, future research should examine the similarities and differences between how social and frugal innovation are practised in emerging markets versus developed markets. Specifically, research can examine the role of entrepreneurs relative to large firms, governments and non-governmental organizations (NGOs) as a source for propagating and practising social and frugal innovation. It can also seek to compare the intellectual property strategies employed by mainstream commercial entrepreneurs for technology and business model innovation with those IP strategies available to and employed by various actors in protecting, promoting and valuing social and frugal innovations. Finally, the role of resource constraints and the use of bricolage and other processes to overcome resource scarcity is a rich avenue for future research.

Empirical/Methodological Issues

This chapter and the theoretical framework we develop offer several empirical and methodological implications for future research. First, the relative paucity of knowledge about social innovation, frugal innovation and the inter-relationship between these two concepts and social inclusion suggests the need for grounded, theory-building research into how entrepreneurs and for-profit and non-profit firms overcome resource constraints and institutional voids to develop highly affordable solutions for large numbers of citizens across geographical and sectoral contexts. Future research in these areas should begin with deep ethnographies of such actors around the world and the strategies they employ over time to achieve their social objectives while remaining financially viable. Second, this chapter and our theoretical framework suggest many opportunities for quantitative research into how innovations for underserved consumers are created and the impact of these markets on social and economic inclusion around the world.

Given that NGOs, startups, multinationals and governments around the world are beginning to develop and implement frugal and social innovations on a large scale in fundamental areas such as energy, health, financial services and education (see Hammond et al., 2007), many opportunities exist for future research to conduct longitudinal field experiments that examine how such innovations impact social and economic inclusion (see Levitt and List, 2009). Given also that many of these innovations are being developed in emerging markets where new policies and institutions are being introduced almost on a daily basis, opportunities arise to exploit such natural experiments to understand how regulatory or technological shocks impact social and frugal innovation and inclusion. Because such field or natural experiments also enable researchers to be present from the birth of a phenomenon, and compare outcomes in treatment relative to control groups in the field, such research also offers the opportunity to make strong causal inferences in real-world environments (see Angrist and Krueger, 2001). While such natural and field experiments are highly influential in development economics (for example, Levitt and List, 2009), hitherto such studies have been relatively rare in business.

Finally, our theoretical framework suggests opportunities for combining qualitative and quantitative techniques in understanding how institutions and human agents (managers, entrepreneurs and policy makers) interact in developing social and frugal innovations to promote social inclusion. Various aspects of institutional work, as well as social and frugal innovation, require actors to use language creatively (Maguire and Hardy, 2009; Maguire et al., 2004; Phillips et al., 2004; Zilber, 2006). Specifically, creating new institutions and reforming current ones requires actors to build a new system of meaning and create a shared sense of purpose. This in turn suggests opportunities for future research to engage with techniques beyond business and management such as from computer science such as natural language processing and big data to understand how such social and frugal innovation is done at scale and how they bring about meaning and sense to institutional change and social inclusion.

CONCLUSION

In this chapter we have sought to present the power and potential of frugal innovation and social innovation to better address the issue of inclusive and sustainable growth around the world. We have outlined how these two types of innovations both independently and together seek to make the process and outcomes of innovation more economically and socially inclusive. We hope that we have laid out a path for researchers to advance theoretical and empirical studies in the area. We also hope that we have provided practitioners and policy makers the means to harness such hybrid models of innovation to resolve the most pressing Grand Challenges of our time.

REFERENCES

Aderhold, J. (2005), 'Gesellschaftsentwicklung am Tropf technischer Neuerungen', in J. Aderhold and R. John (eds), *Innovation. Sozialwissenschaftliche Perspektiven*. Konstanz: UVK, pp. 13–32.

Altenburg, T. (2011), 'Building inclusive innovation systems in developing countries: challenges for IS research', in B.-Å Lundvall, K.J. Joseph, C. Chaminade, and J. Vang (eds), *Handbook of Innovation Systems and Developing Countries: Building Domestic Capabilities in a Global Setting*. Cheltenham, UK and Northampton, MA, USA: Edward Elgar Publishing, pp. 33–56.

Alvord, S.H., L.D. Brown, and C.W. Letts (2004), 'Social entrepreneurship and societal transformation', *Journal of Applied Behavioral Science*, **40**, 260–82.

Angrist, J.D. and A.B. Krueger (2001), 'Instrumental variables and the search for identification: from supply and demand to natural experiments', *Journal of Economic Perspectives*, **15**(4), 69–85.

Austin, J.E. (2000), *The Collaboration Challenge: How Nonprofits and Business succeed through Strategic Alliances.* San Francisco, CA: Jossey Bass Publishers.

Austin, J., H. Stevenson, and J.W. Skillern (2006), 'Social and commercial entrepreneurship: same, different, or both?', *Entrepreneurship Theory and Practice*, **30**, 1–22.

Barré, R. (2001), 'The Agora model of innovation systems: S&T indicators for a democratic knowledge society', *Research Evolution*, **10**, 13–18.

Basu, R.R., P.M. Banerjee, and E.G. Sweeny (2013), 'Frugal innovation: core competencies to address global sustainability', *Journal of Management for Global Sustainability*, **1**(2), 63–82.

Bates, S.M. (2011), *The Social Innovation Imperative: Create Winning Products. Services, and Programs that Solve Society's Most Pressing Challenges*. New York: McGraw-Hill.

Battilana, J. and S. Dorado (2010), 'Building sustainable hybrid organizations: the case of commercial microfinance organizations', *Academy of Management Journal*, **53**(6), 1419–40.

Benford, R.D. and D.A. Snow (2000), 'Framing processes and social movements: an overview and assessment', *Annual Review of Sociology*, **26**(1), 611–39.

Bhatti, Y.A. (2012), 'What is frugal, what is innovation? Towards a theory of frugal innovation', Academy of Management Annual Meeting, 3–7 August, Boston. *Academy of Management Proceedings*, 2012:1 10794. http://dx.doi.org/10.2139/ssrn.2005910

Bhatti, Y.A. (2014), 'Frugal innovation: social entrepreneurs' perceptions of innovation under institutional voids, resource scarcity and affordability constraints', DPhil dissertation, Oxford University.

Bhatti, Y.A. and M. Ventresca (2012), 'The emerging market for Frugal Innovation: fad, fashion, or fit?', SSRN. https://papers.ssrn.com/abstract=2005983

Bhatti, Y., S. Khilji, and R.R. Basu (2013), 'Frugal innovation', in S. Khilji and C. Rowley (eds), *Globalization, Change and Learning in South Asia.* Oxford: Chandos Publishing, pp. 123–45.

Bhatti, Y., A. Taylor, M. Harris et al. (2017a), 'Global lessons in frugal innovation to improve health care delivery in the United States', *Health Affairs*, **36**(11), 1912–19.

Bhatti, Y., M. Prime, M. Harris et al. (2017b), 'The search for the Holy Grail: frugal innovation in healthcare from developing countries for reverse innovation to developed countries', *BMJ Innovations*, **3**(4). http://innovations.bmj.com/cgi/content/abstract/bmjinnov-2016-000186

Bhatti, Y., R. Basu, D. Barron, and M. Ventresca (2018), *Frugal Innovation: Models, Means, Methods.* Cambridge, UK: Cambridge University Press.

Bocken, N.M.P., F. Alison, and J.C. Prabhu (2016), 'Scaling up social businesses in developing markets', *Journal of Cleaner Production*, **139**, 295–308.

Borins, S. (2000), 'Loose cannons and rule breakers, or enterprising leaders? Some evidence about innovative public managers', *Public Administration Review*, **60**, 498–507.

Bornstein, D. (2004), *How to Change the World: Social Entrepreneurs and the Power of New Ideas.* Oxford: Oxford University Press.

Bornstein, D. and D. Davis (2010), *Social Entrepreneurship: What Everyone Needs to Know*. Oxford: Oxford University Press.

Brinckerhoff, P. (2000), *Social Entrepreneurship: The Art of Mission Based Venture Development.* New York: John Wiley & Sons.

Brooks, A. (2008), *Social Entrepreneurship*. Upper Saddle River, NJ: Pearson Prentice Hall.

Cajaiba-Santana, G. (2014), 'Social innovation: moving the field forward. A conceptual framework', *Technological Forecasting and Social Change*, **82**, 42–51.

Cappelli, P., H. Singh, J. Singh, and M. Useem (2010), 'The India way: lessons for the U.S.', *Academy of Management Perspectives*, **24**(2), 6–24.

Cavalli, N. (2007), 'The symbolic dimension of innovation processes', *American Behavioral Scientist*, **50**(7), 958–69.

Chandy, R. and J. Prabhu (2011), 'Innovation typologies', in B. Bayus (ed.), *Wiley International Encyclopedia of Marketing*. Hoboken, NJ: John Wiley & Sons.

Chaudhary, B., A. Modi, and K. Reddy (2012), 'Right to sight: a management case study on Aravind eye hospitals', *International Journal of Multidisciplinary Research*, **2**(1), 447–57.

Christensen, C. (2013), *The Innovator's Dilemma: When New Technologies Cause Great Firms to Fail.* Boston, MA: Harvard Business Review Press.

Cornwell, B. (2007), 'The Protestant sect credit machine: social capital and the rise of capitalism', *Journal of Classical Sociology*, **7**(3), 267–90.

Dart, R. (2004), 'The legitimacy of social enterprise', *Nonprofit Management and Leadership*, **14**, 411–24.

Dees, G. and B.B. Anderson (2006), 'Framing a theory of social entrepreneurship: building on two schools of practice and thought', in R. Mosher-Williams (ed.), *Research on Social Entrepreneurship: Understanding and Contributing to an Emerging Field.* Association for Research on Non-profit Organizations and Voluntary Action (ARNOVA), pp. 36–9.

Dees, G., J. Emerson, and P. Economy (2001), *Enterprising Nonprofits: A Toolkit for Social Entrepreneurs.* New York: John Wiley & Sons.

Dees, J.G. (1996), *Social Enterprise Spectrum: Philanthropy to Commerce.* Cambridge, MA: Harvard Business School Press.

Dees, J.G. (1998), 'Enterprising nonprofits', *Harvard Business Review*, **76**(January–February), 55–67.

DePasse, J.W., A. Caldwell, D. Santorino et al. (2016), 'Affordable medical technologies: bringing value-based design into global health', *BMJ Innovations*, **2**(1). http://dx.doi.org/10.1136/bmjinnov-2015-000069

Desa, G. (2009), 'Mobilizing resources in constrained environments: a study of technology social ventures', PhD Thesis, University of Washington.

Desa, G. (2011), 'Resource mobilization in international social entrepreneurship: bricolage as a mechanism of institutional transformation', *Entrepreneurship Theory and Practice*, **36**(4), 727–51.

Dutz, M. (ed.) (2007), *Unleashing India's Innovation: Toward Sustainable and Inclusive Growth.* Washington, DC: World Bank Publications.

Emerson, J. and F. Twersky (eds) (1996), *New Social Entrepreneurs: The Success, Challenge, and Lessons of Non-Profit Enterprise Creation.* San Francisco, CA: The Roberts Foundation.

Ernst & Young (2011), *Innovating for the Next Three Billion.* London: Ernst & Young.

Etzkowitz, H. and L. Leydesdorff (2000), 'The dynamics of innovation: from national systems and "mode 2" to a triple helix of university–industry–government relations', *Research Policy*, **29**, 109–23.

European Commission (2017), *Frugal Innovation and the Re-Engineering of Traditional Techniques.* Brussels: Directorate-General for Research and Innovation, European Commission. https://publications.europa.eu/en/publication-detail/-/publication/20d6095a-2a44-11e7-ab65-01aa75ed71a1 (accessed 1 August 2017).

Fagerberg, J., D.C. Mowery, and R.R. Nelson (eds) (2005), *The Oxford Handbook of Innovation*. Oxford: Oxford University Press.

Foster, C. and R. Heeks (2013), 'Conceptualising inclusive innovation: modifying systems of innovation frameworks to understand diffusion of new technology to low-income consumers', *European Journal of Development Research*, **25**(3), 333–55.

George, G., A.M. McGahan, and J. Prabhu (2012), 'Innovation for inclusive growth: towards a theoretical framework and a research agenda', *Journal of Management Studies*, **49**(4), 661–83.

Gerometta, J., H. Haussermann, and G. Longo (2005), 'Social innovation and civil society in urban governance: strategies for an inclusive city', *Urban Studies*, **42**(11), 2007–21.

Goldsmith, S. (2010), *The Power of Social Innovation: How Civic Entrepreneurs Ignite Community Networks for Good.* San Francisco, CA: Jossey-Bass.

Govindarajan, V. and R. Ramamurti (2011), 'Reverse innovation, emerging markets, and global strategy', *Global Strategy Journal*, **1**(3–4), 191–205.

Govindarajan, V. and C. Trimble (2012), *Reverse Innovation.* Cambridge, MA: Harvard Business Review Press.

Gulati, R. (2010), 'Management lessons from the edge', *Academy of Management Perspectives*, **24**(2), 25–7.

Gundry, L.K., J.R. Kickul, M.D. Griffiths, and S.C. Bacq (2011), 'Creating social change out of nothing: the role of entrepreneurial bricolage in social entrepreneurs' catalytic innovations', in G. Lumpkin and J.A. Katz (eds), *Advances in Entrepreneurship, Firm Emergence, and Growth.* Bingley, UK: Emerald Group Publishing, pp. 1–24.

Gupta, A. and H. Wang (2009), *Getting China and India Right: Strategies for Leveraging the World's Fastest-Growing Economies for Global Advantage.* New York: John Wiley & Sons.

Hämäläinen, T.J. and R. Heiskala (eds) (2007), *Social Innovations, Institutional Change and Economic Performance: Making Sense of Structural Adjustment Processes in Industrial Sectors, Regions and Societies.* Cheltenham, UK and Northampton, MA, USA: Edward Elgar Publishing.

Hammond, A.L., W.J. Kramer, R.S. Katz, J.T. Tran, and C. Walker (2007), 'The next 4 billion', *Innovations*, **2**(1–2), 147–58.

Hang, C.C., J. Chen, and A.M. Subramian (2010), 'Developing disruptive products for emerging economies: lessons from Asian cases', *Research-Technology Management*, **53**(4), 21–6.

Harris, M., Y. Bhatti, and A. Darzi (2016), 'Does the country of origin matter in health care innovation diffusion?', *Journal of American Medical Association*, **315**(11), 1103–4.

Harris, M., J. Martí, H. Watt, Y. Bhatti, J. Macinko, and A.W. Darzi (2017a), 'Explicit bias toward high-income-country research: a randomized, blinded, crossover experiment of English clinicians', *Health Affairs*, **36**(11), 1997–2004.

Harris, M., Y. Bhatti, and M. Prime (2017b), 'Low-cost innovation in healthcare: what you find depends on where you look', *Journal of the Royal Society of Medicine*, November. https://doi.org/10.1177/0141076817738501

Hart, S.L. (1997), 'Beyond greening: strategies of a sustainable world,' *Harvard Business Review*, **75**(1), 66–76.

Hart, S. and C. Prahalad (2002), 'The fortune at the bottom of the pyramid', *Strategy+Business*, **26**, 54–67.

Hartigan, P. (2006), 'It's about people, not profits', *Business Strategy Review*, **17**, 42–5.

Hartigan, P. and J. Elkington (2008), *The Power of Unreasonable People: How Social Entrepreneurs Create Markets That Change the World.* Boston, MA: Harvard Business School Press.

Hensmans, M. (2003), 'Social movement organizations: a metaphor for strategic actors in institutional fields', *Organization Studies*, **24**(3), 355–81.

Hilgartner, S. and C.L. Bosk (1988), 'The rise and fall of social problems: A public arenas model', *American Journal of Sociology*, **94**(1), 53–78.

Hockerts, K. (2006), 'Entrepreneurial opportunity in social purpose business ventures', in J. Mair, J. Robinson, and K. Hockerts (eds), *Social Entrepreneurship*. London: Palgrave Macmillan, pp. 142–54.

Hoogendoorn, B., E. Pennings, and R. Thurik (2010), *What Do We Know About Social Entrepreneurship: An Analysis of Empirical Research*. Amsterdam: ERIM.

Howaldt, J. and M. Schwarz (2010), *Social Innovation: Concepts, Research Fields and International Trends.* Dortmund, Germany: Sozialforschungsstelle.

Immelt, J.R., V. Govindarajan, and C. Trimble (2009), 'How GE is disrupting itself', *Harvard Business Review*, **87**(10), 56–65.

Jacobi, N. von, D. Edmiston, and R. Ziegler (2017), 'Tackling marginalisation through social innovation? Examining the EU social innovation policy agenda from a capabilities perspective', *Journal of Human Development and Capabilities*, **18**(2), 148–62.

Karamchandani, A., M. Kubzansky, and P. Frandano (2009), *Emerging Markets, Emerging Models: Market-Based Solutions to the Challenges of Global Poverty*. Cambridge, MA: Monitor Group.

Kesselring, A. (2009), 'Social innovation in private companies: an exploratory empirical study', in S. Roth (ed.), *Non-Technological and Non-Economic Innovations: Contributions to a Theory of Robust Innovation*, Bern: Peter Lang, pp. 147–60.

Koh, H. and J. Prabhu (2016), 'Scaling up inclusive markets', *Stanford Social Innovation Review*, Spring, https://ssir.org/articles/entry/scaling_up_inclusive_markets

Lasprogata, G.A. and M.N. Cotten (2003), 'Contemplating "enterprise": the business and legal challenges of social entrepreneurship', *American Business Law Journal*, **41**, 567–95.

Lawrence, T., N. Phillips, and P. Tracey (2012), 'From the guest editors: educating social entrepreneurs and social innovators', *Academy of Management Learning & Education*, **11**(3), 319–23.
Levänen, J., M. Hossain, T. Lyytinen, A. Hyvärinen, S. Numminen, and M. Halme (2016), 'Implications of frugal innovations on sustainable development: evaluating water and energy innovations', *Sustainability*, **8**(1), 4–21.
Levitt, S. and J. List (2009), 'Field experiments in economics: the past, the present and the future', *European Economic Review*, **53**(1), 1–18.
Leydesdorff, L. (2005), 'The triple helix model and the study of knowledge based innovation systems', *International Journal of Contemporary Sociology*, **42**(1), 12–27.
Maguire, S. and C. Hardy (2009), 'Discourse and deinstitutionalization: the decline of DDT', *Academy of Management Journal*, **52**(1), 148–78.
Maguire, S., C. Hardy, and T.B. Lawrence (2004), 'Institutional entrepreneurship in emerging fields: HIV/AIDS treatment advocacy in Canada', *Academy of Management Journal*, **47**(5), 657–79.
Mair, J. and I. Martí (2006), 'Social entrepreneurship research: a source of explanation, prediction, and delight', *Journal of World Business*, **41**(1), 36–44.
Mair, J. and I. Martí (2009), 'Entrepreneurship in and around institutional voids: a case study from Bangladesh', *Journal of Business Venturing*, **24**, 419–35.
March, J. and H. Simon (1958), *Organizations.* New York: Wiley.
McMullen, J.S. (2011), 'Delineating the domain of development entrepreneurship: a market-based approach to facilitating inclusive economic growth', *Entrepreneurship Theory and Practice*, **35**(1), 185–93.
Miller, D. (2009), *Selling Solar: The Diffusion of Renewable Energy in Emerging Markets*. London: Earthscan.
Miller, T., M. Grimes, J. McMullen, and T. Vogus (2012), 'Venturing for others with heart and head: how compassion encourages social entrepreneurship', *Academy of Management Review*, **37**, 616–40.
Moris, F., J. Jankowski, and P. Perolle (2008), 'Advancing measures of innovation in the United States', *Journal of Technology Transfer*, **33**, 123–30.
Moulaert, F., F. Martinelli, E. Swyngedouw, and S. Gonzalez (2005), 'Towards alternative model(s) of local innovation', *Urban Studies*, **42**(11), 1969–90.
Mulgan, G. (2006), 'The process of social innovation', *Innovations: Technology, Governance, Globalization*, **1**(2), 145–62.
Mulgan, G., S. Tucker, R. Ali, and B. Sanders (2007), *Social Innovation: What It Is, Why It Matters and How It Can Be Accelerated.* Skoll Centre for Social Entrepreneurship. http://eureka.sbs.ox.ac.uk/761/1/Social_Innovation.pdf (accessed 28 November 2017).
Mumford, M.D. and P. Moertl (2003), 'Cases of social innovation: lessons from two innovations in the 20th century', *Creativity Research Journal*, **15**(2–3), 261–6.
Munk, N. (2013), *The Idealist: Jeffrey Sachs and the Quest to End Poverty*. New York: Random House Foundation.
Murray, R., J. Calulier-Grice, and G. Mulgan (2010), *Open Book of Social Innovation.* London: The Young Foundation.
Nicholls, A. (ed.) (2006), *Social Entrepreneurship: New Models of Sustainable Social Change*. Oxford: Oxford University Press.
Nicholls, A. and A. Murdock (eds) (2012), *Social Innovation: Blurring Boundaries to Reconfigure Markets.* Basingstoke: Palgrave Macmillan.
Nijhof, A., O. Fisscher, and J.K. Looise (2002), 'Inclusive innovation: a research project on the inclusion of social responsibility', *Corporate Social Responsibility and Environmental Management*, **9**, 83–90.
Nowotny, H., P. Scott, and M. Gibbons (2001), *Re-thinking Science, Knowledge and the Public in the Age of Uncertainty*. London: Polity Press.
Ogburn, W.F. (1937), 'Foreword', in The Subcommittee on Technology to the National Resources Committee (ed.), *Technological Trends and National Policy, Including the Social Implications of New Inventions*, June. Washington, DC: United States Government Printing Office.
Peredo, A.M. and M. McLean (2006), 'Social entrepreneurship: a critical review of the concept', *Journal of World Business*, **41**, 56–65.
Perrini, F. and C. Vurro (2006), 'Social entrepreneurship: innovation and social change across theory and practice', in J. Mair, J. Robinson, and K. Hockerts (eds), *Social Entrepreneurship.* London: Palgrave Macmillan, pp. 57–85.
Phillips, N., T.B. Lawrence, and C. Hardy (2004), 'Discourse and institutions', *Academy of Management Review*, **29**(4), 635–52.
Phills, J.A., K. Deiglmeier, and D.T. Miller (2008), 'Rediscovering social innovation', *Stanford Social Innovation Review*, **6**(4), 34–43.
Porter, M.E. and M.R. Kramer (1999), 'Philanthropy's new agenda: creating value', *Harvard Business Review*, **77**, 121–31.
Porter, M.E. and M.R. Kramer (2011), 'Creating shared value', *Harvard Business Review*, **89**(1/2), 62–77.

Pot, F.W. and F. Vaas (2008), 'Social innovation, the new challenge for Europe', *International Journal of Productivity and Performance Management*, **57**(7), 468–73.
Prabhu, J. (2017), 'Frugal innovation: doing more with less for more', *Philosophical Transactions of the Royal Society*, **375**(2095), 20160372.
Prabhu, J. and S. Jain (2015), 'Innovation and entrepreneurship in India: understanding *Jugaad*', *Asia Pacific Journal of Management*, **32**(4), 843–68.
Prabhu, J., P. Tracey, and M. Hassan (2017), 'Marketing to the poor: an institutional model of exchange in emerging markets', *AMS Review*, **7**(3–4), 101–22.
Prahalad, C.K. (2006), *The Fortune at the Bottom of the Pyramid: Eradicating Poverty Through Profits*. Upper Saddle River, NJ: Prentice Hall.
Prahalad, C.K. and R.A. Mashelkar (2010), 'Innovation's Holy Grail', *Harvard Business Review*, July–August, 1–9.
Prime, M., Y. Bhatti, M. Harris, and A. Darzi (2016), 'African healthcare innovation: an untapped resource?', *World Hospitals and Health Services Journal*, Special issue on Learning from African Innovations, **52**(3).
Prime, M., I. Attaelmanan, A. Imbuldeniya, M. Harris, A. Darzi, and Y. Bhatti (2018), 'From Malawi to Middlesex: the case of the Arbutus Drill Cover System as an example of the cost saving potential of frugal innovations for the UK NHS', *BMJ Innovations*, 30 March. dx.doi.org/10.1136/bmjinnov-2017-000233
Radjou, N. and J. Prabhu (2015), *Frugal Innovation: How To Do Better With Less*. London: Profile Books.
Radjou, N., J. Prabhu, and S. Ahuja (2012), *Jugaad Innovation: Think Frugal, Be Flexible, Generate Breakthrough Growth*. San Francisco, CA: Jossey-Bass.
Ramamurti, R. (2012), 'What is really different about emerging market multinationals?', *Global Strategy Journal*, **2**(1), 41–7.
Rangan, V.K. (2009), *The Aravind Eye Hospital, Madurai, India: In Service for Sight*. Boston, MA: Harvard Business School Publishing.
Roberts, Y. (2008), 'New ways of doing. Social innovation is a new global obsession. It might be a nebulous idea but it has huge potential', *Guardian*, 11 August.
Rogers, E.M. (2003), *Diffusion of Innovations*, 5th edn. New York: Free Press.
Rosenberg, N. (1982), *Inside the Black Box: Technology and Economics*. New York: Cambridge University Press.
Roth, S. (2009), 'Introduction. Towards a theory of robust innovation', in S. Roth (ed.), *Non-Technological and Non-Economic Innovations: Contributions to a Theory of Robust Innovation*. Bern: Peter Lang, pp. 9–28.
Sachs, J. (2005), *The End of Poverty: How We Can Make It Happen in Our Lifetime*. London: Penguin.
Schumpeter, J. (1934), *Capitalism, Socialism and Democracy*. New York: Harper and Row.
Sen, A. (2001), *Development as Freedom*. Oxford: Oxford University Press.
Sharma, A. and G.R. Iyer (2012), 'Resource-constrained product development: implications for green marketing and green supply chains', *Industrial Marketing Management*, **41**(4), 599–608.
Shaw, E. and S. Carter (2007), 'Social entrepreneurship: theoretical antecedents and empirical analysis of entrepreneurial processes and outcomes', *Journal of Small Business and Enterprise Development*, **14**(3), 418–34.
Singh, S.K., A. Gambhir, A. Sotiropoulos, and S. Duckworth (2012), *Frugal Innovation by Social Entrepreneurs in India*. London: Serco Institute.
Soete, L. (2007), 'From industrial to innovation policy', *Journal of Industrial Competition and Trade*, **7**, 273–84.
Stiglitz, J.E. (2007), *Making Globalization Work*. New York: Norton.
Stiglitz, J.E. (2015), *Globalization and Its Discontents*. New York: Norton.
Suter, C. (2010), 'Globalization, economic and social transformation, and inequality: introduction to special issue', *International Journal of Comparative Sociology*, **51**(4), 243–5.
Tellis, G.J., J.C. Prabhu, and R.K. Chandy (2009), 'Radical innovation across nations: the preeminence of corporate culture', *Journal of Marketing*, **73**(1), 3–23.
The Young Foundation (2012), *Social Innovation Overview: A Deliverable of the Project: 'The Theoretical, Empirical and Policy Foundations for Building Social Innovation in Europe' (TEPSIE)*, European Commission – 7th Framework Programme, Brussels: European Commission, DG Research. https://youngfoundation.org/wp-content/uploads/2012/12/TEPSIE.D1.1.Report.DefiningSocialInnovation.Part-1-defining-social-innovation.pdf
Thompson, J. (2002), 'The world of the social entrepreneur', *International Journal of Public Sector Management*, **15**, 412–31.
Tracey, P. and O. Jarvis (2007), 'Toward a theory of social venture franchising', *Entrepreneurship Theory and Practice*, **31**(5), 667–85.
Tracey, P. and N. Phillips (2011), 'Entrepreneurship in emerging markets: strategies for new venture creation in uncertain institutional contexts', *Management International Review*, **51**(1), 23–39.
Tracey, P. and N. Stott (2017), 'Social innovation: a window on alternative ways of organizing and innovating', *Innovation: Organization & Management*, **19**(1), 51–60.
US Census Bureau (2014), 'Income, Poverty and Health Insurance Coverage in the United States: 2013, Press release'. https://www.census.gov/newsroom/press-releases/2014/cb14-169.html (accessed 28 November 2017).

Van de Ven, A.H. (1986), 'Central problems in management of innovation', *Management Science*, **32**(5), 590–607.
Woolridge, A. (2010), 'The world turned upside down. A special report on innovation in emerging markets', *The Economist*, 15 April. http://www.economist.com/node/15879369 (accessed 15 January 2017).
Zeschky, M., B. Widenmayer, and O. Gassmann (2011), 'Frugal innovation in emerging markets', *Research-Technology Management*, **54**(4), 38–45.
Zilber, T.B. (2006), 'The work of the symbolic in institutional processes: translations of rational myths in Israeli high tech', *Academy of Management Journal*, **49**(2), 281–303.

21. Climate change and entrepreneurship

Elizabeth Embry, Jessica Jones and Jeffrey G. York

INTRODUCTION

Human-induced climate change presents one of the greatest managerial challenges of our time (George et al., 2016; Howard-Grenville et al., 2014). Our global society's ecological footprint simply exceeds earth's sustainable carrying capacity. This situation is forecasted to worsen with global economic and population expansion (Pecl et al., 2017). How do organizations then mitigate and combat climate change while still maintaining growth and expansion? The magnitude of the human-induced causes of climate change, the natural disasters that have led to widespread destruction of resources and communities, and the anticipated irreversible negative consequences of excessive carbon emissions (IPCC, 2014a) leave organizations and their leaders uncertain as to how to best address current and future threats. While the need for all actors within society to react to the impacts of climate change is great (Ostrom, 2012), management research has largely focused on regulatory and corporate actors (Hiatt et al., 2015; Reid and Toffel, 2009).

However, policy agreements, such as the Paris Agreement, often fail to be enforceable due to their non-binding nature (Bang et al., 2016). By the time policy goals are agreed upon, the measures will likely not be strong enough to mitigate climate change. This is largely because overarching, national and international policy agreements are broad in their call to action and not specific to local challenges or actions required (Ostrom, 2012; York et al., 2018).

Some have posited that corporations may address gaps created by policy actors; two viewpoints exist for what and how corporations should aim to mitigate the consequences of climate change. The first holds that corporations arguably hold enough power both globally and locally to influence change (Reid and Toffel, 2009). This is largely due to their financial means and influence to mitigate the impacts of climate change and prevent future problems (York and Venkataraman, 2010). The second views corporations as the largest contributors to human-induced climate change (Schaltegger and Hörisch, 2017); therefore, corporations must be responsible to fix and reverse damages. At the surface, corporate social responsibility, corporate greening, and other sustainability initiatives are entering mainstream practice. Yet, such practices and incentives are not sufficient to move large businesses to address the issues of climate change at the substantial level needed (Hockerts and Wüstenhagen, 2010; Pulver, 2007; Wright and Nyberg, 2017). Regardless of the viewpoint, substantive reduction or mitigation of the effects of climate has yet to be realized.

Focusing on governments and corporations to address impacts of climate change overlooks the potential role of entrepreneurs (Dean and McMullen, 2007; Schaltegger, 2002; Schaltegger et al., 2018). Human-induced climate change requires an inclusive approach and ability to think differently about every product, service, process, and system. While the top-down approach as exemplified by regulatory and corporate action is constrained by inflexibility and exclusive practices (Pacheco et al., 2010a; Sine and Lee, 2009), there is a need for influencers outside of such constraints to more completely address impacts of climate change. By engaging entrepreneurs and new ventures in the process of addressing human-induced climate change, an inclusive, bottom-up approach fills in the gaps and accelerates the response.

The field of entrepreneurship is the scholarly examination of how, by whom, and with what affects opportunities to create future goods and services are discovered, evaluated, and exploited (Shane and Venkataraman, 2000; Venkatarman, 1997) and the economic, social, and ecological impacts of such activity. Within this broad field, there is growing interest in social (Mair and Martí, 2006), sustainable (Dean and McMullen, 2007; Shepherd and Patzelt, 2011), and environmental (Lenox and York, 2012; York et al., 2016b) entrepreneurship as unique approaches to address societal and environmental challenges. While these specialty areas enable scholars to engage deeply in a specific research agenda, this chapter focuses on how the broad field of entrepreneurship may play a role in addressing human-induced climate change.

Unconstrained by hierarchy and bureaucracy, entrepreneurs often have the flexibility and creative potential to uniquely address the issues presented by climate change. Entrepreneurship is inherently inclusive unlike corporate or regulatory bodies; there are no constraints as to who an entrepreneur is, or where they are from. Climate change is a transnational issue, and its impacts will be hardest on low- and middle-income countries (IPCC, 2014a). Entrepreneurs from these countries will know firsthand what response is needed and have the cultural competence necessary for effective implementation (Frumkin et al., 2008). Therefore, an effective approach to addressing these impacts must be inclusive and collaborative.

In this chapter, we propose a framework for future research at the nexus of entrepreneurship and climate change. We describe how entrepreneurship may address three overlapping areas of climate change impact: ecological, societal, and health. Ecological impacts result from changes in the natural environment. Societal impacts are the implications of the ecological impacts on communities as humans are forced to adapt. Health implications are the physical and psychological manifestations of the ecological and societal impacts of climate change. We then present the various opportunities for addressing climate change by researching entrepreneurship at the individual, organizational, and institutional levels of analysis. Our hope is that this framework and corresponding theory provide new directions for entrepreneurship scholars to aid in understanding how to address the daunting issue of climate change.

IMPACTS OF CLIMATE CHANGE

Climate change has garnered interest in management journals in recent years (e.g., Ferraro et al., 2015; Howard-Grenville et al., 2014), with work investigating how climate policies impact business practices (e.g., Ansari et al., 2011; Hoffman, 2005) such as corporate reporting (Hahn et al., 2015), governance (Wijen and Ansari, 2007), and responsibilities (e.g., Wang et al., 2016). Although these questions are important for organizational knowledge, this scholarship does little to specifically address how entrepreneurs may address climate change. In order to more clearly identify the causes, consequences, and potential solutions, we identify three specific impacts: ecological, societal, and health. We define climate change impacts as *the manifestations and consequences of climate change on the natural environment, communities and society, and human health.* Next, we define each impact, and explore the challenges and opportunities that each present.

Ecological Impact

Ecological impacts are defined as the *environmental manifestations of climate change* including, but not limited to, increased temperatures, rise of carbon levels, change in sea levels, and a resulting increase of natural disasters. Ecological impacts directly change ecosystems around the world, which have strong negative consequences for the planet's biodiversity. Human approaches to energy, agriculture, water and other activities affect the ways and extent to which climate change will alter the ecosystems we depend on (National Research Council, 2008). Ecological impacts manifest at the local and global level.

Globally, the eight warmest years in the last 100 years have occurred since 1998 (IPCC, 2007). Temperature rise is due to increased production of greenhouse gases, most especially carbon dioxide. Rising temperatures are connected to exposure of air pollution as 87 percent of the world's cities violate the World Health Organization's air pollution guidelines. As such, global exposure to dangerous levels of air pollution has increased by 11.2 percent in the past 20 years (Watts et al., 2018). With the temperature warming, ocean water levels also have changed causing arctic ice to melt, forcing aquatic species to migrate, and contributing to sea level rise.

At the local level, sea level rise has had the greatest impact thus far in the western Pacific. This was a significant factor in the devastation in the Philippines when Typhoon Haiyan surged in 2013 (World Meteorological Organization, 2016b). While such impacts are currently more apparent in the Philippines than they are on the coasts of the United States or other coastal regions, the long-term impacts of sea level rise will be global. These changes are largely attributed to manufacturing and consumption of climate-damaging products at unprecedented rates (IPCC, 2014b). We propose three ways entrepreneurship research can address the ecological impacts of climate change.

First, studying the entrepreneurial process provides opportunities to understand new products, services, and markets for less carbon-intensive forms of energy production. Many entrepreneurs have begun to address this opportunity by increasing alternative available energy options, such as solar, wind, and other renewable energy sources (e.g., Pacheco et al., 2014; Sine and Lee, 2009; York et al., 2016a). Providing access to consistent and clean energy is a significant path to addressing climate change. Thus, understanding how such products and services get into the hands of those in need and what influences widespread adoption is critical for the entrepreneurial process to more effectively address ecological impacts of climate change.

Second, entrepreneurs can also play a role to mitigate environmental destruction, thus ensuring adequate natural resources to absorb carbon emissions. Appropriate property rights can protect natural resources from industrial exploitation and pollution (Anderson and Leal, 2001; Dean and McMullen, 2007). For example, the independently funded Conservacion Patagonia purchased the property rights to 756,000 acres of temperate rainforest in Patagonia, Chile, to ensure that it would not be damaged by the region's industrial growth. Property rights provide an appropriate lens to explore how entrepreneurial actors protect biodiversity (Barbier et al., 2018).

Third, innovation and entrepreneurship focus on the creation of novel products and services. Such processes are critical to develop technologies and solutions focused on mitigating the ecological impacts of climate change. For example, innovations in electric vehicles, artificial intelligence, and building technology may all be harnessed to address climate change; however, this will only occur when entrepreneurial actors translate innovations into new products, markets, and services. Research that explores the innovation process and technology adoption of novel solutions to climate change could help illuminate how, when, and why such efforts succeed.

Studying and addressing the ecological impacts can help to identify entrepreneurial opportunities embedded within the natural consequences of climate change. To explore the broader consequences, we next turn to impacts related to society and health.

Societal Impact

Societal impacts of climate change are defined as *resulting circumstances that force a community to adapt to a change in its physical environment and personal assets*. Societal impacts such as access to food, water, and lodging, separation of family members, and loss of employment or economic assets result in detrimental threats to quality of life and survival. These impacts are often a direct result of the ecological impacts discussed above such as weather-related natural disasters or changes in the growing seasons, which destroy communities or force migration in order for the population to survive.

For example, weather-related natural disasters linked to climate change have increased by 46 percent since 2000 (World Meteorological Organization, 2016a, 2016b). In the United States alone, the cost of physical damage from natural disasters exceeds $40 billion annually (World Meteorological Organization, 2016a) diverting community funds away from other social services and public goods.

Along with physical damage, disasters result in a high rate of migration and displacement. In 2016, there were 24.2 million people newly displaced due to natural disasters (IDMC, 2017). While south and east Asia were most affected due to the large number of vulnerable island states, migration takes place worldwide (IDMC, 2017). Climate change migration also happens due to geographic changes in growing seasons as droughts increase in greater frequency. This migration has led to increased population density and urbanization, which in turn creates pressure for adequate food, housing, and economic opportunity (Schaeffer et al., 2012). While these impacts are daunting, what cannot easily be quantified by dollar amounts is the resulting social challenges of the loss of employment and community. Migration separates families and friends, forcing people to start over in a new region or country, often with a new culture and language.

These impacts present great possibilities for entrepreneurial entrants and enhanced inclusivity, both locally and globally. In the aftermath of natural disasters, new organizations and ventures can form to recover from the physical damage and reform the community that was impacted (Williams and Shepherd, 2016). This work presents opportunities not just for rebuilding physical infrastructure, but also establishing appropriate channels to reuse or recycle damaged goods. Rebuilding and repurposing enables entrepreneurs to envision the use of space and materials differently. This presents the opportunity for both strategic community planning and increased use of alternative energy and materials in the development.

Community planning may also help address the issue of migration and urbanization. Opportunities exist for local entrepreneurs to develop within their community. Local entrepreneurs understand the needs of their community, as well as the culture and environment. This enables them to use their existing knowledge to develop necessary resources and services for the community around them. Additionally, as climate change migrants are often in need of employment, entrepreneurial ventures may enable them to bring their skills and talents to establish programs or goods that fellow migrants would benefit from.

As societal impacts of climate change present opportunities for local entrepreneurship, there are also avenues for global entrepreneurial engagement. Entrepreneurs who are not currently located in the areas responding to a natural disaster or high level of migration can establish systems for moving resources and supplies in or out of the geographic area. They can also mobilize sustainable solutions to keep necessary materials out of landfills and relocate them to communities in need. The creation of global networks and communication channels are needed in response to the impacts of climate change as the communities impacted the most are often in low- or middle-income countries. Thus, the opportunities and response can be on a global scale.

Societal impacts focus on how climate change affects communities through changes such as physical infrastructure, development, migration, and urbanization. These community changes have implications on individuals' health and wellbeing. The next section will specifically look at the human health impacts of climate change.

Health Impact

Human health impacts of climate change are defined as *the physical and psychological manifestations and symptoms resulting from climate change and the resulting changes in vector-borne diseases.* Health impacts are also linked to the population's geographic region and socioeconomic level. The severity of human health impacts of climate change far exceeds advances of modern medicine and public health, and are reported as unequivocal and potentially irreversible (Watts et al., 2018) including infectious disease, chronic disease, and malnutrition.

The spread of infectious diseases is increasing at unprecedented rates. Rather than occurring seasonally, vector-borne diseases are now present year-round due to rising temperatures. For example, the two types of mosquitoes that spread Dengue Fever globally have increased by 9.4 and 11.1 percent since the 1950s.

Rising temperatures have also exposed more than 125 million vulnerable adults to heatwaves in the past 15 years (National Research Council, 2008). The number of heat-related deaths in the United States has risen dramatically in the past 15 years, reaching more than 3.5 people per million (EPA, 2017), not including the number of children worldwide who are also impacted. This spike in deaths is also due to the fact that heatwaves are now year-long occurrences, no longer just between the months of May and September. In addition to death, these heatwaves also lead to exacerbation of chronic diseases and cardiovascular events.

Malnutrition is another major health impact resulting from natural disaster-related injuries and fatalities. The rising temperatures and natural disasters led to a 2 percent decrease of productivity in rural areas in the past year alone with record droughts and devastation (Frumkin et al., 2008). Rural areas, mostly in developing countries, lack the infrastructure to appropriate health and nutrition services. Beginning in 2030, the World Health Organization estimates an additional 250,000 worldwide deaths per year due to malnutrition, malaria, diarrhea and heat stress.

The public health community has now made climate change impacts the top of their agenda. However, these efforts largely focus on effective public health *responses* to these impacts rather than the prevention and sustainable solutions to ongoing climate-related health issues (Frumkin et al., 2008). Health professionals, similar to corporate and regulatory actors, are essential to addressing the health impacts of climate change, yet, the role of new venture creation and entrepreneurship remains overlooked as they pertain to health.

New ventures and technological advances are needed to alleviate physical and psychological suffering due to climate change. While addressing the suffering at hand, there is also a need to innovate to prevent future suffering. For example, practices and programs that are focused on stopping the current spread of diseases must be adapted to the realities of disease transmission with the changing climate. There is also a need for the prevention of future infectious disease, especially in remote and rural areas. Such innovations will require adopting the practices and cultural philosophies of the communities where they will be used.

New ventures are also needed to address the issue of malnutrition more efficiently through creation of new distribution channels that reach areas untouched by governments and corporations. Opportunities also abound in agricultural science to understand possibilities for new crops in different regions with the changing climate. The issue of malnutrition, infectious disease, and chronic diseases present a chance for further studies of opportunity recognition, innovation, and distribution processes.

As discussed with societal impacts, the human health impacts also require collaborative innovations and solutions across industries and communities. This presents a chance to examine how entrepreneurs build trust within communities, especially when they are changing human behaviors and health practices. Success and sustained solutions require high levels of trust, communication, and inclusion of those most vulnerable.

Responding to Climate Change Impacts

While we have presented three climate change impacts as unique, they clearly do not occur in isolation. Ecological, societal, and health impacts are often a result of, or compounded upon one another. Addressing one, two, or all the impacts requires an inclusive response and collaboration on social innovation. This inclusive response could engage entrepreneurs, the actors that have largely been overlooked in the solution to climate change. By focusing on social inclusion, the voices of the vulnerable and most impacted by climate change are present in the innovations that are focused on helping them. As climate change is a global challenge, it requires global citizenship to be a key element of the solution. This means engaging those more affected as well as global citizens to approach the issues from all angles. An innovative and inclusive response to climate change presents new opportunities not previously considered.

As entrepreneurship allows any individual to see climate change as an opportunity to provide a solution, the examination of, and potential solutions to, these impacts should not be limited to a hierarchical perspective based on policy makers or corporations. In order to foster a broader and more inclusive approach, the next section examines three perspectives of entrepreneurship scholarship – individual, organizational, and institutional – as lenses for studies of entrepreneurial action to address climate change. At the individual level, entrepreneurs who are more inclusive have great opportunities to contribute to the mitigation and prevention of the impacts of climate change. At the organizational level, ventures can use social innovation strategies to address the impacts. The process of social innovation around this vast, ambiguous, and intangible problem requires an understanding of how different populations, classes, and races are affected. Thus, social innovation requires collaboration and co-evolution to ensure it makes a difference impacting climate change. Finally, at the institutional level, co-evolutionary perspectives create a chance to inform and improve the work of non-governmental organizations (NGOs), corporations, policy makers, and entrepreneurs. Within each perspective, we examine opportunities to address the impacts of climate change and develop a future research agenda around those opportunities.

A MULTILEVEL FRAMEWORK FOR ENTREPRENEURSHIP RESEARCH ON ADDRESSING CLIMATE CHANGE

Our review of climate change impacts above suggests that while regulatory and corporate actors are central to combating the impacts of climate change, there has not been a systematic attempt to understand the role of entrepreneurial action in such efforts. We now turn to developing a framework to delineate the ways in which entrepreneurial action and research can move towards substantive outcomes related to climate change reduction and mitigation. Our framework assumes that entrepreneurial action focused on the impacts of climate change takes place in inclusive markets. Markets become inclusive places when they are "legitimated arenas for interdependent social and economic activity where formal possibilities align with practical access across gender, race, religion, and social class" (Mair et al., 2012, p. 820). When entrepreneurs and their nascent ventures are more inclusive, they are also more likely to identify socially innovative practices and products that appropriately address the ecological, social, or health impacts of climate change. As individuals perceive opportunities related to climate change, and develop entrepreneurial ventures with appropriate product-market fit, such actors may begin to influence the institutional norms in which we live. Therefore, we argue for the examination of entrepreneurial climate change prevention and/or the alleviation of suffering caused by climate change across multiple levels.

Table 21.1 breaks down the entrepreneurial process into three levels of analysis. At the individual level, we are concerned with who, why, and how entrepreneurs identify inclusive opportunities within climate change impacts. At the organizational level, we focus on whether ventures that incorporate social innovation processes lead to directly addressing one of the three impacts of climate change. Finally, at the institutional level, we discuss how entrepreneurial action embeds and influences the institutional structures that influence climate change and constrain actions to mitigate it. At each of these levels of analysis, we propose how current theoretical lenses related to entrepreneurship may

Table 21.1 Multilevel framework for engaging entrepreneurship scholars to address the impacts of climate change

	Ecological Environmental Manifestations	Social Community and Population Changes	Health Physical and Psychological Symptoms
Individual The Entrepreneur How, when, and why do individuals inclusively create ventures to address climate change impacts?	Motivations driven from changes in consumption Opportunity recognition from natural environment Engagement of the disaster response community in entrepreneurship • Entrepreneurial Identity • Opportunity Development • Cognition	Motivations driven from changes in community dynamics Engagement of migrant and refugee entrepreneurs	Response to disease trends needed in new geographic regions year-round Engagement of the healthcare community in entrepreneurship Adaptation of medical response to those most vulnerable
Organizational New Ventures What new venture processes and actions can help to address climate change impacts?	Changes in resource availability Adoption of new value chains	Signaling legitimacy of new organizations by migrants in community Engagement of existing resources and changing needs in community	Changes in product portfolios and production processes in existing healthcare organizations Adopting cultural competent practices in healthcare delivery to new communities
	• Social Innovation Process • Resource Identification and Acquisition • Product or Process Distribution • Signaling and Legitimacy		
Institutional Organizational Context How do institutions enable or constrain entrepreneurship that mitigates or reduces climate change impacts?	Developing infrastructure to promote responsible use of material goods Establishing community responses to violations	Establishing new community norms for entrepreneurial acceptability Creating an environment that fosters the co-creation of goods and services with migrant community	Creating a culture of preventative health and education Establishing culturally appropriate channels for co-evolution of healthcare service delivery
	• Institutional and Community Structure to Enable/Hinder Social Innovation • Co-evolution of Products/Services and Institutional Structures		

appropriately be extended to better understand climate change mitigation efforts and opportunities.

Individual Level of Analysis: The Entrepreneur

Entrepreneurial action begins with those who recognize or create an entrepreneurial opportunity (Shane and Venkataraman, 2000; Venkataraman, 1997). Only certain individuals are likely to pursue opportunities in the context of climate change mitigation or alleviation. For example, actors focused on building inclusive markets are likely to also see opportunity within climate change impacts. An inclusive entrepreneur advances equitable opportunities through economic growth that benefits every section of society (Mair et al., 2012). If inclusive entrepreneurship leads to more positive outcomes focused on climate change mitigation, future research can explore what makes an entrepreneur more likely to be inclusive. Theories related to identity, opportunity development, and cognitive processes are potential avenues for understanding *how, when, and why do some individuals develop ventures to address climate change impacts?*

First, whether an entrepreneur is inclusive is likely associated with his or her salient identities affiliated with the natural environment and their community. Identity research uses relationships and roles to explain how society shapes social behavior (Mead, 1934; Stryker, 1980). Social identity may connect the entrepreneur to climate change as they, or communities to which they belong, may be directly impacted by one of the climate change impacts. Further, role identities may connect an entrepreneur to an impact of climate change through their public roles with environmental conservation groups, professional occupation, place of residence, or significant experience with a community (Wry and York, 2017).

For example, many environmentalists, medical experts, and activists have shifted to entrepreneurial action in order to make an impact through their technical knowledge, acquired through their voluntary and professional roles. Such experts bring domain-specific knowledge, yet they lack experience in the creation of new ventures. Shane (2000) outlined the three types of entrepreneurial knowledge necessary for successful opportunity exploitation: prior knowledge of markets, knowledge of how to enter the markets, and knowledge of customers and suppliers. There is a need to align non-business-related passion and motivation with entrepreneurial experience and knowledge within existing research (Fauchart and Gruber, 2011; Powell and Baker, 2014, 2017). Thus, there is an opportunity for entrepreneurship scholars to use identity theory to examine the connection between an entrepreneur's social and role identities and their aptitude for creating new ventures that address climate change. This can be done through teleological studies of the development of new ventures in communities impacted by climate change to examine how identity influences and evolves the opportunities pursued.

Second, a critical step of the entrepreneurial process is opportunity development (Shane, 2000; Venkataraman, 1997). Inclusiveness is likely associated with one's ability to identify market opportunities that stem from those suffering from climate change impacts, or replace market opportunities from existing products and services that cause suffering. Individuals exposed to the impacts of climate change have a choice to either sit idle and expect other agencies to solve the problem, or recognize a potential solution to alleviate current suffering or mitigate potential future consequences. Regardless of whether opportunities are found or made (Baron and Ensley, 2006; Sarasvathy et al., 2005), the process by which individuals decide to act is unknown. Future research can examine an individual's behavior to different scenarios to understand what motivates some individuals to action in light of the different climate change impacts. While the impacts of climate change clearly offer third-person opportunities for fostering economic and societal benefits, entrepreneurship scholarship is well suited to examine *how* and *when* and for *whom* these impacts become first-person opportunities (McMullen and Shepherd, 2006).

Third, how an entrepreneur thinks may also influence the likelihood of pursuing inclusive markets. For example, compassion and empathy towards others is likely associated with inclusiveness (e.g., Miller et al., 2012). High levels of empathy drive individuals to opportunities that alleviate others' suffering and motivate them to solve pressing problems (McMullen, 2015). Entrepreneurship research drawing on individual-level theories of personality (Gimeno et al., 1997; Hayton and Cholakova, 2012), orientation (Lumpkin and Dess, 2001), and emotions (e.g., Foo, 2011) could be extended to understanding how some individuals foster new products and markets to address climate change impacts. Future research presents an opportunity to apply cognitive theories of entrepreneurship to entrepreneurs' inclusiveness in the venturing process.

While we believe that these three research areas – identity, opportunity, and cognition – are the primary avenues to mechanisms that drive inclusive entrepreneurs to address climate change, they are not exhaustive. There are likely interactions between an individual's personality and identity. Research examining entrepreneurship at the individual level will need to go across these boundaries to better understand how an inclusive entrepreneur may address the impacts of climate change. For example, prior work has shown how environmentalists may become entrepreneurs (York et al., 2016b) but we know little of how such individuals actually impact the ecological impacts of climate change. Further, how does the social identity of a community member impact the likelihood they will seek to help address the social impacts of climate change? How does the "caregiver" role identity of medical professionals push them towards focusing on climate-driven health impacts versus more lucrative and sure opportunities? Each of these questions has real implications for how individuals become entrepreneurs to address climate change. While the individual entrepreneur clearly influences the organization, social innovation also plays a critical role in addressing climate change at the organizational level.

Organizational Level of Analysis: New Ventures

Once an entrepreneur is in pursuit of a nascent opportunity, the next question arises of how the new venture develops routines, practices, and behaviors focused on reducing or mitigating the impacts of climate change. Scholars from multiple disciplines have focused on social innovation as the creation of products and solutions to combat societal and environmental problems (e.g., Mulgan et al., 2007; Nicholls et al., 2015; Phillips et al., 2017; van der Have and Rubalcaba, 2016). Social innovation is the process of developing and deploying effective solutions to challenging and often systematic issues in support of social progress (Mulgan et al., 2007). However, how new venture behaviors and actions lead to social innovative products and processes is little understood. We believe such an approach holds great promise for understanding *what new venture processes and actions can help to address climate change impacts.*

Entrepreneurial ventures that incorporate social innovation into the venture's routines and practices may be more likely to address climate change impacts. A social innovation approach likely changes how organizations engage in resource acquisition, innovation practices, and overcoming information asymmetries. Research can examine social innovation incorporation by examining organizational forms and foundational attributes. This includes founder network ties (Hallen and Eisenhardt, 2012) and the corporation form such as if it is a registered B-corp (Batillana and Lee, 2014; Conger et al., 2018; Meyer and Rowan, 1977). Additionally, whether the new venture views social innovation as a dynamic capability (e.g., Zahra et al., 2006) or strategic competitive advantage (e.g., Barney, 1991) are fruitful opportunities for research.

First, focusing on the sourcing of an organization's value chain may provide interesting insight to its social innovation practices. For example, local sourcing reduces transportation emissions and packaging materials. This not only reduces the organization's carbon footprint, it also reduces costs for the organization, which may be seen as a capability or strategic competitive advantage. Strategic competitive advantage may also come from local sourcing of human capital while also enabling the growth of local communities (Wiklund et al., 2009). Resource-based view, human and social capital, and dynamic capabilities theorists may be able to explore the question of how socially innovative processes within the value chain of nascent ventures address climate change impacts. Resource acquisition processes localizing the value chain may also establish the use of more sustainable processes and materials.

Second, future research may identify the role of social innovation within the distribution channel of delivering products and services. This connects with the drive for locally sourced value chains and community employment. With local production and focus, there is an opportunity for unique distribution channels to be created. New research can explore the process by which ventures are able to efficiently and uniquely deliver products and services to highly impacted locations, such as providing relief services to a community recently affected by a natural disaster.

Third, social innovation practices are also relevant to research in signaling and legitimacy. Signaling theory in entrepreneurship research often examines how ventures acquire resources through mechanisms of certification (Hsu, 2004), endorsements (Stuart et al., 1999), and market signals (Sanders and Boivie, 2004). Signaling theory has been used in conjunction with institutional theory (e.g., Kirsch et al., 2009), network-based theories (e.g., Hallen and Eisenhardt, 2012), and reputation theories (e.g., Rindova et al., 2007) to examine how signaling complements other actions of the startup firm. The use of multiple theories in this context provides numerous lenses to understand the complex signals the organization may send to resource providers and other audiences. Understanding how practices, products, and services can signal legitimacy not only of the organization, but of the problems presented by climate change, offers an interesting path for future research.

Organizational theories from economics, strategic management, and organizational theory play important roles in understanding how socially innovative products and practices influence organizational behavior and routines. Future research could connect previously understood constructs to specific impacts of climate change. For example, when do organizations with an inherent focus on reducing carbon emissions, such as renewable energy firms, engage in more inclusive social innovations? Conversely, when do social aid organizations, such as economic development NGOs, re-examine the climate impacts of their supplier network and practices? How do health organizations signal to their stakeholders that addressing climate change is intertwined with their mission to address disease? Each of these examples suggest rich paths for future research on the evolution of organizational practices towards addressing climate change.

However, studying organizational-level practices in isolation limits our understanding particularly in the realm of climate change impacts. Because both formal and informal institutions can reinforce or question the practices that have led to climate change, they highly influence what organizations do. We next turn to the interrelationship between institutional opportunities and constraints for entrepreneurial action to address climate change impacts.

Institutional Level of Analysis: The Cultural, Regulative, and Competitive Context

While institutional theorists argue that entrepreneurial action and their ventures can influence both systemic change and the actions of others around them (Tolbert et al., 2011), little is known about how institutional factors either constrain or enable an entrepreneur's ability to address the impacts of climate change. Differences in institutional structures, such as educational, political, family, economic, and religious, are all likely to influence the opportunity to engage in the social innovation process. As entrepreneurs engage in addressing systemic issues associated with climate change, institutional structures will need to evolve and change as well.

Change at the institutional level can be best understood through studying the actor and field interactions that create opportunities or constraints for entrepreneurial action (Battilana et al., 2009; Pacheco et al., 2010b). For example, whether the co-evolution of institutional structures such as social movements and industries influences the ability for entrepreneurial actors to change practices towards climate change mitigation (Pacheco et al., 2014). Further, understanding frame changes (Ansari et al., 2011), institutional work (Lawrence et al., 2009), and other agentic forms of institutional theory such as collective institutional entrepreneurship (Wijen and Ansari, 2007) may shape the communication, collaboration, and awareness of climate change impacts.

Addressing climate change impacts will cross multiple institutional structures; thus, understanding how institutions evolve alongside industries and social movements has important implications. For example, Pacheco et al. (2014) demonstrate how the growth of industries and social movements shifted institutions towards supporting more wind energy in the United States. In this case, the co-evolutionary nature of these institutional forces enabled entrepreneurial activity as the demand for new products and processes in the energy field grew. Future research can test how new products and services addressing climate emerge through co-evolutionary mechanisms across institutional structures. However, research must also further our understanding of the constraining influence of institutional structures in which entrepreneurial activity is halted. Such 'failures' have yet to be studied in institutional entrepreneurship as the outcome of an institutional entrepreneur is the observed systemic change. Understanding when inappropriate regulations inhibit the ability of entrepreneurs to create products and services that address climate change represents a critical opportunity for future research.

Second, institutional factors that inhibit, or enable, entrepreneurs' ability to address climate change are likely contingent upon how climate-related issues are understood within communities (York et al., 2018). Whether and how does an entrepreneur share his or her outcomes with a larger audience through direct interactions and demonstrating the impacts of their work? How does a local entrepreneur's institutional context impact their ability to address one of the climate change impacts? Research on these questions would require teleological data collection from the onset of an entrepreneur's activity. Variables such as information sharing, accessibility, and dissemination may influence public awareness and global citizenship. Little is known about whether these variables enable or constrain entrepreneurial activity, and whether resources are allocated to solving mitigation or prevention of the impacts of climate change.

Not only is the emergence of new industries and institutions important to study, but whether such structures promote cross-institutional rather than segmented actions remains relatively unexplored. Since the impacts of climate change span multiple industries and sectors, there is a need to bring these diverse actors together to connect their experiences, resources, and services. Entrepreneurs are positioned well to drive this connection through their ability to recognize opportunities and flexibility to establish new processes. Future research can examine how different institutional structures enable or hinder cross-sector collaborations around the impacts of climate change, thereby influencing the opportunity for entrepreneurial activity. Institutional-level research can also test how communication and information is shared between the different actors to allow for focused and effective reactions and responses to climate change.

For example, how can entrepreneurs galvanize and evolve community-level norms and thus responses to climate change impacts? How might entrepreneurs re-focus the narrative of ecological impacts towards the creation of new markets and products, rather than regulations? When seeking to address social impacts, research could examine how entrepreneurs evolve community-level logics to understand climate change impacts as opportunities for collective action. Regarding health impacts, institutional-level research could reveal how development policies may constrain the ability for medical care to reach the populations most impacted by climate change.

This section has explored the opportunities to study climate change through addressing entrepreneurship from multiple levels of analysis: the person, the venture, and the context in which they operate. While this beginning is clearly not exhaustive, it aims to be a specific step towards encouraging future research addressing hitherto unaddressed questions.

CONCLUSION

Our hope is that this chapter shows there is a clear need for inclusive entrepreneurship research to address the impacts of climate change. This inclusivity means that there is a role for all researchers in the broad field of entrepreneurship to bring the opportunities and challenges of this work to light. There is a need for entrepreneurship researchers broadly speaking to engage in the issue of climate change, not just those who study environmental or social entrepreneurs. As the impacts of climate change are large and diverse, the response must be equally large and diverse.

To make a daunting and ambiguous issue tangible, we have broken down climate change across categories of ecological, social, and health impacts in the chapter. Within each of these impacts we have examined where there are unique opportunities for entrepreneurial response to current challenges and mitigation of future problems. As these impacts do not happen in isolation, we presented an opportunity model for the field of entrepreneurship to study implications of climate change through an inclusive and socially innovative lens.

This inclusivity also means engaging in transnational work. As impacts of climate change are not restrained by international borders and cultural boundaries, our research should not be either. Through our research and connecting with scholars from other countries and disciplines, there is a chance to broaden understanding of the current success and remaining opportunities for entrepreneurial efforts to address the impact of climate change. This transnational work should especially focus on developing nations as they are not only affected the most by climate change, but also have the greatest percentage of entrepreneurs comprising their economies.

The tools, skills, and resources to bring these entrepreneurial opportunities into reality need to be in the hands of those who are facing the problems. Researchers and academics alone cannot do this. However, we play a unique role in addressing this issue through studying and teaching best practices, and making the tools and skills available. Through the opportunities presented in this chapter, we believe it is possible to address climate change in a more specific and concrete way through entrepreneurial action of all kinds.

REFERENCES

Anderson, T.L. and Leal, D.R. 2001. *Free Market Environmentalism*, revised edn. New York: Palgrave Macmillan.

Ansari, S., Gray, B., and Wijen, F. 2011. Fiddling while the ice melts? How organizational scholars can take a more active role in the climate change debate. *Strategic Organization*, 9(1), 70–6.

Bang, G., Hovi, J., and Skodvin, T. 2016. The Paris Agreement: short-term and long-term effectiveness. *Politics and Governance*, 4(3), 209–18.

Barbier, E.B., Burgess, J.C., and Dean, T.J. 2018. How to pay for saving biodiversity. *Science*, 360(6388), 486–88.

Barney, J. 1991. Firm resources and sustained competitive advantage. *Journal of Management*, 17(1), 99–120.

Baron, R.A. and Ensley, M.D. 2006. Opportunity recognition as the detection of meaningful patterns: evidence from comparisons of novice and experienced entrepreneurs. *Management Science*, 52(9), 1331–44.

Battilana, J. and Lee, M. 2014. Advancing research on hybrid organizing – insights from the study of social enterprises. *Academy of Management Annals*, 8(1), 397–441.

Battilana, J., Leca, B. and Boxenbaum, E. 2009. How actors change institutions: towards a theory of institutional entrepreneurship. *Academy of Management Annals*, 3(1), 65–107.

Conger, M., McMullen, J.S., Bergman, B.J., and York, J.G. 2018. Category membership, identity control, and the reevaluation of prosocial opportunities. *Journal of Business Venturing*, 33(2), 179–206.

Dean, T. and McMullen, J.S. 2007. Toward a theory of sustainable entrepreneurship: reducing environmental degradation through entrepreneurial action. *Journal of Business Venturing*, 22(1), 50–76.

EPA. 2017. Climate Change Indicators of Health Related Deaths. Accessed 17 October 2017, https://www.epa.gov/climate-indicators/climate-change-indicators-heat-related-deaths.

Fauchart, E. and Gruber, M. 2011. Darwinians, communitarians, and missionaries: the role of founder identity in entrepreneurship. *Academy of Management Journal*, 54(5), 935–57.

Ferraro, F., Etzion, D., and Gehman, J. 2015. Tackling grand challenges pragmatically: robust action revisited. *Organization Studies*, 36(3), 363–90.

Foo, M.D. 2011. Emotions and entrepreneurial opportunity evaluation. *Entrepreneurship Theory and Practice*, 35(2), 375–93.

Frumkin, H., Hess, J., Luber, G., Malilay, J., and McGeehin, M. 2008. Climate Change: the public health response. *American Journal of Public Health*, 98(3), 435–45. https://doi.org/10.2105/AJPH.2007.119362

George, G., Howard-Grenville, J., Joshi, A., and Tihanyi, L. 2016. Understanding and tackling societal grand challenges through management research. *Academy of Management Journal*, 59(6), 1880–95.

Gimeno, J., Folta, T.B., Cooper, A.C., and Woo, C.Y. 1997. Survival of the fittest? Entrepreneurial human capital and the persistence of underperforming firms. *Administrative Science Quarterly*, 42(4), 750–83.

Hahn, R., Reimsbach, D., and Schiemann, F. 2015. Organizations, climate change, and transparency: reviewing the literature on carbon disclosure. *Organization and Environment*, 28(1), 80–102.
Hallen, B.L. and Eisenhardt, K.M. 2012. Catalyzing strategies and efficient tie formation: how entrepreneurial firms obtain investment ties. *Academy of Management Journal*, 55(1), 35–70.
Hayton, J.C. and Cholakova, M. 2012. The role of affect in the creation and intentional pursuit of entrepreneurial ideas. *Entrepreneurship Theory and Practice*, 36(1), 41–68.
Hiatt, S.R., Grandy, J.B., and Lee, B.H. 2015. Organizational responses to public and private politics: an analysis of climate change activists and US oil and gas firms. *Organization Science*, 26(6), 1769–86.
Hockerts, K. and Wüstenhagen, R. 2010. Greening Goliaths versus emerging Davids – theorizing about the role of incumbents and new entrants in sustainable entrepreneurship. *Journal of Business Venturing*, 25(5), 481–92.
Hoffman, A.J. 2005. Climate change strategy: the business logic behind voluntary greenhouse gas reductions. *California Management Review*, 47(3), 21–46.
Howard-Grenville, J., Buckle, S., Hoskins, B., and George, G. 2014. Climate change and management. *Academy of Management Journal*, 57(3), 615–23.
Hsu, D.H. 2004. What do entrepreneurs pay for venture capital affiliation? *The Journal of Finance*, 59(4), 1805–44.
IDMC. 2017. *Global Report on Internal Displacement*. Accessed 17 October 2017, http://www.internal-displacement.org/global-report/grid2017/pdfs/2017-GRID.pdf.
IPCC. 2007. Summary for policymakers. In *Climate Change 2007: The Physical Science Basis: Contribution of Working Group I to the Fourth Assessment Report of the Intergovernmental Panel on Climate Change*, ed. S. Solomon, D. Qin, M. Manning, Z. Chen, M. Marquis, K.B. Averyt, M. Tignor, and H.L. Miller. Cambridge: Cambridge University Press, pp. 1–21.
IPCC. 2014a. *Climate Change 2014: Impacts, Adaptation and Vulnerability*. Contribution of Working Group II to the Fifth Assessment Report (AR5). Geneva Intergovernmental Panel on Climate Change.
IPCC. 2014b. Chapter 1: Introductory chapter. In *Climate Change 2014: Mitigation of Climate Change*. Contribution of Working Group III to the Fifth Assessment Report of the Intergovernmental Panel on Climate Change. Cambridge and New York: Cambridge University Press.
Kirsch, D., Goldfarb, B., and Gera, A. 2009. Form or substance: the role of business plans in venture capital decision making. *Strategic Management Journal*, 30(5), 487–515.
Lawrence, T.B., Suddaby, R., and Leca, B. (eds) 2009. *Institutional Work: Actors and Agency in Institutional Studies of Organizations*. Cambridge: Cambridge University Press.
Lenox, M. and York, J.G. 2012. Environmental entrepreneurship. In P. Bansal and A.J. Hoffman (eds), *The Oxford Handbook of Business and the Natural Environment*. New York: Oxford University Press, pp. 70–82.
Lumpkin, G.T. and Dess, G.G. 2001. Linking two dimensions of entrepreneurial orientation to firm performance: the moderating role of environment and industry life cycle. *Journal of Business Venturing*, 16(5), 429–51.
Mair, J. and Martí, I. 2006. Social entrepreneurship research: a source of explanation, prediction, and delight. *Journal of World Business*, 41(1), 36–44.
Mair, J., Martí, I., and Ventresca, M.J. 2012. Building inclusive markets in rural Bangladesh: how intermediaries work institutional voids. *Academy of Management Journal*, 55(4), 819–50.
McMullen, J.S. 2015. Entrepreneurial judgment as empathic accuracy: A sequential decision-making approach to entrepreneurial action. *Journal of Institutional Economics*, 11(3), 651–81.
McMullen, J.S. and Shepherd, D.A. 2006. Entrepreneurial action and the role of uncertainty in the theory of the entrepreneur. *Academy of Management Review*, 31(1), 132–52.
Mead, G.H. 1934. *Mind, Self & Society From the Standpoint of a Behaviorist*. Chicago, IL: University of Chicago Press.
Meyer, J.W. and Rowan, B. 1977. Institutionalized organizations: formal structure as myth and ceremony. *American Journal of Sociology*, 83(2), 340–63.
Miller, T.L., Grimes, M.G., McMullen, J.S., and Vogus, T.J. 2012. Venturing for others with heart and head: how compassion encourages social entrepreneurship. *Academy of Management Review*, 37(4), 616–40.
Mulgan, G., Tucker, S., Ali, R., and Sanders, B. 2007. Social innovation: what it is, why it matters and how it can be accelerated. Skoll Center for Social Entrepreneurship Working Paper.
National Research Council. 2008. *Ecological Impacts of Climate Change*. Washington, DC: The National Academies Press. https://doi.org/10.17226/12491
Nicholls, A., Simon, J., and Gabriel, M. 2015. *Introduction. In Dimensions of Social Innovation, New Frontiers in Social Innovation Research*. Heidelberg: Springer, pp. 1–26.
Ostrom, E. 2012. Nested externalities and polycentric institutions: must we wait for global solutions to climate change before taking actions at other scales? *Economic Theory*, 49(2), 353–69.
Pacheco, D.F., Dean, T.J., and Payne, D.S. 2010a. Escaping the green prison: entrepreneurship and the creation of opportunities for sustainable development. *Journal of Business Venturing*, 25(5), 464–80.
Pacheco, D.F., York, J.G., Dean, T.J., and Sarasvathy, S.D. 2010b. The coevolution of institutional entrepreneurship: a tale of two theories. *Journal of Management*, 36(4), 974–1010.

Pacheco, D.F., York, J.G., and Hargrave, T.J. 2014. The coevolution of industries, social movements, and institutions: wind power in the United States. *Organization Science*, 25(6), 1609–32.

Pecl, G.T., Araújo, M.B., Bell, J.D. et al. 2017. Biodiversity redistribution under climate change: impacts on ecosystems and human well-being. *Science*, 355(6332), 1–9.

Phillips, W., Alexander, E.A., and Lee, H. 2017. Going it alone won't work! The relational imperative for social innovation in social enterprises. *Journal of Business Ethics*, 1–17.

Powell, E.E. and Baker, T. 2014. It's what you make of it: founder identity and enacting strategic responses to adversity. *Academy of Management Journal*, 57(5), 1406–33.

Powell, E.E. and Baker, T. 2017. In the beginning: identity processes and organizing in multi-founder nascent ventures. *Academy of Management Journal*, 60(6), 2381–414.

Pulver, S. 2007. Making sense of corporate environmentalism: an environmental contestation approach to analyzing the causes and consequences of the climate change policy split in the oil industry. *Organization and Environment*, 20(1), 44–83.

Reid, E.M. and Toffel, M.W. 2009. Responding to public and private politics: corporate disclosure of climate change strategies. *Strategic Management Journal*, 30(11), 1157–78.

Rindova, V.P., Petkova, A.P., and Kotha, S. 2007. Standing out: how new firms in emerging markets build reputation. *Strategic Organization*, 5(1), 31–70.

Sanders, W.M. and Boivie, S. 2004. Sorting things out: valuation of new firms in uncertain markets. *Strategic Management Journal*, 25(2), 167–86.

Sarasvathy, S.D., Dew, N., Velamuri, S.R., and Venkataraman, S. 2005. Three views of enterpreneurial opportunity. In Z.J. Acs and D.B. Audretsch (eds), *Handbook of Entrepreneurship Research: An Interdisciplinary Survey and Introduction*, Vol. 1. New York: Springer, pp. 141–60.

Schaeffer, M., Hare, W., Rahmstorf, S. and Vermeer, M. 2012. Long-term sea-level rise implied by 1.5°C and 2°C warming levels. *Nature Climate Change*, 2, 867–70.

Schaltegger, S. 2002. A framework for ecopreneurship. *Greener Management International*, 38, 45–58.

Schaltegger, S. and Hörisch, J. 2017. In search of the dominant rationale in sustainability management: legitimacy- or profit-seeking? *Journal of Business Ethics*, 145(2), 259–76.

Schaltegger, S., Beckmann, M., and Hockerts, K. 2018. Sustainable entrepreneurship: creating environmental solutions in light of planetary boundaries. *International Journal of Entrepreneurial Venturing*, 10(1), 1–16.

Shane, S. 2000. Prior knowledge and the discovery of entrepreneurial opportunities. *Organization Science*, 11(4), 448–69.

Shane, S. and Venkataraman, S. 2000. The promise of entrepreneurship as a field of research. *Academy of Management Review*, 25(1), 217–26.

Shepherd, D.A. and Patzelt, H. 2011. The new field of sustainable entrepreneurship: studying entrepreneurial action linking "what is to be sustained" with "what is to be developed". *Entrepreneurship Theory and Practice*, 35(1), 137–63.

Sine, W.D. and Lee, B. 2009. Tilting at windmills? The environmental movement and the emergence of the US wind energy sector. *Administrative Science Quarterly*, 54(1), 123–55.

Stuart, T.E., Hoang, H., and Hybels, R.C. 1999. Interorganizational endorsements and the performance of entrepreneurial ventures. *Administrative Science Quarterly*, 44(2), 315–49.

Stryker, S. 1980. *Symbolic Interactionism: A Social Structural Version*. Menlo Park, CA: Benjamin-Cummings Publishing.

Tolbert, P.S., David, R.J., and Sine, W.D., 2011. Studying choice and change: the intersection of institutional theory and entrepreneurship research. *Organization Science*, 22(5), 1332–44.

van der Have, R.P. and Rubalcaba, L. 2016. Social innovation research: an emerging area of innovation studies? *Research Policy*, 45(9), 1923–35.

Venkataraman, S. 1997. The distinctive domain of entrepreneurship research. In J. Katz and R. Brockhaus (eds), *Advances in Entrepreneurship, Firm Emergence, and Growth*, Vol. 3. Greenwich, CT: JAI Press, pp. 119–38.

Wang, H., Tong, L., Takeuchi, R., and George, G. 2016. Corporate social responsibility: an overview and new research directions: thematic issue on corporate social responsibility. *Academy of Management Journal*, 59(2), 534–44.

Watts, N., Amann, M., Ayeb-Karlsson, S. et al. 2018. The Lancet countdown on health and climate change: from 25 years of inaction to a global transformation for public health. *The Lancet*, 391(10120), 581–630.

Wijen, F. and Ansari, S. 2007. Overcoming inaction through collective institutional entrepreneurship: insights from regime theory. *Organization Studies*, 28(7), 1079–100.

Wiklund, J., Patzelt, H., and Shepherd, D.A. 2009. Building an integrative model of small business growth. *Small Business Economics*, 32(4), 351–74.

Williams, T.A. and Shepherd, D.A. 2016. Building resilience or providing sustenance: different paths of emergent ventures in the aftermath of the Haiti earthquake. *Academy of Management Journal*, 59(6), 2069–102.

World Meteorological Organization. 2016a. Un/natural disasters: communicating linkages between extreme events and climate change. *The WMO Bulletin*, 65(2).

World Meteorological Organization. 2016b. WMO Statement on the State of the Global Climate in 2016. Accessed 17 October 2017, https://library.wmo.int/opac/doc_num.php?explnum_id=3414

Wright, C. and Nyberg, D. 2017. An inconvenient truth: how organizations translate climate change into business as usual. *Academy of Management Journal*, 60(5), 1633–61.

Wry, T. and York, J.G. 2017. An identity-based approach to social enterprise. *Academy of Management Review*, 42(3), 437–60.

York, J.G. and Venkataraman, S. 2010. The entrepreneur–environment nexus: uncertainty, innovation, and allocation. *Journal of Business Venturing*, 25, 449–63.

York, J.G., Hargrave, T.J., and Pacheco, D.F. 2016a. Converging winds: logic hybridization in the Colorado wind energy field. *Academy of Management Journal*, 59(2), 579–610.

York, J.G., O'Neil, I., and Sarasvathy, S.D. 2016b. Exploring environmental entrepreneurship: identity coupling, venture goals, and stakeholder incentives. *Journal of Management Studies*, 53(5), 695–737.

York, J.G., Vedula, S., and Lenox, M. 2018. It's not easy building green: the impact of public policy, private actors, and regional logics on voluntary standards adoption. *Academy of Management Journal*, 61(4), 1492–523.

Zahra, S.A., Sapienza, H.J., and Davidsson, P. 2006. Entrepreneurship and dynamic capabilities: a review, model and research agenda. *Journal of Management Studies*, 43(4), 917–55.

22. A framework for sustaining hybridity in social enterprises: combining differentiating and integrating

Marya Besharov, Wendy Smith and Tiffany Darabi

INTRODUCTION

Social enterprises – hybrid organizations that pursue social missions through commercial ventures – offer one approach to social innovation (Battilana and Lee, 2014; Smith et al., 2013; Tracey and Stott, 2017). Microfinance organizations create opportunities for people at the bottom of the pyramid to access financial instruments and improve their socioeconomic status (Battilana and Dorado, 2010; Cobb et al., 2016; Zhao and Wry, 2016). Work integration social enterprises create pathways to employment and economic self-sufficiency for the otherwise unemployable (Pache and Santos, 2013b; Smith and Besharov, 2019; Tracey et al., 2011). Other social enterprises create economic opportunities to improve rural or impoverished communities (Slawinski and Smith, 2017; Tracey and Phillips, 2016), address environmental concerns (Jay, 2013), or enhance worker ownership and control (Ashforth and Reingen, 2014).

By combining both social mission and commercial logics in one organization, social enterprises can potentially generate novel solutions to pressing social problems (Battilana et al., 2017). Yet they face challenges in doing so, as the juxtaposition of multiple logics creates tensions and competing demands in macro-level issues of governance, strategy, structure, and stakeholder relationships (Ebrahim et al., 2014; Jay, 2013; Pache and Santos, 2010, 2013b) and in micro-level issues of inter-group dynamics and individual motivations and identities (Ashforth and Reingen, 2014; Besharov, 2014; Miller et al., 2012; Wry and York, 2017).

Paradox theory suggests that organizations can navigate these tensions and sustain dual logics over time by embedding both features that differentiate between logics and features that integrate across logics (Smith and Lewis, 2011; Schad et al., 2016). Differentiating involves surfacing distinctions between each competing demand, for example, through separate subgroups (Ashforth and Reingen, 2014), senior leadership roles (Smith, 2014), or organizational practices (Smets et al., 2015) associated with each side, allowing the organization to focus on the unique demands associated with each logic. Integrating involves reinforcing synergies and linkages across competing demands, for example, through overarching visions (Smith et al., 2010), paradoxical frames (Miron-Spektor et al., 2018; Smith and Tushman, 2005), or shared spaces for negotiation (Battilana et al., 2015), which motivate and create conditions for overcoming potential conflict between logics and encourage novel solutions by addressing both logics simultaneously.

Recent studies of social enterprises have begun to explore how organizations combine features that differentiate and integrate, and the impact of doing so for sustaining dual logics over time (Battilana et al., 2015; Battilana et al., 2017; Besharov, 2014; Smith and

Besharov, 2019). Yet this research remains nascent, and most extant studies describe organizations and their members as either primarily differentiating or primarily integrating social mission and commercial logics (for example, Battilana and Dorado, 2010; Ebrahim et al., 2014; Pache and Santos, 2013a). As a result, we lack a more in-depth and structured understanding of how social enterprises can both differentiate and integrate their dual logics to effectively navigate tensions between them and realize their potential for creating novel solutions to grand societal challenges. Our chapter addresses this issue, integrating insights from paradox theory with social enterprise research to build a framework that demonstrates the value of combining differentiating and integrating and depicts an array of approaches for doing so. Building on this framework, we propose a research agenda to advance insights into the antecedents, moderators, and dynamics of differentiating and integrating in social enterprises, other forms of social innovation, and hybridity more broadly.

THEMES IN SOCIAL ENTERPRISE RESEARCH: FEATURES THAT DIFFERENTIATE AND INTEGRATE DUAL LOGICS

Institutional logics are socially constructed patterns of beliefs and practices that shape cognition and guide action (Friedland and Alford, 1991; Thornton et al., 2012). Scholars have long recognized that logics manifest within organizations through the mental models carried by individual members as well as through organizational features such as routines, practices, and structures (Scott, 2008; Thornton et al., 2012). Increasingly, scholars also recognize the co-existence of *multiple* institutional logics within organizations, such as the dual social mission and commercial logics that characterize social enterprises (Besharov and Smith, 2014). Studies further imply that organizations embedding multiple logics tend to either differentiate these logics or integrate them (Battilana et al., 2017; Greenwood et al., 2011; Kraatz and Block, 2008). Differentiation occurs when separate individuals, structures, and practices serve as carriers of each logic, whereas integration occurs when individuals, structures, and practices represent multiple logics simultaneously. In this section, we draw on extant work describing features at the individual, group, and organizational levels that differentiate or integrate social mission and commercial logics in social enterprises. In doing so, we highlight an underlying assumption in much of the research: that organizations either differentiate or integrate logics rather than combine both approaches – an assumption we will challenge in the following section. Table 22.1 provides a summary.

At the individual level, people tend to be categorized as either predominantly carrying just one logic – that is, differentiating – or predominantly emphasizing both logics – that is, integrating. For example, in her study of a natural foods retailer, Besharov (2014) found that most employees primarily aligned with and enacted either the store's social mission or its business mission, illustrating differentiating, while other employees aligned with and enacted both missions, thereby integrating logics. As research on both identity and institutions shows, the tendency to align with and enact one versus multiple logics emerges from, and is evident in, features such as personal and professional identities (DiBenigno, 2017; Miller et al., 2012; Wry and York, 2017), prior experience and training (Almandoz, 2014; Battilana and Dorado, 2010; McPherson and Sauder, 2013; Pache

Table 22.1 Logic differentiation and integration in social enterprises

Level of Analysis	Key Features	Differentiated	Integrated
Individual	• Professional expertise • Individual identity • Formal/informal roles • Cognitive frames	Individuals carry and enact one logic – either the social mission or the commercial logic. *Example*: "Idealists" carry a social mission logic, "capitalists" carry a commercial logic at Natural Foods (Besharov, 2014).	Individuals carry and enact multiple logics – valuing both the social mission and the commercial logic. *Example*: "Pluralists" carry both social mission and commercial logics at Natural Foods (Besharov, 2014).
Group	• Subgroup identity • Subgroup demographics • Subgroup tasks and responsibilities	Subgroups focus on one logic – either a social mission logic or a commercial logic. *Example*: One subgroup of loan officers at BancoSol carries a banking logic while another carries a development logic (Battilana and Dorado, 2010).	Subgroups focus on multiple logics. Either subgroup members are pluralists carrying multiple logics, or some members carry a social mission logic, others carry a business logic, and others carry both logics. *Example*: The group of loan officers at Los Andes carries both banking and development logics (Battilana and Dorado, 2010). Department members at Natural Foods include idealists, capitalists, and pluralists (Besharov, 2014).
Organizational	• Routines • Practices • Structures • Organizational identity • Stakeholder relationships	Dual logics embodied in separate routines, practices, structures, organizational identities, and/or stakeholder relationships. *Example*: Mobile School creates a social mission unit that provides educational opportunities in low-income neighborhoods, financed by a separate business unit that provides corporate training (Ebrahim et al., 2014).	Dual logics embodied in blended routines, practices, structures, organizational identities, and/or stakeholder relationships. *Example*: VisionSpring integrates social mission and commercial logics through a Bottom of the Pyramid business that provides affordable eyeglasses to the poor and hires low-income women to sell the product (Ebrahim et al., 2014).

and Santos, 2013a), and formal and informal roles (Ashforth and Reingen, 2014). For example, Almandoz's (2014) study of the founding of local, community-oriented banks highlighted founders that differentiated logics. Past experiences in either the nonprofit or financial services sector influenced whether these founders focused on the bank's community or commercial goals when making strategic decisions about financial growth and community needs. Individuals can also serve as pluralists who carry multiple logics simultaneously (Besharov, 2014). For example, Wry and York (2017) note how social entrepreneurs can draw from multiple professional and role identities that span social mission and commercial logics to develop a more integrated understanding of their organizations.

Extending these ideas to the group level, studies depict hybrids in general, and social enterprises in particular, as comprised of subgroups that either differentiate or integrate logics. We define differentiated subgroups as those whose members hold just one logic – either social mission or commercial. For example, Battilana and Dorado (2010) studied two microfinance organizations in Bolivia. One of the organizations, BancoSol, had two distinct subgroups of loan officers. One subgroup included loan officers with backgrounds in social work, sociology, anthropology, and other fields associated with the bank's development focus and social mission logic, while the other subgroup included loan officers with backgrounds in finance, economics, and auditing, consistent with the bank's commercial logic. Ashforth and Reingen (2014) offer another example, noting how members of a natural foods coop split into subgroups that advocated for the idealist and pragmatist sides of the coop's hybrid identity, respectively. In contrast, integrated subgroups include members who carry multiple logics. In some integrated subgroups, all individuals align with both missions. For example, Los Andes, the second microfinance organization studied by Battilana and Dorado (2010), loan officers primarily hired from university graduates with limited work experience in order to more effectively socialize them to adopt mental models and skills that recognized the value and integration of both the social mission and commercial logics. In other cases, integrated subgroups can consist of some individuals carrying a social mission logic, some carrying a commercial logic, and still others carrying both. In her study of the natural foods retailer, for example, Besharov (2014) found that idealists, capitalists, and pluralists worked together in the same departments.

In addition to being carried by individual members and represented across internal subgroups, logics manifest at the organizational level in routines, practices, structures, organizational identities, and other material and symbolic features (Jones and Livne-Tarandach, 2008; Lounsbury, 2007). Institutional theorists argue that logics within a field prescribe particular organizational features, which organizations adopt in order to establish and maintain legitimacy (Thornton et al., 2012). The relationship between field-level logics and organization-level features is particularly evident during periods of change, when organizations alter internal arrangements in response to broader cultural and historical forces that shift dominant logics within a field. For example, Haveman and Rao's (1997) study of the thrift industry shows how organizational practices and structures regarding membership, governance, and technology, as well as the types of products offered, changed as the rise of Progressivism and a growing transient population led to the decline of an institutional logic of mutuality and the ascendance of a logic of bureaucracy. Similarly, Thornton (2002) shows how the demise of an editorial logic and the rise of a market logic in higher education publishing drove the adoption of the M-form organizational structure within publishing firms.

As with research on multiple logics at the individual and group levels, studies at the organizational level generally depict organizational features as either differentiating or integrating multiple logics. Much of the literature emphasizes how field-level features inform the distribution of logics at the organizational level. When separate sets of external stakeholders endorse each logic, organizations more likely develop differentiated features in order to demonstrate clear conformity with these varied stakeholder expectations. For example, Pache and Santos (2013b) show how French work integration social enterprises selectively adopted distinct practices prescribed by different institutional referents associated with their social mission and commercial logics, respectively. In contrast, field-level actors that promote combinations of logics can facilitate integrative organizational features. For example, funding and legitimating agencies such as Ashoka and the Schwab Foundation for Social Entrepreneurship actively support the integration of social mission and commercial logics within organizations.

Across the individual, group, and organizational levels, extant research emphasizes how differentiating or integrating logics in features at one level creates a tendency for a similar relationship between logics in features at other levels, such that organizations as a whole tend to either differentiate or integrate multiple logics. Organizational features are informed by field-level structures, and influence group demographics as well as the mental models carried by members (Jackall, 1988). Similarly, individuals create and enact group and organizational features that reflect the logics they carry (Almandoz, 2014; Colyvas, 2007). Given these reinforcing dynamics, it is perhaps not surprising that scholars implicitly characterize organizations as either differentiated or integrated (Battilana et al., 2012; Ebrahim et al., 2014; Greenwood et al., 2011; see also Albert and Whetten, 1985 who describe hybrid identity organizations as either "ideographic" (differentiated) or "holographic" (integrated)).

In this chapter, we draw from recent research to argue that differentiation and integration of logics can vary both within and across levels, resulting in a more complex distribution of multiple logics within organizations. Individuals can assert agency to alter how logics are embedded in key features at the individual, group, and organizational levels (Lawrence et al., 2011; Zilber, 2002). Asserting agency amidst existing forces is challenging, yet scholars have long recognized that actors can think and act outside of the logics they carry (Friedland and Alford, 1991; McPherson and Sauder, 2013). Social entrepreneurs may be particularly successful in doing so because they tend to operate in emerging fields that juxtapose multiple logics (Dacin et al., 2010; Tracey et al., 2011). In emerging fields, isomorphic, normative, and regulatory pressures have not yet coalesced, giving organizations and their leaders greater latitude to adopt varied internal routines, practices, structures, identities, and other material and symbolic features (Navis and Glynn, 2010). Moreover, the juxtaposition of multiple logics creates a dialectical tension that offers an opportunity for leaders to assert agency and develop novel, creative approaches to organizing (DiMaggio, 1988; Seo and Creed, 2002; Smets et al., 2012). Consistent with this argument, recent studies of social enterprises and other hybrids depict organizations that combine differentiating and integrating. These studies suggest that differentiating and integrating can vary across levels, with features at one level differentiating logics and features at another level integrating logics (Jay, 2013; see also research on ambidexterity, for example, Smith, 2014; Tushman and O'Reilly, 1996). They also suggest that differentiating and integrating can vary across features at a single level such that some individual, group, or organizational features differentiate logics while others integrate logics (Ashforth and Reingen, 2014; Battilana et al., 2015; Besharov, 2014). Other studies have pointed to the potential for differentiating and integrating to occur within the same individuals or the same organizational features (Smets et al., 2015; Smith and Besharov, 2019). In the following section, we explore in more depth various configurations for combining differentiating and integrating, and we draw from paradox theory (Schad et al., 2016; Smith and Lewis, 2011) to help explain how these configurations can benefit social enterprises.

A FRAMEWORK FOR SUSTAINABLE SOCIAL ENTERPRISES: COMBINING DIFFERENTIATING AND INTEGRATING

Although challenging to accomplish, social enterprises can combine differentiating and integrating both within and across individual, group, and organizational levels. Doing so enables organizations to address tensions between their dual logics and sustain hybridity, thereby more effectively facilitating the pursuit of novel solutions to social problems. We draw from paradox theory to explain the dynamics of differentiating and integrating. Paradox theory explores the nature and management of "contradictory, yet interrelated elements that exist simultaneously and persist over time" (Smith and Lewis, 2011, p. 382). Studies suggest that organizations and their leaders can more effectively sustain contradictory yet interrelated elements and navigate tensions between them by both differentiating and integrating (Andriopoulos and Lewis, 2009; Smets et al., 2015; Smith, 2014). Differentiating highlights the unique goals, values, strategies, and practices associated with each logic. However, differentiating without integrating can foster competing subgroups that engage in detrimental conflict (Fiol et al., 2009) and contribute to declining organizational performance (Battilana and Dorado, 2010; Glynn, 2000). Integrating highlights linkages and synergies, while motivating cooperation. Stressing integration without clear differentiation, however, creates the potential for false synergies (Smith, 2014) in which the side with more power takes over (see Huq et al., 2017), resulting in mission drift and loss of hybridity. We elaborate on these processes below. Figure 22.1 depicts our overarching framework and Table 22.2 summarizes internal dynamics and outcomes for alternative configurations of differentiating and integrating.

Differentiating Individual and Group Features While Integrating Organizational Features

When individuals primarily carry either social mission or commercial logics, similarities in values and practices draw members who carry the same logic toward one another and away from those who carry the opposing logic. Over time, informal subgroups associated with each logic are likely to emerge. Subgroups may co-exist peacefully for limited periods of time. However, when resource scarcity or environmental shifts make salient the tensions associated with multiple logics (Smith and Lewis, 2011), subgroup members are likely to feel threatened and respond by seeking to protect their own group's resources, power, and identity, ultimately fostering inter-group conflict (Fiol et al., 2009).

Pairing this differentiation at the individual and group level with differentiated

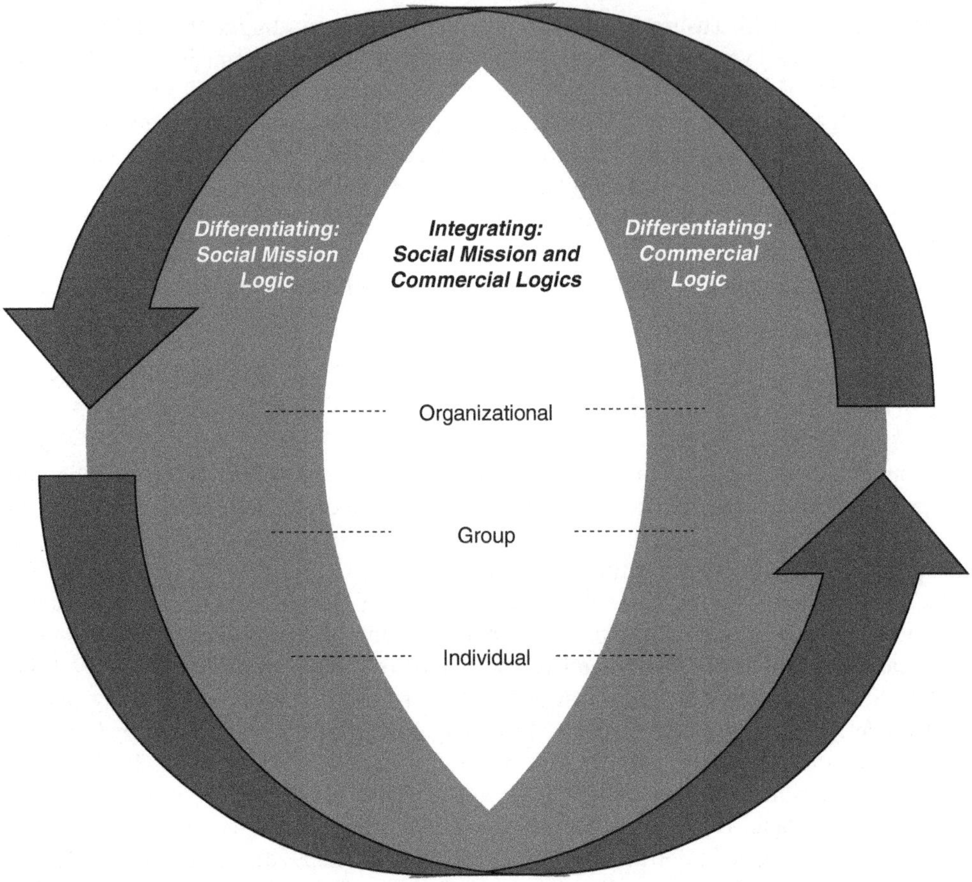

Figure 22.1 A framework for differentiating and integrating in social enterprises

organizational features serves to reinforce the development of subgroup conflict and emphasizes distinctions between individuals who carry opposing logics (see the first row of Table 22.2). As studies of occupational groups in organizations illustrate, it is especially difficult to find common ground when individuals who carry incompatible mental models are in separate formal organizational units with distinct routines and practices (Bechky, 2003b; DiBenigno, 2017; DiBenigno and Kellogg, 2014). Even if subgroups resolve a particular point of tension, distinctions between multiple logics remain. Moreover, inertial forces make organizational arrangements difficult to change (Hannan and Freeman, 1984), and siloed organizational structures reinforce underlying competing demands. As a result, when new tensions emerge, awareness of distinctions between subgroups becomes heightened and members again engage in in-group favoritism and out-group hostility, mutual dis-identification, and battles for jurisdictional control, all of which precipitate additional conflict (DiBenigno and Kellogg, 2014; Fiol et al., 2009; Glynn, 2000). Over time, these dynamics lead to ongoing cycles of tensions, conflict, and mistrust, which become embedded within differentiated hybrids and lead to intractable conflict – protracted clashes that resist resolution (Fiol et al., 2009). For example, Battilana and

Table 22.2 Internal dynamics and outcomes for alternative configurations of differentiating and integrating

Configuration	Internal Dynamics	Outcome	Example
Differentiated features across all levels	Logic conflict occurs between members, who feel threatened, leading to: • in-group favoritism, out-group hostility (Brewer, 1991; Tajfel and Turner, 1986) • mutual dis-identification (Fiol et al., 2009) • battles for jurisdictional control (DiBenigno and Kellogg, 2014) Differentiated organizational features reinforce distinctions between individual members and formal or informal subgroups, making it likely that conflict will escalate and become intractable over time.	Intractable conflict	Banco Sol (Battilana and Dorado, 2010)
Integrated features all levels	Logic conflict occurs within members, who experience ambiguity and ambivalence. Efforts to resolve ambiguity by blending logics lead one logic to become dominant due to: • absence of unique representatives of each logic (Tripsas and Gavetti, 2000) • field-level power dynamics (D'Aunno et al., 1991) Integrated organizational features reinforce logic dominance by making it difficult for actors to recognize the unique features and distinct value of each logic (Janis, 1982; Schweiger et al., 1986).	One logic becomes dominant while the other becomes peripheral	Compartamos (Pache and Santos, 2010)
Differentiated individual and group features; integrated organizational features	When subgroups carry conflicting logics, integrated organizational features minimize threat and promote communication between subgroups, encouraging creative solutions in which both logics are upheld, as evident in research on: • superordinate goals and identities (Sherif et al., 1961; Tushman et al., 2010) • rules and routines (Carlile, 2004) • boundary organizations (O'Mahony and Bechky, 2008) • shared spaces, structures, and tangible objects (Bechky 2003a, 2003b; DiBenigno, 2017)	Incompatible logics maintained in productive tension	"BETA" French Work integration social enterprise (Battilana et al., 2015)
Integrated individual and group features; differentiated organizational features	When all members carry both logics, differentiated organizational features increase members' awareness of the distinct value of each logic, encouraging creative solutions in which both logics are upheld, as evident in research on: • mindfulness (Langer, 1989; Weick et al., 1999) • ambidexterity (Smith and Tushman, 2005) • negotiations (McGinn et al., 2003) • cultural diversity (Ely and Thomas, 2001)	Incompatible logics maintained in productive tension	Cambridge Energy Alliance (Jay, 2013)
differentiated and integrated features at one or more levels	At the individual and group levels, members who carry both logics mitigate tensions between members and groups carrying just one logic or the other (Ashforth and Reingen, 2014; Besharov, 2014). At the organizational level, features that differentiate logics enable members to recognize the unique value of each one, while features that integrate logics encourage synergies between them (Fiol et al., 2009).	Incompatible logics maintained in productive tension	Digital Divide Data (Smith and Besharov, 2019)

Dorado (2010) show how differentiated work practices in the BancoSol microfinance organization, such as administrative procedures consistent with the commercial logic but not the social mission logic, exacerbated conflict between loan officers associated with each logic. As they describe, conflict escalated to the point where it reached "crisis proportions," leading to significant employee turnover and forcing the CEO to resign.

In contrast, combining a differentiated approach at the individual and group levels with integrated organizational features can offset the tendency toward intractable conflict, effectively balancing the differentiation in logics present at the individual and group levels (see the third row of Table 22.2). These features do so by creating an environment that fosters mutual understanding and provides opportunities for confronting and working through tensions between logics (see DiBenigno, 2017). In a study comparing two work integration social enterprises in France, Battilana et al. (2015) found that in both organizations, production supervisors and social counselors formed differentiated subgroups, with production supervisors following the commercial logic and focusing on organizational outputs, while social counselors adhered to the social mission logic and focused on employee development. In the BETA organization, leaders created "spaces of negotiation" that included practices such as mandatory meetings to address inherent conflicts, a formal planning system to schedule and coordinate activities, and a formal appraisal process to surface conflicting goals. By enabling subgroups to address and work through tensions, these spaces of negotiation allowed BETA to achieve both social and commercial success, whereas the ALPHA organization, which did not implement spaces of negotiation, achieved strong social performance but struggled commercially.

In addition to routines and practices, integrative organizational identities can also help bring together disparate groups and prevent conflict from escalating to the point where it becomes counter-productive (Fiol et al., 2009). Foundational research on group conflict shows how the introduction of a superordinate goal, which integrates the varied goals of conflicting subgroups, motivates collaboration, inspires the search for new information, and results in novel, creative problem-solving (Sherif et al., 1961). This work suggests that conflict between subgroups, stemming from differentiation at the individual level, is redirected toward more productive ends when symbolic organizational features, such as goals and identities, are integrated. In particular, as subgroups experience threat, an integrative identity helps minimize the stress and anxiety that arise from threat and helps members be more open and willing to work across subgroups to find creative alternatives that satisfy the groups' competing demands (Fiol et al., 2009).

Integrating Individual and Group Features While Differentiating Organizational Features

When organizational members adhere to competing demands, as is the case when members of a social enterprise carry both social mission and commercial logics, tensions between logics can create feelings of ambiguity and ambivalence (Merton, 1976; Pratt and Praides, 2012; Weigert and Franks, 1989). One way to resolve ambiguity in the face of competing demands is to seek consistency (Cialdini, 1993; Festinger, 1957). In social enterprises and other hybrids, efforts to create consistency and minimize conflict often lead individuals and groups to blend logics (for example, Dalpiaz et al., 2016). Achieving true blending across multiple logics is difficult, however, and efforts to do so can result in individuals and groups unintentionally prioritizing one logic and de-emphasizing the other. This resulting focus on a single logic can occur in part due to the absence of dedicated individuals carrying each logic, which makes it difficult for organizational members to recognize what is distinct and valuable about each one.

The tendency for one logic to become dominant is further reinforced by integrative organizational features (see the second row of Table 22.2). As research on group decision making suggests, absent formal practices, roles, or structures that represent and surface alternative perspectives, one single, initial point of view usually dominates (Janis, 1982; Schweiger et al., 1986). Over time, inertial forces lead the enacted perspective to become embedded in organizational practices, routines, and structures (see Gilbert, 2005; Tripsas and Gavetti, 2000). In hybrids, the result is that organizational features that were once integrated come to embody just one of the organization's logics, with the other logic decoupled from the organizational core and enacted through peripheral and largely symbolic features, if at all (Boxenbaum and Jonsson, 2017; Pache and Santos, 2013b).

Battilana and Dorado (2010) suggest these dynamics in their description of the Los Andes microfinance organization. Los Andes' leaders hired inexperienced members and socialized them to be carriers of a blended logic of operational excellence that combined elements of the banking and development logics on which the organization depended. They also created integrated organizational features, explicitly stating in their annual report that Los Andes sought "to reconcile its social goals with deriving an economic yield" (quoted in Battilana and Dorado, 2010, p. 1430). This strategy appeared to work in the short term, enabling Los Andes to sustain its social mission while also generating a financial profit. However, the authors note that it created a substantial concern over the long term. By pursuing a blended logic of operational excellence, Los Andes risked losing focus on the development logic on which its legitimacy depended. This outcome is evident in other microfinance organizations. At Compartamos in Mexico and SKS Microfinance in India, a commercial banking logic now dominates operations, while the development logic has become peripheral and largely symbolic. These organizations rely on funds from public markets, and, according to observers in the field, they also charge interest rates that enable them to generate increasing profits and engage in marketing and loan collection practices that resemble those of traditional banks (Pache and Santos, 2010). In fact, so many microfinance organizations started to focus only on the banking logic that Mohamad Yunus, known as the father of microfinance, lamented in 2011 that the field was "sacrificing microcredit for megaprofits" (Yunus, 2011).

As the above account suggests, differentiated organizational features can offset the tendency for one logic to become dominant in social enterprises in which members integrate logics (see the fourth row of Table 22.2). When multiple logics are embodied in separate routines, practices, structures, and identities, members are likely to be more aware of each logic's distinct value. While this awareness does not eliminate members' experience of inconsistency, it does enable them to respond to this experience differently, by developing solutions that incorporate both logics rather than unintentionally prioritizing one logic or the other. Several literatures provide insight into the underlying mechanisms through which differentiating encourages solutions that incorporate competing demands. Research on mindfulness suggests increased attention to detail, sensitivity to context, and recognition of novel stimuli encourages creative solutions to problems (Langer, 1989; Weick et al., 1999). In the negotiations field, studies show that when actors obtain information about the distinct interests and needs of their negotiating partner, they are more successful in reaching an agreement that meets the needs of both parties (McGinn et al., 2003). The literature on diversity suggests that recognizing and valuing distinctions associated with different racial and ethnic backgrounds enables work groups to successfully incorporate and learn from the perspectives of culturally diverse members (Ely and Thomas, 2001). In contrast, when work groups attempt to create a common, integrated culture without recognizing the distinct perspectives associated with different racial and ethnic backgrounds, the values and ideas of a single culture or race (usually white) end up dominating (Ely and Thomas, 2001).

Ambidexterity research also highlights the role of differentiation to offset forces for integration and enable organizations to address competing demands (Andriopoulos and Lewis, 2009; Smith and Tushman, 2005). In research on product design firms, Andriopoulos and Lewis (2009) find that the firms most successful in pursuing both exploration and exploitation projects, rather than just one type of project or the other, socialized members to be "practical artists" who combined logics of exploration and exploitation, but then coupled this integration among members with organizational features that differentiated the two activities. Firms developed project portfolios in which some projects involved clearly incremental designs while others called for breakthrough designs. They further delineated distinct exploration and exploitation work phases within projects and established distinct creative and business roles.

Jay's (2013) study of the Cambridge Energy Alliance (CEA) illustrates this configuration in the social enterprise context. Members of the CEA carried both a market and civic logic, illustrating integrative features at the individual level, while external stakeholders such as clients, consultants, and academics tended to represent just one logic or the other, illustrating differentiation in stakeholder relationships at the organizational level. As the alliance struggled to enact both logics and swung from stressing primarily the market logic to emphasizing primarily the civic logic, feedback from external stakeholders called attention to the underrepresented logic, prompting employees to recognize and address tensions between the logics. This process ultimately enabled the CEA to enact both logics simultaneously.

Differentiating and Integrating Within Features

The previous subsections describe individual, group, and organizational features as primarily differentiating or primarily integrating logics, and highlight configurations involving differentiating at one level and integrating at another. However, organizations can also combine differentiating and integrating within levels, such that some individual, group, or organizational features differentiate logics while others integrate logics (see Ashforth and Reingen, 2014; Besharov, 2014; Smets et al., 2015; Smith and Besharov, 2019). As with the configurations described above, doing so has the potential to maintain logics in productive tension while preventing intractable conflict and logic dominance (see the fifth row of Table 22.2). In this subsection, we unpack these dynamics through several illustrative examples.

First, organizations may have some members who adhere to just one logic or the other, while others adhere to both simultaneously. In her study of a natural foods retailer, for example, Besharov (2014) found that the organization included front-line workers who were either "idealists" or "capitalists," carrying the social mission or commercial logic, respectively, but that most managers were "pluralists" who carried both logics simultaneously. When tensions arose between idealists and capitalists, pluralists drew on their integrative mental models to prevent detrimental conflict from emerging. Ashforth and Reingen (2014) show how individuals who are not in formal leadership positions can play a similar role. In the natural foods cooperative they studied, informal subgroups formed around the idealist (social mission) and pragmatist (commercial) sides of the organization. Within each subgroup, some individuals served as "lightning rods" displaying particularly strong commitments to one side or the other, whereas others held less extreme views and helped to manage tensions between the two groups. As these examples illustrate, having some individuals or groups that integrate logics mitigates potentially detrimental conflict between individuals and groups that differentiate logics and instead fosters productive tensions.

Second, the very same individuals could both differentiate and integrate logics. Recent research on the work integration social enterprise Digital Divide Data (DDD) illustrates this more complex distribution of logics within individuals (Smith and Besharov, 2019). While the organization's founder had previous experience and training in both nonprofit and for-profit organizations, most other members of the senior management team and the board had backgrounds and training in either the social mission or commercial logic. Their differentiated professional expertise enabled them to serve as advocates for one mission or the other, raising concerns when practices over-emphasized the alternative. Yet influenced by the founder, these leaders also adopted "paradoxical frames" in which they valued both missions and emphasized synergies and interdependencies between missions, not just distinctions and contradictions. These integrative cognitive frames encouraged leaders to grapple with – rather than avoid – tensions and facilitated an ongoing search for practices that could uphold both missions. In this way, having individual leaders who combined differentiating and integrating prevented intractable conflict and mission drift and fostered productive tensions between logics.

The research on DDD also illustrates the possibility and value of combining differentiation and integration of social mission and commercial logics within organization-level features. DDD leaders created differentiated formal structures, roles, and external stakeholder relationships dedicated to either the social or business mission. Smith and Besharov (2019) refer to these features as "guardrails" because, similar to those on a road, they prevented the organization from drifting too far toward one mission or the other. For example, DDD leaders forged a partnership with a for-profit IT outsourcing firm that supported the business mission by advising on technical and operational issues. Yet leaders also built ties to nonprofit job readiness programs that supported the social mission by selecting and training disadvantaged Cambodians who became DDD's employees. Leaders also produced distinct financial statements to track business and social mission revenues and costs separately, in order to better inform strategic decisions that would enable each one. While the differentiation reflected in DDD's guardrails prevented a single logic from dominating, integration in other organizational features reinforced linkages and synergies between the social mission and commercial logics, fostering productive tensions rather than intractable conflict. For example, leaders adopted an integrated organizational structure in which they pursued the social mission of helping people move out of poverty through the operation of a commercial IT outsourcing business, such that

DDD's employees were also the intended beneficiaries of the social mission. DDD leaders also developed an integrative organizational identity combining social and business objectives. Coupled with leaders' integrative cognitive frames (described above), these integrative organizational features created both actual and perceived interdependence between the two missions and thereby encouraged members to work together to develop practices that could uphold both missions.

Taken together, these configurations of differentiating and integrating offer a framework for sustaining dual logics in social enterprises. As summarized in Figure 22.1 and Table 22.2, our framework depicts varied ways that organizations can combine differentiating and integrating across and within individual, group, and organizational features and explains how doing so fosters productive tensions between logics rather than intractable conflict or mission drift. These ideas raise a number of questions for future research, which we explore in the next section.

DEVELOPING THE FRAMEWORK: AN AGENDA FOR FUTURE RESEARCH

The potential for social enterprises to enable social innovation depends on their ability to sustain social mission and commercial logics over time. In this chapter, we have drawn on paradox theory and recent empirical research on social enterprises to develop a framework for doing so through differentiating and integrating dual logics. Future research can add depth and breadth to our framework in several ways.

Adding Complexity and Nuance

Exploring moderators, antecedents, and dynamic relationships can add nuance to our argument that social enterprises benefit from combining differentiating and integrating. First, research can explore moderating factors that enable the combination of differentiating and integrating in social enterprises. As we noted above, forces at various levels of analysis reinforce one another, creating organizations that primarily differentiate or primarily integrate dual logics. Overcoming these forces requires contexts with weaker normative and isomorphic pressures and greater opportunities for agency. We argued that the relatively nascent state of the field, as well as the juxtaposition of contradictory logics, may afford social enterprises greater flexibility to combine differentiating and integrating compared to other hybrids. However, moderating factors at both the field and organizational levels likely create variance in the extent to which such combinations emerge.

At the field level, mature fields tend to have more specific and rigid stakeholder expectations that become ossified over long periods of time, disrupted by periodic episodes of change (Bodrožić and Adler, 2017). In the social enterprise field, for example, early studies highlight the value of publicly identifying with both social mission and commercial logics (Moss et al., 2011), whereas recent research suggests the value of doing so depends on the extent to which it provides categorical distinctiveness (Gehman and Grimes, 2017). These studies suggest a maturation of the field, which future research can explore in more depth. For example, studies might consider changes in the social enterprise field over time and how these changes influence organization-level variation in differentiating and integrating. In addition to field maturity, studies can also examine the moderating effects of field centralization and regulation (Gehman and Grimes, 2017; Pache and Santos, 2010). Social enterprises in fields that are more regulated or consolidated, such as energy (Jay, 2013) or finance (Battilana and Dorado, 2010), may face more stringent business expectations and greater pressures for both structural and symbolic differentiating of the social mission logic from the commercial logic. In comparison, fields that are more fragmented may enable greater agency, allowing more opportunity for combining differentiating and integrating (Pache and Santos, 2010).

Organization-level factors can also create variation in differentiating and integrating. These may include age and size, as well as the nature of an organization's social or commercial missions. Combining differentiating and integrating in general may be more feasible in smaller and younger organizations as they are less subject to inertial structural and cultural forces that inhibit change (Hannan and Freeman, 1984; Tripsas and Gavetti, 2000). Smaller and younger organizations are also more entrepreneurial, with more direct connections to the founder's vision and values, more intimate ties within local networks, and enhanced bonds of mutual trust amongst employees (Haigh and Hoffman, 2012), all factors that can mitigate detrimental conflict and facilitate dialogue, making nascent social enterprises ripe environments to engage both differentiating and integrating features. The nature of the social mission, particularly the type of beneficiary targeted, may further inform the potential for organizations combining differentiating and integrating. In work integration social enterprises, for example, social mission beneficiaries are the organization's employees, a feature that may facilitate integration through hiring, socialization, and other human resources practices (Battilana et al., 2012). In contrast, for microfinance organizations, social mission beneficiaries are clients, which may enable greater opportunities for structural differentiation within the organization. Research that explores these and other potential moderating conditions can add nuance to our framework.

Second, future studies can further explore antecedents for combining differentiating and integrating in organizations. In particular, the role of paradoxical cognitive frames merits further exploration. Defined as "mental templates in which managers recognize and accept the simultaneous existence of contradictory forces" (Smith and Tushman, 2005, p. 526), paradoxical frames allow individuals to see apparent contradictions as "complementary or reinforcing" (Miron-Spektor et al., 2011), instead of responding to competing demands by becoming defensive and avoidant (Lewis, 2000). They thereby encourage individuals to grapple with rather than avoid strategic contradictions (Miron-Spektor et al., 2018) and to develop novel perspectives on persistent organizational challenges (Lüscher and Lewis, 2008). Given the potential value of paradoxical frames for enabling individuals to manage the competing demands arising from social mission and commercial logics, it will be critical to understand how social enterprises can develop such frames among their members and at what levels of the organization they should do so.

Shifting cognitive frames is challenging, as individuals develop deeply held mental models over time based on their prior personal and professional experiences (Pache and Santos, 2013a; Schein, 2005; Walsh, 1995; Wry and York, 2017). Moreover, paradoxical frames are not simply skills that can be developed but rather mindsets engendered by personal growth (Petriglieri et al., 2011) and the refinement of interpersonal skills and emotional intelligence (Clegg et al., 2002). Yet research in experimental settings shows that mere presence of a paradoxical relationship in task elements can elicit the adoption of paradoxical frames and enhance creativity (Leung et al., 2018; Miron-Spektor et al., 2011). Future research can further unpack the opportunities and challenges inherent in engendering paradoxical frames amongst existing organizational members as opposed to hiring new members who already embrace paradoxical frames.

Relatedly, future research can explore the organizational roles in which paradoxical frames are of greatest value to enable particular configurations of differentiating and integrating. Extant research emphasizes the value of paradoxical frames among leaders, including board members (Ebrahim et al., 2014) and senior managers (Smith, 2014; Smith and Besharov, 2019; Smith and Tushman, 2005; Smith et al., 2012). Other studies imply that paradoxical frames might be of value among middle managers or front-line employees. For example, Besharov (2014) found that when front-line managers in a natural foods retailer perceived synergies between the firm's social and business missions, while also recognizing their distinctions and contradictions, they could more effectively mitigate tensions between employees who primarily differentiated the two missions. Building on this work, studies can explore the role and value of paradoxical frames at multiple organizational levels and consider how their presence at one level might compensate for their absence at other levels.

A third key area in which future research can add depth to our framework involves dynamics over time. Research on social enterprises and other hybrids points to shifts in organizational features over time in response to changing internal and external dynamics (Ashforth and Reingen, 2014; Dalpiaz et al., 2016; Jay, 2013; Ramus et al., 2017), and Smith and Besharov's (2019) research on DDD unpacks how ongoing adaptation is critical to sustaining hybridity. Future research can build on these emerging insights to examine whether and how organizations adapt configurations of differentiating and integrating as they evolve and grow. One way this may occur is through the emergence and spread of paradoxical frames, as we discussed above. Such changes may be conscious and purposeful, as in cases of planned organizational change (for example, Fiol, 2002). Yet they also likely emerge through unintentional and unconscious processes, as organizational members infuse their daily actions with unique meanings based on their perceptions of organizational arrangements at the day-to-day task level (Zilber, 2002). Examining both types of processes as they unfold over time will add depth to our existing model.

Differentiating and Integrating Beyond the Social Enterprise Context

Future research can also explore the applicability of differentiating and integrating to other forms of social innovation and to hybridity more generally. In this chapter, we focused on differentiating and integrating within social enterprises, which explicitly and intentionally combine social mission and commercial logics within a single organization. While social enterprises are increasingly common, they are not the only organizational form for pursuing social innovation. We focus here on two alternatives that Tracey and Stott (2017) highlight: social intrapreneurship and social extrapreneurship.

Social intrapreneurship involves developing novel solutions to societal challenges from within the boundaries of established organizations, where there may be differential power afforded to social and commercial demands and where responsibility for managing each tends to be bifurcated among varied leaders (Tracey and Stott, 2017). For example, in traditional for-profit organizations, the role of social innovation could vary from central and integrated in organizational strategy to peripheral and decoupled (Weaver et al., 1999). Yet even where social innovation is core, pressures to generate profits may lead social problems to be viewed as commercial opportunities (Tracey and Stott, 2017), facilitating differentiation of social mission from commercial logics while impeding integration. Exploring processes and conditions that enable a balance of differentiating and integrating is therefore a particularly important question for future research seeking to understand how social intrapreneurship initiatives can sustain dual logics.

Social extrapreneurship involves inter-organizational actions that develop novel solutions to societal challenges by combining ideas, people, places, and resources across organizational boundaries (Tracey and Stott, 2017). For example, Engineers Without Borders collaborates with firms, government organizations, and non-governmental organizations (NGOs) to address the infrastructure challenges facing impoverished countries while also building a network of engineers from around the world committed to the ethical and environmental dimensions of engineering design (Tracey and Stott, 2017). Recent research on businesses and NGOs engaged in cross-sectoral partnerships in India suggests the value of paradoxical thinking in social extrapreneurship (Sharma and Bansal, 2017), indicating there is much potential to explore the applicability of our framework to this form of social innovation.

Second, moving beyond social innovation, studies can explore the applicability of our framework to other types of hybrid organizations, including universities (Albert and Whetten, 1985), arts organizations (Glynn, 2000), and biotechnology firms (Powell and Sandholtz, 2012) among others (see Battilana et al., 2017). In particular, it may be useful to consider how our framework applies to hybrids that vary in the compatibility and centrality of the logics they combine (Besharov and Smith, 2014). In social enterprises, social mission and commercial logics tend to be central to organizational functioning, yet also to offer seemingly incompatible prescriptions for action. In other types of hybrids, centrality may be lower and compatibility higher, raising questions about the value of combining differentiating and integrating in such contexts.

Finally, we encourage research that moves beyond dualities to examine differentiating and integrating in settings with a plurality of logics, echoing other recent calls to examine settings in which three or more competing demands are at play (Besharov and Smith, 2014; Greenwood et al., 2011; Smith and Tracey, 2016). Organizations increasingly adopt a "triple bottom line" of people, planet, and profits, an approach which adds an environmental logic to the combination of social mission and commercial logics found in many social enterprises. For example, renewable energy cooperatives combine community, environmental, and market logics in their effort to develop economically profitable and environmentally sustainable local energy solutions (Mitzinneck and Besharov, 2018). With a plurality of logics, the number and complexity of approaches to combining differentiating and integrating increases significantly. For example, organizations could differentiate two logics from one another while integrating one or both of them with a third logic. Would such configurations enable the benefits of combining differentiating and integrating as described in our framework, or is it necessary to differentiate and integrate across all three logics? Similarly, would the negative impact of only differentiating or only integrating be amplified when three or more logics are involved?

As social innovation initiatives become increasingly complex and ambitious in their scope, addressing these questions is all the more important. We hope our chapter provides a starting point and roadmap for this work.

REFERENCES

Albert, S. and D.A. Whetten (1985), "Organizational identity", in L.L. Cummings and B.M. Staw (eds), *Research in Organizational Behavior*, Vol. **7**, Greenwich, CT: JAI Press, pp. 263–95.
Almandoz, J. (2014), "Founding teams as carriers of competing logics: when institutional forces predict banks' risk exposure", *Administrative Science Quarterly*, **59** (3), 442–73.
Andriopoulos, C. and M.W. Lewis (2009), "Exploration-exploitation tensions and organizational ambidexterity: managing paradoxes of innovation", *Organization Science*, **20**, 696–717.
Ashforth, B.E. and P.H. Reingen (2014), "Functions of dysfunction: managing the dynamics of an organizational duality in a natural food cooperative", *Administrative Science Quarterly*, **59** (3), 474–516.
Battilana, J. and S. Dorado (2010), "Building sustainable organizations: the case of commercial microfinance organizations", *Academy of Management Journal*, **53** (6), 1419–40.
Battilana, J. and M. Lee (2014), "Advancing research on hybrid organizing. insights from the study of social enterprises", *Academy of Management Annals*, **8** (1), 397–441.
Battilana, J., M. Lee, J. Walker and C. Dorsey (2012), "In search of the hybrid ideal", *Stanford Social Innovation Review*, **10** (3), 50–5.
Battilana, J., M. Sengul, A.C. Pache and J. Model (2015), "Harnessing productive tensions in hybrid organizations: the case of work integration social enterprises", *Academy of Management Journal*, **58** (6), 1658–85.
Battilana, J., M. Besharov and B. Mitzinneck (2017), "On hybrids and hybrid organizing: a review and roadmap for future research", in R. Greenwood, C. Oliver, T. Lawrence and R. Meyer (eds), *The SAGE Handbook of Organizational Institutionalism*, Vol. 2, London: Sage, pp. 133–69.
Bechky, B.A. (2003a), "Object lessons: Workplace artifacts as representations of occupational jurisdiction", *American Journal of Sociology*, **109** (3), 720–52.
Bechky, B.A. (2003b), "Sharing meaning across occupational communities: the transformation of understanding on a production floor", *Organization Science*, **14** (3), 312–30.
Besharov, M.L. (2014), "The relational ecology of identification: how organizational identification emerges when individuals hold divergent values", *Academy of Management Journal*, **57** (5), 1485–512.
Besharov, M.L. and W.K. Smith (2014), "Multiple institutional logics in organizations: explaining their varied nature and implications", *Academy of Management Review*, **39** (3), 364–81.
Bodrožić, Z. and P.S. Adler (2017), "The evolution of management models: a neo-Schumpeterian theory", *Administrative Science Quarterly*, **63** (1), 85–129.
Boxenbaum, E. and S. Jonsson (2017), "Isomorphism, diffusion and decoupling: concept evolution and theoretical challenges", in R. Greenwood, C. Oliver, T. Lawrence and R. Meyer (eds), *The SAGE Handbook of Organizational Institutionalism*, Vol. 2, London: Sage, pp.79–104.
Brewer, M. (1991), "The social self: on being the same and different at the same time", *Personality and Social Psychology Bulletin*, **17** (5), 475–82.
Carlile, P.R. (2004), "Transferring, translating, and transforming: an integrative framework for managing knowledge across boundaries", *Organization Science*, **15** (5), 555–68.
Cialdini, R. (1993), *The Psychology of Influence*, New York: William Morrow & Co.
Clegg, S.R., J.V. da Cunha and M.P. e Cunha (2002), "Management paradoxes: a relational view", *Human Relations*, **55** (5), 483–503.
Cobb, J.A., T. Wry and E.Y. Zhao (2016), "Funding financial inclusion: institutional logics and the contextual contingency of funding for microfinance organizations", *Academy of Management Journal*, **59** (6), 2103–31.
Colyvas, J.A. (2007), "From divergent meanings to common practices: the early institutionalization of technology transfer in the life sciences at Stanford University", *Research Policy*, **36** (4), 456–76.
Dacin, P.A., M.T. Dacin and M. Matear (2010), "Social entrepreneurship: why we don't need a new theory and how we move forward from here", *Academy of Management Perspectives*, **24** (3), 37–57.
Dalpiaz, E., V. Rindova and D. Ravasi (2016), "Combining logics to transform organizational agency: blending industry and art at Alessi", *Administrative Science Quarterly*, **61** (3), 347–92.
D'Aunno, T., R.I. Sutton and R.H. Price (1991), "Isomorphism and external support in conflicting institutional environments: a study of drug abuse treatment units", *Academy of Management Journal*, **34** (3), 636–61.
DiBenigno, J. (2017), "Anchored personalization in managing goal conflict between professional groups: the case of US Army mental health care", *Administrative Science Quarterly*, **63** (3), 526–69.
DiBenigno, J. and K.C. Kellogg (2014), "Beyond occupational differences: the importance of cross-cutting

demographics and dyadic toolkits for collaboration in a US hospital", *Administrative Science Quarterly*, **59** (3), 375–408.
DiMaggio, P.J. (1988), "Interest and agency in institutional theory", in L.G. Zucker (ed.), *Institutional Patterns and Organizations: Culture and Environment*, Vol. 1, Cambridge, MA: Ballinger Publishing, pp. 3–21.
Ebrahim, A., J. Battilana and J. Mair (2014), "The governance of social enterprises: mission drift and accountability challenges in hybrid organizations", *Research in Organizational Behavior*, **34**, 81–100.
Ely, R.J. and D.A. Thomas (2001), "Cultural diversity at work: the moderating effects of work group perspectives on diversity", *Administrative Science Quarterly*, **46** (2), 229–73.
Festinger, L. (1957), *A Theory of Cognitive Dissonance*, Evanston, IL: Row, Peterson.
Fiol, C.M. (2002), "Capitalizing on paradox: the role of language in transforming organizational identities", *Organization Science*, **13** (6), 653–66.
Fiol, C.M., M.G. Pratt and E.J. O'Connor (2009), "Managing intractable identity conflicts", *Academy of Management Review*, **34** (1), 32–55.
Friedland, R. and R.R. Alford (1991), "Bringing society back in: symbols, practices and institutional contradictions", in W.W. Powell and P.J. DiMaggio (eds), *The New Institutionalism in Organizational Analysis*, Chicago: University of Chicago Press, pp. 232–63.
Gehman, J. and M. Grimes (2017), "Hidden badge of honor: how contextual distinctiveness affects category promotion among certified B corporations", *Academy of Management Journal*, **60** (6), 2294–320.
Gilbert, C.G. (2005), "Unbundling the structure of inertia: resource versus routine rigidity", *Academy of Management Journal*, **48** (5), 741–63.
Glynn, M.A. (2000), "When cymbals become symbols: conflict over organizational identity within a symphony orchestra", *Organization Science*, **11** (3), 285–98.
Greenwood, R., M. Raynard, F. Kodeih, E.R. Micelotta and M. Lounsbury (2011), "Institutional complexity and organizational responses", *Academy of Management Annals*, **5**, 317–71.
Haigh, N. and A.J. Hoffman (2012), "Hybrid organizations. The next chapter of sustainable business", *Organizational Dynamics*, **41** (2), 126–34.
Hannan, M.T. and J. Freeman (1984), "Structural inertia and organizational change", *American Sociological Review*, **49**, 149–64.
Haveman, H.A. and H. Rao (1997), "Structuring a theory of moral sentiments; institutional and organizational coevolution in the early thrift industry", *American Journal of Sociology*, **102** (6), 1606–51.
Huq, J.L., T. Reay and S. Chreim (2017), "Protecting the paradox of interprofessional collaboration", *Organization Studies*, **38** (3–4), 513–38.
Jackall, R. (1988), *Moral Mazes: The World of Corporate Managers*, New York: Oxford University Press.
Janis, I. (1982), *Groupthink: Psychological Studies of Policy Decisions and Fiascoes*, Boston, MA: Houghton Mifflin.
Jay, J. (2013), "Navigating paradox as a mechanism of change and innovation in hybrid organizations", *Academy of Management Journal*, **56** (1), 137–59.
Jones, C. and R. Livne-Tarandach (2008), "Designing a frame: rhetorical strategies of architects", *Journal of Organizational Behavior*, **29** (8), 1075–99.
Kraatz, M. and E. Block (2008), "Organizational implications of institutional pluralism", in R. Greenwood, C. Oliver, R. Suddaby and K. Sahlin-Andersson (eds), *Handbook of Organizational Institutionalism*, London: Sage, pp. 243–75.
Langer, E. (1989), *Mindfulness*, Boston, MA: Addison-Wesley.
Lawrence, T., R. Suddaby and B. Leca (2011), "Institutional work: refocusing institutional studies of organization", *Journal of Management Inquiry*, **20** (1), 52–8.
Leung, A., S. Liou, E. Miron-Spektor et al. (2018), "Middle ground approach to paradox: within- and between-culture examination of the creative benefits of paradoxical frames", *Journal of Personality and Social Psychology*, **114** (3), 443–64.
Lewis, M. (2000), "Exploring paradox: toward a more comprehensive guide", *Academy of Management Review*, **25** (4), 760–76.
Lounsbury, M. (2007), "A tale of two cities: competing logics and practice variation in the professionalizing of mutual funds", *Academy of Management Journal*, **50** (2), 289–307.
Lüscher, L.S. and M.W. Lewis (2008), "Organizational change and managerial sensemaking: working through paradox", *Academy of Management Journal*, **51** (2), 221–40.
McGinn, K.L., L. Thompson and M.H. Bazerman (2003), "Dyadic processes of disclosure and reciprocity in bargaining with communication", *Journal of Behavioral Decision Making*, **16** (1), 17–34.
McPherson, C.M. and M. Sauder (2013), "Logics in action: managing institutional complexity in a drug court", *Administrative Science Quarterly*, **58** (2), 165–96.
Merton, R.K. (1976), *Sociological Ambivalence and Other Essays*, New York: Simon & Schuster.
Miller, T.L., M.G. Grimes, J.S. McMullen and T.J. Vogus (2012), "Venturing for others with heart and head: how compassion encourages social entrepreneurship", *Academy of Management Review*, **37** (4), 616–40.

Miron-Spektor, E., F. Gino and L. Argote (2011), "Paradoxical frames and creative sparks: enhancing individual creativity through conflict and integration", *Organizational Behavior and Human Decision Processes*, **116** (2), 229–40.

Miron-Spektor, E., A.S. Ingram, J. Keller, W.K. Smith and M.W. Lewis (2018), "Microfoundations of organizational paradox: the problem is how we think about the problem", *Academy of Management Journal*, **61** (1), 26–45.

Mitzinneck, B.C. and M.L. Besharov (2018), "Managing value tensions in collective social entrepreneurship: the role of temporal, structural, and collaborative compromise", *Journal of Business Ethics*, https://doi.org/10.1007/s10551-018-4048-2.

Moss, T.W., J.C. Short, G.T. Payne and G.T. Lumpkin (2011), "Dual identities in social ventures: an exploratory study", *Entrepreneurship Theory and Practice*, **35** (4), 805–30.

Navis, C. and M.A. Glynn (2010), "How new market categories emerge: temporal dynamics of legitimacy, identity, and entrepreneurship in satellite radio, 1990–2005", *Administrative Science Quarterly*, **55** (3), 439–71.

O'Mahony, S. and B.A. Bechky (2008), "Boundary organizations: enabling collaboration among unexpected allies", *Administrative Science Quarterly*, **53** (3), 422–59.

Pache, A.C. and F. Santos (2010), "When worlds collide: the internal dynamics of organizational responses to conflicting institutional demands", *Academy of Management Review*, **35** (3), 455–76.

Pache, A.C. and F. Santos (2013a), "Embedded in hybrid contexts: how individuals in organizations respond to competing institutional logics", in M. Lounsbury and E. Boxenbaum (eds), *Institutional Logics in Action, Part B*, Bingley, UK: Emerald Group Publishing, pp. 3–35.

Pache, A.C. and F. Santos (2013b), "Inside the hybrid organization: selective coupling as a response to competing institutional logics", *Academy of Management Journal*, **56** (4), 972–1001.

Petriglieri, G., J.D. Wood and J.L. Petriglieri (2011), "Up close and personal: building foundations for leaders' development through the personalization of management learning", *Academy of Management Learning & Education*, **10** (3), 430–50.

Powell, W.W. and K.W. Sandholtz (2012), "Amphibious entrepreneurs and the emergence of organizational forms", *Strategic Entrepreneurship Journal*, **6** (2), 94–115.

Pratt, M.G. and C. Praides (2012), "Just a good place to visit? Exploring positive responses to psychological ambivalence", in K.S. Cameron and G.M. Spreitzer (eds), *The Oxford Handbook of Positive Organizational Scholarship*, New York: Oxford University Press, pp. 924–37.

Ramus, T., A. Vaccaro and S. Brusoni (2017), "Institutional complexity in turbulent times: formalization, collaboration, and the emergence of blended logics", *Academy of Management Journal*, **60** (4), 1253–84.

Schad, J., M.W. Lewis, S. Raisch and W.K. Smith (2016), "Paradox research in management science: looking back to move forward", *Academy of Management Annals*, **10** (1), 5–64.

Schein, E.H. (2005), "From brainwashing to organizational therapy: a conceptual and empirical journey in search of 'systemic' health and a general model of change dynamics", *Reflections*, **6** (8–10), 1–14.

Schweiger, D.M., W.R. Sandberg and J.W. Ragan (1986), "Group approaches for improving strategic decision making: a comparative analysis of dialectical inquiry, devil's advocacy, and consensus", *Academy of Management Journal*, **29** (1), 51–71.

Scott, W.R. (2008), "Lords of the dance: professionals as institutional agents", *Organization Studies*, **29** (2), 219–38.

Seo, M.G. and W.E.D. Creed (2002), "Institutional contradictions, praxis, and institutional change: a dialectical perspective", *Academy of Management Review*, **27** (2), 222–47.

Sharma, G. and P. Bansal (2017), "Partners for good: how business and NGOs engage the commercial–social paradox", *Organization Studies*, **38** (3–4), 341–64.

Sherif, M., O.J. Harvey, B.J. White, W.R. Hood and C.W. Sherif (1961), *Intergroup Conflict and Cooperation: The Robbers Cave Experiment*, Norman, OK: University of Oklahoma Book Exchange.

Slawinski, N. and W.K. Smith (2017), "Inviting engagement with paradox: how leaders of social enterprises communicate complexity", Memorial University of Newfoundland, Working paper.

Smets, M., T. Morris and R. Greenwood (2012), "From practice to field: a multilevel model of practice-driven institutional change", *Academy of Management Journal*, **55** (4), 877–904.

Smets, M., P. Jarzabkowski, G.T. Burke and P. Spee (2015), "Reinsurance trading in Lloyd's of London: balancing conflicting-yet-complementary logics in practice", *Academy of Management Journal*, **58** (3), 932–70.

Smith, W.K. (2014), "Dynamic decision making: a model of senior leaders managing strategic paradoxes", *Academy of Management Journal*, **57** (6), 1592–623.

Smith, W.K. and M.L. Besharov (2019), "Bowing before dual gods: how structured flexibility sustains organizational hybridity", *Administrative Science Quarterly*, **64** (1), 1–44.

Smith, W.K. and M.W. Lewis (2011), "Toward a theory of paradox: a dynamic equilibrium model of organizing", *Academy of Management Review*, **36** (2), 381–403.

Smith, W.K. and P. Tracey (2016), "Institutional complexity and paradox theory: complementarities of competing demands", *Strategic Organization*, **14** (4), 455–66.

Smith, W.K. and M.L. Tushman (2005), "Managing strategic contradictions: a top management model for managing innovation streams", *Organization Science*, **16** (5), 522–36.
Smith, W.K., A. Binns and M.L. Tushman (2010), "Complex business models: managing strategic paradox simultaneously", *Long Range Planning*, **43** (2), 448–61.
Smith, W.K., M.L. Besharov, A.K. Wessels and M. Chertok (2012), "A paradoxical leadership model for social entrepreneurs: challenges, leadership skills, and pedagogical tools for managing social and commercial demands", *Academy of Management Learning & Education*, **11** (3), 463–78.
Smith, W.K., M. Gonin and M.L. Besharov (2013), "Managing social-business tensions: a review and research agenda for social enterprise", *Business Ethics Quarterly*, **23** (3), 407–42.
Tajfel, H. and J. Turner (1986), "The social identity theory of intergroup behavior", in S. Worchel and W.G. Austin (eds), *Psychology of Intergroup Relations*, Chicago: Nelson, pp. 7–24.
Thornton, P.H. (2002), "The rise of the corporation in a craft industry: conflict and conformity in institutional logics", *Academy of Management Journal*, **45**, 81–101.
Thornton, P.H., W. Ocasio and M. Lounsbury (2012), *The Institutional Logics Perspective: A New Approach to Culture, Structure and Process*, New York: Oxford University Press.
Tracey, P. and N. Phillips (2016), "Managing the consequences of organizational stigmatization: identity work in a social enterprise", *Academy of Management Journal*, **59** (3), 740–65.
Tracey, P. and N. Stott (2017), "Social innovation: a window on alternative ways of organizing and innovating", *Innovation*, **19** (1), 51–60.
Tracey, P., N. Phillips and O. Jarvis (2011), "Bridging institutional entrepreneurship and the creation of new organizational forms: a multilevel model", *Organization Science*, **22** (1), 60–80.
Tripsas, M. and G. Gavetti (2000), "Capabilities, cognition, and inertia: evidence from digital imaging", *Strategic Management Journal*, 18, 1147–61.
Tushman, M.L. and C.A. O'Reilly III (1996), "Ambidextrous organizations: managing evolutionary and revolutionary change", *California Management Review*, **38** (4), 8–29.
Tushman, M., W.K. Smith, R. Wood, G. Westerman and C. O'Reilly (2010), "Organizational design and innovation streams", *Industrial and Corporate Change*, **19** (5), 1331–66.
Walsh, J.P. (1995), "Managerialand organizational cognition: notes from a trip down memory lane", *Organization Science*, **6** (3), 280–321.
Weaver, G.R., L.K. Trevino and P.L. Cochran (1999), "Integrated and decoupled corporate social performance: management commitments, external pressures, and corporate ethics practices", *Academy of Management Journal*, **42** (5), 539–52.
Weick, K.E., K.M. Sutcliffe and D. Obstfeld (1999), "Organizing for high reliability: processes of collective mindfulness", *Research in Organizational Behavior*, **21**, 81–123.
Weigert, A. and D. Franks (1989), "Ambivalence: a touchstone of the modern temper", in D. Frank and E.McCarthy (eds), *The Sociology of Emotions: Original Essays and Research Papers*, Greenwich, CT: JAI Press, pp. 205–27.
Wry, T. and J.G. York (2017), "An identity-based approach to social enterprise", *Academy of Management Review*, **42** (3), 437–60.
Yunus, M. (2011), "Sacrificing microcredit for megaprofits", *The New York Times*, 15 January, p. A23.
Zhao, E. and T. Wry (2016), "Not all inequality is equal: deconstructing the societal logic of patriarchy to understand microfinance lending to women", *Academy of Management Journal*, **59** (6), 1994–2020.
Zilber, T.B. (2002), "Institutionalization as an interplay between actions, meanings, and actors: the case of a rape crisis center in Israel", *Academy of Management Journal*, **45** (1), 234–54.

23. Organizing for global change

Yves Plourde

INTRODUCTION

There is no shortage of global issues. From hunger to climate change to nuclear war, the *Encyclopedia of World Problems and Human Potential* lists approximately 12,000 world problems in 320 categories. These global issues have been identified by some 75,000 international non-governmental organizations (NGOs) as grand challenges because they involve a significant threat to human life. Many of these grand challenges are systemic and structural, so that despite their urgency there is a tendency to deny that they even exist, and this leads to paralysing social and political dynamics. Finding adequate explanations for what causes world problems involves thinking outside these paralysing dynamics, and solving them requires 'significant changes in the way society evolves, how its structures are modified, its ethical norms revisited' (Moulaert et al., 2013, p. 13). For this type of social innovation to be possible, numerous actors – many of whom have important differences in worldviews and interests – have to collaborate. The goal of global change organizations is to help overcome these differences and to make this collaborative work successful.

Global Change Organizations

Global change organizations are 'organizations committed to serve as agents of change in the creation of environmentally and socially sustainable world futures' (Cooperrider and Dutton, 1999, p. 12).They include NGOs like Greenpeace, corporations like Tesla, social enterprises like the Grameen Bank and intergovernmental organizations like the World Bank.[1] They may have different visions of how to change global structures, but they all share the same goal of finding viable solutions to global problems.

In addition to a focus on global problems, global change organizations share a number of other characteristics. According to Cooperrider and Dutton (1999, p. 12), they attempt to create 'innovative social-organizational architectures that make possible human cooperation across previously polarizing or arbitrary constraining boundaries', and they are committed to empowering people to take their destiny into their own hands. Moreover, pursuing activities that cross national borders, they function outside the state and are not constrained by a geographic space. Often they are also cross-sectorial. Indeed, Cooperrider and Dutton (1999, p. 12) emphasize that 'many of the most significant global change organizing innovations involve partnerships bridging sectorial boundaries in new hybrid forms of business'. For example, there may be intergovernmental collaboration, or governmental organizations may work together with private sector volunteer groups.

Global change organizations do not all use the same tools nor do they all tackle problems the same way. NGOs can use their influence to persuade actors in a position of power to help find solutions to the problems perceived as the most salient or to inform the general public about how to make a difference. They can also build on their social capital to promote innovative partnerships. For-profit corporations can lobby governments for more stringent regulations, commercialize novel technologies to solve a focal problem or allocate some of their most valuable resources to efforts to solve important environmental and/or social problems as part of a corporate social responsibility initiative. Intergovernmental organizations can set the agenda for countries and provide them with advice on best practices for addressing global problems. Regardless of the tools at the disposal of global change organizations, having an impact remains their main goal. Yet it can be extremely difficult to find viable solutions to issues as complex as the ones discussed here. To see how global change organizations can use their tools more effectively, we need to look more closely at how global change occurs.

How Global Change Occurs

The type of change that I discuss in this chapter is primarily transformational as opposed to incremental (Micelotta et al., 2017). Transformational change occurs when shared understandings are overturned or significantly altered. At the global level, international institutions play the most important role when it comes to defining these shared understandings, for they provide 'relatively stable sets of related constitutive, regulative, and procedural norms and rules that pertain to the international system, the actors in the system, and their activities' (Duffield, 2007, p. 2). Norms can be formal, as in the case of agreements or treaties set in place by intergovernmental organizations that 'prescribe, proscribe, and/or authorize behaviors' (Koremenos et al., 2001, p. 762).[2] They can also be informally 'recognized patterns of behavior or practice around which expectations converge' (Young, 1982, p. 277). In certain cases, however, global change may require the creation of new institutions because of the absence of shared understandings.

Systemic change at the international level can occur in many different ways. It can involve a 'top-down' approach when an initiative is led by an international organization or institution. For instance, the adoption of the Montreal Protocol successfully addressed the issue of chlorofluorocarbons, for it led to their being banned because of their harmful effect on stratospheric ozone (Haas, 1992). Similarly, over 150 countries signed the Convention on Biodiversity to coordinate a coherent response to the loss of biodiversity. Yet top-down initiatives remain imperfect. Decisions to adopt, modify or eliminate international regulations depend on a political process that remains fragile because of the different resources, interests and identities of the various institutional actors involved (March and Olsen, 1998). Moreover, the adoption of agreements at intergovernmental organizations involves a 'two-level game', both at the intergovernmental organizations themselves and in the member countries, because the governments who have a formal voice at these organizations are also accountable to their constituents (Putnam, 1988). This makes the adoption of new international agreements an arduous process that can extend over several years, if not decades. Finally, once an agreement has been adopted, there is no guarantee that it will be implemented, for the influence of these organizations remains limited.

Systemic change can also occur through bottom-up initiatives led by actors with much less power than intergovernmental organizations. These initiatives are ways for innovation to be diffused across scales (Westley et al., 2011; Westley et al., 2014). Westley et al. (2011, p. 767) emphasize that high impact change 'demands innovation across multiple scales'.

Individuals or groups first initiate an invention or idea on a microscale, and then little by little it is incorporated into a problem domain on a mesoscale, until in the end large institutions are also transformed. Westley et al. (2014, p. 237) use the term 'scaling up' to describe this process of 'identifying opportunities and barriers at broad institutional scales, with the goal of changing the system that created the social problem in the first place'. For them, this term is particularly appropriate 'for situations where an organization aims to affect everybody who is in need of the social innovation they offer, or to address the institutional roots of a problem' (p. 237). Scaling up occurs not only when NGOs or social enterprises attempt to effect change, but also when corporations join together to pursue a common cause. For example, multinational corporations (MNCs) can create a 'coalition of the greater good' by agreeing to adopt best practices to fight corruption at a global level. They can also act as agents of change by diffusing new methods and technologies that radically change the landscape (Eden and Lenway, 2001).

Organizing for Global Change

Organizing for global change means coordinating actions to eliminate the underlying causes of global problems. This type of coordination is above all a form of sense-making (Cooperrider and Dutton, 1999). The latter is at the origin of the human response to global problems because 'it sets the frame for decision-making, becomes the basis for envisioning possible futures, creates the communication context for linking with others, and is itself transformed in the designs and processes of organizing' (Cooperrider and Dutton, 1999, p. 11). The type of organizing that I focus on in this chapter is formal because global organizations possess certain capabilities that make it easier for them to have a global impact. In particular, they are able to draw from a broader resource pool, they have the network necessary to coordinate actions globally, and they can use their size and influence to scale up successful initiatives rapidly. Nevertheless, within the various structures of a global organization minds and ideas must be connected efficiently to ensure that actors possess the right frames, that they can envision possible futures with viable outcomes, and that they have the right organizational context to transform potentially successful projects into concrete systemic change. In the next section, I present some of the issues confronted by global change organizations when they attempt to achieve their goals.

ORGANIZING FOR GLOBAL CHANGE: THREE IMPORTANT CHALLENGES

Global change organizations – and organizations in general – are a 'kind of social actor capable of behaving in a purposeful, intentional manner' (King et al., 2010). Yet being international is no guarantee that an organization can successfully address global problems. Indeed, many international NGOs simply replicate their innovations across locations to affect more people and to cover a larger geographic area without impacting the broader system underlying the issue that they are addressing, a strategy that Westley et al. (2014, p. 237) describe as 'scaling out'. When they adopt this strategy, organizations fail to align their goals with their global reach. In line with this observation, this section focuses on three challenges associated with organizing for global change: making sense of global problems, developing a coherent action plan to deal with them and creating the conditions to address them effectively and repeatedly.

Making Sense of Global Problems and Determining Which Ones to Target

A problem can be well documented at the international level without there being a consensus among international organizations that it is 'global'. The complexity of global problems can lead to divergent interpretations of how widespread they are and of what they actually consist in as 'global' problems. Part of this complexity has to do with their scale, which challenges the ability of individuals and organizations to make sense of them (Bansal et al., 2018; Gibson et al., 2000). Problems may not be visible to all organizational members, or some members may only have a partial view of them. This can create variations in the perception of the urgency to act that create important obstacles to discussion between organizational members. These variations in perception can be compounded by the fact that members are in different locations, so that both their understanding of the problem and their sense of its urgency may be highly equivocal (Weick and Van Orden, 1990). For instance, the effects of climate change are different in California and in Europe. California may have drought and wild fires, whereas Europe may endure colder winter temperatures than in the past. Different local experiences of global problems can delay action until more information becomes available. They can also lead to the misidentification of problems and to an inaccurate understanding of them. On the other hand, problems may be correctly identified but appear so overwhelming that they defy solution, so that allocating time and resources to address them may seem like a waste of time (Weick, 1984). Finally, there may not be enough information available to determine whether perceived problems are real problems. This has been the case for the issue of the environmental impact of genetically modified organisms, with precaution prevailing in Europe while the US moves forward with the technology. In short, global problems are not necessarily seen as such by actors who focus on specific aspects of them without seeing the bigger picture.

Global problems cannot be addressed effectively before actors have made sense of them. Sense-making is an interactive process (Gray et al., 2015; Kudesia, 2017) that results in the creation of frames (Cornelissen and Werner, 2014; Sandberg and Tsoukas, 2015). The latter are 'schemata of interpretation' (Goffman, 1974, p. 21) that serve as filters for information. They matter because once an issue has been framed, the interpretation is shared across an organization through its communication channels, and this impacts the search for solutions (Ocasio, 1997). Thus, failing to categorize problems as 'global' limits the ability of organizations to collect and interpret information about them, especially when this information comes from different locations. It also limits their ability to identify the transformations required to address them effectively.[3] Giving a narrow focus to problems does not preclude change, but it does limit its scale, making it more likely that band-aid solutions are introduced instead of systemic transformations with the potential to alleviate or even to eliminate problems in the long term. Therefore, sense-making and the constant adaptation of frames, to take into consideration additional information as it becomes available, are essential to the success of actions undertaken to address global problems.[4]

Making Sense of Potential Actions and the Time Frame for Undertaking Them

The second challenge faced by global change organizations is determining what actions to undertake. Developing solutions to global problems involves examining all the potential actors and what they have the ability to do, but actions are actor-specific to the extent that they are rooted in organizational contexts and decision-making processes. Making sense of potential actions depends on the tools at the disposal of an organization, its position in the landscape and what it interprets as a viable solution to the targeted problem. Tools for action vary with the missions of organizations and the assets at their disposal. A corporation may be able to use its financial resources, its geographic scope and its innovation capabilities to develop market-based solutions that allow it to address a problem while at the same time generating enough revenues and profits to satisfy its shareholders. An NGO may have to use research, education, lobbying or even protests and direct actions to raise awareness about a problem and persuade others to act.

Regardless of the primary mission of an organization and the options available, deciding on a course of action is a challenge. For a car manufacturer aiming to produce emission-free vehicles, it may be a question of finding the right technology. For an NGO aiming to combat climate change, it may be a question of choosing which institutions to target and determining how to encourage them to act. In both instances, deciding on a course of action is a sense-making exercise whose outcome determines how the organization uses its time and resources.

Moreover, actions that address global problems do not need to be global. Because of globalization, legislation in one country can have an impact on economic activity in other countries. For instance, the decision of the State of California to implement more stringent regulations to reduce the fuel consumption of cars has affected the auto industry in other states and countries because California is an important market for car manufacturers. All around the world, car manufacturers have adapted their research and development efforts accordingly, and this has led to the availability of more fuel-efficient cars in most markets. Similarly, in their fight against genetically modified organisms, NGOs initially limited their actions to Europe, but because of the importance of international trade in the agricultural sector, the adoption of a moratorium on importing genetically modified food into Europe forced other countries, particularly in Africa, to comply with new regulations. It is clear that globalization now offers NGOs and corporations a wide range of alternatives to initiate the systemic transformations necessary to address global problems.

Whatever course of action is chosen by an organization, timing matters because it can make or break innovation (Griffith, 1999). Timing has to do with the potential openness to new solutions and to ideas that involve thinking outside the box. As Moulaert et al. (2013, p. 17) emphasize, social innovation 'takes place through windows of opportunity for social creativity along lines of life, lines of Imagination, lines of bringing in assets for a better future'. Events such as environmental disasters can provide opportunities for advancing a cause, as long as an organization is ready to act quickly. Other opportunities can emerge when concern about a focal issue increases as a result of political circumstances that make governments more attentive. This is also true at the global level where crises can create political opportunities for encouraging international institutions to put a problem on their agenda (Joachim, 2003).

Determining the actions needed to address global problems requires flexibility and adaptation, for each step in the sense-making process can elicit reactions and uncover new issues that were not initially seen. The complexity of global problems and the reluctance of human beings to change make the task of transforming international institutions a long-term endeavour. Solutions may seem too expensive. Vulnerabilities in the system may render small victories meaningless. Some solutions may even create new problems.[5] And because it is rare for global problems to be completely eradicated, there is almost always the question of what to do next to address them.

Creating the Conditions for Effectiveness

The third challenge concerns the conditions for effectiveness.[6] To be effective, organizations must be able to identify problems, develop viable solutions to them and undertake actions that can transform these solutions into systemic change. In light of the challenges presented above, this means creating an organizational context that fosters the development of numerous capabilities. An effective organization must be able to focus on the long term, to identify and make sense of cues signalling problems and to think creatively about potential solutions. It must also be able to navigate through divergent interests to mobilize actors from different horizons.

The conditions for effectiveness are intimately linked to the design, the structures, the processes and the practices of an organization. An organizational structure that encourages discussion and that gives members a distinct, stable sense of who they are and what they represent provides greater opportunities for bringing about global change (Weick, 1999). An effective organizational structure should also value the use of data, favour ways to make cues more visible, enable resilience in the face of interpretative interruptions and encourage interactions across the organization (Weick, 1999). The ultimate goal is to create an organization that embraces top-down and bottom-up processes of change to promote the most effective actions for addressing problems.

THE CASE OF GREENPEACE

To illustrate the crucial importance of the three challenges presented above, I shall revisit three episodes in the history of Greenpeace, an international NGO whose primary mission is to shape the future by actively promoting the idea of a greener planet. As a social movement and as an international NGO, Greenpeace has campaigned actively – and sometimes successfully – to bring about change related to a number of global issues. It has been an active voice on every issue from the proliferation of nuclear technologies to the protection of whales to climate change. Beginning in 1971 as a local protest movement against the nuclear testing conducted by the US Navy in Amchitka, Alaska, Greenpeace became a formal international organization in 1979. From there the organization slowly evolved into a key player in international politics. Indeed, it has been involved in the establishment of a number of international agreements, including the Moratorium on Commercial Whaling, the London Dumping Convention and the Convention on Biodiversity. Its explicit focus on global issues, its long-time commitment to global change and its successful track record on environmental protection make Greenpeace a prime example of a global change organization.

Although Greenpeace has been involved in raising awareness about global problems since its early days, this focus has not always been explicit. The three episodes that I present in this section highlight some of the challenges that Greenpeace has faced in its efforts to develop the organizational competencies necessary for bringing about global change. The first episode is connected to the organization's involvement in the issue of commercial whaling. It illustrates the challenge of making sense of global change. The second episode is connected to the shift in scale that occurred at Greenpeace in the late 1980s and the early 1990s. It illustrates the challenge of making sense of global problems. The third episode is connected to Greenpeace's quest to become a more effective 'global influence', an ongoing concern for the organization's leadership. It illustrates the importance of effectiveness.

Episode 1: Making Sense of Global Change

The first episode took place from 1974 to 1982 and resulted in the adoption of a ten-year moratorium on commercial whaling by the International Whaling Commission (IWC), the international organization founded in 1947 to establish quotas on the number of catches made by whalers. Participation in the IWC is on a voluntary basis so that only member countries are bound by its decisions. Greenpeace's role in changing the whaling regime has been recognized by a number of observers of the IWC. There are two fundamental ways in which the organization made a difference. First, it helped make the whale a symbol of environmental protection (Kalland, 1993). Second, it influenced the adoption of the moratorium on commercial whaling by encouraging new countries to join the IWC (Petersen, 1992; Skodvin and Andresen, 2003). Through this twofold contribution, it brought about global change. Yet the potential outcome of the actions undertaken was not obvious for Greenpeace leadership at the time that the events took place.

The moratorium on commercial whaling came into effect in 1982, but the depletion of whale stocks had been observed decades earlier. By the 1960s, it was already clear that stocks were depleting fast and that whaling posed a fundamental threat to the species (Petersen, 1992; Stoett, 1997). Yet taking action to protect the whales remained difficult. One key problem was that any IWC vote to change the whale protection regime had to obtain a three-quarters majority, and that there were still enough member countries opposed to the reduction of quotas to make it difficult to muster that level of support. Another key problem was that the general public was largely unaware of the issue. The first step taken by Greenpeace was to decide to tackle the issue. Given the interests of group members and the challenge of raising public awareness of an issue so distant from the everyday reality of the majority of citizens, the decision to tackle it was fraught with uncertainty (Weyler, 2004). Nevertheless, the group accepted the challenge and conducted its first anti-whaling intervention in 1975, when Greenpeace members went on an expedition off the coast of California to locate whalers. Spotting a group of Russian whalers, they positioned themselves in small inflatable boats between the whalers and their prey. The goal was to film their intervention and distribute the footage to the media so that the public could see the inhumanity of whaling first hand in the graphic images broadcast in television reports. The strategy proved highly successful, and other groups soon picked up on the issue and started protesting against governments that supported commercial whaling.

The dramatic tactic of chasing the whalers at sea led some observers to describe

Greenpeace as more effective at protecting the whales than the IWC itself (Mandel, 1980). Yet not enough member countries were mobilized to bring about effective change. Moreover, largely in favour of commercial whaling, Japan was working behind the scenes to ensure that there would be no change to the whaling regime, inviting new countries – including some that were landlocked – to join the IWC and vote against the moratorium on whaling in exchange for subsidies and foreign aid. This meant that Greenpeace had to continue looking for new strategies. After having attended the IWC as an observer for a few years, and following discussions with other NGOs, the idea of imitating Japan's strategy emerged (McTaggart, 2002). Using the same underhanded approach as Japan, Greenpeace and a few other NGOs spent two years convincing non-member countries to join the IWC and vote in favour of a moratorium, even going so far as to pay the membership fees for some of these countries.

Despite considerable disagreement within the organization about how to proceed, Greenpeace ultimately adopted this approach. For it to be successful, however, Greenpeace leadership had to find a way to leverage the organization's scope to maximize the impact. The solution was to shift from engaging in local action targeting individual countries like Japan and Norway to engaging in global action that focused on convincing IWC members with hesitations about the moratorium and bringing in new members already opposed to whaling. This change in strategy involved a complex process of negotiation and coordination. Indeed, many organizational members found it counterintuitive and were strongly opposed to it. Nevertheless, Greenpeace's direct involvement in IWC politics ultimately led to the adoption of the moratorium on commercial whaling.

Although protecting the whales is a relatively clear-cut issue, Greenpeace still struggled to bring about the type of change required to address it. Greenpeace's first successful battle to impact an international institution illustrates the challenges faced by organizations striving to effect systemic transformations. It also illustrates the role of sense-making and the value of organizing for global change. Over the course of its long campaign to protect the whales, Greenpeace had to shift its focus from raising public awareness about the issue to changing the norms and regulations that apply to the whaling industry internationally. In other words, Greenpeace leadership had to begin by making sense of the problem and by collecting evidence that could be shared with actors outside of the organization, so that they too could make sense of the problem. This was achieved through Greenpeace interventions at sea and through the protests that various affiliated groups organized in North America, Europe and Oceania. Greenpeace leadership then had to make sense of the international system that needed to be changed, the system overseen by the IWC, because raising awareness about the necessity of protecting the whales had not sufficed to bring about effective action to protect them. Greenpeace succeeded in making sense of this international system by participating in the IWC as an observer. This participation broadened the organization's overall understanding of what was at stake and allowed it to see why, despite strong opposition to commercial whaling worldwide, the IWC was unable to take the necessary measures to address the issue. Next, Greenpeace leadership had to develop an action plan to bring about change at the IWC. This required making sense of the political strategy adopted by Japan to further the interests of the whaling industry so that it could be turned against the whaling industry and used as a political strategy to protect the whales. Finally, Greenpeace leadership had to make sense of the numerous issues related to organizing effective actions to accomplish this goal.

Episode 2: The Shift in Scale

The second episode was connected to a shift in scale that occurred when Greenpeace stopped focusing on local problems in various specific countries and began to concentrate instead on what were described as 'real global problems'. Up until 1986, local Greenpeace groups determined the national priorities of the organization and there was limited focus on global issues. The turning point came with the bombing of the *Rainbow Warrior*, an event that put Greenpeace on the radar of charitable donors interested in supporting global causes (Dale, 1996; Zelco, 2013). The cost for Greenpeace was increased scrutiny, but this forced the organization to be more explicit about its focus on global problems. In October 1986, Greenpeace Chairman and International Executive Director David Fraser McTaggart wrote in a letter to board members and trustees that it was essential to distinguish between global problems and 'real' global problems.[7] By the latter, he meant problems like the greenhouse effect, the worldwide depletion of marine life and the long-term destruction of the stratospheric ozone layer. McTaggart's efforts culminated in the publication of the *Long-Term Plan* in 1988, which formalized the list of issues targeted by the organization.

The original intent of the shift in scale was to take advantage of Greenpeace's geographic scope and its global capabilities to redirect attention to the most important issues that the organization could impact, which also meant preventing affiliates from prioritizing problems that were primarily of interest to their local supporters.[8] Scaling up ambitions was not easy. Members disagreed about the global problems that needed to be addressed and about what could be realistically achieved given the organization's resources and expertise and the interests of specific affiliates. There were some epic internal battles, but the end result was a list of global problems and measures to address them that indicated to members who they were as an organization.

The shift in scale that occurred at Greenpeace during the 1980s was extremely important for the organization's future. It had an enduring impact on Greenpeace priorities because it involved identifying key issues that the organization continued to target during the next few decades. Again, it is important to stress that many members had strong hesitations about the shift in scale. While identifying 'real' global problems might appear an easy task, it took the organization almost two years to select the issues that it wanted to focus on. Moreover, many of the issues selected never became priorities. Some were debated for several years before Greenpeace acted on them. Others became priorities for the secretariat but not for members at other levels of the organization. This episode clearly indicates that when organizations endeavour to transform themselves, in order to address global issues more effectively, they have to ensure that the sense-making process is an inclusive exercise involving all those who will be impacted by the outcome of the change initiative.

Episode 3: The Search for Effectiveness

The third episode is connected to Greenpeace's efforts between 1992 and 1994 to become more effective. At the time, the organization was struggling to meet the objectives tied to its new priorities, the 'real' global problems that it had selected to target. Several Greenpeace affiliates were having difficulty convincing local supporters and donors to accept issues like climate change. Some affiliates were refusing to adopt the organization's new priorities and were continuing to focus on issues with more local appeal. The struggle led to a full-blown crisis when money started to fall short. Driven by a strong desire to have a global impact, most members embraced the higher aims of the organization, but there was little agreement about the means to achieve global change. To resolve this issue, members initiated discussions about how to be more effective as an organization. A consensus emerged that it was important to seize opportunities arising from unforeseen events and to draw on the work of all affiliates to determine what type of national and international interventions are effective in campaigns addressing global issues.[9] More than anything else, members stressed that Greenpeace had to be more inclusive in order to succeed as an organization. At the same time, everyone knew that this was easier said than done.

In the years that followed, Greenpeace launched the Programme of Reforms, a restructuring plan to make the organization more effective at influencing international institutions. The Programme built on previous discussions from the 1992–94 period and on Greenpeace's 1995 intervention against Shell's plan to dispose of the Brent Spar oil storage buoy in the North Sea, an intervention that brought Greenpeace back to the forefront in the struggle to protect the environment.[10] The restructuring gave a new role to the international secretariat. It now had the task of creating conditions that favoured the scaling up of the most successful local initiatives.[11] As a result of the organizational changes that began to be introduced in 1995, Greenpeace improved its capacity to create global change. For the 1995–2004 period, it reported 42 instances of global change, some in the practices of MNCs and others in those of international organizations, a sharp increase over the 1985–94 period for which the organization reported only seven successful attempts to bring about global change.[12] The success of the restructuring plan is supported by the data on membership and income, both of which rose until 1991, declined from 1991 to 1998 and then began to increase again in 1998. According to internal reports, these organizational changes also helped Greenpeace benefit from better public perception of its contribution to society, a key indicator of NGO performance (Mitchell and Stroup, 2017).

The various new structures, processes and practices that were adopted during these years cannot be discussed in detail here. However, it is important to emphasize that the 'new' Greenpeace encouraged all members to engage in action to address global problems, and that it promoted interactive communication between all organizational levels and locations to improve its ability to make sense of problems and to move quickly to seize opportunities. This involved making the organization more egalitarian in terms of listening to the diversity of member voices. At the same time, there was agreement about the need to promote a strong sense of organizational identity, a need that was encapsulated in the unifying phrase 'one Greenpeace'. Focusing on global problems, while remaining open to the possible viability of various solutions, was central to this organizational identity. Everyone belonged to one and the same organization, but members were offered more flexibility in order to encourage creativity in the search for solutions.

Although these changes improved the capability of Greenpeace to leverage its geographic scope to address global problems, the question of effectiveness remains an ongoing concern for the organization's leaders. The strategy for improving effectiveness reflected the geopolitical context of the 1990s and the organizational tools that were then available. Nevertheless, there is a consensus among past and current Greenpeace leaders that the problem of organizational effectiveness can never be fully resolved. Today there is more concern with establishing external connections than with issues related to internal organization. Greenpeace is seeking to build stronger alliances with other groups, it is promoting the values of inclusiveness and diversity, and it is providing training in methods and techniques for taking effective action to help others develop the skills to launch their own initiatives for global change.

RESEARCH AGENDA

In the early 1990s scholars anticipated that global change would accelerate exponentially both as an international social phenomenon and as a new field of academic research. Cooperrider and Pasmore (1991, p. 1037) went so far as to predict that 'the 1990s [would] be known as the decade of global social innovation'. History suggests that they were wrong, for problems such as poverty, famine and global warming continue to be prime concerns not only for global change organizations but also for academic researchers (Buckley et al., 2018; Howard-Grenville et al., 2014). In this chapter, I have presented some of the challenges faced by global change organizations and I have argued for the need to examine how they can improve their ability to identify and make sense of global problems, how they can determine the best action plan for addressing them, and how they can structure their activities more effectively to bring about systemic transformations of international practices and institutions.

Greenpeace has been used to illustrate the challenges faced by global change organizations, but this in no way implies that the systemic transformations required to address global problems would be possible without the participation of multiple actors (Ansari et al., 2013; Ferraro et al., 2015). Global social innovation must be inclusive, although it is important to stress that this inclusiveness can have different forms. For instance, it may be the case that providing greater access to information would help solve many global problems. Almost 50 percent of the world's population does not have access to the Internet, and this leads to social exclusion. At the same time, some populations have been economically excluded from globalization and simply do not have the necessary resources to access modern telecommunications technologies. Thus, making sense of global problems related to social and/or economic exclusion is not only a matter of identifying who needs to be targeted, it also requires developing adequate interpretations of the causes of this exclusion. Organizing for global change is directly related to inclusiveness because depending on how activities are organized, they can either include or exclude the persons most affected by the change. To be inclusive, global change organizations must ask difficult questions about whom to target and about whom to include in their interventions. Most importantly, they must adopt strategies to address global problems in ways that include those who are directly confronted by them. A starting point, both for practitioners in the field and for academic researchers, is to map the systems that need to be transformed and to identify the actors and the processes involved as well as the systemic impediments that are preventing change from occurring.[13]

This chapter has focused on the general theme of organizing for global change. Because non-profit and for-profit organizations both function as social systems, their approaches to organizing for global change share important similarities. Yet the triggers for focusing on specific global problems are often different at non-profit and for-profit organizations, and these two types of organization do not always promote the same kinds of innovation. Below I provide a research agenda that takes into account the challenges discussed above as well as the specific characteristics of each type of organization.

NGOs and Organizing for Global Change

Unbeholden to shareholders, NGOs have explicit goals, their unique mission being to bring about the changes necessary to achieve these goals. This makes them one of the most common types of global change organizations. However, even for international NGOs, a focus on global issues may be difficult to maintain (Bansal et al., 2018; Tarrow and McAdam, 2005). Research on NGOs has focused on the most conspicuous aspects of their actions and interventions instead of on the link between their structures and their effectiveness (Lambell et al., 2008; Teegen et al., 2004). More research needs to be done on this link. Since NGOs have ambitious goals, but limited resources, they must use these resources creatively in order to be successful, and this makes them highly interesting as organizations. To understand how NGOs function, researchers should begin by examining their internal sense-making processes. How they make sense of problems and adapt their interpretive frames and their actions to those of other organizations and stakeholders may be directly related to their valorization of inclusiveness.

How a focus on global problems can be shared across an organization to mobilize action and encourage the search for creative solutions is another important theme for research. Indeed, this theme is particularly relevant because conflicts about means and ends are common at NGOs. Given that the fundamental allegiance of their members is to the cause, not to the organization (Pache and Santos, 2010), conventional mechanisms of control like centralizing decision-making or formalizing procedures for decision-making are unlikely to work well at NGOs. Creating shared goals and shared values may be a way to overcome this challenge, assuming that organizational members can agree on what those goals and values should be. Research on improving the capability of NGOs to leverage their scope would provide valuable insights into organizing for global change.

Finally, NGOs often struggle to measure impact. The latter can be measured through tangible changes like the adoption of international agreements, but such events are relatively rare. Moreover, even when agreements can be reached, they do not necessarily lead to systemic transformation. Because impact is difficult to measure, NGOs often base their measure of it on a perception of effectiveness rather than on tangible outcomes (Mitchell and Stroup, 2017). This is another issue that deserves attention from researchers. Indeed, exploring new ways to measure the impact of the actions and interventions of NGOs would be relevant both from a theoretical and from a practical standpoint.

Corporations and Organizing for Global Change

Corporations are important drivers of innovation, and they can play a prominent role in bringing about systemic transformation. For example, Tesla has succeeded in making electric cars a realistic alternative to cars with internal combustion engines. Together with its Solar City venture, which pairs the energy sourcing power of houses and cars to create an integrated system of energy production and consumption, Tesla's innovation in the auto sector gives it the potential to generate the kind of systemic transformation that could have a sustainable impact on climate change. While such innovations are at the forefront of global change, their success depends on inclusiveness, for the latter is a necessary condition for effective global change. For Tesla, inclusiveness meant sharing some of its technologies with other car manufacturers so that they could embrace similar objectives. But inclusiveness is not only about creating and sharing new technologies, it is also about improving the lives of the four billion human beings who find themselves at the so-called 'bottom of the pyramid'. Ensuring that these human beings reap some of the benefits of global change is a necessary path for the future growth of corporations because these human beings live in the regions of the world undergoing the greatest population growth. In other words, favouring inclusive global change is a way for corporations to ensure that they have future markets for their products and services.

There are wide-ranging possibilities for research on the role that corporations can play in bringing about global change. In addition to examining issues that corporations share with NGOs, such as the challenge of motivating people to commit to their goals and the complexity of scaling up the most promising ideas, questions can also be raised about the connection between the for-profit mission of corporations and their potential to bring about global change. Corporations may aim to have a global impact, but the constraints imposed by the necessity to seek profits may create tensions between business goals and the aspiration to become a catalyst for systemic transformation. Given that global change can wreak havoc on decades-old business models, corporations may have hesitations about launching innovations that could hurt the bottom line. Some are better than others at managing the tensions between profitability and long-term change for the good. Researchers need to provide more accounts of corporations that have succeeded in finding creative solutions to these tensions and allowed global change to become part of their business model.

The role of inclusiveness in corporate efforts to bring about global change is another issue that deserves attention from researchers. Internally, inclusiveness means giving more weight to less powerful voices without deep historical roots in the organization so that they can join the conversation and play a more prominent role in making sense of problems and developing solutions. Some research has started to focus on how such actors can obtain the attention of corporate headquarters (see, for example, Bouquet and Birkinshaw, 2008a, 2008b) and on the processes involved in directing the attention of corporations to global issues (see, for example, Bouquet and Birkinshaw, 2011; Bouquet et al., 2009). Recently, some corporations have actively sought to change the balance of power so that more weight can be given to the specific views and interests of corporate locations that have traditionally had little visibility. However, it is important not to conflate the promotion of increased visibility with the effort to create the conditions for real inclusiveness. The latter entails inviting actors who were previously excluded to begin participating in sense-making and decision-making. But how do corporations manage the additional information that these voices bring to strategic discussions? How do they resolve the conflicts that can emerge from the consideration of a diversity of viewpoints and interests? By addressing these and other questions, researchers would shed new light on the challenges faced by corporations when they attempt to create global change and on ways for them to cope with these challenges.

Finally, corporations do not have to focus on global issues in order to help bring about systemic transformation at the global level. Initiatives such as ensuring that remote areas of wealthy nations like Canada and the US have the telecommunications infrastructure to stay connected to what is happening in the world are also part of organizing for global change. Focusing on local problems is a way for corporations to promote the inclusiveness that is necessary to address global problems. For instance, some of IBM's clients are among the biggest firms on the planet, and its focus on break-through innovations has involved launching a number of initiatives that draw on artificial intelligence and block-chain technologies to help address global issues related to health and poverty. Yet IBM also addresses local issues like increasing the yield of farmland in India and helping the Indian government establish a goods and services taxation system. The underlying logic is that local and/or national initiatives are necessary to address global problems. But how can corporations encourage such initiatives without losing sight of the bigger picture? And how do they determine which ones will have the greatest global impact? In short, researchers need to examine the interplay between the local and the global objectives of corporations to improve our understanding of its impact on the contribution of corporations to global change.

Interactions Between Categories of Actors and Organizations

Global change requires a great amount of cooperation, especially at the international and the interorganizational levels (Bilimoria et al., 1995). Making sense of potential solutions to global problems is above all an interactive process involving actors with different and sometimes conflicting agendas (Gray et al., 2015). In these interactions, every actor has a role to play. The media can diffuse information about the nature of a global problem and its gravity (Waisbord, 2015) that creates a narrative shaping the worldwide search for potential solutions. International organizations can adopt new agreements and find innovative ways to ensure that they are successfully implemented. Through legislation, governments can introduce solutions to global problems nationally. Corporations can propose market-based innovations that have a global impact. There is no doubt that the multiplicity of actors and possible interactions between them deserves the attention of researchers interested in global change.

When corporations, governments and NGOs collaborate on global change projects, they are confronted by numerous challenges. A burgeoning literature is focusing on ways to ensure that such collaboration succeeds in overcoming these challenges (see, for example, Dahan et al., 2010; Kourula and Laasonen, 2010). From a sense-making perspective, however, many questions remain: When should organizations partner? When should they seek allies? Whom should they choose to work with? How should they approach potential partners and allies? These are all important questions because collaboration has an impact on how organizations conceptualize global problems and potential courses of action to address them. In terms of capability, some organizations are better at building partnerships and alliances than others, and this has an impact on their effectiveness. Researchers need to determine what makes these organizations different from other ones. Most importantly, they need to identify the specific capabilities required to make interorganizational collaboration a powerful tool for global change.

Cooperrider and Dutton (1999, pp. 20–1) emphasize that interactions between categories of actors can lead to new organizational arrangements: 'whether termed strategic bridging institutions, social movement organizations, public–private partnerships, regimes, networks, referent organizations, or locally-globally linked NGOs, virtually all involve organizational arrangements that use resources and/or governance structures from more than one existing organization'. Many recent initiatives to address climate change or to alleviate poverty offer examples of hybrid forms of organization (Battilana and Dorado, 2010; Jay, 2013). This suggests that researchers should pay more attention to alternative ways of organizing for global change. Among other issues, they should examine the effectiveness of temporary organizations, the organizational benefits of Internet platforms, and the norms and rules for collaborative action involving a multiplicity of organizations (Bowen et al., 2018).

Finally, we should not dismiss the role that confrontation plays in bringing about global change. Activism that favours confrontation can involve the vilification of actors who are resisting global change, which can sometimes have a beneficial impact (Reinecke and Ansari, 2015). It can lead to the emergence of new organizational forms (Rao et al., 2000) and to the success or failure of radical innovations (Rao, 2009). But when should organizations adopt confrontational strategies instead of a more diplomatic approach to change? How can they determine whether or not confrontation will be effective? And once they have opted for a confrontational intervention, how should they prepare for it? These are all questions that deserve further research.

NOTES

1. According to Cooperrider and Dutton (1999), labour unions, human rights organizations and socio-political movements for independence were all predecessors of global change organizations.
2. It is important to recognize that although norms and rules can be formal, international regulations are often considered soft because they depend on the willingness of states to comply with them.
3. For example, if an organization identifies whaling as the cause of the depletion of whale stocks, it is likely to target the International Whaling Commission (IWC), the organization that establishes the worldwide quotas for whaling. On the other hand, if it identifies the pollution of the oceans as the cause of the problem, it is likely to undertake actions that focus on reducing this pollution. In the latter case, the identification of the structures that need to be changed and the actions that should be undertaken are more complex because they require a closer examination of the sources of this pollution.
4. To change the bigger picture, an organization has to make a shift in scale (Tarrow and McAdam, 2005, p. 123). This shift then has to be shared across the organization in order for the latter to go from scaling out to scaling up (Westley et al., 2014). Still, making sense of problems is not just about interpreting the problems themselves. It also involves determining which ones should be focused on given the organization's past commitments, its current engagements, and its resources and capabilities. In addition, an organization has to determine what it can realistically achieve.
5. For instance, the exploitation of workers in some African diamond mines, where the diamonds are often referred to as 'blood diamonds', is partly caused by the demand for these precious stones. Yet prohibiting the purchase of diamonds from these regions is a false solution because part of the problem is poverty. If buyers stop acquiring diamonds, the workers may end up in a worse situation. To address the problem adequately, there is a need to analyse the value chain, to educate customers and to implement mechanisms to track the process leading from the extraction of the diamonds to their purchase. This is a good example of how making sense of global problems involves making sense of local problems and their connection to the broader system.
6. While effectiveness is a somewhat loose concept for the analysis of global change organizations, I argue that to be effective, global change organizations must be able to modify and adapt structures and systems at various levels repeatedly.
7. Source: Letter from David McTaggart to the board members and trustees, Greenpeace International (Amsterdam) Archives, Folder 209, International Institute of Social History, Amsterdam, Netherlands.

8. Source: Stitching Greenpeace Council annual general meeting, minutes 1986, p. 22, Greenpeace International (Amsterdam) Archives, Folder 209, International Institute of Social History, Amsterdam, Netherlands.
9. Source: Stitching Greenpeace Council annual general meeting, minutes 1993, pp. 19–20, Greenpeace International (Amsterdam) Archives, Folder 237, International Institute of Social History, Amsterdam, Netherlands.
10. The Brent Spar campaign was a joint initiative between the Greenpeace regional offices in Germany, the Netherlands and the UK. It was largely an unexpected success for Greenpeace, and it tried to learn from the experience. In the years that followed, it promoted the development of locally driven initiatives that could be 'scaled up' internationally.
11. Source: Stitching Greenpeace Council annual general meeting, minutes 1998, p. 16, Greenpeace International (Amsterdam) Archives, Folder 245, International Institute of Social History, Amsterdam, Netherlands.
12. During the 1995–2004 period, Greenpeace continued to target intergovernmental organizations, but it also began to target MNCs. Nevertheless, the focus remained on intergovernmental organizations. Greenpeace reports that during the 1985–94 period it was involved in the creation of six international agreements, but that in the 1995–2004 period it was involved in the creation of 23.
13. For example, whenever Greenpeace tackles an issue, it creates a map identifying all the activities and practices connected to the issue and all the potential stakeholders. For whaling, this map included consumers (for example, the military organizations that use whale oil to lubricate cannons and the members of the general public who eat whale meat), workers in the whaling industry and countries with a stake in the industry. To transform the system, Greenpeace started by focusing on changing laws to make the international trade in whale meat illegal. This isolated Japan because once the new laws were in effect, only the Japanese fleets could capture the whales to be sold on the Japanese markets. Thus, by breaking the system, Greenpeace allowed a new system to emerge.

REFERENCES

Ansari, S., Wijen, F. and Gray, B. (2013), 'Constructing a climate change logic: an institutional perspective on the "Tragedy of the Commons"', *Organization Science*, **24**(4), 1014–40.

Bansal, P., Kim, A. and Wood, M. (2018), 'Hidden in plain sight: the importance of scale on organizations' attention to issues', *Academy of Management Review*, **43**(2), 217–41.

Battilana, J. and Dorado, S. (2010), 'Building sustainable hybrid organizations: the case of commercial microfinance organizations', *Academy of Management Journal*, **53**(6), 1419–40.

Bilimoria, D., Cooperrider, D.L., Kaczmarski, K., Khalsa, G., Srivastva, S. and Upadhayaya, P. (1995), 'The organization dimensions of global change: no limits to cooperation', *Journal of Management Inquiry*, **4**(1), 71–90.

Bouquet, C. and Birkinshaw, J. (2008a), 'Managing power in the multinational corporation: how low-power actors gain influence', *Journal of Management*, **34**(3), 477–508.

Bouquet, C. and Birkinshaw, J. (2008b), 'Weight versus voice: how foreign subsidiaries gain attention from corporate headquarters', *Academy of Management Journal*, **51**(3), 577–601.

Bouquet, C. and Birkinshaw, J. (2011), 'How global strategies emerge: an attention perspective', *Global Strategy Journal*, **1**(3–4), 243–62.

Bouquet, C., Morrison, A.J. and Birkinshaw, J.M. (2009), 'International attention and multinational enterprise performance', *Journal of International Business Studies*, **40**(1), 108–31.

Bowen, F.E., Bansal, P. and Slawinski, N. (2018), 'The scale of environmental issues in corporate collective actions', *Strategic Management Journal*, **39**, 1411–36.

Buckley, P.J., Doh, J.P. and Benischke, M.H. (2018), 'Towards a renaissance in international business research? Big questions, grand challenges, and the future of IB scholarship', *Journal of International Business Studies*, **48**(9), 1045–64.

Cooperrider, D.L. and Dutton, J.E. (1999), 'No limits to cooperation: an introduction to the organizational dimensions of global change', in D.L. Cooperrider and J.E. Dutton (eds), *Organizational Dimensions of Global Change: No Limits to Cooperation*, Thousand Oaks, CA: Sage, pp. 1–36.

Cooperrider, D.L. and Pasmore, W.A. (1991), 'Global social change: a new agenda for social science?', *Human Relations*, **44**(10), 1037–55.

Cornelissen, J.P. and Werner, M.D. (2014), 'Putting framing in perspective: a review of framing and frame analysis across the management and organizational literature', *Academy of Management Annals*, **8**(1), 181–235.

Dahan, N.M., Doh, J.P. and Yaziji, M. (2010), 'Corporate-NGO collaboration: co-creating new business models for developing markets', *Long Range Planning*, **43**(2–3), 326–42.
Dale, S. (1996), *McLuhan's Children: The Greenpeace Message and the Media*, Toronto: Between the Lines.
Duffield, J. (2007), 'What are international institutions?', *International Studies Review*, **9**(1), 1–22.
Eden, L. and Lenway, S. (2001), 'Introduction to the symposium: the Janus face of globalization', *Journal of International Business Studies*, **32**(3), 383–400.
Ferraro, F., Etzion, D. and Gehman, J. (2015), 'Tackling grand challenges pragmatically: robust action revisited', *Organization Studies*, **36**(3), 363–90.
Gibson, C.C., Ostrom, E. and Ahn, T.K. (2000), 'The concept of scale and the human dimensions of global change: a survey', *Ecological Economics*, **32**, 217–39.
Goffman, E. (1974), *Frame Analysis: An Essay on the Organization of Experience*, London: Harper & Row.
Gray, B., Purdy, J.M. and Ansari, S. (2015), 'From interactions to institutions: microprocesses of framing and mechanisms for the structuring of institutional fields', *Academy of Management Review*, **40**(1), 115–43.
Griffith, T.L. (1999), 'Technology features as triggers for sensemaking', *Academy of Management Review*, **24**(3), 472–88.
Haas, P.M. (1992), 'Banning chlorofluorocarbons: epistemic community efforts to protect stratospheric ozone', *International Organization*, **46**(1), 187–224.
Howard-Grenville, J.A., Buckle, S.J., Hoskins, B.J. and George, G. (2014), 'Climate change and management', *Academy of Management Journal*, **57**(3), 615–23.
Jay, J. (2013), 'Navigating paradox as a mechanism of change and innovation in hybrid organizations', *Academy of Management Journal*, **56**(1), 137–59.
Joachim, J. (2003), 'Framing issues and seizing opportunities: the UN, NGOs, and women's rights', *International Studies Quarterly*, **47**, 247–74.
Kalland, A. (1993), 'Management by totemization: whale symbolism and the anti-whaling campaign', *Arctic*, **46**(2), 124–33.
King, B.G., Felin, T. and Whetten, D.A. (2010), 'Finding the organization in organizational theory: a meta-theory of the organization as a social actor', *Organization Science*, **21**(1), 290–305.
Koremenos, B., Lipson, C. and Snidal, D. (2001), 'The rational design of international institutions', *International Organization*, **55**, 761–99.
Kourula, A. and Laasonen, S. (2010), 'Nongovernmental organizations in business and society, management, and international business research: review and implications from 1998 to 2007', *Business & Society*, **49**(1), 35–67.
Kudesia, R.S. (2017), 'Organizational sensemaking', in *Oxford Research Encyclopedia of Psychology*, Oxford: Oxford University Press, pp. 1–47.
Lambell, R., Ramia, G., Nyland, C. and Michelotti, M. (2008), 'NGOs and international business research: progress, prospects and problems', *International Journal of Management Reviews*, **10**(1), 75–92.
Mandel, R. (1980), 'Transnational resource conflict: the politics of whaling', *International Studies Quarterly*, **24**(1), 99–127.
March, J.G. and Olsen, J.P. (1998), 'The institutional dynamics of international political orders', *International Organization*, **52**(4), 943–69.
McTaggart, D.F. (2002), *Shadow Warrior: The Autobiography of Greenpeace International Founder David McTaggart*, London: Orion.
Micelotta, E., Lounsbury, M. and Greenwood, R. (2017), 'Pathways of institutional change: an integrative review and research agenda', *Journal of Management*, **43**(6), 1885–910.
Mitchell, G.E. and Stroup, S.S. (2017), 'The reputation of NGOs: peer evaluations of effectiveness', *Review of International Organizations*, **12**(3), 397–419.
Moulaert, F., MacCallum, D. and Hillier, J. (2013), 'Social innovation: intuition, precept, concept, theory and practice', in M. Frank (ed.), *The International Handbook on Social Innovation: Collective Action, Social Learning and Transdisciplinary Research*, Cheltenham, UK and Northampton, MA, USA: Edward Elgar Publishing, pp. 13–24.
Ocasio, W. (1997), 'Towards an attention-based view of the firm', *Strategic Management Journal*, **18**(Summer Special Issue), 187–206.
Pache, A.-C. and Santos, F. (2010), 'When worlds collide: the internal dynamics of organizational responses to conflicting institutional demands', *Academy of Management Review*, **35**(3), 455–76.
Petersen, M.J. (1992), 'Whalers, cetologists, environmentalists, and the international management of whaling', *International Organization*, **46**(1), 147–86.
Putnam, R.D. (1988), 'Diplomacy and domestic politics: the logic of two-level games', *International Organization*, **42**(3), 427–60.
Rao, H. (2009), *Market Rebels: How Activists Make or Break Radical Innovations*, Princeton, NJ: Princeton University Press.
Rao, H., Morrill, M. and Zald, M.N. (2000), 'Power plays: how social movements and collective actions create new organizational forms', *Research in Organizational Behavior*, **22**, 239–82.

Reinecke, J. and Ansari, S. (2015), 'Taming wicked problems: the role of framing in the construction of corporate social responsibility', *Journal of Management Studies*, **53**(3), 299–329.
Sandberg, J. and Tsoukas, H. (2015), 'Making sense of the sensemaking perspective: its constituents, limitations, and opportunities for further development', *Journal of Organizational Behavior*, **36**(S1), S6–S32.
Skodvin, T. and Andresen, S. (2003), 'Nonstate influence in the International Whaling Commission, 1970–1990', *Global Environmental Politics*, **3**(4), 61–86.
Stoett, P.J. (1997), *The International Politics of Whaling,* Vancouver: University of British Columbia Press.
Tarrow, S. and McAdam, D. (2005), 'Scale shift in transnational contention', in Della Porta and S. Tarrow (eds), *Transnational Protest and Global Activism*, Lanham, MD: Rowman and Littlefield, pp. 121–47.
Teegen, H., Doh, J.P. and Vachani, S. (2004), 'The importance of nongovernmental organizations (NGOs) in global governance and value creation: an international business research agenda', *Journal of International Business Studies*, **35**(6), 463–83.
Waisbord, S. (2015), 'Three challenges for communication and global social change', *Communication Theory*, **25**(2), 144–65.
Weick, K.E. (1984), 'Small wins: redefining the scale of social problems', *American Psychologist*, **39**(1), 40–9.
Weick, K.E. (1999), 'Sensemaking as an organizational dimension of global change', in D.L. Cooperrider and J.E. Dutton (eds), *Organizational Dimensions of Global Change*, Thousand Oaks, CA: Sage, pp. 39–56.
Weick, K.E. and Van Orden, P.W. (1990), 'Organizing on a global scale: a research and teaching agenda', *Human Resource Management*, **29**(1), 49–61.
Westley, F., Olsson, P., Folke, C. et al. (2011), 'Tipping toward sustainability: emerging pathways of transformation', *Ambio*, **40**(7), 762–80.
Westley, F., Antadze, N., Riddell, D.J., Robinson, K. and Geobey, S. (2014), 'Five configurations for scaling up social innovation: case examples of nonprofit organizations from Canada', *Journal of Applied Behavioral Science*, **50**(3), 234–60.
Weyler, R. (2004), *Greenpeace: An Insider's Account,* Richmond, BC: Raincoast Book Distribution.
Young, O.R. (1982), 'Regime dynamics: the rise and fall of international regimes', *International Organization*, **36**(2), 277–97.
Zelco, F. (2013), *Make it a Green Peace: The Rise of Countercultural Environmentalism*, New York: Oxford University Press.

PART VI

NETWORKS AND SOCIAL CHANGE

24. Collaborative governance

Ann Florini

Three strands of social innovation are converging into a new way for societies to govern themselves and for the world as a whole to cope with transnational challenges: cross-sector collaborations across governments, businesses, and civil society groups. This "collaborative governance" goes beyond the traditional governmental hierarchies and market-based approaches. It has become a key social innovation intended to address problems ranging from infrastructure to poverty, hunger, financial instability, and climate change.

The three sets of practices that are giving rise to this innovation in governance come from different but increasingly overlapping realms:

- Public management and administration, once purely the province of government, is becoming an arena of "shared discretion" (Donahue and Zeckhauser, 2011). National and local governments are collaborating with relevant private sector and civil society actors in local and national problem-solving, and the public administration literature is exploring the conditions under which collaborations arise and how they function.
- Over the past two decades, pushed in part by privatization of what had been governmental responsibilities and partly by growing societal expectations of business behavior, corporate social responsibility (CSR) has transformed from corporate philanthropy into a deep reconsideration of the roles of business in providing public goods and self-regulating (Zadek, 2001, 2004). As businesses navigate this unfamiliar terrain, they find themselves drawn into partnerships with civil society organizations and governments. The business management literature, particularly in such journals as the *Journal of Business Ethics*, has investigated the roles that business actors play in partnerships, as well as the conditions under which private firms benefit from such participation.
- International relations in both theory and practice has expanded beyond government-to-government interactions to encompass a plethora of multi-stakeholder collaborations (Khagram, 2006). These collaborations build on the growing global "webs" of interconnection among actors from all sectors to complement the "chessboard" of traditional inter-governmental ties (Slaughter, 2017).

Such cross-sector collaboration to address social challenges began having significant impacts in the 1980s. It has grown substantially since then, attracting the attention of scholars and policymakers alike. Now, it is seen as essential to achievement of global goals, as prominently encapsulated in such major international agreements as the 2015 Sustainable Development Goals and the 2015 Paris climate change accords, both of which explicitly emphasize cross-sector partnership (Florini and Florini, 2017). As Ansell and Gash (2017, p. 17) explain, "In the past, governments, international organizations, local communities, and foundations have often turned to collaborative governance as a last resort when other strategies have failed. More recently, they have begun to envision collaborative governance as a more proactive policy instrument on a grander scale."

This chapter explores this rapidly growing phenomenon: what is meant by collaborative governance, why it is happening, and the state of scholarship on the topic. It finds that considerable progress has been made in understanding when and why collaborative approaches emerge and how they function, but that much remains to be done in evaluating the impact of collaborative governance efforts. It ends with a call for a scaled-up research agenda in keeping with the scale, promise, and potential pitfalls of this major social innovation.

DEFINING GOVERNANCE

To understand collaborative governance, we start by defining the second half of the term. Governance is not equivalent to "what governments do." But what exactly is it?

The *Oxford Handbook of Governance* has fun with the definition:

> Governance is said to be many things, including a buzzword, a fad, a framing device, a bridging concept, an umbrella concept, a descriptive concept, a slippery concept, an empty signifier, a weasel word, a fetish, a field, an approach, a theory and a perspective. (Levi-Faur, 2012, p. 3)

But editor David Levi-Faur then gets serious about tracing the complex history of this complex concept. He makes note of two points particularly relevant to the collaborative governance discussion: the standard description of "modes" of governance distinguishing between hierarchy, markets, and networks as means of control and organization (p. 5) and the argument that authority is increasingly shifting in how it is institutionalized: "upward (to the regional, transnational, intergovernmental, and global), downward (to the local, regional, and the metropolitan) and horizontally (to private and civil spheres of authority)" (p. 6). All this points to governance as something done by many actors in addition to governments, and by various means beyond governmental hierarchies of control. But what is it that those actors actually do when they are governing?

One common, and useful, way to define governance is to draw on collective action theory and the theory of public goods. In this way of thinking, governance comprises all the various ways in which groups of people set and enforce rules needed to enable that group to achieve desired outcomes (Florini and Sovacool, 2009). Those rules are necessary for two reasons that make it impossible for groups to rely solely on the "invisible hand" of market forces to supply all that society demands.

First is the "public goods" problem (Samuelson, 1954). Markets are extraordinarily good at producing many goods and services that people want, but they fail when the incentives of producers and consumers do not align. For such goods and services as effective protection of property rights, provision of basic education for all, or national defense, no producer has an adequate incentive to produce. This is because once the goods or services exist, everyone can free-ride, consuming them without paying directly for them. I benefit from my country's national defense and rule of law systems even if I avoid contributing my share of the taxes that pay for them. That leaves dutiful taxpayers resentful and looking for their own ways to free-ride. The technical term for such goods and services is "public goods": products and services that are non-excludable (once they exist, no consumer can be excluded from consuming them) and non-rival in consumption (no one's consumption interferes with the ability of other consumers to consume them) (Hardin, 1982; Olson, 1965; Ostrom, 1990, 1992). Governance is required to ensure their production, either coercively (such as governmental imposition of taxes with effective enforcement) or via agreements that participants are willing to honor.

Governance to provide public goods requires multiple steps for collective action to overcome the free-rider problem: agreement on what goods or services are to be produced – the agenda; negotiation of rules about how to get the public goods provided and who will pay; implementation of the rules, and systems for monitoring and enforcement of the rules. Every step of collective action has significant challenges that, as we shall see below, apply equally if not more so when governance occurs via cross-sector collaboration.

Notably, the agenda for what should count as a public good, as opposed to a private good that market forces should provide, is frequently and often bitterly contested. Water provision is a good example: water consumption is both excludable and rival in consumption, so many argue that it should be supplied by markets rather than governments. But when markets fail to do so, it is often because the underlying systems needed to supply water at scale have elements of public goods, such as the need to provide water to people too poor to pay market rates. The United Nations' Sustainable Development Goals call for cross-sector collaboration in large part because the goals have this mixed quality for which both public and private sectors could logically contribute.

Second, governance is also needed to address the externalities inherent in the activities of business and society. Externalities are simply incidental, unintended consequences and can be either negative or positive. When negative, such as pollution, governance is needed to stop the generator of that negative externality from producing it. When positive, governance may be desired to ensure that it continues to be produced. Governance to address externalities can take the form of government regulation (rules that threaten punishment if a factory continues to pollute). But governance to manage externalities can also occur via voluntary agreements among firms to refrain from using cheaper production processes that generate negative externalities, such as human trafficking that emerges in a supply chain labor force in response to cost-cutting pressures. Because the private sector is rarely well set up to create and enforce such standards on its own, frequently such arrangements are negotiated between businesses and civil society groups to set standards for business practices.

DEFINING COLLABORATIVE GOVERNANCE

With governance defined as provision of public goods and management of externalities, we can move on to the collaborative element. Not all interactions across government, business, and civil society add up to collaborative governance. Other types of interactions include philanthropic, adversarial, or purely contractual arrangements in which all decision-making authority remains in the hands of one party. The focus in this chapter, in contrast, is on "problem-solving" partnerships in which decision-making authority is significantly shared across the collaborators from different sectors: what Donahue and Zeckhauser (2011) refer to as "shared discretion."

Collaborative governance thus refers to governance that may or may not involve government, but specifies deliberate sharing of authority among actors from at least two of the three sectors. It is thus narrower than the broad field of governance. Notably, the collaborative governance literature in all three fields – public administration, management theory, and international relations – adopts similar definitions of each sector, implicitly or explicitly. The public sector is government, usually focused on the executive branch. The private sector is generally assumed to be the Western publicly traded corporation with diffuse ownership, with little attention to other modes of for-profit activity such as the family-owned business or state-owned enterprises. Civil society could mean anything from trade unions to religious groups, but attention generally focuses on legally registered non-governmental organizations (NGOs).

Some of the public administration literature initially kept government in the driver's seat. Ansell and Gash (2008, p. 544), for example, distinguish collaborative governance from the more familiar adversarial or managerial forms of government-led governance. But they still see government as driving the process: "a governing arrangement where one or more public agencies directly engage non-state stakeholders in a collective decision-making process that is formal, consensus-oriented, and deliberative and that aims to make or implement public policy or manage public programs or assets" (Ansell and Gash, 2008, p. 547). Similarly, Donahue and Zeckhauser (2011, p. 4) define it as "carefully structured arrangements that interweave public and private capabilities on terms of *shared discretion*" (italics in original) to serve as a force multiplier for government efforts.

But other public administration scholars have not seen a need to limit the purview to government-driven collaborations. In an article that helped to define the field a decade ago, Bryson et al. (2006, p. 44) define cross-sector collaboration as "*the linking or sharing of information, resources, activities, and capabilities by organizations in two or more sectors to achieve jointly an outcome that could not be achieved by organizations in one sector separately*" (italics in original). They note that the purpose of such collaboration is the creation of public value in circumstances where a single sector has already failed or is likely to fail to create such value – in other words, governance beyond government.

And unsurprisingly, the literature from the international relations and global governance fields, where no single government is in charge, is less prone to put government first in collaborative governance. As globalization integrated the world more rapidly and deeply than existing inter-governmental structures could manage, international relations scholars developed a deep interest in non-governmental governance (Rosenau and Czempiel, 1992).

"Global governance" is the term for efforts to manage or solve border-spanning problems. Most of humanity's major challenges, from climate change to financial instability, inherently require decision-making that crosses national boundaries – not something that territorially based nation states, jealous of their sovereign prerogatives, are well set up to do. One means is via inter-governmental treaties (often a slow and painstaking process). Another is delegation to inter-governmental organizations such as the United Nations (UN) (which is so starved of resources and independent authority that its capacity for action is extremely limited).

Given the notable lack of success of such methods of governing the world, international relations and global governance scholars have been turning their attention to the growing importance of "non-state" actors – that is, all the private firms and civil society groups that populate the governance scene with real influence on how governance happens. NGOs push issues onto the global agenda, monitor the behavior of countries and businesses, and may even participate directly in official negotiations (Florini, 2003 [2005]). Global governance merges into collaborative governance as state and non-state actors increasingly work directly together in a bewildering array of partnerships (Waddell and Khagram, 2007). The business sector sometimes makes its own rules to regulate its own activities (Braithwaite and Drahos, 2000; Cutler et al., 1999; Haufler, 2001). The business management literature mostly addresses the conditions under which businesses benefit, in standard business terms, from participation in partnerships. In keeping with rational choice theory, it asserts that business is motivated by risk (reputation and regulatory) and reward (the prospect of financial gains).

Simon Zadek, who has written on collaborative governance from both the business management and global governance perspectives, defines it as "the process by which multiple actors, including public and private institutions, come together and evolve, implement, and oversee rules, providing long-term solutions to pervasive challenges" (2006, p. 3). Cashore (2002) has championed the importance of "non-state market-driven" (NSMD) systems of private collaborative governance as a means of compensating for governmental regulatory failures. NSMD systems, by focusing on forcing changes in private supply chains to improve the social and environmental impacts of market behaviors, have the potential to challenge state regulatory authority. This is collaborative governance because it involves both firms and civil society in the classic governance functions of rule-making and enforcement, but it often does not rely on formal governmental participation. As Bernstein and Cashore (2007, p. 347) elaborate, "NSMD systems encourage compliance by recognizing and tracking, along the market's supply chain, responsibly produced goods and services. They aim to establish 'political legitimacy' whereby firms, social actors, and stakeholders are united into a community that accepts 'shared rule as appropriate and justified'" (see also Auld et al., 2009).

From these literatures, three conditions emerge as key to what makes something an instance of collaborative governance:

1. At least two of the three sectors (government, the private sector, and civil society) participate. Civil society is sometimes further subdivided into academia, media, NGOs, political parties, and so on.
2. The intended purpose of the collaborative is to create public value, not merely private returns.
3. The collaborators share authority – these are not hierarchical arrangements in which one party tells the others what to do.

The "shared discretion" and "public value" parts of the definition have clearly taken hold, as a recent definition from Torfing (2016) suggests: "a pluricentric mode of governance that brings together a diversity of public and/or private actors in more or less institutionalized arenas of negotiated interaction, which contribute to the production of public value through formulating and implementing public policy and regulation or through producing and delivering particular solutions and services." And scholars have written extensively about how and why the notion of creating public value is relevant for business leaders in an era of rising societal expectations (Moore and Khagram, 2004).

The primacy of governmental roles in collaborative governance, however, is still contested, with perhaps a growing acceptance that government remains key. As a recent review by Marques (2017b, p. 24) notes, scholarship increasingly "argues that states occupy a much more essential role than the literature to date has suggested." The global governance literature had led the way in considering governance beyond government as global interdependence surged in the 1980s and 1990s despite the anarchic structure of world order in which there is no central public actor tasked with governing the rest. But specific examinations of transnational collaborative governance tend to find that many if not most successful multi-stakeholder initiatives are led by governments and are not viable without strong government roles (Marques, 2017b).

EXPLAINING THE RISE OF COLLABORATIVE GOVERNANCE

Why are we seeing the rise of cross-sector collaboration in governance? After all, every land surface in the world, other than Antarctica, is divided into territories controlled by national governments tasked with making and enforcing rules. But governance by government alone has run into multiple problems. Many national governments lack the capacity and resources to govern in the public interest. This is most clearly true in failed and failing states, by definition. But increasingly governments in more established countries are stressed as well, as globalization increases the demands on governments and reduces their ability to exert full control within their borders (Florini, 2003 [2005], pp. 61–88).

Proponents argue that cross-sector collaborative governance is desirable because it can encompass a greater diversity of skill sets and resources in problem-solving and can generate a wider range of solutions. Rationales are both functional (the explosion of "wicked" problems creates complexity beyond government capacity; "glocalization" requires deep transborder collaboration that the inter-governmental system is unable to muster) and ideological in calling for shifts in how governance is done (the push toward a more limited role for government starting in the 1980s and the current debates over the social legitimacy of various forms of capitalism and business).

Those rationales have found a ready audience, with thousands of instances of collaborative governance efforts emerging around the world. Scholars have investigated collaborations that play key governance roles in a wide range of arenas: providing transnational business regulation in the absence of a coherent inter-governmental process able to do so (Abbott et al., 2016; see also Eberlein et al., 2013); bolstering more effective, accountable, and inclusive national public governance (Brockmyer and Fox, 2015); and delivering basic services (Beisheim et al., 2014).

The collaborative turn in governance is both reflected and fostered by a series of international negotiations and agreements. In 1992, the UN Conference on Environment and Development set an agenda for the twenty-first century, Agenda 21, that encouraged the "active involvement of the non-governmental organizations and other groups" (Paragraph 1.3) in its implementation, with a section on "strengthening the role of major groups," including NGOs and business, in the "effective implementation of the objectives, policies and mechanisms agreed to by Governments in all programme areas of Agenda 21" (Chapters 23–32). Ten years later, the next global summit for sustainability, the 2002 World Summit on Sustainable Development (also known as the Johannesburg Summit or the Earth Summit) emphasized cross-sector collaboration as a key means of reaching global goals. In 2015, the world's governments adopted a set of Sustainable Development Goals that set an ambitious agenda to 2030 whose realization would depend heavily on collaborative governance. The 17th and last of the goals describes how the rest of the goals are to be achieved:

> 17.16: Enhance the global partnership for sustainable development, complemented by multi-stakeholder partnerships that mobilize and share knowledge, expertise, technology and financial resources, to support the achievement of the sustainable development goals in all countries, in particular developing countries.
> 17.17: Encourage and promote effective public, public-private and civil society partnerships, building on the experience and resourcing strategies of partnerships.

But why should firms and civil society organizations take part in tasks that previously fell to governments? Civil society includes a vast array of NGOs focused on advocating for changes in public policy and service delivery, so their involvement is a logical extension of their *raison d'être*. But business generally is focused on generating and capturing private returns, not public value, so its participation requires more explanation.

The private sector is often willing to participate for a number of reasons (Florini, 2013). One is to create "soft" regulation in which it has a voice as a means of fending off "hard" regulation that government might impose if it did not receive cooperation from the business sector. Another motive for the private sector is reputational risk: a firm may legally get away with polluting or using slave labor in its supply chains, only to face severe economic consequences from consumers or investors when such behavior comes to light. Yet firms may not know how to manage such externalities and may need the expertise to be found in government or civil society. A third and increasingly important motivation is the growing recognition on the part of major firms that their business models are severely threatened by the world's failure to regulate and provide public goods, that is, to manage physical and social ecosystems in such a way as to create the enabling conditions for the private sector to flourish. Thus, the business sector faces intense pressures to help in these governance tasks.

One recent and somewhat stunning development emphasizes the extent of those pressures. On 16 January 2018, Larry Fink used the occasion of his annual letter to chief executive officers (CEOs) to issue an extraordinary challenge (Fink, 2018). Given that Fink is the founder, chairman, and CEO of BlackRock, Inc., the world's largest money management firm with some $6 trillion in assets – that is, the world's largest private investor – a challenge from him is one that publicly traded firms take seriously. In the letter, Fink argued that publicly traded firms have been too focused on quarterly results and have not properly engaged with shareholders on strategies for long-term value creation that take into account broad structural trends "from slow wage growth to rising automation to climate change." Fink went on to note that stakeholders from investors, consumers, and communities

> are demanding that companies exercise leadership on a broader range of issues. And they are right to: a company's ability to manage environmental, social, and governance matters demonstrates the leadership and good governance that is so essential to sustainable growth, which is why we are increasingly integrating these issues into our investment process.

THEORIZING COLLABORATIVE GOVERNANCE

Three somewhat overlapping scholarly communities in business and management, government and public administration, and international relations/development/global governance all have extensive literatures around a set of theoretical questions about changing processes of governance beyond government. They also address key questions of interest to practitioners concerning the design, governance, meta-governance, and impact of cross-sector collaborations under various conditions. However, there is much more in the literature on formation and processes – why collaborations start and how they do and should work – some on metrics and accountability, and least on impacts and effectiveness.

The literature has grown rapidly since the 1990s and has become far too extensive to be covered in detail here. Useful starting points for a deeper dive into the literature, in addition to the specific works cited in this chapter, include the *Annual Review of Social Partnerships* produced by the Cross-Sector Social Interaction (CSSI) network of scholars and the *Journal of Business Ethics*.

Out of the vast literature, a few key works have had particular influence or are useful sources for tying together broad scholarly developments. For example, Bryson et al. (2006) was a highly influential article that drew on an extensive survey of the literature to that point to develop 22 propositions about the conditions under which cross-sector collaborations may develop and may succeed. With regard to global governance, Avant et al. (2010) have called attention to the identities of specific governors (both state and non-state), pushing the international relations field beyond its usual focus on intergovernmental processes. Kahler's (2009) work on networked politics is helping to create relevant theoretical frameworks, as elaborated in policy-relevant ways by Slaughter (2017). Scholars of international development have joined the party (see, for example, the special issue of *Public Administration and Development*, 2011, 31(1), and particularly Brinkerhoff and Brinkerhoff, 2011). A comprehensive survey of the management and international business literature on the interaction between business and NGOs assesses six categories: NGO activism; NGO–business partnerships; multi-sectoral partnerships; global governance and standardization; national-level governance; and company stakeholder management (Kourula and Lassonen, 2010).

Several key questions dominate the literature:

- Much has been written on power and resource asymmetries among the collaborators and steps that can be taken to overcome such differentials to prevent hierarchy and exploitation (for example, Ansell and Gash, 2008; Gray and Purdy, 2018, chapter 7; Purdy, 2012).
- Accountability, both internally among collaborators and to external stakeholders, features prominently as a concern (Zadek, 2006). Emerson and Nabatchi (2015, p. 220) argue that "The participants must reconcile at least four levels of accountability: (1) to the organization or constituency they represent, (2) to their own values and their professional training and ethics, (3) to the CGR [collaborative governance regime] itself, and (4) to the broader public interest."
- Organizational systems and capacity are key issues in the literature (Ansell and Gash, 2017).

- Individual capacity to create, manage and participate in collaborative governance has recently emerged as a focal area (Florini, 2018; MacDonald and Stadtler, 2017).

To address these questions, multiple theoretical lenses are deployed. Indeed, a particularly noteworthy aspect of collaborative governance scholarship is its interdisciplinary strength, drawing upon numerous strands of social science theory to investigate governance broadly. In his analysis of the capacity of governance networks to foster collaborative innovation that solves societal problems, Torfing (2016, p. 14) lays out a lovely if partial summary of the range of relevant bodies of theory. Although his focus is specifically on public innovation, his overview points to the range of theories applicable for scholarship on any component of collaborative governance:

> *Public administration theory* helps us understand the shifting conditions for innovation in the public sector, and *public management research* sheds light on how collaborative innovation processes are managed . . . *discourse theory* provides an analytical tool for analyzing the discursive construction of problems, solutions, and decision-making premises and for studying how actors with diverging interests are kept together by common narratives and story lines that may create a momentum for change. Collaborative innovation is not only framed by different discourses but also conditioned by *institutional frameworks* of rules, norms, and cognitive scripts. This recognition is captured by different forms of historical and sociological institutionalism that help us understand the institutional embeddedness of collaboration innovation and the impact of institutional design on processes, outputs, and outcomes. Institutions facilitate and constrain the processes of collaborative innovation, but they do not tell us much about what actually happens in the processes that lead to innovation. Here *learning theory*, with its emphasis on motivation, creativity, and transformative learning, provides some important insights, and there has been a growing interest in collective learning processes in social systems such as workplaces. *Complexity theory* has its strength in relation to grasping the dynamic, iterative, and adaptive character of such systems. Last but not least, *theories of collaborative network governance* help us understand why and how a plethora of social and political actors interact and collaborate in complex and learning-based processes that are framed by discourses and conditioned by institutions. Governance network theory also allows us to understand how relatively self-governing governance networks can be metagoverned in order to spur collaboration, creativity, and innovation.

Two forms of theory appear to be the most extensively used: network theory and institutionalism. As Bryson et al. (2006, p. 52) note:

> Many public management scholars view these collaborations as "networks," use network theory to ground research questions, and situate their research within recent work on policy implementation tools. This perspective offers a rich theoretical base focused on structural variables, but it tends to disregard three critical components of cross-sector collaboration: (1) an appreciation of the uniqueness and differential strengths and weaknesses of governments, nonprofit organizations, businesses, and communities; (2) ongoing process dimensions, including leadership broadly defined; and (3) the dynamic nature of collaborative development. On the other hand, scholars who focus on collaborations as collective action solutions to public problems offer less theoretically grounded research but rich material on process dimensions, sources of ambiguity within collaborative work, and finding that can more easily be translated to the world of practice.

Institutionalism in various forms is commonly used as a theoretical starting point. Here, a particularly important new book is Gray and Purdy (2018). Although they refer to "multi-stakeholder partnerships" (MSPs) rather than "collaborative governance," they are discussing the same types of phenomena. They use an institutional theory lens to conceptualize partnerships as a new form of social organizing that have arisen in response to changing conditions within institutional fields. Institutional fields are defined as "evolving and often contentious social orders characterized either by common or conflicting interpretations of the purposes, relationships and rules of interaction within the field." These new organizational forms can effect change in those institutional fields, negotiating shared norms and practices to govern partners' interactions in that field.

ASSESSING THE IMPACT OF COLLABORATIVE GOVERNANCE

As the above discussion indicates, substantial scholarly progress has been made in understanding the conditions under which actors elect to engage in collaborative governance and the processes that they should follow to enjoy legitimacy and accountability within the collaboration. But many questions remain to be addressed.

Perhaps the most important immediate issue in collaborative governance research concerns the question of impact. As Marques (2017a, p. 18) notes, "While such partnerships continue to be touted by some scholars, policy-makers and companies as one of the most innovative solutions to social and environmental problems, there is a glaring lack of evidence regarding their effectiveness, particularly at the transnational level." Ansell and Gash (2008, p. 549) note that of the 137 cases in the extensive literature they review, very few studies say much about governance outcomes.

But the question of whether collaborative governance works turns out to be a complex question. One issue is to define the set to be assessed, in order to be able to go beyond individual case studies and draw broader lessons. Collaborative governance arrangements are now numerous and varied, but no estimates of who and how many exist that would support systematic assessment.

The most extensive evidence on impact to date is found with regard to the set of collaborations that are public–private partnerships (PPPs) for infrastructure projects (Jomo et al., 2016). One reason for the emphasis in the UN Sustainable Development Goals on cross-sector collaboration is the overwhelming financial and practical need for private sector engagement in infrastructure around the world. The Addis Ababa Action Agenda (AAAA) that came out of the Third International Conference on Financing for Development (Addis Ababa, 13–16 July 2015) noted that "both public and private investment have key roles to play in infrastructure financing, including through . . . public private partnerships" (paragraph 48, AAAA). But the AAAA also advised caution in creating and implementing such partnerships, which have at best a mixed track record.

On the surface, PPPs for infrastructure seem logical as a way to combine the best of government, with its attention to the public interest, and the resources and efficiency mindset of business, to produce better quality services at lower cost. Such partnerships fall somewhere between standard government procurement and complete privatization. The public sector determines what infrastructure is needed, and turns to the private sector for some combination of financing, designing, building, and operating. Ownership may be shared or turned over to the private sector, which then receives revenues from government payments, user fees, or both. These PPPs could be (but often are not) structured to meet the "collaborative governance" terms of shared discretion in public value creation.

In a superb synthesis of research on the performance of infrastructure PPPs to date,

KS Jomo and colleagues (2016) find numerous problems in both the conceptualization and the implementation of these partnerships.

One key conceptual issue for infrastructure partnerships is that it is not clear why private sector involvement would necessarily lower costs or improve the quality of service. On the financing side, public sector borrowing costs are usually lower, not higher, than those of the private sector. The transaction costs of negotiating complex public–private agreements can be considerable. Most important, as Jomo et al. (2016, p. 12) note,

> the terms "cost" and "quality of service" require interpretation in a broader sense, with the former taking into account not just the financing, transactions and operational costs of a project, but also its longer-term fiscal implications (including the risks of any contingency liabilities) and the latter taking due note of efficiency gains, as well as the social, economic and environmental objectives embodied in the 2030 Agenda for Sustainable Development.

The empirical question is therefore whether private sector efficiencies are actually sufficient to compensate for these costs in a way that produces substantial public value.

As this suggests, PPPs for infrastructure are prone to what Donahue and Zeckhauser (2011, pp. 48–58) refer to as "payoff discretion." The "shared discretion" in decision-making that Donahue and Zeckhauser champion turns out on closer examination to mean what they call "production discretion" – that is, shared authority on how best to get the public value generated. But collaborations, particularly in infrastructure, are vulnerable to rent-seeking, clearly bad for the public value goals of collaborative governance. The purpose of a PPP is to create more value than the government could produce acting alone or using a tightly structured contract. Who captures that extra value – the public, the government, or the private sector? The private sector's incentive is to engage only in such partnerships in which it can earn market returns, and it will attempt to capture as much of the total financial return as possible. Government oversight is required to ensure that discretion over the distribution of that payoff serves public, not only private, interests. Yet Jomo et al. (2016) find that inappropriate risk-sharing arrangements, in which the government promises excessive support should the project not prove profitable for any of a broad range of reasons, often leave government holding the bag. This is particularly true in developing countries where the infrastructure needs are greatest but governmental regulatory capacity is most lacking.

There is also the issue of project selection. The private sector is generally interested only in the most profitable elements of the most profitable projects, such as advanced urban hospitals rather than national health systems. Private partners have every incentive to try to persuade government to distort its spending accordingly.

Given these grounds for concern, what does the evidence tell us about the impact of infrastructure PPPs? Jomo et al. (2016) make a convincing argument that the empirical case favoring PPPs for infrastructure in the literature has been based on assessments that were too narrowly focused in comparison to the public value goals of collaborative governance. Few studies have attempted to consider this broader way of thinking about costs and benefits. When they do, they may find that projects that otherwise appear successful in the narrow sense may be so costly to the government as to threaten to bankrupt a country, as Oxfam (2014) found in assessing an ostensibly successful hospital PPP in Lesotho that was eating up more than half of the country's health budget.

In short, the best known form of public–private collaboration, PPPs for infrastructure, often fall short in meeting the first part of the basic definition of collaborative governance: effective shared discretion in decision-making. When discretion *is* shared, it may be payoff discretion rather than production discretion, to use the Donahue and Zeckhauser (2011) terminology. And most evaluations to date do not consider the most critical questions: who if anyone in the public benefitted, the distributional consequences, fiscal effects, or long-term impacts. So it remains unclear whether such partnerships generally meet the second part of the collaborative governance definition: successful creation of significant public value.

The other well-defined set of collaborative governance cases are the partnerships that registered with the UN in conjunction with the World Summit on Sustainable Development in 2002. This summit was focused on the predecessor agenda to the Sustainable Development Goals, known as the Millennium Development Goals because they were adopted in 2000 for implementation out to 2015. The 2002 World Summit became known as the "partnership summit" for its encouragement of cross-sector collaborations as key means for implementing the Millennium Goals. Nearly 300 partnerships were announced at the summit and many more registered thereafter. This set of collaborative efforts had little in common other than the fact of registering. They covered a wide range of issues, places, types of collaborating institutions, and goals. Nonetheless, they did provide a defined set that could be evaluated for impact.

The results of that evaluation are not pretty:

> First, on analyzing the sample of 340 partnerships after more than five years since inception, approximately 38 percent show low levels or no measurable output. Moreover, roughly 42 percent (86) of the partnerships with measurable output engage in activities without direct relation to their publicly stated goals and ambitions . . . Summing up, of these numbers, 211 partnerships are inactive, lack any outputs, or fail to match their stated ambition with their observed activities. (Pattberg and Widerberg, 2016, p. 44)

These results are almost comical in their clarity. Doing nothing, or nothing related to the stated goals of the collaboration, makes it easy for researchers to assess impact – or lack thereof.

But other collaborative examples have demonstrated much more activity, addressing everything from health to energy to security. The InterSector Project, which focuses on the United States, has detailed case studies on some 40 partnerships.[1] The Cross Sector Social Interactions scholarly community, drawn mostly from business schools, has an *Annual Review of Social Partnerships* with information on many more.[2] What is known about the impacts of all of these?

This question of impact brings us to the chronic problem that the international development field has long faced. In development, evaluation is a much-contested arena with many metrics but little consensus. Does success mean producing output for given inputs, meeting specific targets (outcomes), or measurably improving the lives of intended beneficiaries (impacts)? Similarly, collaborative governance arrangements could be held accountable primarily internally or externally (Zadek, 2006). Success with an internal accountability focus would mean that the collaborating entities are all satisfied. Success with an external focus would require the harder measurement of societal impact – which then raises challenging issues of what impact should reasonably be expected from a given collaboration and who gets to define that choice of reasonable impact.

A 2016 special issue of the *Journal of Business Ethics* set out to suggest approaches to theoretical generalizations on partnership impact assessment that could go beyond the case studies that have dominated the literature to date. The overview article (van Tulder et al., 2016) helpfully connects the partnership and development impact assessment literatures in a thorough analysis of the questions raised above. It then devises a guide to further research in the form of four "impact loops" that address different elements of the collaborative governance impact question (van Tulder et al., 2016, pp. 11–12):

- First-order impact loops look inside the partnership at individual participants to focus on questions of operational efficiency and direct effects on mindsets and employee engagement among participating organizations. Given that many businesses first enter into partnerships with governments and NGOs to provide their employees with opportunities to "do good," assessing what happens to employee mindsets matters to the future of collaborative governance.
- Second-order impact loops function at the organizational level, where research can assess the tactical level of project performance, questions of the legitimacy of the collaboration among those organizations, and the effects of the particular tools of partnership management in use. Much of the collaborative governance literature focuses at this level, trying to understand what management practices and mechanisms have what impact on project performance.
- Third-order impact loops aim to investigate whether changed outcomes can be attributed to a specific partnership, and conversely whether a collaboration is achieving its stated mission. Does the collaboration accomplish its declared specific missions, and if so is it thereby adding public value? At this level, questions of attribution become challenging, but unavoidable.
- Fourth-order impact loops raise the big question of what systemic impacts particular instances of collaborative governance are having. As van Tulder and colleagues (2016, p. 12) note, "Fourth-order impact effects refer to the overall added value captured by the partnership. It includes all the stages from input to impact and assessing the full extent of the partnership's contribution to the (social) issue."

THE RESEARCH AGENDA FOR COLLABORATIVE GOVERNANCE

In short, a prime component of the research agenda for collaborative governance should focus on the impacts of collaborative governance. But the research agenda also should include at least five other items that have as yet received relatively little attention:

- The potential for collaborative governance to foster social inclusion.
- Coordination among collaborative governance initiatives in a given issue area.
- The political economy of collaborative governance.
- The changing nature of the private sector and its roles in collaborative governance.
- The fragmentation versus emergent governance argument.

Collaborative Governance and Social Inclusion

An explicit aim of much of collaborative governance is to include voices that are not normally part of governance conversations. Ideally, those voices should include all stakeholders, including any intended targets and beneficiaries of collaborations. In practice, however, collaborative governance has a more mixed track record, one which has recently begun to attract much-needed scholarly attention.

As Pouliot and Therien (2018, p. 171) note, "the practice of launching multistakeholder partnerships allows for non-hierarchical, results-centered collaborative schemes that nonetheless rest on arbitrary processes of self-selection and a certain degree of normative homogeneity." Their review of the politics of global governance innovations, including cross-sector collaborations, points to the beginnings of a research agenda on the conditions under which collaborations counter or simply replicate existing patterns of inclusion, exclusion, and power. And they make the crucial point that "powerful actors strive to preserve their domination by limiting access to decision-making, while peripheral and subordinate players want to open up the political game," with the struggle often framed as efficiency versus democratization (Pouliot and Therien, 2018, p. 165).

Coordinating Collaborative Governance

A given issue area may have many collaborations involving different (if sometimes overlapping) participants and goals. In practice, there is a trend toward collaboration "platforms" that aim to coordinate among such initiatives. This trend toward institutionalization among institutional innovations is only beginning to receive significant scholarly scrutiny, although it has powerful implications for the likelihood of progress in any given issue area (Ansell and Gash, 2017; Florini and Pauli, 2018). How can and should we evaluate the workings of and needs for meta-collaborations?

The Comparative Political Economy of Collaborative Governance

The roles of and relationships among government, business, and civil society vary greatly from country to country, with significant implications for how collaborative governance is conceptualized and practiced, and even whether it is possible at all. The literature to date is heavily Western-centric in its assumptions and case selection. It tends to assume that all societies are organized into similar easily measured categories of public sector, for-profit private sector, and civil society. There is little work to date on how and why cross-sector collaboration unfolds in countries where sectors are less distinct and defined. Are state-owned enterprises or government-linked corporations public or private, or are new categorizations needed? Nor is there much attention yet to the possibility that sectors may play different roles than in the conventional Western understanding. For example, are civil society organizations autonomous as in the West, or are they primarily an arm of the government with delegated authority as in China? Do Asia's family conglomerates collaborate differently than publicly traded multinational corporations (MNCs)?

Changing the Private Sector

Much of the literature addresses the challenges of aligning interests between entities concerned with public welfare and businesses concerned with profit maximization. But profit maximization is just one goal around which business can be organized. Although by definition the private sector needs to earn sufficient financial returns to keep operating, there is no law of nature that says that profits must be maximized, especially in the short term. BlackRock CEO Larry Fink's letter to corporate leaders in early 2018 calling for greater social responsibility in business practice is just one of many indications that the clash of purposes between public and private sectors could evolve (Roche and Jakub, 2017).[3] Firms that partner closely with the other sectors may find it easier to make the transition to operating in compliance with what appears to be new terms for the social license to operate.

Fragmenting or Flourishing?

With so many cross-sector partnerships underway, does the exploding number of collaborative governance arrangements constitute fragmentation of governance or the development of a comprehensive "bottom-up" system of governance that will complement the formal governmental and inter-governmental systems? It is possible that the multitudinous partnerships are beginning to generate positive "governance externalities" that emerge from the accumulation of partnerships around specific issues and organizations in which social capital is formed at scale and across multiple issues and places. But is it equally possible that the proliferation of partnerships reflects and will exacerbate efforts by many actors to ensure that they each have a forum in which their separate interests can prevail? Some of the global governance literature is just beginning to explore this conundrum (Hale and Held, 2017), but the meta-studies of meta-studies are yet to be done.

CONCLUSION

Our standard concept of governance leads us astray in an age of complexity. We model governance on what we think national governments do: setting and enforcing rules by which everyone agrees to – or is forced to – abide. But with a few key exceptions, governance needs to foster transformation of whole systems, a task beyond the scope of conventional rule-making.

The complex nature of our biggest challenges does not lend itself to one-size-fits-all hierarchal rules that must be enforced by some external coercive elements. In complex systems, unlike simple or merely complicated ones, the sum of the parts differs fundamentally from the characteristics of any individual components. Just as one cannot predict the behavior of a school of fish from knowing everything about one single member of the species, one cannot know how a national economy or polity will behave even from knowing extraordinary details about the behavior of individual firms, consumers, or voters. Such complexity characterizes a growing share of the issues requiring governance, from the economy to the environment to everything that matters in our longing to create a just, stable, prosperous, and sustainable society.

The complex and urgent governance agenda is generating a vast array of cross-sector collaborations that aim to provide public goods and manage externalities. In the language of complexity theory, collaborative governance is an adaptive response to the need for collective action in conditions of complexity, where traditional hierarchical rule-making is inadequate to cope with the need for flexibility and rapid response in the face of rapid non-linear change (Colander and Kupers, 2014).

Despite the emergence of large literatures across multiple disciplines that have made significant progress on many questions, the remaining research agenda is both vast and vital if we are to assess the degree to which we are seeing the emergence of a new era for governance. Are collaborative governance regimes merely a transitional phenomenon filling in for governments, as governments slowly develop greater capacity to govern at home and cooperate effectively across borders? Or are we seeing the beginnings of a secular shift to a wholly new form of either domestic or cross-border governance of collective action problems – or both?

On the applied front, practitioners can pick up these themes to make progress toward determining not just what *is* happening but what *should* be done to ensure we end up with a desirable and effective form of governance. Given the profusion of innovations and experiments around the world that are now striving to realize transformational change, a broad policy debate on the desirability of collaborative governance in its many incarnations is long overdue. What are the legitimate goals for which collaborative governance should aim, and how should these be decided? What standards and benchmarks should be used to measure progress? How can all stakeholders enjoy appropriate protections and hold collaborators accountable? Under what conditions, if any, is collaborative governance the kind of governance we want?

NOTES

1. See http://intersector.com/case-library/, accessed 24 October 2017.
2. http://www.cssicommunity.org/arsp, accessed 24 October 2017.
3. See also the extensive work on the growth of a "fourth sector" of mission-driven business at fourthsector.net.

REFERENCES

Abbott, Kenneth W., Jessica F. Green, and Robert O. Keohane (2016), "Organizational Ecology and Institutional Change in Global Governance," *International Organization* 70(Spring), 247–77.

Ansell, Chris, and Alison Gash (2008), "Collaborative Governance in Theory and Practice," *Journal of Public Administration Research and Theory* 18, 543–71.

Ansell, Chris, and Alison Gash (2017), "Collaborative Platforms as a Governance Strategy," *Journal of Public Administration Research and Theory* 28(1), 16–31.

Auld, Graeme, Cristina Balboa, Steven Bernstein, and Benjamin Cashore (2009), "The Emergence of Non-State Market-Driven (NSMD) Global Environmental Governance: A Cross Sectoral Assessment," in Magali A. Delmas and Oran R. Young (eds), *Governance for the Environment: New Perspectives*, Cambridge: Cambridge University Press, pp. 183–218.

Avant, Deborah D., Martha Finnemore, and Susan K. Sell (eds) (2010), *Who Governs the Globe?*, Cambridge: Cambridge University Press.

Beisheim, Marianne, Andrea Liese, Hannah Janetscheck, and Johanna Sarre (2014), "Transnational Partnerships: Conditions for Successful Service Provision in Areas of Limited Statehood," *Governance* 27(4), 655–73.

Bernstein, Steven, and Benjamin Cashore (2007), "Can Non-State Global Governance be Legitimate? An Analytical Framework," *Regulation and Governance* 1(4), 347–71.
Braithwaite, John, and Peter Drahos (2000), *Global Business Regulation*, Cambridge: Cambridge University Press.
Brinkerhoff, Derrick, and Jennifer Brinkerhoff (2011), "Public–Private Partnerships: Perspectives on Purposes, Publicness and Good Governance," *Public Administration and Development* 31(1), 2–14.
Brockmyer, Brandon, and Jonathan Fox (2015), *Assessing the Evidence: The Effectiveness and Impact of Public Governance-Oriented Multi-Stakeholder Initiatives*, London: Open Society Foundation Transparency and Accountability Initiative.
Bryson, John, Barbara C. Crosby, and Melissa Middleton Stone (2006), "The Design and Implementation of Cross-Sector Collaboration: Propositions from the Literature," *Public Administration Review*, December, 44–55.
Cashore, Benjamin (2002), "Legitimacy and the Privatization of Environmental Governance: How Non–State Market-Driven (NSMD) Governance Systems Gain Rule-Making Authority," *Governance* 15(4), 503–29.
Colander, David, and Roland Kupers (2014), *Complexity and the Art of Public Policy*, Princeton, NJ: Princeton University Press.
Cutler, Clair A., Virginia Haufler, and Tony Porter (eds) (1999), *Private Authority and International Affairs*, New York: State University of New York Press.
Donahue, John D., and Richard J. Zeckhauser (2011), *Collaborative Governance: Private Roles for Public Goals in Turbulent Times*, Princeton, NJ: Princeton University Press.
Eberlein, Burkard, Kenneth W. Abbott, Julia Black, Errol Meidinger, and Stepan Wood (2013), "Transnational Business Government Interactions: Conceptualization and Framework for Analysis." http://digitalcommons.osgoode.yorku.ca/scholarly_works/3, accessed May 2018.
Emerson, Kirk, and Tina Nabatchi (2015), *Collaborative Governance Regimes*, Washington, DC: Georgetown University Press.
Fink, Larry, (2018), "Annual Letter to CEOs: A Sense of Purpose." https://www.blackrock.com/corporate/en-us/investor-relations/larry-fink-ceo-letter.
Florini, Ann (2003), *The Coming Democracy: New Rules for Running a New World*, Washington, DC: Island Press, reprinted in 2005, Washington, DC: Brookings Press.
Florini, Ann (2013), "Global Companies and Global Society: The Evolving Social Contract," in John Mikler (ed.), *The Handbook of Global Companies*, Chichester: Wiley Blackwell, pp. 335–50.
Florini, Ann (2018), "Professionalizing Cross-Sector Collaboration to Implement the SDGs," in Homi Kharas and John MacArthur (eds), *Summits to Solutions: Innovations in Implementing the Sustainable Development Goals*, Washington, DC: Brookings Press, pp. 106–25.
Florini, Ann, and Markus Pauli (2018), "Big Business for Small Farmers? The Sustainable Development Goals and Cross-Sector Partnerships in Asian Agriculture," Paper presented at the annual convention of the International Studies Association, panel on Powering Ahead?: Multi-Stakeholder Initiatives and the Future of Global Governance, San Francisco, 4 April.
Florini, Ann, and Benjamin K. Sovacool (2009), "Who Governs Energy? The Challenges Facing Global Energy Governance," *Energy Policy* 37, 5239–48.
Florini, Karen, and Ann Florini (2017), "It's Not Just About Paris: International Climate Action Today," *Foreign Service Journal* 94(6), July/August, 26–31.
Gray, Barbara, and Jill Purdy (2018), *Collaborating for the Future: Multistakeholder Partnerships for Solving Complex Problems*, New York: Oxford University Press.
Hale, Thomas, and David Held (2017), *Beyond Gridlock*, Cambridge: Polity Press.
Hardin, Russell (1982), *Collective Action*, Baltimore, MD: Johns Hopkins University Press.
Haufler, Virginia (2001), *Public Roles for the Private Sector: Industry Self-Regulation in a Global Economy*, Washington, DC: Carnegie Endowment for International Peace.
Jomo, KS, Anis Chowdhury, Krishnan Sharma, and Daniel Platz (2016), "Public–Private Partnerships and the 2030 Agenda for Sustainable Development: Fit for Purpose?" United Nations Department of Economic & Social Affairs, DESA Working Paper No. 148 ST/ESA/2016/DWP/148, February.
Kahler, Miles (ed.) (2009), *Networked Politics: Agency, Power, and Governance*, Ithaca, NY: Cornell University Press.
Khagram, Sanjeev (2006), "Possible Future Architectures of Global Governance: A Transnational Perspective/Prospective," *Global Governance* 12, 97–117.
Kourula, Arno, and Salla Lassonen (2010), "Nongovernmental Organizations in Business and Society, Management, and International Business Research: Review and Implications From 1998 to 2007," *Business & Society* 49(35), 35–67.
Levi-Faur, David (2012), "From Big Government to Big Governance," in David Levi-Faur (ed.), *Oxford Handbook of Governance*, Oxford: Oxford University Press, pp. 3–18.
MacDonald, Adriane, and Lea Stadtler (2017), "It's More Than the Reading Assignment: Skillsets and

Competencies for Effective Cross-Sector Collaboration," *Annual Review of Social Partnerships*, November, 45–52.
Marques, Jose Carlos (2017a), "From Compilation to Insights," *Annual Review of Social Partnerships* 12, 18.
Marques, Jose Carlos (2017b), "The Public–Private Governance Nexus: New Perspectives on MSI Performance and State Agency," *Annual Review of Social Partnerships* 12, 23–4.
Moore, Mark H., and Sanjeev Khagram (2004), "On Creating Public Value: What Business Might Learn from Government About Strategic Management," Harvard University Corporate Social Responsibility Initiative, March.
Olson, Mancur (1965), *The Logic of Collective Action: Public Goods and the Theory of Groups*, Cambridge, MA: Harvard University Press.
Ostrom, Elinor (1990), *Governing the Common: The Evolution of Institutions for Collective Action*, Cambridge: Cambridge University Press.
Ostrom, Elinor (1992), "The Rudiments of a Theory of the Origins, Survival, and Performance of Common Property Institutions," in Daniel W. Bromley (ed.), *Making the Commons Work: Theory, Practice, and Policy*, San Francisco, CA: ICS Press, pp. 293–318.
Oxfam (2014), "A Dangerous Diversion: Will the IFC's Flagship Health PPP Bankrupt Lesotho's Ministry of Health?" Oxfam Briefing Note, https://wwwcdn.oxfam.org/s3fspublic/file_attachments/bndangerousdiversionlesothohealthppp070414en_0.pdf, accessed May 2018.
Pattberg, Phillip, and Oscar Widerberg (2016), "Transnational Multistakeholder Partnerships for Sustainable Development: Conditions for Success," *Ambio* 45, 42–51.
Pouliot, Vincent, and Jean-Philippe Therien (2018), "Global Governance in Practice," *Global Governance* 9(2), 163–72.
Purdy, J.M. (2012), "A Framework for Assessing Power in Collaborative Governance Processes," *Public Administration Review* 72(3), 409–17.
Reinecke, Wolfgang (1999), "The Other World Wide Web: Global Public Policy Networks," *Foreign Policy* 117, 44–57.
Roche, Bruno, and Jay Jakub (2017), *Completing Capitalism: Heal Business to Heal the World*, Oakland, CA: Berrett-Koehler Publishers.
Rosenau, James, and Ernst-Otto Czempiel (1992), *Governance Without Government: Change and Order in World Politics*, Cambridge: Cambridge University Press.
Samuelson, Paul A. (1954), "The Pure Theory of Public Expenditure," *Journal of Economics and Statistics* 36(4), 387–9.
Slaughter, Anne-Marie (2017), *The Chessboard and the Web: Strategies of Connection in a Networked World*, New Haven, CT: Yale University Press.
Torfing, Jacob (2016), *Collaborative Innovation in the Public Sector*, Washington, DC: Georgetown University Press.
van Tulder, Rob, M. May Seitanidi, Andrew Crane, and Stephen Brammer (2016), "Enhancing the Impact of Cross-Sector Partnerships: Four Impact Loops for Channeling Partnership Studies," *Journal of Business Ethics* 135, 1–17.
Waddell, Steve and Sanjeev Khagram (2007), "Multi-stakeholder Global Networks: Emerging Systems for the Global Common Good," in Pieter Glasbergen, Frank Biermann and A.P. Mol (eds), *Partnerships, Governance and Sustainable Development: Reflections on Theory and Practice*, Cheltenham, UK and Northampton, MA, USA: Edward Elgar Publishing, pp. 261–87.
Zadek, Simon (2001), *The Civil Corporation*, London: Earthscan.
Zadek, Simon (2004), "The Path to Corporate Responsibility," *Harvard Business Review* 82(12), December, 125–32, 150.
Zadek, Simon (2006), "The Logic of Collaborative Governance," Harvard Corporate Social Responsibility Initiative Working Paper 17.

25. Inclusive innovation through alliance networks

Arno Kourula

INTRODUCTION

Grand societal challenges cross national boundaries and can affect all organizational forms. Management scholars have recently started paying more attention to these challenges, ranging from modern slavery (Crane, 2013) to income inequality (Cobb, 2016), and from climate change (Howard-Grenville et al., 2014) to the potential disruptive impacts of artificial intelligence on employment (George et al., 2014). Grand challenges are seen as 'formulations of global problems that can be plausibly addressed through coordinated and collaborative effort' (George et al., 2016). At the same time, we see a strong rise in sustainable innovation to address these concerns, often taking the form of collaboration across societal sectors and sometimes with unexpected allies (Adams et al., 2016; Stephan et al., 2016). Thus, collaboration and innovation will be key elements in addressing grand societal challenges.

While traditionally we have looked to governments to address grand challenges in concerted efforts, the interest in (and criticism of) market-based initiatives and inclusive innovation is on the rise. Inclusive innovation is typically understood as involving business-led or business-like approaches to support excluded populations. Nonetheless, the broader notion of inclusive development encompasses 'marginalized people, sectors and countries in social, political and economic processes for increased human well-being, social and environmental sustainability, and empowerment' (Gupta et al., 2015, p. 546). To achieve inclusive development, different actors need to come together to form networks of action. One prominent form of such collaboration is the alliance network. These types of alliances are particularly interesting as they are increasingly used to address challenges such as energy, climate change, poverty and labor conditions, but are simultaneously complex to manage or orchestrate. These forms of alliances have only recently emerged as a phenomenon of analysis and sustainability related examples include industrial symbiosis (Paquin and Howard-Grenville, 2013) and zero-carbon built environments (Rydin, 2013). Research on inclusive development networks, focusing on excluded populations is still scarce, but offers a fruitful research opportunity.

This chapter focuses on this particular form of collaboration aiming at inclusive innovation and sustainable development: alliance networks. In particular, we utilize the concept of organizational roles within alliance networks (Peterman, 2013; Peterman et al., 2014; Peterman et al., 2015). While the analysis of interorganizational relations (Lumineau and Oliveira, 2018; Parmigiani and Rivera-Santos, 2011) and interorganizational networks (Majchrzak et al., 2015; Phelps et al., 2012; Provan et al., 2007) has been a wide cross-disciplinary research endeavor for decades, this chapter focuses specifically on collaborative alliances that aim to address innovation for sustainable development.

The Collaboration Imperative

We have experienced a tremendous rise in interest and practice around collaborating for social, inclusive and sustainable development. At the global level, perhaps the strongest signal of this are the Sustainable Development Goals (SDGs), a set of 17 goals devised as a United Nations-led multi-stakeholder initiative tackling grand challenges (see George et al., 2016). The final goal of the SDGs explicitly focuses on collaboration, problem-solving and implementation through partnerships. While the SDGs tackle four P's – people, planet, prosperity and peace – arguably the most important one of these P's is the fifth one – partnerships (Kolk, 2016; Kolk et al., 2017). At the national level we tend to emphasize the need for government to adopt a broader portfolio of activities, going beyond legal, regulatory and economic means towards informational, partnering and hybrid forms of engagement (Steurer, 2010).

At the interorganizational level, a wide literature has explored partnerships across the societal sectors of government, corporations and civil society (Gray and Stites, 2013; Selsky and Parker, 2005). A key challenge for cross-sector partnerships are the different motivations, resource levels and activities of the different actors involved. While these partnerships or alliances are often dyadic in nature, we are also seeing a rise in multi-organization cross-sector partnerships. More complex partnerships typically involve a facilitating organization playing the role of a 'bridge' (Parmigiani and Rivera-Santos, 2011). Furthermore, at this interorganizational level of analysis, a substantial literature has explored voluntary private regulation, such as corporate self-regulation and multi-stakeholder initiatives (Bartley, 2007; Fransen and Kolk, 2007; King and Lenox, 2000; Sharma and Bansal, 2017; Turcotte et al., 2014). Examples include larger general initiatives such as the United Nations Global Compact and the ISO 26000 sustainability standard, and more focused international standards such as the Forest Stewardship Council and the Roundtable for Sustainable Palm Oil.

Collaboration has also been examined to a large extent from the corporate lens. Social and sustainable entrepreneurs are typically seen as change-makers that engage with a wide variety of stakeholders to try to simultaneously create value for the venture and for society (Cohen and Winn, 2007; Mair and Martí, 2006, 2009). A wide scholarship on corporate social responsibility (CSR) has offered important insights about related theories (Frynas and Yamahaki, 2016; Garriga and Melé, 2004), the link to financial performance (Carroll and Shabana, 2010; Margolis and Walsh, 2003) and its international dimensions (Kolk, 2016; Pisani et al., 2017). CSR can be seen as a collaborative market-based approach (or a form of voluntary governance) linked to sustainable development. Within studies focusing on the organizational and corporate perspective, a wider stream of research on sustainability-oriented innovation has emerged (Adams et al., 2016; Stephan et al., 2016).

Collaboration Beyond Markets and Hierarchy

Traditionally, we have looked to government-led hierarchical solutions such as legislation and regulation and, more recently, market-based approaches such as corporate innovation to solve societal challenges (Adams et al., 2016; Pisani et al., 2017). In the past two decades, we have seen a rise in network forms of engagement for inclusive, social and/or sustainable innovation. Table 25.1 describes the basic mode, government role and

Table 25.1 Governance through hierarchy, networks and markets

	Hierarchy	Network	Market
Mode	Rules	Relations	Prices
Government role	Enforcer	Collaborator	Encourager
Outcomes	Standards	Knowledge sharing	Incentives

Source: Adapted from Peterman et al. (2014), based on Powell (1990).

outcomes of networks in comparison to hierarchies and markets. The basic functioning of hierarchical, network and market-based approaches are different, but these tools should be seen as complementary to address grand challenges. Networks are particularly well suited for knowledge sharing, but as they are relationship-based also involve a lot of trust-based interaction and social expectations.

The form of sustainable development and inclusive innovation through networks is varied, especially if alliance networks are broadly understood as cooperative and voluntary knowledge sharing and development arrangements between three or more organizations. In this chapter, we focus on larger alliance networks related to inclusive and sustainable development. Next, we turn to introducing interorganizational networks more broadly, and examining inclusive innovation networks more specifically.

INCLUSIVE INNOVATION THROUGH ALLIANCE NETWORKS

Interorganizational networks are a vital tool to achieve inclusive innovation and sustainable development. Several recent reviews of interorganizational relations and network studies provide an overview of the state of the field. Within network studies, we will argue that the notion of an organizational role can be particularly fruitful to determine organizational participation and outcomes as well as network-level dynamics and outcomes of alliances.

Networks and Inclusive Innovation

Several reviews of network studies and interorganizational collaboration more broadly have been published within fields such as management, sociology and political science. Parmigiani and Rivera-Santos (2011) offer a meta-review of various forms of interorganizational collaboration including alliances, joint ventures, vertical relationships, franchising, cross-sector partnerships, and different types of networks, associations and consortia. Müller-Seitz (2012) reminds us to take into consideration key aspects of the network to be able to understand its leadership. Sydow et al. (2016) offer a range of insights and examples of managing interorganizational relations. Majchrzak et al. (2015) review existing qualitative case studies of interorganizational collaborations to understand the dynamics taking place within these types of arrangements. In an early study in the field of networks, Tracey and Clark (2003) explore the role of alliances and networks in creating clusters of innovation. The authors emphasize the importance of network structure and geography. In their review, Provan et al. (2007) focus on the level of analysis of the entire network. Finally, Phelps et al. (2012) explore how management, psychology, sociology and economics have defined and analysed knowledge networks.

Within network literature, alliance networks are seen as an innovative tool to address social and environmental challenges. They are understood as a longer-term form of voluntary cooperation between organizations involving substantial sharing and co-development (see Gulati and Gargiulo, 1999). Alliance networks allow participants to gain legitimacy, knowledge and market power as well as speed up technological development by pooling risks (Eisenhardt and Schoonhoven, 1996; Möller and Svahn, 2006; Robertson et al., 1996). The purpose of interorganizational alliance networks is to diffuse both public and private goods in areas too complex for any single organization to handle on its own (Provan and Lemaire, 2012). As alliance networks are becoming an essential tool to address grand challenges (Feldman, 2012; Rydin, 2013; Wassmer et al., 2014), it is important to study the roles that different organizations adopt within these networks.

Organizational Roles in Alliance Networks

Organizational roles in networks have often been explored in a loosely defined way. Nonetheless, a handful of studies have systematically analysed organizational roles, moving us closer to a definition of this concept. An early study depicted roles of non-governmental organizations (NGOs) in relation to industry within the environmental movement in the United States. In this study, Hoffman (2009) used network analysis to identify what he called Mediators, Bridges, Independents, Captives and Isolates. These roles were largely defined by network position, that is, the network ties of the organization. However, the roles of environmental NGOs also correlate with their drivers (so-called bright green organizations tend to engage with industry, while dark green NGOs are more adversarial) and resources (that is, funding and membership).

Bertels et al. (2014) continue on NGO roles with a more extensive analysis of heterogeneity within challenger environmental movements in the United States. Using an institutional work lens and a combination of qualitative and quantitative data, the authors define a role through social position within the network, organizational identity, and the type of work or activities implemented within a network. The roles identified are called Portal, Coordinator, Member, Fringe Player and Purist.

Paquin and Howard-Grenville (2013) explore organizational roles within a network but focus on the central role of the network orchestrator. The work involved in adopting this role consists of assembling and developing the network, in this case a national industrial symbiosis program in the United Kingdom. The key finding of the study in terms of enacting this role is that over time serendipitous encounters tend to be replaced by more purposeful coordination or relationship building. Unlike Hoffman (2009) and Bertels et al. (2014), focusing on the enactment of a particular central role as Paquin and Howard-Grenville do can bring important insight on how networks can and should be managed.

Building on the above-described recent foundational studies on organizational roles and our ongoing research on this topic (cf. Peterman et al., 2014, 2015), we can arrive at a definition of the key elements of a role. Peterman et al. (2014, 2015) define a role to consist of three key interrelated elements: the drivers of an organization to participate within the

Source: Adapted from Peterman et al. (2014, p. 1074; 2015).

Figure 25.1 Conceptual framework of key elements defining an organizational role

network, the organizational resources applicable to the network, and the relationships to other actors within the network. These are depicted in Figure 25.1.

Obviously, organizational drivers in the sense of motives to participate in a particular inclusive and sustainable development network are important. As an example of a systematic analysis of firm drivers for ecological responsiveness, Bansal and Roth (2000) describe the firm motivations of competitiveness, legitimation and environmental responsibility. Within alliance networks, a range of concurrent motives can drive firm action including ethics, legitimacy, knowledge gain, competition, risk sharing and stakeholder pressure related elements (see, for example, Ahuja, 2000; Eisenhardt and Schoonhoven, 1996; Möller and Svahn, 2006; Robertson et al., 1996).

Organizational resources are taken to mean resources that the organization possesses independently from the network. They are seen to consist of financial, personnel, technical, physical and reputational capabilities that the organization possesses applicable to the area of relevance of the network (see Barney, 1991; Hart, 1995). It is important to highlight that the resources need to be able to be leveraged within the particular network. For instance, if a network is about access to energy of local marginalized communities, resources are understood to be the financial, personnel, technical ones that apply only to the area of access to energy for local marginalized communities.

In terms of network ties, previous research has emphasized their importance for decades (see, for example, Ahuja et al., 2012; Burt, 1976). As the previous subsection reviews, a wide literature on networks has explored the importance of relationships between organizations, typically from a structural perspective. Both the scope of network ties as well as the depth of the relationship or tie in terms of knowledge sharing can be important (in determining a role). In addition, network analysis is not merely concerned with analysing the existence and/or strength of particular ties, but also to understand the position that an organization plays within the wider structure. For instance, whether the organization is central or peripheral and how well it connects other organizations with each other can become important.

Ultimately, these three elements can be explored independently, but when examined in combination, that is, as a role, we can start seeing patterns of activities developing. In the next subsection, we illustrate the notion of organizational roles using an interorganizational alliance network, the Better Buildings Alliance, in the area of sustainable innovation.

Case: Roles in the Better Buildings Alliance

Peterman and colleagues (Peterman, 2013; Peterman et al., 2014) provide a good example of an interorganizational alliance network in the area of business sustainability. The authors examine a network that later became called the Better Buildings Alliance. This decade-long multibillion dollar investment by the US government aims at improving the energy efficiency of buildings. As buildings and their construction represent 36 percent of global final energy consumption and account for nearly 40 percent of total direct and indirect CO_2 (carbon dioxide) emissions (International Energy Agency, 2019), the energy efficiency of buildings has wide-ranging societal implications. At the time of analysis, the Better Buildings Alliance included 153 governmental organizations, corporations and associations (now over 200) (Peterman et al., 2014). The alliance comprised three separate but interconnected networks in the areas of retail, real estate and healthcare (later also including higher education and hospitality). The aim of the alliance was to produce environmental knowledge in the form of scientific knowledge, standards, prototypes and best practices.

The key insight of the study and the authors' subsequent work is to examine how a combination of organizational drivers, resources and network ties can be understood as the organization's role. Peterman et al. (2014) focus on governmental roles and find that the eight public sector organizations analysed adopted very different roles labeled Commissioner, Interpreter, Marketer and User. Thus, using the notion of organizational roles, we are able to understand the plurality of engagement forms the government has within this particular alliance. While typically we assign specific tasks, such as regulation, to government actors and examine them as monoliths, by looking at multiple public sector actors in one setting we can better understand their actions. In the study, some governmental actors such as the Department of Energy had significant resources whereas others such as the General Services Administration, which manages and supports the basic functioning of federal agencies, had important deficits in research and development capabilities. The motives also varied widely, for example, research laboratories wanted to primarily access and analyse real world data whereas the Department of Energy was seeking to develop new standards. While the Department of Energy was the Commissioner of this particular hierarchical network, other public sector actors were much less connected to other organizations within the Better Buildings Alliance. It is through analysing the drivers, resources and network ties of organizations that we can understand why they are participating in the network, how they behave within the network and what they get out of the network. These patterns can be understood as roles, which exhibit consistent behavior at the organizational level and have important consequences for gaining knowledge. At the network level, analysing constellations of roles brings us both a structural and relational understanding that is crucial to be able to manage or orchestrate such networks.

BIG UNDEREXPLORED THEMES AND QUESTIONS IN INCLUSIVE INNOVATION

While networks and related dynamics have been explored for decades, organizational roles within alliance networks is an emerging research area. Recently, Lumineau and Oliveira (2018) have argued that we have several blind spots in researching interorganizational relations more generally. These include taking a single-party focus, assuming uniform relationships between parties and focusing on a single level of analysis. We offer the notion of an organizational role as a relational concept and a bridge between the organizational and network levels of analysis.

Sustainability and inclusive innovation are an excellent context to explore organizational roles due to their complexity and dynamism. Box 25.1 lists underexplored themes in the area of interorganizational roles in alliance networks. Specific issues, for example, specific SDGs, get more attention than others (Kourula et al., 2017). While this is known, we do not have a clear idea about the processes of prioritization and marginalization of issues and related power dimensions within sustainability networks. Ultimately, the interaction between the individual, organizational, interorganizational and institutional levels within alliances will be a crucial theme to explore further. We also know little about how different types of organizations (for example, by societal sector) adopt different roles within alliance networks and the related necessary institutional logics and work. We have very few comparative analyses of alliances or cross-alliance activity to determine organizational role adoption. Similarly, we would need to explore how roles within alliances develop over time to understand alliance network related role phenomena. Finally, the geographic dimension of roles in inclusive development alliances is a fruitful theme for further exploration.

Box 25.2 lists big underexplored questions about interorganizational roles in inclusive innovation and distinguishes them by level of analysis: institutional, network, organizational and individual.

Based on Box 25.2, we can notice that several questions are still open for investigation. To some extent, recent research has explored similar questions, but in other contexts than alliance networks. Ultimately, the key aspect of a research agenda for the future on roles in interorganizational alliance networks is to understand the multilevel nature of this phenomenon.

BOX 25.1 BIG UNDEREXPLORED THEMES ABOUT INTERORGANIZATIONAL ROLES IN INCLUSIVE INNOVATION

1. Issues addressed: Sustainable Development Goals (SDG).
2. Multilevel interaction within alliances (individual, organizational, interorganizational and institutional).
3. Role constellations and role adoption by different types of organizations.
4. Comparative assessment of alliances and cross-alliance activity.
5. Development of roles within alliance networks over time.
6. The geography of roles in inclusive development alliances.

BOX 25.2 BIG UNDEREXPLORED QUESTIONS ABOUT INTERORGANIZATIONAL ROLES IN INCLUSIVE INNOVATION

Institutional level	1. How do alliance networks interact with other institutional structures? 2. How can we achieve the most appropriate combination of hierarchical, network and market-based programs? 3. How is the combination of programs linked to outcomes such as innovation, inclusiveness, effectiveness, efficiency, impact and sustainability? 4. Is the existence of competing alliance networks beneficial for inclusive innovation? 5. How does knowledge transfer across alliance networks?
Network level	1. How do alliance networks form, evolve and cease to exist over time? 2. Do the above happen differently for inclusive innovation alliance networks in comparison to other network forms? 3. What is the optimal constellation of roles to make alliance networks inclusive? 4. What is the most effective constellation of organizational roles for innovation and knowledge sharing? 5. What kind of roles do different types of actors (for example, public sector, corporate and civil society) adopt within inclusive innovation networks? 6. How does marginalization take place in alliance networks? 7. Do different types of networks (for example, small or large, homogeneous or heterogeneous, issue-based and/or industry-centered, national versus international) organize and operate differently?
Organizational level	1. What role(s) should an organization adopt in an alliance network? 2. How do organizational drivers, resources and network ties interact with each other? 3. Which kinds of roles lead to which kinds of organizational outcomes within alliance networks? 4. What are the barriers for an organization to adopt and change its role in an alliance network? 5. How do organizations manage their portfolio of roles in multiple networks?
Individual level	1. How do individuals perceive organizational roles within alliance networks? 2. What are the cognitive limitations of individuals to understand larger networks? 3. How can individual representatives of organizations avoid network fatigue (that is, time and effort going into participating in multiple alliance networks)?

AN AGENDA FOR FUTURE RESEARCH

As we aim to further develop research on interorganizational roles in alliance networks, we can look to several research streams for insights, each typically focusing on particular levels of analysis.

Organizational Roles in Innovation

Different streams of literature examine inclusive innovation and sustainable development primarily in an organizational-centric or dyadic interorganizational manner. Particularly prominent streams of literature include social entrepreneurship, CSR and cross-sector partnerships. Social entrepreneurship literature has typically explored the identities, drivers, activities and outcomes of change agents aiming to implement business models beneficial for both the firm and society as a whole (Mair and Martí, 2006). Due to this actor-centric perspective, entrepreneurial environments and networks have received much less attention. The intermediary roles played and the institutional work conducted by entrepreneurs in relevant networks is a very fruitful avenue of research (cf. Armanios et al., 2017).

A wide literature has addressed the notion of CSR (for example, Margolis and Walsh, 2003; Pisani et al., 2017). Similar to social and sustainable entrepreneurship, this literature tends to be actor-centric deemphasizing the importance of context. CSR literature has tended to adopt a stakeholder relations frame to understand relationships with external parties (Parmar et al., 2010; Pisani et al., 2017), but we should move from understanding relationships to exploring roles within networks (Kourula et al., 2011). In addition to an inside-out perspective, this would also allow an outside-in perspective to evaluate corporate participation in networks.

Within the emerging literature of organizational roles within networks that this chapter addresses, there are multiple open questions. While Peterman and colleagues (Peterman et al., 2014, 2015) define a role to consist of organizational drivers, resources and relationships to other actors within the network, the interaction of these elements is still to be fully explored. Additionally, we know little about how firms and other types of organizations manage their roles within a network of the portfolio of roles across different sustainability programs. Managing a portfolio of roles in sustainability-oriented alliance networks may have similarities with managing a portfolio of traditional business alliances, but not necessarily due to the often pre-competitive nature of sustainability networks. These networks are often strongly oriented towards collaboration and knowledge sharing, instead of proprietary information. While stakeholder management is a broad field, we know little about role management. What is particularly interesting is that organizations in networks can identify and aim to adopt a particular role, but also try to promote or hinder other organizations' adoption of their roles.

The outcomes of role-based activity perhaps need the most attention, particularly from the perspective of innovation. While, for instance, the number of prototypes tested, technologies implemented, standards adopted and programs launched are clear outcome measures of network participation, there would need to be a clear link between the adoption of a particular role and the type of benefits gained due to this action. As we are still trying to define and clarify what an organizational role is, the outcomes have still not explicitly been explored.

Majchrzak et al. (2015) and Phelps et al. (2012) note that one of the most interesting avenues for future research is the individual-level cognitive processes related to participation in networks. For instance, we know little about how individual representatives within organizations perceive the entire network they are participating in. As information, existing relationships and participation levels vary widely, cognitive perceptions are going to be an important element of organizational roles. While often organizational role adoption is a purposive process, some organizational roles can be assigned without much strategic thought. Furthermore, barriers to participation in different networks, such as what can be termed 'network fatigue' (for example, lower participation motive due to participation in multiple – too many – networks), have not been explored yet.

Orchestrating Alliance Networks for Social Impact and Inclusiveness

At the network level, we can gain several insights from the vast network literature (Gulati and Gargiulo, 1999; Phelps et al., 2012; Provan et al., 2007). If we focus specifically on a role-based understanding of networks, we can explore role-based processes and dynamism. Networks will involve a range of role conflicts and contests, which have received limited attention (Peterman et al., 2015). Networks can be managed and orchestrated only to a certain degree. One of the most important questions for orchestrating networks is to try to determine what kind of role constellations lead to what kind of network outcomes. We are seeing the development of a wide variety of networks: led by government agencies, companies, NGOs or a combination of these; and local, national and regional networks. The key challenge is to determine how broad a sustainability network should be and who should take the lead. The core participants and roles are likely to be already determined in the network shaping phase.

Ultimately, what matters are the processes and outcomes of sustainability related alliance networks. These networks can have as objectives the creation of new knowledge, the development of industry standards and/or the commercialization of innovative technologies. While these innovative outcomes can be measured, the inclusiveness of the process is rarely discussed. To really have an impact on the marginalized, inclusive innovation approaches need to be designed with the most marginalized and vulnerable populations in mind. In practice, this seems to be more of an afterthought. What is more, the limitations of networks as a tool for inclusive and sustainable innovation and development need to be determined. These approaches will work and develop in interrelated ways with hierarchical and market-based tools and as such it is the effectiveness and impact of the whole system of approaches that matters.

A Broader Call for Management Scholars

In addition to the above-described avenues for future research, it is important to acknowledge some important deficiencies of management scholarship's attempt to address inclusive innovation and development. First, there is a very strong focus on social and environmental sustainability, while marginalization and empowerment and human well-being for all are often ignored (Kourula et al., 2017). Second, within the exploration of inclusive development, specific topics such as poverty (in the form of bottom/base of the pyramid) have received much attention (Kolk et al., 2014), while others such as modern slavery (Crane, 2013) call for further exploration. Third, for a variety of reasons, specific geographical locations such as developing countries tend to receive little scholarly attention (Pisani et al., 2017), although interest is increasing (Kolk and Rivera-Santos, 2018). Finally, to address these concerns we have a long way to go to develop interdisciplinary insights in inclusive development (Kolk et al., 2017; Kourula et al., 2017).

All things considered, through an in-depth examination of organizational (typically corporate) activities across different levels of analysis, management scholars have a lot to offer to our understanding of inclusive innovation and development. Interorganizational roles within alliance networks are a particularly fruitful area of scholarly exploration and impact.

ACKNOWLEDGMENTS

This chapter is inspired and based on collaborative work with Dr Andrew Peterman, Professor Raymond Levitt, Dr Markus Paukku and Professor Mikko Koria. I thank them for our insightful discussions on organizational roles and their valuable contributions in furthering this research field.

REFERENCES

Adams, R., Jeanrenaud, S., Bessant, J., Denyer, D. and Overy, P. (2016), 'Sustainability-oriented innovation: a systematic review', *International Journal of Management Reviews*, **18** (2), 180–205.

Ahuja, G. (2000), 'Collaboration networks, structural holes, and innovation: a longitudinal study', *Administrative Science Quarterly*, **45**, 425–55.

Ahuja, G., Soda, G. and Zaheer, A. (2012), 'The genesis and dynamics of organizational networks', *Organization Science*, **23** (2), 434–48.

Armanios, D.E., Eesley, C.E., Li, J. and Eisenhardt, K.M. (2017), 'How entrepreneurs leverage institutional intermediaries in emerging economies to acquire public resources', *Strategic Management Journal*, **38** (7), 1373–90.

Bansal, P. and Roth, K. (2000). 'Why companies go green: a model of ecological responsiveness', *Academy of Management Journal*, **43** (4), 717–36.

Barney, J. (1991), 'Firm resources and sustained competitive advantage?', *Journal of Management*, **17** (1), 99–120.

Bartley, T. (2007), 'Institutional emergence in an era of globalization: the rise of transnational private regulation of labor and environmental conditions', *American Journal of Sociology*, **113** (2), 297–351.

Bertels, S., Hoffman, A.J. and DeJordy, R. (2014), 'The varied work of challenger movements: identifying challenger roles in the US environmental movement', *Organization Studies*, **35** (8), 1171–210.

Burt, R.S. (1976), 'Positions in networks', *Social Forces*, **55**, 93–122.

Carroll, A.B. and Shabana, K.M. (2010), 'The business case for corporate social responsibility: a review of concepts, research and practice', *International Journal of Management Reviews*, **12**, 85–105.

Cobb, J.A. (2016), 'How firms shape income inequality: stakeholder power, executive decision making, and the structuring of employment relationships', *Academy of Management Review*, **41** (2), 324–48.

Cohen, B. and Winn, M. (2007), 'Market imperfections, opportunity and sustainable entrepreneurship', *Journal of Business Venturing*, **22** (1), 29–49.

Crane, A. (2013), 'Modern slavery as a management practice: exploring the conditions and capabilities for human exploitation', *Academy of Management Review*, **38** (1), 49–69.

Eisenhardt, K.M. and Schoonhoven, C.B. (1996), 'Resource-based view of strategic alliance formation: strategic and social effects in entrepreneurial firms', *Organization Science*, **7** (2), 136–50.

Feldman, D.L. (2012), 'The future of environmental networks – governance and civil society in a global context', *Futures*, **44** (9), 787–96.

Fransen, L.W. and Kolk, A. (2007), 'Global rule-setting for business: a critical analysis of multistakeholder standards', *Organization*, **14** (5), 667–84.

Frynas, J.G. and Yamahaki, C. (2016), 'Corporate social responsibility: review and roadmap of theoretical perspectives', *Business Ethics: European Review*, **25**, 258–85.

Garriga, E. and Melé, D. (2004), 'Corporate social responsibility theories: mapping the territory', *Journal of Business Ethics*, **53**, 51–71.

George, G., Haas, M.R. and Pentland, A. (2014), 'Big data and management', *Academy of Management Journal*, **57** (2), 321–5.

George, G., Howard-Grenville, J., Joshi, A. and Tihanyi, L. (2016), 'Understanding and tackling societal grand challenges through management research', *Academy of Management Review*, **59** (6), 1880–95.
Gray, B. and Stites, J.P. (2013), *Sustainability Through Partnerships: Capitalizing on Collaboration*, London, ON, Canada: Network for Business Sustainability.
Gulati, R. and Gargiulo, M. (1999), 'Where do interorganizational networks come from?', *American Journal of Sociology*, **104** (5), 1439–93.
Gupta, J., Pouw, N.R.M. and Ros-Tonen, M.A.F. (2015), 'Towards an elaborated theory of inclusive development', *European Journal of Development Research*, **4**, 541–59.
Hart, S.L. (1995), 'A natural-resource-based view of the firm', *Academy of Management Review*, **20** (4), 986–1014.
Hoffman, A.J. (2009), 'Shades of green', *Stanford Social Innovation Review*, Spring, 40–49.
Howard-Grenville, J., Buckle, S.J., Hoskins, B.J. and George, G. (2014), 'Climate change and management', *Academy of Management Journal*, **57** (3), 615–23.
International Energy Agency. (2019), 'Energy efficiency: buildings', https://www.iea.org/topics/energyefficiency/buildings/, accessed 13 May 2019.
King, A. and Lenox, M.J. (2000), 'Industry self-regulation without sanctions: the chemical industry's Responsible Care program', *Academy of Management Journal*, **49** (1), 698–716.
Kolk, A. (2016), 'The social responsibility of international business: from ethics and environment to CSR and sustainable development', *Journal of World Business*, **51**, 23–34.
Kolk, A. and Rivera-Santos, M. (2018), 'The state of research on Africa in business and management: insights from a systematic review of key international journals', *Business & Society*, **57** (3), 415–36.
Kolk, A., Rivera-Santos, M. and Rufin, C.R. (2014), 'Reviewing a decade of research on the "base/bottom of the pyramid" (BOP) concept', *Business & Society*, **53** (3), 338–77.
Kolk, A., Kourula, A. and Pisani, N. (2017), 'Multinational corporations and the Sustainable Development Goals: perspectives on a collaborative agenda', *Transnational Corporations*, **24** (3), 9–32.
Kourula, A., Paukku, M. and Koria, M. (2011), 'The multiple levels and actors in corporate social responsibility: a role management approach', Paper presented at 27th European Group for Organizational Studies (EGOS) Colloquium, Gothenburg, Sweden, 7–9 July.
Kourula, A., Pisani, N. and Kolk, A. (2017), 'Corporate sustainability and inclusive development: highlights from international business and management research', *Current Opinion in Environmental Sustainability*, **24** (1), 14–18.
Lumineau, F. and Oliveira, N. (2018), 'A pluralistic perspective to overcome major blind spots in research on interorganizational relationships', *Academy of Management Annals*, **12** (1), 440–65.
Mair, J. and Martí, I. (2006), 'Social entrepreneurship research: a source of explanation, prediction and delight', *Journal of World Business*, **41** (1), 36–44.
Mair, J. and Martí, I. (2009), 'Social entrepreneurship in and around institutional voids', *Journal of Business Venturing*, **24** (5), 419–35.
Majchrzak, A., Järvenpää, S.L. and Bagherzadeh, M. (2015), 'A review of interorganizational collaboration dynamics', *Journal of Management*, **41** (5), 1338–60.
Margolis, J.D. and Walsh, J.P. (2003), 'Misery loves companies: rethinking social initiatives by business', *Administrative Science Quarterly*, **48**, 268–305.
Möller, K. and Svahn, S. (2006), 'Role of knowledge in value creation in business nets', *Journal of Management Studies*, **43** (5), 985–1007.
Müller-Seitz, G. (2012), 'Leadership in interorganizational networks: a literature review and suggestions for future research', *International Journal of Management Reviews*, **14** (4), 428–43.
Paquin, R.L. and Howard-Grenville, J. (2013), 'Blind dates and arranged marriages: longitudinal processes of network orchestration', *Organization Studies*, **34** (11), 1623–53.
Parmar, B.L., Freeman, R.E., Harrison, J.S., Wicks, A.C., Purnell, L. and de Colle, S. (2010), 'Stakeholder theory: the state of the art', *Academy of Management Annals*, **4** (1), 403–45.
Parmigiani, A. and Rivera-Santos, M. (2011), 'Clearing a path through the forest: a meta-review of interorganizational relationships', *Journal of Management*, **37** (4), 1108–36.
Peterman, A. (2013), 'The roles within: building energy conservation in the United States through alliance networks and other voluntary strategies', Doctoral dissertation, Stanford University, Civil and Environmental Engineering.
Peterman, A., Kourula, A. and Levitt, R. (2014), 'Balancing act: government roles in an energy conservation network', *Research Policy*, **43** (6), 1067–82.
Peterman, A., Kourula, A. and Levitt, R. (2015), 'Roles within the structure: interorganizational roles in an environmental alliance network', in *Proceedings of 75th Academy of Management (AOM) Annual Meeting*, Vancouver, Canada, 7–12 August.
Phelps, C., Heidl, R. and Wadhwa, A. (2012), 'Knowledge, networks, and knowledge networks: a review and research agenda', *Journal of Management*, **38** (4), 1115–66.

Pisani, N., Kourula, A., Kolk, A. and Meijer, R. (2017), 'How global is international CSR research? Insights and recommendations from a systematic review', *Journal of World Business*, **52** (5), 591–614.
Powell, W. (1990), 'Neither market nor hierarchy: network forms of organization', *Research in Organizational Behavior*, **12**, 295–336.
Provan, K. and Lemaire, R.H. (2012). 'Core concepts and key ideas for understanding public sector organizational networks: using research to inform scholarship and practice', *Public Administration Review*, **72** (5), 638–48.
Provan, K., Fish, A. and Sydow, J. (2007), 'Interorganizational networks at the network level: a review of the empirical literature on whole networks', *Journal of Management*, **33** (3), 479–516.
Robertson, M., Swan, J. and Newell, S. (1996), 'The role of networks in the diffusion of technological innovation', *Journal of Management Studies*, **33** (3), 333–59.
Rydin, Y. (2013), 'The issue network of zero-carbon built environments: a quantitative and qualitative analysis', *Environmental Politics*, **22** (3), 496–517.
Selsky, J.W. and Parker, B. (2005), 'Cross-sector partnerships to address social issues: challenges to theory and practice', *Journal of Management*, **31** (6), 849–73.
Sharma, G. and Bansal, P. (2017), 'Partners for good: how business and NGOs engage the commercial–social paradox', *Organization Studies*, **38** (3–4), 341–64.
Stephan, U., Patterson, M., Kelly, C. and Mair, J. (2016), 'Organizations driving positive social change: a review and an integrative framework of change processes', *Journal of Management*, **42** (5), 1250–81.
Steurer, R. (2010), 'The role of governments in Corporate Social Responsibility: characterising public policies on CSR in Europe', *Policy Sciences*, 43 (1), 49–72.
Sydow, J., Schüssler, E. and Muller-Seitz, G. (2016), *Managing Inter-organizational Relations: Debates and Cases*, London: Palgrave.
Tracey, P. and Clark, G.L. (2003), 'Alliances, networks and competitive strategy: rethinking clusters of innovation', *Growth and Change*, **34** (1), 1–16.
Turcotte, M.F., Reinecke, J. and den Hond, F. (2014), 'Explaining variation in the multiplicity of private social and environmental regulation: a multi-case integration across the coffee, forestry and textile sectors', *Business and Politics*, **16** (1), 151–89.
Wassmer, U., Paquin, R. and Sharma, S. (2014), 'The engagement of firms in environmental collaborations: existing contributions and future directions', *Business & Society*, **53** (6), 754–86.

26. Social entrepreneurs as network orchestrators: a framework and research agenda on networks and leadership in the context of social innovation

Christian Busch and Harry Barkema

INTRODUCTION

Social networks are crucial in the context of social innovation, as tackling grand challenges in environmental sustainability, education and poverty alleviation usually requires partnerships across sectors (George et al., 2012; Waitzer and Paul, 2011). Over the last few decades, extensive research about the role of networks in commercial venture creation and development has been produced in the literature in both sociology (e.g., Chiesi, 2007; Powell et al., 2005) and management (e.g., Batjargal et al., 2013; Khayesi et al., 2014). However, despite the importance of specialized networks for different geographical locations, for different phases of development and for different organizational objectives and business models, we know surprisingly little about network development and transition in the context of social innovation (Barkema et al., 2015; Battilana and Lee, 2014).

Social innovation has been defined as "new ideas that address unmet social needs – and that work" (Mulgan et al., 2007a, p. 2). These "ideas" can take the shape of actions, systems, processes, services, rules, regulations and business models (Nicholls et al., 2015). Social enterprises – enterprises with an embedded social purpose and the underlying motivation to create social change – are often the vehicles that enact social innovation ideas (Austin et al., 2006; Dacin et al., 2011; Mair and Marti, 2006; Nicholls et al., 2015). Social enterprises play a potentially important role when states and markets fail to address fundamental human needs. Today, social enterprises are becoming more and more relevant as governments, donors and businesses increasingly partner up to tackle social and economic inequality. They differ from commercial enterprises with respect to goals, ways of coordination and distribution of benefits (Austin et al., 2006) and, thus, potentially develop different types of networks than commercial ventures. Therefore, there is a clear need for understanding how and why social enterprises develop networks for important social outcomes such as social inclusion.[1]

The purpose of this chapter is to review the network literature relevant to social innovation and to suggest potential avenues for further research. We develop a framework of *Transformative Network Orchestration* that helps to anchor social networks – and the related leadership approaches – in the context of social innovation. The framework addresses a gap in our collective understanding of how networks evolve in the context of social innovation and opens up intriguing avenues for further inquiry.[2]

EMERGING THEMES

Social entrepreneurship has been anchored in a number of disciplines, including entrepreneurship, organizational theory and non-profit management (e.g., Battilana et al., 2015; Rivera-Santos et al., 2015). While there has been much debate about its exact demarcations, there is broad consensus in the literature that social entrepreneurship refers to an entrepreneurial activity with an embedded social purpose and with the underlying drive to create social value (Austin et al., 2006). Thus, social enterprise "performance" is usually related to social value creation, which can be conceptualized and measured related to outcomes and/or outputs. This includes measures such as improvement of individuals' capabilities, local capacity built, and number of projects taken over by other actors (Bagnoli and Megali, 2009; Sen, 1999).[3]

As in commercial ventures, networks are essential for social ventures (Dufays and Huybrechts, 2014; Lyon and Fernandez, 2012). However, for two major reasons the networks of social ventures can be expected to develop differently from those of commercial ventures.[4] First, given the often low purchasing ability of their customers, social ventures often need funders to finance delivery of direct service. Thus, funders are often considered as primary clients (Austin et al., 2006). However, access to investment capital is scarce due to limited measurability, long return cycles and high fragmentation of the marketplace and other pertinent issues (Kohler, 2011). Thus, social enterprises tend to turn toward a broader set of foundations, philanthropists, investors and governments, resulting in a further diversification of stakeholders (Austin et al., 2006). Given the often limited potential of financial returns, these stakeholders typically demand non-financial benefits, such as particular reporting procedures (Jacokes and Pryce, 2010).

Second, the personal, end-connected nature of local interaction is often entrenched in a social enterprise's business model, as a deep, local embedding is necessary to develop effective solutions to societal problems, which are usually context-specific and complex (Beckmann and Zeyen, 2014). In addition, as social issues, such as structural inequality or social exclusion, often require a large variety of actors to join forces, many of the required resources tend to lie outside the social venture's direct control (Alvord et al., 2004; Dacin et al., 2011). From early on, social enterprises thus have to engage in a deep dialectic with a broad range of actors, articulating shared goals and deciding upon norms (Austin et al., 2006; Dacin et al., 2011). For example, Wheeler et al. (2005), studying 50 cases of social ventures in developing countries, concluded that achieving an increase in social value necessitated building ties with different stakeholders like governments simultaneously, as only then sufficient access to the variety of relevant assets, such as human capital, was possible.

Thus, networks and their effective coordination are a main element for survival and value creation (Light, 2008; Wheeler et al., 2005). However, while recent research in the context of social innovation has led to intriguing findings, it has been unclear how and why social networks evolve in this context (Barkema et al., 2015; Busch, 2014; Light, 2008). Thus, below we review relevant theory on networks and entrepreneurship for application in the context of social innovation, develop a related framework and discuss promising avenues for further research.

Social Networks and Orchestration

Social networks are understood as sets of actors and the ties that connect them (Brass et al., 2004), while social capital has been understood as the value that is embedded in those (Putnam, 2000). Previous research can broadly be divided into a stream focusing on network structure and a stream focusing on network governance and content.

Network structure

Network structure is concerned with the patterns of indirect and direct ties – the properties of the network as a whole (Hoang and Antoncic, 2003). Measures that have been employed to uncover structural patterns include network centrality, density and actor type (Easter and Conway Dato-on, 2015; Powell et al., 2005).

Network centrality refers to the position of an actor within the broader configuration of the network (Powell et al., 2005). Central positions allow for easier information access and reputation and status increases, as actors often attempt to attach to more central others due to higher expected benefits (Powell et al., 2005; Shipolov and Li, 2008). This leads to organizations that are involved early becoming more central over time, resulting in a bigger overall network size of relevant actors (Paquin and Howard-Grenville, 2012; Powell et al., 2005). Network density reflects the numbers of strong and weak ties between actors in a network. Strong ties are characterized by frequent and prolonged interaction, reciprocal services and emotional intimacy, while weak ties loosely connect various actors in arm's-length relationships (Granovetter, 1973).

The type of actors can include family, friends, customers, suppliers, distributors, investors and numerous other associations (Maurer and Ebers, 2006). The corresponding types of ties can range from fundraising, franchising, to grant-making partnerships (Easter and Conway Dato-On, 2015; Kohler, 2011). The multiplicity of ties is particularly relevant in the context of social innovation, where often a multitude of partners need to be engaged on different levels to tackle complex and intractable social issues (Light, 2008).

Network governance

Network governance refers to the content and control of resources that are exchanged within a social network (Hoang and Antoncic, 2003). This can include access to information and opportunities, emotional support, resources, and reputational and signaling content (Brass et al., 2004).

Given that stakeholders influence and are influenced by the actions of focal ventures in the network, stakeholder governance can be an important determinant (Maurer and Ebers, 2006) or moderator (Stam and Elfring, 2008) of a firm's performance. The multiplicity of stakeholders of social enterprises makes network governance particularly challenging in the context of social innovation, as discussed below.

Network orchestration

Given the importance of networks to venture development and performance, research has focused more and more on intentional network orchestration – the set of actions undertaken by a firm as it seeks to create and extract value from the network (Dhanaraj and Parkhe, 2006; Nambisan and Sawhney, 2011). As organizations face dissimilar resource requirements and challenges in different growth phases, an enterprise's ability to accommodate shifting demands by adjusting social networks over time is important to reach its objectives (Martinez and Aldrich, 2011; Maurer and Ebers, 2006). The entrepreneurship and innovation literature has thus suggested that enterprises evolve via progressive phases (Hite and Hesterly, 2001; Light, 2008; Paquin and Howard-Grenville, 2012).

Scholars have therefore increasingly studied how networks change over time (e.g., Maurer and Ebers, 2006) and how they can be proactively orchestrated (e.g., Nambisan and Sawhney, 2011), highlighting the importance of agency and *leadership* (Fleming and Waguespack, 2007). While the exact names, delineations and number of phases vary, they usually encompass an early *startup phase* (e.g., "opportunity recognition"; "emergence"), as well as a *growth phase* (e.g., "expansion") (Hite and Hesterly, 2001; Jacokes and Pryce, 2010; Light, 2008; Maurer and Ebers, 2006). Different phases hold dissimilar comparative advantages when it comes to the resource challenges of access, availability and uncertainty (Hite and Hesterly, 2001).[5]

Startup phase Ventures in early phases usually identify the opportunity and idea and launch the product and/or company (Maurer and Ebers, 2006). Newly created firms often lack critical resources to ensure survival – thus, uncertainty is high and legitimacy, reputation and market knowledge are usually lower than in later growth phases (Hite and Hesterly, 2001). The founder's social network and the firm's network at this point are often virtually synonymous (Hite and Hesterley, 2001; Paquin and Howard-Grenville, 2012). Bricolage – making the best out of whatever is at hand – plays a crucial role in this early phase (Baker and Nelson, 2005).

Social ventures usually start out with the ambition to tackle a social need, which defines the opportunity scope (Austin et al., 2006; Bull et al., 2008). A core challenge at this point is gaining acceptance in the market and among partners, given that as a new player, usually there is no proven track record (Jacokes and Pryce, 2010). Similar to commercial ventures, after some time, social ventures tend to "launch" the product and/or embark on the legal creation of the firm (Light, 2008). This includes recruiting the core team, acquiring physical capital and endowing social networks (Leadbeater, 1997). Bricolage – often in coordination with the respective local community – is particularly relevant for social ventures, as their customers often have a limited purchasing ability (Busch and Barkema, 2017; also see Alvord et al., 2004).

Thus, early phase social ventures imagine and discover the opportunity for change and take the first steps in this direction (Jacokes and Pryce, 2010; Light, 2008).

Growth phase In later phases (here collectively referred to as "growth phase"), commercial ventures start making strategic decisions to intentionally develop beyond mere sufficiency and survival (Hite and Hesterly, 2001; Kazanjian and Drazin, 1989). Growth necessitates broader resources, and networks often become more diverse (Hite and Hesterly, 2001).

Social ventures often follow a similar course (Leadbeater, 1997; Light, 2008).[6] The growth phase involves expanding the venture and acquiring new projects, users and partners (Leadbeater, 1997; Jacokes and Pryce, 2010). Combined with increased environmental uncertainty (due to yet unchartered territories and ambiguous institutional environments) this necessitates even broader resources (Light, 2008; Mair and Marti, 2009). Over time, social ventures start to institutionalize the venture and its idea and often aim to drive ecosystem change. Replication approaches such as social franchising often become important in this phase (e.g., Beckmann and Zeyen, 2014; Light, 2008; Weber et al., 2012).

Thus, social ventures in the growth phase often aim to develop their breadth and/or depth of impact (Bloom and Smith, 2010; Desa and Koch, 2014).

Network leadership

Network development often depends on individual agency and leadership (Light, 2008). Given that (social) innovation activities are fluid and less defined than traditional firm boundaries, they are often shaped by leaders' architectural and structural decisions and often influenced by their followers' choices of where to focus their efforts (Fleming and Waguespack, 2007). The most challenging role for a leader of fluid organizational forms is to integrate and bind stakeholders together by creating and occupying relevant network positions, for example, acting as boundary spanners (Fleming and Waguespack, 2007).

Recent studies have shown that charismatic and transformational leadership are particularly important in the social innovation context (see, e.g., Barkema et al., 2014). However, we know surprisingly little about how social organizations and their leaders navigate social networks, opening up intriguing questions for further research.

While the phase logic discussed above partly applies in the social context, social enterprises often develop different networks than commercial ventures. Thus, below we draw on the social innovation and entrepreneurship literature to "fill in the blanks" and develop a framework of network evolution and transition in the context of social innovation.

CONCEPTUAL FRAMEWORK: *TRANSFORMATIVE NETWORK ORCHESTRATION*

In this section, we will integrate the networks and leadership approaches discussed above into the social innovation context, develop a related conceptual framework and then, in the following section, suggest avenues for further research.

Startup Network (Startup Phase)

Social ventures usually start out with a social goal, defining the scope and operations and thus the range and variety of resource needs (Austin et al., 2006; Bull et al., 2008). Often the larger the scope of the social goal(s), the more (diverse) resources a social venture might need in order to be successful. The core challenge in this phase is gaining acceptance in the market and among partners (Jacokes and Pryce, 2010). Furthermore, newly created firms often lack critical resources to ensure survival – thus, networks play a crucial role to ensure initial viability. Below we discuss the evolving network structure and governance in the context of social innovation.

Network structure

In early phases, social entrepreneurs often draw on a variety of stakeholders to formulate the social value proposition and to reconcile the values and ideas of (potential) funders, customers and local communities (Bull et al., 2008). Ventures at this point often foster dense sets of connections, resulting in networks that are primarily based on socially embedded ties. Like commercial ventures, network cohesion is often based on norms of shared cognitive schema. Social ventures often already early on in their development assume a central network position to be able to formulate a convincing social value proposition and align stakeholder values and interests (Austin et al., 2006; Light, 2008). In order to effectively tackle the customers' needs and to develop community buy-in, local community members are frequently involved in product development, at times as members of the founding team. These strong local community ties can increase legitimacy through (perceived) increases in accountability and reliability.

Due to constraints on funding and incentives, social entrepreneurs often leverage volunteers to fill key functions, for example, as fundraisers, service providers or staff (Alvord et al., 2004). The lack of investor capital is related to limited measurability, long return cycles and high fragmentation of the marketplace, as well as lack of extrinsic incentives such as stock options (Kohler, 2011). Social ventures thus turn toward a broader set of philanthropists, foundations and governments for their capital needs, which leads to a further diversification of stakeholders (Austin et al., 2006). In lieu of direct financial returns, these funders and volunteers often demand non-financial benefits such as board positions, cooperative exchanges or particular reporting requirements (Jacokes and Pryce, 2010).

Network governance

In the startup phase, cohesive governance structures along opportunity, resource, political and emotional support dimensions accompany the above network. In this early phase, entrepreneurs rely on emotional support from interpersonal relationships, as resources are mobilized from neighbors, friends and family (Light, 2008). Opportunities are often drawn from the dense network both with respect to tangible resources and intangible needs and social entrepreneurs in this phase regularly benefit from in-depth information flows to build up their value proposition (Light, 2008). Face-to-face relations between volunteers and other stakeholders act as inexpensive monitoring and a sanctioning mechanism that coordinate the resource flows (Beckmann and Zeyen, 2014). The resulting dialectic can at times lead to mission expansion or mission drift, as founders are often pressed toward growing the solution, or changing it toward funders' goals (Austin et al., 2006).

Social ventures in this early phase frequently employ bricolage (Bacq et al., 2015). Engaging local (and often previously undervalued) partners in "making do by applying combinations of the resources at hand to new problems and opportunities" (Baker and Nelson, 2005, p. 333) is invariably critical for the co-creation of local solutions related to social change, and fosters social inclusion (Bacq et al., 2015; Busch and Barkema, 2017). Bricolage allows enterprises to access resources as well as discover new ideas (Bacq et al., 2015). Given the usually low purchasing power of clients and the limited access to conventional funding sources, bricolage is particularly salient in the context of social organizations. It has been shown that bricolage in early phases of social venture development can have positive effects due to a bias for action, rather than waiting for resources to come along (Bacq et al., 2015).

Thus, from the very early stages of development, social ventures need to engage in a dialectic with a variety of stakeholders (Austin et al., 2006).

Growth Network (Growth Phase)

In the growth phase, social ventures require networks that support expanding or adapting an organization's output to better match the magnitude of the social need or problem being tackled (Weber et al., 2012). As such, growth networks allow for breadth and depth of impact, as ventures in the growth stage attempt to expand geographic reach and/or the scope of the product or service (Desa and Koch, 2014). Breadth-impact networks help an organization increase its capacity to serve its membership base or geographic area via approaches such as social franchising (Beckmann and Zeyen, 2014). Depth-impact networks help expand the number and type of product/service activities (Desa and Koch, 2014). It follows that network structure and governance are increasingly arranged to allow for the scaling of social impact (Waitzer and Paul, 2011; Weber et al., 2012), as discussed below.[7]

Network structure

In this phase, social ventures often leverage the social, financial and human capital of network partners to address resource scarcity challenges and to scale up (Beckmann and Zeyen, 2014). Ventures use approaches such as social franchising to develop strong local relationships while expanding (Beckmann and Zeyen, 2014). Rather than continuing to rely on neighbors and friends, similar to commercial enterprises, social enterprises increasingly depend on professional accountants, lawyers, government agencies, capital providers, customers and suppliers (Light, 2008). Social ventures may turn toward a large variety of sources of capital, such as governments or foundations for grants, or social venture funds for investment. A previously organic network becomes more intentionally managed; the exploitation of structural holes is emphasized over cohesion; and primarily socially embedded ties are complemented with arm's-length relations (Busch, 2014). Over time, given the complexity of social issues and need for systemic solutions, successful (scaled) social ventures often aim to navigate whole ecosystems, enhancing the scale and scope of activities and solutions (Beckmann and Zeyen, 2014; Yu, 2015). Network structures are often adjusted to accommodate operational difficulties, insufficient distribution channels and the purchasing (in)ability of beneficiaries (Bloom and Smith, 2010). Network governance approaches are often adapted accordingly.

Network governance

A core governance challenge for growing social ventures is to maintain a focus on their social mission and customers while generating benefits for other stakeholders (Austin et al., 2006). While fundraising and securing financing play recurring and prominent roles across the whole life cycle, capital access is particularly salient during expansion. Governance structures at this phase tend to focus on resource mobilization and political support in lieu of opportunity recognition or emotional support. Governance structures need to balance a big-group logic (e.g., governing franchise-driven organizations) with a small-group cohesiveness (e.g., governing local community partners) (Beckmann and Zeyen, 2014).[8] Successful social ventures often support partners in the ecosystem with access to different types of resources, and alliances may be selected for mission alignment, rather than for efficiency (Bloom and Smith, 2010). Coordination with municipalities, government or political parties often increases due to heightened emphasis on systemic change.

Thus, the reasons for why networks change over time can be found in the changing resource needs and institutional contexts (Mair and Marti, 2009). The networks that are needed in early phases are not sufficient in later phases, where more dispersed, diverse resources are required. A social venture trying to navigate new network partnerships is faced with different network configurations that offer different optimizations of network structures and governance. In order for the venture to navigate over time, it needs to be sensitive to the needs of existing stakeholders, while identifying opportunities with new stakeholders. How does a social venture navigate partnerships as it grows its social impact?

Transformative network orchestration explains the reconfigurations of network structures and governance as social ventures and their impact evolve over time. Below, we will discuss two example mechanisms that have emerged from recent inductive studies that illustrate this overarching process/capability. These orchestration mechanisms may occur sequentially or in parallel and include various feedback loops that depend on the respective resource needs, which are driven by market, mission and opportunity changes.

Network Orchestration

Benevolent disembedding

Social enterprises gain large parts of their legitimacy by understanding and catering to local needs and often rely on the respective local community for the framing of their value proposition (Light, 2008). Their operating model is usually based on a "small-group" logic, grounded in a cultural and social context (Beckmann and Zeyen, 2014). The move toward expansion requires different stakeholder networks and governance, and it is often necessary to reach compromises that satisfy the multitude of relevant stakeholders (Light, 2008).

At the same time, social inclusion and the related deep, local embeddedness – for example, with regard to local norms – might constrain intentional network management; the advantage of being entrenched in local communities to access resources might turn into a liability in constraining the adaptation of the network, for example, when family members, friends or local community members claim benefits (Khayesi and George, 2011). Particularly in more collectivistic contexts, challenges such as (over-) embeddedness (e.g., Granovetter, 1985; Khayesi and George, 2011), social liability and maintenance costs (e.g., Khayesi et al., 2014) play a major role. Therefore, once enterprises start growing, they often need to decouple from the local context to avoid network inertia.

In the context of commercial ventures, a number of disembedding mechanisms have been discussed. These include hiring employees of other ethnicities (e.g., Granovetter, 1995), such as more non-family ties in the network (e.g., Khayesi et al., 2014), accumulating non-shareable durable goods at the expense of shareable durable goods (e.g., Di Falco and Bulte, 2011), focusing on non-kin customers to make denying credit easier (e.g., Granovetter, 1995), facilitating exit routes for companies or individuals and pruning by disbanding interlocks (e.g., Davis, 2016; Hernandez et al., 2015). These mechanisms are essentially about avoiding or cutting ties – thus, limiting social liability.

However, these simple disembedding mechanisms might not work well for social enterprises because a social enterprise's legitimacy is often based on its local embedding, making the process of disembedding more complex (Light, 2008). Social enterprises often develop particularly multiplex relationships with stakeholders; this multiplexity leads to higher tie embeddedness, as usually mutual obligations and expectations are imbued on different levels. This might increase the possibility of cognitive and relational lock-in.[9] Thus, social enterprises often have difficulties employing simple disembedding mechanisms and many social enterprises that aim to scale never do so.

Transformative network orchestration via mechanisms such as benevolent disembedding soothes the move from the startup phase to the growth phase, helping the social venture satisfy the multitude of relevant stakeholders (Busch and Barkema, 2016). Busch and Barkema (2016), in a study of six social enterprises in Kenya, showed how social ventures kept close local ties while disembedding. Instead of using simple decoupling mechanisms such as avoiding or cutting ties (see Davis, 2016; Granovetter, 1995; Hernandez et al., 2015), social enterprises decoupled while providing value to their local ties. Consistent with their social objectives and legitimacy, they turned potential social liabilities into neutral or even positive social capital.

Thus, social ventures often need to balance staying embedded and catering to local social needs with the emerging need to scale and disembed – we term this mechanism *benevolent disembedding*.

Transformative network leadership

Developing a business model that accounts for local norms, cultures and context and includes policymakers, regulators and other stakeholders becomes a challenge when a social venture aims to expand (Beckmann and Zeyen, 2014; Weber et al., 2012; Wheeler et al., 2005). At the same time, in order to be able to initiate social change, social enterprises often venture into new areas and thus need to engage with a broad range of (new) stakeholders. This is facilitated by *leadership* – a social process that engages stakeholders and the respective community (Day, 2000; Leitch et al., 2013).

We know from the innovation literature that the responsibility for (social) innovation – for good or bad – often lies squarely on the shoulders of leaders (Smith and Tushman, 2005). Transformational and charismatic leadership theories (Bass and Riggio, 2006) may inform the social innovation context on how to motivate group members and create personal commitment to a vision or collaboration. Specifically, *transformational leadership* has been linked to outcomes such as innovative behavior and performance via generating confidence among stakeholders and encouraging them to suggest innovative ideas (Kang et al., 2015). Transformational leaders motivate followers through their idealized influence ("charisma"), individual consideration and intellectual stimulation and often encourage stakeholders to alter the environment (Bass and Riggio, 2006).

Leadership is particularly effective if a task is challenging, if conditions or directions are uncertain, if short-term results cannot be measured and monetized through financial rewards or when faith or moral convictions of team members can be mobilized (Shamir et al., 1993). These are precisely the conditions that are present in the context of social innovation. Leadership thus becomes an important factor to navigate interdependencies, motivation and cooperation in this context.

Transformational leaders are likely to reach central positions in networks because they tend to use intrinsic means to motivate stakeholders (Jung et al., 2003; Kang et al., 2015). Indeed, recent findings of a longitudinal qualitative study at two of the most innovative organizations in India, Tata (producers of the Tata Nano) and Mjunction, revealed that charismatic leadership in the context of social innovation can be crucial

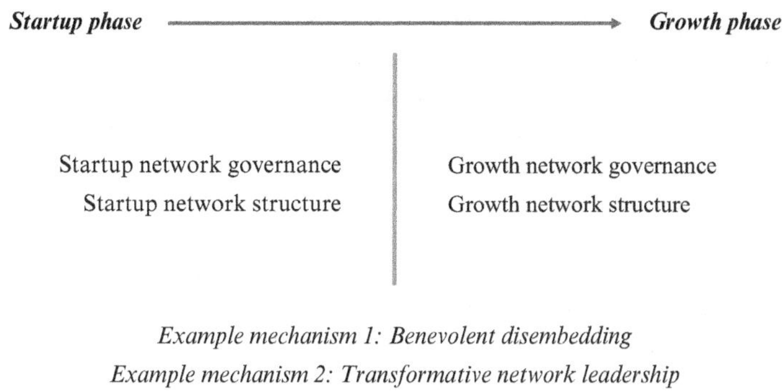

Figure 26.1 Conceptual framework: transformative network orchestration

(Barkema et al., 2014). In a similar vein, Busch and Barkema (2016) showed how social enterprise leaders can navigate whole ecosystems. They found that social enterprises *enabled co-creation ecosystems* via strengthening their customers' capacity to self-help and enhancing the context of social action. Shifting the perspective from resource-constrained environments as liabilities to troves of resourcefulness not only led to a shift of mindsets but also enhanced social inclusion by integrating previously undervalued people into the value chain. The social ventures *aligned the ecosystem* via establishing a dominant narrative and leveraging social control mechanisms. A social enterprise in Kenya, for example, became an active part of the value chains of its partners. By selling beehives to farmers and then buying back the honey and further helping farmers with financing the beehives via third parties, developing farmer capacity beyond the immediate "value capture" area of the social enterprise, they enabled a whole *transformative ecosystem*.

Thus, rather than developing dependency mechanisms, barriers to imitation and monetization mechanisms (e.g., Williamson and de Meyer, 2012), transformational leadership in the context of social innovation can support whole transformative ecosystems. We thus label this mechanism *transformative network leadership*.

Our discussion suggests a conceptual model as depicted in Figure 26.1. The *transformative network orchestration* framework depicts the process of engaging stakeholders in network growth and transition in the context of social innovation. Startup network structure and governance evolve into growth network structure and governance, driven by the (illustrative) mechanisms of *benevolent disembedding* and *transformative network leadership*. We define this *transformative network orchestration* as "the ability to effectively build, manage, govern and adapt networks for social change." This capability in earlier phases can be embodied by key individuals and teams such as the original founder(s), while in later stages it evolves more and more into an organizational capability.

Implications

In all, the *transformative network orchestration* framework indicates how and why social ventures navigate and transition their networks over time. Transitioning includes overcoming challenges related to institutionalizing and coherently communicating an idea, aligning a variety of potentially conflicting stakeholder expectations and disembedding from negative ties to avoid lock-in and network inertia.

Nahapiet and Ghoshal (1998), in their landmark paper on social capital, discussed four conditions that need to be in place for the effective combination and exchange of resources and, thus, the leveraging of social networks. These are the existence of the opportunity to exchange, the expectancy of value arising out of the exchange, the motivation of the engaged parties and the capability to combine information or expertise. However, while these conditions can help explain why social ventures are able to leverage their networks at a given point in time, they cannot explain why over time these conditions change (e.g., why a government might be unsupportive at the early phase of a venture, but champion it at later phases) and how and why these conditions can be proactively initiated or changed by social enterprises.

We suggest that *transformative network orchestration* can help explain this gap. The transformative leadership of a social entrepreneur/enterprise can "motivate" crucial stakeholders (e.g., employees, the government) to engage; can proactively create a narrative to show potential value of the collaboration ("value expectancy"); and can sustain the relationships necessary to combine experience and information. *Transformative network orchestration* is thus a necessary condition/capability for effectively building and leveraging social networks over time and at scale in the context of social innovation. It allows social ventures to develop, integrate and adapt their networks based on their respective needs.

An important implication of this discussion is that successful social enterprises might neither be only "brokers," connecting previously disconnected actors as "the third who enjoys" (see Burt, 1997; Obstfeld, 2005) nor only "integrators," bringing people together to fill structural holes as "the third who joins" (see Obstfeld, 2005; Xiao and Tsui, 2007), but rather be *transformative network orchestrators*, combining elements of both. This more holistic perspective focuses on orchestrating, enabling and transforming ecosystems, rather than on individual relationships or simple self-interest-driven (innovation) networks.

Thus, *transformative network orchestration* elucidates how a social venture can balance network structure and governance processes when navigating network partnerships, enabling a trust-based system that *transforms* rather than *monetizes* the broader ecosystem (Busch and Barkema, 2016). In doing so, network orchestration can be important for facilitating social inclusion not only as an outcome but also as a built-in process: for example, by integrating the poor as contributors, rather than treating them as "beneficiaries" without an effective role in the value chain. However, a socially inclusive orchestration process can hinder growth if it results in over-embeddedness, and thus requires mechanisms such as *benevolent disembedding.*

Importantly, the broader theme of enterprises facing tensions between social and financial objectives extends far beyond social enterprises. Given that commercial companies increasingly aim to create social value (see, e.g., recent work on "inclusive business model innovation," "business model innovation at the base of the pyramid" and "sustainable enterprises" such as Ansari et al., 2012; Eccles et al., 2014; George et al., 2012; Prahalad, 2004; Seelos and Mair, 2007), the implications of our discussion extend to other organizational forms. For example, commercial companies that operate in collectivistic low-income contexts might face similar challenges to the ones discussed above, such as limited purchasing ability of customers and the primacy of social relationships. This indeed is a major underlying assumption of this chapter: enterprises are not strictly social or financial, but often aim to balance a multitude of objectives. This indicates that commercial companies might (need to) employ similar tactics such as those used by social enterprises discussed in our study if they are to be effective in the context of social innovation.

The social venture context thus can be used to illustrate broader phenomena pertinent in the field of social innovation and organizational effectiveness, such as methods of coordination, multiplicity of goals and distribution of benefits. This is particularly relevant in more collectivistic contexts, where frequently social welfare and social capital are as important as financial capital (Ansari et al., 2012; George et al., 2012).

Next, we explore the intriguing avenues for further research that emerge from our discussion.

AVENUES FOR FURTHER RESEARCH

The themes discussed above open up intriguing avenues for further research.

Social Networks

There is a clear need for understanding how networks for social innovation develop over time. Further research could zoom in on each of the themes discussed above. For example, researchers could employ an inductive case study approach to investigate network evolution in different social innovation contexts and investigate what drives changes in the related network structures and governance mechanisms, as well as how these network elements might change over time. Under what conditions are social enterprises able to disembed while keeping local goodwill? What are the underlying mechanisms? What are the different factors that determine the efficacy of network orchestration in these contexts? Why are they (not) effective? What are the role of leaders' previous experience, education, personality type and skillsets in relation to social innovation networks? How could new technologies such as social media be used to map and enforce network constellations? Finally, what are the interdependencies between social networks and the social and/or financial performance of social ventures? For example, based on the literature on networks, one might assume that more successful social enterprises are more likely to attract better partners – but is that equally the case in the context of social innovation? In addition, deductive research could develop and test a number of hypotheses based on the above framework.

More specifically, at present there is still little (novel) management theory on non-Western settings, especially with regard to (in-) effective networks in poverty settings (George et al., 2016). This opens up a number of intriguing avenues for further research. Low-income contexts in South Asia and sub-Saharan Africa, for example, often manifest uncertainty due to the relatively fragile formal institutional frameworks, frequently necessitating (social) entrepreneurs to rely on informal networks (Barkema et al., 2015). In addition, networks may work very differently in these settings – for example, due to tribal dynamics. These settings thus provide an interesting context to explore relationships between networks, institutions and social innovation outcomes. For example, how do institutional changes interact with the social networks of social enterprises? How and why do social entrepreneurs adjust to institutional changes that affect the context of social innovation?

In these "extreme contexts" (Eisenhardt et al., 2016), the use of mixed methods might be particularly effective. For example, inductive qualitative longitudinal studies could help develop much-needed theory, complemented with a deductive quantitative longitudinal study to test emerging theories. The mixed methods approach allows the researcher to combine variance theorizing ("what works") with process theorizing ("how it is done"). We suggest the use of longitudinal data to observe how processes unfold over time and to capture the often complex longer-term outcomes.

In-depth qualitative research plays a particularly important role in these contexts, as studying (social) organization in extreme settings is very different from the (Western) setting from where traditional management theories originate and because in-depth local exposure is needed to uncover locally valid concepts and theories (Barkema et al., 2015). Non-Western settings are interesting both as intriguing research sites as well as a basis for developing evidence-based knowledge that can make a true difference. Collaborating with local researchers that speak the local language and have an appreciation of the respective local context might enhance the probability (and validity) of potential contributions.

Furthermore, given that commercial enterprises increasingly integrate social and environmental impact at the core of their business models (Eccles et al., 2014; George et al., 2012), the above-discussed insights could be tested in the context of social innovation projects at large multinational companies. For example, under which conditions do social innovation projects of multinational companies (e.g., in low-income contexts) scale up via local partnerships? Busch and colleagues interviewed and studied 16 of the world's leading chief executive officers (CEOs) as identified by *Harvard Business Review*'s "CEO Ranking 2016." Tentative results indicate that social and environmental impact has been increasingly embedded at the core of these traditionally more commercially focused organizations. Interestingly, the United Nations' *Sustainable Development Goals* framework is being used by many executives to develop a "north star" and to derive tangible performance measures related to social and environmental impact, and organizations are increasingly aiming to develop into *Impact Organizations* (Busch et al., 2018).[10]

However, while "public–private-partnerships" and "collaboration" played a major role in organizations' social innovation projects, the question of how social innovation can be navigated, particularly with local partners in poverty contexts turns out to be a major challenge for many of them (also see George et al., 2012). Further research could look into how large organizations might be able to learn from the network orchestration efforts of social enterprises, who often have a deep understanding of local communities (Light, 2008). In particular, researchers could look into which of the governance approaches and network structures discussed above might apply to organizations moving toward social or environmental impact. How are networks adjusted in contexts of a broad range of pre-existing "commercial" relationships that might suffer from network inertia? How and why do social intrapreneurs within larger organizations navigate old and new relationships for social innovation? Which types of leadership traits are needed for these network orchestrations?

Network Orchestration and Social Inclusion

Network orchestration can be an important process facilitating social inclusion (Busch and Barkema, 2017). Mechanisms such as *transformative network orchestration* can make groups of people within a society feel valued and important if they are integrated as contributors rather than "beneficiaries." However, this also opens up questions for further research, such as: Which types of network activities and mechanisms are enhancing social inclusion, which ones have unintended consequences?

For example, while the inclusion of vulnerable people in the value chain might lead to positive outputs (e.g., job creation), unintended longer-term implications might evolve (e.g., destabilization of previously integrated community structures). Thus, further research could look at questions such as: Under which conditions does network orchestration facilitate social inclusion? Adjacent questions could look into the question of when social inclusion of one group might lead to social exclusion of another, and which mechanisms might be more effective for social inclusion, which ones less so. For example, while bricolage-based scaling might be an effective way to engage large groups of previously undervalued people, we know little about the conditions under which this might (or might not) hold true.

Social Innovation Communities

A related theme pertains to the engagement of civil society in social innovation. A potential approach emerging as a way to address many of the challenges of social innovation is social innovation communities (Toivonen, 2016). Social innovation communities are collections of individuals, often from diverse fields, that are bound by informal relations and with an interest in social innovation and/or social and human capital development (Toivonen, 2016). Communities such as Sandbox Network, the Global Shapers and Ashoka aim to foster a spirit of positive innovation and are often based on proxy trust – trust is extended to members that one does not yet know. Could weak ties function as "quasi-strong ties" in these environments? Could "proxy trust" be developed to allow weak ties to work as if they were strong ties? And what is the role of community identity in relation to these questions?

Scholars could draw on the literature on communities of practice (e.g., Wenger, 2000), theories of social movements (e.g., Rao, 2008) and case studies of social innovation communities to distill the mechanisms by which social communities can address the challenges related to social innovation – such as developing trust-based ecosystems and communities. Related questions could focus on the role of leaders in this context: Do the assumptions regarding leadership in traditional innovation communities (e.g., Fleming and Waguespack, 2007) fully apply in the context of social innovation communities? If yes, how? If not, why not? In particular, we know little about the effects of transformational leadership and its influence beyond direct reports, and the role of leaders in forming unconventional innovation communities and/or social capital is severely under-researched (Leitch et al., 2013). Hence, studying the interaction of leadership and social innovation communities could be fruitful.

Replication

As increasing the well-being of its target population and initiating wider social change is at the core of many a social enterprise's mission, scalability is often a major objective (Dees et al., 2004; Weber et al., 2012).[11] Tackling social problems, including deep-rooted inequalities in education, health and living standards, requires the development of solutions that can be scaled quickly and cost-effectively in different settings (Seelos and Mair, 2007). However, while there are many examples of social innovations that have been successful on a local scale, taking these innovations into other contexts via local partnerships has proved highly challenging, particularly given that social problems manifest themselves differently in different places (Beckmann and Zeyen, 2014). Intriguingly, despite its importance, rigorous research on how social organizations in resource-constrained environments scale is scarce, and elucidating the mechanisms behind scaling in the context of social innovation leaves much space for further research and substantial contributions.

The replication/adaptation literature (e.g., Chliova and Ringov, 2017; Sutter et al., 2014) might have relevant input on how organizations replicate proven practices while being receptive to local partners and their context. The interplay of replication and adaptation is especially relevant in the social sector because social enterprises often operate across very different contexts (Beckmann and Zeyen, 2014). For social organizations, replication approaches like social franchising can overcome resource scarcity issues and help adapt to the local context by involving local individuals or organizations and their networks and resources (Ahlert et al., 2008). This is particularly salient in low-income contexts, where apart from intriguing exceptions such as the global development organization, BRAC, examples of organizations that have successfully scaled are scarce. Indeed, we know surprisingly little about how and under which conditions replication really works in resource-constrained environments (Chliova and Ringov, 2017).

This opens up intriguing avenues for further research. For example, what are the tradeoffs between replication and adaptation in the context of social innovation? What are the moderating variables that might indicate where and when accurate replication (or adaptation) is most applicable? Which factors and contingencies might affect the impact of replication on social outcomes? Why? How do organizations transfer knowledge to partners, such as local franchisees or the government? Further research could, for example, dive deeper into the qualities of the respective knowledge that is transferred, as well as the related outcomes.

Bricolage

While much of this chapter has focused on the acquisition of partner resources, often the (at times under-appreciated) resources that are already at hand (e.g., in the respective local community) are essential (Baker and Nelson, 2005), particularly in the context of social innovation (Bacq et al., 2015; Busch and Barkema, 2017). For example, former drug dealers might have previously channeled their energy in ways that were not socially beneficial – but given their resourcefulness, local embeddedness and authority, they have the potential to be potent "champions" for social innovation projects (Busch and Barkema, 2017). However, while the important role of bricolage in the social innovation context and with regard to social inclusion has been established, it is unclear if (and if so, under which conditions) bricolage can be scaled (Bacq et al., 2015; George et al., 2012).

Recent papers have shown that bricolage – which has traditionally been thought of as less scalable – can indeed be scalable (Busch and Barkema, 2017). Busch and Barkema (2017) show that via the use of particular heuristics (e.g., "mindful transfer"), bricolage can be scaled via local partners. Looking at local communities and individuals as potential co-creators – rather than "beneficiaries" or "victims" – goes a long way to avoid incentivizing a handout mentality and instead focus on developing buy-in, dignity, local empowerment and true social inclusion. This also points to the importance of looking at different variants of co-creation – bringing different parties together in order to jointly produce a mutually valued outcome. Future research could explore under which conditions this particular form of co-creation is possible – could, for example, large organizations take on a scaling bricolage approach? Which role does technology, such as social media, play in this process?

Last but not least, organizational development often happens without the respective individuals proactively thinking about each step. Further research could look into the role of (cultivating) serendipity in the social innovation process or for social outcomes. Given that in the intricate context of social innovation we often do not know which challenges we will face next, often an organization's best option might be to cultivate an environment that makes positive coincidences more likely to happen. How can we develop these conditions for serendipity? Which types of approaches facilitate, which ones hinder serendipity? For example, Busch et al. (2018) show how practices such as "project funerals" can cultivate, accelerate and sustain "positive coincidences," and facilitate an evolving capability: *curating serendipity*. Further research could elucidate the different conditions and mechanisms behind the facilitation of serendipity in the context of social innovation.

This chapter has focused on the social innovation process and its enactment via social enterprises. However, in order to truly understand the context of social innovation and to be able to develop strong theory that is helpful to academia and practice alike, elucidating the *actual* (as opposed to "envisioned") social outcomes such as social inclusion is crucial. Thus, below we will briefly discuss potential areas of research pertaining to social outcomes.

Social Outcomes

Social outcomes are often socially constructed; they are likely to differ across contexts and stakeholder groups and the end state and the changes required to reach it are often uncertain and evolve over time (Zollo et al., 2016). Thus, there is no one "golden bullet" for conceptualizing and measuring social outcomes and the fundamental assumption that organizations with social goals necessarily have positive "social impact" has been challenged (Karnani, 2007; Shakya and Rankin, 2008). Empirical evidence from the fields of development, anthropology and increasingly management suggests that anticipated social outcomes often do not materialize or are in fact often detrimental (Karnani, 2007; Shakya and Rankin, 2008). For instance, micro-finance schemes are detrimental if the poorest women in a group get ostracized for not being able to repay their part of the group loan (Shakya and Rankin, 2008), and programs benefiting Muslim boys may hurt Muslim girls (Nambissan, 2012).

Thus, the "impact" of organizations with social goals is more complex than one might assume at first glance and it is essential to look at research questions and lenses that allow us to understand the *actual* social outcomes. Thus, research questions could include: When is social "change" a true improvement for the target population and when is it simply changing without improvements? What are the potential *unintended consequences* of aiming to increase social value? The "dark side" of social innovation – for example unintended consequences – is an important area of further research. Work in anthropology (e.g., Huang, 2018) might have interesting pointers on the dynamics behind the potential reinforcement of existing inequality and power structures through social innovation.

Research on *proactive behavior* – self-initiated and future-oriented action that aims to change and improve the situation or oneself – could be interesting to integrate into the social innovation context, as proactivity has been linked to innovation and change (Crant, 2000; Grant and Ashford, 2008). A focus on proactivity might help us understand the longer-term outcomes of social interventions on the individual level (e.g., related to the development of individual capacity and capabilities; also see Nussbaum, 2011; Sen, 1999). Important research questions follow from these: How do social organizations influence proactive motivation (see, e.g., Parker et al., 2010)? In the context of education, for instance, little is known about the types of behaviors or actions that teachers might engage in that trigger and stimulate proactivity among children. Likewise, do these same behaviors and actions replicate in other contexts? How can organizations such as social incubators or governments facilitate proactive behavior?

Another approach to elucidate important social outcomes such as social inclusion is social capital. Social capital has often been conceptualized as a by-product of problem solving, or as an antecedent of the scaling of social impact – but it can also be an important outcome in itself. However, many projects particularly in poverty contexts have been shown to merely draw from or even destroy, rather than enhance, social capital (Ansari et al., 2012). Much work remains to be done on how social capital among the poor can be developed at scale, and it is an interesting lens to understand the complex social forces in the context of social innovation (George et al., 2012). How do different forms of social capital (e.g., bridging versus bonding social capital) interact over time in this context? How might technology like social media influence the "natural" boundaries of social capital? Is it possible that the cognitive and temporal limits of social capital can be relaxed given the new types of technology that allow for connecting often and with more people?

At the same time, the critical approach to social capital (e.g., Bolin et al., 2004) has highlighted the flipside of social capital. For example, criminal gangs or extremists are often encouraged by strong bonding social capital and groups that are based on strong social capital but do not bridge to others can become isolated and disenfranchised from exactly those groups with whom bridging ought to occur (Bolin et al., 2004). This raises the question: How could these potential hazards and potential negative implications of social capital be reduced? Under which conditions does social capital turn into a liability in the context of social innovation and how could this be overcome?

CONCLUSION

This chapter started out with the question of how and why social ventures develop their networks over time. Our *transformative network orchestration* framework distills core areas of research in the areas of networks, entrepreneurship and leadership and their potential application in the social innovation context.

We hope that researchers and practitioners alike will find this framework useful as a guiding structure to develop future research in this intriguing context. In a world where many solutions to societal issues require cooperation between private, public and voluntary sectors, social ventures as hybrid organizations illustrate phenomena that are widely applicable in the context of social change.

The responsibility of researchers extends to elucidating the actual outcomes of social innovation – including potential unintended consequences. Social innovation is not an end in itself, but the means toward achieving a more just, dignified and inclusive world. With the increasing attention to the normative dimension of business, our hope is that this research will help us inform and build organizations that enable people to become who they are truly capable of becoming. This will not only be fruitful on the aggregate societal level but also facilitate building organizations that are fit for the future – treating clients as potential co-creators rather than as "beneficiaries."

ACKNOWLEDGMENTS

We would like to thank Sarah Ashwin, Tim Weiss, Tuukka Toivonen, Rainer Busch, Gerry George, Stuart Hart, Juliane Reinecke, Janet Berkovitz, Geoffrey Desa, Malte Busch, Nicolas Friederici and the participants of a paper session at the Academy of Management conference 2015 for their valuable insights on previous versions of this chapter.

NOTES

1. Social inclusion is the act of making all groups of people within a society feel valued and important (Collins English Dictionary, 2019).
2. We define *transformative network orchestration* as "the ability to effectively build, manage, govern and adapt networks for social change."
3. Instruments to measure social inclusion and/or social integration include the *Social Inclusion Questionnaire User Experience* (Mezey et al., 2013); the *Social Inclusion Scale* (Secker et al., 2009); and the *Social Integration Survey* (Kawata and Revicki, 2008).
4. As we will discuss below ("further research"), the fact that commercial organizations increasingly integrate social and environmental goals at the core of their organizations makes the task of understanding networks in the sphere of social innovation all the more important and topical.
5. In order to not get trapped in deterministic, prescriptive, or "linear" notions and to keep parsimony, we thus clustered the phases into early "startup" and later "growth" phases, allowing for variation and iteration.
6. In this chapter, we focus on enterprises that *aim to grow.* Of course, some social ventures do not aim to grow and stay local by choice.
7. Network development often happens without the protagonist proactively thinking about each step and often dots are connected at hindsight.
8. A *small-group* or *microcosm* logic focuses on social interactions that are characterized by personal, face-to-face relationships and information norms. *Macro-cosms* ("*big-group* logic"), in turn, refer to the interactions that take place in society at large – in which interaction is rule-connected rather than end-connected (Beckmann and Zeyen, 2014).
9. Lock-in refers to the inability to cut old ties in favor of new ones (Maurer and Ebers, 2006). A similar phenomenon can be observed for commercial ventures in (collectivistic) low-income contexts, where social capital and communal well-being is often as important if not more so than financial capital (see below).
10. *Impact Organizations* are defined as "organizations reconciling financial and social impact at the same

strategic level," viewing social and financial objectives not as potentially conflicting (or "paradoxical"), but rather as potentially dialectical and mutually reinforcing (Busch et al., 2018). The emerging "enlightened self-interest" of market participants potentially results in an "enlightened self-interest-based model of capitalism."

11. We understand *scalability* as the ability to increase the impact that an organization produces to better match the magnitude of the social need it seeks to address (Mulgan, 2007b; Weber et al., 2012).

REFERENCES

Ahlert, D., M.H. Ahlert, H. Duong Dinh et al. (2008), *Social Franchising: A Way of Systematic Replication to Increase Social Impact*, Berlin: Bundesverband Deutscher Stiftungen.

Alvord, S.H., D.L. Brown and C.W. Letts (2004), "Social entrepreneurship and societal transformation", *Journal of Applied Behavioral Science* **40** (3), 260–82.

Ansari, S., K. Munir and T. Gregg (2012), "Impact at the 'BoP': the role of social capital in capability development and community empowerment", *Journal of Management Studies* **49**, 813–42.

Austin, J., H. Stevenson and J. Wei-Skillern (2006), "Social and commercial entrepreneurship: same, different, or both?", *Entrepreneurship Theory and Practice* **30** (1), 1–22.

Bacq, S., L.F. Ofstein, J.R. Kickul and L.K. Gundry (2015), "Bricolage in social entrepreneurship: how creative resource mobilization fosters greater social impact", *The International Journal of Entrepreneurship and Innovation* **16**, 283–9.

Bagnoli, L. and C. Megali (2009), "Measuring performance in social enterprises", *Nonprofit Voluntary Sector Quarterly* **40**, 149–64.

Baker, T. and R.E. Nelson (2005), "Creating something from nothing: resource construction through entrepreneurial bricolage", *Administrative Science Quarterly* **50**, 329–66.

Barkema, H.G., C. Coleridge, F. Qin, J. Smit and D. Stam (2014), "Business model innovation: team networks and leadership", Working paper, London School of Economics and Political Science.

Barkema, H.G., X.P. Che, G. George, Y. Luo and A.S. Tsui (2015), "West meets East: new concepts and theories", *Academy of Management Journal* **58**, 460–79.

Bass, B.M. and R.E. Riggio (2006), *Transformational Leadership*, 2nd edn, London: Routledge.

Batjargal, B., M.A. Hitt, A.S. Tsui, J.L. Arregle, J.W. Webb and T.L. Miller (2013), "Institutional polycentrism, entrepreneurs' social networks and new venture growth", *Academy of Management Journal* **56**, 1024–49.

Battilana, J. and M. Lee (2014), "Advancing research on hybrid organizing: insights from the study of social enterprises", *Academy of Management Annals* **8**, 397–441.

Battilana, J., M. Sengul, A. Pache and J. Model (2015), "Harnessing productive tensions in hybrid organizations: the case of work integration social enterprises", *Academy of Management Journal* **58**, 1658–85.

Beckmann, M. and A. Zeyen (2014), "Franchising as a strategy for combining small and large group advantages (logics) in social entrepreneurship: a Hayekian perspective", *Nonprofit & Voluntary Sector Quarterly* **43**, 502–22.

Bloom, P.N. and B.R. Smith (2010), "Identifying the drivers of social entrepreneurial impact: theoretical development and an exploratory empirical test of SCALERS", *Journal of Social Entrepreneurship* **1** (1), 126–45.

Bolin, B., E. Hackett, S. Harlan et al. (2004), "Bonding and bridging: understanding the relationship between social capital and civic action", *Journal of Planning Education and Research* **24**, 64–77.

Brass, D.J., H.R. Galaskiewicz, W.P. Greve and A. Tsai (2004), "Taking stock of networks and organizations: a multilevel perspective", *Academy of Management Journal* **47** (6), 795–817.

Bull, M., H. Crompton and D. Jayawarna (2008), "Coming from the heart (the road is long)", *Social Enterprise Journal* **4** (2), 108–25.

Burt, R.S. (1997), "The contingent value of social capital", *Administrative Science Quarterly* **42**, 349–65.

Busch, C. (2014), "Substantiating social entrepreneurship research: exploring the potential of integrating social capital and networks approaches", *International Journal of Entrepreneurial Venturing* **6** (1), 69–84.

Busch, C. and H.G. Barkema (2016), "How and why does the network of social entrepreneurs in low-income contexts influence performance?", *Academy of Management Proceedings*, Vol. 2016, No. 1, 30 November. https://doi.org/10.5465/ambpp.2016.12573abstract.

Busch, C. and H.G. Barkema (2017), "Scaling bricolage in the context of deep poverty", *Academy of Management Proceedings*, Vol. 2017, No. 1, 30 November. https://doi.org/10.5465/ambpp.2017.11768abstract.

Busch, C., C. Gyori and L. Sharp (2018), "Purpose activation", in C. Gyori, L. Sharp, C. Busch and M. Brahman (eds), *North Star Journey: Purpose-Driven Leadership in the 21*st *Century*, Washington, DC: Leaders on Purpose, pp. 20–34.

Chiesi, A.M. (2007), "Measuring social capital and its effectiveness: the case of small entrepreneurs in Italy", *European Sociological Review* **23** (4), 437–53.

Chliova, M. and D. Ringov (2017), "Scaling impact: template development and replication at the base of the pyramid", *Academy of Management Perspectives* **31**, 44–62.
Collins English Dictionary (2019), "Social inclusion", https://collinsdictionary.com/dictionary/english/social-inclusion.
Crant, J.M. (2000), "Proactive behavior in organizations", *Journal of Management* **26**, 435–62.
Dacin, T., P.A. Dacin and P. Tracey (2011), "Social entrepreneurship: a critique and further directions", *Organization Science* **22** (5), 1203–13.
Davis, J.P. (2016), "The group dynamics of interorganizational relationships: collaborating with multiple partners in innovation ecosystem", *Administrative Science Quarterly* **35**, 128–52.
Day, D. (2000), "Leadership development: a review in context", *Leadership Quarterly* **11** (4), 581–611.
Dees, J.G., B.B. Anderson and J. Wei-Skillern (2004), "Scaling social innovation: strategies for spreading social innovations", *Stanford Social Innovation Review* **1**, 34–43.
Desa, G. and J.L. Koch (2014), "Scaling social impact: building sustainable social ventures at the base-of-the-pyramid", *Journal of Social Entrepreneurship* **5**, 146–74.
Dhanaraj, C. and A. Parkhe (2006), "Orchestrating innovation networks", *Academy of Management Review* **31** (3), 659–69.
Di Falco, S. and E. Bulte (2011), "The dark side of social capital: kinship, consumption and savings", *Journal of Development Studies* **47**, 1128–54.
Dufays, F. and B. Huybrechts (2014), "Connecting the dots for social value: a review on social networks and social entrepreneurship", *Journal of Social Entrepreneurship* **5**, 214–37.
Easter, S. and M. Conway Dato-On (2015), "Bridging ties across contexts to scale social value: the case of a Vietnamese social enterprise", *Journal of Social Entrepreneurship* **6** (3), 320–51.
Eccles, R.G., I. Ioannou and G. Serafeim (2014), "The impact of corporate sustainability on organizational processes and performance", *Management Science* **60** (11), 2835–57.
Eisenhardt, K.M., M.E. Graebner and S. Sonenshein (2016), "Grand challenges and inductive methods: rigor without rigor mortis", *Academy of Management Journal* **59**, 1113–23.
Fleming, L. and D.M. Waguespack (2007), "Brokerage, boundary spanning and leadership in open innovation communities", *Organization Science* **18**, 165–80.
George, G., A.M. McGahan and J. Prabhu (2012), "Innovation for inclusive growth: towards a theoretical framework and a research agenda", *Journal of Management Studies* **49** (4), 661–83.
George, G., C. Corbishley, J.N.O. Khayesi, M.R. Haas and H. Tihanyi (2016), "From the editors", *Academy of Management Journal* **59**, 377–93.
Granovetter, M.S. (1973), "The strength of weak ties", *American Journal of Sociology* **78** (6), 1360–80.
Granovetter, M. (1985), "Economic action and social structure: the problem of embeddedness", *American Journal of Sociology* **91**, 481–510.
Granovetter, M. (1995), "The economic sociology of firms and entrepreneurs", in A. Portes (ed.), *The Economic Sociology of Immigration: Essays on Networks, Ethnicity and Entrepreneurship*, New York: Sage, pp. 128–65.
Grant, A. and S.J. Ashford (2008), "The dynamics of proactivity at work", *Research in Organizational Behavior* **28**, 3–28.
Hernandez, E., W.G. Sanders and A. Tuschke (2015), "Network defense: pruning, grafting and closing to prevent leakage of strategic knowledge to rivals", *Academy of Management Journal* **58**, 1233–60.
Hite, J.M. and W.H. Hesterly (2001), "The evolution of firm networks: from emergence to early growth of the firm", *Strategic Management Journal* **22** (3), 275–86.
Hoang, H. and B. Antoncic (2003), "Network-based research in entrepreneurship: a critical review", *Journal of Business Venturing* **18** (2), 165–87.
Huang, J.Q. (2018), "The ambiguous figures of social enterprise: gendered flexibility and relational work among the iAgents of Bangladesh", *American Ethnologist* **4**, 603–16.
Jacokes, J. and J. Pryce (2010), "The life cycle of social enterprise financing", in Social Enterprise Alliance (ed.), *Succeeding at Social Enterprise – Hard-Won Lessons for Non-Profits and Social Entrepreneurs*, San Francisco, CA: Jossey-Bass, pp. 23–45.
Jung, D.I., C. Chow and A. Wu (2003), "The role of transformational leadership in enhancing organizational innovation: hypotheses and some preliminary findings", *Leadership Quarterly* **14**, 525–44.
Kang, J.H., G.T. Solomon and D.Y. Choi (2015), "CEO's leadership styles and managers' innovative behavior: investigation of intervening effects in an entrepreneurial context", *Journal of Management Studies* **52**, 531–54.
Karnani, A. (2007), "Doing well by doing good – case study: 'Fair & Lovely' whitening cream", *Strategic Management Journal* **28**, 1351–7.
Kawata, A.K. and D.A. Revicki (2008), "Reliability and validity of the social integration survey (SIS) in patients with schizophrenia", *Quality of Life Research* **17**, 123–35.
Kazanjian, R.K. and R. Drazin (1989), "An empirical test of a stage of growth progression model", *Management Science* **35**, 1489–505.
Khayesi, J.N.O. and G. George (2011), "When does the socio-cultural context matter? Communal orientation

and entrepreneurs' resource accumulation efforts in Africa", *Journal of Occupational and Organizational Psychology* **84**, 471–92.
Khayesi, J.N.O., G. George and J. Antonakis (2014), "Kinship in entrepreneur networks: performance effects of resource assembly in Africa", *Entrepreneurship Theory and Practice* **38**, 1323–42.
Kohler, J. (2011), *Coordinating Impact Capital: A New Approach to Investing in Small and Growing Businesses*, Santa Clara, CA: Santa Clara University Press.
Leadbeater, C. (1997), *The Rise of the Social Entrepreneur*, London: Demos.
Leitch, C.M., C. McMullan and R.T. Harrison (2013), "The development of entrepreneurial leadership: the role of human, social and institutional capital", *British Journal of Management* **24**, 347–66.
Light, P.C. (2008), *The Search for Social Entrepreneurship*, Washington, DC: Brookings Institution Press.
Lyon, F. and H. Fernandez (2012), "Strategies for scaling up social enterprise: lessons from early years providers", *Social Enterprise Journal* **8** (1), 63–77.
Mair, J. and I. Marti (2006), "Social entrepreneurship research: a source of explanation, prediction and delight", *Journal of World Business* **41** (1), 36–44.
Mair, J. and I. Marti (2009), "Social entrepreneurship as institution building", in E. Robinson (ed.), *International Perspectives on Social Entrepreneurship Research*, Basingstoke: Palgrave Macmillan, pp. 144–59.
Martinez, M.A. and H.E. Aldrich (2011), "Networking strategies for entrepreneurs: balancing cohesion and diversity", *International Journal of Behavioral Research* **17**, 7–38.
Maurer, I. and M. Ebers (2006), "Dynamics of social capital and their performance implications: lessons from biotechnology start-ups", *Administrative Science Quarterly* **51** (2), 262–92.
Mezey, G., S. White, A. Thachil, R. Berg, S. Kallumparam, O. Nasiruddin, C. Wright and H. Killaspy (2013), "Development and preliminary validation of a measure of social inclusion for use in people with mental health problems: the SInQUE", *International Journal of Social Psychiatry* **59**, 501–7.
Mulgan, G., S. Tucker, R. Ali and B. Sander (2007a), *Social Innovation: What It Is, Why It Matters and How It Can Be Accelerated*, Oxford: Skoll Centre for Social Entrepreneurship.
Mulgan, G., R. Ali, R. Halkett and B. Sanders (2007b), *In and Out of Sync: The Challenge of Growing Social Innovations*, London: NESTA.
Nahapiet, J. and S. Ghoshal (1998), "Social capital, intellectual capital and the organizational advantage", *Academy of Management Review* **23**, 242–66.
Nambisan, S. and M. Sawhney (2011), "Orchestration processes in network-centric innovation: evidence from the field", *Academy of Management Perspectives* **25** (3), 40–57.
Nambissan, G.B. (2012), "Business as usual? Private schools for the poor", *Economic & Political Weekly* **47**, 24–36.
Nicholls, A., J. Simon and M. Gabriel (2015), "Introduction: dimensions of social innovation", in A. Nicholls, J. Simon and M. Gabriel (eds), *New Frontiers in Social Innovation Research*, London: Palgrave, pp. 1–26.
Nussbaum, M. (2011), *Creating Capabilities: The Human Development Approach*, Cambridge, MA: Belknap.
Obstfeld, D. (2005), "Social networks, the tertius iungens orientation and involvement in innovation", *Administrative Science Quarterly* **50**, 100–30.
Paquin, R.L. and J. Howard-Grenville (2012), "Blind dates and arranged marriages: longitudinal processes of network orchestration", *Organization Studies* **34**, 1623–53.
Parker, S.K., U.K. Bindl and K. Strauss (2010), "Making things happen: a model of proactive motivation", *Journal of Management* **36**, 827–56.
Powell, W.W., D.R. White, K.W. Kogut and J. Owen-Smith (2005), "Network dynamics and field evolution: the growth of inter-organizational collaboration in the life sciences", *American Journal of Sociology* **110** (4), 1132–205.
Prahalad, C.K. (2004), *The Fortune at the Bottom of the Pyramid: Eradicating Poverty Through Profits*, Upper Saddle River, NJ: Wharton School Publishing.
Putnam, R. (2000), *Bowling Alone: The Collapse and Revival of American Community*, New York: Simon & Schuster.
Rao, H. (2008), *Market Rebels: How Activists Make or Break Radical Innovations*, Princeton, NJ: Princeton University Press.
Rivera-Santos, M., D. Holt, D. Littlewood and A. Kolk (2015), "Social entrepreneurship in sub-Saharan Africa", *Academy of Management Perspectives* **29**, 72–91.
Secker, J., S. Hacking, L. Kent, J. Shenton and H. Spandler (2009), "Development of a measure of social inclusion for arts and mental health project participants", *Journal of Mental Health* **18**, 65–72.
Seelos, C. and J. Mair (2007), "Profitable business models and market creation in the context of deep poverty: a strategic view", *Academy of Management Perspectives* **21** (4), 49–63.
Sen, A. (1999), *Development as Freedom*, 1st edn, New York: Oxford University Press.
Shakya, Y.B. and K.N. Rankin (2008), "The politics of subversion in development practice: an exploration of microfinance in Nepal and Vietnam", *Journal of Development Studies* **44**, 1214–35.

Shamir, B., R.J. House and M.B. Arthur (1993), "The motivational effects of charismatic leadership: a self-concept based theory", *Organization Science* **4**, 577–94.
Shipolov, A.V. and S.X. Li (2008), "Can you have your cake and eat it too? Structural holes' influence on status accumulation and market performance in collaborative networks", *Administrative Science Quarterly* **53**, 73–108.
Smith, W.K. and M.L. Tushman (2005), "Managing strategic contradictions: a top management model for managing innovation streams", *Organization Science* **16**, 522–36.
Stam, W. and T. Elfring (2008), "Entrepreneurial orientation and new venture performance: the moderating role of intra- and extra-industry social capital", *Academy of Management Journal* **51** (1), 97–111.
Sutter, C.J., G.M. Kistruck and S. Morris (2014), "Adaptations to knowledge templates in base-of-the-pyramid markets: the role of social interaction", *Strategic Entrepreneurship Journal* **8**, 303–20.
Toivonen, T. (2016), "What is the social innovation community? Conceptualizing an emergent collaborative organization", *Journal of Social Entrepreneurship* **7**, 49–73.
Waitzer, J.M. and R. Paul (2011), "Scaling social impact: when everybody contributes, everybody wins", *Innovations* **6** (2), 143–55.
Weber, C., A. Kroeger and K. Lambrich (2012), "Scaling social enterprises – a theoretically grounded framework", Paper presented at the Academy of Management Conference, Boston.
Wenger, E. (2000), "Communities of practice and social learning systems", *Organization* **7** (2), 225–46.
Wheeler, D., K. McKague, J. Thomson, R. Davies, J. Medalye and M. Prada (2005), "Creating sustainable local enterprise networks", *MIT Sloan Management Review* (Fall), 33–40.
Williamson, P.T. and A. de Meyer (2012), "Ecosystem advantage: how to successfully harness the power of partners", *California Management Review* **55**, 24–46.
Xiao, Z. and A.S. Tsui (2007), "When brokers may not work: the cultural contingency of social capital in Chinese high-tech firms", *Administrative Science Quarterly* **2**, 1–31.
Yu, X. (2015), "Social entrepreneurship in China's non-profit sector: the case of innovative participation of civil society in post-disaster reconstruction", *China Perspectives* **3**, 53–61.
Zollo, M., E.L.M. Bettinazzi, K. Neumann and P. Snoeren (2016), "Toward a comprehensive model of organizational evolution: dynamic capabilities for innovation and adaptation of the enterprise model", *Global Strategy Journal* **6**, 225–44.

27. Empowerment, social innovation and social change

Helen M. Haugh and Maggie O'Carroll

INTRODUCTION

Scholarly interest has turned to the societal challenges of inequality (Tilly, 1998), poverty (Thorp et al., 2005) and social exclusion (Colquitt and George, 2011) and a growing body of research claims that system-wide transformations are required to address such grand challenges (Seyfang and Haxeltine, 2012). Throughout their lives, women are treated differently and lag behind men in many domains (OECD, 2013, 2017) – they are denied access to education, employment and political participation (Duflo, 2012). Such disadvantages, however, are not exclusive to women from developing nations and significant gender disparities exist across the globe in educational achievement and career progression, earnings and employment conditions, entrepreneurship, financial literacy and economic empowerment, and representation in family, community and political decision-making (OECD, 2017). Intersectional stigmatization by nationality, ethnicity and displacement renders men, as well as women, socially excluded and powerless in the context of both developed and developing nations. Social innovation to instil empowerment responds to such inequality, disadvantage and social exclusion by developing new products, services and programmes that promote social inclusion and advocate for social change (Phills et al., 2008).

The United Nations frames social inclusion as promoting *a society for all* in which policies to eradicate poverty, create employment, uphold human rights and principles of equity and equality are fundamental (United Nations, 2010). Many countries have introduced social inclusion policies that focus on human identity and wellbeing (Berman and Phillips, 2000; Saraceno, 1997). The essential elements of wellbeing include access to material goods such as food and shelter, as well as opportunities to meaningfully participate in social life, such as education, work, politics and cultural activities (Collins, 2003). To achieve a state of wellbeing individuals must be empowered to pursue their chosen goals in relation to such non-material aspects of life.

Strategies to promote social inclusion focus on protecting political, civil and human rights, enacting anti-discrimination legislation and progressive social policies, and redistributing opportunity through education, training and employment (Lister, 1998). In relation to employment, social inclusion comprises more than securing paid work – the quality of work is also important. Low paid and dirty work may reduce economic marginality but not lead to social inclusion (Atkinson, 1998). Nor does unemployment equate with social exclusion – participation in voluntary, familial and unpaid care work may reduce social isolation and foster community cohesion (Levitas, 1998). But how does one go about fostering social inclusion in societies responsible for creating social exclusion in the first place? We turn to empowerment to address this conundrum.

EMPOWERMENT

Empowerment is a broad concept that refers, in general, to gaining influence over events and outcomes of importance. To be empowered means to understand and have influence over the personal, social, economic and political forces that impact on one's life (Kabeer, 1999; Schulz et al., 1995). Broadly, empowerment is summarized as any action that promotes the participation of people, organizations and communities in gaining control over their life in both their community and larger society. This perspective of empowerment focuses on being empowered to act and bring about change, not as the capacity to dominate others (Wallerstein and Bernstein, 1988, p. 380). Empowerment is thus concerned with differences in people's capacity to make choices (Kabeer, 1999, 2005a) and stems from inequalities in access to 'opportunities and rewards for different social positions or status within a group' (Mair et al., 2016, p. 2021).

While definitions of empowerment are numerous, Kabeer's frequently employed definition suggests that empowerment is a tripartite configuration of agency, resources and achievements (Kabeer, 1999). Agency describes the ability to define goals and act upon them (Kabeer, 1999, p. 438). In practice, agency is manifest in the ability of individuals or collectives to make meaningful decisions in the face of prevailing power structures. Second, resources comprise the material and non-material assets through which agency may be exercised. Access to resources is determined by the institutional rules and norms in play that, somewhat inevitably, vary between sites and contexts (Kabeer, 1999). The power structures that control access to resources are vested in regulatory, cultural and social institutions which, in some contexts, restrict access to resources by specific groups. For example, irrespective of gender, access to resources by stigmatized groups, such as refugees, is tightly controlled by regulatory, cognitive and normative institutions (de la Chaux et al., 2018). Agency and resources together constitute capabilities, namely, the potential that people have for living the life they want. The third component of empowerment is achievement, namely, the outcome(s) of combining agency and resources in activities to generate social change. When empowerment is instilled the impacts are deemed to include positive self-image, self-confidence, the ability to think critically, group cohesion and fostering decision-making and action (Amin et al., 1994; Kabeer, 1999; Schulz et al., 1995). In contrast, when the failure to achieve one's goals is attributed to the constraints on the ability to choose, then this is taken to be the manifestation of disempowerment (Kabeer, 1999, p. 438).

Reading across the literature, we find that four characteristics of empowerment are evident from extant research and, further, that each characteristic has implications for social inclusion. First, empowerment is processual and comprises movement along a continuum towards becoming more empowered (Jackson et al., 1989; Labonte, 1990; Schulz et al., 1995). For a person to become empowered means being able to progress from being denied the ability to make choices towards acquiring such ability (Kabeer, 1999). Second, empowerment is agentic in that a person takes control over personal processes, or a community is in command of community processes (Dohmwirth and Hanisch, 2018; Hjorth, 2003; Schulz et al., 1995). Third, empowerment is multidimensional (Mosedale, 2005; Zimmerman, 2000; Zimmerman and Rappaport, 1988). The dimensions include different levels, such as individual, organizational and community (Dohmwirth and Hanisch, 2018; Schulz et al., 1995) which in turn are connected to society, and different domains of empowerment, for example, personal, social, economic and political (Schulz et al., 1995). Finally, and following on from multidimensionality, attempts to measure empowerment are fraught with definitional and measurement challenges (Narayan-Parker, 2005). A recent review article noted that while increasing the economic status of women is understood to be a pathway to improving reproductive health outcomes, connecting health and economic interventions in practice was rare (Grown et al., 2016). We next consider social innovation and empowerment.

SOCIAL INNOVATION AND EMPOWERMENT

Social innovation is defined as 'introducing new products, processes or programs that profoundly change the basic routines, resource and authority flows or beliefs of the social system in which the innovation occurs' (Westley and Antadze, 2010, p. 2). Examples of social innovations include programmes that promote furniture recycling (Tremblay and Gutberlet, 2012), community-owned and tenant managed housing (Howell, 2016) and work integration (Pache and Santos, 2013), as well as projects concerning local food production, food banks and access to microcredit (Church and Elster, 2002; Sanyal, 2009). Social innovation seeks to disrupt basic beliefs by challenging the 'social system and social institutions that govern people's conduct by affecting the fundamental distribution of power and resources' (Wesley and Antadze, 2010, p. 3). The effectiveness of social innovation is assessed in terms of individual, community and societal impact and durability. Since empowerment may be realized at individual, collective and system levels, social innovation has the potential to instil empowerment. We employ the label *emancipatory social innovation* to describe new socially and environmentally useful products, services and programmes that directly and indirectly empower beneficiaries.

Emancipatory social innovations originate from a range of sources, including for example, government programmes (Onyejekwe, 2001), corporations (Scott et al., 2012), business incubators (Nicholls and Murdoch, 2012) and social entrepreneurs (Witkamp et al., 2011). While the efficacy of such sources for emancipatory social innovation is yet to be established, grassroots solutions tend to be closely embedded in the interests and values of communities (Seyfang and Smith, 2007) and are thus likely to be more efficacious than top-down initiatives. Since grassroots initiatives are led by activists and social entrepreneurs (Seyfang and Smith, 2007; Witkamp et al., 2011), they will be anchored in the established regulatory, cognitive and normative institutions that they directly seek to change. Culturally embedded emancipatory social innovation(s) is thus sensitive to long held values and beliefs that, although slow to change, may be supported to shift over time.

MEASURING EMPOWERMENT

Although lacking an agreed definition and standardized measurement techniques, measuring empowerment provides a way to facilitate comparisons over time, between locations, demonstrate the impact of specific interventions and draw out the implications for policy and practice (Kabeer, 1999). Alongside empowerment initiatives, the practices involved in evaluating the extent to which interventions instil empowerment 'brings the voice of disempowered citizens to those who have power' (Miller and Campbell, 2006, p. 297) and opens up possibilities for change. Across different contexts and cultures, empowerment is argued to be an isomorphic construct that retains the same basic meaning across the levels of analysis (Maynard et al., 2012) which we consider next.

Individual

Individual empowerment (Zimmerman, 1990) refers to a person's life decisions such as self-efficacy, personal competence (Schulz et al., 1995, p. 310) and the capacity for self-help (Withorn, 1980). At the personal level, empowerment also considers awareness of the social and political context, and the development of skills needed to bring about social change (Kieffer, 1984). An empowered person is aware of their personal agency and possesses the capacity to act accordingly (Miller and Campbell, 2006). Techniques to evaluate individual empowerment have been created to measure generic empowerment, such as the Women's Empowerment and Agriculture Index (Alkire et al., 2013) and the Oxfam Guide to Measuring Women's Empowerment (Lombardini et al., 2017), as well as specific empowerment dimensions such as the Social and Health Assessment Instrument (Berg et al., 2009) and the Warwick-Edinburgh Mental Well Being Scale (Putz et al., 2012).

Organization

In organizations, empowerment involves delegating decision-making authority to the lowest employee level as a means to increase employee motivation (Seibert et al., 2004). Typical practices to increase employee empowerment include creating structures that diffuse authority and developing policies to embed employee empowerment. Such empowerment initiatives are introduced to enhance employee performance, wellbeing and positive attitudes (Maynard et al., 2012). Empowered organizations are those that have influence over their environments and the ability to affect the distribution of social and economic resources (Schulz et al., 1995). Empowered groups and organizations are sufficiently confident to compete effectively for resources and influence policy and gain from being networked to others (Miller and Campbell, 2006). As with measuring individual empowerment, several organizational-level frameworks have been developed, for example, the Empowerment Barometer (Blanchard et al., 1995).

Community

At the community level, individuals, groups and organizations influence empowerment by shaping access to social, economic and political resources (Schulz et al., 1995). Using Kabeer's definition of empowerment, community empowerment is the process of gaining influence over conditions that matter to people who share neighbourhoods, workplaces, experiences or concerns. Through community participation, individuals and groups are able to mobilize efforts towards social and political change (Laverack, 2001, 2005). While standardized measures of community empowerment are available, such as the community efficacy scale developed by Zimmerman and Rappaport (1988), the evaluation of the extent of community empowerment tends to be dominated by qualitative case study research that uncovers the mechanisms that connect programmes and projects to social change outcomes (for a review, see Miller and Campbell, 2006). In the next section we build and develop a new framework to categorize extant empowerment research.

FRAMING EMPOWERMENT, SOCIAL INNOVATION AND SOCIAL CHANGE

From our review of the empowerment and emancipatory social innovation literatures we advance a new framework that extends prior reviews (e.g., de Bruin et al., 2007) and brings together disparate domains of inquiry. The framework employs the distinction between empowerment dimensions of agency, resources and achievements (Kabeer, 1999), empowerment domains (Schulz et al., 1995) and emancipatory social innovation. The framework is presented in Table 27.1 and discussed below. For each principal domain we summarize empowerment pathways and present an illustrative case study.

Personal Empowerment

The large volume of empowerment research has considered a wide range of domains in which people may become empowered. To organize this literature our framework distinguishes between physical, psychological and intellectual empowerment. In each category we offer examples of disempowerment and explain how to connect agency, resources, achievements and social change. To illustrate the three dimensions of personal empowerment we discuss Camfed, a registered charity and international non-profit organization established in 1993 to support girls access to primary and secondary education and empower young women to develop as leaders of change in their communities (https://camfed.org).

Physical: Abuse

We adopt a female perspective for abuse, namely, all forms of physical cruelty and violence. For women, poor reproductive health and wellbeing, lack of fertility control and family size, and child health are all associated with disempowerment (Kabeer, 1999). For example, although the ability to manage menstrual health with adequate knowledge, safety and dignity and without stigma is an essential human right, millions of girls and women in low-resource contexts are not well prepared for menstruation. Their rights are compromised if they are required to be isolated from their family, avoid work, withdraw from activities, school, and face physical risks because of a basic physiological process (Keith, 2016; Philipps-Howard et al., 2015; Wilson et al., 2014). Such physical risks spill over into psychological disempowerment resulting from fear, shame, lack of self-esteem and confidence. In addition, it is well documented that females are highly vulnerable to gender-based violence including harassment, physical assault and rape (Keith, 2016). Emancipatory social innovations to overcome abuse include increasing access to professional advice, support, the provision or access to appropriate products and services, and interventions to advance personal, social, economic and political empowerment (Schuler et al., 1996; Sen, 1999).

Table 27.1 Analytical framework for emancipatory social innovation

Domain		Personal		Social	Economic	Political
Category	Physical	Psychological	Intellectual			
Denied the ability to make choices	*Abuse*: Lack of reproductive health and fertility control, domestic violence, infant mortality and childhood disease	*Oppression*: Mental health disorders, unquestioned acceptance of subordinate status	*Ignorance*: Poor access to education, low human capital	*Isolation*: Low social capital, restricted family and social networks	*Poverty*: Low income, lack of sustainable livelihood	*Powerlessness*: Lack of political representation and participation
Agency* *The ability to define goals and act upon them	Fertility regulation, critical awareness of personal safety and risk, reduce or delay sexual and drug risks	Identity formation, gender awareness, joint family decision-making	Develop positive attitudes towards education and training, joint family decisions about children's education	Group identity and affiliation, joint family decision-making in meaningful life choices	Employment, new venture creation, purchase decisions concerning home and consumer durables	Participation in community, local and national governance structures, advocacy for social change
Access to resources	Medical practitioners, health and social care workers, health care products and services	Mental health practitioners, community groups	School attendance, vocational training	Family, community groups, social media	Wage employment, career development, new venture finance, business training and support	Organizations, institutions, networks, social media
Achievements and social change	Better sexual and reproductive health and rights, personal safety, improved life expectancy, infant survival and immunization	Instil self-efficacy, sense of hope, improved mental wellbeing	Advance knowledge, skills, literacy, numeracy, access to information technology	Engender trust, collective efficacy, change social norms	Critical awareness of financial independence, control over wage and enterprise income, flexible working	Political participation, increased control over distribution of social and economic resources, policy and institutional change
Examples of Emancipatory Social Innovation						
Camfed	✓	✓	✓	✓	✓	
Grameen Bank	✓	✓	✓	✓	✓	✓
Kuapa Kokoo		✓	✓	✓	✓	✓
Lijjat Papad		✓	✓	✓	✓	✓

Psychological: Oppression

The positive aspect of agency refers to the ability to make choices even in the face of opposition from others (Kabeer, 2005a). The negative aspect refers to the capacity of actors to have power over others through, for example, authority, violence, coercion and subjugation. Implicit power over others may be embedded in social and cultural norms that lead subordinates to accept their oppressed status. Thus, although opportunities to make choices exist, they are not 'seen to exist' and therefore cannot be acted upon (Kabeer, 2005a, p. 14). For example, access to education and employment opportunities in the formal economy may be limited by cultural conditions that subordinate specific groups distinguished by gender (Datta and Gailey, 2012) or ethnicity. Emancipatory social innovations to overcome psychological disempowerment are linked to programmes that develop coping skills (Chesler and Chesney, 1988), confidence (Kieffer, 1984) and self-efficacy (Bandura, 1982).

Intellectual: Ignorance

There is strong evidence that access to education develops cognitive ability, and the capacity to critically reflect and act on the conditions of one's life (Kabeer, 2005a). Women in many developing countries, however, lack access to formal education (Onyejekwe, 2001). Education increases the likelihood that women will look after their own and their children's wellbeing, participate in a wider range of household decisions, and be less likely to suffer from domestic violence and better able to deal with public officials (Kabeer, 2005a, pp. 16–17). Intellectual disempowerment may also be associated with refugee status, irrespective of gender. Emancipatory social innovations to overcome intellectual disempowerment include programmes, information dissemination and the promotion of role models to change negative perceptions to positive societal attitudes to universal access to education and training.

Camfed

The charity Camfed works in Zimbabwe, Zambia, Ghana, Tanzania and Malawi, all countries in which education is not freely available, girls are often excluded from education or are forced to drop out due to a variety of reasons including lack of family income to pay school fees, the tradition of early marriage, teenage pregnancy and ill health from HIV/AIDS. Camfed operates within a wider social and economic context in which poverty has been identified as one of the greatest barriers to accessing education and where in sub-Saharan Africa, 28 million girls are out of school. The charity has supported over 1.5 million children to access education and is working towards reversing the fact that over 58 million girls and boys will probably never have access to any form of education (UNICEF, 2016).

The focus of Camfed is to facilitate access to education as an essential route to empowering women and girls by equipping them with the knowledge, skills and self-confidence necessary to enable them to fully participate in community, economic and political life. The charity website describes female education as a silver bullet with the capacity to impact positively in areas such as reducing child and maternal mortality, accelerating economic development, and helping communities to address climate change.

The Camfed business model comprises distinct, yet interrelated, activities: supporting access to primary education by providing funds to schools to cover pupil fees; training for Parent Support Groups and promoting volunteer activities and enabling access to and sustainability within the secondary education cycle for girls by funding school uniform costs; paying boarding fees and training Teacher Mentors to support girls' personal and social development; and providing access to a network of Camfed alumni offering peer support and leadership role models to help support progression and pathways to economic independence.

The emancipatory social innovations in the Camfed business model are the activities to unlock female potential, tackle inequality and transform communities and economies. Camfed describes the emphasis on female education as a starting point for social change with the aim of igniting wider social movements where women and girls hold leadership roles, community resources are catalysed to create future leaders and change agents, and opportunities are exploited to achieve systemic change.

Social Empowerment

Isolation

Instilling personal empowerment has been linked to the development of social networks, support and information (Chesler and Chesney, 1988). Grassroots community development projects respond by providing opportunities to increase interpersonal trust as well as engagement in education and infrastructure projects (Janssens, 2010). Women are known to depend more on informal networks than men since they have less access to formal organizations and economic assets (Agarwal, 2000). Emancipatory social innovations to overcome social disempowerment include community interventions, such as microfinance, that enable women to build social networks and increase influence in the family (Sanyal, 2009). In addition, social isolation may be decreased by increasing access to paid work, entrepreneurship and involvement in cooperative organizational structures (Datta and Gailey, 2012). While the participatory governance structure of cooperative organizations increases the opportunities for women to meet and interact with other women outside their family relations, such benefits are not necessarily gender specific. Cooperative ownership structures contribute to economic empowerment by encouraging members to invest in the cooperative and save for the future. Members also benefit from cooperative share ownership when dividends are distributed.

Kuapa Kokoo Cooperative

The farmer cooperative Kuapa Kokoo (http://www.kuapakokoo.com) demonstrates how emancipatory social innovation has been deployed to progress social, and economic, empowerment. Kuapa Kokoo was established in Ghana in 1993 in response to legislative and policy changes that led to the partial liberalization of the international cocoa trade. The Ghanian government's structural adjustment programme transformed Ghana's cocoa market from a state industry to a mixed ownership industry that allowed private licensed companies to compete in buying and transporting cocoa from smallholder farms to auction and processing centres. The partial liberalization of the cocoa industry presented both opportunities and risks to individual cocoa farmers and the wider cocoa farming community. The Kuapa Kokoo cooperative facilitated the accrual of a range of benefits directly to smallholder farmers, such as collective bargaining power, subsidized resources and credit extension services. Participation in the Kuapa Kokoo cooperative therefore provided the means for greater collective control and influence, and increased the flow of financial and other resources to small-scale producers.

The emancipatory impact of Kuapa Kokoo was subsequently increased by the creation of four additional entities. First, the Kuapa Kokoo Farmers Union (KKFU), established in 1995, was instrumental in securing the first Fairtrade certified smallholder farmers organization in West Africa. Achieving Fairtrade certification status was fundamental to opening, growing and sustaining access to international markets for smallholder farmers to supply quality and ethically produced cocoa beans. Following the success of the KKFU, the Kuapa Kokoo Farmers Trust (KKFT) was established to distribute all general income generated from the sale of cocoa. The distribution of these funds provides the core investment for a range of community-based education, health clinics, water infrastructure and gender equality programmes. Third, the Kuapa Kokoo Credit Union (KKCU) was created to provide access to productive and provident loan finance and to encourage a savings culture among members. The purpose of productive loans is to maintain or start new farms and provident loan finance is made available to members for personal use, such as medical expenses and school fees. Finally, to increase the volume of profit from cocoa farming, fully utilize the KKFU knowledge of the chocolate market and create other income streams to invest in social programmes, the KKFU established a separate company, Divine Chocolate, to market their own brand of chocolate in Europe and America. Divine Chocolate is owned by smallholder farmers and this ensures that farmers receive a better price for their cocoa, provides additional income to invest in community projects, and company ownership gives farmers a share of the profits and a stronger voice to effect change in the cocoa industry.

Economic Empowerment

Poverty

The empowerment potential of income earning opportunities, particularly for women, has stimulated much debate (Kabeer, 2005a; Kantor, 2003). Income may be generated from access to paid employment and career progression from either working in, or away from, the home (Kantor, 2003), and from exploiting entrepreneurial opportunities. While home-based work is considered less empowering than other forms of work (Kantor, 2003), when the income earned is essential to household survival the source of income is able to negotiate greater family respect, influence in family decision-making, broaden their social networks and leave abusive marriages (Kabeer, 2005a). However, income generation without any redistribution of household tasks is unlikely to instil empowerment since it leads to work intensification, particularly for women (Calás et al., 2009). Emancipatory social innovations to instil economic empowerment include work and workplace adaptations to accommodate personal, social and cultural constraints (Haugh and Talwar, 2016), and entrepreneurship education and support (Scott et al., 2012). While the main goal of collateral free loans to the poor is to help improve earnings and self-employment, other personal, social and political goals, such as access to family planning, raising consciousness, education and leadership development, are simultaneously and interactively stimulated by such loans (Amin et al., 1994, p. 556).

Grameen Bank

The Grameen Bank (http://www.grameen.com/), initially conceived by Muhammad Yunus in 1974, was established to make small loans to be used as start-up capital for new small businesses. The Grameen Bank was formally registered in 1983 and as of 2017, there were more than 2,600 branches, 9 million borrowers, with a repayment rate of 99.6 per cent of which 97 per cent of the borrowers are women. Grameen is active in 97 per cent of the villages of Bangladesh and is a globally recognized microcredit model serving poor communities.

The Grameen Bank operates in a sphere where globally over 4 billion people living in developing economies do not have access to financial services and the commercial banking structures struggle to serve poor households due to a variety of factors such as insufficient loan collateral, the high administration cost of processing small loans, the combination of low literacy and documentation requirements, and geographic isolation of borrowers.

Financial inclusion is a key factor in economic development and poverty reduction yet the poor, women, youth and rural residents tend to face greater barriers to accessing financial services (WBGFD, 2014). There is a considerable evidence base that demonstrates poor communities benefit enormously from a comprehensive package of financial services and access to finance is linked with economic growth, job creation and personal empowerment. The emancipatory social innovation of the Grameen business model has promoted social financial inclusion through research, practice and awareness raising, inspired similar financial inclusion initiatives in more than 40 countries around the world and has actively worked with stakeholders to address entrenched financial exclusion.

Political Empowerment

Powerlessness

The final domain in the framework we propose is political disempowerment, namely, the patterns by which power and resources are distributed. Institutions establish the distributional rules of the game and since social change involves changing such rules, it cannot proceed without political change. Democracy and participation provide opportunities to empower those stakeholders not usually given a voice in organizations (Tremblay and Gutberlet, 2012) and communities (Dohmworth and Hanisch, 2018). Strategies to overcome political disempowerment include interest representation in local and national governments (Kabeer, 2005a) and the creation of participatory organizational structures such as cooperatives (Datta and Gailey, 2012; Laverack, 2005; Mayoux, 1995) and self-help and loan groups (Kabeer, 2005b). The interconnectedness of different empowerment domains is further emphasized in that participation in groups also helps to build individual psychological wellbeing and social capital among members (Datta and Gailey, 2012; Sanyal, 2009).

Lijjat Papad

The Indian women's cooperative Shri Mahila Griha Udyog Lijjat Papad (Lijjat Papad) exemplifies large-scale and multifaceted emancipatory social innovation. Lijjat Papad was founded in Mumbai in 1995 with the explicit goal to empower women by creating employment opportunities through the manufacturing and sale of various bread, food and domestic cleaning products. More than 22 million people live in Mumbai and 70 per cent live in slums. Slum communities have limited access to electricity, clean water, food, educational opportunities and employment and it is within that context that seven women founders used their domestic cooking skills to generate income to support themselves and their families. However, the cooperative does not identify as an organization for poor, needy women or women from a specific class, Lijjat Papad promotes the ideals of personal dignity, empowerment and respect. Lijjat Papad is one of the most successful cooperatives in India with annual sales exceeding 5.5 billion rupees and with over 81 branches and 27 divisions (Datta and Gailey, 2012).

The cooperative is grounded in the Sarvodaya philosophy that emphasizes the decentralization of power, and employs cooperative principles to instil individual and community empowerment. Lijjat Papad is built around a system of shared values in which all members own the cooperative and therefore any profits, or losses, are shared equally among the members. Any woman pledging to adopt Lijjat Papad values and with respect for producing a quality product can become a member and thus a co-owner. The governance structure and operating model comprise strategic and local committees which collectively and consensually make and implement all decisions. This approach places influence and decision-making power in the hands of women members. While men cannot become members of the cooperative, they may participate without voting rights.

The philosophy of Lijjat Papad's institutional design enhances empowerment at an individual and community level, for example, production is carried out in thousands of individual homes and this contributes to the distributive model of female leadership and control. The long-term goal of Lijjat Papad is to replace the politics of power with cooperation and economic empowerment.

CAUTIONARY EMPOWERMENT TALES

The analytical framework presented above portrays a positive perspective of the emancipatory potential of social innovation and we now critically reflect on the challenges associated with instilling emancipatory impact. The emancipatory pathways described in the framework suggest a linear progression from less to more empowerment. However, the pathways to empowerment may be non-linear, controversial, subjective, and can be reversed (Jaumier, 2017; Tremblay and Gutberlet, 2012). Overturning the normative societal acceptance of inequality and exclusion (Mair et al., 2016, p. 2021) is unlikely to proceed unchallenged. The socially constructed and maintained categories of oppressed groups are taken-for-granted ordering of reality and, unless challenged, perpetuate the status quo. Although gaining access to resources is a key component of empowerment (Kabeer, 1999), securing access to resources is no guarantee of social change (Calás et al., 2009) since culturally embedded norms may continue to limit agency, choices and the capacity to make decisions (Sen, 1999). Similarly, although participatory governance structures open opportunities for empowerment, they do not automatically empower women and may empower some groups but not all (Dohmwirth and Hanisch, 2018). Participatory governance structures may also act as a brake on scaling empowerment

(Jaumier, 2017; Jones and Kalmi, 2012; Tremblay and Gutberlet, 2012) because of the administrative complexity of managing member involvement in decision-making. Finally, the difficulties described earlier that are associated with measuring empowerment means that the impact of empowerment initiatives has yet to be fully established. While interventions may have decreased maternal mortality and increased school enrolments, the impact on women's employment, property rights and meaningful political participation has been slower (Grown et al., 2016). Despite such challenges, the empowerment potential of emancipatory social innovation offers many opportunities for future research, several of which we outline in the final section of this chapter.

RESEARCH AGENDA

In this chapter we introduced the concept of emancipatory social innovation to describe new socially and environmentally useful products, services and programmes that directly and indirectly advance empowerment. In addition, we created a novel framework to elucidate multiple empowerment pathways and employed four case studies to illustrate the empowerment pathways in practice. The empowerment pathways also provide routes and mechanisms for addressing individual societal detachment and fostering social inclusion. In this final section we develop eight suggestions to advance future emancipatory social innovation research.

1. *Social innovation opportunity recognition.* Opportunity recognition is fundamental to innovation and entrepreneurship (Shane and Venkataraman, 2000), however, when society values some groups above others, this may impact on emancipatory social innovation opportunity recognition in two ways. Groups that are disempowered may be alerted to finding socially innovative ways of meeting their needs which remain unsatisfied by mainstream products and services. Conversely, disempowered groups may lack the confidence to engage in social innovation opportunity recognition and exploitation. Unpacking the connections between disempowerment, self-perception and emancipatory social innovation opportunity recognition would elaborate current theoretical explanations of mainstream opportunity recognition and exploitation.
2. *Empowerment transitions.* Transition theory considers the need for system change process that is oriented towards human wellbeing and sustainability. The theory 'develops the notion of sociotechnical niches as protected spaces where new sociotechnical practices can develop' (Seyfang and Haxeltine, 2012, p. 383). A sociotechnical niche is considered in relation to dominant practices and creates opportunities to investigate how actors and intermediary organizations might grow the niche and eventually replace the dominant regime (Geels, 2005). Transition agents serve as global carriers of new standards, practices and social networks which inform, and are informed by, local projects. Three processes account for successful niche growth: managing expectations, building social networks and learning. Future research could employ transition theory to examine how emancipatory social innovations diffuse, or fail to diffuse, from niche to the mainstream.
3. *Emancipatory social innovation experimentation.* Although there are a few examples, the positive reporting bias means that it is usually stories about successful

emancipatory social innovations that are told. This reporting, however, is myopic as much can be learned from why social innovations fail, or fail to diffuse. In transition theory (Seyfang and Haxeltine, 2012) a niche provides a safe space for experimentation and thus considering transition theory in the domain of social innovation 'failures' would offer opportunities for theorizing about productive emancipatory social innovation processes, diffusion and translation.

4. *Systemic empowerment.* Institutional conditions collectively serve to instil, constrain or extinguish empowerment. For example, it was found that in the context of rural poverty in which women-only cooperatives are promoted without offering additional development opportunities for men, the empowering effects remain limited to increased leadership abilities (Dohmwirth and Hanisch, 2018) and in some cases the empowerment benefits are deemed to be minimal (Mayoux, 1995). Investigating the relationships between systemic disempowerment and the efficacy of emancipatory social innovation would advance knowledge on diffusing and scaling empowerment.
5. *Emotions and empowerment.* Scholarly interest in emotions and institutions has noted how compassion differentiates social from commercial entrepreneurs (Miller et al., 2012). Research that explores how emotions that have traditionally assumed to be negative, such as conflict and resistance, may be instrumental to achieving positive empowerment outcomes would enrich our understanding of emotions and institutional stasis and change. For example, theoretical advances to explain the impact on institutional change of displayed and hidden emotional responses to abuse, oppression, ignorance, isolation, poverty and inequality.
6. *Methodological considerations.* Assessing the empowerment impact of emancipatory social innovations can be accomplished in both quantitative and qualitative research designs. For example, the impact on school attendance of social innovation for menstrual hygiene, such as reusable sanitary products, lends itself to experimental method (Wilson et al., 2014). Yet social programmes to alleviate poverty increasingly involve a range of integrated services that seek to engender empowerment across personal, social, economic and political spheres (Amin et al., 1994). This makes the specification of the combinations of causal factors that impact on empowerment difficult to isolate. Future research that employed qualitative content analysis (QCA) would advance understanding of the multiple pathways between emancipatory social innovation and empowerment. Demonstrable and meaningful connections between social innovation, empowerment and social change have yet to be established and it is not clear whether and how different forms of empowerment lead to each other.
7. *Empowering marginalized social groups.* While much research has investigated gender and empowerment, the extent to which extant theory is generalizable to other stigmatized groups remains puzzling. Setting aside the methodological barriers that prevent gaining access to hard to reach groups, such as people bonded into modern slavery, the homeless and stateless, how such groups become empowered would inform our current understanding of empowerment pathways. Further, the empowerment paradox created by the exclusion of groups, such as men, from emancipatory social innovations oriented to empowering women would benefit from further examination.
8. *Intersectionality.* The multidimensional nature of empowerment may explain why intersectionality has yet to appear in the management literature. Intersectionality describes how overlapping oppressive institutions, such as sexism, racism, homophobia

and socioeconomic class, cannot be explained without reference to each other and, further, that the impact of intersectionality is coalescence into new forms of discrimination. If the methodological challenges could be overcome, research that investigated how new groups are either accepted or oppressed would illuminate how disempowerment takes root. The closed circle of empowering one group at the expense of another may be opened if research uncovers how to empower new groups, and ultimately reduce the need for emancipatory social innovation.

CONCLUSION

To be empowered means not being prevented from participating in society by exclusionary or discriminatory institutions and practices, and being able to act in accordance with one's goals and preferences. The case studies we presented illustrate how empowerment can be advanced by removing exclusionary constraints, providing equal access to opportunities and implementing proactive policies of affirmative action. By advancing empowerment these practices also strengthen social capital, community cohesion and collectively foster social inclusion. Whereas high levels of inequality and social exclusion undermine both social and economic development, the diffusion of emancipatory social innovations shares the benefits of practical and workable solutions with individuals, communities and societies. The impact then of emancipatory social innovation is the creation of more equitable societies in which opportunity for all is an achievable goal.

REFERENCES

Agarwal, B. (2000), 'Conceptualising environmental collective action: why gender matters', *Cambridge Journal of Economics*, **24**(3), 283–310.

Alkire, S., R. Meinzen-Dick, A. Peterman et al. (2013), 'The Women's Empowerment in Agriculture Index', *World Development*, **52**(1), 71–91.

Amin, R., A.U. Ahmed, A.J. Chowdhury and M. Ahmed (1994), 'Poor women's participation in income-generation projects and their fertility regulation in rural Bangladesh: evidence from a recent study', *World Development*, **22**(4), 555–65.

Atkinson, A.B. (1998), 'Social exclusion, poverty and unemployment', in A.B. Atkinson and J. Hills (eds), *Exclusion, Employment and Opportunity*, London: Centre for Social Exclusion, pp. 1–20.

Bandura, A. (1982), 'Self-efficacy mechanism in human agency', *American Psychologist*, **37**(2), 122–47.

Berg, M., E. Coman and J.J. Schensul (2009), 'Youth action research for prevention: a multi-level intervention designed to increase efficacy and empowerment among young urban youth', *American Journal of Community Psychology*, **43**(3–4), 345–59.

Berman, Y. and D. Phillips (2000), 'Indicators of social quality and social exclusion at national and community level', *Social Indicators Research*, **50**(3), 329–50.

Blanchard, K.H., J.P. Carlos and W.A. Randolph (1995), *The Empowerment Barometer and Action Plan*, Escondido, CA: Blanchard Training and Development.

Calás, M., L. Smircich and K. Bourne (2009), 'Extending the boundaries: reframing "entrepreneurship as social change" through feminist perspectives', *Academy of Management Review*, **34**(3), 552–69.

Chesler, M. and B. Chesney (1988), 'Self-help groups: empowerment attitudes and behaviours of disabled or chronologically ill persons', in H.E. Yuker (ed.), *Attitudes Towards People With Disabilities*, New York: Springer, pp. 230–45.

Church, C. and J. Elster (2002), *The Quiet Revolution*, Birmingham: Shell Better Britain.

Collins, H. (2003), 'Discrimination, equality and social inclusion', *Modern Law Review*, **66**(1), 16–43.

Colquitt, J.A. and G. George (2011), 'Publishing in AMJ: topic choice', *Academy of Management Journal*, **54**(3), 432–5.

Datta, P.B. and R. Gailey (2012), 'Empowering women through social entrepreneurship: case study of a women's cooperative in India', *Entrepreneurship Theory and Practice*, **36**(3), 569–87.
de Bruin, A., C. Brush and F. Welter (2007), 'Advancing a framework for coherent research on women's empowerment', *Entrepreneurship Theory and Practice*, **31**(3), 323–39.
de la Chaux, M., H. Haugh and R. Greenwood (2018), 'Organizing refugee camps: "respected space" and "listening posts"', *Academy of Management Discoveries*, **4**(2), 155–79.
Dohmwirth, C. and M. Hanisch (2018), 'Women and collective action: lessons from the Indian dairy cooperative sector', *Community Development Journal*, **53**(4), 675–93.
Duflo, E. (2012), 'Women empowerment and economic development', *Journal of Economic Literature*, **50**(4), 1051–79.
Geels, F. (2005), 'Processes and patterns in transitions and systems innovations: refining the co-evolutionary multi-level perspective', *Technological Forecasting and Social Change*, **72**(6), 681–96.
Grown, C., T. Addison and F. Tarp (2016), 'Aid for gender equality and development: lessons and challenges', *Journal for International Development*, **28**(3), 311–19.
Haugh, H. and A. Talwar (2016), 'Social entrepreneurship and social change: the mediating role of empowerment', *Journal of Business Ethics*, **133**(4), 643–58.
Hjorth, P. (2003), 'Knowledge development and management of urban poverty alleviation', *Habitat International*, **27**(3), 381–92.
Howell, K. (2016), 'Building empowerment in market-based redevelopment: changing paradigms for affordable housing and community development in Washington, DC', *Community Development Journal*, **52**(4), 573–90.
Jackson, T., S. Mitchell and M. Wright (1989), 'The community development continuum', *Community Health Studies*, **8**(1), 66–73.
Janssens, W. (2010), 'Women's empowerment and the creation of social capital in Indian villages', *World Development*, **38**(7), 974–88.
Jaumier, S. (2017), 'Preventing chiefs from being chiefs: an ethnography of a cooperative sheet-metal factory', *Organization*, **24**(2), 218–39.
Jones, D. and P. Kalmi (2012), 'Economies of scale versus participation: a cooperative dilemma?', *Journal of Entrepreneurial and Organizational Diversity*, **1**(1), 37–64.
Kabeer, N. (1999), 'Resources, agency and achievements: reflections on the measurement of empowerment', *Development and Change*, **30**(3), 435–64.
Kabeer, N. (2005a), 'Gender equality and women's empowerment: a critical analysis of the third millennium development goals 1', *Gender and Development*, **13**(1), 13–24.
Kabeer, N. (2005b), 'Social exclusion and citizenship: the wider impacts of microfinance', in J. Copestake, M. Greeley, S. Johnson, N. Kabeer and A. Simanowitz (eds), *Money With a Mission*, London: ITDG, pp. 94–125.
Kantor, P. (2003), 'Women's empowerment through home-based work: evidence from India', *Development and Change*, **34**(3), 425–45.
Keith, B. (2016), 'Outlook on reproductive health', PATH, Seattle. https://www.path.org/publications/files/RH_outlook_mh_022016.pdf (accessed 15 November 2017).
Kieffer, C. (1984), 'Citizen empowerment: a developmental perspective', *Prevention in Health Services*, **3**(2–3), 9–36.
Labonte, R. (1990), 'Empowerment: notes on professional and community dimensions', *Community Health Studies*, **8**, 66–73.
Laverack, G. (2001), 'An identification and interpretation of the organizational aspects of community empowerment', *Community Development Journal*, **36**(2), 134–45.
Laverack, G. (2005), 'Using a "domains" approach to build community empowerment', *Community Development Journal*, **41**(1), 4–12.
Levitas, R. (1998), *The Inclusive Society? Social Exclusion and New Labour*, Basingstoke: Macmillan.
Lister, R. (1998), 'From equality to social inclusion: New Labour and the welfare state', *Critical Social Policy*, **18**(2), 215–25.
Lombardini, S., K. Bowman and R. Garwood (2017), 'A "how to" guide to measuring women's empowerment: sharing experience from Oxfam's impact evaluations', Oxford: Oxfam. https://policy-practice.oxfam.org.uk/publications/a-how-to-guide-to-measuring-womens-empowerment-sharing-experience-from-oxfams-i-620271 (accessed 1 March 2019).
Mair, J.H., M. Wolf and C. Seelos (2016), 'Scaffolding: a process of transforming patterns of inequality in small-scale societies', *Academy of Management Journal*, **59**(6), 2021–44.
Maynard, M.T., L.L. Gilson and J.E. Mathieu (2012), 'Empowerment – fad or fab? A multilevel review of the past two decades of research', *Journal of Management*, **38**(4), 1231–81.
Mayoux, L. (1995), 'Alternative vision or utopian fantasy? Cooperation, empowerment and women's cooperative development in India', *Journal of International Development*, **7**(2), 211–28.

Miller, R.L. and R. Campbell (2006), 'Taking stock of empowerment evaluation. An empirical review', *American Journal of Evaluation*, **27**(3), 296–319.
Miller, T.L., M.G. Grimes, J.S. McMullen and T.J. Vogus (2012), 'Venturing for others with heart and head: how compassion encourages social entrepreneurship', *Academy of Management Review*, **37**(4), 222–7.
Mosedale, S. (2005), 'Assessing women's empowerment: towards conceptual framework', *Journal of International Development*, **17**(2), 243–57.
Narayan-Parker, D. (2005), *Measuring Empowerment: Cross-Disciplinary Perspectives*, Washington, DC: World Bank.
Nicholls, A. and A. Murdoch (2012), *Social Innovation: Blurring Boundaries to Reconfigure Markets*, Basingstoke: Palgrave Macmillan.
OECD (2013), *Recommendation of the Council on Gender Equality in Education, Employment and Entrepreneurship*, Paris: Organisation for Economic Co-operation and Development.
OECD (2017), *Gender Recommendations – Some Progress on Gender Equality but Much Left to Do*, Paris: Organisation for Economic Co-operation and Development.
Onyejekwe, C.J. (2001), 'Micro-finance and economic empowerment: women's cooperatives in Nigeria', *Asian Journal of Women's Studies*, **7**(4), 70–89.
Pache, A.-C. and F. Santos (2013), 'Inside the hybrid organization: selective coupling as a response to conflicting institutional logics', *Academy of Management Journal*, **56**(4), 972–1001.
Philipps-Howard, P.A., G. Otieno, B. Burmen et al. (2015), 'Menstrual needs and associations with sexual and reproductive risks in rural Kenyan females: a cross-sectional behavioural study linked with HIV prevalence', *Journal of Women's Health*, **24**(10), 801–11.
Phills, J.A., K. Deiglmeier and D.T. Miller (2008), 'Rediscovering social innovation', *Stanford Social Innovation Review*, **6**(4), 34–43.
Putz, R., K. O'Hara, F. Taggart and S. Stewart-Brown (2012), *Using WEMWBS to Measure the Impact of Your Work on Mental Wellbeing: A Practice-Based User Guide*, Coventry Wellbeing Project. http://www.corc.uk.net/media/1244/wemwbs_practitioneruserguide.pdf (accessed 1 March 2019).
Sanyal, P. (2009), 'From credit to collective action: the role of microfinance in promoting women's social capital and normative influence', *American Sociological Review*, **74**(4), 529–50.
Saraceno, C. (1997), 'The importance of the concept of social exclusion', in W. van der Beck, L. Maesen and A. Walker (eds), *The Social Quality of Europe*, The Hague: Kluwer Law International, pp. 157–64.
Schuler, R., S.M. Hashemi, A.P. Riley and A. Akhter (1996), 'Credit programs, patriarchy and men's violence against women in rural Bangladesh', *Social Science in Medicine*, **43**(12), 1729–42.
Schulz, A.J., B.A. Israel, M.A. Zimmerman and B.N. Checkoway (1995), 'Empowerment as a multi-level construct: perceived control at the individual, organizational and community levels', *Health Education Research: Theory and Practice*, **10**(3), 309–27.
Scott, L., C. Dolan, M. Johnstone-Louis, K. Sugden and M. Wu (2012), 'Enterprise and inequality: a study of Avon in South Africa', *Entrepreneurship Theory and Practice*, **36**(3), 543–68.
Seibert, S.E., S.R. Silver and W.A. Randolph (2004), 'Taking empowerment to the next level: a multiple-level of empowerment, performance and satisfaction', *Academy of Management Journal*, **47**(3), 332–49.
Sen, P. (1999), 'Enhancing women's choices in responding to domestic violence in Calcutta: a comparison of employment and education', *European Journal of Development Research*, **11**(2), 65–86.
Seyfang, G. and A. Haxeltine (2012), 'Growing grassroots innovations: exploring the role of community-based initiatives in governing sustainable energy transitions', *Environment and Planning C, Government and Policy*, **30**(3), 381–400.
Seyfang, G. and A. Smith (2007), 'Grassroots innovations for sustainable development: towards a new research policy and agenda', *Environmental Politics*, **16**(4), 584–603.
Shane, S. and S. Venkataraman (2000), 'The promise of entrepreneurship as a field of research', *Academy of Management Review*, **25**(1), 217–26.
Thorp, R., F. Stewart and A. Heyer (2005), 'When and how far is group formation a route out of chronic poverty?', *World Development*, **33**(6), 907–20.
Tilly, C. (1998), *Durable Inequality*, Berkeley, CA: University of California Press.
Tremblay, C. and J. Gutberlet (2012), 'Empowerment through participation: assessing the voices of leaders in recycling cooperatives in Sao Paulo, Brazil', *Community Development Journal*, **47**(2), 282–302.
UNICEF (2016), *The State of the World's Children. A Fair Chance for Every Child*, New York: United Nations Children's Fund.
United Nations (2010), *Analysing and Measuring Social Inclusion in a Global Context*, New York: United Nations.
Wallerstein, N. and E. Bernstein (1988), 'Empowerment education: Freire's ideas adapted to health education', *Health Education Quarterly*, **15**(4), 379–94.
WBGFD (2014), *Global Financial Development Report. Financial Inclusion*, The International Bank for Reconstruction and Development, Washington, DC: World Bank.

Westley, F. and N. Antadze (2010), 'Making a difference. Strategies for scaling social innovation for greater impact', *The Innovation Journal: The Public Sector Innovation Journal*, **15**(2), article 2.
Wilson, E., J. Reeve and A. Pitt (2014), 'Education, period. Developing an acceptable and replicable menstrual hygiene intervention', *Development in Practice*, **24**(1), 63–80.
Withorn, A. (1980), 'Helping ourselves: the limits and potential of self-help', *Social Policy*, **11**, 20–27.
Witkamp, M.J., R.P. Raven and L.M. Royakkers (2011), 'Strategic niche management of social innovations: the case of social entrepreneurship', *Technology Analysis and Strategic Management*, **23**(10), 667–81.
Zimmerman, M.A. (1990), 'Taking aim on empowerment research: on the distinction between individual and psychological conceptions', *American Journal of Community Psychology*, **18**(1), 169–77.
Zimmerman, M.A. (2000), 'Empowerment theory: psychological, organizational and community levels of analysis', in J. Rappaport and E. Seidman (eds), *Handbook of Community Psychology*, New York: Kluwer Academic, pp. 43–64.
Zimmerman, M. and J. Rappaport (1988), 'Citizen participation, perceived control and psychological empowerment', *American Journal of Community Psychology*, **16**(5), 725–50.

Index